THE CAMBRIDGE HISTORY
OF
BRITISH FOREIGN POLICY

IN THREE VOLUMES
VOLUME THREE

THE CAMBRIDGE HISTORY

OF

BRITISH FOREIGN POLICY

1783–1919

EDITED BY

SIR A. W. WARD, Litt.D., F.B.A.

AND

G. P. GOOCH, M.A., Litt.D.

VOLUME III

1866–1919

1970

OCTAGON BOOKS

New York

First published 1923

Reprinted 1970
by permission of Cambridge University Press

OCTAGON BOOKS
A Division of Farrar, Straus & Giroux, Inc.
19 Union Square West
New York, N. Y. 10003

Reproduced from a copy in the Yale University Library

Library of Congress Catalog Card Number: 70-119436

PREFACE

THE concluding Volume of this *History* may seem to some of our readers to make its appearance too soon, seeing that on many of the transactions narrated or questions discussed in it the time has not yet arrived for expressing a definitive judgment. Public archives are thrown open, and private memoirs made known in rapid succession, to a breathless world; and at the very moment when this Preface is being written, the Foreign Policy of our country, seemingly at a standstill of unprecedented perplexity, may be on the eve of changes not less momentous than any discussed in the ensuing pages. But there can be no reason for abandoning the conviction with which this work was first taken in hand, that a study of British Foreign Policy, based on authentic documents, is indispensable for an insight, however incomplete, into the problems engaging that Policy at the present day, and that the existing responsibilities of its conductors to the welfare of our nation and empire, and to the Peace of the World, cannot be dissociated from the lessons taught by history as to the endeavours and the failures of the past. Moreover, since the period of European and World politics falling under the particular range of our Third Volume may fairly be described as a period of Congresses and Conferences, designed to adapt the international relations between the Powers Great and Small to changes brought about by conflicts between Alliances formed in the interests of particular States, so the future may have in store an age in which those interests will be reconciled under the control of other interests common to the whole body of States and peoples, and in subjection to the predominant interest of them all—the Peace of the World. The establishment and development of such a system, only partially and tentatively antici- pated in the efforts and experiments of previous periods, will in that event inevitably become the cardinal task of British Foreign Policy. For Great Britain and her empire cannot stand aside or play a merely acquiescent part. They have been called by their history to the position of the foremost among European World Powers, and are consequently authorised to take a leading part in working out what promises to be the next chapter in the destinies of the World.

The present Volume has, like its predecessors, benefited by the interest taken in the progress of this *History* as a whole by friends and well-wishers, among whom we should specially like to repeat our acknowledgments to Lord Fitzmaurice, to the Right Hon. Sir Ernest Satow, G.C.M.G. and to Dr H. Hall, late Assistant Keeper of the Public Records. The private papers of the late Sir Andrew Buchanan, G.C.B., with the loan of which we were favoured by his relatives, and more especially Mr Henry Mellish, of Hadsock Priory, Worksop, have continued to be serviceable. They include a Correspondence extending from November 9th to December 15th, 1870, concerning the repudiation by Russia of the obligations imposed upon her by the Convention of March 30th, 1856, together with certain Letters of the previous October, showing Sir Andrew to have been fully aware already at that time, and even earlier, of Prince Gorchakoff's intention to press the wishes of Russia upon the European Powers at the earliest opportunity. The Wallace Papers, the generous loan of which to us for the purposes of this work, has already been gratefully recorded, contain a number of Letters belonging to the period from June, 1894, to March, 1896, to Sir D. M. Wallace, from Sir Valentine Chirol, when correspondent of *The Times* at Berlin, which are of singular interest and have of course been referred by us to their writer, the distinguished contributor of Chapter IV to the present Volume.

As Mr Algernon Cecil's summary analysis in the Table of Contents will show, the Chapter (VIII) on *The Foreign Office* in this Volume, from its own point of view, covers the whole ground of our work. Its proper place seemed, therefore, to be at the end of the narrative chapters (including the *Epilogue*, which deals, for many reasons in summary fashion, with the course of the World War and the circumstances and conditions of the Peace which brought it to a close). The complex task of critically surveying a field at once so wide and in several respects so contentious called for independence of judgment as well as fulness of knowledge. In acknowledging the advantages derived by our contributor from distinguished expert information and counsel, we desire, on his behalf as well as on our own, to state explicitly that no responsibility of any sort rests with those to whose assistance he is indebted. With this proviso, we are requested by Mr Algernon Cecil to acknowledge the kind assistance of the Earl of Balfour, K.G., late Secretary of State for Foreign Affairs and Chancellor of our University, the late Lord Sanderson, G.C.B., Lord Carnock of Carnock, G.C.B., G.C.M.G., Sir Algernon

Law, K.C.M.G., C.B., Sir W. E. Davidson, K.C.M.G., C.B., the Marquis of Lansdowne, K.G., the Right Hon. Lord Robert Cecil, M.P., Lord Eustace Percy, M.P., Lady Gwendolen Cecil, and others.

Our thanks are again due to Miss A. D. Greenwood, a historian in her own right, for supplying the Index to this Volume as she has to its predecessors; to Mr A. T. Bartholomew, Assistant Librarian of the University, for varied help, and to Miss Pate, for her indefatigable aid in preparing this Volume for the Press.

Finally, in once more recording our gratitude to the Syndics of the University Press, and to the whole body of its workers, for entering upon and carrying through the publication of this *History*, we cannot but call to mind at least one side of the very serious difficulties with which of late they have had to meet in all their undertakings. In the Preface to our Second Volume we referred to the lamented death of the late Secretary of the Syndicate, Mr A. R. Waller, whose work has since been taken up by a trusted successor. More recently, the death of the University Printer, Mr J. B. Peace, Fellow of Emmanuel College, has inflicted another grievous loss upon our Press and the University whose best interests it serves. May we add that the sorrow which these events have caused throughout the Press, and the sympathy with which has been shared by the University at large, attest the intimacy of cooperation long notable in the history of an institution indissolubly bound up with the past, present and future of Cambridge?

A. W. W.
G. P. G.

March, 1923

CORRIGENDA

VOL. II.

p. 16, l. 11 from bottom. For *Chapter III* read *Chapter VI*.
p. 430 note. For *C. IX* read *C. VIII*.
p. 525, note 1, line 2. For *ceded in return* read *retained possession of*.

VOL. III.

p. 203, line 27. For *as* read *at*.
p. 505, line 4. For *of Belgium* read *to Belgium*.
p. 538, line 9. For *Kamel* read *Kemal*.
p. 556, line 9. For *between* read *with*.

CONTENTS

BOOK IV

FROM THE THIRD MINISTRY OF LORD DERBY TO THE FIRST MINISTRY OF LORD SALISBURY, 1866–1886

CHAPTER I

NEUTRALITY, 1866–1874

A. NEUTRALITY IN CONTINENTAL AFFAIRS
1866–1874

By C. R. M. F. CRUTTWELL, M.A.
Fellow and Tutor of Hertford College, Oxford

B. SEA-POLICY AND THE ALABAMA CLAIMS

By Professor J. E. G. DE MONTMORENCY, M.A., LL.D., Peterhouse
Quain Professor of Comparative Law in the University of London

CHAPTER II

FORWARD POLICY AND REACTION
1874–1885
By WILLIAM HARBUTT DAWSON

BOOK V

THE SECOND AND THIRD SALISBURY
ADMINISTRATIONS AND AFTER
1886–1907

CHAPTER III

IMPERIAL POLICY IN THE OLD AND THE NEW WORLD
1885–1899

By WILLIAM HARBUTT DAWSON

I. FRONTIER DISPUTES IN CENTRAL ASIA

CONTENTS

CHAPTER IV

THE BOER WAR AND THE INTERNATIONAL SITUATION
1899–1902
By SIR VALENTINE CHIROL

CONTENTS

CHAPTER V

CONTINENTAL AGREEMENTS

1902–1907

By G. P. GOOCH, M.A., Trinity College; LITT.D.

BOOK VI

BEFORE AND IN THE WORLD WAR
1907–1919

CHAPTER VI

TRIPLE ALLIANCE AND TRIPLE *ENTENTE*
1907–1914

By G. P. GOOCH, Litt.D.

CHAPTER VII

EPILOGUE. THE WAR AND THE PEACE
1914–1919

By G. P. GOOCH, LITT.D.

CHAPTER VIII

THE FOREIGN OFFICE

By ALGERNON CECIL, M.A., New College, Oxford

---

[1] The *Duke of Wellington* acted as Foreign Secretary for a few months from Nov. 15, 1834 to April 1835.

CONTENTS xix

BOOK IV

FROM THE THIRD MINISTRY OF LORD DERBY TO THE FIRST MINISTRY OF LORD SALISBURY, 1866–1886

SECRETARIES OF STATE FOR FOREIGN AFFAIRS

July,   1866: Lord Stanley (Earl of Derby).
December, 1868: Earl of Clarendon.
July,   1870: Earl Granville.
February, 1874: Earl of Derby.
April,   1878: Marquis of Salisbury.
April,   1880: Earl Granville.
June,   1885: Marquis of Salisbury.

UNDER-SECRETARIES OF STATE FOR FOREIGN AFFAIRS

Right Hon. Edmund Hammond (afterwards Lord Hammond) (*Permanent*).

*July,   1866: Edward Christopher Egerton.
*December, 1868: Arthur John Otway (afterwards Right Hon. Sir Arthur).
July,   1869: Hon. Thomas Charles William Spring Rice (*Assistant*).
August,   1870: Odo W. L. Russell (afterwards Lord Ampthill) (*Assistant*).
*January, 1871: George H. C. Byng, Viscount Enfield (afterwards Earl of Strafford).
October,   — : Charles Stuart Aubrey Abbott, Lord Tenterden (*Assistant*).
October,   1873: The same (*Permanent*).
October,   1873: Thomas Villiers Lister (afterwards Sir Villiers Lister) (*Assistant*).
*February, 1874: Hon. Robert Bourke (afterwards Lord Connemara).
July,   1876: Sir Julian (afterwards Lord) Pauncefote (*Assistant*).
*April,   1880: Sir Charles (afterwards Right Hon. Sir C.) Dilke, Bart. (*Parliamentary*).
September, 1882: Sir Julian (afterwards Lord) Pauncefote (*Permanent*).
October,   — : Philip W. (afterwards Lord) Currie (*Assistant*).
*January, 1883: Lord Edmond George Petty Fitzmaurice (afterwards Lord Fitzmaurice) (*Parliamentary*).
*June,   1885: Right Hon. Robert Bourke (afterwards Lord Connemara) (*Parliamentary*).

* *Parliamentary.*

CHAPTER I

NEUTRALITY, 1866–1874

A. NEUTRALITY IN CONTINENTAL AFFAIRS, 1866–1874

I. *The Austro-Prussian War and the Conference of London*, 1866–1867

THE year 1866 opened ominously for European diplomacy. It became increasingly clear that the relations between Austria and Prussia had grown worse instead of better after the Convention of Gastein (August 14th, 1865). This Convention had, it is true, appeared most objectionable to the British Government, based, as it was, on the mere principle of force; but it had not even the virtue of providing for an agreement between the two countries. In Bismarck's words, it had merely "papered over the cracks"; and the paper was already wearing very thin. The arrangement by which Austria administered Holstein and Prussia Schleswig must speedily come to an end, and only two solutions were possible. Either the Duchies must enter into the Germanic Confederation, which Prussia would not permit, or they must be annexed to Prussia, to which Austria could not be expected to grant a peaceable consent. Lord Russell's Government had, therefore, to face the probability of an Austro-Prussian war, for which the pretext was ready at hand; and the results of which, even if Europe as a whole was not involved, would certainly not be restricted to a final settlement of the Schleswig-Holstein question.

Neither Lord Clarendon nor Lord Augustus Loftus, the British Ambassador at Berlin, had any doubts as to the intentions of Bismarck to force a war, with the object of destroying the existing Germanic Confederation for the benefit of Prussia. The difficulty lay, however, in discovering any effectual method of preventing war. British diplomacy, acting in conjunction with France, had been signally unsuccessful on the occasions of the Polish rising (1863) and the Schleswig-Holstein War (1864). The main results had been to make Bismarck serenely contemptuous, and to render both Great Britain and France unwilling to risk any further failures in common. Moreover, the Foreign Office had an acute distrust of the character and methods of Drouyn de Lhuys, on whose retirement Lord Cowley wrote, in September, 1866, that "it will certainly not cause regret...as I have never been able to place complete reliance on the accuracy of his statements[1]." Finally, it was certain that, in any question affecting the reconstruction of Germany, it would be quite impossible for the Emperor Napoleon to act with the measure of disinterestedness which alone could give any concerted action the possibility of success. It does not indeed appear that Lord Clarendon had any idea of the extent to which the Emperor Napoleon had fettered his freedom of action by his interviews with Bismarck at Biarritz (October, 1865); but he believed that, although the Emperor would shrink from war in deference to the wishes of the Chamber and the commercial classes in France, he would not be averse from fishing in troubled waters.

The task, therefore, of endeavouring to avert war rested on the British Government alone. On February 28th, 1866, the Ministerial Council held at Berlin determined not to modify the Prussian demands on Austria, and virtually adopted Bismarck's view that the Schleswig-Holstein question was only a part of the larger problem of German Reconstruction which logically required, as a preliminary, a war with Austria. Direct negotiations with Italy were immediately commenced, which were concluded by the offensive and defensive Alliance of April 8th.

These actions naturally succeeded, as they were intended to do, in alarming Austria, who, early in March, proceeded to reinforce her troops on the Bohemian and Galician frontiers. The work of mediation was thus seriously compromised, before it had actually begun. Lord Clarendon lost no time; on March 18th he suggested that "Prussia, before going to war, should bear in mind the agreement entered into by the Congress of Paris, to refer disputed questions to a friendly Power"; and indicated that, if the King of Prussia should ask for the good offices of the British Government, they would be given, in conjunction if possible with other Powers. Bismarck replied in the tone which he consistently adopted throughout the negotiations; and cast the whole responsibility on Austria. The conduct of the Prussians had been throughout scrupulously correct: they had always closely observed the Convention of Gastein, which Austria had "shamefully violated"; any military precautions which they had taken were only an inadequate defensive reply to those already set on foot by Austria, who by making them proved her intention of evading her treaty obligations by force. He made, however, the admission that, in view of Austria's conduct, 'the whole Prussian nation was now unanimous in regarding annexa-

[1] From Lord Cowley, No. 235, September 2nd, 1866.

tion (of the Duchies) as a vital question, whether regarded in its military or political aspect[1]"; and that the proposal of convoking the Estates of the Duchies in order to decide on their future destiny was, in consequence, inadmissible as they would probably adhere to the Duke of Augustenburg. Clarendon replied by directly traversing these statements, and declaring that Austria neither wanted war nor was preparing for it. In a conversation with Count Bernstorff on April 4th[2], he showed how completely he understood Bismarck's position. "Count Bismarck," he told the Prussian Ambassador, "was not an ordinary Minister; he exercised supreme power, he dictated the policy of Prussia which was territorial aggrandisement, he was a man of purpose and that which he announced he was likely to execute. War with Austria had become necessary for his position and his designs, and Austria was right in preparing to repel the blow that might at any moment be aimed at her by Prussia." He told Bernstorff with passion that Bismarck was engaging his country in the greatest of all wrongs, unjustifiable war, which he was certain would not have been contemplated by the King, a sincere Christian and a man of the highest honour, if the whole truth had been made known to him.

Such an appeal was not, however, likely to influence Bismarck, who was then presented with a suggestion that both Prussia and Austria should disarm. Bismarck, at first, promised that disarmament should proceed *pari passu* in both countries; but, finally (on April 26th), he declared that Prussian action must be contingent on the complete disarmament of Austria against Italy also: with the result that within a week general mobilisation was in progress in all three countries. Since General de La Marmora had, with singular frankness, repeatedly told the British Minister at Florence that "as soon as war was declared between Austria and Prussia he would declare it against Austria[3]," this condition, which Bismarck had sought to impose, offered the clearest proof both of the identity of interest between Prussia and Italy and of the determination of the former to push the dispute to extremes without further loss of time. The chance that war might be avoided by any agreement or compromise was now exceedingly slight; for, as the history of the nineteenth century has shown, the almost inevitable sequel of mobilisation is war. The Emperor Napoleon, however, whose efforts had hitherto been mainly confined to clearing the way to war

[1] Clarendon to Loftus, No. 33, March 24th, 1866.
[2] Clarendon to Loftus, No. 42, April 4th, 1866.
[3] Clarendon to Loftus, No. 81, April 29th, 1866.

for two of the prospective combatants, pressed forward a proposal for a European congress. It is doubtful whether the Emperor expected, either that a congress would be held, or that, if held, it would be successful in averting war; but it could not do France any harm, and would give the French Representative an opportunity of explaining more precisely what the Emperor had meant by his pointed reference at Auxerre, on May 6th, to the detestation with which he and the majority of French people regarded the Treaties of 1815, "*dont on voudrait faire aujourd'hui l'unique base de notre politique extérieure.*"

Clarendon doubted, from the outset, whether a congress offered a reasonable prospect of effecting the purpose for which it would be convoked. He objected that it would be powerless to enforce its decisions, and again suggested the employment of the means recommended by the Paris Protocol of 1856. Great Britain, France and Russia should appeal jointly to the prospective combatants to resume the *status quo*. The French thought that better results would be achieved by presenting a programme which had been settled in advance by the three Powers, and was accompanied by a joint declaration of their "firm intention" to solve the international difficulties in the direction of peace. Clarendon considered that the words "firm intention" might suggest a course of action which his Government did not intend to pursue, while the French argued, with some force, that to make it clear from the outset that no armed intervention was contemplated under any circumstances would ensure the futility of any offer of mediation.

The proposal for a congress was finally accepted by Great Britain and Russia, and invitations were sent out on May 24th. They were addressed to the Germanic Confederation as well as to the three principal parties to the dispute, and the object to be attained was thus defined. "It is proposed in the interests of peace to settle by means of diplomacy the question of the Elbe Duchies, that of the Italian dispute and, thirdly, that of the reforms to be introduced into the Federal Pact, as far as they may affect the balance of power in Europe." The vague phrase, "the Italian dispute," was understood to include the Venetian question, but expressly to exclude all discussion respecting the guarantee of the Temporal Power of the Pope. No preliminary condition of demobilisation was insisted upon, but a hope was expressed that military preparations would be suspended while the congress was sitting. Prussia and Italy accepted without conditions. Bismarck, as always, was careful to act with formal correctness towards Europe; and the event proved that he was right in taking the apparent risk of seeing his plans overthrown. For Austria accepted only with a proviso which was regarded by the inviting Powers as a refusal. She demanded that the congress should exclude from its deliberations any arrangement which would give to any one of the States invited any accession of territory or any increase of power. This condition excluded any arrangement such as the proposal—privately favoured by Clarendon—by which Austria would cede Venetia to Italy, and would renounce any claims to the Elbe Duchies in favour of Prussia, while receiving Silesia in exchange from the latter Power. Austria had definitely determined not to cede Venetia without war; though the Secret Treaty concluded with the Emperor Napoleon on June 12th showed that, at the moment, she considered her interests in Germany more vital than those in Italy, as she undertook to cede Venetia, if successful in conquering Silesia. Clarendon had strongly warned Austria against refusal; since, in contrast with the acceptance of the two other Powers, it would throw upon her the technical responsibility for the ensuing rupture, and divert public opinion abroad from the Prussian designs. British opinion had, in fact, been deeply exasperated against Prussia, and Bernstorff had constantly, during the spring, warned his Sovereign of the general hostility which he encountered in London.

The last steps to war were now speedily taken. On June 7th Prussian troops entered Holstein in answer to the proclamation by which Gablenz, the Austrian Commander, had convoked the Estates of the Duchy. On June 10th, Bismarck proclaimed his far-reaching aims by publishing the draft of a new Federal Constitution for Germany, from which Austria was to be excluded.

The neutrality of Great Britain in the ensuing struggle had been generally accepted as a matter of course both at home and abroad. It is true that the Queen had expressed her opinion, in a Memorandum written at her desire on March 30th, that Austria should be given armed support; while Lord Russell had also inclined to the same view, if Austria had been prepared to sacrifice Venetia. But no Cabinet, of whatever party complexion, would have advised participation in a war in which no British interests were directly affected—and least of all the discredited and moribund Liberal Administration, which, on June 19th, actually resigned office, in consequence of a defeat in the House of Commons in Committee on the Reform Bill. This resignation aroused the indignation of the Queen, whose intense interest in the struggle, due to both political and personal reasons, made her consider the crisis at home as inconsiderable, especially when viewed in the light of the general apathy in the country towards Reform. Lord Russell, however, declined to accept her view that he was acting inconsistently with the duty which he owed herself and the country, and refused to reconsider his resignation.

She then endeavoured, but without success, to induce Clarendon to remain at the Foreign Office as a member of the Conservative Government which Lord Derby finally succeeded in forming on July 6th. It was, indeed, unfortunate that a change of Government should have taken place at this moment. The new Ministry, faced by a minority of 70 in the House of Commons, could not expect to speak with authority abroad. But the accession of Lord Stanley to the Foreign Office brought no change to British policy. He was, it is true, comparatively inexperienced, exceedingly cautious and unwilling to commit himself or the country; and the Queen had suggested the fear, on his appointment, that he might be inclined to go too far in the line of non-intervention. Nor can his temperament, as sketched by Disraeli a year later, be said to suggest the qualities requisite in a successful diplomatist. He wrote to the Queen (August 16th, 1867) that "although Lord Stanley is of a reserved and rather morose temper, and will not go out of his way to confess that he has been in error, he is really *au fond* truthful and impartial, and, if convinced that he has erred or miscalculated, is never blind to the result, and often unavowedly, to a certain degree perhaps unconsciously, will assuredly modify his conduct." Yet it is impossible to see how Clarendon could have enabled the country to play a more active and influential part in the settlement which followed.

For the rapidity and completeness of the Prussian triumph made any attempt at mediation between the victor and the vanquished completely futile, unless backed by a determination to employ force, as the Emperor Napoleon found to his cost. Moreover, no British statesman of either party seems to have had any clear idea as to what resettlement of Germany would be compatible or incompatible with British or European interests. It was generally assumed that Prussia was simply following her traditional method of territorial aggrandisement and that, if successful, she would swallow up some more pieces of Germany; but, until the terms of peace were presented to Austria, no one, with the exception of Sir Robert Morier[1], seems to have

[1] See *Memoirs and Letters of Sir R. Morier*, vol. II. ch. xix.

perceived clearly that the aim of Bismarck was to create a united Germany, or to have considered how the new creation would affect the Balance of Power in Europe. It was indeed recognised that the Germanic Confederation, as part of the Vienna Settlement, was legally under the guarantee of the Signatory Powers, and that any alteration might be held to require their preliminary assent. Curiously enough, Russia, without whose consent, given or implied, Bismarck could never have embarked on the War, proposed a joint declaration by Great Britain, France and Russia, to the effect that Prussia could neither dissolve the Germanic Confederation nor form another without the consent of all the Great Powers[1]. Russia cannot have wished to preserve the existing Germanic Confederation, and was probably anxious to discover what would be the attitude of the British Government. Lord Stanley, while declining the Russian proposal, stated that armed intervention would be in any case impossible. The policy of the Government, in short, was to wait on events—and, indeed, no other policy was at the moment possible—but no attempt was made to think out what changes would be desirable for British interests in Central Europe, and what would be the position in the new European system of an Austria deprived of influence both in Italy and Germany, and of a united Germany controlled by Prussia.

Disraeli was, indeed, beginning to point out to his countrymen that British Foreign Policy was growing to be imperial rather than European. In his speech on reelection he said:

"The abstention of England from any unnecessary interference in the affairs of Europe is the consequence, not of her decline of power but of her increased strength. England is no longer a mere European Power; she is the metropolis of a great maritime empire, extending to the boundaries of the furthest ocean. It is not because England has taken refuge in a state of apathy that she now almost systematically declines to interfere in the affairs of the Continent of Europe. England is as ready and as willing to interfere as in old days when the necessity of her position requires it. There is no Power, indeed, that interferes more than England. She interferes in Asia, because she is really more an Asiatic Power than a European. She interferes in Australia, in Africa, and New Zealand, where she carries on war often on a great scale. Therefore, it is not because England does not recognise her duty to interfere in the affairs of the Continent of Europe that persons are justified in declaring that she has relinquished her imperial position, and has taken refuge in the *otium cum dignitate* which agrees with the decline of life, of power, and of prosperity. On the contrary, she has a greater sphere of action than any European Power, and she has duties

---

[1] From Buchanan, unnumbered, July 7th, 1866.

devolving upon her on a much larger scale. Not that we can ever look with indifference upon what takes place on the Continent. We are interested in the peace and prosperity of Europe, and I do not say that there may not be occasions on which it may be the duty of England to interfere in European wars."

The emphasis in this passage is obviously laid rather on the point that the interests of the empire are not primarily European, than on the prior truth that its security rests on the existence of a favourable Balance of Power in Europe.

The Government found no difficulty in meeting the terms of the Treaty of Prague with a ready acquiescence. The Queen had, indeed, shown much concern at the plight of the fugitive King of Hanover, but was persuaded by Disraeli and the King of Prussia that it would be unwise to permit him to find a refuge in England. When Russia proposed to Prussia that a European congress should be held to discuss the post-War settlement, Lord Stanley declined to support the Russian demand, and it was not seriously pressed. He had already stated in the House of Commons (July 20th) that he could not see how the establishment of a strong compact Power in northern Germany would be either a detriment or a menace to Great Britain, whatever it might be deemed to be by other Powers. From these last words it is clear that British anxieties were beginning to be diverted from Prussia towards the probable attitude of France.

When Thiers exclaimed in the French Chamber, "It is France that has been defeated at Sadowa," he was emphasising two points whose overwhelming importance appealed instinctively to French public opinion. That duality in Germany, whose existence the French had always regarded as a pledge of their security or an opportunity for their advantage, was gravely threatened. It is true that the Treaty of Prague permitted to any future Confederation of the southern States "an international independent existence"; but how were they to be prevented from falling under the exclusive influence if not the direct control of Prussia? Moreover, Prussia herself, the triumphant head of the new centralised North-German Confederation, had added to her dominions 4,000,000 inhabitants. The Emperor Napoleon, after the failure of the Benedetti negotiations, made it clear by parting with Drouyn de Lhuys (September 1st, 1866), that he intended, at least for the present, to accept the Treaty of Prague, and that, if territorial compensation was to be sought for France, it would not be looked for in German territory. The alarm which Disraeli expressed in a letter to Lord Stanley (December 30th, 1866) as to the existence of secret French designs against the independence of Belgium was, indeed, well justified, as was proved by the subsequent publication by Bismarck of the draft Treaty, in Benedetti's handwriting, which provided for the French annexation of that country. (The vigilant anxiety of British Ministers for the integrity of Belgium during the next four critical years will be considered later, in connexion with the steps taken to secure it during the Franco-Prussian War.)

The Emperor Napoleon, however, in order to satisfy public opinion, and in particular the indignation of the Army, which was intense, required some immediate and tangible territorial advantage. In February, 1867, he entered into negotiations with Bismarck and the King of the Netherlands for the transfer to France of the grand-duchy of Luxemburg. This territory, although quite small in both extent and population, offered considerable advantages. Its strategic value was high: in French hands it would render extremely difficult any hostile advance through Belgium, while facilitating a French advance down the valley of the Moselle towards Coblenz. The Emperor declared to Lord Cowley that he required it solely for the security of France, and not from any prompting of *amour propre*. Further, the position of the grand-duchy after the War was extremely anomalous. Previously a member of the then dissolved Germanic Confederation, it formed no part of that Confederation's North-German successor; but its fortress was still garrisoned by Prussian troops under Treaties concluded between Prussia and Holland in 1816 and 1856. Its Sovereign was the King of the Netherlands; but the grand-duchy enjoyed a separate existence; its inhabitants were believed to have French sympathies, and the King, who needed money, was supposed to be ready to part with it[1]. Bismarck appeared to entertain no objection to the transfer, provided that the bargain was kept secret until its completion. Lord Stanley, when consulted on the subject by the French Ambassador, replied that the French acquisition seemed to him a cheap price for ensuring the Peace of Europe; and there seemed no reason to suppose that any objections would be made by Austria or Russia, the other guarantors of the Treaties of 1839, by which the grand-duchy was assigned to the King of the Netherlands. To the dismay of the British Government, the proposed transfer, which had

---

[1] The French Ambassador told Lord Stanley that it was only at the request of the King of the Netherlands that France had entered into the negotiations. (To Cowley, No. 109, April 10th, 1867.)

seemed a promising means for preserving peace between France and Germany, suddenly developed into an imminent threat of war. The question was raised in the *Reichstag* on April 1st, probably without the connivance of Bismarck, who had consistently warned Benedetti of the dangers of premature publicity. Bismarck immediately gave expression to the outburst of national feeling in Germany, and declared that the Emperor Napoleon's attitude had caused "the question to become one of German national honour; the position of Prussia in Germany is involved, and that is well worth fighting for[1]." In point of fact, neither Bismarck nor the Emperor desired a war at this moment, and the acquisition of the grand-duchy was no longer left open to France, since the King of the Netherlands refused his consent so soon as he became aware of the state of German feeling on the subject. But, considering the relations between the two Governments and the feelings of the two nations, it was exceedingly difficult to avoid war without calling in the offices of a third party. Thus, Bismarck, when writing to Bernstorff and using the words quoted above, threw out a hint that he would not object to see the question discussed by a European congress; and the French Ambassador, on April 12th, appealed to the good offices of Great Britain, while giving Lord Stanley to understand that the danger to France lay in the occupation of the fortress by the Prussian garrison, whose withdrawal might make a friendly arrangement possible[2]. The question was thus reduced to the narrow limit as to whether Prussia should or should not maintain in the fortress a garrison, whose presence, as Bismarck afterwards admitted, was not, in his opinion, legally justified, though it suited him at the moment to maintain that the Treaty of 1816 between Prussia and Holland was a complete justification of it. On April 19th, Lord Stanley telegraphed to Lord A. Loftus:

"If the question is really reduced to these limits, it is deserving the consideration of Prussia whether she should not make so small a sacrifice· since her hesitation to do so would seem to countenance the notion that she wishes to keep Luxemburg for aggressive purposes against France and so to justify the urgency of the French Government to obtain security in that quarter. France is understood only to seek such security without insisting on any other point in regard to Luxemburg than that it should not be used for hostile purposes against herself. Speak in this sense to Count Bismarck and ascertain his views. Her Majesty's Government would

---

[1] To Cowley, No. 92, April 5th, 1867, giving the substance communicated to Stanley by Bernstorff of a despatch from Bismarck.
[2] To Cowley, No. 111, April 12th, 1867. "Most confidential."

see with deep regret the breaking out of a war for an occasion apparently so trifling, which could not but retard the consolidation of Germany."

After another week of negotiation, during which Austria actively used her influence to preserve the peace, the hesitations of Bismarck were overcome. He declared that Prussia accepted a conference, at which she could make concessions to Europe and Holland on behalf of peace, which she could not make to France, and on this account could not accept any preconcerted basis for the conference. Lord A. Loftus, however, confidently stated that Prussia would accept the neutralisation of the grand-duchy and withdraw her garrison, if the fortress were placed under a European guarantee[1]. On the same day, he confirmed and expanded this acceptance in a telegram to Bernstorff in which he stated that Prussia was "prepared to concede the evacuation and rasing of the fortress, if the Conference expresses the wish that she should do so, and at the same time gives a European guarantee for the neutrality of Luxemburg, such as now exists in the case of Belgium." Such a declaration removed all serious obstacles to the meeting of a conference. But Lord Stanley was extremely uneasy at the thought of "giving any fresh guarantee in the actual state of public opinion which prevails in this country[2]." The existing responsibilities of Great Britain with regard to Belgium had already aroused his apprehension, and he had written to Disraeli:

"I am ready to go as far as may be necessary in support of Belgium, short of giving an absolute pledge to fight for its independence. Suppose we gave such a pledge, that France and Prussia came to an understanding, Russia and Austria standing aloof, where should we be?[3]"

He, accordingly, suggested as a basis for the proposed treaty that, as Luxemburg was already guaranteed to the King of the Netherlands by the Treaties of 1839, he should engage not to alienate it without the consent of all the Powers[4]. When this proposal proved generally unacceptable, he suggested that Luxemburg might be declared neutral, without being the subject of a special guarantee. It was, however, evident that Bismarck would not consent to a conference, unless the neutrality of Luxemburg were guaranteed by all the Powers. Lord Stanley was therefore compelled to abandon his objections. The Conference met on May 7th in London, and was attended by Plenipotentiaries from all the Powers who had signed the Treaties of 1839,

---

[1] From Loftus, No. 181, April 27th, 1867.
[2] To Cowley, No. 189, April 27th, 1867.
[3] Buckle, *Life of B. Disraeli, Earl of Beaconsfield*, IV. 471.
[4] To Cowley, No. 227, May 3rd, 1867.

and from Italy, who thus received that formal recognition of her status as one of the Great Powers to which Cavour had looked forward as the logical sequel to the appearance of the Piedmontese Representatives in Paris in 1856. It was agreed that the Prussian garrison should be withdrawn from the fortress of Luxemburg, which was to be demolished. The grand-duchy itself was declared to be a perpetually neutral State, and its neutrality was placed "under the sanction of the collective guarantee of the Powers signing the present Treaty, with the exception of Belgium, which is itself a neutral State" (Article II, Treaty of London). Moreover, Luxemburg, unlike Belgium, was placed under no obligation to defend her neutrality, and was indeed prevented from doing so, since by Article III the King of the Netherlands as Grand-duke undertook to maintain no fortresses within the territory, and only so many troops as were necessary for the preservation of order. In view of the demand made by Bismarck that the conference should give "a European guarantee for the neutrality of Luxemburg such as now exists in the case of Belgium," it is important to ascertain what obligations British statesmen, then and subsequently, considered themselves to be assuming. Lord Stanley told the House of Commons that he had assented to this provision with more doubt and anxiety than he had ever felt on any public question, but asserted that the guarantee involved only a "limited liability"; while Lord Derby amplified his son's language in the House of Lords (July 4th, 1867) by emphasising the difference between a collective and a separate and several guarantee:

"A several guarantee binds each of the parties to do its utmost individually to enforce the observance of the guarantee. A collective guarantee is one which is binding on all the parties collectively; but which, if any difference of opinion should arise, no one of them can be called upon to take upon itself the task of vindicating by force of arms."

A collective guarantee, thus interpreted, implies no more than an engagement by each of the Signatory Powers to respect the neutrality of a State so guaranteed, with the liberty, but not the obligation, to regard any violation as a *casus belli*; the British Government had therefore, in reality, pledged itself no further than it would have done by Lord Stanley's first suggestion, which not only Prussia but the other Powers represented at the Conference had declared insufficient. Lord Derby proceeded to point out that the Treaties of 1839, on the other hand, provided Belgium with a separate guarantee from each of the five Signatory Powers, and that Prussia must have been well aware of the difference between the two engagements when she signed the Treaty of London. This interpretation of the practical difference between the two Treaties seems to have been accepted as a matter of course by British statesmen. Viscount Grey, at the outbreak of War in 1914, treated it as a matter of common knowledge that Great Britain was bound to engage in a single-handed defence of Belgium, but was not so bound in the case of Luxemburg. A comparison, however, of the text of the two Treaties, of 1839 and 1867, by no means bears out this clear distinction, from which such vitally important results have flowed. Article II of the Treaty of London of 1839 speaks simply of "the guarantee" of the Signatory Powers—omitting the word "collective" but not inserting the word "joint and several." But this latter is a technical diplomatic term, which was actually inserted in the Treaty signed by Great Britain, Austria and France on April 14th, 1856, by which "the high contracting parties guarantee, jointly and severally, the independence and the integrity of the Ottoman Empire." Such an omission, therefore, makes it appear that legally the value of the guarantee of 1867 was precisely that of the guarantee of 1839; that Prussia was justified in supposing that she had actually obtained the result that had been implied in her demands; and finally that, if the guarantee to Luxemburg meant only what Lord Derby asserted, then that to Belgium had no higher legal value. The practical difference between the two may be considered to amount to this: Great Britain would always regard the violation of Belgium neutrality as a *casus belli*, because she would always view the integrity and independence of Belgium as a vital interest[1], and could always render that country direct assistance by sea; whereas neither of these considerations applied to Luxemburg.

The Queen pointed out with truth to Disraeli that, while the British action in preventing war had restored to the country much of its lost prestige, yet the most likely method of provoking the violation of a neutral State was to use language which suggested that Great Britain regarded her guarantees as a dead letter. In point of fact, a vigorous British protest was lodged when, in December, 1870, Bismarck declared that Prussia no longer felt bound to respect the neutrality of Luxemburg, in view of the use which the French had been permitted to make of the grand-duchy for military purposes.

---

[1] Compare the language used by Gladstone in the House of Commons, August, 1870: "We have an interest in the independence of Belgium which is wider than that which we may have in the literal operation of the guarantee."

As Bismarck in reply stated that he had no intention of denouncing the Treaty of London, nor entertained any design of annexing Luxemburg, the matter was allowed to drop.

II. *The Abyssinian Expedition*, 1868

Although the Conservative Government during the remainder of its tenure of office were not faced with any further complications in Europe, it won, deservedly, great credit for its successful handling of the Abyssinian Expedition, of which the object was to release the British captives whom Theodore, the Negus, or supreme King, of the country, had detained in his hands since November, 1863. Theodore, who maintained with difficulty and great cruelty the position which he had usurped in 1855, had been in the habit of seeking the society of British Consuls at Massowah, who had been appointed since 1848 for the protection of British trade with Abyssinia and the countries adjacent thereto. They had no official status in the country, since Theodore had always refused to ratify a Treaty which Consul Plowden had negotiated with his predecessor, providing for mutual representation. But Consul Plowden, who had become one of the King's most intimate friends, was killed while assisting him against a rebellion in Abyssinia; and his successor, Cameron, in spite of warnings from Lord John Russell as to his not holding the position of a diplomatic Representative, also spent much of his time at Theodore's Court. In the spring of 1863, Cameron forwarded to the Foreign Office a letter from the King to Queen Victoria proposing an Embassy and an alliance against the Turks, although he had been expressly warned that no Embassy would be received from him until he had given up his hostile designs against Turkey and Egypt. This letter remained unanswered, and Theodore retaliated by throwing Cameron into prison. Apart from the slight to his vanity, the King seems to have feared that Great Britain would join Egypt in an attack on his independence, and discovered a further grievance in the fact that Abyssinian pilgrims to Jerusalem were being treated by the Turkish authorities as Turkish subjects, whereas he considered that Lord Malmesbury had promised them in 1852 the protection of the British Consul[1]. He was confirmed

---

[1] Lord Malmesbury's actual Instructions had been that, while the British Government could not undertake officially to protect Abyssinians residing in Turkish territory, yet the British Consul was, in case of need, to use his good offices on their behalf "as members of a Christian Church in spiritual communion with the Established Church in this Country."

in his suspicions by an intercepted despatch to Cameron, which ordered the latter to return at once to Massowah and to cease from interfering in Abyssinian affairs. Ten European missionaries, of whom two were women, were joined with Cameron in captivity, and were treated intermittently with extreme cruelty: they believed themselves to have excited the King's displeasure by commenting unfavourably on his wholesale massacre of rebels. In 1865, the captives still remained in Theodore's hands, and public opinion began to demand that effectual steps should be taken to secure their release. An abortive attempt had been made in February to use the Abouna, or Christian Bishop, of the country as an intermediary for the purpose. Lord Russell rejected the notion of force, writing on June 8th: "I cannot think that it would be wise to send a military expedition to attack the King of Abyssinia. I know not how we could reach him in that way"; and decided to send an official British Mission. Accordingly, Rassam, an Armenian by birth who had received an English education, and held the post of First Assistant to the Resident at Aden, was sent to Massowah, with a letter from Queen Victoria to Theodore, affecting not to know of Cameron's imprisonment and promising that the King should be permitted to send an Embassy when the Consul had returned to England. In September, 1865, Rassam received an invitation from Theodore to proceed to Abyssinia, and after many delays was received, on February 7th, 1868, by the King, who immediately released Cameron and all the other prisoners. Rassam was delighted; "Nothing" he wrote, "could exceed King Theodore's courteous and polite behaviour"; and the whole matter seemed to be successfully concluded. On April 13th, however, the King suddenly ordered the rearrest of the liberated prisoners, and placed Rassam and the remainder of his Mission under confinement. Theodore, whose diseased mind was influenced by an intense suspiciousness bordering on insanity, apparently believed that, if he allowed his captives to leave the country, the British Government would on their safe return send an expedition to attack him. He, therefore, determined to retain them as hostages until he had a satisfactory reply to his original offer of an alliance with the Queen, and to take advantage of the opportunity for procuring from England a number of skilled artisans, desired by him for the development of his country. The Government, with extraordinary forbearance, acting on the advice of the Resident at Aden, Colonel Merewether, who was then in London, advised the Queen to give an audience to the German missionary who brought Theodore's demand to England, and sent presents of machinery for Theodore to Aden, together with a number of artisans, who had been induced to go to Abyssinia by a guarantee against financial loss given by the Government. Theodore, however, returned no answer to the intimation that they would be placed at his disposal when the captives reached Aden; but merely removed these to the inaccessible and rockbound fortress of Magdala. In October, 1866, Lord Stanley asked the War Office to consider the possibilities of a military expedition; though expressing his real feelings in a letter to Disraeli: "I sincerely hope the W.O. will find the country inaccessible. I think they will." No further action was taken until April, 1867, in the belief that Theodore, who was surrounded with rebels, might be overthrown and the captives in consequence released. On April 16th, Lord Stanley forwarded through Aden an ultimatum to Theodore, warning him that, if the prisoners were not restored within three months from the despatch of the letter, all friendship between him and the Queen must cease. No answer was returned by him to this communication. On August 19th, it was decided that an Expedition should be immediately despatched from Bombay, the Governor of that province having already drawn up plans under the Instructions of Sir Stafford Northcote, Secretary of State for India. The Instructions given to Sir Robert Napier, who was placed in command of this force, show extremely clearly the objects which the Government had in view. His primary object was to be to secure the release of Cameron, Rassam and all the other official persons detained by Theodore, and he was, also, to use his best endeavours to secure the release of all other Europeans in captivity, whether British citizens or not, though he was not to prolong the Expedition for that purpose. Theodore was not to be deprived of any portion of his territory, nor to be forced to make any concession, pecuniary or other. While Napier might take advantage of the existence of any hostility to the King in Abyssinia, he was not to wage war in order to set up a pretender in a country where there were really no British interests to promote. If Theodore fell into the hands of the Expeditionary Force, he was to be sent to Bombay. Lord Stanley concluded by remarking that, "Her Majesty's Government have no concern with what might befall Abyssinia by the removal of Theodore from the country. The lesson to be taught to rulers of his character and their peoples is that wanton outrages to British Subjects will sooner or later bring down upon the perpetrators of them signal retribution." It is not within the scope of the present work to describe the Expedition, which was handled throughout with the greatest ability and met with a complete and almost bloodless success. Theodore, who had taken no notice of a last warning letter sent him by the Khedive of Egypt after the Expedition had actually started, recognising the impossibility of resistance, killed himself in Magdala, on the day before the British troops entered and found the prisoners all unharmed (April 13th, 1868). Within a week they were beginning their withdrawal from Abyssinian territory.

Great Britain had acted in this protracted affair with a combination of extreme patience and rapid energy. Four years had elapsed between the imprisonment of Cameron and the entrance of British soldiers on Abyssinian soil; but within five months they had overcome all the geographical and climatic difficulties, and were masters of a fortress, which all who were acquainted with it had described as impregnable. It is certain that the impression of irresistible power produced in India, where the Expedition had been organised, powerfully enhanced British prestige, which Sir Henry Rawlinson so aptly described as "the power which enables us to achieve very great results with very small means at our immediate disposal." Disraeli was fully justified in calling the attention of Parliament to the disinterestedness which had throughout characterised our action. When the Expedition was starting, he had stated that its object was "not to obtain territory, not to secure commercial advantages, but for high moral causes and for high moral causes alone." On its completion, he repeated that,

"when it was first announced that England was about to embark on a most costly and perilous expedition, merely to vindicate the honour of our Sovereign, and to rescue from an unjust but remote captivity a few of our fellow-subjects, the announcement was received in more than one country with something like mocking incredulity. But we have asserted the purity of our purpose. In an age accused, and perhaps not unjustly, of selfishness, and a too great regard for material interests, it is something, in so striking and significant a manner, for a great nation to have vindicated the higher principles of humanity. It is a privilege to belong to a country which has done such deeds."

The mass of papers preserved among the records of the Expedition, which emphasise the importance of developing British trade in Abyssinia and describe the richness of the mineral deposits, prove that Ministers did not adhere to their disinterested policy from lack of inducements to depart from it.

III. *The Franco-German War*, 1870

The Abyssinian success, however, did not prevent the Liberals from obtaining a large majority in the new electorate at the General Election held in the autumn of that year (1868). Gladstone became head of a powerful and active Government, and Lord Clarendon returned once more to his old post. But the latter appointment was not made until objections from a most unexpected quarter had been overcome. In 1866, the Queen had been so unwilling to part with Clarendon as Foreign Secretary as to write that she "cannot express *too strongly* her *hope* and earnest wish that Lord Clarendon may find himself enabled to accede to the proposal, which the Queen knows Lord Derby will make to him, of remaining in his present office" (June 28th, 1866). But, two years later, we find from Lord Halifax's *Journal*[1] that she desired to place an absolute veto on his name for that post. An entry there, for November 26th, states that

"The essential part of the Queen's message was her objection to Clarendon as Foreign Secretary. She told Charles[2] that he was the only one of her Ministers who had ever been impertinent to her, and that she could not submit to him in the position of Foreign Secretary which brought him into such constant communication with herself; that he was too intimate with the Queen of Holland and was influenced by her, and that his opinions against the German unity and views of Russia, which she considered so right and necessary, rendered him unfit for that post on public grounds. She said that both Clarendon and Lowe were very sarcastic, and she did not like such people in intimate communication with her."

It was fortunate that the Queen's opposition, which appears at bottom to have rested on some personal pique, was overcome. Lord Clarendon was the only British diplomatist who possessed a European reputation; and so far was he from desiring to break the continuity of our Foreign Policy that he tells us himself that on taking office he had "a long official talk with Stanley, who was most friendly and communicative. I did not detect a shade of difference of opinion between us[3]." In fact, the Memorandum which was presented by Gladstone to General Grey for the information of the Queen (April 17th, 1869) furnishes an exposition of the principles which should govern the relations of Great

---

[1] Quoted in Sir H. Maxwell's *Life of Lord Clarendon*, II. 353.
[2] General the Hon. Charles Grey, her Private Secretary.
[3] Sir H. Maxwell's *Life of Lord Clarendon*, II. 355.

Britain to Europe very similar to that laid down by Disraeli in his speech quoted above[1]. He writes:

"I do not believe that England ever will or can be unfaithful to her great tradition, or can forswear her interest in the common transactions and the general interests of Europe. But her credit and her power form a fund which, in order that they may be made the most of, should be thriftily used...."

And he adds:

"As I understand Lord Clarendon's ideas, they are fairly represented by his very important diplomatic communications since he has taken office. They proceed upon such grounds as these: That England should keep entire in her own hands the means of estimating her own obligations upon the various states of facts as they arise; that she should not foreclose and narrow her own liberty of choice by declarations made to the Powers, in their real or supposed interests, of which they would claim to be at least joint interpreters; that it is dangerous for her to assume alone an advanced, and therefore an isolated position, in regard to European controversies; that, come what may, it is better for her to promise too little than too much; that she should not encourage the weak by giving expectations of aid to resist the strong, but should rather seek to deter the strong by firm but moderate language from aggression on the weak; that she should seek to develop and mature the action of a common, or public or European opinion, as the best standing bulwark against wrong, but should beware of seeming to lay down the law of that opinion by her own authority, and thus running the risk of setting against her, and against right and justice, that general sentiment which ought to be, and generally would be, arrayed in their favour. I am persuaded that at this juncture opinions of this colour being true and sound, are also the only opinions which the country is disposed to approve. But I do not believe that on that account it is one whit less disposed than it has been at any time, to cast in its lot upon any fitting occasion with the cause it believes to be right."

Meanwhile, the relations between France and Prussia remained inevitably the central problem of European diplomacy. The publication by Bismarck (March, 1867) of the Treaties of Alliance with the southern States, and the wave of national excitement which swept all over Germany at the time of the Luxemburg incident, proved how shadowy were the guarantees of the Treaty of Prague for the independent existence of the south, and suggested that the surest method of cementing a German Unity, which to all impartial observers now seemed inevitable, would be a war against France for an object common

[1] See for this letter or memorandum Lord Morley's *Life of Gladstone*, II. 316–318, where it is described as "in truth a sort of charter of the leading principles of Mr Gladstone's foreign policy at the moment when he first incurred supreme responsibility for our foreign affairs."

to all Germans. Many reasons combined to draw closer the relations between Great Britain and France. Lord Clarendon was a personal friend of the Emperor Napoleon, who regarded him with complete confidence[1]; while Lord Lyons proved an extremely able successor to Lord Cowley, who had shown himself during his fifteen years of office (1852–67) to be the most effective of contemporary British Ambassadors. The Emperor, throughout all the windings of his policy, attached the highest importance to preserving British friendship. Clarendon regarded the continuance of the Napoleonic empire as the only guarantee against the evil of high tariff walls between the two countries, and was suspicious of the transformation into a Parliamentary system which was gradually taking place in the government of France[2]. Further, he hoped to prevent the Emperor from either tampering with the independence of Belgium, or making war on Prussia to secure popular opinion for the support of his tottering dynasty. In its continuance he had little confidence, and he expressed his opinion, in August, 1869, that the French "will drift into a Republic before another year is over." As to the unification of Germany, he did not believe it to be imminent, but expected that it would prove a gradual and inevitable process.

"I agree with you (he wrote to Lyons, March 3rd, 1870) that Prussia will never declare that she will not complete the unity of Germany, because she looks on it as inevitable. Nothing, as the King himself said to me, can prevent the gravitation of the weak towards the strong, but that it would not take place in his life, possibly not in that of his son. France if not grown wiser by that time will probably consider it as a *casus belli*...and she would weld all Germany together as one man if she attempted by force to prevent Bavaria, Württemberg and Baden from joining the North, when they had determined that it was for their own interest to do so."

There was little interchange of real confidence between Berlin and London; although Clarendon did not believe that Prussia meant war, he felt the deepest distrust of Bismarck, whom he had described in 1864 as "a man without faith or law." He saw clearly that, while

[1] Cf. Lord Lyons to Lord Stanley, October 20th, 1868. The Emperor told Clarendon in strict confidence of a proposal which he had not, he said, mentioned even to his Ministers. Men of weight (*des hommes sérieux*) had proposed a Confederation between the south-German States and Switzerland. (See Lord Newton, *Lord Lyons*, I. 204.)

[2] See Lyons's letter to Clarendon, December 3rd, 1869: "I am afraid we shall never again, either in political or commercial affairs, have as good times as we had under the personal power of the Emperor—by *we* of course I mean the English"; to which Lord Clarendon replied: "I quite agree with you that we shall never have such good times again under a Parliamentary instead of a personal régime." (Lord Newton, *Lord Lyons*, I. 240–1.)

France and Prussia persisted in their competition of armaments, peace must remain at the mercy of an incident, so soon as one or other party believed itself to be momentarily possessed of a clear superiority. The King of Prussia had always, in spite of his real desire for peace, shown himself no less unapproachable than Bismarck on this subject; but the Emperor Napoleon, with whom the Foreign Secretary had a conversation in September, 1869, proved more sympathetic. The rural population, the solid prop of the French empire, was growing more and more restive under the burden of taxation and conscription; and, so early as April, 1868, the Emperor's Government had informally suggested to Lord Stanley that Great Britain might "give advice" to Prussia on the subject of disarmament, which he had refused to do. The newly formed Ministry, which under Ollivier was to reconcile responsible government with the empire, made another essay in the same direction through La Valette, the French Ambassador at London (January 26th, 1870). Clarendon agreed to enter into the design, though it was clear that its handling required the most delicate tact. For, as Ollivier told Lord Lyons (January 30th) it was essential that the French Government should not be in any way compromised; since, "under present circumstances a public rebuff from Prussia would be fatal." "Un échec," he said, "c'est la guerre." He hoped, therefore, that Prussia might be led to agree with France on a simultaneous disarmament, or at least to receive a proposal from her in a friendly spirit. After obtaining the approval of the Queen and the Prime-Minister, but without communicating the matter to the Cabinet, Clarendon sent a Memorandum (February 2nd) which Lord A. Loftus was instructed to lay before Bismarck in strict confidence. This document, after pointing out the destructive and anachronistic burden which the enormous standing armies of Europe imposed on civilisation, suggested that Prussia, better than any other Power, might undertake to modify this system. Clarendon, therefore, hoped that, in spite of the King's "parental feeling and affection for his army," Bismarck would recommend to him a partial disarmament. The moment seemed highly propitious, as France had "never been more peacefully inclined than at the present time, under a responsible government which cannot make war for an idea, because it represents a nation that is determined to maintain peace so long as there is no just cause for war, and because the Emperor entirely shares the feelings of his people." He concluded by expressing his conviction that the French Government would raise no opposition to a reduction of the Army pari passu with Prussia.

In point of fact, the moment was very unpropitious for opening this question with Bismarck, who was becoming increasingly anxious as to whether the Treaties with the south-German States, his principal pledge of security, would be renewed when they expired in 1871. The fall of the Hohenlohe Cabinet in Bavaria (February 14th) and the unconcealed hostility of the King of Würtemberg, showed how substantial were his reasons for uneasiness. Moreover, as he pointed out with force in a conversation with Lord A. Loftus (February 5th) Prussia's geographical position made the taking of any initiative in the reduction of armaments far less feasible for her than for Great Britain. "Our position," he said, "is an exceptional one. We are surrounded by three great empires with Armies as large as our own, any two of whom might combine against us." He further remarked that Prussia's military strength was an advantage to Great Britain, as the events of 1869 had shown, when an occupation of Belgium would have taken place, had it not been known at Paris that Prussia would join in the defence of that country. He declared that he did not dare even to name the subject of Clarendon's letter to the King, "much less show it to His Majesty. He would get into a fury and immediately think that England was trying to weaken Prussia in the interests of France."

Daru, the French Foreign Minister, on hearing the substance of Bismarck's objections, expressed his determination to disarm, whether Prussia did so or not, and to propose to the Emperor a reduction of the yearly contingent from 100,000 to 90,000 men, which reduction he would have suggested to be even larger, if the accounts of Prussian intentions were more satisfactory (February 10th). This step would, he thought, furnish Clarendon with a powerful argument for persevering in his endeavours to work on Prussia. Clarendon was not discouraged, and renewed his attempt in a letter to Lord A. Loftus on March 9th. He tried to convince Bismarck that Prussia had nothing to fear from any of the three empires which surrounded her. Austria "could not, even on the most pressing emergency, bring 200,000 men into the field. Her finances are dilapidated and her internal disorganisation affords just cause for alarm." Bismarck had dwelt on the "hostility of the Muscovite party towards Germany and on the dislike of the Tsarevitch to everything German" which must cause a great change in the relations between Prussia and Russia after the death of Alexander. Clarendon replied that

"Count Bismarck must know better than myself that Russia has long since, and wisely, ceased to aim at influence in Germany or intervention in German affairs, and that all her energies are now directed eastwards, with a view of extending her territory and her commerce in Asia. Whatever sentiments may be suggested in other quarters by a rapid development of the present feeling of Russia, which has the entire support of public opinion in that country, it appears certain that Germany can have no danger to guard against from Russia, whatever may be the personal feelings or opinions of the reigning Sovereign."

In this assumption, Clarendon was hardly expressing his real feelings, since he had already told Lord Lyons that he believed it to be true that the Tsarevitch and the Slav races were very hostile to Germany. He proceeded to emphasise the importance of the reduction in the French Army to which the Emperor had assented, and added: "I venture to think that the present state of opinion in France, founded as it is upon a true estimate of French interests, is a more solid guarantee than any that the respective Governments of France and Germany could effect for their own security." His practical proposal, derived from a suggestion by Daru, was in favour of a general disarmament.

"The military forces of the great Continental Powers have a certain proportion to each other; in order to maintain that proportion, very heavy burdens are imposed upon each country; but if, by common agreement, each reduces its army by a certain number of men, the same proportions will be maintained, while the burdens, which are fast becoming intolerable, will be alleviated."

In reply, Bismarck naturally controverted the extravagant expectations which Clarendon based on the present disposition of the French people. In conversation with Lord A. Loftus (March 12th) he said that, "although the nation was now pacific, you know as well as I do that a war cry can be raised in France, on any emergency, and at the shortest notice. If...the present Constitutional government had been three years instead of three months in existence, then there would be some chance for its duration and for the maintenance of peace." At the present moment, he observed, there was a party anxious to restore the previous state of things, a personal government. That party included the Empress Eugénie, and they would not be sorry to divert the public attention from home affairs by raising some questions of foreign policy. Bismarck, however, on this occasion did not refuse to bring the matter to the notice of the King, and appeared to be less decidedly opposed to any disarmament. But any hope that King William might view the project with a favourable eye was quickly dashed. He stated his objections with a conclusive simplicity which made it impossible to continue the negotiations. The German Army could only be reduced in two ways: either by changing its legislative basis, and thereby its whole character, or by reducing the period of military service to two and a half years. The former method was impossible; the latter had been the subject of a five years' struggle between the King and his Parliament, and he would rather give up his Throne than yield on it. Moreover, as Bismarck had foretold, the King regarded the proposal as put forward in the interests of France, and as showing no regard for the safety of Prussia.

It is not surprising that this attempt should have failed. The whole interchange of views rested on a basis of unreality. The one supreme difficulty which barred the way to mutual confidence between France and Germany was never mentioned. Yet it was perfectly clear—to French and German as well as to disinterested observers—that the tension between the two countries must continue, until either France was satisfied that Prussia had no design of uniting Germany, or until Prussia was satisfied that France would not oppose such a Union by force. The character of an intrigue was thus inevitably thrust upon the negotiations themselves. The French Government was desperately anxious that Bismarck should not know that they had anything to do with the proposal, since such knowledge might lead to immediate war; while Bismarck, in return, professed great eagerness that the French Government should not be acquainted with it.

The preparations for a plebiscite which was to ratify the recent Constitutional changes in France provoked the uneasiness of Lyons, who feared that a failure or a small majority might turn the minds of the Ministers to war. Writing to Clarendon on May 6th, he said:

"With reference to Loftus's despatch, I sincerely hope that his most confidential informant is not so well informed as he represents himself to be, and that no change is really contemplated in the *status quo* of Hesse and Baden. It would be quite a mistake to suppose that this is a moment at which it would be safe to defy France. On the contrary, a war unmistakably provoked by Prussia would be hailed by many as a welcome diversion from internal difficulties. So far as I can judge, *Ollivier is not the man to shrink from one.*"

The overwhelming majority, however, which Ollivier's "devouring activity" secured two days later seemed a pledge of renewed confidence, and the last month of Clarendon's life offered no premonitions of the coming storm. He died suddenly on June 27th, only ten days before the Hohenzollern candidature became publicly known.

Lord Clarendon owed his great reputation at home and abroad less to his achievements than to his character. Passionately attached to peace—the French called him "*le commis voyageur de la paix*"—he was constantly to see wars gathering before his eyes, which his best efforts failed to prevent; of all his public utterances none is so firmly enshrined in the popular mind as his statement in 1854: "We are drifting into war." His personal reputation reached its height at the conclusion of the Congress of Paris, in which he had become the most prominent and popular figure. The Queen expressed a general feeling when she wrote: "We congratulate him on the success of his efforts in obtaining the peace, for to him alone it is due; and also to *him alone* is due the dignified position which the Queen's beloved country holds, and which she owes to a straightforward, steady and unselfish policy throughout." His European position was established, and was never afterwards shaken. Lord Augustus Loftus has described him as possessing all those qualities which mark the ideal diplomatist: "Courteous and dignified, with charming manners, he won the regard and confidence of all with whom he came in contact. Firm and courageous, with consummate judgment, he was neither open to flattery nor to the influence of fear." Gladstone dwelt on "his unswerving loyalty, his genial temper, his kindness ever overflowing in acts yet more than in words, his liberal and indulgent appreciation of others"; and estimated him to have been the "very easiest and most attractive" of all his colleagues in the Cabinet. His broad sympathies, and his effortless power of being happily at home in any society invested him with that personal attractiveness which helps in so important a measure to smooth the path of diplomacy. It is perhaps true that he was a better judge of men than of events, and that while he "understood how to dash off in a few daring if slightly contemptuous phrases the main features of a political situation and the leading traits of the European statesmen whom he had known," he was less successful and possibly less interested in forecasting the future developments of Europe. His influence was increased by his rare personal detachment: he was so far from desiring office that he accepted its burdens only with increasing reluctance, and has been well described as having been a member of successive Cabinets simply because he had proved himself indispensable. One of the highest compliments ever paid him was that posthumously bestowed by Bismarck, who told Lord Clarendon's daughter in 1871 that he was never in his life more glad to hear of anything than of her father's death, because if he had lived he would have prevented the War.

Lord Granville, whose very first duty in taking office was to attempt this task, had many of the personal qualities of his predecessor. He, too, was noted for his tactful, courteous and conciliatory address, which made him for more than thirty years so successful a leader of the Liberal minority in the House of Lords. He even surpassed Clarendon in the unusual command which both possessed of the French language. His previous direct experience of the Foreign Office amounted to less than three months; succeeding Palmerston, after the dismissal of the latter in December, 1851, he won the complete approval of Lord John Russell, who, on his retirement, expressed the somewhat extravagant belief that "the country will lose one of the best Foreign Secretaries it ever had." During the eighteen years which elapsed before his resumption of the office, Lord Granville had, however, exerted at intervals a remarkable influence over the course of British Foreign Policy. In 1856, he had been sent to Russia immediately after the conclusion of the Crimean War, as head of a Special Mission to attend the Coronation of the Tsar. The Queen, who placed entire confidence in his sagacity and moderation, twice employed him, when President of the Council, as her mouthpiece in the Cabinet to combat the views of Palmerston and Russell. In 1859, she urged upon him, in a private communication, the duty of controlling the Italian sympathies of his colleagues; and in 1864, in a still more urgent appeal, she begged him to prevent the country's becoming involved in the Schleswig-Holstein War. In September, 1862, he had, on his own initiative, taken the leading part in defeating the proposal made by Palmerston for a joint intervention with France in the American Civil War. He was, therefore, regarded in 1870 as the natural and inevitable successor to Clarendon. But his achievements were not equal to the expectations of his friends. Faced as he was throughout his two subsequent periods of office (1870–74, 1880–85) by a constant series of difficult problems directly affecting British interests, the responsibilities of office bore very heavily upon him. He was constantly (though often unjustly) accused of indifference or of imperfect sympathies; and, in the long run, his lack of decision contributed to involve the country in misunderstandings with several of the Great Continental Powers.

On the afternoon of July 5th, Granville, who was to receive the Seals next day, had a conversation at the Foreign Office with Hammond, the Permanent Under-Secretary. The latter assured him that he had never during his long experience known so great a lull in foreign affairs. This unforgotten false prophecy cannot be held to convict British diplomacy of any peculiar ignorance; for it was only on the 3rd that Paris knew definitely of the acceptance by Prince Leopold of

Hohenzollern-Sigmaringen of the offer of the Spanish Crown. It rather proves the extraordinary success with which Bismarck had matured his plan in secret. It is not necessary or indeed relevant to enter into a full discussion of the methods by which the Prince's reluctance to grant his consent was overcome. The full extent of Bismarck's responsibility for the decision, which could only be suspected in 1870, has gradually become known through a series of subsequent revelations. The British Government could only base its policy on such information as was obtainable at the time. The deposition of Queen Isabella on September 30th, 1868, had created a *de facto* republic in Spain, from which Marshal Prim, who had induced the Cortes to pass a monarchical Constitution, wished to rescue his distracted country as soon as possible. He had not been actuated by hostility towards France in the invitation to Prince Leopold, who was related to the Emperor Napoleon both by birth and marriage, and whose elder brother, Charles, had ascended the Roumanian throne in 1866 with the Emperor's goodwill. But Leopold proved very cautious. Although Lord A. Loftus reported that the Prince was being mentioned in diplomatic circles as a possible candidate so early as October, 1868, he was not finally persuaded to accept until June 21st, 1870, when the King of Prussia gave his reluctant assent. The Spanish Cortes had been kept sitting in order to proceed with the election; but, owing to a telegraphic error in the date announced for the return to Madrid of the Envoy, Salazar, who was bringing the acceptance with him, they were adjourned without proceeding to a vote. This small mistake of a clerk had very important consequences. Bismarck had hoped to keep the entire question secret until France could be confronted with a *fait accompli*. In that case, only two practical alternatives would have been open to her: either to accept Prince Leopold of Hohenzollern as King of Spain—a humiliation and a prospective menace which the condition of French feeling at the moment would hardly have endured—or to make war on both Germany and Spain together, it being exceedingly improbable that a people proverbially proud like the Spanish would have consented to drop their elected King at the bidding of a foreign Power.

But, as a matter of fact, the secret began to leak out in Madrid. The Emperor Napoleon had expressed his suspicions to the Duc de Gramont, the French Foreign Minister, so early as June 17th; but had been reassured by Mercier, the French Ambassador at Madrid, on June 25th, who wrote that if the candidature was really a subject for negotiation, it was kept very secret and suspected by no one, and, on July 1st, that he had still not heard a word of it. Next day, Prim somewhat shamefacedly informed him of Leopold's acceptance; it would not, he knew, be agreeable to the Emperor, but then he had no other alternative. Spain could not be left a prey to revolution, and Leopold would make an ideal King. Mercier warned him with great vigour and gravity that the news would produce an "extraordinary effect" in France, and that public opinion would view it as a "real provocation." Ollivier and Gramont, acquainted with the news of the 3rd, were stiffened in their resolution next day by the almost unanimous voice of the Press, and by the affectation of complete ignorance, which they disbelieved, at Berlin. When Lyons saw Gramont and Ollivier on the 5th, their language was perfectly definite and firm. Gramont exclaimed: "To this France will not resign herself, and when I say that we shall not resign ourselves to it, I mean that we shall not permit it; and we shall use our whole strength to prevent it." The proposal was not only an insult, but a positive danger to France. It would paralyse 200,000 French troops in case of a war with Prussia. Leopold was a member of a family which had shown peculiar devotion to the head of the House of Hohenzollern. His brother Charles had acted under the direction of Bismarck when he accepted the Throne of Roumania; he had begun to build up a military State there, and would use his army for any purpose which Prussia might require[1]. Such were the arguments which were presented as the French justification. Prim, when conversing with Mercier (July 2nd) had ridiculed the importance of the dynastic danger; a King of Spain, he said, will always be a Spaniard; but subsequent events have shown that Gramont was justified in believing that family relationships between rulers may still play a considerable part in determining the policy of European States in both peace and war. On the 6th, Gramont read in the Chamber a Declaration, the terms of which had been concerted by the Council of Ministers. It stated that respect for the sovereignty of Spain did not oblige France to allow a foreign Power, by placing one of its princes on the throne of Charles V, to shift the existing Balance of Power in Europe to the detriment of France and to endanger her interest and honour. The Government hoped that the wisdom of the German and the friendship of the Spanish people would prevent this project from being carried into execution; but, if this should be the case, they would do their duty without hesitation or weakness.

[1] From Lord Lyons, No. 685, July 5th, 1870; Nos. 697–8, July 7th, 1870.

The Emperor and Ollivier, at least, seem to have used this strong language with the object not of precipitating, but of preventing, war; for, on the same evening, the French Ambassador asked Lord Granville if the British Government would advise the abandonment of the candidature at Berlin and Madrid. When Gladstone had first heard the news, he had, while expressing his disapproval, said that he was not disposed to interfere with the liberty of the Spanish people to choose their own Sovereign. But both he and Granville readily assented to the request made for their good offices. They deprecated the language which Gramont had used; they did not admit that Leopold's nomination to the Spanish Throne was "a matter of such importance to a great and powerful nation like France as to warrant carrying to extremes a natural feeling of resentment[1]"; but they perceived that the strict secrecy in which the affair had been matured made the issue exceedingly dangerous. A telegram was at once despatched to Layard at Madrid, ordering him to "use every pressure which will not offend the Spanish Government, but will in your judgement promote the abandonment of the project." But no representations appear to have been sent to Berlin until the 9th, as Lord Granville's despatch, though written on the 6th, was delayed for the approval of a Cabinet meeting held on the former date. Lord A. Loftus was instructed to avoid any appearance of dictating either to Spain or to Prussia; to assume that the King of Prussia had not sanctioned the project, the secrecy of which was, so far as it went, a just cause of offence to France; and to point out the dangers which it would involve to Spain, Prussia and Prince Leopold himself.

Meanwhile, in spite of the commencement of French military preparations, there seemed good reasons for believing that war would be averted. On July 8th, Gramont told Lyons that "a voluntary renunciation on the part of the Prince would be a most fortunate solution of a difficult and intricate question, and he begged Her Majesty's Government to use all their influence in bringing it about[2]." The Emperor Napoleon, on the same day, sent a secret message to the King of the Belgians urging him to put pressure upon Prince Leopold to withdraw; and in equal secrecy gave his personal approval to Strat, the Roumanian Agent, who had been induced by the Spanish Ambassador at Paris to go to Sigmaringen on the same errand. Thus,

---

[1] To Lord Lyons, No. 13, July 6th, 1870; No. 19, July 9th, 1870; and to Lord A. Loftus, July 6th, 1870.
[2] From Lord Lyons, No. 708, July 8th, 1870.

from all quarters, both official and unofficial, a converging pressure was being employed to obtain the result suggested by Gramont. Nor was it ineffectual, for on July 12th, Prince Anthony telegraphed to Madrid withdrawing the candidature of his son. But by this time the French Government had changed its position, or rather had reverted to that which it had adopted in instructing (July 7th) Benedetti to negotiate at Ems directly with the King of Prussia. Gramont had, in a confidential letter, instructed Benedetti to obtain a declaration from the King that his Government disapproved of Prince Leopold's acceptance and ordered him to revoke his unauthorised decision; by this means alone could France be satisfied and war avoided. But on the 8th, in conversation with Lyons, this was put forward as only the one of two alternatives: the other being pressed upon the attention of the British Government as a "most fortunate solution." On July 9th, however, Benedetti extracted from King William the information that he had known of Leopold's candidature, and had not withheld his assent, though he maintained that he had acted simply in his capacity as head of the Hohenzollern family. The news seemed to Ollivier most ominous[1]; after a Council of Ministers Gramont told Lyons, on July 10th, that "the affair is now, beyond all controversy, one between France and the King"; that, therefore, it was necessary for its satisfactory conclusion for Prince Leopold to withdraw "on the advice of the King of Prussia." Granville does not appear to have perceived the importance of this enlarged demand, and to have confidently expected that the news of Leopold's renunciation on the 12th would satisfy France. But Gramont was far from being satisfied. He acknowledged, indeed, to Lyons (July 12th) that Spain was now out of the dispute; but said that the answer of the King was neither courteous nor satisfactory. The Government was placed in a very embarrassing position; for public opinion was so much excited that the Ministry would probably be overthrown, if they announced next day in the Chamber that the affair was settled, without having obtained some more complete satisfaction from Prussia. Gramont was peculiarly irritated by his knowledge that King William had privately advised Leopold to retire[2], though he had refused when conversing with Benedetti to give such advice. Such an attitude really shows, as Lyons pointed out, that the King's intentions were pacific, and he warned Gramont that if war

---

[1] See his note to Gramont on the night July 9–10th: "*La dépêche Benedetti est fort claire; elle confirme tous mes pressentiments et dès maintenant la guerre me paraît imposée; il n'y a plus qu'à s'y résoudre intrépidement et virilement.*"

[2] In a letter sent to Prince Anthony by Colonel Strantz on July 11th.

broke out now "all Europe would say that it was the fault of France; that France rushed into it without any substantial cause—merely from pride and resentment," and that Prussia might well expect to rally all Germany in defence against such an attack[1]. So soon as Lord Granville learnt this, he telegraphed at midnight, July 12th–13th, to instruct Lyons to renew his representations before the Council of Ministers was held, and to remind Gramont that the British Government had intervened at the request of France, and that their efforts could not have been more promptly and energetically employed, and to impress upon him the immense responsibility which would rest on France, if she should seek to enlarge the grounds of the quarrel.

As the Ministers were in session when Lyons received the telegram, he embodied the substance in a letter which was handed to Gramont at the Council table (July 13th). But France was already committed. Ollivier, on hearing of the renunciation, considered that peace was now assured, and the Emperor at first agreed with him; but the Empress and various Deputies of the Right so worked upon his vacillating mind, during the afternoon of the 12th, that Gramont was authorised at 7 p.m. to send to Benedetti a telegram containing the words: "In order that this renunciation by Prince Anthony may produce its full effect, it seems necessary that the King of Prussia should be associated with it, and should give us the assurance that he will not authorise this candidature in future." Ollivier had, in fact, been simply ignored by the Emperor; and his attempt, in a second despatch to Benedetti, to narrow the scope of the guarantees demanded arrived too late. Benedetti had acted with great promptitude, and had seen the King early in the morning of the 13th. The latter categorically refused to give the required promise, and declined the request of the Ambassador for a second audience, at which he intended to act on his modified instructions; but sent word later by his aide-de-camp, Prince Radziwill, that he gave his full and unreserved approval to the renunciation made by Leopold. Meanwhile, Lyons still hoped during the 13th that peace might be preserved. The Council of Ministers had neither called out the reserves nor issued an ultimatum to Prussia, and Gramont had merely announced to the Chamber that the negotiations with Prussia were not yet concluded. Gramont, it is true, maintained a very stiff attitude. He told Lord Lyons that

from Prussia France had obtained nothing, absolutely nothing.... Surely, it is but reasonable that France should take some precautions against

[1] From Lord Lyons, No. 738, July 12th, 1870.

a repetition of what had occurred when Prince Leopold's brother went off to Bucharest. It was not to be supposed that France would run the risk of Prince Leopold suddenly presenting himself in Spain and appealing to the chivalry of the Spanish people. Still, France did not call upon Prussia to prevent the Prince's going to Spain: all she desired was that the King should forbid him to change his present resolution to withdraw his candidature. If His Majesty would do this, the whole affair would be absolutely and entirely at an end.

He then asked whether France could count on the good offices of the British Government in obtaining this prohibition from the King. Thus Gramont made his third *volte-face* to the Ambassador within five days; each time he had added something to his original demand, and each time he had protested that he had nothing else to ask.

Lyons, without committing himself, forwarded this new suggestion to the Foreign Office; and it was considered next day at a Cabinet Meeting. It was decided that Gramont's new demand was inadmissible; but another attempt was made to preserve peace by a communication handed to Bernstorff which ran as follows:

"We recommend to Prussia that as the King consented to the acceptance and thereby in a certain sense became a party to the arrangements, so he might with perfect dignity communicate to the French Government his consent in like manner to the withdrawal of the acceptance, if France should waive her demand for an engagement covering the future. Such a communication at the suggestion of a friendly Power would be a further and the strongest proof of the King's desire for the maintenance of the peace of Europe."

The proposal was at the same time sent to Paris. But it arrived too late to have a chance of acceptance in either country. For, on the previous evening, Bismarck, who strongly disapproved of the King's negotiation with Benedetti, and had threatened to resign if he received the Ambassador again, took advantage of the discretionary power allowed him by the King and published the Ems telegram. He so rearranged the wording as to make it appear that, in consequence of Benedetti's offensive importunity, the King had been compelled to repel him by a public slight. This version of the telegram was not only published in the newspapers, but sent officially to the Prussian Diplomatic Agents abroad. The French Council of Ministers met on the afternoon of the 14th and called out the reserves. But, momentarily shrinking from a war which now stared them in the face, they assented to the proposal of the Government, that France should appeal to a European Congress to give a formal recognition to the principle of international law, which, it was stated, forbade princes connected with any of the reigning Houses of the Great Powers from accepting a foreign Throne, without the preliminary assent of all. The two further Councils held on the evening of the 14th and morning of the 15th, influenced partly by the furious excitement shown in the Press and in the streets, partly by a despatch from Vienna, which suggested that Bavaria would remain neutral, hesitated no longer, but decided to demand from the Chamber a vote of credit for 50,000,000 francs, which was justified by a statement amounting—as Ollivier admits— to a declaration of war. After recounting the course of Benedetti's negotiations, it asserted that the King's refusal to give the required guarantees, although regrettable, had not led to a rupture of negotiations; but that his refusal to see the Ambassador, which had been officially communicated to foreign Governments, rendered further attempts at conciliation undignified and imprudent. Granville made a last desperate appeal to the two Governments, in accordance with the Paris Protocol of 1856, to have recourse to the good offices of some friendly Power acceptable to both before proceeding to extremities; but it met with no more success than Lord Clarendon's similar effort in 1866. War was formally declared by the French on July 19th. Great Britain entered into a difficult and much resented neutrality.

It has been maintained by both Bismarck and Ollivier that Great Britain might have prevented the War. The former said to Lord A. Loftus: "Great Britain should have forbidden France to enter on war. She was in a position to do so, and her interests and those of Europe demanded it." No importance can be attached to this charge, when it is remembered that Bismarck has himself admitted in his *Recollections* his intense desire for the War; besides indicating in a moment of frankness that Clarendon was the only man whose influence over the Emperor Napoleon could have averted it. Ollivier based his belief on different grounds. He wrote that

The English Cabinet did not realise the decisive influence which it could exert; in short, it could, if it had so desired, have prevented the War. It had only to say: 'An international rule which we created in the case of Belgium and bowed to in the case of Greece, forbids every Great Power to place one of its members on a foreign throne, without the consent of Europe. We consider that under the present circumstances which threaten the peace of the world, a Conference should assemble to examine the validity of this rule and to decide in what way it is to be applied to the case of the candidature to the Spanish Crown[1].'

Such a proposal, he believed, which, coming from France, would have

[1] *L'Empire Libéral*, xv. 156.

met with the refusal of Prussia, would have met with success if made by Great Britain. Ollivier, however, assumes the very point at issue. If the British Government had recognised the existence of such a rule, the procedure which he recommended might have been appropriate; but both Gladstone and Lord Granville made it perfectly clear throughout the negotiations that they did not claim to interfere in any way with the free exercise of the right of national self-determination by either Spain or Prussia; if they recommended the withdrawal of Prince Leopold's candidature, it was simply because such a candidature was at the moment injudicious, not because it offended against international law. The cases of Belgium and Greece, which Ollivier cites as precedents, are hardly even analogies. Each of these countries had been erected into an independent State by the Great Powers; each was subjected to a special régime, Belgium being neutralised under the guarantee of the five Great Powers, and Greece being guaranteed as a Constitutional monarchy by Great Britain, France and Russia. It is no doubt true that every Power has always held itself absolutely free to object to any dynastic change in the case of another, and if necessary to push this objection to the point of war; but such an action would be taken in the interests of the Power concerned, or, if in the interests of Europe, in order to secure the Balance of Power, not in order to preserve international law from violation. Further, the candidature was not itself the cause of war, for the candidature had been withdrawn. If, at the suggested congress, France had put forward the further demand for guarantees, it would certainly have been refused by Prussia, and the negotiations would have been left at precisely the same stage as they had actually reached on July 12th. Nor, finally, is there any justification for the allegation afterwards made by Disraeli that the British remonstrances had been lacking in energy. If Ollivier had been in real instead of nominal control, war would not have broken out; but the Emperor and Gramont changed their policy without Ollivier's knowledge, and they obstinately persisted in their provocative action in spite of Granville's most urgent warning, delivered at the Council Table in the middle of their deliberations. It is useless to speculate whether Clarendon would have been more successful, for his personal influence over the Emperor had died with him. The Cabinet could not have exerted stronger pressure on France except by uniting with the other Powers in a collective protest; but such a united action was as impossible in the existing diplomatic grouping of Europe as was any collective mediation to enforce peace during the course of the War itself. The only other alternative—that of declaring that, if France engaged in an unjustifiable war, Great Britain would range herself as a belligerent on the side of Prussia—would not have met with the support of any section of public opinion.

The first and most important problem which confronted the British Cabinet was that of the neutrality of Belgium. The independence and integrity of that country had been an almost uninterrupted source of anxiety during the four preceding years. At the time of the Austro-Prussian War the Belgian Minister had expressed his anxiety to Lord Stanley[1]. He said that the country was prosperous and contented under a popular King, and that no French party existed; but that his Government had been urged more than once to obtain some confirmation or fresh sanction for the guarantees of 1839. This was not his own opinion, since he thought that no fresh Treaty could strengthen the obligation under which the Powers already lay; but he admitted that Belgium had been alarmed by a statement made by a personage of importance—not connected with the British Government—that Great Britain would stand aloof, if Belgium was attacked. Lord Stanley agreed that the existing guarantees could not be strengthened by a new Treaty, and said that the greatest danger to Belgium would be the existence of a strong party hostile to its independent nationality within the country itself; inasmuch as there would always be in England a strong feeling against a rupture with France, any such division of opinion in Belgium might plausibly be adduced as an argument that the existing guarantees should not be held applicable. The Belgian Minister asked if the British Government would let Napoleon know that an attack on Belgium would eventually bring about a rupture with France; to which Lord Stanley replied that he believed that Lord Clarendon had already given such an assurance and that "the views of the present and late Government were on that point the same." Lord Cowley took the opportunity on August 10th of emphasising these views to Drouyn de Lhuys, who, in a conversation about French "compensations" had cynically remarked that "as far as he was aware no sacrifice would be asked from Belgium." On the 14th, Drouyn de Lhuys enclosed a letter, written by the Emperor's order, in which he disavowed all intention of demanding from Belgium the frontiers of 1814[2]. Only two days later, Rouher sent Instructions

[1] To Lord Cowley, p. 57, July 20th, 1866.
[2] From Lord Cowley, No. 166, August 14th, 1866: "*Mon cher Ambassadeur, L'Empereur me charge de vous écrire que, si vous venez à Paris il vous verra avec plaisir, que cependant il croit inutile que vous vous dérangiez si votre visite n'a pour but que*

to Benedetti to obtain Bismarck's consent to the annexation of Belgium;
and he fulfilled these Instructions by drawing up and leaving with
Bismarck the draft of a Treaty by which France was to assent to a
federal union between north- and south-Germany in return for
Prussian military assistance "in case His Majesty the Emperor of the
French should be obliged by circumstances to cause his troops to enter
Belgium and to conquer it." This transaction remained unknown to
the British Government, though Disraeli suspected its existence. In
April, 1867, Beust had proposed as a solution of the Luxemburg
Question that Belgium should receive the grand-duchy and cede to
France the frontiers of 1814—a proposal which Belgium had, with
British support, resisted.

These continual suggestions among the Great Powers for trafficking
in Belgian territory caused keen alarm to Queen Victoria; especially
as Lord Stanley was inclined to minimise the extent of British responsibilities. She impressed upon Disraeli that:

"Prussia isn't likely to violate either the neutrality of Luxemburg or the
independence of Belgium—indeed, she has no interest to do so—unless
she sees reason to believe that England means her guarantee of both these
objects to remain a dead letter; in which case she might think it to her
interest to come to an agreement with France, fatal to the independence
of the rest of Europe."

It was hardly possible even for the Emperor Napoleon to renew
negotiations with Bismarck for compensations after the humiliating
failure to obtain Luxemburg[1]. Lord Stanley had shrewdly penetrated
the intentions of the Emperor, when he spoke of the danger of the
formation of a French party within the country itself; for the imperial
policy was now one of peaceful penetration, politically and above all
economically. The inspired French Press had, in 1868, again raised
the often discussed problem of a Franco-Belgian customs union, but
at the end of the year a serious practical question arose between the
two countries. The French Eastern Railway Company had already
made an arrangement which gave it the right of exploiting the

de lui demander s'il compte revendiquer la partie des frontières de 1814 qui appartient
aujourd'hui à la Belgique; que je puis vous rassurer complètement à cet égard que les
forteresses de Philippeville et de Marienbourg, appartenant à un état neutre, ne menacent
plus nos frontières, et que, quant aux autres parties de territoire qui ne sont pas à la
Belgique, ce n'est ni par intimidation ni par violence qu'il désire une ratification (sic) de
frontières, mais par une entente amicale avec les parties interessées. Voilà textuelement
ce que j'ai pour instructions de vous dire....Drouyn de Lhuys."
    [1] There is no doubt that Bismarck was intentionally inaccurate in giving the
summer of 1867 as the date of the Draft Treaty in his telegram to Bernstorff of
July 28th, 1870.

Guillaume-Luxemburg line, which served the grand-duchy. The Eastern Company further entered into secret negotiations for acquiring the two adjacent Belgian railways. Such an amalgamation was highly objectionable to Belgium, as the Eastern Company had behind it a French State guarantee, and would be able to control the most important industrial region in Belgium round Liége. The Belgian Government therefore passed (February 23rd, 1869) a law forbidding the transfer of any Belgian railway without the authorisation of the Government. The Emperor chose to regard this action as a proof of hostility towards France, concerted with Prussia, and entertained serious thoughts of war[1]. He had hoped that this project of railway amalgamation would lead to a close union between the two countries; hinting through his agent, La Guerronière, who had been appointed French Minister at Brussels, that since 1866 former Treaties had no more than an "ideal value," and that Belgium must henceforward "lean towards France." Gladstone and Bright were believed to be firm partisans of non-intervention, while the Alabama question seemed likely to embroil Great Britain with the United States. The use of such language naturally confirmed the Belgian Government in the conviction that, under the guise of a commercial transaction, an attack was being made on the neutrality of the country. Queen Victoria, always intensely preoccupied with Belgium, had urged Clarendon (January 14th) to make it known that any proceedings which seemed to threaten Belgian independence or neutrality "would bring England at once into the field." Gladstone agreed that "the independence of Belgium was an object of the first interest to the mind of the British people," and hoped that it would be made clear to France that "the suspicion even of an intention on the part of France to pay less respect to the independence of Belgium than to the independence of England would at once produce a temper in the country which would put an end to the good understanding and useful and harmonious cooperation of the two governments." But Clarendon was able by friendly pressure to induce the parties to agree (March 21st) on examining the whole economic relations between the two countries by a Franco-Belgian Commission. Frère-Orban, the Belgian Prime-Minister, repaired to Paris to carry through these negotiations, which proved very thorny, as the Emperor seemed determined to press his original demands. Clarendon, throughout, urged Belgium to come to an agreement with

[1] See his letter to Marshal Niel, February 19th, 1869, quoted in Ollivier, *L'Empire Libéral*, XI. 375.

France, provided that this did not involve the transfer of the railways, which would prevent Belgium from remaining its own master[1]. He deprecated the Belgian proposal to call upon the guarantors of 1839 to decide the question, except as a last extremity, in the event of a definite rupture of negotiations. On the other hand, he warned the French Ambassador in unmistakable terms (April 22nd) that, if Frère-Orban quitted Paris without an arrangement having been reached, the results might prove more serious to the Emperor than to Belgium. The incident finally terminated in a Protocol signed on April 27th, which provided for the appointment of the Commission agreed upon, and definitely rejected the projects of the Eastern Company. Bismarck afterwards claimed to Lord A. Loftus that, "although there had been no direct understanding with England, it was felt and known at Paris that Prussia would have supported England, if action had been taken. It was this knowledge that warded off action, and Belgium was saved." This statement was misleading, since Napoleon was prepared to face Prussian hostility in the matter, under the impression that such a *casus belli* would not unite German sentiment. It is true that Bismarck had made it clear that Prussia would join with Great Britain; but it was British, not Prussian, action which exercised the decisive influence over the Emperor.

IV. *The Franco-German War and the Conference of London*, 1871

At the outbreak of war in 1870, both France and Germany expressed their intention of respecting Belgian neutrality. But the publication by Bismarck, on July 25th, of the Benedetti Treaty considerably diminished the value of their assurances, and produced a strong feeling that Great Britain should take immediate steps to secure the enforcement of the guarantee. Since each of the belligerents hastened to lay on the other the blame for a document which, as each declared, embodied the policy of his adversary, it was easy to obtain from both a further pledge for Belgium's security. Gladstone differed from the view expressed by Lord Stanley in 1867, that no new Treaty could strengthen the existing guarantees. "The sole or single-handed defence of Belgium," he wrote on August 4th to Bright, "would be

---

[1] The result of the Eastern Company's control of the Luxemburg lines was clearly shown in 1870, when the Luxemburg Government excused unneutral proceedings which had taken place on their territory by disclaiming all responsibility for a railway directed solely by a foreign Company, whose employés were also foreigners. (Despatch of Servais, *Ministre d'État* of the grand-duchy, to Bismarck, December 14th, 1870.)

an enterprise which we incline to think Quixotic; if these two great military Powers combined against it—that combination is the only serious danger; and this it is which by our proposed engagements we should I hope render improbable to the very last degree." Accordingly, Treaties were signed (August 9th) with both belligerents, each of whom undertook to join Great Britain in defence of Belgian neutrality against the other; Great Britain not engaging to take part in any general operations of the War beyond the limits of Belgium. These Treaties were to remain in force for one year after the conclusion of peace.

During August, the British Government took the leading part in forming what the French incorrectly called the League of Neutrals. Its genesis and scope can be best described in the language used by Granville to Lyons[1]:

" M. de Lavalette informed me to-day that the French Government had reason to suppose that Prince Gortchakoff had informed the Russian Chargé d'affaires in Paris that England had agreed with Italy that neither party should abandon its neutrality without announcing its determination to the other, and that the British Government proposed similar arrangements should be made between the Great neutral Powers and those of the second order."

The Emperor of Russia, the telegram went on to say, had given his complete adhesion to the proposal.

" M. de Lavalette asked me whether the fact stated by Prince Gortchakoff was true—what was the nature of the engagement referred to, whether it was made and whether it was proposed afterwards to make it general.

I replied that the statement was substantially true—that the nature of the engagement was what it purported to be—that there was to be no treaty nor protocol, but merely an interchange of despatches, which however had not yet taken place, and it was under consideration to make such an arrangement general. The proposal arose as follows. Several Powers, I said, since the beginning of the war, have proposed that a combined neutrality should be made of all the neutral Powers. His Majesty's Government have always objected to any formal compact, although professing their desire to exchange freely ideas which would tend to circumscribe the war or which would lead to any prospect of peace.

The Italian Government last week informed me that it was still desirous of maintaining neutrality, but that pressure was applied to it from more quarters than one, which made it difficult for it to do so; and it applied to Her Majesty's Government to give it some assistance. I replied that I still objected to any formal engagement; but that, if it would be of any use to the Italian Government to interchange an assurance that Great Britain and Italy would not depart from their neutrality without announcing to each other their intention, I was ready to do so.

[1] To Lord Lyons, No. 242, August 18th, 1870.

I told M. de Lavalette further that I have informed the Russian Government of what had passed...and have asked it whether some such arrangements between neutral Governments might not be useful to the lesser Governments who desired to maintain their neutrality, and that the Russian Government had assented...."

Such a proposal was in fact addressed to all the European States, and met with general assent. Austria, indeed, wished to widen the scope of the understanding by an agreement between neutrals not to take isolated steps towards mediation; as she was determined not to move on her own single initiative, owing to the belief that Prussia would not accept her mediation as impartial, and to her fear of Russia. She finally, however, agreed to the British proposal on September 9th. Granville himself was firm in his intention to take part in no mediation either collective or individual, unless it seemed to offer a solid hope of success. He refused, on August 17th, an appeal by Italy, who, alarmed at the rapid successions of German victories, offered to agree beforehand to any conditions which Great Britain might propose to maintain the integrity of France. Nor was he shaken, when the Provisional Government, which had risen to power on the ruins of the empire (September 4th) sent over Thiers, who visited all the neutral Great Courts in succession, to implore mediation with all the impetuous eloquence for which he was famed. He urged, in three successive interviews (September 13th–16th), every argument which might induce Great Britain to help a country which had overthrown the responsible authors of its defeat. "It was not," he said, "for the interest of England that a dishonourable peace should be patched up which would leave France weak and irritable, unable to assist England, but ready for every occasion for recovering her lost prestige"; while again he urged the warning that "there was nothing that North Germany, with a population of 60 millions, could not do, acting as a machine and led by such a man as Count Bismarck." Granville replied, very coldly, that

We had done all in our power to obtain peace; we went beyond what we had a right to do in urging Spain to abandon a candidate whom she had a right fully to choose. We succeeded in removing the ground of quarrel. But the French Government had not been satisfied, and, leaving us on one side, had hastened to declare hostilities. From the first, we told all who pressed us that it was not our intention to offer ourselves as mediators, unless we had reason to believe that mediation would be acceptable to both parties, and that there seemed to be a basis on which both belligerents would agree to negotiate; but that by all we could learn such a state of things had not arisen.

He told Thiers, further, that he believed

it would be much easier for the King and Bismarck to agree to conditions
which the army and Germany might not consider to be ample, if the
concession was made spontaneously and not upon the advice of a neutral,
who had taken no part in the difficulties of the war.

Granville was, moreover, of opinion, as he afterwards told the Provisional Government, that their refusal to cede "an inch of their soil
or a stone of their fortresses" was an obstacle in the way of peace.
Acting on this belief he, after a protracted struggle in the Cabinet,
defeated Gladstone's "effort to speak with the other neutral Powers
against the transfer of Alsace and Lorraine without reference to the
populations[1]." Gladstone continued to press his views with the
greatest persistency; the matter, he contended, "involves considerations of legitimate interest to all the Powers of Europe. It appears to
bear on the Belgian question in particular. It is also a principle likely
to be of great consequence in the eventual settlement of the Eastern
question." In any case, whether mediation were practicable or not,
he declared that, if no voice were previously raised against an enforced
transfer, "it will in my opinion be a standing reproach to England,"
and finally prophesied to Lord Granville (December 20th, 1870) that
he feared "this violent laceration and transfer is to lead us from bad
to worse, and to be the beginning of a new series of European complications." But no British protest was made against the cession,
notwithstanding the unanimous and touching declaration of the Deputies
from Alsace-Lorraine in the National Assembly at Bordeaux (February
16th, 1871). Gladstone's forebodings have been fulfilled to the letter,
for, in the words of President Wilson[2]: "The wrong done to France
by Prussia in 1871, in the matter of Alsace-Lorraine...unsettled the
peace of the world for nearly fifty years." It was not because the
remainder of the Cabinet approved of Bismarck's intentions that they
prevented the action desired by Gladstone; but because they believed
that any protest would by its futility simply exacerbate the conflict.
Armed mediation, in which Russia would not have joined, they
believed—and probably with justice—would have created great danger
of a universal European conflagration. It is possible, however, that
British remonstrances might have had some effect on Prussia after the
denunciation of the Black Sea Clauses by Russia; as Odo Russell's
negotiations with Bismarck showed him to be at that time desperately

[1] Entry in Gladstone's Diary, September 30th, 1870, quoted by Morley, *Life
of Gladstone*, II. 346.
[2] Point viii.

anxious to prevent the extension of the War. The French themselves were to blame for losing the last opportunity of putting their case before the representatives of Europe by omitting to send a Plenipotentiary to the London Conference, until after the Preliminaries of Peace had been signed. For Granville had let it be known, in spite of Bismarck's opposition, that, when he presided over the Conference,

"if at the end of the Conference or even after one of its sittings the French Plenipotentiaries should wish to take advantage of the presence of the Plenipotentiaries to bring any subject before them, in that case it would not be my duty to interfere.... I cannot concur in Prince Bismarck's view, if it be his view, that the Conference remains a Conference after it has been adjourned or closed. No special character attaches to the place where it may be held. The Conference ceases as soon as it is formally adjourned or closed. Every Plenipotentiary is freed from any restriction which may have been imposed...and is at liberty to address any one or more of those who may still remain or are willing to listen[1]."

The aim of Granville was simply to remain impartial throughout the struggle; and, as is inevitable when the most violent passions are aroused, he was exposed to the continual reproaches of both parties. His reply to Bernstorff's remonstrance against the unrestricted export of coal and warlike stores to France explains his attitude in a few words. "It seems hardly to admit of doubt that neutrality, when it once departs from strict impartiality, runs the risk of altering its essence, and that, the moment a neutral allows his proceedings to be biassed by predilection for one of the two belligerents, he ceases to be a neutral." In pursuance of this view, he was always ready to facilitate meetings between Representatives of the two belligerents to discuss an armistice; but, except in one instance, he resolutely refused to express any opinion on the conditions of peace. The reduction of the indemnity demanded from France from six to five milliards of francs was, partly at least, due to the representations of the British Government.

The neutrality to which Russia had committed herself had a very different object in view from that sought by Granville. Germany had been able to embark on the War in the confident expectation that Austria would be mobilised because of her fear of a Russian attack, if she threw in her lot with France. Lord A. Loftus had been fully justified when he expressed his confidence that Bismarck had no fear of the Russian policy towards Prussia, so long as the Tsar lived and Gortchakoff remained Minister (March 12th, 1870). But Russia's

[1] To Odo Russell, No. iii, February 25th, 1871.

friendly attitude was not inspired by a disinterested desire to promote the Union of Germany. The Tsar had felt bitterly the humiliation imposed on his country by the clauses of the Treaty of Paris which provided for the neutralisation of the Black Sea, and he constantly expressed the view that their existence "was a blot on his reign." Indeed, such a limitation of the free exercise of sovereignty by a Great Power did not carry with it the promise of permanence. Lord Palmerston, its principal author, used, with extraordinary levity, to tell Russian statesmen when they objected that the provisions could not last, that they would "last ten years[1]." Whenever any question arose in the Near East which required the collective action of the Powers, the Foreign Office was preoccupied with the fear that Russia would demand the revision of the Treaty of Paris. It was certain that Prussia attached no importance to the Black Sea Clauses which Bismarck afterwards described as "politically absurd, and therefore in the long run impossible." So early as August, 1866, Lord Cowley reported that the French Ambassador at Petrograd

appeared to think that Prince Gortchakoff has profited by the opportunity to express the expectation of the Russian Government that if they are silent in the subject of the territorial acquisitions now made by Prussia, they may count on the goodwill of Prussia in obtaining a modification of the Treaty of 1856, whenever a favourable occasion may present itself. Baron Talleyrand even hints that a secret treaty may have been signed to that effect[2].

It is improbable that, either then or subsequently, any such formal compact was made between the two Powers; but Bismarck has himself stated that he took the initiative in 1870 in sounding Gortchakoff and promising him the support of Prussia[3].

The Russian action, however, did not take the form, which respect for international law would have dictated, of demanding from the co-Signatories of the Treaty of Paris the desired modification. Certain

[1] See Granville's speech in the House of Lords, February 14th, 1871: "General Ignatieff told me that he remarked to Lord Palmerston, 'These are stipulations which you cannot expect will last long,' and Lord Palmerston replied, 'They will last ten years'; and his despatch to Sir A. Buchanan, British Ambassador at Petrograd, No. 303, November 13th, 1870. Confidential." Baron Brunnow said in conversation: "He had warned Lord Palmerston that it could not last, and Lord Palmerston said it would last ten years."
For what follows cf. *Correspondence respecting the Repudiation by Russia of the Obligations of the Treaty of March 30th, 1856. Private. Printed for the use of the Foreign Office.* (A copy of these is preserved among the papers of Sir A. Buchanan.)
[2] Lord Cowley, No. 191, Confidential, August 21st, 1866.
[3] Bismarck's *Reflections and Reminiscences* (English Translation), II. 114.

Russian military preparations which had been noticed during October, 1870, made the Turks fear that some violent *coup* might be imminent; they were inclined, however, to believe that the Russian intention was to occupy that portion of Bessarabia, the cession of which in 1856 had deprived Russia of control over the mouth of the Danube. But, on October 29th, immediately after the fall of Metz had rendered it absolutely impossible for France to throw in her lot with Great Britain, and made it probable that Peace would be speedily concluded, Gortchakoff despatched to the Russian Representatives abroad a Circular, in which he distinctly denounced Clauses XI, XIII and XIV of the Treaty of Paris. The Tsar, he declared, could "no longer hold himself bound by the stipulations of the Treaty of March, 1856, as far as they restrict his sovereign rights in the Black Sea." This repudiation he endeavoured to justify by two arguments. The Tsar could not "admit, *de jure*, that treaties violated in several of their essential and general clauses should remain binding in other clauses directly affecting the interests of his Empire." He referred, in particular, to the union of Moldavia and Wallachia in 1866 under Prince Charles of Hohenzollern, which, accomplished through revolution, had received the implied sanction of the Powers. Neither could he admit, "*de facto*, that the security of Russia should depend on a fiction which had not stood the test of time." Great Britain and France, he pointed out, had concentrated naval forces in the Mediterranean, Turkey was at liberty to maintain a navy in the Straits; and the introduction of ironclads "unknown and unforeseen" in 1856 still further imperilled the Russian position in the Black Sea. When Sir A. Buchanan at Petrograd heard of the Circular, he immediately, without waiting for Instructions from his Government, wrote to Gortchakoff that he would expect to receive orders to ask for his passports and to leave immediately. But the Cabinet was by no means inclined to take any action which would precipitate a rupture, and would either involve Europe in a general war or leave Great Britain to fight Russia single-handed. The reply to Russia, therefore, took the form of a despatch to Buchanan, which, though firm in its language, contained nothing in the nature of an ultimatum. Granville refrained from discussing whether the Russian desire to be freed from the restrictions of the Treaty was in itself reasonable or not. He confined himself to elaborating the single point, that no single Power can free itself from any of the stipulations of a treaty except by obtaining the previous consent of the co-Signatories. The effect of unilateral denunciation, such as Gortchakoff claimed the power of exercising, "is to bring the entire authority and efficacy of treaties under the discretionary control of each one of the Powers who may have signed them; the result of which would be the entire destruction of treaties in their essence." Gortchakoff had declared that Russia fully adhered to the general principles of the Treaty of Paris; but, "however satisfactory this may be in itself, it is obviously an expression of the free will of that Power which it might at any time alter or withdraw." It was, therefore, "impossible for Her Majesty's Government to give any sanction, on their part, to the course announced by Prince Gortchakoff." The final paragraph, however, suggested a more conciliatory attitude by the remark that, if Russia had requested the Signatories of the Peace of Paris to examine

"whether anything has occurred which could be held to amount to an infraction of the Treaty, or whether there is anything in the terms which, from altered circumstances, presses with undue severity upon Russia, or which, in the course of events, had become unnecessary for the due protection of Turkey, Her Majesty's Government would not have refused to examine the question in concert with the co-Signatories to the Treaty."

Granville was less reserved in an interview with Brunnow on the following day. The Russian Ambassador had known nothing of the Circular beforehand[1], and regarded the British reply as both "sudden" and "unexpected." He complained that it had not opened with an acknowledgement of the Tsar's assurance that he meant to observe the principal stipulations of the Treaty. "Was it possible," Granville replied, "that the Government of a great country should express satisfaction with an assurance from the head of another State because, when denouncing a portion of his treaty obligations, he said that he did not denounce them all?" Brunnow could only observe that "the value of treaties, particularly in late times, depended much on their longevity" —a side-allusion to the recent Treaties for the protection of Belgium, which the Russians chose to regard as a tacit admission that the obligations assumed by the Powers in 1839 could no longer be considered binding. Brunnow, who "was much perturbed and sometimes angry" during this interview, asked whether he should prepare for departure, but was told by Lord Granville that "the imperial Government had

---

[1] To Buchanan, No. 303, Confidential, November 13th, 1870. "I told Baron Brunnow that, although of course he would not and could not admit it, I was sure he disapproved the Circular as much as I did. Baron Brunnow confessed that it had taken him as much by surprise as it had done me; that, if he had had the misfortune of being Foreign Secretary, he should have first negotiated with Turkey and then with the other parties to the Treaty." (This passage is omitted in the final draft of the despatch.)

taken one step and we another, and I did not wish to anticipate any event."

The British attitude for the moment was deliberately calculated to leave Russia in uncertainty as to our intentions. "Promising peace is as unwise as to threaten war," was the expression used by Lord Granville to the Prime-Minister. The practical question to be decided was this: if the country went to war with Russia, who would be its allies and who its opponents? The resentment in Turkey, the country most directly affected by the Circular, was great, and was increased by the offensive cynicism of Gortchakoff's explanatory Despatch, in which he assumed that he was doing the Porte a service by removing the main cause of friction between it and Russia. Sir H. Elliot, the British Ambassador, had indeed prophesied, a few days before the news became public, that Turkey would undoubtedly fight[1]. He wrote, without qualifications, that

"the neutralisation of the Black Sea is a bulwark as strong and more reliable than the signed guarantes of all the Great Powers of Europe. If it were not for it, Turkey would be almost helpless at the mercy of Russia. ...The Turkish statesmen are so fully convinced of this and feel so keenly that if there should once be a powerful Russian fleet on that sea, after the completion of the railway system has rendered easy the rapid concentration of the enormous military forces of the Empire, it will be in the power of the Russian Government to strike a fatal blow at the independence of the Sultan, at any moment when the Allies of the latter are unable to come forward to his assistance. They would rather fight now for that neutralisation, which they regard as their best ally, than passively await the greater danger, which will threaten them when they have it no longer to trust to."

But when Turkey was actually faced with the event, the problem did not solve itself with the same simplicity. The Russian move had placed her in the necessity of declaring and waging an offensive war, which would suit neither her disordered finances nor her military capacity. She would probably have been willing to proceed to extremities, if Great Britain and Austria would have given their simultaneous support. As it was, the Turkish Ambassador in Vienna remarked plaintively to Beust: "The Porte derives little comfort from alternate assurances that each of her Allies is willing to help her, if the other will only set the example, whilst the peril of her position is daily increasing[2]."

Feeling within the Austro-Hungarian empire was in fact bitterly

---

[1] From Elliot, No. 254, October 30th, 1870.
[2] From Bloomfield, No. 203, Confidential, November 24th, 1870.

divided. The hatred which the Hungarians felt towards Russia, their ruthless conqueror in 1849, was still unabated. Andrássy, the Foreign Minister, told Bloomfield in great excitement that, "so far as Hungary was concerned, he should be ready for action at once, the sooner the better, for Russia was not so well prepared for war as was generally supposed...[1]." But the Slav races and the Czechs in particular were no less violently in favour of Russia; while the German element, with its representative, the Imperial Chancellor Beust, was eager for a conciliation. Such fundamental divisions necessarily limited Austrian policy. Moreover, Beust himself had never concealed his view that the restrictive clauses had "placed Russia in the Black Sea, in a situation unworthy of a Great Power," and had actually proposed in January, 1867, the convocation of a congress, which would agree to free her from those disabilities. His reply to the Circular, therefore (November 10th), though vigorous in wording, contained no express refusal to sanction the course adopted by Russia. Gortchakoff, Buchanan wrote to Granville, would find this reply "easy to answer."

Italy, which frankly subordinated its policy to that followed by Great Britain and Austria, could be relied on to cooperate in any steps which would prevent the general peace from being disturbed.

France, entirely powerless in a military sense, had received the news with general satisfaction, "as likely to lead to European complications which will stop Prussia[2]." Thiers at once urged on Lyons that "England, Austria, Italy, Turkey and Spain should now unite with France to check the aggression of Prussia and Russia," and thought "that without war this would lead to a Congress in which all Europe would settle the terms of peace." This view, although perfectly natural to French statesmen in their present extremity, was not very helpful to Granville, as its motive was plainly to bring about that collective mediation to which he had repeatedly refused his sanction.

It was, in fact, clear, as Granville had seen from the commencement of the crisis, that the attitude of Prussia would play the decisive part in determining that of Austria and Italy, and that Prussia's intentions could be extracted from Bismarck alone, since both Thile at Berlin and Bernstorff at London confined themselves to colourless expressions of surprise at the Russian action. Accordingly, Odo Russell was at once (November 11th) despatched to Prussian headquarters at Versailles as a Special Envoy to Bismarck. His Instructions were

[1] From Lord Bloomfield, No. 200, Confidential, November 23rd, 1870.
[2] From Lord Lyons, No. 1803, Confidential, November 14th, 1870.

very general, as the first object of the Cabinet was to gain such information as would enable them to decide on their next move. The Chancellor had maintained complete silence, doubtless in the belief that the Circular would, after a preliminary protest, be tacitly accepted. His only concern was to circumscribe the War, and to prevent any European interference between France and Germany. Moreover, the military situation was, at the moment, causing the German Staff some anxiety; for Orleans, reoccupied by the French on November 10th, still remained in their hands, and seriously menaced the investment of Paris. The Cabinet had made an excellent choice in their Envoy. The combination of frankness and subtlety in Odo Russell's character appealed to Bismarck, who afterwards treated him, during his tenure of the Embassy at Berlin (1871–84), with an esteem and intimacy accorded to no other British diplomatist. Two interviews took place between them, on November 21st. In the former, Bismarck simulated surprise at the Russian Circular and entire disapproval of the method and the time chosen by the Russian Government; but expressed himself as unable to interfere or even answer the Circular for the present. He strongly recommended that a conference should be held at Constantinople before resort to hostilities. But, in the evening, Russell, who had convinced himself that the Chancellor respected strength above everything else, boldly out-stepped his Instructions and told him bluntly that the question "was of a nature in its present state to compel us, with or without allies, to go to war with Russia." The conversation was prolonged till midnight; but before it closed Bismarck "came round to the British point of view, and felt that in our place he could not recede[1]." He now offered to take the initiative of proposing a conference at Petrograd, at which the question might be peacefully settled. The way of peace was soon afterwards made easier for the Cabinet by a despatch from Gortchakoff, which was communicated to Lord Granville on November 25th. It was effusive in its protestation of friendship, and while not explicitly withdrawing in any way from the attitude of the Circular, attenuated the effects of the denunciation of the Treaty into "the abrogation of a theoretical principle without immediate application."

It was now time to decide between three alternative courses of action: either to go to war against Russia with the possible support of Turkey, which was becoming the more doubtful in consequence of Bismarck's efforts to induce that Power to come to a separate under-

[1] Letter to Lord Granville, November 30th, 1870.

standing with Russia; or to accept the Circular, which Lord Granville's despatch of the 10th had categorically refused to do; or, finally, to enter into a Conference. Bismarck's proposal, as it stood, was inadmissible; for, as Granville caustically told Bernstorff, it "only stated that if we would ask the Prussian Government they would ask Russia to agree to a conference to be held at St Petersburg, whence the Circular, which had caused so painful an impression had emanated, with a view apparently to giving, with the support of Prussia, to Russia all that she desired[1]." But Bismarck made no difficulty in agreeing to the required modifications. Invitations to the conference were to be sent "on the express understanding that it should be in no way prejudiced by any previous assumption as to the result of its deliberations"; but the British Government "would feel bound, in concert with the other Powers, to weigh with fairness and without bias any claims which Russia might advance and any proposals which she might make[2]." A very conciliatory despatch to Buchanan (November 28th) stated that if Gortchakoff's refinements on the Russian Circular, quoted above, "are to be construed into an announcement that Russia has formed and stated her own opinion of her rights, but has no intention of acting in conformity with it without due concert with the other Powers, they go far to close the controversy in which the two Governments have been engaged." Austria and Italy readily agreed; Turkey was anxious to receive an assurance that the deliberations of the conference would be confined to the Black Sea Question. Granville pointed out that the terms of the invitation made it impossible to come to any definite agreement beforehand as to what matters should be discussed, but agreed that it would be most inadvisable to extend the scope of the deliberations. France, at first, refused on the ground that the proposal emanated from Prussia; then endeavoured to make her acceptance contingent on the prior enforcement of an armistice on Prussia by the neutral Powers, and the inclusion in the deliberations of the Conference of the conditions of peace between the two belligerents, and finally, after accepting the conference, was not represented at it till its penultimate meeting (March 13th, 1871)—owing to lengthy disputes between Bismarck and Favre, as to the method by which the latter should obtain the necessary safe-conduct from Paris.

The Conference, which met on January 17th, 1871, prolonged its six sessions over a period of two months. Its labours produced three

[1] To Loftus, No. 324, November 24th, 1870.
[2] To Russell, November 25th, 1870.

positive results. At the first formal meeting all the Plenipotentiaries agreed to a Protocol by which they recognised "that it is an essential principle of the law of nations that no Power can liberate itself from the engagements of a Treaty, nor modify the stipulations thereof, unless with the consent of the Contracting Powers by means of an amicable arrangement." This Declaration amounted to a withdrawal by Russia from the claim put forward in the Circular, and was indeed a logical corollary of the British proviso that the Conference should meet without any previous assumptions as to its results. It also removed the obligation, which legally bound Great Britain to go to war to prevent any infringement of the Treaty of Paris, by making it appear that no infringement of the Treaty had taken place. But the subsequent history of Europe fails to justify the assertion that the Declaration has added any additional security to the sanctity of Treaties.

"In diplomacy," as Bismarck was fond of saying, "one hand must wash the other." After signing Granville's Protocol, the Plenipotentiaries proceeded to abrogate, in accordance with Russian demands, the three Clauses of the Treaty of Paris which provided for the neutralisation of the Black Sea. Finally, Turkey was granted a corresponding advantage. While the principle of closing the Straits to warships was maintained, the Sultan was allowed the power to open them "in time of peace to the vessels of war of friendly and allied Powers, in case the Sublime Porte should judge it necessary in order to secure the execution of the stipulations of the Treaty of Paris." This liberty would have proved of service to Turkey, had she wished at any time to engage her Allies in a war with Russia, as it would have enabled her to reinforce the Turkish Black Sea Fleet before war had been declared. If, however, her object was, not war, but negotiations backed by force, the entry of a foreign fleet into the Bosphorus would be calculated to precipitate the very crisis which she desired to avoid. To assert that Granville's diplomacy had resulted in giving the command of the Black Sea to Turkey seems a great exaggeration of language[1]. So long as the entrance into the Black Sea in the event of war between Turkey and Russia remained in Turkish hands, a British fleet could always pass into and control that sea as it did in 1854; the revision of the clause merely rendered it less probable that the Turkish fleet would suffer defeat or destruction before the arrival of allied reinforcements.

The removal of the neutralisation had, in fact, little influence on the relations between Russia and Turkey. It failed, on the one hand,

[1] See Lord Fitzmaurice, *Life of Lord Granville*, II. 76.

to produce that improvement of relations which Gortchakoff professed to anticipate. The neutralisation had been itself an effect, not a cause, of their mutual hostility. While the Christian populations under the Porte could still complain with justice of misgovernment and oppression, and were steadily progressing, through the self-consciousness of nationality, towards fitness for an independent existence, over which Russia expected to exercise an exclusive influence, the relations between her and Turkey inevitably grew worse instead of better. Both Lord Stanley and Lord Granville were oppressed by the immense responsibility devolving upon Great Britain as a guarantor of the integrity of Turkey by the Tripartite Treaty of 1856, and perceived its provisions to be obsolete, since their enforcement would, in practice, be impossible[1].

But, on the other hand, the Russian freedom of action in the Black Sea did not, as Elliot gloomily prophesied, leave Turkey almost helpless. On the contrary, the War of 1877–78 was not decided or even appreciably affected by naval operations, but by the final success of the Russians in capturing Plevna and forcing the barrier of the Balkans[2].

Great Britain emerged from this dangerous crisis as satisfactorily as could be expected, and probably with less discredit abroad than at home. Here, public opinion, which is seldom impressed by the niceties of diplomatic formulae, was convinced that the country had surrendered to the threats of Russia; for it was impossible to deny that, what Russia had demanded, she had obtained. Thus, the hatred and fear of Russia, which had begun to die down after the Crimean War, received a strong stimulus, and manifested itself in 1878 with a violence and intensity which have become proverbial. The attention of the country was diverted from the significant part played by

[1] Lord Stanley said in 1867 to the French Ambassador: "It was dangerous to seem to negotiate with the Porte on a reciprocal basis of good government by it and obedience by the subjects, as we could not possibly guarantee the latter half of the bargain. Maladministration was not the primary cause of the discontent which had its root in feelings of nationality and religion, which the best Government could not wholly remove and which indeed with increasing prosperity was likely to grow stronger." (To Cowley, March 11th, 1867.) Granville wrote to Elliot (No. 208, Confidential, October 6th, 1870): "I have already told the Turkish Ambassador that I could not give assurances as to future contingencies. Would it not be more friendly to say more and to point out that there are contingencies in which Turkey must feel, now that she could not rely on our aid, and to impress upon her that her real safety will depend upon the aspirations and feelings of the populations over which she rules?"...

[2] See, as to Russia's tentative efforts, down to 1908, to secure complete freedom of navigation in the Black Sea, A. Stern, "Zur Geschichte der Meerengenfrage," in *Wissen und Leben*, XVI. 6 (Zurich, 1923).

Bismarck. He had throughout dominated and directed the policy of Europe; he had successfully maintained the diplomatic isolation of France, and had created the German empire, at the very time when the Conference was engaged in its deliberations. Up to 1870, his policy had aimed with extraordinary success at obtaining from Europe the necessary liberty of action by which Prussia made Germany; henceforward, he was so to direct and manipulate diplomatic conditions in Europe as to maintain intact the supremacy in Europe which Germany had already won. The position of the Chancellor was not, indeed, to remain for long so unassailable as to justify Odo Russell's estimate, in 1872, that "Napoleon was not more powerful than Bismarck is at this moment." But the centre of power and diplomacy had, without dispute, been transferred to Berlin. British statesmen, like all others, had to shape their policy in accordance with their views of the future position and intentions of Germany. Bismarck had already told Odo Russell confidentially at Versailles, "that his ambition for Germany was an alliance with England and Austria in preference to a Russian alliance; but he did not see his way to it yet[1]"; and he multiplied his expressions of goodwill, when the Special Envoy had become the Ambassador at Berlin. It was easy to believe that Bismarck was expressing his real feelings; for the prospective advantages to Germany were obvious. She would hope to guarantee all that she had won, and to perpetuate the isolation, and therefore the helplessness, of France. But Great Britain could expect no corresponding reciprocity. It was certain, as Bismarck himself admitted, that Germany would never, by acceding to the Tripartite Treaty, become a guarantor of the integrity of Turkey; it was most unlikely that she would even agree on any joint policy in the Near East, which might bring her into antagonism with Russia. In fact, the Liberal Government during its last three years of office, occupied with the Alabama Arbitration abroad and with its comprehensive legislative programme at home, stood entirely aloof from a Europe which was beginning to feel its way towards an inevitable new grouping of its Powers.

B. Sea Policy and the Alabama Claims, 1861–1907

The "Alabama Claims," the Treaty of Washington concluded between Her Britannic Majesty and the United States of America on May 8th, 1871, and the International Arbitration which, in pursuance of that Treaty, decided those claims, constituted a group of events

[1] From Russell, No. 16, Secret, December 1st, 1870.

which formed not only a definite stage in the evolution of British Foreign Policy in relation to the Law of the Sea, but also a turning-place in the history of that Law. The policy of the dominant Sea-Power was, and is, something more than the policy of a single nation. Despite the accidents of events and the errors of individual statesmen, that policy presents an organic growth of principles rather than the selfish policy of an individual Power. Those principles, in ever-growing measure, have represented what has been accepted as the inevitable relationship of neutrals with belligerents, of neutrals with neutrals and (in time of peace) of all nations with one another. Sooner or later, a complete doctrine of Neutrality was destined to emerge, and the rapid transformation of the character of Sea-Power, as the result of new methods of propulsion introduced about the middle of the nineteenth century, made it certain that it could not be long delayed. The North American Civil War, which began in April, 1861, as the consequence of the Secession from the Union in November, 1860, of seven States—South Carolina, Florida, Mississippi, Alabama, Georgia, Louisiana and Texas—under the designation of "The Confederate States of North America," created conditions which could not but result in war at sea. The Seceding States in the spring of 1861 were joined by the States of Virginia, North Carolina, Tennessee and Arkansas. The United States of America, after a century of extension and consolidation, were reft asunder. A vast unbroken region in central and southern North America from Mexico northward to the Potomac River asserted with ample arms and a solid political organisation the right of self-determination and independence. It was neither a revolt nor a revolution. It was a deliberate setting-up of a new national hearth. The northern region of the great republic—"the North," as it was called—decided at all costs to maintain the Union; and in this country there was a political and social repercussion of the terrible struggle which was raging in the vast areas of North America. Great Britain, on the question of principle, was split in twain, and the cleavage became clearly apparent in the light of the early successes of the secessionists. Each of the antagonists strove to lean upon Great Britain, their mother-country. The North looked for moral support not only in respect to the doctrine of National Unity and all that it meant to civilisation, but also in respect to the great policy (of which Great Britain was the protagonist) of the extirpation of Slavery[1]. The South looked for the material support of Great

---

[1] See J. L. Motley's letter to the Duke of Argyll of June, 1861, *Autobiography and Memoirs of the Eighth Duke of Argyll*, II. 173.

Britain and relied on the economic difficulties and disasters caused by the interruption of the supplies of cotton to the manufacturers of the Northern counties. The cleavage of English opinion took unexpected lines. The starving operatives of the north of England, whose material interests lay with the success of the apparently triumphant Secessionists, repudiated the "Slave States" and gave the North their moral support. Disraeli held the same view and gave no support to the South. On the other hand, Gladstone was so impressed with the doctrine of self-determination in the form which it had then assumed as to declare, in the autumn of 1862, that Mr Jefferson Davis "had made an army and had made a navy, and, what was more, had made a Nation." So late as the summer of 1863, Gladstone affirmed that the maintenance of the Union was impossible. A steady foreign policy in these circumstances was difficult to maintain and liable to strange deflexions. It was destined to turn ultimately on Gladstone's statement that the south "had made a Navy."

For British statesmen, the problem, when stripped of all its passions and conflicting sympathies, was a problem of sea-policy. If this had not been plain from the first—and it cannot be denied today that Lord John Russell was ill-advised and obstinate in his early dealings with the question—Liverpool soon made it plain. The coming of the War found this western seaport teeming with the rich and unscrupulous agents of the Confederate States. Into Liverpool there had drifted, as by the influence of some economic magnet, hundreds of British and American sea-adventurers of every kind, but, for the most part, of the old piratical type. The quays of Liverpool hummed with rumours of sea-adventure; and the things that the British Government did not know, that the Custom-House officials and their London chiefs did not choose to know, were the common talk of every marine-store dealer in the famous seaport. The naval side of the War developed with great rapidity. In April, 1861, the Confederates secured Fort Sumter (at the north of Charleston Harbour), the military arsenal of Harper's Ferry on the Potomac, and the naval arsenal at Norfolk. On April 15th, the President of the United States called out the militia, and, on April 17th, Jefferson Davis (who had been elected President of the Confederate States in February) issued a counter-proclamation inviting applications for letters of marque and reprisals against the United States. Lincoln's inevitable answer, two days later, was to declare a blockade of the Seceding States. Confederate vessels were captured and condemned, and the Supreme Court held that "a state of war" existed. In these circumstances, the British Government had no alternative. On May 14th, 1861, a Proclamation of Neutrality was issued with the necessary reference to the Foreign Enlistment Act, 1819. Great offence was given to the North by this action; but, in fact, a similar course had been followed by the United States in the Canadian Rebellion of 1837, and, moreover, a recognition of a state of war did not involve any recognition of Independence[1]. On June 1st, the British Government forbade any belligerent warships to carry prizes into any harbour of the empire, and, on January 31st, 1862, excluded all ships of war from the Bahama Islands and forbade any ship of war to stay more than twenty-four hours in any other imperial port. The Government, moreover, in its anxiety to avoid any charge of favouring the Confederate States, recognised from the first the blockade of a coast line of 3000 miles declared by Lincoln, though in truth it was, for a considerable time, by no means effective.

It was at this stage that Liverpool became the storm-centre of British policy. It was the interest of the cotton trade to make the blockade of the Southern ports ineffective. It was the business of the blockading forces to make this blockade effective. In the case presented on the part of the British Government to the Tribunal of Arbitration, constituted under Article I of the Treaty of Washington, it was contended that

the right of blockade is a belligerent right, and the enforcement of it belongs to the belligerent and not to neutral powers. That blockades to be binding must be made effective by the blockading power, is a settled and salutary rule; and this indeed is the sole protection of neutrals against an undue and extravagant extension of the right of blockade. It follows, of necessity, that to the exertions of the blockading Power, and to those alone the task of making them effective must be left.

It will be desirable to examine this declaration of policy in the light of Anglo-American relations; but, first, it is necessary to refer in bare outline to the facts which gave rise to the Alabama Claims and to the subsequent tendencies of British and American policy.

In June, 1862, it became clear that Liverpool had determined to break the blockade not only by running cargoes but by strengthening the Confederate fleet. In a strong letter to Lord Russell, dated June 23rd[2], C. F. Adams, the United States Minister in London, referred to the case of the gunboat *Oreto* (which became the *Florida*) in the Confederate

[1] See *The Education of Henry Adams, an Autobiography*, p. 153. (Constable, 1919.)
[2] Papers presented to Parliament, 1872.

service, which had been built at Liverpool, and sailed thence in March, 1862; and to a sister ship—"a new and still more powerful war steamer"—then within nine or ten days of completion. This was the 290th ship laid down in the building-yards of Messrs Laird at Birkenhead. It was admittedly "a ship of war." When completed and armed, "she will be a most formidable and dangerous craft, and, if not prevented going to sea, will do much mischief to our commerce. The persons engaged in her construction say that no better vessel of her class was ever built."

No one in Liverpool doubted the destination of "No. 290," and the password among the crew, who were enlisted from July, 1862, was "290"; but Adams merely asked the British Government for "such action as may tend, either to stop the projected expedition, or to establish the fact that its purpose is not inimical to the people of the United States." On June 25th, Lord Russell replied, "I have lost no time in referring the matter to the proper Department."

Delays, due to bad fortune or carelessness and to the amazing view of the Commissioners of Customs, that "at present there is not sufficient ground to warrant the detention of the vessel," were tolerated by Lord Russell. However, all the necessary evidence was submitted to him by Adams on July 24th, including an opinion from one of the most eminent of English lawyers, R. P. Collier, K.C., who stated that "it appears difficult to make out a stronger case of infringement of the Foreign Enlistment Act, which, if not enforced on this occasion, is little better than a dead letter[1]."

There can be no doubt that Lord Russell ought to have acted at once on such evidence and on such an opinion. His vacillation, perhaps, reflected the cleavage of national opinion and the view held by a section of the nation that it was perfectly legitimate to ride through the policy of the Foreign Enlistment Act of 1819 on purely technical grounds. In June, Lord Russell ought to have taken immediate action. On July 24th he had his last opportunity, but did nothing for four days. He then wrote, on July 28th, to Adams that the papers had been referred to the Law Officers of the Crown. There were delays in securing this opinion, due to the illness of one of the Law Officers; but the opinion, when it came, entirely confirmed the opinion of Collier. The delay, however, hardly mattered; for No. 290,

---

[1] Sir Robert Collier was Solicitor-General from October, 1863, and was appointed Attorney-General in 1868. In 1885 he was created Lord Monkswell. (Lord John Russell was created Earl Russell on July 30th, 1861.)

on the fatal July 28th, went for a trial trip out of the Mersey, from which she never returned. She was joined by most of her crew in a bay on the Welsh coast, sailed round the north coast of Ireland and arrived at the island of Terceira (among the Azores) on August 20th. There she was met by a British barque loaded with guns and war material, and later by the S.S. *Bahama,* bringing Captain Semmes, more guns and the rest of the crew. Here *The Alabama* was equipped outside the three-mile limit, and, on Sunday, August 24th, 1862, she was commissioned by the authority of the Confederate States Government and began the devastating cruise of twenty-two months, which ended in her destruction on Sunday, June 19th, 1864, off Cherbourg, by the U.S.S. *Kearsage.* It is not necessary here to retell the story of the *Alabama,* or to estimate in detail the great losses that she inflicted on the loyal subjects of the United States Government. These were the fruit of Lord Russell's vacillation. An acute observer declared that his four days of indecision cost England a million sterling a day[1]. Lord Russell, in his *Recollections,* accepted full blame. He wrote:

" I assent entirely to the opinion of the Lord Chief Justice of England that the *Alabama* ought to have been detained during the four days I was waiting for the opinion of the Law officers. But I think that the fault was not that of the Commissioners of Customs, it was my fault as Secretary of State for Foreign Affairs[2]."

It is unnecessary, as it would be painful, further to recall Lord Russell's explanations of his error and his account of his belated efforts to stop the *Alabama* at Liverpool, Queenstown and Nassau. Adams's moderation of tone in the face of great provocation offers a model for Ambassadors. He contented himself with writing, on September 30th:

" The extent to which Her Majesty's Flag and some of her ports have been used to the end of carrying on hostile operations is so universally understood that I deem it unnecessary further to dwell upon it. But, in the spirit of friendliness with which I have ever been animated towards Her Majesty's Government, I feel it my duty to omit no opportunity of urging the manifestation of its well known energy in upholding those laws of neutrality upon which alone the reciprocal confidence of nations can find a permanent base."

[1] Lord Houghton (in Fitzmaurice's *Granville*), II. 81. See also Mr Sidney Low and Mr L. C. Sanders' *History of England during the Reign of Victoria,* p. 264. There are many records of the cruise of the *Alabama.* Very vivid accounts by eyewitnesses were published in *The Century* magazine for March, 1886. The account of life on board by one of the hands is a horrible picture of a pirate crew of earlier centuries, a gang of murderous ruffians. On the other hand, the account given by the First Officer of the ship is much more favourable. Probably, the truth lies between these two accounts.
[2] See also *The Education of Henry Adams,* p. 150.

Adams, in this sentence, removed the whole subject of sea-policy from the arena of local politics and passion to the region of history, tradition and reasonableness. He knew, as possibly Lord Russell's legal advisers at that time did not know, that there was a continuity of British and American policy in relation to neutrality which could or should be the only test of the troubles involved in the losses that British carelessness had imposed on his sorely tried republic. It is in this connexion noteworthy that, in answer to his further letter of November 20th, 1862, dealing with the relations of the two countries on the subject of neutrality from the latter part of the eighteenth century, Lord Russell offered to amend the Foreign Enlistment Act, 1819: an offer that was carried into effect in 1870.

The difficulties of policy that have for more than a century beset the accepted doctrine of Neutrality have been almost entirely due to the tardiness in the emergence of that doctrine. It was first enunciated in 1793 by the United States of America in Jefferson's famous proclamation; but it was limited by the fact that, at that date, the international rules relating to Contraband and Blockade in restraint of belligerent trade had reached a definite form, and the doctrine of Neutrality was so framed as not to interfere with these rules. Jefferson declared in 1793

that a neutral nation must, in all things relating to the War, observe and enact impartiality towards the parties; that favours to one to the prejudice of the other would import a fraudulent neutrality, of which no nation would be the dupe; that no succour should be given to either unless stipulated by treaty, in money, arms, or anything else directly bestowing favour.

This development of the views of Gentilis in the seventeenth century, and of Vattel and Rousseau in the eighteenth, carried with it two implications. It is the neutral Sovereign and not the Sovereign's subjects whom the rule or doctrine binds, and, therefore, while enlistment in neutral territory, and the arming of vessels in neutral waters are alike unlawful, yet the neutral Sovereign has no duty to restrain his subjects from trade with any belligerent or any fellow neutral. These implications follow at once from Rousseau's doctrine that nations, not nationals, are at war. In policy these implications have survived, though Rousseau's doctrine finally disappeared in the Five Years' War that ended in November, 1918. Jefferson laid special stress, in ominous words, on this right of nationals to trade:

" American citizens have always been free to make, vend and export arms. It is the constant occupation and livelihood of some of them. To suppress their calling, the only means, perhaps, of their subsistence, because a war exists in foreign and distant countries, in which they have no concern, would scarcely be expected. It would be hard in principle and impossible in practice."

This doctrine or policy and its implications were never overlooked in England or in America. The duty of the neutral Sovereign was conscientiously enshrined in the American Neutrality Acts of 1794 and 1818, and the British Foreign Enlistment Acts of 1819 and 1870, the latter being the direct fruit and a step towards the peaceful settlement of the Alabama Claims. The rights of the neutral nationals were already enshrined in the rules of law which, from the days of Lord Stowell to our own, have been steadily evolved with the intention of giving reality to those very rules relating to Contraband and Blockade, which have made anything in the nature of absolute or true Neutrality impossible. Had the doctrine of Neutrality emerged before the doctrines of Contraband and Blockade, the duty of a neutral Sovereign to restrain his subjects in the pursuit of trade in goods that are essential to the maintenance of a war might have been enunciated; but the policy of successive neutrals during successive Wars made this impossible. Hugo Grotius, in 1625, laid down the complete doctrine of Contraband, including the doctrine of Pre-emption that played so great a part in the War of 1914. Grotius, in effect, declared that no person belonging to a non-belligerent State has the right to play the part of a belligerent. If he does so he must share the fate of a belligerent in respect to goods useful in war. Such goods included goods *ancipitis usus*, goods capable of a double purpose and in fact useful in war. The belligerent who might suffer injury has full rights of self-protection; and, even if the shipper is innocent and has no noxious purpose, yet the goods may be seized, subject, in certain circumstances, to restitution. The Treaty of Whitehall between England and Sweden in 1661 practically adopted the doctrine of Grotius, and the English Courts crowned the list of Contraband contained in that Treaty by a recognition of this practice of Preemption.

So the Anglo-American doctrine of Contraband arose, whereby Absolute and Conditional Contraband were recognised and special cases of necessary seizure were met by the recognition of the equitable practice of Compensation or Pre-emption. The Continental Powers for the most part rejected this conception of Conditional Contraband. Yet the practice by which the capture of goods *ancipitis usus* involves compensation where a guilty mind cannot be brought home to the shipper was a fair answer to Continental objections, while it brought in for trial all real cases of Contraband. This doctrine was fully at work before Jefferson enunciated his theory of Neutrality; but the policy of the Washington Government in 1793 gave permanence to the practice that the neutrality of a Power is consistent with the assiduous belligerency, at their own risk, of its subjects. If the doctrine of Wolff rather than that of Vattel had been adopted in 1793, the United States and Great Britain would have decided to police their own subjects and have thus ended many temptations to war.

The question of Blockade is not less important. Blockade springs from the idea of Siege. No neutral could cross the lines of a besieged city, even if the lines of investment were on the sea; and this led to what Grotius called the Closure of Ports. In 1584, and again in 1630, the Dutch had declared certain ports closed, and, though an effort was made to limit in practice such closure to Contraband, yet after 1700 it was well recognised that all commerce could be legitimately excluded from a port definitely invested by sea. The principle is that a non-belligerent shall not be allowed to supply any goods that will tend to prolong the resistance in any defined area. The Blockade must be recognised, must be effective and one that does not distinguish between neutrals. In these circumstances, a belligerent has a right to condemn the ship, and probably the cargo, of any non-belligerent who seeks to succour a blockaded enemy. Blockade and Contraband are penal measures against the subjects of neutral Powers who, for their own profit, decide to intervene in a war. The Washington Administration in 1793 adopted for the benefit of their own subjects a policy of Neutrality which included a law of Contraband and Blockade invented to penalise subjects of neutral Powers intervening in a war. The United States might have forbidden its subjects to traffic in Contraband, or to run cargoes through blockaded areas. This would have been a step forward; but, so soon as the policy of 1793 had been adopted by England as well as by America, the doctrine had to be carried to its logical conclusion.

This conclusion was foreseen by Lord Stowell and Sir William Grant during the Napoleonic Wars. The doctrine of Continuous Voyage, which sprang from what is known as the Rule of the War of 1756, extended the rule as to Contraband to cases where the goods were colourably consigned to a neutral port, this being merely a stage on the journey to the belligerent forces. Lord Stowell held that the real destination was the test. No doubt there was a question as to whether the test was the real destination of the ship or of the goods. But Dr Westlake has rightly pointed out[1] that Lord Stowell never committed himself to the view that the real destination was that of the ship. Such a conclusion would have been a logical absurdity, since the question of guilt lies with the shippers. The American judges during the War of Secession were not likely to be misled on this point, and, in the case of the *Peterhof*[2], the Supreme Court boldly and without hesitation applied the doctrine of Continuous Voyage to the transport of goods. The Court gave the doctrine its legal extension to a doctrine of Continuous Transport, whether by sea or land, when the goods were shipped with the guilty intention of supplying the enemy with Contraband. The British Courts during the War of Secession expressly recognised this developed doctrine of Contraband and applied it during the War of 1914 with further logical extensions. The devices of non-neutral shippers were endless, and the range of Contraband became practically endless. In order to make the doctrine of Non-access complete, the British Government claimed so to apply the doctrine of Continuous Transport as to allow the capture of cargoes consigned to neutral ports "to order" or to an unknown consignee, while the doctrine was carried to the length that all Contraband goods were shut out from a neutral country, which was proved to be sending supplies to the belligerent. All this was the logical and inevitable extension of the policy adopted by Jefferson in 1793; and all this would have been avoided, had the doctrine that a neutral nation must police its own nationals been adopted at that date.

At the time when the Alabama Claims were accruing this growth of policy was in active process, and North and South alike were watching the development of that policy with eager eyes. It was unfortunate that, at such a time, British statesmanship should not have perceived the line that lay between the duty of neutral Governments not to intervene in a war and the right of neutral nationals, at their own risk, so to intervene, and should have confused the notions of a ship as a Contraband article and of a ship as an illegal expedition. The line of distinction was clear enough, had British statesmen known the history of the policy and of the doctrine which it was their duty to apply in the case before them.

The reaffirmation of the principle of the Union in North America,

[1] *International Law*, part II. p. 296.
[2] 5 Wallace 28 [1866].

at vast cost in lives and treasure, created on the other side of the Atlantic a Power that had been integrated and become strong in the furnaces of fratricidal war. In a sense, modern America dates from the successful emergence of the re-united States from a struggle that threatened its life. It emerged triumphant, but through the nation there thrilled a deep dislike and distrust of Great Britain, of the mother-country who was believed to have failed them in their distress. Such a belief was ill-founded, for errors of judgment are not errors of heart; but the belief grew and was grafted into earlier griefs and became a kind of national tradition, fostered, as it is even still to some extent fostered, by school histories which all true American historians condemn. Lord Russell's vacillation and defective knowledge of history bore bitter fruit that was still ripening so late as the year 1914; but some part of the harvest came to sudden maturity immediately after the conclusion of the War of Secession in 1869. American statesmen and journalists alike were determined to make the case of the *Alabama* and her sister ships a test of the future relations between the two countries; and a growing party, flushed with victory, were not only tempted but anxious to try conclusions by war with the mother-country. Such a feeling was by no means universal; yet the peace party would not have been strong enough to preserve peace, had statesmanship proved incapable of finding a *via media*. Mr Lucien Wolf, in his *Life of the First Marquess of Ripon*, goes so far as to say that, towards the end of 1870, "war with America had become almost a question of opportunity and the opportunity was ominously nigh[1]."

The wiser and greater minds on both sides of the Atlantic were, however, in no mood for a repetition of 1812. In 1869, John Lothrop Motley, despite President Grant's instinctive dislike of him—a dislike that extended to anyone that Grant could not understand[2]—had been sent as Minister to the Court of St James; and he was no war-maker. Henry Adams was then in London, seeking an opportunity to discuss the Alabama Claims with the British Ministers. The younger Adams looked on the Claims, so he says, as his own special creation, "discussed between him and his father long before they had been discussed by Government." He, too, was no more of a war-maker than his father. The crash of the War of 1870 gave time for the wiser minds to think. President Grant, so long as there was peace, wanted peace. He would have been very dangerous if war had actually begun, or if

[1] *Life of the First Lord Ripon*, by Lucien Wolf, 1921, I. 237.
[2] *The Education of Henry Adams*, p. 276.

he had thought that it must begin; but war was not his goal. He had no goal except to let things drift. "Grant had no objects, wanted no help, wished for no champions. The Executive asked only to be let alone. This was his meaning when he said: 'Let us have peace[1].'"

The only danger was, lest the policy of drifting should lead to the cataracts. It was the business of Hamilton Fish, the Secretary of State, to watch the drifting; and he was as little of a war-maker as Adams or Motley. Yet the position was dangerous and the danger was intensified by the very simplicity of General Grant, whose message to Congress on December 5th, 1870, on the relations between the two countries was by no means friendly. Fortunately, the British Government had already perceived the dangers of the position. The Foreign Enlistment Act of 1870 had been passed and on November 19th, the Cabinet had considered a Memorandum, drawn up by Lord Tenterden of the Foreign Office, in which it was asserted that "as a matter of national exigency there must be a friendly adjustment of American claims[2]." The American Senate seemed inclined to determine the President's policy of drift into a very unfriendly direction. Lord Clarendon had accepted an Arbitration Treaty proposed by the American Government. This the Senate had thrown out, and it was therefore useless to suggest that the Alabama Claims should be submitted to arbitration. The mystery which has hitherto wrapped the almost unexpected *rapprochement* reached by the two Governments has been cleared up by Mr Lucien Wolf from the confidential documents to which he had access for the purposes of his *Life of Lord Ripon*[3]. Lord Tenterden proposed to the Cabinet a way out of the *impasse*. He suggested that the two Governments should appoint High Commissioners to consider outstanding matters relating to Canadian Fisheries and allied subjects, and that the proposal should emanate from the British Government in such a form as to lead the United States Government to accept it on condition that the Alabama Claims should be included. Sir John Rose, a Canadian lawyer and statesman, who had settled in England, but had large business interests in America, was sent to Washington to sound the Government and to discuss the question with Hamilton Fish. The latter had no desire for war and, indeed, earnestly wished for reconciliation; but it was necessary that he should satisfy the potential War Party. He was, therefore, inclined to insist on expressions of regret and compensation;

---

[1] *The Education of Henry Adams*, p. 267.
[2] *Life of the First Lord Ripon*, I. 238.   [3] *Ibid.* I. 240.

but he did not press this. He, no doubt, felt that the British Government would go as far as possible in their desire for peace, and that a hint in the right direction was, as it proved to be, sufficient. The business was rapidly carried through. On January 26th, 1871, a Note was addressed to the United States Government proposing a High Joint Commission on Canadian Fisheries and similar questions. On January 30th, Fish asked that the Alabama Claims should be included in the reference. This was conceded by the British Government on February 1st, and on February 3rd the American acceptance of the British proposal was officially notified. Any American was plainly at liberty to affirm the simple truth that the British Government had yielded to the demand of the United States Government and had referred the Alabama Claims, without a moment's delay, to the Joint High Commission. It is not often that secret diplomacy has so successfully applied methods resembling those of the nursery to the pride of nations.

The British Commissioners were skilfully chosen. They were Lord de Grey and Ripon, representing the Government, Sir Stafford North-cote, representing the Opposition, Sir Edward Thornton, the British Minister at Washington, Sir John Macdonald, Prime-Minister of Canada, and Professor Montague Bernard who, as Chichele Professor of International Law at Oxford, knew something of the history of the Anglo-American doctrines of Neutrality, Blockade and Contraband. Lord Tenterden, who invented the fair and simple device, was the appropriate Secretary. The understood process was followed, when, at the third sitting of the Joint Commission, the Alabama Claims came up for discussion. On April 8th, Lord de Grey expressed "the regret felt by Her Majesty's Government for the escape of the *Alabama* and other vessels from British ports and for the depredations committed by these vessels."

It was the truth, and Fish accepted it from his heart "as a token of kindness[1]." Then the bomb fell. The American Government laid its cards on the table and proposed that Great Britain should pay as compensation an agreed gross sum, or, *alternatively*, that the question of liability should be referred to a competent tribunal; but that, in any event, the following principles should be applied to the decision as to the Claims:

"1. Any Great Maritime Power with a strong Government possessed of the material resources requisite to enable it to perform its duties, is

[1] *Despatches from the High Commissioners*, April 8th and 10th, 1871.

bound to use active diligence in order to prevent the construction or getting out, arming, equipping or augmenting the force, within its jurisdiction, of any vessel whereby war is intended to be carried on upon the ocean against a Power with which it is at peace, during hostilities between that Power and its insurgent citizens who have been recognised as belligerents by such Great Maritime Power.

2. When such vessel shall have escaped, such Power is bound to use like diligence to correct and detain her when she comes again within its jurisdiction.

3. Such Power is further bound to instruct its naval forces in all parts of the globe to arrest and detain vessels so escaping, whenever found upon the High Seas.

4. Any Power failing to observe either of the rules of international law above described, is justly to be held responsible for the injuries and depredations committed and damages occasioned by such vessels."

The British Commissioners were placed in a difficult position. The American proposals, as they stood, clearly could not be accepted; and yet to break off the labours of the Commission by a definite refusal was an impossible alternative. In these circumstances, the Commissioners, led by Lord de Grey, advised the Cabinet by telegram on March 15th[1] to accept the best that could be wrung from the American Representatives: namely, that the American proposals as amended by agreement should be an Instruction to an Agreed Tribunal. The Cabinet had assumed that all would go well and that the British Commissioners would secure with ease a solution that would reestablish cordial relations. Everything had been done to secure this. The Foreign Enlistment Act, 1870, though of course it was not international law, had carried English Municipal Law into an equality with the American Law, and beyond that no agreement could go. The American proposals, as they stood, were totally inadmissible, and the question before a distraught Cabinet was how far the principle of amendment could be trusted. Lowe, Cardwell and Goschen were opposed to any agreement. Forster and Sir Roundell Palmer were firmly in favour of the proposed compromise. Gladstone, Lord Kimberley and Lord Halifax were doubtful but were in favour of an agreement. Lord Hartington was silent and doubtful[2]. Commonsense carried the day—commonsense and trust in the carefully-chosen Commissioners. The Government agreed to the principles as amended, while insisting that no

[1] *Life of Lord Ripon*, I. 245.
[2] See Letters of Lord Granville and W. E. Forster to Lord de Grey, *Life of Lord Ripon*, I. 246–7.

such principles were in force when the *Alabama* Claims arose[1]. Thus, the fateful agreement was made and the reliance upon Lord de Grey and his colleagues was well justified. The Americans had asked more than they expected to secure, and so obvious was this that they abandoned three-quarters of their original demands, and the rules of guidance for the Tribunal of Reference went little beyond the rules of the British Foreign Enlistment Act of 1819[2]. Had the American Commissioners asked for less, they would have secured more. The Treaty of Washington was signed on May 8th, and approved by the Senate on May 22nd, 1871. It must have created considerable satisfaction in America to know that Lord Russell declared this a British surrender, though, on June 12th he withdrew his hostile motion in the House of Lords. Indeed, the whole transaction was designed to save the feelings of everyone. Lord de Grey, writing at the beginning of June to Lord Granville, stated that it was necessary "to reconcile by some compromise more ingenious than elegant the conflicting desires of the Senators, President and Canadians, without letting go the substantial objects we had in view."

Those objects were legitimate and desirable: the preservation of peaceful relations and also of a sound policy of neutrality. It was no easy task, and furnished a notable illustration of Ovid's maxim—*obsta principiis*. In this case, the remedy seemed likely to come too late. Commonsense had to work in an atmosphere laden with fire-damp. No protocols of the daily proceedings were taken, and the agreed summaries throw little light on the struggle; and therefore, as Sir Stafford Northcote wrote to Lord Granville, "the history of our exploit will never be written as it deserves to be, and de Grey will never get all the credit he deserves for his strategy.... I have told you already how much de Grey has impressed us all by his judgment, tact and temper, and by the high tone he has maintained all through the affair[3]." Lord de Grey carried the Davy lamp which in a very dangerous atmosphere made progress possible and creditable to Americans and English alike.

The Three Rules contained in the Treaty of Washington ran as follows:

"A Neutral Government is bound:

First, to use due diligence to prevent the getting out, arming or equipping within its jurisdiction of any vessel which it has reasonable grounds to believe is intended to cruise, or to carry on war against a Power with which it is at peace; and also to use like diligence to prevent the

[1] Despatch from the High Commissioners, April 5th, 1871. See *Life of Lord Ripon*, I. 249.   [2] Letter from Lord Tenterden of March 6th, 1871.
[3] *Life of Lord Ripon*, I. 251. Fitzmaurice, *Granville*, II. 87, 89.

departure from its jurisdiction of any vessel intended to cruise or carry on war as above, such vessel having been specially adapted, in whole or in part within such jurisdiction, to warlike use.

Secondly, Not to permit or suffer either belligerent to make use of its ports or waters as the base of naval operations against the other, or for the purposes of the renewal or augmentation of military supplies or arms, or the recruitment of men.

Thirdly, to exercise due diligence in its own ports or waters, and as to all persons within its jurisdiction, to prevent any violation of the foregoing obligations and duties."

These Rules were, in the words of the Washington Treaty, adopted by the British Government "in order to evince its desire of strengthening the friendly relations between the two countries and of making satisfactory provision for the future."

The High Contracting Parties, therefore, agreed "to observe these rules as between themselves in the future and to bring them to the knowledge of other maritime powers, and to invite them to accede to them."

The First Rule hardly went beyond the Foreign Enlistment Act, 1819; but Dr Westlake considers that the Second and Third Rules in effect extended to territory and were not limited to "ports and waters[1]."

The British Government were not, however, out of the troubled waters. In 1869, Charles Sumner, in the debates on the Reverdy-Johnson Convention, had put forward as part of the Alabama Claims, claims in respect of the remote consequences of the depredations committed by the *Alabama*, the *Florida*, the *Georgia* and the *Shenandoah*. The Commissioners had assumed that these Indirect Claims had been abandoned, and, on June 12th, 1871, Lord Granville stated that they had disappeared under the limited reference to the Arbitrators. Lord Cairns, however, held that the Treaty justified the American demands[2]. The point was a very fine one. In a despatch from the British Commissioners of March 8th, 1871, it was stated that the United States Government did not put forward the Indirect Claims, and that this was an important concession. In the signed Protocol, it was stated that the Indirect Claims might be revived in the event of a non-settlement. Language, indeed, could hardly have made it plainer that these far-reaching Claims were excluded from the Arbitration; but they were in fact put forward in the American Case of December 15th, 1871. The Cabinet and the country were deeply moved. Russell, Lowe, Cardwell, Goschen and Gladstone insisted on

[1] *International Law*, vol. ii. War, p. 222.
[2] Wolfe, p. 252. Buckle, *Beaconsfield*, v. 178.

our withdrawal from the Arbitration, and even Granville rightly became doubtful of American goodfaith. On the other side, Hamilton Fish attempted to justify the Claims on the ground that the amicable settlement in question referred to the first alternative in the original American proposal, and not to the case of an arbitration. His position was arguable, but really untenable, and the outburst of public opinion in England made it clear to American statesmen that to press these Claims was to ruin all. General Schenck, the American Minister in London, tried once again to revert to the first alternative and secure a direct settlement without an arbitration. Sir Stafford Northcote, in an interview, made it clear that this was impossible, and on April 24th, 1872, General Schenck was given to understand that a way out must be found, or the Treaty was at an end[1]. Fish found the way out. He decided to "ride off upon an adverse decision of the Arbitrators"; and, once again, the essential commonsense of pacific Ministers found a method of saving national pride and of preserving the Treaty. It was definitely understood that the Arbitrators would rule out these Indirect Claims, and it is not surprising to find that the records of the Arbitration register this interesting fact. Secret diplomacy has been much condemned; but it is only fair to say that it was secret diplomacy, and secret diplomacy of almost childlike simplicity, that placed finally the relations of Great Britain and the United States of America on a basis which not even the shock of the War of 1914 could unsettle. The Arbitrators were duly appointed by Great Britain, the United States of America, Brazil, Italy and Switzerland in accordance with the Treaty of Washington, and the Tribunal of the Arbitration duly met at Geneva. After no less than thirty-two sessions, their decision was formulated, on September 14th, 1872. Great Britain had to pay, in respect to the devastations of the three ships (the *Alabama*, the *Florida* and the *Shenandoah*), damages amounting to 15,500,000 dollars. It is not necessary here to deal with the proceedings or the legal arguments[2].

Policy ends, or should end, when the Court takes seisin of a case. It is only necessary to notice two points. The first needs no further comment: the Tribunal ruled out the Indirect Claims. The second concerned the construction that the Tribunal put upon the words "due diligence" in the first Rule of reference. Though the question of construction could not affect the agreement to submit the Alabama

---

[1] Fitzmaurice, *Granville*, II. 64.
[2] See Westlake, *u.s.*, also *Cambridge Modern History*, XII. 16–22, and legal authorities collected by L. Oppenheim, *International Law*, § 335. See also J. B. Moore, *Arbitrations* (I. 653–9) and Phillimore, *International Law* (III. § 151 *a*) for the text of this record.

Claims to the Tribunal, the British Government declined, and inevitably declined, to be bound in future by this construction. The Tribunal held that the due diligence of a nation must be in proportion to the risks to which either belligerent may be exposed from failure to fulfil the obligations of neutrality on his part. Professor Oppenheim points out that, had this been generally accepted, "the most oppressive obligations would have become incumbent upon neutrals." He adds that no such general acceptance has taken place and that "due diligence" must have its regular meaning in municipal law, namely such diligence as can reasonably be expected when all the circumstances and conditions of the case are taken into consideration[1]. With this exception, the First Rule was adopted by the Second Hague Conference of 1907: the words, "to employ the means at its disposal," being substituted for "to use due diligence." Hence, the sole difficulty arising out of the Arbitration has disappeared.

"These Alabama Rules," says Dr Westlake, "will always be memorable in the history of international law, not only as having been the means of settling a threatened dispute, but as a first and not unsuccessful attempt to supply some of the *axiomata media* which Bacon taught the necessity of interposing between the first principles and the detailed results of any science, and the want of which is conspicuous in the theory of neutral duties."

The Rules, the Treaty of Washington and the subsequent Arbitration at Geneva represent also the climax of a Sea-policy of Neutrality which, even if it is not consistent with the highest peace policy, brought finally together the two greatest maritime nations in the world. After Geneva, the common elements of this policy were so fully understood, that in the most crucial moments of stress between belligerent Great Britain and neutral United States in 1915, Mr Bryan, the Secretary of State, in writing to the Chairman of the Senate Committee on Foreign Relations, frankly declared that

some of the doctrines, which appear to bear hardly upon neutrals at the present time, are analogous to, or outgrowths from, policies adopted by the United States of America when it was belligerent. The Government, therefore, cannot consistently protest against the application of rules which it has followed in the past, unless they have not been practised as heretofore[2].

Such a communication between two great Departments of American Government was the direct fruit of the wisdom with which Lord Granville, Lord Selborne, Lord Ripon and Sir Stafford Northcote repaired the shortcomings of Lord Russell and brought back Sea-policy into the lines of reasonableness and tradition.

[1] *International Law*, § 363.
[2] *State Department Publication*, January 24th, 1915.

CHAPTER II

FORWARD POLICY AND REACTION, 1874–1885

I. Forward Policy in Central Asia, 1874–1880

STATESMEN in India, though differing on some fundamental questions of foreign policy, were at all times agreed in regarding the North-west Frontier as the Empire's greatest source of anxiety, and Afghanistan, lying as it did between two great rival Powers, as the weakest link in an imperfect chain of defence. A succession of Viceroys, from Canning onwards, taught by the bitter lesson of 1838–42, had adhered to the conservative policy of letting Afghanistan alone, deeming active intervention so hazardous as to be justified only by the avoidance of still greater risks. Opposed to this school of thought was the "forward" party, represented particularly in military circles, which wished to anticipate a development of events already assumed to be inevitable, and at once bind all the frontier rulers and chiefs to the British Government by means of alliances, missions and, where necessary, subsidies in the form of money and material of war.

The problem of the North-west Frontier became serious only after the annexation of Sind (1843) and the Punjab (1849) had brought the Indian empire to the belt of territory beyond which lay Afghanistan. Although not forming part of Afghanistan, this territory was inhabited by tribes, more or less lawless, who accepted its ruler as suzerain and rendered to him some sort of feudatory service. There were two obvious methods of regulating British relations with the Ameer and his dependencies. One was to assert political influence by force, and the alternative was to trust to the moral effect of a friendly understanding, formally defined. The former of these lines of policy had been tried in 1838 with disastrous results; and its failure ensured the adoption of the second, which was consistently followed for over thirty years. British garrisons were stationed at strategical points as near to Afghanistan as was prudent; but to respect the independence of the Ameer's dominion and refrain from interference in its internal affairs was still regarded as an axiomatic principle of British Policy.

The accepted bases of the political relations of Great Britain with Afghanistan were contained in Treaties and Agreements of 1855, 1857, 1869, and 1873. By a Treaty of March 3rd, 1855, concluded with Dost Mohammad Khan during the governor-generalship of Lord Dalhousie by Sir John Lawrence, as Chief Commissioner of the Punjab, the East India Company undertook to respect the independence of the territories then in the Ameer's possession "and never to interfere therein"; while the Ameer gave a pledge that he would be the friend of the Company's friends and the enemy of its enemies. By a Treaty of 1857, arising out of the Anglo-Persian War, a subsidy was promised to Dost Mohammad for the period of the War, and he agreed to the residence at Kabul, Kandahar, Balkh and elsewhere of British officers for controlling its employment, as well as to the maintenance of a Vakeel at Peshawur. The officers were to be withdrawn on the cessation of the subsidy; but the Ameer was to receive henceforth at Kabul a permanent Vakeel, appointed by the British Government, but not a British officer, and he was still to be represented by a Vakeel at Peshawur. Both Agents were duly appointed; but the Ameer's was withdrawn in 1858 and not replaced.

Dost Mohammad died in 1863, leaving a large legacy of trouble for his kingdom in the shape of sixteen sons, many of whom were, at one time or another, mixed up in the internecine disputes of the succeeding two decades—some as active claimants to the Throne. He had named his third son, Shere Ali, as his successor, and the elder brothers gave a grudging assent. Although in continual conflict with his own kin, Shere Ali maintained his position for fifteen years with but one break, and during the whole of that time was able to count on British support.

While Great Britain had been advancing towards Afghanistan from the south, Russia had been approaching ever nearer from the north; and, to make the resulting situation the more perplexing, there were no exact frontiers, for these had changed continually with the fortunes of war. Already in 1867, Sir John Lawrence, who followed Lord Elgin, suggested to the Home Government that it would be wise to make some communication on the Frontier question to Petrograd in order to obviate possible misunderstanding in the future. The Government replied that they entertained no anxiety regarding Russia's movements, and that the establishment under her auspices of order and civilisation in backward regions was to be preferred to the continuance of the existing state of unsettlement and anarchy. These were likewise Lawrence's views, though his foresight went further. It is customary to identify him in a special manner with the policy described by himself as one of "masterly inactivity." Beyond doubt, he was hostile to any measure that suggested aggression or encroachment, or threatened to weaken the confidence of the Afghans —and herein he was maintaining an old tradition of proved wisdom. While, however, he was far from regarding the Russian advance as a necessary menace, and while he recognised it as no less inevitable and natural than the corresponding advance of British authority on the other side of Afghanistan, he also saw that it contained the possibility of danger. For that reason, he was eager to come to an understanding with Russia as to the limits within which the spheres of influence of the two countries should extend, and the transgression of which by Russia should, in his view, involve her in "war with England in every part of the world." He thought the time had come for this understanding, when, after absorbing successively Tashkand and Khokand, Russia in 1868 occupied Samarkand. As regards Afghanistan, however, he favoured to the end a policy of non-intervention, commended by a money subsidy and the provision of arms to the Ameer as before, with an undertaking that Great Britain would support his independence so long as she could count on his fidelity.

The policy of Lawrence was in the main followed by the Earl of Mayo (1868–72), though with a concurrent slackening of the Ameer's attachment and cordiality. Having been given money, Shere Ali demanded more and more of it, and complained when it was not forthcoming. It was hoped that a meeting between the Viceroy and the Ameer, which took place at Amballa (March 27th–29th, 1869), would restore the earlier confidence. Shere Ali, professing fear of Russia, formally asked for a guarantee of his independence and security, the recognition of his younger son, Abdulla Jan, as his successor, assistance in the form of arms and ammunition as might be needed, and a fixed yearly subsidy. The Indian Government opposed, and the Home Government rejected, the demand for an unconditional guarantee, and their attitude was approved by both political parties at the time; but the Viceroy was authorised to promise the Ameer money, arms, and ammunition at the full discretion of his advisers. Interpreting his Instructions narrowly, as he was bound to do, all Lord Mayo could promise was that the Ameer's applications for assistance would be received always "with consideration and respect." The question of the Succession was evaded.

The caution and reserve shown by his Ally disappointed the Ameer, whose alarm, though it may have been exaggerated, was not difficult to understand. The Home Government had themselves begun to perceive the importance of coming to a clearer understanding with Russia. Just before the Amballa meeting, Lord Clarendon had discussed the Central Asian Question with Baron Brunnow and suggested "the recognition of some territory as neutral between the possessions of England and Russia, which should be the limit of those possessions and should be scrupulously respected by both Powers." Brunnow communicated with Prince Gortchakoff, who replied that the idea of maintaining between the two empires in Asia "a zone to preserve them from contact" had always been favoured by the Tsar. He also gave the assurance that the Tsar regarded Afghanistan as "completely outside the sphere within which Russia may be called upon to exercise her influence." The assurance was deemed satisfactory, but insufficient. In the past, there had never been any reluctance on Russia's part to disclaim the intention of further advance in Central Asia, or even to disown the inconvenient action of zealous soldiers on the spot, eager to make reputations for themselves. Nevertheless, in spite of all assurances and disclaimers, Russia had, in fact, continued to go forward; and where she went she invariably remained.

It will always be a point of dispute how far the suspicion of Russian designs, which was diligently fostered by a powerful party in England throughout the 'seventies, accentuated the very danger against which it was directed. Russia had, of course, just the same right to approach Afghanistan from the one side as Great Britain had from the other. If the interests of the Indian empire called for a policy of annexations and protectorates, so did those of the Russo-Asiatic empire; and the reasons which operated in the one case applied equally in the other. When this has been said, however, it must be allowed that Russian diplomacy was not as straightforward as it might have been; and the habit of the Tsar's advisers of carrying on two policies, the one at Petrograd, official and conciliatory, and the other in Central Asia, unofficial and at times aggressive, yet open to repudiation at discretion, inevitably increased distrust.

The principle of a neutral zone having been accepted, the boundary of Afghanistan had to be fixed. The Oxus was taken as the general northern line, a final Agreement to that effect being reached in January, 1873, at which time Russia gave positive assurances, not only that the Emperor did not intend to take Khiva, but that orders had been issued to prevent such a step.

Lord Northbrook was now Viceroy, having succeeded Lord Mayo, who was assassinated in February, 1872. Like his predecessor, North-brook was a safe man, in whose character the English qualities of slow-going caution and sterling commonsense were shown at their best. Above all, he had a passion for justice and fair-dealing. It was his conviction that, in political relations, Eastern ideas and practices should be met with Western, and that, if the European could not compete with the Oriental in duplicity and intrigue, he could meet him successfully with the more generous weapons of frankness and honesty. His successful administration in India, however, synchro-nised with a relapse in external relations. Ground was lost in Afghanistan, and, while the British blamed the Ameer, the Ameer blamed the British. The Seistan boundary settlement of 1873 sorely displeased Shere Ali, who felt—as many Anglo-Indians felt with him —that in that transaction his interests had been sacrificed to the cause of Anglo-Persian amity. He, also, harped continually upon the question of a guarantee and resented its not being offered to him in the form which could alone remove his legitimate anxiety. In 1870, General Kaufmann, Governor-General of Russian Turkestan, had addressed a letter of courtesy to the Ameer, who had replied to it in terms approved by the Viceroy. Two years later, Kaufmann pro-posed a regular exchange of correspondence between himself and Kabul, and thereby alarmed the Ameer, who was not relieved by the Indian Government's assurance that Russia had promised to regard his country as outside the sphere of her influence.

For Russia was still pressing on. Not only did she retain Samar-kand, after occupying it avowedly as a temporary measure, but, in August, 1873, she obtained the cession of Khiva by treaty. This proceeding led Lord Granville to send to the British Ambassador at Petrograd a despatch in which, while deprecating a too close enquiry into how far the Treaty was in accord with Russia's past assurances, and disclaiming the exaggerated apprehensions current in England, he stated it to be increasingly desirable that a clear and frank under-standing as to their relative spheres of interest should "continue" to exist between the two countries.

In his alarm, the Ameer now not only asked for a larger subsidy, more arms and ammunition, help in building forts on the Northern Frontier, and for the recognition of his favourite son as successor, but demanded an assurance that he would be able to count on British help in the event of his territory being invaded. In October, the Viceroy conferred with the Afghan Foreign Minister at Simla, but failed to satisfy him. He was authorised to give the assurance that the British Government would afford the Ameer assistance in the event of unprovoked aggression, so long as he followed their advice in foreign affairs; but it was made clear that they reserved the right to judge whether and when help should be given. Any unconditional guarantee of protection was positively refused. To the last, Lord Northbrook declined to share the fears of Russian designs which periodically perturbed a section of the public at home. "We are quite comfortable in India, but England is all in a flutter," he wrote home in 1873, on the occasion of one of these alarms. He was of Lawrence's opinion, however, that the weakness of Great Britain's position consisted in the fact that she had not made sufficiently clear to the Russian Government the paramount importance for her of intimate relations with Afghanistan and the danger of any disturbance of the frontier of that State. "I go heartily with Lord Lawrence and against fuss and interference," he wrote so late as January, 1875; "but there is a point upon which I would fight, and I should let the Russians understand this very clearly."

The Gladstone Administration resigned in February, 1874, and in the succeeding Cabinet of Disraeli Lord Derby was for four years Foreign Secretary, and Lord Salisbury, for the same time, Secretary for India. Gladstone's defeat led to his abandonment of the leadership of his party and practically—though he continued to represent his old constituency—to his temporary retirement from political life. Not all his colleagues lamented this self-effacement; yet the absence of his steadying influence, his instinctive regard for the moralities of national life, his warm humanitarian sympathies, and his lynx-eyed scrutiny of the blunders and foibles of his opponents was a great loss to the House of Commons, and in Foreign Affairs it meant the withdrawal of a wholesome check upon the actions of a statesman who was irresistibly attracted to ambitious designs.

In his appeal to the nation in the general election, Disraeli had blamed the outgoing Government for showing too little energy in Foreign Affairs, and too much in domestic legislation. That order of things it was his intention to reverse. For twenty years Disraeli, both as statesman and writer, had been educating his party to the recognition of Great Britain's wider imperial destiny. Having now behind him a compliant House of Commons and a consistently sympathetic House of Lords, he lost no time in putting his ideas into practice. It was his ambition to revive the spacious days of Elizabeth; Great

Britain's influence should again be felt to furthest Thule. Without her word nothing should be done in Europe, for he was determined to win for his country the place in Continental politics which Germany under Bismarck was usurping. Still more distinctly, he aspired to make his country, instead of Russia, the imperial mistress of the East. Long ago, indeed, he had conceived of her as less a European than an Asiatic Power[1]. The accomplishment of designs so bold involved a reorientation of Great Britain's Foreign Policy and a change of emphasis in her relations with several of the Powers. It was a tribute to his remarkable will-power and concentration of purpose that he succeeded so easily in winning his party for a transformation so fundamental and so contrary to long tradition.

There was no immediate change of policy in India, though strong influences at once became active to that end at home. In particular, Sir Bartle Frere, ex-Governor of Bombay, and now a member of the Indian Council, falling back upon a minute of Sir Henry Rawlinson's of 1868, succeeded in convincing the Secretary of State of Russia's sinister designs and in winning his acceptance of Rawlinson's specific for frustrating them. This was the appointment of a British Resident, in addition to the existing native Agent in Afghanistan, to be stationed, first at Herat, but later at Kabul. Lord Salisbury formally made himself the mouthpiece of the "forward" school by a despatch addressed to the Viceroy on January 22nd, 1875, which he reinforced by private letters. In this document, fateful because it led to the abandonment of the old prudent policy, and the opening of a new era of rash experiment and daring adventure, it was stated that the Government had anxiously followed the course of events in Central Asia, and particularly on the frontiers of Persia and Afghanistan, and were impressed by the need for precautionary action. It was felt that the information which reached the Indian Government as to what passed in Afghanistan and on its frontiers was neither sufficient nor trustworthy, and that there was reason to suspect that the Ameer controlled that information at will. In order to remedy this evil, the Viceroy was directed to "take measures, with as much expedition as the circumstances of the case permit, for procuring the assent of the Ameer to the establishment of a British Agency at Herat"; and it was added that, when this had been done, a similar step might be desirable in regard to Kandahar—but not to Kabul, on account of "the difficulties which are interposed by the fanatic violence of the people."

---

[1] Speech at Aylesbury, July 13th, 1866.

Neither then nor later, however, did Lord Salisbury take seriously the alleged menace of a Russian advance upon India; what he chiefly feared was that Russia might seek to foment Afghan hostility against Great Britain, with the object of supplanting British influence at the Ameer's Court.

Lord Northbrook lost no time in telegraphing (February 18th) that in the opinion of his Government "the time and circumstances appeared unsuitable for taking the initiative in the matter," and that the Ameer might be unwilling to allow a British Agent to reside at Herat without harbouring disloyal intentions to the British Government. He, therefore, asked for discretion as to the time and opportunity of giving effect to his Instructions. Lord Salisbury sanctioned a delay of three or four months. In the following month, and again in June, the Viceroy reported that the opinion of the officers of the Punjab was averse to any pressure being applied to the Ameer in the way and for the purpose proposed. The attitude of the Indian Government was not, however, absolutely negative, for, in view of the situation which would arise if Russia occupied Merv, it was suggested that such a step would make it necessary to give to the Ameer additional assistance and more specific assurances that Great Britain would help him to defend Afghanistan against attack from without; and that then would be the proper time to establish a British Resident at Herat, as part of a new treaty arrangement.

In his reply (November 19) Lord Salisbury confessed to serious apprehension of Russian aggression. A short time before, in fact, a Russian Agent had been received at Kabul for the first time, and thenceforward there was a more or less regular exchange of courtesies between the emissaries of the Government of Turkestan and the Ameer. By the end of 1875, Russia was, also, completing the subdual and annexation of Khiva and Khokand, and the early appropriation of Merv seemed certain. Adhering as firmly as before to the proposal of a British Agency, the Indian Secretary, on behalf of the Government, now instructed Lord Northbrook to find without avoidable delay "some occasion for sending a mission to Kabul and to press the reception of this mission very earnestly upon the Ameer." It was to be the object of the Mission to arrange for the stationing of British officers in his kingdom. In their reply (January 28th, 1876) the Viceroy and Council still resisted the proposal by an argument which went to the extreme limits of official prudence, ending with the grave warning: "We deprecate, as involving serious danger to the peace of

Afghanistan and to the interests of the British Empire in India, the execution under present circumstances of the Instructions conveyed in your Lordship's despatch." Several months before this, Lord Northbrook had written to Lord Salisbury, in a private letter (September 30th, 1875): "My firm opinion is that to do anything to force him (the Ameer) to receive agents of ours in his country against his will is likely to subject us to the risk of another unnecessary and costly war in Afghanistan before many years are over."

It was now too late for any counsels of prudence to have effect. At home, the "forward" party was in full hue and cry. A "spirited Foreign Policy" was the parole of the day. A beginning had been made in Europe, and the continuation was to be in Asia. Convinced that his work in India was done and his influence with the Home Government undermined, Lord Northbrook resigned in November; and he returned to England in the following spring.

Some time before this, the Prime-Minister had given two fresh proofs of his wish to strengthen British prestige in India. In the autumn of 1875, the Prince of Wales, at his suggestion, paid a visit of several months to India and there met the chief native rulers. Early in the following year, he sprang on the Houses of Parliament a proposal to confer upon the Queen a distinct title in virtue of her Indian dominion. The proposal was not popular in the country; but, since the Queen was known to favour it, the necessary Bill met with little opposition, though the undertaking was given that the new title should not be used in the United Kingdom. On the first day of 1877, the Queen was accordingly proclaimed at Delhi and other Indian cities as "Empress of India" (*Kaisar-i-Hind*).

The new Viceroy appointed was Lord Lytton, then British Minister at Lisbon[1]. If the offer of the position was a great surprise to him, as he has recorded, it was no less such to the public. Lord Lytton's distinction had been rather literary than political. Although he had many qualities of statesmanship, and in particular the rare gift of imagination, he had never touched questions of high politics, he had had little or no experience of parliamentary life, and to this particular office, as he admitted to Disraeli, he came with "inexperience of all administrative business and ignorance at the outset of Indian affairs[2]."

[1] Disraeli offered the Viceroyalty to Lord Lytton in a letter of November 23rd, 1875, and he left England on March 1st following.
[2] Letter to Disraeli of December 1st, 1875. *Lord Lytton's Indian Administration*, p. 3. (In the following August Disraeli was raised to the peerage as Earl of Beaconsfield.)

Lord Lytton, however, was not required to have an Indian policy; one had been prepared for him in advance, and he was merely selected as the likeliest instrument for executing it. Sir A. C. Lyall, his first Foreign Secretary, spoke of him as having come to India "more as a Government official than as an Oriental ruler." He was to inaugurate the "forward" movement which Lord Northbrook had for a time delayed, and he carried his Instructions with him in the form of an elaborate Memorandum. While these Instructions were perfectly explicit as to the object in view, they left him a wide discretion as to the methods by which this object was to be attained. Briefly, he was to concede the demands made by the Ameer in 1869 and 1873, and, in particular, to insist upon the reception of a British Mission in return.

For a short time longer, events in Europe held back active measures. There, the attention of the British and Russian Governments was concentrated upon an Eastern problem nearer home, and, throughout the whole of the year 1876, because approaching this problem from different angles and with different motives, the two Governments had barely succeeded in maintaining the appearance of harmony. In a great empire like that of Great Britain, Indian and Colonial Policy has perforce to march together in close step with general Foreign Policy; and while difficulties were increasing in Europe the time was inopportune for precipitating complications in Asia. Meanwhile, his knowledge of the preoccupations of the British Government and of the delicate relations in which Great Britain stood to Russia encouraged in the Ameer an attitude of greater independence. Reports of his growing disaffection began to alarm the Indian Government, and when, early in 1877, he was alleged to have preached a *jihad* against British rule in India and to have opened direct communications with the Russian authorities, contrary to his bond, formal complaint was made to his advisers.

An open breach with Russia occurred when, after the abortive Constantinople Conference, she declared war on Turkey (April 24th, 1877), claiming a justification which the British Government denied. In that War, as in the succeeding Peace settlement[1], Great Britain's influence was thrown wholly on Turkey's side. Russia, therefore, only followed the rules of fair fighting when she decided that, as her opponent had struck her in one place, she would strike back in another. The later developments of the Eastern controversy thus

[1] Cf. *infra*, pp. 140–2.

produced violent repercussions in Central Asia, and their gravity was not lessened by the fact that Russia's action there was tactical rather than part of a deeply laid scheme of territorial aggression[1].

Twelve days after his first meeting with the Indian Council, then far from sympathetic, Lord Lytton took the first step in the pursuance of the policy entrusted to him, when, through the Commissioner at Peshawur, he informed the Ameer of the intention to depute a Special Envoy to wait upon him at an early date, with a view to notifying the Queen's Imperial title and his own assumption of office. In his reply (May 22nd), the Ameer declined a conference, on the ground that it could serve no purpose, unless the Indian Government had something new to say, which went beyond the conversations at Simla. Answering a further letter, the Ameer so far relented as to propose that the British native Vakeel at Kabul should be called to Simla, to report upon affairs at that Court, and should thereafter communicate to him the views and wishes of the British Government. This meeting took place on October 6th, and the result was to show the Ameer to be in a bad humour and dissatisfied with many things which the British Government had done or omitted to do. He still brooded over the refusal of the more definite alliance for which he asked in 1873, and he had come to the conclusion that the British Government cared for him only in so far as they were enabled by his help to serve their own interests. He objected to the despatch of a mission to Kabul on the threefold ground: that he expected no practical result from it, that it would inflame native feeling, and that Russian counteraction would be the inevitable consequence. It was, nevertheless, clear that the Ameer was willing to receive any amount of subsidy, and that, if an alliance could but be shaped to his liking, he would rather admit British officers than forfeit it, provided the British Government would recognise his younger son, Abdulla Jan, as his successor, and not otherwise interfere in the internal affairs of Afghanistan. Lord Lytton offered to meet the Ameer on both points, and practically to accept his 1873 demands, the details to be arranged at a conference. By this time, he had broken down opposition in the

[1] Describing in a letter to the Queen (July 22nd, 1877) the measures which were to be taken if war broke out with Russia because of her apprehended occupation of Constantinople, the Prime-Minister wrote: " It is Lord Beaconsfield's present opinion that in such a case Russia must be attacked from Asia, that troops should be sent to the Persian Gulf, and that the Empress of India should order her armies to clear Central Asia of the Muscovites, and drive them into the Caspian. We have a good instrument for this purpose in Lord Lytton, *and indeed he was placed there with that view*." (*Life of Benjamin Disraeli, Earl of Beaconsfield*, VI. 155.)

Council, and was able to report to Lord Salisbury that he anticipated "no further opposition in carrying out my views."

The Conference was held at Peshawur in January, 1877, the Indian Government being represented by Sir Lewis Pelly and the Ameer by his Minister Syud Noor Mohammad and the Mir Akhor Ahmed Khan, whose powers were *ad referendum*. The discussions dragged on for a long time. There was agreement on many points; but, when the question of despatching Missions was raised, the negotiators at once found themselves in front of a dead wall. Then, the Viceroy addressed to the British Envoy a long letter (March 3rd) of which the object was to stimulate the Ameer's wish for an alliance by convincing him that at present the British Government were under no obligations to him. It cannot be said that this reasoning was altogether free from sophistry, and its effect was necessarily unfavourable. Lord Lytton contended that, under the Treaty of 1855, the Government had "contracted no liabilities whatever on behalf of the Ameer," not even reciprocating his pledge to be "the friend of its friends and the enemy of its enemies." Nevertheless, the Treaty certainly bound the Government to respect the territories then in the Ameer's possession and to maintain "perpetual peace and friendship" with Afghanistan—commitments capable of a very restricted, but also of a very wide, interpretation. Lord Mayo's undertaking of 1869 had gone further, while the Simla Agreement of 1873, though it gave only a conditional promise of help in the event of foreign aggression, in reality involved a moral and even a political obligation which the British Government would have ignored at their peril.

It was, of course, competent for Great Britain at any time to denounce her Treaties altogether in due form, as a preliminary either to the conclusion of a new agreement or to the entire abandonment of conventional relations with Afghanistan. But confidence in her good faith was certain to be weakened by an attempt to prove that the engagements which had existed for twenty years, though meaning much to the Ameer, meant nothing at all to his supposed friend and ally. It was an inauspicious fact that Lord Lytton showed so little readiness to view the question from the standpoint of a ruler as proud, suspicious, self-willed, and masterful as himself. If obligations which the Ameer had held to be, though insufficient, at least genuine so far as they went, were to be robbed of all value, it was hardly reasonable to expect him to enter with fervour into a new agreement which might be diluted at a future date in a similar manner.

A white light is thrown upon the frame of mind in which Lord Lytton proceeded with his task by a passage in a letter which he addressed a little later to Captain Cavagnari, the new British Agent at Peshawur (May 19th, 1877):

> *Me judice*, the radical defect in the conduct of our past relations with Shere Ali is that the *tone* of it has never been in wholesome accordance with the realities of our ‘relative positions—the weakness of his position and the strength of our own....We can get on without Shere Ali; he cannot get on without us. Ere long he must either go to shipwreck altogether, or else return to the old moorings on the Peshawur side in a temper chastened by sharp experience[1].

The fact is that, from the beginning, Lord Lytton was determined to drive the Ameer; never once did he seriously try to lead him.

The Government at home had, so far, cordially approved all the Viceroy had done. "We must completely and unflinchingly support Lytton," Lord Beaconsfield wrote to the Foreign Secretary (April 1st, 1877); "we chose him for this very kind of business." The support which the Viceroy received from home at this juncture was, indeed, so unreserved as to encourage him to greater independence of action than he had yet dared to assert.

While large events were shaping themselves in Afghanistan, a smaller "forward movement" was carried out with complete success in another part of the same frontier. Energetic soldiers like Colonel Sandeman and Colonel Roberts had long been reconnoitring on the borders of Baluchistan. Lord Northbrook had sanctioned overtures to the friendly ruler of that State, with a view to bringing him formally under British influence; and Sandeman was engaged on this business when Lord Lytton arrived. Eventually, by the Treaty of Jacobabad, concluded with the Khan of Khelat (December 8th, 1876) Baluchistan passed under British protection, and the right was obtained to station British troops at Quetta. British influence was also strengthened in Chitral and Gilgit in the north at the same time.

The incident did not improve the Ameer's humour or facilitate the proceedings at Peshawur. In the midst of the Conference, too, his Minister Syud Noor Mohammad, who had arrived there sick, died (March 26th). The consequence was the suspension of the negotiations, and Sir Lewis Pelly left Peshawur on April 12th without

---

[1] *Lord Lytton's Indian Administration*, p. 162. In the same work is quoted a letter of August 27th, 1876, in which Lord Lytton says of the Ameer: "A tool in the hands of Russia I will never allow him to become. Such a tool it would be my duty to break before it could be used."

a treaty. Hereupon, the British native agent at Kabul was withdrawn, and for some months there was a complete break in political relations between the Governments of India and Afghanistan, though news from Kabul continued to trickle through the receiving office at Peshawur.

The negotiations which had ended so unsatisfactorily left both sides with full liberty to go their own way, and both claimed and exercised this liberty. For a time, Lord Lytton applied himself to the task of working out an alternative solution of the Afghan Question —the method of disintegration. Fearing that Shere Ali had irretrievably slipped out of his hands, he contemplated the division of his kingdom, thus rendering him impotent for harm.

Soon events in Europe made their influence felt. Smarting under the humiliations which she had there sustained at Great Britain's hands, Russia did not hesitate to make the most of her advantages in Central Asia. In the summer of 1878, news was received of active Russian plottings in Kabul. In July, General Stoletoff, bearing letters from General Kaufmann, made his way to the Ameer's capital, where he was cordially received. If, as is maintained, he took back with him a formal Treaty of Alliance, it was a paper arrangement, for it did not help Afghanistan in its later difficulties. Convinced that the time for resolute action had now come, Lord Lytton, by urgent entreaty, obtained the Government's permission to insist on the immediate reception of a British Mission. Hitherto, the door into Afghanistan had been closed by prejudice, and bolted and barred by suspicion and fanaticism. Now he was resolved to force it, though he well knew the dangers which lurked behind, for some of his most experienced advisers had repeatedly warned him of them.

The Envoy chosen was Sir Neville Chamberlain, who was to be accompanied by Major Cavagnari[1]; Major St John, Captain Hammick, and a medical officer, with Kazi Syud Ahmed, and a sufficient escort. It was necessary that the Ameer should be informed in advance by a native emissary, in order to prepare the way and to allow of the necessary arrangements being made for the quiet passage of the Mission through Afghan territory. The departure of this advance agent was delayed owing to the death of the heir-apparent, Abdulla Jan (August 17th), and he reached Kabul only on

---

[1] The testimony of this gallant officer was quoted by the Indian Government, in a despatch of June 7th, 1875, in support of its contention that the Ameer would be "most unwilling to receive a British agent at Herat."

September 10th. The Ameer received him ungraciously and firmly declined the proffered overtures.

In the meantime, the Mission had set out. Travelling by the Khyber Pass route, it had no sooner reached the outpost of Ali Masjid, at the entrance to the defile, than it came to a standstill. There, the commander of the fort refused permission to pass his lines. In reply to protest, he said that he had no authority from the Ameer to allow the Mission to go forward, and that in its absence further progress would if necessary be resisted by force. When parley, expostulation and threat proved unavailing, the Mission returned to Peshawur (September 23rd).

The news of the rebuff offered to the Mission met with a mixed reception from the British Cabinet. The action of the Russian Agent and of the Ameer was, of course, irregular and aggravating; but the Viceroy's impulsive method of countering it was felt to be indiscreet and inopportune. For, at this time, the two Governments in Europe, their dispute over the Eastern Question having been adjusted, seemed at last in a fair way of coming to a complete understanding on the Question of Central Asia. Accordingly, Lord Beaconsfield and Lord Salisbury (Foreign Secretary since March), who managed the more important Foreign Affairs in partnership, were both opposed to the idea of rash reprisals. The former was certainly in no mood for a second rupture with Russia, after the first had been healed so satisfactorily. He did not forget that the Treaty of Berlin, quite recently concluded (July 13th), had been represented by him as an all-round settlement with Russia in Asia as well as in Europe. The country had responded enthusiastically to his *Ave* "Peace with honour!" when he returned from Berlin; "but if they find there is no peace they will soon be apt to conclude there is also no honour[1]." He was, therefore, disposed at first to condemn the Viceroy's impetuous action as spoiling the good work which he and his lieutenant had accomplished in Berlin.

Headstrong counsels abounded at that time. "Jingo" voices in India and at home were calling in chorus for the immediate chastisement of a half-savage ruler who had proved truculent as well as treacherous. Without any concession to passion, however, there were grave political considerations which made it difficult to overlook the affront. Western authority in Oriental countries is based on the principle that prestige is power. Many moderate men, free from

[1] Letter of September 17th, 1878.

any feeling of vindictiveness, believed that, if it were to go forth in the East that a border-chief could with impunity set at defiance Great Britain and the Envoy of the Empress-Queen, the British tenure of India might not be worth a year's purchase. Rejecting the Viceroy's request for permission to adopt forcible measures, however, the Cabinet decided to continue the military preparations; but, in the meantime, to try the effect upon the Ameer of another message, the text of which, for caution's sake, was to receive its explicit approval before despatch. This letter, as authorised by the Secretary of State on October 31st, and delivered to the Afghan commander at Ali Masjid on November 2nd, demanded from the Ameer an apology and an undertaking to receive a permanent British Mission within his territory, failing which his intentions were to be regarded as hostile and he was to be treated as a declared enemy of Great Britain.

No reply to the British ultimatum having been received within the time limit fixed (November 20th), three British forces of invasion were set in motion simultaneously. The northern force, under General Browne, moved on the Khyber Pass, taking the obstructive fort of Ali Masjid and then Jellalabad, so clearing the way to Kabul; the centre column, under Sir Frederick Roberts, followed the Kurum Valley, capturing the Peiwar Khotel after a sharp engagement; while, in the south, Generals Biddulph and Stewart operated, the former advancing from Quetta to Pishin, which he occupied without resistance, while the latter took command there of the Kandahar expeditionary force, which he brought to its destination on January 9th, 1879. Shere Ali had, in the meantime, fled from Kabul into Afghan Turkestan (where he died in February), leaving in command his son Yakoob Khan, whom he had liberated after long imprisonment. On the last day of the month, his belated reply to the ultimatum was received: no apology was tendered, but he agreed to a British Mission. No attempt was made by the Russians to increase the invaders' difficulties. On the outbreak of hostilities the Kabul Mission withdrew into its own territory, and, when the Ameer appealed for assistance, he received only the good advice to make peace.

Authority having been thus asserted, peace was offered to Afghanistan on terms which practically realised the Salisbury-Lytton programme. Unfortunately, it had to be concluded with the makeshift ruler, Yakoob Khan, in default of anyone holding authority by the known will of the Afghan people. It was signed on behalf of the Queen by Cavagnari, who was associated with the "forward" policy from the beginning to its tragic *dénouement*. By the Treaty of Gandamak (May 26th), the Ameer agreed to conduct his foreign relations in accordance with the advice and wishes of the British Government, to enter into no engagements with foreign States, and not to take up arms against any such States except with British concurrence. Kandahar and Jellalabad were to be returned to the Ameer so soon as his Government was reestablished; but Great Britain was to acquire certain frontier districts and to retain control of the Khyber Pass and the Pishin, Sibi and Kurum districts. On the other hand, the British Government were to have a Resident in the country, with the right of stationing British Agents to such parts of the Afghan frontier as occasion might require, so as to guarantee Afghanistan against unprovoked foreign aggression, and to pay a regular and increased subsidy.

No time was lost in accrediting a British Envoy to the new Ameer. Yakoob Khan had suggested Kabul as the place of residence, and Sir Lewis Cavagnari, having been chosen for the post, arrived there with his suite on July 24th. The reception of the Mission was "everything that could be desired[1]"; and Cavagnari's first month in the Afghan capital confirmed the first favourable impressions. A letter from him of August 30th to the Viceroy, though not making light of a difficult and still obscure position, seemed confident and betrayed no anxiety. At the end of the letter he regretted that the entry of the Mission into Kabul had been ignored by the Press at home, and added his fear that "the British public require a blunder and a huge disaster to excite their interest." The fear was to be justified. Three days later, the Residency was attacked by a body of mutinous Afghan troops from the Herat garrison, and the members of the Embassy were brutally massacred.

The effect of the crime in India was stupefying, while a cry of horror went through England. Stunned though he was by a disaster which seemed to turn the proud boast of "Peace with honour" into a cruel jest, Beaconsfield in that trying crisis exercised statesmanlike restraint. Not once did he lose head or nerve, or palter to the barbarous cry for crude revenge. It was clear that the Treaty of Gandamak must be regarded as null and void, and new arrangements devised in its place. If Yakoob remained faithful and the Sirdars rallied to him, Beaconsfield thought Great Britain ought not to abandon him; if,

---

[1] Letter of Cavagnari to Lord Lytton, July 24th, 1879. (*Lord Lytton's Indian Administration*, p. 342.)

however, the Ameer was dead or had fled, the right course would be to consolidate the military frontier, and retain Kandahar; though, for the rest, Afghanistan might be left to fall into pieces, if it must, and be partitioned amongst feudatory chiefs. This was, in effect, the policy of "disintegration" upon which Lord Lytton had long before been prepared to fall back, if all methods of conciliating the Ameer and converting him into a trustworthy ally failed.

A long and toilsome road had still to be trodden, before the situation in Afghanistan became sufficiently clear to make possible the adoption of any kind of policy for the regulation of the country's future relations with India and Great Britain. Of the ensuing War the most notable incident was General Roberts's brilliant march to Kabul, which he entered on October 12th. Yakoob Khan had already surrendered himself to the British camp with his Ministers. As the result of a strict legal investigation, he was acquitted of complicity in the massacre, but was held to be culpable in that he had not interposed effectively for the protection of the Mission as he might have done. Such of the ringleaders in the massacre as could be brought to justice were put to death.

Yakoob was not loth to abdicate, and he was sent into India for safety. His departure was the signal for a revolt throughout the Kabul region which was not suppressed until the end of December. Throughout 1880, however, there was intermittent fighting in the frontier districts. Word had gone forth from the India Office in London, which now allowed itself to be entirely led by the Viceroy, that Afghanistan was no longer to exist as a united dominion. Lytton's idea was the formation of a new western kingdom, with Kandahar as its capital, covered by a British cantonment at Pishin, and constituting a tributary State of the Indian empire; and, in April, Shere Ali, a cousin of the late Ameer, was experimentally appointed Governor of this territory.

Before further progress with the settlement of the country could be made on these lines, political events at home created a new situation. Encouraged by the success of the Ministerial candidates in two bye-elections, Lord Beaconsfield dissolved Parliament in April. The election was fought over the clear issue of Foreign and Colonial Policy, and the result showed that swing of the pendulum which is so characteristic of British political opinion. Once more, the nation proclaimed its distrust of any extreme course of policy and its instinctive preference for the line of caution and safety. In all the three kingdoms, in counties and boroughs alike, the Government suffered a crushing defeat. For the Prime-Minister the result was a final fall, and it says much for the chivalry of English party life that the sympathies of not a few of his political opponents accompanied the old master of statecraft, enfeebled, disillusioned, and broken, into his lonely retirement at Hughenden, where he died a year later (April 19th, 1881).

The work of settlement and reorganisation was completed under the viceroyalty of the Marquis of Ripon. For, with right feeling and great good sense, Lord Lytton decided not to outstay in office the renunciation and reversal of his policy, and he resigned with the Government to whose confidence he owed a dramatic, if trying, experience. It was impossible to restore without modification the *status quo ante bellum*. The idea of annexation was abandoned, and it was decided to evacuate Afghan territory and leave the Afghans as much as possible to themselves—which was all they asked. A timely auxiliary appeared in the person of Abdur Rahman (son of Shere Ali's half-brother Mahommad Afzul Khan), who had just returned from exile in Russian territory. On July 22nd, 1880, he was installed Ameer in Kabul, after his acceptance of the arrangements made by the Treaty of Gandamak, with two exceptions: Kandahar was to be under a separate ruler, and the admission of a British Resident was not to be pressed, though it was suggested that by mutual agreement a Mohammadan Agent of the British Government might be stationed at Kabul for convenience of intercourse. Subject to his compliance with these conditions, the Ameer was to receive a guarantee against external aggression.

The retention of Kandahar was not of long duration. While the negotiations with Abdur Rahman were in progress, Ayoob Khan, a younger son of the late Ameer, who had asserted himself at Herat, began an advance on the town. General Burrows set out thence to oppose him, but suffered a disastrous reverse at Maiwand (July 27th). Kandahar being hard pressed, General Roberts, with 10,000 picked men, carried out between August 11th and 31st his famous march of 313 miles from Kabul to the beleaguered city, before the walls of which he engaged and routed the aggressor (September 1st). The subsequent withdrawal of the British garrison from Kandahar again encouraged Ayoob Khan, who had reestablished himself at Herat, to attempt its capture, and in the following July he succeeded. In September, however, Abdur Rahman, having consolidated his position, defeated the pretender and chased him across the frontier, thus making himself master of the whole of Afghanistan.

II. The Reopening of the Eastern Question, 1875-1877

A. *The Revolt in Herzegovina and Bosnia, 1875-1876*

At the beginning of the 'seventies, almost the entire Balkan peninsula, from the Mediterranean to the southern and south-eastern frontiers of Austria-Hungary, with the exception of Greece, still continued under either the direct sovereignty or the suzerainty of Turkey. Roumania, formed out of the provinces of Moldavia and Wallachia in 1861, Servia, a principality since 1830, and Montenegro had alike obtained virtual autonomy, though they were still tributary States. Hellas was a kingdom, but only in parts; for a large *irredenta*, including Thessaly and Epirus, remained outside the limits of the monarchy, as determined in 1830. The European empire directly subject to the Sultan comprised Bulgaria, Roumelia, Bosnia and Herzegovina, Albania, Thessaly, Epirus, Thrace, and Macedonia.

Within these still centrally governed provinces there existed great diversity both of race and religion, and the broad rule everywhere applied that, while the adherents of the Moslem faith practically escaped oppression, they systematically oppressed their neighbours. The Christian populations were deprived of the commonest liberties and rights of citizenship, as understood in Western countries; they enjoyed very inadequate protection before the law; the small peasantry laboured under bad land-laws; taxation was everywhere arbitrary, exorbitant, and ruthlessly enforced. Inter-racial rivalry strengthened the hands of the Turkish rulers, who played off one people and one faith against another, having learned by long experience that, in proportion as the subject populations were divided, it became easier to misgovern them with impunity.

Lord Aberdeen had predicted that the Crimean War would secure the Peace of Europe for a quarter of a century. It was hoped that Turkey would take to heart the need for internal reform, the duty of which had so often been impressed upon her. She did little or nothing; and, where bad political conditions do not become better, they usually become very much worse. The harshness of Turkish rule underwent no alleviation in the Balkans, and, in the absence of Constitutional government, revolt was the only vent for pent-up discontents.

In July, 1875, news reached the Governments of Europe that the Christian population of Herzegovina, exasperated by the extortions of the tax-gatherers, had risen in revolt. For a time, the news attracted little attention, and it was assumed that the outbreak would exhaust itself in the usual way. Instead of this, the movement spread to Bosnia, and it was soon seen that the Porte had to deal with an insurrection of a dangerous type. In one of their proclamations, the insurgents declared their determination "to win liberty or to die to the last man." From the first, Servia and Montenegro were profuse of sympathy with their kinsfolk, and much surreptitious support found its way to the seat of disturbance; but strong hands restrained them from joining in the quarrel.

Russia and Austria-Hungary were particularly interested in the welfare of the Balkan populations—the former as the head of the Slavic family of nations and the self-constituted protector of the Christian races living under Ottoman rule, the latter as a semi-Slavic State sensitive to every outside movement directed towards the extension of the Panslavic idea. Russia was not inclined to interpose in the insurrection, so long as it seemed to be prospering, since it was her policy to encourage the autonomy of the Slavic provinces of the Ottoman empire in the hope that they would look to her for more direct protection. To Austria the insurrection was unwelcome for two reasons. Not only was it a menace to her own tranquillity and security, but Count Andrássy, who had succeeded Count Beust in the control of Foreign Affairs in 1871, had long cherished the hope of seeing the revolted provinces pass one day under Habsburg rule.

Without Bismarck's quick sagacity, Andrássy was not less clear and deliberate in his aims than the German Chancellor had been, and, when it seemed necessary, as unscrupulous as he in his choice of means. His paramount concern was Austria's self-preservation, and, if the annexation of Bosnia and Herzegovina was part of his Balkan policy, he sought aggrandisement, not for its own sake, but as a safeguard against disintegration. To make Austria more Slavic seemed to him the only alternative to her becoming less so. Nevertheless, he had no wish to see the Ottoman empire violently dissolved. It was no part of his plan that Austria should even play the part of a gendarme in Turkey, and for the present he was unwilling either to take or to sanction any step that would weaken her. His line of action as regarded the coveted provinces in particular was, instead of driving out the Turks, to support them in possession so long as they showed themselves amenable to reasonable influence, but to supplant them so soon as, owing to their own folly or weakness, their position became untenable[1]. In no event was he prepared to tolerate the creation on Austria's frontiers of a strong Slavic State, whether in the form of a Greater Servia or in that of a Greater Montenegro.

Germany's attitude towards the Balkan Question, on the other hand, was one of entire detachment and freedom from sentiment. Bismarck would rather have seen the Christian subjects of the Sultan governed well than ill, and he preferred peace to war, almost as much in other countries as in his own; but the only question that was vital to him was the interest of Germany, and that interest required the maintenance of good relations between all three Eastern Powers.

The relation of Great Britain to Turkey was still that of a more or less candid friend, deeply concerned to preserve the Ottoman empire from dissolution, yet conscious that this purpose could only be attained in so far as Turkey showed the will and the power to reform herself. The positive side of this policy had not of late been urged with undue emphasis. The British Representative at Constantinople at that time was Sir Henry Elliot, who since 1867 had wielded an influence recalling in some respects that of Stratford Canning, that earlier "voice of England in the East." His position was unique. In that home of intrigue and insincerity, where suspicion, jealousy, backbiting, and calumny then made up a large part of the substance of political life, only a man of strong character and unsullied probity could hold his own with dignity, and this Elliot succeeded in accomplishing[2]. Keeping aloof from all scheming, he as a consequence enjoyed the confidence of all the schemers, and even of the chief of them, his Russian rival, Ignatieff, who was distrusted as much by the Porte as by his diplomatic colleagues, now habituated to their *doyen's* vanity, unveracity, and deceit.

After Elliot and Ignatieff hardly any other diplomat seriously counted at Constantinople. The German and Austro-Hungarian Ambassadors cooperated more or less closely with their Russian colleague; such weight as France carried at the time usually went to the British side, for Elliot had done his best to encourage cordial relations between that Power and the Porte, thus securing support for his efforts to

---

[1] See Wertheimer, *Graf Julius Andrássy, sein Leben und seine Zeit*, II. 260–1.

[2] A letter written early in 1878 to Lord Derby by Sir Austen Henry Layard, Elliot's successor, soon after his arrival at Constantinople, is interesting as containing an experienced English diplomatist's clear-cut first impressions of political life there. "One lives here," he said, "in an atmosphere of intrigue, corruption, and rascality that only those who have personal experience of the place can appreciate. It is Byzantium over again. The threatened fall of the Turkish empire can be sufficiently accounted for by this state of things" (February 20th, 1878).

counteract anti-Turkish influence. The Italian Ambassador was also a safe auxiliary.

No foreign Representative enjoyed so largely, and none deserved so well, the confidence which was reposed in Elliot by Sultan, Grand-Vizier, and Ministers alike. No important foreign, and few domestic, decisions were taken without consultation with him, and it is creditable to his candour and judgment that he could be relied on to give—if not always with sufficient decision—the advice which the circumstances demanded[1]. He was in truth a constant and trusted power behind the Throne. To the Grand-Viziers he openly spoke of himself as "a friend of Turkey," and this attitude found its complement in bitter hostility to, and unreasoning distrust of, Russia—sentiments which he did his utmost to foster at home.

Nevertheless, it is questionable whether Elliot's absorbing attachment to Turkey and her interests was really advantageous either to that country or to his own, inasmuch as it inevitably blinded him to Turkish shortcomings. Further, by acting as the Porte's unofficial adviser, he did much to undermine the independence of the Sultan and his Ministers, who gradually came to look to Great Britain for guidance and support as of right, so that their sense of responsibility was weakened, together with their capacity and will to act vigorously in any emergency.

In accordance with his Instructions, Elliot's influence was directed towards restricting the area of disturbance and persuading the Porte to lose no time in restoring order and removing the causes of discontent. He held strongly to the opinion that the Sultan should be left to quell the disturbance without interference of any kind from the outside, and for this opinion he won both Lord Derby, the Foreign Secretary, and the Prime-Minister. Instead of taking steps to redress the grievances underlying the revolt, the Porte as usual did nothing, even for a time making no attempt to restore order. From the first, it had regarded the whole movement as insignificant and negligible, like a moorland fire that would burn itself out in a night. Meanwhile, the insurrection spread, and volunteers from Dalmatia, Servia, and Montenegro threw themselves in increasing numbers into the struggle with the common enemy. The subject soon found its way into the House of Commons, where there was much plain speaking about the slow progress of reform in Turkey, insomuch

---

[1] "Upon questions of importance it is to Great Britain and not to Russia that the Porte turns for counsel." Elliot to Lord Derby, July 4th, 1875.

a system of provincial self-government was to be introduced. In the absence of any guarantee that its promises would be translated into fact this document excited no enthusiasm.

The Vienna deliberations ended in the Andrássy Note, which was communicated to the Powers on December 30th. The Eastern Powers proceeded on the assumption that the Sultan would be amenable to friendly advice, and accordingly disclaimed any idea of wanton or offensive interference in the internal affairs of Turkey. The Note expressed apprehension that the insurrection would spread to Bulgaria and Crete in the spring, and that, eventually, Servia and Montenegro would join it, a fear justified by the event. In the interest of pacification, therefore, it proposed the granting of complete religious liberty to the two provinces, the abolition of the system of tax-farming, the application of the proceeds of direct taxes levied in the provinces to the purposes of their respective populations, under the control of representative bodies constituted in the sense of the imperial firman of December 12th, the creation of a special Mission, composed of Mussulmans and Christians in equal numbers, to control the execution of the reforms proposed by the Powers or promised by the Porte, and the amelioration of the condition of the rural population.

In his reception of the Andrássy Note Lord Derby, for once, threw off the influence of the Ambassador in Constantinople. Recognising that a stand had to be made, sooner or later, against the Porte's policy of inactivity and procrastination, he favoured the prompt acceptance of the Note with its consequences. "It is too late," he wrote to the Prime-Minister (January 1st, 1876), "to stand on the independence and dignity of the Sultan. A Sovereign who can neither keep the peace at home nor pay his debts must submit to some disagreeable consequences." Disraeli agreed to support the Note, influenced by the Powers' request that he would do so, but equally by the fear that if Great Britain refused to join them the Eastern Powers would act without her. The result was that the Note secured the support of an undivided Concert. The Sultan accepted it with bland acquiescence, as he had accepted similar expostulations before, and treated it with the old indifference. Both the imperial firman and the Note were stillborn.

Soon events occurred which gave a n w turn to the development of the Eastern problem and the relations of the Powers towards it. On May 6th, the German and French Consuls at Salonica were murdered in a Mussulman riot. Prompt recompense and the punishment of the criminals were demanded of the Sultan, and, after the usual prevarication and delay, were alike conceded. Early in the same month, the Tsar, with his Chancellor Gortchakoff, passed through Berlin, and the occasion was taken for a second Conference between the chief Ministers of the Eastern Powers. The result was a bolder restatement of the Andrássy Note in the form of the Berlin Memorandum of May 13th. It was the governing idea of the authors of this document that in the settlement of Bosnia and Herzegovina was to be found the key to the peace of the Balkans in general. They accordingly proposed that Turkey should conclude an armistice with the insurgents for two months, and that, in the interval, attempts at a reconciliation should be made by applying the principles of the Andrássy Note. Should no satisfactory results follow, the three Powers were to be free to resort to more effectual measures—a veiled threat suggestive rather of Gortchakoff than of either Andrássy or Bismarck. Andrássy returned to Vienna confident, as he told the Delegations there on May 18th, that European peace was assured "as far as human foresight could perceive." The efficacy of the Memorandum depended, however, upon two factors: first, its acceptance by the other Powers, without which its proposals could have no chance of enforcement, and then the willingness of Turkey to act upon it. France and Italy accepted, but Great Britain rejected, the proposals, holding, rightly or wrongly, that the proper order of events was, first, the suppression of the insurrection, and then the concession by Turkey of such reforms as circumstances might require. In coming to this decision the Government reflected the opinion of the Ambassador in Constantinople, who, in his turn, was in constant communication on the subject with the Grand-Vizier.

If one effect of the British Government's action at this point was to encourage Turkey in obstinacy, another was to throw her still more upon Great Britain's hands and support. It is not too much to say that, from that time forward until the eve of the settlement of the Eastern Question, the main lines of Turkish policy were determined in London. The political and moral responsibility which fell upon the British Government and nation in consequence was incalculable. Henceforth, it was impossible to shake the Sultan's faith that Great Britain stood behind him, ready to protect him to the last extreme against the designs of his enemies; and this faith encouraged the Porte again and again in opposing the collective pressure of the Powers.

The British Government's action in rejecting the Berlin Memorandum was severely judged abroad both then and later, and Bismarck, Gortchakoff and Andrássy[1] alike attributed to it the entrance of Servia on the scene and the far more serious developments which followed. At home, opinion was divided. The violent pro-Turkish party, which saw the menace of Russian aggression in every attempt to induce the Sultan to govern his subjects with justice and clemency, applauded the Cabinet. Nevertheless, not a few of the Prime-Minister's followers entertained serious misgivings concerning the wisdom and morality of the policy which he was pursuing. In the Cabinet he had a majority on his side; but the strongest of his colleagues, if not absolutely hostile to him, were still halting between two opinions[2]. On the other hand, the view that a valuable opportunity of rendering a great service to the cause of civilisation had been wilfully sacrificed was held by statesmen so far apart in their general view of the Eastern Question as Gladstone and Stratford de Redcliffe. Granville, though his hands were tied by the fact that he had been already head of the Foreign Office and would probably return to it, contended that, even granting the Government to have been justified in rejecting the Memorandum, they were wrong in failing to produce alternative positive proposals of their own.

In the meantime, the Sultan experienced in Constantinople in his own person the lawlessness and violence which he had so long condoned and protected in other parts of his empire. On May 10th, nationalist riots broke out in the capital, the Ministry fell to cries of "Turkey for the Turks," and the place of the Sultan's reactionary advisers was taken by reformers. At the end of the month (May 30th), Abdul Aziz was deposed, and his nephew, Murad II, was proclaimed as his successor "by the will of God and by general consent." A week later, the ex-Sultan committed suicide. Murad's reign proved brief and inglorious, for he was a weakling, fit only to be the puppet of schemers. On August 31st, he, too, was deposed, and his death by suicide or murder followed shortly afterwards.

The new Sultan was Abdul Hamid II, who inherited an impecunious treasury, an empire torn asunder by discontent and revolt, and the reproaches of the greater part of the civilised world. Nevertheless, all the Powers, with the exception of Russia, wished to give the new ruler a chance of proving voluntarily his good intentions,

---

[1] See particularly Wertheimer, *Graf Julius Andrássy*, II. 318 and III. 1.
[2] Cf. *Life of Robert, Marquis of Salisbury*, II. 80.

and the Berlin Memorandum was withdrawn. Disraeli acclaimed this proceeding as a justification of his Government's policy of abstention, and could proudly boast: "All the Great Powers, Russia included, seem anxious to defer to England, and something like the old days of our authority appear to have returned[1]."

Fresh fuel was added to the insurrectionary fires at this time. At the beginning of July, Servia, and a month later Montenegro, declared war against their ancient enemy. Both States hoped to emerge from the struggle with frontiers enlarged at Turkey's expense. For Servia, however, though a Russian general commanded her army and many Russian officers enlisted in it as volunteers, the war was a succession of humiliating defeats, more galling to the Tsar than the disobedience of his *protégé*.

In the desperate hope of stemming a movement which had now passed the assigned limits, Gortchakoff proposed that the revolted provinces should be granted autonomy, though still under Turkish suzerainty; and, contrary to Elliot's advice, Lord Derby favoured the idea, though not Gortchakoff's further suggestion that both Servia and Montenegro should receive an increase of territory. Andrássy refused to agree to any change of status in the provinces which would stand in the way of their later absorption in the Austrian monarchy; he also objected to an enlarged Servia, though willing to buy Montenegro's goodwill by an extension of frontier. A reconciliation of views was reached, however, as a result of a Conference between the Russian and Austro-Hungarian Emperors and their leading Ministers at Reichstadt on July 8th. It was there agreed that, if Turkey were beaten, Serbia and Montenegro should receive an increase of territory, while the bulk of Bosnia and Herzegovina should be annexed by Austria, Russia acquire Bessarabia and territory in Asia Minor, Bulgaria, Roumelia, and Albania become independent, Thessaly and Crete be added to Greece, and Constantinople become a free city.

B. *The Bulgarian Atrocities*, 1876

While Europe was still painfully exercised over the Bosnian insurrection, a further shock was administered to it by an outburst of barbarism in another part of European Turkey. Bulgaria was an unprogressive province of the empire, whose population indulged in no grandiose dreams of independence, and would, with good govern-

---

[1] *Life of Beaconsfield*, VI. 37.

ment, have proved a bulwark of peace and order in the midst of an unstable political system. Of late years, this province had on the whole received tolerable treatment, and the Sultan's action in making the Exarchate independent of the Greek Patriarchate had been greatly appreciated as a recognition of Bulgarian nationality. For some years, revolutionary propagandism had been carried on stealthily and on a small scale by a committee, composed for the most part of middle-class politicians of advanced views; but there had been little or no response from the people at large.

Nevertheless, letters sent by the Constantinople Ambassador to the Foreign Office in October, 1875, reported signs of unrest and of a temper which might with provocation give rise to anxiety. Elliot, to his credit, promptly warned the Porte of this ferment, and strongly urged the removal of the Bulgarian grievances before disaffection spread. To make matters worse, in the same month massacres of Bulgarians, accompanied by floggings, outrages on women, and the pillaging of houses, were committed by Mussulmans in the Adrianople and other districts. By the end of the year, a vague apprehension gained currency that more serious events would happen in the spring.

One of the centres of discontent was the Tatar-Bazardjik district, in the sandjak of Philippopolis, and here the spirit of revolt took shape, on May 2nd, 1876, in excesses committed by armed bands of Christian Bulgarians, on whom the Mohammadans retaliated with savage ferocity. Of these events Elliot received information, as well as of one or two similar outbreaks, and of the arming of Bashi-Bazouks and others, who had been guilty of excesses in their turn. As before, when the Bosnian insurrection broke out, he had besought the Porte not to put the Bashi-Bazouks in the way of temptation[1]. He now duly reported the disturbances to his Government, taking care—accustomed as he was to see Muscovite intrigue everywhere—to suggest that Russia was at the bottom of the mischief; and he wrote with satisfaction of the prompt steps which were being taken to suppress it. For a moment, there seemed a likelihood of a widespread rising, and the portents were gloomy.

But it was not till six months after he had heard of the first outbreak that the Ambassador and the British public learned from the London *Daily News* what had since occurred, and now came

---

[1] From October 1875 onward he was constantly urging the Porte to keep a firm hand upon them, and each time he received fair assurances which proved to be worthless.

to be known as the Bulgarian Atrocities, which were, in an unprecedented way, to stir the indignation of this country. For once, the Sultan and his advisers had not been taken by surprise. They had been often and severely reproached for their ineffectual attempts to stamp out the Herzegovinian insurrection while it was still under control, and they determined not to commit the same mistake again. Without waiting to parley with the rebels, the Government let loose in the disturbed district bands of Bashi-Bazouks under the nominal command of Achmed Aga and Mohammad Aga, who speedily restored quiet on a plan of their own. Falling upon one disaffected town, that of Batak, these irregulars brutally murdered all but 2000 of its 7000 inhabitants. Slaying, mutilation, pillage, violation, burning, perpetrated with every refinement of cruelty and barbarity which fiendish ingenuity could devise, continued day and night, and within a month 12,000 Christians had been done to death.

A copy of the despatch of our Vice-Consul at Adrianople which contained an account of the Atrocities had been sent to our Consul-General at Constantinople, but it does not appear what had become of the duplicate sent to the Embassy there. On the other hand, the report had been seen by the correspondent of *The Daily News*, in whose columns the substance of it was published on June 23rd. Several days later, questions were asked on the subject in the House of Commons; whereupon, relying on Elliot's incomplete reports, and on the fact that the first published accounts of the Atrocities had appeared in a leading Opposition newspaper, Disraeli referred to the horrors as "to a large extent inventions," and professed to regard the allegations against the Turks as part of the political capital of unprincipled critics. For his early sceptical attitude the Prime-Minister cannot, in the circumstances, be fairly condemned: he spoke and judged according as he knew, and at that time he never suspected that the half had not been told him.

As to their inadequacy, Elliot's despatches speak for themselves. On June 8th, after the revolt had been suppressed and a whole population had been wiped out, he informed Lord Derby regretfully that "cruelty and in some places brutality" had occurred. He refused, however, to credit the worst reports, as being exaggerations, but added that there was "evidence that the employment of Circassians and Bashi-Bazouks has led to the atrocities which were to be expected." Six days later, he forwarded a Consul's account of the cruelties, but discounted it. "No doubt," he wrote, "many of the revolting details that are given are either purely imaginary or at least grossly exaggerated." He even threw doubt on *The Daily News'* stories by the suggestion that they owed their origin to ill-informed American missionaries, "good men but ultra-Bulgarians," and by inference certain to exaggerate. As confirmation of the worst stories accumulated, he had to let in the light; but he did it gradually, screening the eyes of British Ministers from the full glare so long as possible.

Before a month had passed, Disraeli was bitterly complaining behind the scenes that the Foreign Office, owing to its "mismanagement" and "the ineptitude of its agents," was serving the Government badly and "letting him down," since the information supplied to him was proving "neither ample nor accurate[1]." At the very time that the Government were still endeavouring to discredit the independent reports which had reached England and to diminish their effect on the excited public mind, Consular reports which went far towards a complete confirmation of them were reaching the Constantinople Embassy, and the Ambassador, the scales now fallen from his eyes, was urgently imploring the Porte to put an end to the orgies of murder and lust. When fuller facts reached the Foreign Office, far too tardily, Lord Beaconsfield[2] for a time feared the publication of the despatches on the ground that it would involve "a great exposure of our diplomatic system abroad and at home," since both Elliot and his Department "had shown a lamentable want of energy and deficiency of information throughout[3]."

These strictures on the Ambassador were again, in the circumstances, justifiable. Elliot did not, and could not, deny that excesses had taken place; but, by throwing doubt here and suggesting reservation there, he succeeded in taking the sting out of the earlier reports, with the result that the Government were misled and the public deceived. When, however, being in full command of the facts, he began to take the Atrocities seriously, it was too late to undo the harm which had been wrought by his previous supineness and unwillingness to credit the facts[4]. It may be true that many of the

[1] Letter to Lord Derby, July 14th, 1876.
[2] Disraeli was created Earl of Beaconsfield on August 21st, 1876.
[3] Letter to Lord Derby, August 7th, 1876.
[4] Beaconsfield wrote of Elliot on August 15th, 1876, when the results of Mr Walter Baring's investigation ·ere coming in: "His conduct has seriously compromised and damaged the Government, and the more that is done now by him to redeem the situation, the more evident he makes it that all this should have been done months ago. Exertions which are made in August to counteract the mistakes of May can achieve no reputation; as a public servant the nation has utterly

individual instances of brutality reported were either exaggerated or imaginary, but it is equally true that incidents identical in character occurred again and again during the Terror through which the Bulgarians passed in May and June.

No one can read the despatches, little warmed by any wholesome indignation, which passed from the Constantinople Embassy to the Foreign Office at that time, without feeling that the national reputation was seriously compromised. There had been a serious decline from the humanitarian tradition represented by Palmerston when it was possible for a town-crier to proclaim in the streets of Adrianople, in spite of its manifest absurdity, the shameless falsehood that the Bashi-Bazouks who were being called up for service would be remunerated by the British Government.

Lord Derby's influence at that time was, as Gladstone wrote, "good, but there has been too little of it." The Foreign Secretary had early instructed Elliot to demand the suppression of the excesses and the punishment of the criminals, and, from June forward, he was constantly urging the Ambassador to lift up his voice against the murderers and spare not[1]. His honest indignation was in strong contrast to Elliot's early reserved and halting censures.

When at last W. Baring, Second Secretary of the Constantinople Embassy, after a full investigation on the spot, presented his report (September 1st), there was no longer any possibility of whitewashing the Turks. The quintessence of this document was contained in the sentence: "The manner in which the rising was suppressed was inhuman in the last degree (the horrors probably surpassing those committed in 1863 by the Russians in Poland), fifty innocent persons suffering for every guilty one." He estimated that 12,000 Christians had been massacred, and 58 villages destroyed, in the sandjak of Philippopolis, while only 200 Mussulmans had lost their lives. He, also, reported that "the vast majority of the Mussulman population look upon the perpetrators of the horrors not as criminals but as heroes, who for their praiseworthy efforts to extirpate a noxious condemned him" (*Life of Beaconsfield*, VI. 49). For the circumstances in which the Adrianople Vice-Consul's despatch failed to reach the Ambassador, and its existence remained unrevealed till a much later date, see Sir H. Elliot's *Recollections* (1922), p. 260 and Introduction; comparing also the letter of Mr R. H. Francis in *The Times Literary Supplement*, May 4th, 1922.

[1] *E.g.* letters of August 8th and 29th, and September 15th. In the second of these, he tells Elliot that "the impression produced here by events in Bulgaria has completely destroyed sympathy with Turkey. The feeling is so universal and so strong that if Russia were to declare war against the Porte Her Majesty's Government would find it practically impossible to interfere."

race have deserved well of their country," and added that the Government "did much to encourage this idea by dealing out with a liberal hand decorations and rewards to such miscreants as Achmed Aga[1]." Nevertheless, by the end of September no attempt had been made to punish the criminals, though 2000 Bulgarians had been arrested for alleged complicity in the incipient revolt. Elliot completely endorsed Baring's report.

The Bulgarian Atrocities gave to Mr Gladstone an unexampled opportunity for one of those impassioned appeals to the moral sense of the community into which he was wont to put the full force of a highly emotional nature. The Queen had been indignant with the stories which had slowly filtered through from Bulgaria and had urged her Prime-Minister to throw more warmth into his condemnation of the brutalities. Lord Beaconsfield, however, had compromised himself by his too flippant scepticism. After having deprecated the stories as evil exaggerations, on the strength of official information, it was difficult for him to go back upon his words in public, whatever he might do in private; what he had said he had said, and, the credit of his Government being at stake, he left the subject alone. So it came to pass that the political advantage of a great moral movement rested with his rival. In September Gladstone published his famous "Bulgarian Horrors" pamphlet, which contained a damning and unanswerable indictment of Turkish misrule, and pointed to the ejection of the Turk from Bulgaria, "bag and baggage," as the only possible remedy[2].

The pamphlet had an immediate and unexampled effect; but the agitation reached its climax when the resting Achilles left his tent early in December and threw himself into the open fray. The old British enthusiasm for the cause of "oppressed nationalities" broke out like a storm and swept the country from south to north; and constituencies which, more than a century before, had rung with the cry

---

[1] Someone took care that the Blue Book containing the report on the Atrocities was translated for the Sultan's edification.

[2] Gladstone proposed to apply this "bag and baggage" ejection to the province, and not (as Lord Beaconsfield among others represented) to European Turkey as a whole, as Sir Stratford Canning had suggested in 1821. The famous passage runs: "Let the Turks now carry away their abuses in the only possible manner, namely by carrying off themselves. Their Zaptiehs and their Mudirs, their Bimbashis and their Yuzbashis, their Kaimakams and their Pashas, one and all, bag and baggage, shall, I hope, clear out of the province they have desolated and profaned" (*The Bulgarian Horrors and the Question of the East*). "Lord Granville thought the passage too strong and wanted it out of the pamphlet" (Lord Morley's *Life of Gladstone*, II. 550).

"Wilkes and liberty!" now echoed to "Gladstone and emancipation!" The agitation may have been overdone; but the impulses underlying it were real and generous, and for a time British life was lifted out of the atmosphere of dull routine and mere material preoccupations[1]. Only London seemed to be little affected by the moral outburst, while the greatest enthusiasm was shown in the reserved, yet highly emotional, North.

After the rebellion in Bulgaria had been crushed and Turkey was able to give undivided attention to the prosecution of the War, the Servian rising had no longer even the remotest chance of success. Not for the first or last time in their history, the Serbs had to confess, in the words of their Prime-Minister, Ristich, the spokesman of the Greater Servian movement, "*Nous avons fait une grande illusion.*" For months, armistice and peace negotiations were carried on between Turkey and the Powers, of whom Great Britain acted as an informal mandatory. The Porte sought to impose severe conditions; but to these not even Lord Beaconsfield would listen, holding that the "atrocities" created a justification for pressing the Porte to a degree beyond what had hitherto been contemplated. Conscious, however, of the difficulty of holding the balance between Russia and Austria-Hungary, neither of whom he trusted, he contemplated, in October, a treaty with Germany for a *bon accord*, which was to be something less than an alliance, with a view to maintaining the territorial status in the Balkans, in the belief that it would secure Great Britain against Russia and Germany against France. But the idea failed to find favour with the Cabinet.

Finally, Great Britain put forward as reasonable bases for the conclusion of an armistice, which it was hoped would prove the precursor of a settled peace, the restoration of the *status quo ante bellum* in Servia and Montenegro, autonomy for Bosnia and Herzegovina, and guarantees against future administrative abuses in Bulgaria. Austria's agreement to these proposals was only obtained after the idea of autonomy had been so diluted that it had dwindled into a mere reform of local administration. Still the Porte held out, though Elliot had urged the Sultan to place himself unreservedly in the hands of the mediating Powers, since Her Majesty's Government

[1] In the Public Record Office are preserved six large volumes of resolutions of protest against the Bulgarian Atrocities addressed to the Foreign Secretary from September onward. They came from political meetings, representing all parties, town and village meetings, municipal and other local government councils, labour organisations, meetings of agricultural labourers, and religious bodies of all kinds.

would then be "able to exercise a salutary influence in the decisions to be come to[1]." It was only after Lord Derby had warned Turkey that, if she rejected the terms proposed, others more onerous would be pressed on her by force, and had instructed Elliot to leave Constantinople failing her compliance, and after Russia had demanded an unconditional armistice on pain of immediate declaration of war, that the Porte yielded.

C. *The Constantinople Conference, 1876*

Just before the suspension of hostilities, the British Government had decided to invite the Treaty Powers to meet in conference at Constantinople with a view to discovering conditions for a general settlement of the Balkan troubles. Gladstone called the decision "the best thing the Government have yet done in the Eastern Question." Lord Derby had been eager to anticipate action in Petrograd, fearing that if Russia took the initiative she would wish to lay down the basis of discussion, with the result that Austria, whose cooperation in resistance to any attempt upon the integrity of the Turkish empire was so important, might decline to take part. All the Powers accepted the invitation.

The British Ambassador at Constantinople had discouraged the idea of a conference at that stage, convinced that it would wish to probe inconvenient subjects. A conference might have to come after peace had been established; but, even so, he urged that it should be limited to the question of the revolted districts[2]. By that time, however, Lord Derby had emancipated himself from the influence of an adviser whose persistent pro-Turkish sympathies seemed altogether to incapacitate him from taking a European view of what was a European problem and was becoming more so every day. Elliot had done his best, it is true, to speed up Turkey in the matter of the reforms, and had failed. Considering how strongly the Porte believed that it had a permanent lien on British sympathy and support, his failure was perhaps inevitable, and was not discreditable to him. He laid himself open to just criticism, however, in that, with little or no reason for confidence in Turkey's willingness to act, he had nevertheless based all his recommendations on the assumption that she would act, and had succeeded in persuading the Government to orientate their attitude from the same fallacious point of view. His policy of

[1] Letter of September 14th, 1876.
[2] Letter to Lord Derby, September 4th, 1876.

non-intervention and leaving Turkey to reform herself as and how she would had broken down, and, excepting himself, no one had any longer a word to say for it. When in September Musurus Pasha, on behalf of his Government, protested to Lord Derby against diplomatic interposition in the affairs of Bosnia and Herzegovina as an infringement of the Sultan's rights, the Foreign Secretary answered that the Powers had never abandoned their right to urge upon the Sultan the proper treatment of his Christian subjects, and that recent events had shown the exercise of this right to be more necessary than ever before.

The attitude of Russia was changing from one of impatience and irritation into one of a frank disposition to war. Whether the world believed him or not, the Tsar had hitherto consistently professed pacific intentions; now, a distinctly warlike spirit came over him. Convinced that he was called upon to play the *rôle* of Protector of the Christian populations, and that envious rivals were attempting to frustrate his mission, he listened more readily than before to the suggestions of Ignatieff and the Moscow Pan-Slavist party. That he was honestly concerned to remove British suspicions of his ultimate aims, which he somewhat bitterly resented, cannot be doubted. To Lord Augustus Loftus he said at Livadia (November 5th): "*Avant tout, imprimez-vous trois points. Le testament de Pierre le Grand n'existe pas; je ne ferai jamais des conquêtes aux Indes; je n'irai jamais à Constantinople.*" Even, he said, if necessity should oblige him to occupy a portion of Bulgaria, "it would only be provisionally and until peace and the safety of the Christian population were secured."

All such assurances failed to convince Lord Beaconsfield. Speaking at the Lord Mayor's banquet on November 9th, 1876, he uttered a boastful challenge of which the application could not be mistaken. "If," he said, "England were to go to war in a righteous cause, her resources would prove inexhaustible. She is not a country that, when she enters into a campaign, has to ask herself whether she can support a second or a third campaign. If she enters a campaign she will not terminate it until right is done." On the following day, without knowledge of this threat, the Tsar declared, in the presence of notables of Moscow, that unless Turkey ceased to make war upon her own subjects and agreed to accept reforms at the bidding of the Powers collectively, he would intervene alone and compel her by force of arms. There was a certain justification for Russia's disposition to take matters into her own hands, and it consisted in the fact that she was negotiating on unequal conditions. She knew that in dealing with Turkey she was dealing with two Powers at once, since behind the Porte in counsel, influence, and interest stood Great Britain.

The Conference met from December 12th to January 20th, 1877. Lord Salisbury had been chosen as the British Plenipotentiary, with Sir Henry Elliot as prompter and *adjoint*. Than Lord Salisbury no better choice could have been made. He was neither a pro-Turk nor an anti-Russian, but simply an unemotional, unbiassed, clear- and just-minded British statesman, who was concerned to draw from an honest sifting of the facts of a difficult problem honest conclusions, and to act upon them. The apparent hopelessness of Ottoman rule had convinced him that nothing could be done for the Christian races without the application to the Porte of strong pressure perfectly definite in its purpose; and, though he was as yet quite as much opposed as was the Prime-Minister himself to the dissolution of the Turkish empire, he was free from preconceived views as to how far interference with its internal organisation should go. To decide that question was the main object of the Conference.

Lord Beaconsfield took accurate measure of the Conference when he wrote to the British Plenipotentiary: "It will consist of a meeting between you and Ignatieff. It is possible that the meeting may have results." Before it assembled, the Foreign Secretary submitted to the participating Governments a series of propositions, by way of defining the scope and purpose of its deliberations. They included (1) the independence and the territorial integrity of the Ottoman empire; (2) a declaration that the Powers would not seek for any selfish terri- torial advantage, exclusive influence, or commercial concessions[1]; (3) as the bases of pacification, the general observance of the *status quo* in Servia and Montenegro, and an undertaking by the Porte to grant to Bosnia and Herzegovina a system of local institutions giving to the population some control over their affairs and guarantees against the exercise of arbitrary authority, with no question, however, of the actual establishment of a tributary State; guarantees of a similar kind to be provided against maladministration in Bulgaria; the reforms already agreed to by the Porte to be included in the administrative arrangements for Bosnia and Herzegovina, and, so far as they might be applicable, in those for Bulgaria. These propositions found general

---

[1] A similar declaration had been made on September 17th, 1840, in the Protocol for the Pacification of the Levant, and again on August 3rd, 1860, in connexion with the Pacification of Syria, greatly to the regret of France.

acceptance, and, together with the Andrássy Note, they governed the proceedings of the Conference throughout.

On the suggestion of the Prince of Wales, Lord Salisbury travelled to Constantinople by way of Paris, Berlin, Vienna and Rome, for the purpose of conferring with the leading statesmen in these capitals, a wise precaution discouraged by the Foreign Office. The Prime-Minister, however, had urged his representative to trust his own intuitions rather than the promptings of "Tenterdenism[1]"; and this preliminary round of visits unquestionably strengthened his position and made clearer to him both the problems with which he had to deal and the difficulties in the way of their practical solution. He found Bismarck even more doubtful of success than Beaconsfield; his distrust of Andrássy was increased; and the suspicion which he had already formed, that the principal obstacle to a satisfactory settlement would be Turkey and not Russia, was strongly confirmed[2].

The Plenipotentiaries met for preliminary deliberation from December 12th to 22nd, and on the 23rd the Porte's representatives were invited to confer upon the proposals which had been drawn up, Safvet Pasha, the Foreign Minister, now acting as President of the Conference. Perhaps no important joint deliberation of the Great Powers has been characterised, on the whole, by a readier spirit of accommodation than was shown by the Constantinople Conference. The secret of the harmony which prevailed throughout its proceedings lay in the fact that the assembly was singularly well balanced, and that its members were honestly determined to seek and find a practical basis of agreement promising success to the purpose which all the Powers had in view.

At the outset, Lord Salisbury gave, both to the Conference and to the Porte, a full assurance that, while his Government would not join in any measure of active coercion against Turkey, they would in no way protect her from the consequences of resistance to the reforms which might be proposed. Ignatieff began by countering the British propositions with a scheme for the reorganisation of a Greater Bulgaria as an autonomous territory, still under Turkish suzerainty, but administered by Christian Governors, to be nominated by the Porte subject to the assent of the Powers. Turkish troops were to continue in the province, but in cantonments, and the importation

---

[1] Lord Tenterden was the, somewhat pragmatical, Permanent Secretary of the Foreign Office at the time. See *Life of Salisbury*, II. 95.

[2] Letters to Lord Derby, November 9th and 26th. *Ibid.* II. 92 and 102.

of Circassians was to cease[1]. The execution of these reforms was to be supervised by an International Commission, supported by forces—Belgian or Italian—sufficient to impose its decisions and to preserve tranquillity. Although this scheme failed to meet with much favour, some of its proposals were embodied in the programme of reforms which was submitted to the Porte when the full Conference began its sessions.

This programme underwent much modification in the course of the ensuing negotiations; and in its final form it proposed a rectification of frontiers for Montenegro, to be decided by an International Commission, and the recognition of the *status quo ante bellum* in Servia, subject to the settlement of frontier difficulties on the Bosnian side by a Commission. With reference to Bosnia, Herzegovina and Bulgaria, governors-general (*valis*) were to be appointed for the first five years by the Porte after prior agreement with the Powers; with redivision of the provinces for administrative purposes and the creation of provincial and local bodies, taxation reforms, including the abolition of tax-farming, the reorganisation of the judicial system, and the appointment by the Powers of two Commissions of Control, to watch over the execution of the regulations and to assist the local authorities.

On the day of Turkey's entrance into the Conference (December 23rd) a Constitution was proclaimed for the empire (Midhat Pasha, the Young Turk leader, had just become Grand-Vizier). Laudable though this step was, there was no mistaking its real purpose, which was to justify the Porte in rejecting the reforms upon which the Powers were agreed and, in other words, in scouting the Conference as superfluous. For a month, the Plenipotentiaries of the Powers, Lord Salisbury (who did not share Elliot's trust in Midhat) among the most earnest and urgent of them, endeavoured to persuade the Porte to accept the joint programme of reforms, but in vain. That the British Plenipotentiary was severely handicapped by the lukewarmness of Sir Henry Elliot, the "friend of Turkey," who applied the brake whenever possible, is certain[2]. Sir William White, who was

[1] See letters from Sir H. Elliot to Lord Derby as to the Circassians, *e.g.*: "After the great Circassian immigration, many of that lawless people were very imprudently established in colonies close to the Serbian frontier" (September 21st, 1875); and "Circassian villages are simply depôts of plunder in which the local authorities, even if they have the will, have not the power to make any effectual search" (December 3rd, 1875).

[2] In reporting to Lord Beaconsfield on January 15th his intention to leave Constantinople if the final terms were not accepted by the Porte, Lord Salisbury complained that Elliot refused to promise to leave at the same time. "This," he

diplomatically engaged in Constantinople at the time, suggests that the British Embassy staff, immoderately pro-Turkish in sympathies, likewise did its utmost to defeat Salisbury's statesmanlike endeavours[1].

In addition to these auxiliaries, however, the Porte had at its disposal still more effectual weapons of obstruction of its own. Every sort of prevarication, subterfuge, and chicane was employed by the shiftiest minds in Constantinople in the attempt, first to delay, and then to wreck, the work of the Conference. Proposals accepted one day were rejected the next; an assent which when given had seemed clear and unambiguous was soon explained to mean something quite different, and in fact to be no assent at all. Even though at one time the Porte announced its acceptance of the proposals in principle, when it came to the discussion of details objection was offered to the entire scheme. All sorts of counter-proposals were produced; but they simply amounted to turning the positive measures of the Powers into flat negations. When Salisbury warned the Grand-Vizier in grave language of the "extreme danger" which he was running, that Turkey stood absolutely alone, and that if war broke out she might find herself exposed to aggressive action from other States, Midhat only replied that if it were the will of God that the empire should fall he would be resigned to that fate; but he would not capitulate upon the question of reform.

All through the stubborn contest of wits and diplomatic strategy, the Turkish Ministers were imploring Lord Salisbury, in the name of traditional friendship, to detach himself from his colleagues; and, when these attempts failed in Constantinople, Musurus Pasha and a Special Envoy, in the person of Odian Effendi, tried in London to influence, first, Lord Derby and then, behind his back, the Prime-Minister—in each case with the same result. In the plainest and firmest language possible, Lord Derby refused to deviate from the policy agreed upon by the Powers and warned the Envoy that, if Turkey found herself at war with Russia, Great Britain would not raise a finger to help her. Odian Effendi replied that Turkey had

said, "will make our success much more unlikely. It will be treated as justifying the rumours that he represents a different policy from the Conference, and that the British Government will not support me." It appears that at Salisbury's request an Instruction was sent that the two Delegates should leave together. See also letters from the German Ambassador in Paris to Prince Bismarck (January 6th, 1877), and from the German Ambassador in Constantinople to the Foreign Office in Berlin (January 14th, 1877) in *Die Grosse Politik der europäischen Kabinette, 1871–1914*, II. 121, 123–5.

[1] For evidence on this head see *Life of Salisbury*, II. 117, 120–3; also *Sir William White, his Life and Correspondence*, by H. S. Edwards, pp. 116–18.

600,000 men under arms and did not fear a struggle with Russia. Somehow and somewhere, the Sultan's advisers at that time found encouragement sufficient to convince them that the British Government were "bluffing" and playing fast and loose with the other Powers, and would at the critical moment turn round and desert them[1].

The last word of the Plenipotentiaries was spoken on January 15th, and the Porte was given until the 17th to make up its mind. On the preceding day, a meeting of the Grand Council, consisting chiefly of State dignitaries and officials, met to pass judgment upon the Powers' proposals. According to Lord Salisbury, the Sultan was now won over. The Grand-Vizier, however, was opposed to the reforms, and he so represented them to the Council as to secure an emphatic repudiation. Such a decision was at least a relief to the Plenipotentiaries, since they now knew where they stood and were at liberty to return home. The Porte's final attempt at compromise was a plea for just one year more, in which to convert the Ottoman deserts into smiling places. It ignored the fact that it had had fifty years' grace already, and had abused instead of using it. Lord Salisbury crystallised the result of the four weeks of futile negotiations in the words: "The Porte only proposes to execute its former promises; it refuses to promise anything new or to give any guarantee for the future," while the Italian Plenipotentiary's comment was: "They put us off with good intentions where we think it necessary to have realities."

On January 22nd Lord Salisbury had to make to Lord Derby the sorrowful confession: "The principal object of my mission, the conclusion of a peace between Russia and Turkey, has not been attained." So far did the Porte's defiance go that its Representatives ostentatiously absented themselves from the general meeting of the Conference on the previous day. The fact, however, that peace was not assured meant that war must almost inevitably ensue.

As Lord Beaconsfield had predicted, two men had dominated the Conference, Lord Salisbury and Ignatieff—yet not as antagonists or

---

[1] A telegram sent by Lord Salisbury to Lord Derby on January 8th, 1877, several days after the reception of the Special Envoy in London, shows that he was mystified by what was taking place, for the Grand-Vizier had just told him that he believed that he could "count upon the assistance of Lord Derby and Lord Beaconsfield." Lord Derby replied (January 9th) that he had warned Musurus Pasha in a contrary sense, adding: "It is not in my power to speak more plainly than I have done on this subject, and I feel satisfied that no language different to this is being held by any person connected with Her Majesty's Government." See also *Life of Salisbury*, II. 112 and 127.

even rivals, but as reasonable coadjutors emulating each other in the furtherance of a great task of civilisation[1]. If the repute of Great Britain as the friend of "oppressed nationalities" had been compromised by her cool reception of the Berlin Memorandum, it was abundantly redeemed by the bold and consistent attitude of her Plenipotentiary at Constantinople. While Lord Beaconsfield approached the Eastern Question from the purely political standpoint, as one of power and prestige, and gave to British interests, real or imaginary, almost exclusive consideration, Lord Salisbury saw in addition the moral and humanitarian issues which were involved, and viewed the question in its larger European relations. Undeterred by the knowledge that the Prime-Minister unfairly suspected him of pressing the Porte unduly[2], he persisted in this attitude to the end, fully justifying Gladstone's judgment of him as a statesman who "has no Disraelite prejudices, keeps a conscience, and has plenty of manhood and character[3]." As the head of a Cabinet, Lord Beaconsfield was a hard taskmaster, and when he was in a fault-finding mood his tongue had the edge of a file. The other and more generous side of his character was shown by his chivalrous greeting when his Envoy returned to England, disappointed and disillusioned[4].

Though the Conference had resulted in a deadlock, it had had the result of strengthening Russia's position just in proportion as

[1] On January 19th, 1877, Lord Salisbury wrote to Lord Carnarvon that the failure of the Conference had been due, in the first instance, to the Turkish Government's belief in Russia's weakness, and, in the second, to the impression conveyed in the same quarter, that his views were not really those of the British Government. (*Life*, II. 123.)

[2] "Salisbury seems most prejudiced and not to be aware that his principal object in being sent to Constantinople is to keep the Russians out of Turkey, not to create an ideal existence for Turkish Christians" (Letter of Lord Beaconsfield to Lord Derby, December 28th, 1876). Lord Beaconsfield's judgments were notoriously very impetuous and in consequence erratic. In the same letter he wrote of Lord Salisbury: "He is more Russian than Ignatieff: *plus Arabe que l'Arabie*. While Russia, I believe, is meditating and preparing compromise, and the Porte not disinclined to that, Salisbury sees only obduracy and war." Yet within fourteen days he wrote, in another temperamental letter (January 8th, 1877); "Salisbury succeeded in moderating the Russians, and I have done my best to moderate the Turks." The truth was that someone had conveyed to the Porte the suggestion that Russia really disliked the prospect of war, which was a fact, and would bear a good deal of squeezing. The moderation was on her side, not on that of the Turks.

[3] Letter of December, 1876, quoted in Lord Morley's *Life of Gladstone*, II. 560.

[4] "I hope you will not permit the immediate result of the Conference unduly to oppress you. Trust me, before very long you will bless the day which permitted you to obtain such a mastery of men and things, and especially as connected with the East, as this momentous enterprise has afforded to you." (Letter of February 6th, 1877, *Life of Beaconsfield*, VI. 114.)

that of Turkey had been weakened by her obstinacy and short-sightedness. In spite of the suspicion under which she had entered the Conference, it was admitted that Russia had honestly and temperately striven for a *modus vivendi*, and that for the failure to discover one no blame attached to her. Cleared, to that extent, in the eyes of Europe, she now endeavoured to induce the Powers to acknowledge her as their mandatory in a further attempt to bring the Porte to reason. Wisely or not, their consent was withheld.

III. THE RUSSO-TURKISH WAR AND THE TREATY OF SAN STEFANO, 1877–1878

After the abortive Constantinople Conference, conversations were continued for a time in London, and on March 31st the Powers laid before the Porte a Protocol, requiring the adoption of measures for the amelioration, without further loss of time, of the condition of the Christian populations in the European provinces of the empire. The warning was added, that any neglect to carry out the undertakings demanded would be deemed incompatible with the interests of the Powers, as of Europe in general, and would cause them to consider what steps the consequent situation might call for. Turkey was, also, urged to negotiate with Russia at once, with a view to mutual demobilisation, so soon as peace had been concluded with Montenegro.

The Porte replied (April 9th, 1877), protesting against this further admonition as an unjustifiable encroachment upon the Sultan's sovereignty and independence. It was willing to meet the Powers on some points, but on all that it deemed vital it was inflexible. It repudiated any outside right to interfere in Turkish affairs in future, but, while refusing to yield to force, reaffirmed its intention to carry out its own reforms. The answer was regarded as a challenge to Russia; the British Ambassador in Constantinople so described it to the Grand-Vizier, who admitted that it had been designed to bring matters to a crisis and force Russia to make a full disclosure of her intentions. There was, in fact, an influential war party in the Sultan's *entourage*, and the Mussulman population in the provinces was eager to cross swords again with the old enemy. Lord Derby in London and the British Ambassador in Constantinople did their best to persuade the Porte to accept the Protocol, but in vain; for it was a settled principle of Turkish policy always to offer to do something less than the situation required. When, at last, the Sultan, overcoming the resistance of the war faction, agreed to invite the mediation of the Powers, it was too late; for Russian troops were already crossing the Pruth and the Asiatic frontier of Turkey.

A drastic solution of the Eastern imbroglio had now become inevitable. In spite of all his public declarations to the effect that the maintenance of the independence and complete integrity of the Ottoman empire was a fundamental principle of British policy, even Lord Beaconsfield had, in private intercourse, already abandoned that position. There was, indeed, a large element of opportunism in the policy which he was pursuing, nor could it be pretended that he knew from the beginning how far, or even in what precise direction, that policy would take him. The arena of diplomatic conflict was for him more or less new ground, and the experience of the past afforded but little help towards any constructive solutions of the problems which had arisen. His attitude on the territorial question in particular was for a long time undecided and obscure, and changed continually. While labouring under the irritation caused by the Bulgarian Atrocities, he had been prepared to neutralise Constantinople with its vicinity and make it a free port "in the custody and under the guardianship of England, as the Ionian Isles were[1]." Immediately before the Constantinople Conference, he thought of purchasing from Turkey a port on the Black Sea—Batoum, Sinope, or Varna—as a means of neutralising Russian action[2]. In a letter written to the Foreign Secretary when the Conference was over, he adroitly analysed "the famous phrase 'integrity and independence,'" and drew the conclusion that an empire might retain its integrity even though its limits were curtailed, and that the continuance of sovereign power was independent of any question of territorial area[3]. "If war begins," he wrote to Lord Derby a few days later, "I think it will end in partition."

War actually began on April 24th, and therewith the Ottoman political system passed again into the crucible. Russia had already concluded a Convention with Austria-Hungary (January 1st) by which Servia, Montenegro, and the strip of territory lying between these two States and forming the sandjak of Novi-Bazar, were, in the

---

[1] Letter to Lord Derby, September 4th, 1876.
[2] Conversation with Gathorne Hardy, November 28th, 1876. *Gathorne Hardy, First Earl of Cranbrook: a Memoir*, I. 377.
[3] "England and Austria and France will assert their integrity, and expect it to be acknowledged, though they have all of them lost more provinces than Turkey." Letter of January 29th, 1877.

event of hostilities, to be treated as neutral. A supplementary Convention, of March 18th, determined the territorial changes upon which the two Powers were to insist if the dissolution of the Turkish empire followed. Austria was to receive, in permanence, Bosnia and Herzegovina with a population of a million and a quarter, while Novi-Bazar was to be divided between Servia and Montenegro. Russia was to receive Bessarabia from Roumania, and to have discretionary power to make acquisitions in Asia Minor. The Convention thus yielded to Austria-Hungary, without that Power needing to draw the sword or to mobilise a single battalion, all that Andrássy wished. On April 16th, Russia concluded a further Convention with Roumania, permitting the passage of an army of invasion through that State, while the Tsar pledged himself to maintain and defend its existing integrity. At the end of the month, Montenegro resumed hostilities as Russia's ally.

In a Circular Letter addressed to the Powers, Gortchakoff claimed justification for the action taken, on the ground that the Porte had refused to listen to reason. "Nothing remains," he added, "except to let this state of things continue, or to obtain by force what the Powers have failed to obtain by persuasion." In his reply to this letter, Lord Derby declined to admit that the Porte's answer of April 9th "removed all hope of deference on its part to the wishes and advice of Europe and of security for the application of the suggested reforms," and disputed the assumption that the course which Russia was following was "in accordance with the sentiments and interests of Europe."

The British Government declared their intention to observe neutrality, so long as the interests held to be vital to Great Britain were respected. These were stated to be the maintenance of complete freedom of communication between Europe and the East by means of the Suez Canal; the exclusion of Egypt from the sphere of military operations; and the recognition by Russia of the inviolability of Constantinople and the navigation of the Bosphorus and the Dardanelles. Gortchakoff furnished assurances upon all these points. The acquisition of Constantinople in particular, he said, was outside the purview of the Tsar, who recognised that its destiny was in any case a question of common interest which could only be regulated by an *entente générale*, though he was of opinion that, in the event of change of tenure, it should not pass into the hands of any European Power. In a conversation with Lord Derby on June 8th, Count Schouvaloff made the further offer that, assuming the neutrality of the Powers, if Turkey sought peace before the Russian armies had crossed the Balkans, this line should not be passed and hostilities should cease on certain conditions. These conditions, with the single exception of the extent of the future Bulgaria, were more favourable to Turkey than those which were imposed on her by the Powers a year later.

It cannot be said that Russia, in entering the War, attracted much sympathy except from the Slavic world and those spheres of Western, and particularly Anglo-Saxon, opinion which may be described as anti-Turkish in principle. Even in this country, although Gladstone had recently roused public feeling against the Turk, there was a strong wing of the Liberal party which declined to approve any action that might embarrass the Cabinet at such a time. When the eloquent tribune proposed to challenge the Government's policy, his intention was diplomatically countered by the joint efforts of his colleagues Lord Granville and Lord Hartington, who were not convinced that the nation was so profoundly moved by indignation against Turkey as the author of *The Bulgarian Horrors* believed[1]. On the other hand, the Russophobes were clamouring for war. Nowhere did the war passion find such marked expression as in the metropolitan zone.

Most people in Russia believed that the War would be a mere promenade for their armies; but they were soon to be undeceived. Roumania furnished the master-key to the field of operations, since she lay between the Russian frontier and the Danube, beyond which stretched Bulgaria and the Balkans, with Turkey proper on the southern side. The principality was still a vassal State of the Ottoman empire; and Turkey, regarding the Russian Convention with Roumania as a violation of the Treaty of Paris, began at once the bombardment of Kalafat, on the Danube. Hereupon, Prince Charles formally declared war, and simultaneously his country's political independence (May 21st).

Another month passed before Russian troops, under General Gurko, crossed the Danube at two places—in the north-east in the Dobrudja and opposite Sistova, in Bulgaria. Reaching the Balkans, the invading army forced the Shipka Pass, and its progress was, for a time, so rapid that a continuous march to Adrianople and even Constantinople seemed probable. With a change in the Turkish military

---

[1] Lord Hartington, with blunt commonsense, uttered a truth generally applicable to rhetorical politicians when he said of Gladstone that he refused to understand that not all the people who listened to and admired his speeches agreed with them.

command a turn in the fortunes of war supervened, and the Russian armies were thrown on the defensive, Gurko suffering a serious defeat at Stara Zagora, south of the Shipka, and being driven back to the mountains, while Osman Pasha occupied Plevna, and, digging himself in, held the Russian hosts at bay. Further advance became impossible until this strong position had been reduced, and its siege began on July 20th

From May onwards, Lord Beaconsfield and the Foreign Secretary had been eagerly pressing upon Andrássy the expediency of a common policy; and, on July 26th, a verbal agreement was arrived at—the Prime-Minister called it "a moral understanding"—affirming solidarity of interests and pledging the two Governments to identical, but separate, diplomatic action, and, should their interests be endangered, to subsequent united military measures. They agreed to oppose the exercise of an exclusive protectorate by any Power over the Christian populations of the Balkans, and to demand the cooperation in the determination of the terms of peace of all the Signatories to the Treaty of Paris; Russia was not to be allowed acquisitions of territory on the right bank of the Danube or to occupy Constantinople; the existing arrangements as to the Dardanelles were to be maintained; and no great Slavic State was to be established in the Balkans to the prejudice of its neighbours. Andrássy was, nevertheless, as resolute as ever to keep out of the War. He explained his Government's policy in the words (June 22nd): "*Mettre à l'abri nos intérêts sans nous exposer à la nécessité de devoir les sauvegarder les armes à la main—tel a été dès le début de la crise, tel reste le but constant de nos efforts.*" Meeting Bismarck in September, Andrássy told him of the agreement, and was assured that he had acted wisely in concluding it.

When the siege of Plevna, marked by many heroic onslaughts heroically repelled, had lasted for four months, General Todleben, the defender of Sebastopol, resorted to close investment, and, on December 10th, Osman Pasha surrendered with his gallant army. In the meantime, the Russians and their Allies won new successes in other parts of the theatre of war. Every attempt of the Turks to capture the Shipka Pass had failed. To the westward, the Montenegrins had defeated the enemy in the Zeta valley and captured Nikshich, after a siege of four months. Servia joined forces in December and was fighting with greater credit than in the late War. In Asia Minor, the campaign had gone altogether against the Turks, and Kars had been captured by Loris Melikoff, a General of Armenian extraction.

By this time, an ugly temper had seized hold of a large part of the British people, and, in proportion as the successes of the Russian arms multiplied, the desire for war increased. On the other hand, the Cabinet, which had been divided on Eastern policy from the beginning, was becoming daily more difficult to control. A section, which took its cue from Lord Derby, was determined not to have war at any price; Lord Salisbury represented a moderating middle party, and was against war at the present moment[1]; while among the remaining Ministers were several bitter Russophobes, though at that stage hardly one of them seriously contemplated the prospect of hostilities. With the war party in the country Lord Beaconsfield himself was widely supposed to be in sympathy, the truth being that, while he welcomed its vociferous support, he never allowed it to influence his action or his judgment.

It is now known that it was not the power behind the Throne, but the Throne itself, which was at that time most eager for war[2]. Nevertheless, for the Queen's combative attitude her Prime-Minister must be held essentially responsible. He had worked so strongly and persistently upon her feelings and prejudices that, in the end, he had infused in her a far greater distrust of, and hostility to, Russia than he had himself ever entertained. Lord Beaconsfield's principal concern at that time was that Russia should not occupy Constantinople. So early as June, he had asked the Porte to invite the presence of the British fleet there, and had even offered to occupy the Gallipoli peninsula for the duration of the War, if a proposal to that effect were formally made to him. So determined was he to keep the Russians away from the capital that, when he found its occupation to be regarded by Lord Derby, and also by Lord Salisbury, as Russia's good right in virtue of her military success, he persuaded the Queen to tell the Foreign Secretary that it was her wish that it should not be permitted, and led her to believe that Great Britain's entrance into the struggle would be a necessary consequence of the act.

When, however, it became necessary to restrain the Queen's eagerness for resolute counter-action in Turkey's behalf, the task proved difficult. In reply to her appeal (June 27th) for prompt measures with a view to checking Russia's forward march—"Be bold!...pray

---

[1] See his letter to Beaconsfield of December 24th, 1877, in *Life of Salisbury*, ii. 169.
[2] The story, which is one of the most curious in our modern political history, is fully told in the sixth volume of the *Life of Beaconsfield*.

act quickly!"—the Prime-Minister, while "sympathising with all Your Majesty's feelings in the present critical state of affairs," pointed out that military expeditions took time and that the occupation of the Dardanelles or any part of the Turkish empire was impossible without the Porte's permission, which would be given only if Great Britain assumed the character of Turkey's ally; while, as for a declaration of war against Russia, "there are not three men in the Cabinet who are prepared to advise that step." Palmerston, in his day, systematically kept the Queen in ignorance of important State documents. It might, perhaps, have been well if, on some delicate questions of policy, Lord Beaconsfield had told his Sovereign either more or less than he did, and avoided the consequence of communications made to her in one sense being interpreted in quite another. So far did he, at that time, share with the Sovereign the management of affairs of State that he reported to her upon the votes of his colleagues in Cabinet, and classified them according to their support of "her" policy, as he professed to regard it, while the Queen, in return, praised or blamed her Ministers accordingly.

On the fall of Plevna, Turkey and her friends in England knew that the end could not be far off, and panic was as great in London as in Constantinople. On December 12th, the Porte appealed to the Powers to mediate with the enemy; but they declined. At the end of the month, Great Britain was asked to perform that service, and she put the belligerents into direct communication; for the Tsar refused to negotiate through any third party. In the meantime, his armies were still advancing victoriously. Recrossing the Balkans, Gurko took, in succession, Sofia (January 3rd, 1878) and Philippopolis (January 16th–17th), inflicting a signal defeat on Suleiman Pasha, while Skobeleff and Radetzky captured an entire Turkish army at Senova, near the Shipka Pass (January 9th).

Peace now became indispensable for Turkey, whose armies, demoralised by a succession of defeats and retreats, were incapable of resisting the Russian march to Constantinople. On January 20th, Adrianople was occupied by Russian troops—for the second time in half a century. The Serbs and Montenegrins were, also, multiplying their successes, the former occupying the old Servian town of Nisch and the latter capturing Spizza, Antivari, and Dulcigno (January 18th), thus satisfying for the present the old Montenegrin longing for an outlook on the sea.

The visible and ostensible attitude of the British Government had hitherto been one of patient vigilance, though much scheming had been going on behind the scenes. Now that Turkey was beaten and at the mercy of her enemies, Russophobe passions again flared up dangerously. Parliament was called together earlier than usual, and this added greatly to the public excitement. Though still a united body, however, the Cabinet was far from being of one mind. More than ever, it was the Prime-Minister's object to prevent the occupation of Constantinople. With this purpose in view, the Government had, for months, been entreating the Sultan to allow a British squadron to enter the Dardanelles; but he had declined, resentful that his old ally, while so ready with advice, had given him no real help. When Plevna fell and the way to the south lay open, Lord Derby pressed the Russian Government to give an undertaking that no attempt would be made to occupy the capital or the Dardanelles, and was told that to seize Constantinople had never been the Tsar's intention, but that, if Turkey insisted on protracting the War, he would claim the complete freedom of action which is the right of every belligerent State. A renewed promise was, however, made, that British interests, as already defined, would be respected, and it was added that, if other interests were involved and were now clearly specified, the Tsar would endeavour to bring them into accord with those of Russia.

At a Cabinet on January 12th, Lord Beaconsfield proposed that the fleet should be sent to the Dardanelles, a measure to which Lords Derby and Carnarvon offered strong opposition. A split was only prevented by the adoption of Lord Salisbury's amendment to ask Turkey's sanction to the movement of the British fleet—which was refused—and to request an undertaking by Russia that she would not occupy Gallipoli. Impatient at the influences which seemed to be restraining her trusted Minister, the Queen, in a letter written at this time, denounced "the great barbarians" (the Russians), the "low tone" of a country which was not sufficiently enthusiastic for war, and the Cabinet itself, of which she was "utterly ashamed"; and even talked of abdication (January 10th, 1878).

On January 23rd the peace-loving section of the nation heard with alarm that the Mediterranean squadron had been ordered to proceed through the Dardanelles to Constantinople. The decision to adopt this strong measure brought to a head the growing division in the Cabinet. Lord Derby and Lord Carnarvon tendered their resignations, but, the order being countermanded, the Prime-Minister persuaded the former to stay. There was little generosity in the act; for though he was now satisfied that his hesitating colleague could no longer do harm in the Cabinet, Lord Beaconsfield greatly feared that he might do harm outside. The Queen gave reluctant consent to Derby's remaining. As a further precautionary step, a vote of six millions for military preparations was asked for.

A war spirit without parallel since the Crimean campaign, taking the new-fangled and ugly form of "Jingoism," was now abroad, and the Armistice of Adrianople (January 31st) failed to allay the fever, since in spite of it the Russian troops continued to advance. It was clearly Russia's aim to force Turkey to accept conditions of peace before the Powers could intervene. To complicate the situation, the Greeks, who had long been eager to enter the fray, were now threatening to throw in their lot with the victorious Power, hoping to share in the division of the spoils. It was largely owing to British pressure and promises that they were restrained.

For several weeks longer, war between England and Russia seemed to hang upon a thread. On February 7th, intense excitement was caused in London by the report, received by way of India, that Russian troops had reached Constantinople. The Queen urged an immediate declaration of war, and, on being told that the situation did not justify so extreme a measure, was disappointed and again talked of laying down her "thorny crown[1]"; whereupon Lord Beaconsfield imparted to her the obvious fact, insisted on by Lord Derby and Lord Salisbury from the first, that "it was never in the power of a neutral State to prevent the entry of the Russians into Constantinople." The Cabinet decided, however, on the Prime-Minister's proposal, to despatch a division of the fleet to Constantinople "for the protection of life and property," and to invite the other neutral Powers to take similar action. The report which led to this decision proved to be unfounded; but it made the passing of the vote of credit a mere matter of form. The British fleet moved forward accordingly, in spite of Turkish protests, while Russia's reply was to advance further towards the capital. Just two years before, Gladstone had wished to despatch vessels of war to Constantinople by way of menace to Turkey.

Turkey's faith that Great Britain would extricate her from difficulty had been rudely shaken, though the Sultan had still a good friend in the British Ambassador. Sir Henry Elliot had been removed

[1] Letter to Lord Beaconsfield, February 9th, 1878.

to Vienna at the end of 1877, and his place had been taken by Sir A. H. Layard, whose views were as antagonistic to Russia as his own. The policy carried on in Constantinople was in consequence but little affected. Layard fanned the dying embers of hope, so long as he dared, without adding new fuel in the shape of actual assurances which he had no authority to give or power to substantiate. On January 7th, the Grand-Vizier had startled him by a "vehement and bitter" condemnation of Great Britain's alleged faithlessness and treachery. After exemplifying her alleged deceit, he added, "Such is the justice and humanity of England. She has abandoned her old and faithful ally, and leaves us to be crushed by her and our implacable enemy, because forsooth a few Bulgarians were killed[1]." He even said that he was now in favour of turning from Great Britain, and settling with Russia on the best terms he could get. The outburst was not quite just, but it was far from being altogether the contrary. For years, Turkey had been regarded in London almost as a vassal of the British Crown, and the control of the Porte's Foreign Policy might be said to have passed into British hands. The Turk had been so long tutored and patronised, protected and pampered, that his self-reliance and power of initiative were sapped, and in a time of supreme crisis there was left in him no residue of vigour or power of resistance. Yet now, after almost the last vertebra of backbone had been taken out of him, he was expected to stand upright and play his part like a man.

So late as February, the Sultan, who had already offered to place his fleet at Great Britain's disposal, was still begging that his old ally would help him "with men, money or in any other way," so as to enable him to defend his capital, which he declared the Russians should enter only over his dead body. When the British Government were importuned to say their last word on the subject (February 12th) Lord Derby instructed Layard, in a despatch which received its final form from the Prime-Minister's hand, to inform the Porte that they were "not prepared under existing circumstances to incur the responsibility of advising an armed resistance to the entry of Russian troops into Constantinople." The cold comfort was added that such action by Russia would be a violation of the Armistice, which would entitle the Porte to protest, though it was to be presumed that "armed resistance would be fruitless and disastrous." Being requested, hereupon, to remove Russia's justification for advancing on the capital by withdrawing the British fleet from Constantinople waters, or,

[1] Letter to Lord Derby, January 8th, 1878.

alternatively, to come out into the open as Turkey's ally and assist her in repelling the enemy, the British Government flatly refused to do either (February 18th).

Thus, at the last, Turkey's eyes were opened to the real position. Trusting to a hundred signs and intimations, she had reposed in Great Britain a blind confidence, staking everything on British attachment and friendship. Now, she learned that the only tie between the two informal Allies was that, not of Turkish, but of British, interests. As these latter, however, were not endangered, a *casus foederis* was held not to exist.

The Government still used their best endeavours to keep the Russians away from the capital; but it must be gravely doubted whether the idea of helping Turkey to resist them had ever been seriously entertained. This position was beyond a doubt correct. What exposed the Cabinet to reproach was the fact that it should have allowed its position and intentions to be at any time open to misunderstanding. The episode of Denmark and Schleswig-Holstein had been repeated, not to England's credit.

Lord Beaconsfield had yet to satisfy his followers in the country. Behind him, egging him on, was a shouting rather than fighting majority of the nation, whose roused emotions he had made no attempt to restrain, and who had called for the translation of his many bold words into equally bold deeds. He had, however, landed himself on the horns of a dilemma. He had raised the expectation that the occupation of Constantinople would be regarded as a *casus belli*; but now, when the danger seemed imminent, he had to admit that Russia was quite within her rights. In this predicament of his own causing, he sought and obtained from Russia an undertaking that she would not occupy Gallipoli, on condition that Great Britain refrained from landing troops on Turkish territory either in Europe or Asia (February 19th). A little later, he suggested to the Cabinet an idea which he had privately ventilated before—the purchase of some point of Turkish territory which might be "conducive to British interests": a Black Sea port and a commanding position on the Persian Gulf were mentioned. The Quixotic notion of a Mediterranean League, which Italy and Greece, France and Austria were to join, for securing the independence of that sea and frustrating Russian aggression, was also seriously discussed. No one appears to have asked what motive France could have for entering an organisation so unequally balanced, or how it could exist without her.

On March 3rd, Peace Preliminaries were signed on behalf of the belligerent Powers by General Ignatieff and Safvet Pasha at San Stefano. The terms were not communicated to the British Government until the 23rd; but, on the 8th, the Cabinet resolved that in the event of their "compromising the maritime interests of Great Britain in the Mediterranean, a new naval station in the east of the Mediterranean must be obtained, and if necessary by force." This assertion of the doctrine of might as against that of right was to be applied to the injury of the very State whose independence and integrity Great Britain was at that moment professing to protect against a Power which had defeated it in fair warfare.

Two years earlier, when the Eastern Question was beginning to look serious, the Prime-Minister had written (May, 1876): "Whatever happens we shall certainly not drift into war, but go to war, if we do, because we intend it." The words faithfully define his policy; but it must be added that he did not go to war, because he never intended to do so. A study of the diplomatic despatches and conversations which passed between the Foreign Office and the Porte at that time, and of Lord Beaconsfield's concurrent correspondence with the Queen, his colleagues, and his friends, makes it impossible to resist the conclusion that all the admonitions, remonstrances, and veiled threats which were addressed to Russia on the subject of Constantinople were a gigantic piece of bluff[1]. Lord Beaconsfield was, of course, determined to prevent the occupation of the capital if it were by any means possible, and in support of his assurances to the Queen on the subject he went as far towards an open breach with Russia as he dared; nevertheless, there is no justification for supposing that he was ever prepared to go to war on this issue alone, but every reason to conclude that he was ready, if the fortunes of diplomacy went against him, to accept accomplished facts and make the best of them. That he went even so far as he did was due to his knowledge that it was safe to apply to Russia, in her then exhausted state, a very strong degree of pressure. Raouf Pasha, the Turkish Minister of War, who was sent on a mission to Petrograd in March, brought home the assurance that the military authorities there were thoroughly alarmed by the prospect of a war with Great Britain.

---

[1] The biographer of Lord Salisbury records that "at a later period he came to doubt whether there had been substantial grounds for the charge" made by Liberal politicians that Beaconsfield had "the intention of manoeuvring England into a war in defence of Turkey," though both he and Lord Carnarvon had for a time believed it. *Life of Salisbury*, II. 137.

At a Cabinet held on March 27th, the Prime-Minister proposed the immediate calling-out of the Reserves and the despatch of a large native force from India, with a view to occupying ports in the Levant commanding the Persian Gulf and the country round Bagdad, so as to neutralise the Russian conquests and influence in Armenia[1]. In the event, this proposal of the forcible occupation of the territory of a friendly Power was not carried out; but, towards the end of May, an Indian expeditionary force of 7000 native troops was landed at Malta, from which garrison it happily became unnecessary to move it. Lord Derby was the only dissentient from the decision, and he now definitively resigned. In so doing he merely withdrew from an intolerable position; for his place in the Administration had almost become that of a Minister without portfolio. On March 8th the Prime-Minister had informed the Queen that the Cabinet had "taken the management of the Foreign Office into its own hands." For some time, he had, practically, himself acted as Foreign Secretary, so far as the Eastern Question was concerned; while Lord Derby's functions were those of an executive officer and more or less friendly critic. Lord Salisbury received the vacant office, the reversion of which he had expected for some time.

All this time, *pourparlers* of a different kind were proceeding in two directions. At the end of January, a busy exchange of diplomatic Notes between London and Vienna began. Lord Beaconsfield sprang on the Cabinet the proposal of a defensive alliance with Austria-Hungary, and Lord Carnarvon alone opposed it. Negotiations were accordingly resumed with Andrássy on the basis of the "moral understanding" of the preceding July, but for a long time without definite result. Andrássy had not abandoned the hope of coming to a satisfactory agreement with Russia. He was as indisposed to hostilities as ever, and was not convinced that Great Britain would fight in any event; hence he had hitherto played for delay. The publication of the terms of peace, however, compelled him to come to a definite decision: his first comment on the San Stefano Treaty was: "Russia has played us false." Simultaneously, there had been negotiations on the subject

---

[1] Cyprus and Alexandretta appear to have been suggested as suitable for occupation. Lord Derby left a Memorandum of the proceedings of this Cabinet in which Lord Beaconsfield's speech advocating the seizure of Turkish territory without permission was summarised as follows: "An emergency has arisen: the balance of power in the Mediterranean is in danger; every State must now look to its own interests.... Proposes to communicate with the Porte, to guarantee the revenues now received, so that they shall not lose. This does not involve alliance with the Porte. Nor is it inconsistent with anything we have done."

of a Conference of the Powers. So soon as it became certain that the War would end in Russia's favour, Great Britain and Austria-Hungary had given both the belligerent Powers to understand that no modification of the Treaties of 1856 and 1871 would be regarded as valid without consultation with the Signatory States. Accordingly, early in February, Andrássy sounded the Powers as to their willingness to confer on the subject, and all agreed with or without condition. The British Government made their participation dependent upon the submission of the entire Treaty to the free judgment of the Powers—a condition to which Russia demurred.

The Treaty of San Stefano was a forced contract, and its territorial provisions went far towards justifying those who had suspected Russia of pursuing interested ends under the pretence of performing a disinterested public duty. The principal proposal was to create a Greater Bulgaria as an autonomous principality, covering broadly, by the incorporation of Roumelia and the larger part of Macedonia, the territory lying between the Danube, the Black Sea, and the Aegean. Little more was to be left to Constantinople than Epirus, Thessaly, Thrace and the peninsula of Chalcis. The proposal was, in effect, the revival of the medieval Bulgarian empire, as it existed before the Turkish Conquest. A Russian Commissioner was to assist in the organisation of the new system of administration and to supervise it for two years. Servia was to receive a considerable increase of territory (including the old town of Nisch) together with independence, and her liability to pay tribute to Turkey was to be cancelled. Montenegro, which the Tsar had always specially favoured, was to be trebled in size and doubled in population by the absorption of districts of Herzegovina, Albania, and the sandjak of Novi-Bazar. It was to retain Nikshich, Spizza, Antivari, and Dulcigno, which had been occupied during the War; and its political independence, which had existed in practice for many years, was now to be formally recognised. It was proposed that the original recommendations relating to Bosnia and Herzegovina which the Powers had urged on the Porte at the Constantinople Conference (implying a limited autonomy) should be at once enforced, subject to such modifications as the Russian, Turkish, and Austro-Hungarian Governments might deem needful. Reforms were also to be introduced in Crete, Epirus, Thessaly, and other parts of European Turkey, and security and good government were to be assured to the Armenians. In general, Russia was liberal in the grant of Constitutions to the Balkan territories, though as yet without Constitutional government herself.

Roumania fared worst under the Treaty, though she had rendered Russia invaluable assistance during the War, and, at one time, had stood between the great Muscovite Power and imminent disaster. She was to receive political independence, but was to retrocede to Russia southern Bessarabia[1], in exchange for a portion of the Dobrudja, which was to be taken from Turkey in part payment of the War indemnity. Russia required for herself, in addition, Ardahan, Kars, Bayazid, and Batoum in Asia Minor, with a strip of Asiatic coast. The indemnity was fixed at 1410 million roubles, commutable in territory to the extent of 310 millions. Further, the Bosphorus and the Dardanelles were to remain open, in time of war as of peace, to the merchant vessels of neutral States bound to or from Russian ports.

In its territorial aspects, the Treaty of San Stefano was dictated by an almost exclusive consideration for certain favoured Slavic States. Russia showered favours upon the races which she had drawn, or hoped to retain, under her Protection, but did little for those outside the range of her influence. Thus, the national claims of Greece were altogether ignored. The Treaty was further vitiated by the worst defect of most former Treaties of conquest: in that it bartered human beings like chattels and placed large populations under alien rule, not only against their will, but with total disregard of ethnical or historical claims.

Petitions promptly rained upon the British Government from aggrieved nationalities—Turks, Roumanians, Greeks, Albanians—protesting against arrangements so inequitable and begging for their revision. Roumania was prepared to join in war against Russia at once, if Great Britain would take the lead. To representations from these quarters Lord Beaconsfield and the new Foreign Secretary were not indifferent; but the considerations which chiefly weighed with them were the danger to the Ottoman empire of a Greater Bulgaria subject to control from Petrograd, and the menace to British interests in Asia Minor. Austria was equally opposed to the Treaty as ignoring her claims in regard to Bosnia and Herzegovina, preparing the way for the creation of a powerful Slavic State on her borders, and, in

[1] Lord Beaconsfield suggested this restitution in a letter written to Lord Derby in the preceding September.

consequence of the proposed enlargement of Bulgaria, blocking the road to Salonica, the ultimate goal of Habsburg ambitions. Even France was alarmed by the prospect of a Russian naval base on the eastern side of the Mediterranean; and an attempt made at that time to float a Russian loan on the Paris market failed.

The first important official act of the new Foreign Secretary was the issue to the Powers of a Circular Note (April 1st) criticising the proposals of the San Stefano Treaty, and stating the attitude and policy of the British Government with perfect definiteness and clarity. This Note, the main propositions in which he had submitted to the Prime-Minister in a letter of March 21st, was in substance a challenge to Russia in the name of all the Powers which were prepared to take their stand on the maintenance of the existing Balance of Power, whether in Europe or Asia Minor, and the binding force of international treaties. Lord Salisbury recalled the fact that, in the Declaration annexed to the First Protocol of the London Conference of 1871, the Signatory Powers affirmed it to be "an essential principle of the law of nations that no Power can liberate itself from the engagements of a treaty, or modify the stipulations thereof, unless with the consent of the Contracting Powers, by means of an amicable arrangement." It was impossible, he said, without violating the spirit of this Declaration, to acquiesce in the withdrawal from the cognisance of the Powers of any Articles in the Treaty of San Stefano which modified existing arrangements or were inconsistent with them.

Coming to the details of the Peace Preliminaries, he indicated the British Government's suspicion of the creation, in the proposed Greater Bulgaria, of a powerful Slavic State, possessing harbours on the Euxine and the Aegean, and controlled by Russia, which would thereby obtain "a preponderating influence over both political and commercial relations in those seas." It was also objected that the territorial severance from Constantinople of the Greek, Albanian and Slavic provinces which were still to remain under the government of the Porte would create constant administrative difficulty and embarrassment, and not only weaken the Porte itself politically, but expose the inhabitants of the provinces to the danger of anarchy. The indemnity was criticised from the standpoint of its form rather than of its amount, since it was to be open to Russia to commute part of it into territory or leave it as an unredeemed liability—a provision capable of proving a powerful instrument of coercion.

Turkey having frustrated the objects of the Powers as agreed upon at the Constantinople Conference, he admitted that large changes might now be necessary in the Treaties by which south-eastern Europe had hitherto been ruled, since "good government, assured peace, and freedom for populations to whom these blessings have been strange," were still the objects of Great Britain's earnest concern. His Government would, therefore, have willingly entered a congress in which the stipulations contained in the Preliminaries of Peace could have been examined as a whole, "in their relation to existing treaties, to the acknowledged rights of Great Britain, and to the beneficent ends which the united action of Europe has always been directed to secure." They were unable to take part in a congress whose deliberations were to be restricted in the manner proposed by Prince Gortchakoff.

Both as an exposition of policy and a *pièce justificative*, the Salisbury Circular was a State document of great ability and power, and the praise awarded to it by Lord Beaconsfield, whose part in its production was merely that of *retoucheur*, was well deserved. The Porte had already asked the British Government to help it to obtain modifications of the Treaty in regard to the limits of Bulgaria (which it wished to restrict to the territory between the Danube and the Balkans), the Armenian cessions, and the indemnity, and a promise had been given accordingly.

In an elaborate reply (April 9th) Gortchakoff challenged the British Government to abandon their negative standpoint and say not merely what they did not want, but what they wanted, seeing that matters could not remain as they were. Every Power taking part in the congress, he promised, would have the same complete freedom of action which Russia claimed for herself. He contended that the proposed Greater Bulgaria was merely a development of the State which was contemplated by the Conference of Constantinople, and justified the retrocession of Roumanian Bessarabia as the reversal of an intolerable decision which was forced on Russia in the time of her impotence. Cessions of territory, he added, were a natural consequence of war, and if England had wished to spare Turkey she should have joined Russia, as she was twice invited to do, in bringing to bear upon the Porte such pressure as would have averted hostilities.

Turkey concluded peace with Servia a little later, but continued on a war footing as regards Montenegro.

IV. The Berlin Congress and its Issues, 1878-1880

A. *The Berlin Congress*, 1878

Lord Beaconsfield claimed that the Salisbury Circular had "put the country on its legs again." It certainly clarified the European situation and brought all the Powers to a sense of actualities. At Petrograd and in at least one other imperial capital, where conviction had hitherto been lacking, it was recognised that the British Cabinet had decided to make a firm stand in the defence of interests which it honestly believed to be menaced by Russia's action. From this time onward, the Eastern crisis showed signs of abatement, and diplomacy passed into smoother waters.

In a letter written a few days after the signing of the San Stefano Treaty, Lord Beaconsfield claimed that Great Britain was strong enough to have a policy of her own and to carry it through—a policy of which the purpose should be to "vindicate and assert her own rights and interests"; and he protested: "we must think less of Bismarcks and Andrássys and Gortchakoffs, and more of our own energies and resources[1]." In truth, he had gained powerful auxiliaries in the persons both of the German and Austro-Hungarian Foreign Ministers. In his relations to the Powers principally concerned, Bismarck had hitherto "hedged"; now, he took a more decided stand on the side of Great Britain and Austria, and in token of his change of mind began to show an unwonted zeal in the cause of conciliation.

The proposal of a conference of the Ambassadors, originally planned for Vienna, had in the meantime grown into something larger. Gortchakoff had suggested that the conference should be composed of the leading Ministers of the Powers, as Plenipotentiaries, for he intended to take part himself; and Bismarck, accustomed to decide questions of policy *proprio motu*, agreed, for once, with the Russian Chancellor. This larger view prevailing, Berlin was by general consent accepted as the meeting-place of what was now described as a Congress. There remained the British Government's objection to sending Plenipotentiaries to Berlin or elsewhere, merely to confirm a series of *faits accomplis*. They claimed, with perfect justification, that the Treaty of San Stefano should be submitted in its entirety to the jurisdiction of the Powers, whose duty and right it would be to determine how far it was inconsistent with the Treaty of 1856 and the Protocol of 1871, and to approve or reject any departures from these

[1] Letter of March 8th, 1878.

agreements according to their full discretion. Gortchakoff wished merely to communicate the Treaty to the Congress, leaving to each Power represented there full liberty of judgment and of action (*la pleine liberté de ses appréciations et de son action*). Such a concession, however, ignored the question in dispute, since it implied that Russia would not regard herself as bound, in case of disagreement, to abide by the decision of the other Powers. This evasion of the condition of their acceptance of the Congress only strengthened the British Cabinet's conviction of its importance. Finally, Gortchakoff cut short the dispute with the curt intimation that the Russian Government "leaves to the other Powers the liberty of raising such questions as they may think fit to discuss, and reserves to itself the liberty of accepting or not accepting the discussion of these questions."

The deadlock which ensued was resolved by a secret understanding between the two Governments. Holding tenaciously to the view that the Congress, if held at all, must possess unlimited jurisdiction, and convinced that no good could come of a series of roaming discussions directed to vague and undefined objects, the British Foreign Secretary conferred with the Russian Ambassador with a view to ascertaining how far the Treaty of San Stefano might be brought into line with the views of his Government, and so serve as the basis of a general agreement. The result was the conclusion of the Salisbury-Schouvaloff Convention of May 30th, by which the two Powers agreed upon the broad lines of a settlement mutually acceptable. In reality, the difficulties between them proved easy of adjustment. Russia was told that Great Britain cared little about Servian and Montenegrin questions, provided her views in regard to Bulgaria and the proposed annexations in Asiatic Turkey were fairly met. In the end, the idea of a Greater Bulgaria was abandoned, the territory south of the Balkans being left to Turkey, while Russia's acquisition of Bessarabia and of certain points in Armenia, including Batoum, was to stand. Turkey's promises to Russia in regard to Armenia were to be made to Great Britain, also, who was likewise to have a voice in determining the future organisation of the Greek provinces of European Turkey. Moreover, Russia renounced the idea of commuting any part of the war indemnity into a further acquisition of territory.

The Secret Convention was divulged in the columns of a London newspaper by the malfeasance of a copying clerk in the Foreign Office, employed on the transcription of confidential State documents at the pay of eightpence an hour. The Prime-Minister's annoyance at the disclosure turned to dismay when he learned that the Foreign Office had decided to expose itself by prosecuting the offender.

The practice of secret diplomacy never exercised the Chanceries of Europe more assiduously than during the few weeks immediately preceding the Berlin Congress. Great Britain, Russia, Austria-Hungary and Turkey were all engaged simultaneously in concluding surreptitious conventions and treaties. While negotiating with Russia, Lord Salisbury was bargaining with Andrássy, whom Gortchakoff was known to be making strong efforts to capture. Ever since the conclusion of the Declaration, or "moral understanding," of July, 1877, the British Government had been pressing Andrássy to enter into a more binding agreement. In diplomatic usage, a reciprocal Declaration is a treaty with the strings untied; and he was now determined to tie the strings. Neither Lord Salisbury nor Lord Beaconsfield trusted Andrássy, and it was their lack of confidence in him, caused by his refusal to enter into a definite self-commitment, that had induced them to fall back on the Anglo-Russian Convention[1]. Even during the negotiations now begun, Lord Salisbury believed that Andrássy might at any time turn round and come to an agreement with Russia, providing for the partition with her of the Balkan peninsula by a line running from Servia to the Gulf of Rendina. On the other hand, Andrássy had heard with alarm of the negotiations between London and Petrograd, and was anxious to know what they meant. Bismarck shared his apprehensions, and on May 25th urged Lord Salisbury not to come to any agreement with Russia that would be prejudicial to Germany's Ally.

After much pressure on Lord Salisbury's part, and much wavering on Andrássy's, an understanding was reached. Lord Salisbury defined the broad object of British policy in European Turkey at that time in a letter to our Ambassador at Vienna, wherein he told him that "all practicable support should be given to the races which are likely to act as a barrier to the advance of the Slavonic Power." These races were, preeminently, the Turks and the Greeks. On May 27th, while

---

[1] In a letter to Elliot at Vienna of June 3rd, 1878, Lord Salisbury wrote: "The necessity for a special agreement on the part of Her Majesty's Government with Russia would not have arisen, if the Austrian Government had responded at an earlier period to the overtures which have been repeatedly made to them by Her Majesty's Government to come to an agreement for the full cooperation of Austria and England in dealing with the state of things resulting from the War between Russia and Turkey. Her Majesty's Government have never been able, notwithstanding the assurances which they have on various occasions received from Count Andrássy, to acquire the conviction that Austria might not altogether desert them, and they have accordingly been forced to provide against that contingency."

at Petrograd Schouvaloff was commending the draft Anglo-Russian Convention to the Tsar, Lord Salisbury sent to Vienna another draft Convention for Andrássy's consideration. The principal stipulations were that the two Powers were to insist on the Balkan range as the boundary of Bulgaria, Roumelia continuing under the political and military supremacy of the Sultan; the duration of the Russian occupation of Bulgaria was to be limited to six months from the signature of the definitive Treaty; European was to be substituted for Russian supervision of Bulgarian reorganisation; while Great Britain was to support any propositions which Austria might make at the Congress with respect to Bosnia and, generally, as to the future frontiers of Servia and Montenegro, yet to be under no engagement to go to war on the question of the precise boundaries of these two States. It was understood that Austria had no immediate wish to annex Bosnia and Herzegovina, but was only concerned to bring them within her undisputed sphere of influence, perhaps to the extent of occupation for purely administrative purposes. A Convention embodying the above provisions was signed in Vienna on June 6th.

One other Secret Treaty was concluded by the British Government on the eve of the Congress; it related to the integrity of the Sultan's dominions in Asia. The tripartite Treaty of April 25th, 1856, gave Great Britain the right to ask France to cooperate in preventing any appropriation of Turkish territory. But France, conscious of liabilities nearer home, had throughout made it clear that in no circumstances would she fight on our side, much less on our behalf, against Russia. If, however, Great Britain undertook to perform police duty for Turkey in Asia Minor single-handed, it followed that she could fairly claim permission to adopt whatever measures might seem necessary to the due discharge of that task. By a Convention of June 4th, signed in Constantinople by Sir A. H. Layard and Safvet Pasha, Great Britain entered into a defensive alliance with Turkey, pledging herself to defend by force of arms the Asiatic dominions of the Sultan, as they might be fixed by the Congress, should any attempt be made upon them by Russia. In return, the Sultan undertook to introduce reforms, to be agreed upon later between the two Powers, into the government of these territories and for the protection of the Christian and other subjects of the Porte in them, and further to "assign the island of Cyprus to be occupied and administered by England," in order to enable her to "make necessary provision for executing her engagement."

The Anglo-Russian Convention having been divulged prematurely, it became a question whether the complementary agreement with Turkey should be frankly published at once or be disclosed at some opportune moment as the proceedings at the Congress developed. For the present, it was kept back, though Russia was told of its purport. Some weeks later, Lord Salisbury also informed Waddington, the French Foreign Minister, of the conclusion of the Convention and the reasons for it. For Great Britain the security of the Indian empire was a paramount concern; that security required the maintenance of an open way through Asia Minor and the Middle East, and therewith the continuance of Turkish power there. Cyprus had been acquired as a base from which assistance would be given to Turkey in case of need, since Malta was too far distant for the purpose. Nevertheless, he added that "whenever Russia shall, for whatever reason, return to her Asiatic frontier as it existed before the last war, Great Britain would immediately evacuate the island" (July 7th, 1878). In order to lighten the shock of the revelation, Lord Salisbury told Waddington that "advisers of no mean authority" had urged the British Government to appropriate a far larger slice of Turkish territory—to wit, Egypt, or at least the borders of the Suez Canal, and even parts of Asia Minor, but that, out of regard for French susceptibilities, they had virtuously declined these suggestions.

The disclosure created in France alarm and resentment, and also a feeling that Great Britain had not acted straightforwardly. Although, as Waddington wrote, France in entering the Congress had "expressly excluded from discussion the state of things existing in the Lebanon, the Holy Places, and Egypt," the British Government was appropriating an island "situated in the most favourable strategic and maritime position for commanding at once the coasts of Syria and of Egypt[1]." The French Government asked, as a condition of continued harmonious cooperation, that the British Government should offer an assurance that there would be no interference with the spheres of interest of the two countries in the valley of the Nile; and this assurance Lord Salisbury gave as regarding not only Egypt, but Palestine and Syria. He even let it be known that Great Britain would raise no objection if France were, in her turn, to take Tunis[2].

[1] Despatch of Waddington of July 21st, 1878.
[2] A year later (March, 1879), Lord Salisbury suppressed the British Consulate-General in Tunis and reduced it to a Consulate of the second class, which meant the recall of an energetic official who, in the eyes of France, had been too zealous in the protection of British interests.

At home, the Convention was variously judged. The Liberal party as a whole condemned it as a dangerous leap in the dark, while the Ministerialists applauded it and upbraided the Government for not having taken a larger portion of the Ottoman empire while they were about it.

So soon as he knew that Great Britain and Russia were ready for debate, Bismarck issued invitations to the Congress of Berlin, whose first session was held on June 13th, 1878. All the Great Powers, together with Turkey, sent as Plenipotentiaries leading Ministers of State, and the Ambassadors accredited to the German imperial Court were attached to the Congress as Special Envoys. Great Britain was represented by Lord Beaconsfield[1], Lord Salisbury and Lord Odo Russell, whose intimate relationship with the German Chancellor was of great assistance to his colleagues; and the other leading Plenipotentiaries were: for Germany, Prince Bismarck and Prince Hohenlohe-Schillingsfürst (afterwards Chancellor); for Russia, Prince Gortchakoff and Count Schouvaloff; for Austria-Hungary, Count Andrássy and Count Karolyi; for France, M. Waddington; for Italy, Count Corti; and for Turkey, Alexander Karatheodori Pasha and Mehemet Ali Pasha, the former of Greek, the latter of German, extraction. None of the small States whose interests were to be adjudicated upon was allowed Representation; but Delegates from Roumania and Greece were heard when questions affecting these countries arose. The presidency fell as a matter of course to Bismarck.

The British Plenipotentiaries proceeded to the scene of their labours well supported by material and moral auxiliaries, and in a very confident mood. "We have," Lord Salisbury wrote to Lord Lyons (June 5th), "assembled a powerful fleet at Portsmouth, and we have six or seven first-rate ironclads to do what may be necessary in the Mediterranean, besides smaller ships." Better still, the Government's relations with Bismarck were "particularly good." Lord Lyons was to be trusted to keep the temperature of Paris cool, and to see that the statesmen there "confined themselves to epigrams." By reason of ill-health, Beaconsfield had intended to take part in

---

[1] Desirous though she was that the Prime-Minister should represent Great Britain at the Congress, the Queen had scruples on the score of his health, and for that reason would have preferred a nearer city, Brussels, The Hague or Paris, as the meeting-place. If, however, Beaconsfield was seriously handicapped by his 73½ years, still more so, with his 80 years, was Gortchakoff, who had to make a land journey of equal length. Both of these veteran statesmen had, accordingly, to divide their stay in Berlin between the Congress room and the quiet of their hotels.

only the early sessions of the Congress, leaving Lord Salisbury, in whose judgment and loyalty he had perfect confidence, to "complete all the details of which he is consummate master[1]"; but he remained in Berlin to the end. Never did a Power attend an international Court of arbitration so panoplied by prior treaty guarantees, commitments and reservations as Great Britain in entering the Congress of Berlin. Lord Beaconsfield said truly, "We have made our book with Austria, and Turkey is in our pocket." Protected by agreements with both belligerents and also with the only neutral Power directly concerned in the future organisation of the Balkans, the British Plenipotentiaries could enter upon the negotiations with composure, since what was lost in one direction was certain to be gained in another. The general lines which were to be followed by them were laid down in a series of Instructions sent to Lord Odo Russell at Berlin on June 8th. Any proposals legitimately tending to benefit and strengthen the Austro-Hungarian monarchy were to be supported. Great Britain was to "go far" towards meeting Russia in regard to her acquisitions in Asia, and in particular to allow her to retain Batoum, Kars, and Ardahan, inasmuch as "the other Powers would not be likely to care." There was to be no active interposition by Great Britain in matters not directly concerning her, and, in particular, she was not to "intervene conspicuously" in relation to the frontiers to be assigned to Servia and Montenegro and the arrangements which might be proposed as to Bosnia and Montenegro; but support was to be given to measures for ensuring the welfare and good government of the populations concerned. The general policy to be followed as to Turkey was to be one of consideration for her interests; Bulgaria was not to be allowed to extend south of the Balkans, and the future organisation of that territory was stated to be the part of the Treaty which affected England most closely.

From first to last, the Congress resolved itself into an intellectual tourney between three outstanding figures, Beaconsfield, Gortchakoff, and Bismarck; and all three men were in the doctors' hands. Never did weary Titans acquit themselves more gallantly. Bismarck feared that the British Plenipotentiaries had come in an aggressive mood, and might put forward demands so extreme that, rather than comply with them, Russia would prefer to go to war. Even the tradition of the Congress as handed down represents Lord Beaconsfield and Gortchakoff as stripped gladiators, confronting each other with tense

[1] Letter to the Queen, May 31st, 1878.

muscles and glaring eyes. The picture is remote from the truth. They were rivals; but their rivalry was that of clever chess-players, sedate, polite, and good-humoured, each straining resolutely for his own hand, but always with perfect loyalty to the rules of the game. Beaconsfield was for a time something of an enigma to Bismarck, who, himself the author of so many *coups*, was always in fear that the inscrutable English statesman with the oriental face and temperament would spring a dramatic surprise upon the Congress. He touched a weak point in British diplomacy when he discovered that Beaconsfield and his adjutant, Lord Salisbury, were not in all points agreed, the latter clearly not sharing the Prime-Minister's extravagant Russophobia and more disposed than his colleague to bring a European, international mind to the judgment of the problems in hand.

Fortunately for the British view of things, the opinion was current in Russian circles that Great Britain was prepared at any time to withdraw from the Congress if her demands were too brusquely handled; for the effect was to make Russia cautious. The Russian Plenipotentiaries, however, had another reason for circumspect procedure; for they soon made the disconcerting discovery that their country had few friends in the Congress, since the San Stefano Treaty was held to belie all its past professions of unselfish purpose. Andrássy claimed that by the Congress he had put Russia "in the prisoner's box"; and in the Berlin negotiations she was unquestionably regarded as a suspect whose designs called for close scrutiny, while the mutual orientation of the Powers was distinctly to her disadvantage. Great Britain and Austria-Hungary systematically worked together, and France and Italy, alike distrustful of Russia's ambition to become a Mediterranean Power, were usually to be found in their company. Germany, true to Bismarck's promise, played the part of the "honest broker," and succeeded in it so well that, when the Congress was over, both Great Britain and Russia claimed its decisions as a triumph for their respective purposes. Next to the success of his mediatory offices, Bismarck's great concern was that Turkey should not, by her old tricks of procrastination, equivocation, and intrigue, repeat the fiasco of the Constantinople Conference. The Turkish Delegates were soon to learn that they had come to Berlin not to carry on negotiations, but to accept dictation[1].

The order of procedure was that all questions were introduced

---

[1] "Bismarck sits upon the Turks mercilessly," Lord Salisbury wrote home on June 22nd.

publicly and then, in appropriate cases, negotiated, and if possible settled, privately between the countries chiefly concerned. True to his rule of putting first things first, Bismarck asked the assembled Plenipotentiaries to begin their discussions with the Sixth Article of the Treaty of San Stefano, dealing with Bulgaria, since the success or failure of the Congress depended on its coming to an agreement on the future extent and organisation of this particular territory. On this subject, the Treaty of Berlin, which embodied the decisions of the Plenipotentiaries (July 13th), simply gave concrete form to the general principles affirmed in the Anglo-Russian Convention. It provided that Bulgaria should be cut in two, exclusive of Macedonia, which was disregarded in the new arrangements. The northern, and larger, portion was to be an autonomous principality, tributary to Turkey, bounded by the Danube, the Black Sea (with an outlet at Varna), the Balkans, and the frontiers of Servia, its ruler to be "freely elected by the population and confirmed by the Porte with the consent of the Powers." South of the Balkans, the province of Eastern Roumelia was to be formed, with administrative autonomy and a Christian Governor-General, but subject to the political and military authority of the Sultan; its future government was to be organised by a European Commission (Articles I–XXII).

Austria, according to this plan, received a mandate empowering her to occupy and administer Bosnia and Herzegovina, subject to Turkish suzerainty (Article XXV); and, since it was a part of her bargain with Great Britain that the Russian design of creating a chain of Slavic States stretching across the Balkan peninsula should be frustrated, it was decided that the sandjak of Novi-Bazar should not be divided between Servia and Montenegro, as Russia desired, but be garrisoned by Austria, in accordance with her wish, without prejudice to Turkish sovereignty. In the private negotiations with the Porte which Austria, with British support, had carried on in Constantinople before the opening of the Congress, the cession of the provinces "*en toute propriété*" had been asked for; but this claim was abandoned. Austria was, however, to take over from Montenegro the Dalmatian port of Spizza.

Something had to be done for Servia, Montenegro and Roumania; and, though Lord Beaconsfield had little sympathy with these rebellious tributary States, it was one of the ironies of the peace settlement that more concern was shown for their welfare by Great Britain and Austria than by Russia herself. Servia was to receive full independence with an increase of territory, but was refused any access to the Adriatic (Articles XXXIV–XLII). Montenegro was, also, to become a sovereign State, and was doubled in size, and furnished with an outlet to the sea at the Bay of Antivari; but she was to return Dulcigno to Turkey and, as already stated, to cede Spizza (Articles XXV–XXXIII).

Roumania could hardly have received harsher treatment, had she fought against Russia instead of on her side. She was, indeed, declared independent; but she was required to return the Bessarabian territory which had been transferred from Russia to Moldavia in 1856, and was assigned, instead, the sterile tract of the Dobrudja, inhabited by an alien population (Articles XLIII–XLVI).

The Greek Delegates present in Berlin were heard on their country's behalf, and put forward a strong claim to consideration, pointing to the passive attitude of Greece during the troubles of the last three years and the mischief which she might have done, if she had entered the War. They asked for a large increase of adjacent territory, together with Crete. The Powers, however, merely urged the Porte to accept a rectification of the frontier in Thessaly and Epirus (13th Protocol and Article XXIV). In Crete, the Porte undertook to apply conscientiously the Organic Statute of 1868, with such amendments as might be called for (Article XXIII).

Albania was still treated as the Cinderella of the Balkans. The province lost territory to Servia and Montenegro, and its claim to independence, and even its petition for a Christian Governor, fell on deaf ears.

In Asiatic Turkey, Russia acquired Ardahan, Kars, and Batoum, the last-named subject to the condition, spontaneously offered by Gortchakoff, that it should be a "free port, essentially commercial"—a condition repudiated eight years later by Russia without the assent of the other Powers. On the other hand, she renounced the acquisitions of Erzeroum, Bayazid, and the valley of Alaschgerd (Articles LVIII–LX).

A stipulation, short but definite, was devoted to Armenia, for whose welfare Great Britain had tacitly made herself responsible by the Convention of June 4th. This stipulation bound the Porte to introduce "without further loss of time such ameliorations and reforms as are called for by the local conditions of the provinces inhabited by the Armenians, and to take measures to protect them against the Circassians and Kurds." The measures adopted were to be announced periodically to the Powers appointed to supervise their execution

(Article LXI). Of the Christians of Macedonia there was no mention. New provisions for the regulation of the navigation of the Danube were introduced (Articles XLVI–LVII), and the Signatory Powers declared that the Treaty of Paris of 1856 and the London Protocol of 1871 remained in full force, except in so far as any of their provisions were annulled or modified by the new Treaty (Article LXIII).

In closing the Congress on July 13th, Bismarck paid a well-deserved tribute to "the spirit of conciliation and mutual goodwill which has animated all the Plenipotentiaries," and added: "The Congress has deserved well of Europe. If it has been impossible to fulfil all the aspirations of public opinion, history will, at all events, do justice to our intentions and to our work."

On the whole, the Treaty of Berlin might fairly be claimed as a triumph for Anglo-Austrian policy: it remained for later years to show whether the Treaty could be regarded as a vindication of that policy. It would be wrong to say that it showed no concern for the victims of Turkish misrule. It averted from the Balkan States and provinces the horrors of a further conflict between Russia and Turkey; it removed many abuses and wrongs which had long and vainly cried for remedy; it did justice to the political aspirations of races whose advance on the road to independence had for generations been slow and halting, converting three tributary States into free principalities, creating a new tributary principality, and alleviating the hard yoke of Ottoman rule over peoples for whose complete emancipation the time was not yet ripe,—achievements which directly benefited, in the aggregate, eleven millions of people. Nevertheless, the underlying motive in the case of most of the negotiating Powers was not, in the phraseology of Napoleon III, the "pensée humanitaire," but the "pensée politique"; and the result was only a temporary settlement based on political expediency. Lord Beaconsfield had entered the Congress holding a power-of-attorney for Turkey, Bismarck with a watching brief on behalf of Austria and, in a secondary degree, of Russia; but the wider standpoint of the European nations and of civilisation at large was without special representation, though the force of circumstances prevented it from being altogether overlooked. Lord Beaconsfield said at a later date that, next to serving Turkey, he had aimed at shattering the *entente* of the three empires; and he maintained that he had succeeded in the task[1].

[1] See letter of November 4th, 1880, to Sir H. D. Wolff, quoted in his *Rambling Recollections*, II. (1908), 265.

Lord Beaconsfield returned to England claiming that he had brought back from Berlin "Peace with honour," and that the Treaty of Berlin and the Anglo-Turkish Convention had together removed from Europe and the British empire all occasion of distrust and alarm. He had, however, to meet many reproaches from the more unreasoning of his pro-Turkish followers, and their complaint that the Ottoman empire, whose integrity was to have been preserved at all costs, had nevertheless been partitioned. He ridiculed the idea that there had been any partition at all. A country might lose provinces, he replied, but that was not partition. "A Power which calls one of the strongest cities in the world its own, has still at disposal an army and a fleet, and rules over twenty million people, cannot be described as a Power whose territory has been partitioned[1]." Those who deplored the cessions of Turkish territory in Asia were reminded that Russia, after all, had won the War, and that international usage recognised the right of conquest; and he added—with his eyes directed more to Central than to Near Asia—a much-needed rebuke to the intemperate Chauvinists who saw in the expansion of Great Britain's Eastern rival nothing but greed and menace: "Asia is large enough for both of us. There is no reason for these constant wars, or fears of wars, between Russia and England."

Nevertheless, no solemn international covenant has been so systematically and openly infringed and ignored, in part by the Signatory Powers themselves, as the Treaty which was concluded in Berlin in July, 1878, "in the name of Almighty God." Large States and small States have one after another overridden and evaded stipulations objectionable to them. Within seven years (1885), Bulgaria violated the Treaty and defied the Powers by absorbing Eastern Roumelia. A year later (July, 1886), Russia repudiated the conditions under which Batoum had been assigned to her—a proceeding indulgently tolerated by all the Powers except Great Britain, on whose behalf Lord Rosebery protested vigorously against it as a dangerous violation of the sanctity of treaty engagements which would tend to make future international agreements difficult and to cast doubt on those already concluded. Greece received far less territory than was designed for her by the 13th Protocol of the Congress, and had to wait for forty years for more generous treatment. The Porte made no effort to reform the government of Crete, with the result of repeated insurrections, leading to the transference of the island to the custody of

[1] Speech in the House of Lords, July 19th, 1878.

the Powers in 1898. Further, in total disregard of the reaffirmation of the integrity of the Ottoman empire by Article LXIII of the Treaty, France seized Tunis in 1881; and from 1882 onwards the authority of Great Britain step by step superseded the dominion of Turkey in Egypt and the Soudan provinces. Later (1908) Austria, with the connivance of Germany, arbitrarily converted the occupation of Bosnia and Herzegovina into formal annexation. Within times still more recent (1912), the Balkan States took into their own hands the repartition of European Turkey, the Powers refraining from active interference; while Italy possessed herself by force of Tripoli (1912). In spite of the provisions laid down in their favour at Berlin nothing was done for the good government and security of the Armenians, who continued to be given over to oppression, pillage, and massacre.

B. *First Overtures for an Anglo-German Alliance*, 1879

The issue of the Berlin Congress did much to revive for a time the political influence of Lord Beaconsfield at home, which had shown signs of decline, and, had he dissolved Parliament immediately after his return, while his laurels were still green, he would probably have received a striking reaffirmation of national confidence. Even Gladstone believed that the country was still with his rival. But, though a master of political strategy, Beaconsfield forgot that the British nation likes its emotions to be taken by storm, and made the fatal mistake of giving it time to reflect. When an appeal was made to the constituencies nearly two years later, the reaction was in full flood, and the sand-castles of a flamboyant imperialism were swept away.

On the other hand, Andrássy returned to Vienna to find his Balkan policy criticised with extreme bitterness by those who had hitherto been his loyal supporters. Only at the Emperor's urgent wish did he remain in office until the aftermath of problems incidental to a great territorial readjustment should have been cleared away. Shortly before his retirement, he concluded with Bismarck the Dual Alliance which formed the basis of the later Triple Alliance. The more the Tsar reflected upon the Berlin settlement, the more he was convinced that he had been out-manœuvred, and that Germany had failed in her duty to an old Ally. His resentment found sharp expression when, in the course of the succeeding boundary negotiations, he came to the conclusion that Germany was still of set purpose using her influence against Russia and Russian interests. In some brusque letters, he accused William I of want of loyalty, and, reminding him of the service which he had rendered to Germany in 1870, bade him mend his ways.

Bismarck had said to Gortchakoff during the Berlin Congress: "Do not compel me to choose between Russia and Austria-Hungary." Apart from this outbreak of pique, the fact that Andrássy had made a mysterious journey to Petrograd, suggesting the possibility of an Austro-Russian agreement, which it was expedient to circumvent, and the further suspicion that Russia was beginning to reciprocate the advances long attempted by France, convinced Bismarck that the best days of the Triple *Entente* were over, and that for future security Germany must look to a new combination. A Convention concluded at Vienna on October 7th, 1879, providing for a Defensive Alliance between the German and Austro-Hungarian empires, to meet the contingency of an attack upon either of these Powers by Russia, was his answer to the Tsar's menace. Francis Joseph welcomed the Dual Alliance warmly; but William I accepted it with reluctance, conscious that it foreboded the rupture of an old dynastic tradition, and, contrary to Bismarck's wish, he insisted on informing the Tsar of the existence, though not of the provisions, of the Convention[1].

While the negotiations with Andrássy were still in progress, Bismarck endeavoured to bring Great Britain into the same partnership. Four years before, in the year of the war-scare which marked the alienation of Gortchakoff and brought Russia and France nearer together, he had sent his confidant Lothar Bucher to London, to explore the possibility of forming a more intimate friendship in that quarter. The result appears to have been negative; but, from that time, Bismarck dropped hints to the British Ambassador in Berlin on the same subject, and during the Congress he sounded both Lord Beaconsfield and Lord Salisbury, receiving encouragement from the former. During his intercourse with Beaconsfield he had come to regard Great Britain in a new light. Her Prime-Minister's bold proclamation of an imperialistic policy, as evidenced by the Suez Canal shares purchase and the firm stand which he had made against Russia both in Europe and Central Asia, suggested to him that Great Britain was destined to play again her old part in foreign affairs and that the days of non-intervention were ended. An alliance of the two military empires with the strongest of naval Powers would be a perfect realisation of his ideal of a "coalition *à trois*."

[1] Bismarck's *Gedanken und Erinnerungen*, II. p. 248.

On September 26th, 1879, Count Münster visited the Prime-Minister at Hughenden, bringing with him a proposal of an alliance. He asked that the communication might be regarded, for the time, as a personal one, and said that the manner of its reception would determine whether it would be repeated in official form, adding that Bismarck had not as yet mentioned the subject to the Emperor. Beaconsfield was reminded that, three years earlier, Bismarck had already made suggestions of the kind through the British Ambassador in Berlin; and it was now hinted to him that if an alliance had been concluded earlier, the Eastern complications and the Russo-Turkish War might not have occurred. In its absence, Germany had been compelled to fall back upon Russia; but that makeshift had now failed. Of the immediate future Bismarck drew a lurid forecast. "Russia is preparing to attack Austria; the peace of the world will be threatened; it is in the nature of things that it will not be a localised war; it will be a great and general war. Peace is necessary to Germany; no country more desires or requires peace. To secure it, he proposes an alliance between Germany, Austria and Great Britain[1]." It was suggested that, while under the arrangement proposed Germany would enjoy security against any war of aggression aimed against her, Great Britain would receive support for her policy and interests in the Levant and the East generally[2].

Beaconsfield assured the Envoy that he personally welcomed these overtures, and obtained permission to confer with the Queen and also with the Foreign Secretary, then abroad. In communicating with both he favoured a sympathetic attitude. To Salisbury he said that the German alliance would be likely to be popular; for the country would regard it as a natural sequence to the Government's past attitude of suspicion towards Russia as a Power from which menace to the Empire was one day to be feared. The Queen was not indisposed to respond to Bismarck's advances, provided there were no alienation of France; but Salisbury was sceptical and suspected that Bismarck wished to use Great Britain as a merely temporary convenience. On Beaconsfield's suggestion, it was arranged that the Foreign Secretary should

---

[1] *Life of Beaconsfield*, VI. 488, and *Life of Salisbury*, II. 364-5.

[2] The editors of *Die Grosse Politik der europäischen Kabinette*, 1871-1914, take the view that the object of Bismarck's overtures was only to ascertain what the attitude of Great Britain would be in the event of Germany declining to give unreserved support to Russia's Eastern policy and losing her friendship in consequence, and it is true that Count Münster's Instructions went no further than this. The Ambassador also reports that the suggestion of an alliance came from Lord Beaconsfield. *Die Grosse Politik*, etc. IV. 3-14.

discuss the question privately with the German Ambassador; and this was done at Hatfield on October 15th, a week after the signing of the Austro-German Treaty. As a result of a frank exchange of views, Salisbury now formed the conclusion that the urgency of the German overtures had diminished since Count Münster had first begun them. Thereupon, he gave an assurance that in the event of a Russian attack on Germany and Austria British goodwill and assistance might be relied on, while, as for France, he said that Bismarck might feel sure that Great Britain would not allow an attack on Germany through Belgium, and he was also confident that she would even be able to restrain any French Government from joining Russia against Germany[1].

No more definite approach to an alliance appears to have been made on either side, and it is possible that Bismarck, discouraged by the absence of a more cordial response in the first instance, had already cooled down on the subject and looked for no practical result. Twelve days after the Hatfield conversation, Count Karolyi, the Austro-Hungarian Ambassador, informed Salisbury confidentially of the conclusion of the Dual Alliance, but made no allusion to the question of Great Britain's adhesion to it.

It is quite evident that Beaconsfield experienced a sense of keen relief at not having been pressed to return a positive answer to Bismarck's offer. For, as he wrote to the Queen (November 5th), "it would have been a difficult and even dangerous affair to have altogether rejected the contemplated alliance." In the circumstances, his satisfaction at the time that Great Britain was still "as free as air, and this, too, without showing any want of sympathy with the Austro-German views," was legitimate[2]. The Queen's comment on the episode, suggestive of a return of her former statesmanlike grip of realities, was, "We are well out of it." The words aptly describe the feeling which must have come over Bismarck himself, when in the general election of the following April the British nation pronounced emphatic condemnation upon all "spirited" Foreign Policy and sent the Beaconsfield Administration into retirement. The Triple Alliance was completed, two years later, by the adhesion of Italy (May, 1882).

---

[1] *Life of Salisbury,* II. 367–9.
[2] Nevertheless, according to a German diplomatist, who took part in more than one later attempt to draw his country and Great Britain closer together, Lord Beaconsfield, shortly before the fall of his Ministry, sketched the outlines of an Anglo-German alliance for Bismarck's examination. See Hermann Freiherr von Eckardstein, *Diplomatische Enthüllungen zum Ursprung des Weltkrieges,* p. 13. Cf. *infra,* pp. 276 ff.

C. *The Execution of the Treaty of Berlin*, 1878–1880

As was to be expected, Turkey was in no hurry to execute the Treaty, and, at the beginning of September, two months after its signature, Bismarck, pressed by France, whom he was desirous of conciliating, suggested the issue of an Identic Note to the Porte on the subject. The British Government, while declaring their intention to see the Treaty enforced, thought such action premature, and failed to make allowance for the Sultan's difficult position. This was, also, the view of other Powers, and Bismarck himself accepted it. When nine months had passed and the Porte had still taken no steps to draw up the Constitutions required by Article XXIII for Crete and other portions of European Turkey, Salisbury (on August 7th) made immediate and strong representations at Constantinople, recognising (as he wrote to our Ambassador there) that "the Sultan's inclination to come to an agreement and our power of insisting will diminish with each succeeding month"; but they had little effect.

The beneficiary States which were able to rely on their own strength speedily made good their treaty rights. Under the Anglo-Turkish Convention, Great Britain occupied Cyprus in July, 1878, and placed the island under a High Commissioner, the Turkish tribute being fixed at £92,800. Nearly three years later (February, 1881), during negotiations with Turkey as to the Greek frontier, Mr (afterwards Viscount) Goschen, then British Envoy Extraordinary at Constantinople, proposed that the island should be given back to the Porte as a makeweight; but the idea did not spread beyond the inner circle of the Cabinet, where it found no favour.

Austrian troops promptly entered the provinces of Bosnia and Herzegovina (July 29th), heralded by a proclamation stating that they did so "for the better preservation of order and tranquillity." Mohammadan risings at once followed, and a large army had to be employed in their suppression. The military occupation of the sandjak of Novi-Bazar was effected in September of the following year. Turkey retained all other jurisdiction, administrative, judicial and financial; and, on the whole, this experiment in dual control, on a small scale, worked smoothly and efficiently, the only disturbing influence being the Greater Servian agitation encouraged from the outside.

The spring of 1879 had arrived before practical progress was made in fixing the frontier between Bulgaria and Eastern Roumelia, and the Russian Government was anxious that the task should be completed before the time came for the withdrawal of the Tsar's troops. Major-General Hamley was the British Commissioner, and his Instructions were to secure for Turkey such a frontier as she would be able to defend, fortify, and garrison. Before the frontier was settled, there were frequent bickerings between the Commissioners on both sides; and in January, 1879, Gortchakoff, in an arrogant despatch, charged the British Government with deliberately impeding progress. Salisbury had no difficulty in proving that the delay in question was due to the action of the Russian agents, who had assured the inhabitants of Eastern Roumelia that the arrangements made by the Treaty of Berlin were merely temporary, and that the province would after all be joined to Bulgaria. A friendly understanding, taking the form of reciprocal pledges to enforce the Treaty provisions without fear or favour, facilitated the remainder of the frontier negotiations; and, early in June, the British Commissioner was able to report to Lord Salisbury that the result of his efforts had been "as advantageous to the defence of Turkey as could be desired."

For a time, Russian influence was supreme in the principality. The first ruler, Prince Alexander of Battenberg, a dashing young Prussian officer who had fought in the late War, was a nephew of Tsar Alexander II. Russian Ministers were imposed on him, and Russian officers were freely seconded to his army. Before long, however, the Bulgarians began to question the advantage of being emancipated from one Power in order to be yoked to another; and, in 1883, the Prince rid himself of his foreign advisers, though Russian intrigue continued active in the country.

Although for a time defeated, the cause of Bulgarian Union was kept alive by agitation both in the principality and in the severed province. The movement was, also, encouraged by much petty tyranny and *chicanerie* on the part of the Suzerain Power and its agents, and by resentment at the Porte's jealous and short-sighted policy in keeping Bulgarians out of the Roumelian administrative service. When the Liberal party came to power in Great Britain in the spring of 1880, the cause of Union received new stimulus, and on May 31st Sir William White, our Diplomatic Agent at Bucharest, warned Lord Granville that active measures might be expected at any time. The plan matured only five years later. On September 18th, 1885, the Turkish Governor-General of Eastern Roumelia was deposed by a band of military officers and despatched to Constantinople, and the Union of the province with Bulgaria under Prince Alexander was proclaimed. With great lack of discretion, the Prince accepted the proffered extension of his rule without consulting Turkey, his Suzerain, Russia, his Protector, or the Signatory Powers collectively. The Sultan protested and made defensive preparations, but did nothing further. What was more surprising was the attitude of the two Powers which had so bitterly wrangled over the question of a Greater Bulgaria in 1878. While Lord Salisbury (now Foreign Secretary in his own first Government), so soon as he had ascertained that the Powers were not conjointly disposed to reestablish the Treaty *status* by force, decided to support the Union, Russia refused to assent to an arrangement which she had vainly endeavoured to carry out seven years before.

Though so far bloodless, the *coup d'état* occasioned violent repercussions throughout the Balkan peninsula. Greece and Servia at once demanded territorial compensation at the expense of Turkey, and the Cretans again proclaimed Union with the Hellenic kingdom. King Milan of Servia (who had assumed the royal status in March, 1882) rashly declared war against his neighbour; but within a week (November 14th–20th) his kingdom lay prostrate at Bulgaria's feet. Only Austria's intervention prevented the Bulgarians from making a triumphant entry into Belgrade. The Treaty of Bucharest (March 3rd, 1886) restored the *status quo*. A little later, the Personal Union of Bulgaria and Eastern Roumelia was recognised by the Powers, the Sultan appointing Prince Alexander Governor-General of the detached province. Greece was prevented from attacking Turkey by the stern action of the Powers, France alone standing aloof. It was by the firm attitude adopted first by Lord Salisbury and later, on his relinquishment in 1886 of the Foreign Office, by the Earl of Rosebery, that the restless little State was held in check. When the Government of M. Delyanni refused to comply with the demand for disarmament, a blockade of the Greek coasts was instituted by five of the Powers, France abstaining. Delyanni's resignation eased the situation, and by the capitulation of Tricoupis, his successor, the blockade was raised and peace was preserved (June 6th, 1886).

No sooner had Prince Alexander of Bulgaria's new *status* been confirmed by the Powers than he laid down, not unwillingly, a somewhat thorny Crown (September 7th, 1886). His successor was Prince Ferdinand of Saxe-Coburg-Gotha, who was elected by the Grand Sobranje on July 7th, 1887, though without receiving recognition by the Powers until February, 1896.

While the early readjustments under the Treaty of Berlin were in progress, a Liberal Government came into power in England (April, 1880), animated by a stronger desire to see the provisions of the Treaty put into force. Lord Granville returned to his old post at the Foreign Office. He was not a man of rapid decisions; but he was conscious of the responsibility of his party and the country to the populations which had been freed from Turkish rule, and determined that the Porte should honour its many pledges. Its inertia was, however, still blocking the way, wherever the apathy or indecision of the Powers allowed it, and the suspicion was widespread that the British Government and their Representative in Constantinople were no longer favourable to the exercise of pressure.

Sir A. H. Layard's past attitude was inconsistent with zealous acceptance of the ideas represented by the new Ministry. Once before, in a critical time, Great Britain had spoken to Turkey with two voices, and the result had been disastrous. He was, therefore, given leave of absence until another Embassy could be found for him, and Goschen was sent to Constantinople as Special Ambassador and Plenipotentiary, with a view to the adjustment of the Greek and Montenegrin frontier questions and the securing of better conditions for Armenia.

The Greeks had wished to begin the retracing of their northern frontier almost before the signatures to the Treaty were dry, and had to be reminded that, as the arrangement proposed was dependent on moral suasion, the first step must be to come to an amicable understanding with the Porte. A long time was spent in futile negotiations, Turkey objecting that, while she had originally been asked to give Greece an inch, she was now called upon for an ell: the promise of a frontier rectification had become a demand for a province. Hereupon, France, who had played a very insignificant part in the Berlin Congress and the events which led up to it, seldom exposing herself to odium from any side and never to the remotest possibility of danger, posed for a time as the champion of the rights of the Hellenic race. But no sooner had it become plain that zealous support of the Greek claims would bring her into antagonism with Turkey, than she fell back into her old passive attitude. At that time, France was preparing to seize Tunis, and this fact, known only to herself, indisposed her to ruffle the Porte unnecessarily. In March, 1880, since no progress had been made, Salisbury proposed the appointment of an international commission for investigating the question on the spot and making definite recommendations to the Powers. A change of Government having occurred immediately afterwards, Granville suggested, instead, a conference in Berlin; and to this the Porte agreed.

When the recommendations of the Conference were communicated to the disputant States (July 15th), Turkey declined to accept them, and the deadlock continued. Invited by Granville to advise on further action, Bismarck suggested that the Plenipotentiaries should negotiate with the Porte in Constantinople as to a fresh frontier in Thessaly, but substituting Crete for the portions of Epirus conditionally awarded by the Treaty of Berlin, so as to avoid trouble with the Albanian Mussulmans there. The Plenipotentiaries met on February 20th, 1881, Goschen taking a leading part as British Representative. In a Collective Note addressed to the Greek Government on April 7th, the Powers assigned to Greece Thessaly and the district of Artis in Epirus, but made no mention of Crete. This arrangement gave Greece something less than the Berlin decision, and, as it left out of account a considerable Hellenic population in Epirus, it created no enthusiasm; but the Greek Government agreed to accept it, as did the Porte, and, with the signing of the Turco-Greek Convention of May 24th, a stormy dispute was for a time disposed of.

To the new Liberal Government fell likewise the initiative in the settlement of the Montenegrin frontier difficulty. In conformity with Article XXXII of the Treaty, Montenegro duly withdrew her troops from Dulcigno, and she was able to take peaceable possession of the territory assigned to her on the Herzegovina frontier; but not so in the case of that granted to her in compensation at the expense of Albania. A stalwart but lawless people, who feared civilisation far more than oppression, since against the latter they had always been able to defend themselves, the Albanians objected to the seizure of any of their lands, murdering the Sultan's first Envoy and refusing to obey the second; and fighting between them and the Montenegrins followed. The Powers suggested the cession of a different district, and the Porte agreed; but no sooner had the Turkish troops been withdrawn from it than the Albanians took possession, and there was reason to believe that they did so as part of a pre-arranged plot. Hereupon, the Ambassadors' Conference held in Berlin in June, 1880, recommended that Montenegro should receive back Dulcigno with the seaboard as far as the Bojana. However, Turkey objected, and encouraged the Albanians to revolt; and, in consequence, the British Government in September proposed the somewhat stale, but usually effectual, device of a naval demonstration, in support of a Montenegrin advance to the port by land. This time, the threat failed to move the Sultan, and it was only when the alternative occupation of the prosperous port of Smyrna, with the sequestration of its customs revenue, was proposed, and the case became one of losing both daughter and ducats, that he yielded. It was not difficult to eject the Albanian garrison from Dulcigno, when its presence was no longer desired; and Montenegro entered into possession peaceably on November 27th, the Allied fleets withdrawing several days later.

Little was done under the provisions of the Treaty of Berlin which called for the introduction of administrative reforms. In October, 1878, indeed, Crete received a Constitution, known as the Pact of Halepa; but, after an insurrectionary outbreak in the following year, the Sultan repealed it, and placed the island under a Mussulman Governor-General; so that for another decade Turkish rule continued as before. The Armenians fared even worse. Article LXI of the Treaty required the prompt introduction by the Porte of reforms in the provinces inhabited by them. Sir A. H. Layard did his best to persuade the Porte to fulfil its obligation, but without success; and, on June 11th, 1880, the Powers served on it an Identic Note calling attention to the deplorable condition of the provinces and demanding the execution of the Treaty provisions. An evasive reply was returned to this letter on July 5th, and, as nothing was done, a Collective Note was addressed to the procrastinating Government on September 7th, repeating the demand for action in more peremptory terms—but still without result. The zeal of the Powers in the cause of oppressed nationalities had now begun to cool down; and the later history of these unhappy outcasts of Christendom was darkened by periodical outrages and massacres in which Turk and Kurd surpassed their worst records of savagery.

The fate of the Macedonians, who were thrust back under Turkish rule owing to the defeat of Russia's plan of a Greater Bulgaria, was in its way equally deplorable. Though not expressly mentioned in the Treaty, Macedonia was intended to benefit by the general stipulation on the subject of administrative reforms contained in Article XXIII. The purpose of this Article was not fulfilled, and the province became the cockpit of Balkan strife. All the adjacent States—Servia, Bulgaria, Greece—were intent upon expansion, and, inasmuch as Macedonia was the natural outlet for their ambitions, its frontiers were periodically raided by its neighbours. Turkey seemed to humour each of the rivals in turn, yet succeeded in retaining undivided possession of the contested territory.

V. The Reorganisation of Egypt: the Dual Control, 1875–1880

Since the Great Powers confirmed Mehemet Ali in the hereditary Governor-Generalship—the title *Khedive* was not regularised till 1866 —Egypt had enjoyed an increasing measure of independence, though the Sultan's suzerainty remained unimpaired and was jealously re-asserted in successive firmans. British influence vied with French in the Viceroy's counsels, yet, faithful to the tradition which Palmerston had done so much to strengthen, without any attempt at aggression or needless interference. Not wishing to enter Egypt herself, and de-termined to bar entrance to any other Power, it was Great Britain's policy to maintain the Sultan's rights and to strengthen his Viceroy's position. Recognition of the fact that the nearest highroad to India lay through Egypt became, with the construction of the Suez Canal, the primary consideration of British statesmen; yet, neither before nor after the accomplishment of that undertaking, did concern for British interests exclude genuine solicitude for the country's pros-perity and better government.

If, at any time, the voice of Great Britain can be said to have been clearly predominant at Cairo, it was in the middle of the century, under Said Pasha. That farsighted ruler died in January, 1863, giving place to Ismail, whose career of reckless extravagance proved his own and his country's undoing. Said Pasha had left a public debt heavy in proportion to the national resources; for, while borrowing freely he had made insufficient provision for meeting the exorbitant charges of his foreign creditors. Whatever folly was to be laid to his account in this respect was, however, surpassed by the wastrel Ismail, whose master-passions were self-indulgence and prodigality. Inheriting a debt of three and a quarter million sterling, he succeeded in increasing it step by step, until it amounted to fifteen pounds a head in a popula-tion composed in the main of small and impecunious peasants and oppressed labourers.

Ismail was a man of considerable parts, with bold ideas and not unwholesome ambitions. From the first, he showed great eagerness to enlarge his rights and jurisdictions as tributary ruler, and, by means of his success in ingratiating himself with the Sultan, he usually obtained what he wanted. From each visit to Constantinople he returned with a new firman making some addition to his preroga-tives, though inevitably also to the tribute payable to the Suzerain.

These larger powers, which a careful ruler might have exercised with great public advantage, were not an unmixed good for the country; for the more independent Ismail became, the more he indulged in rash expenditure and the deeper he sank in debt. Much of his expenditure was, of course, incurred on account of public works of greater or less value; but, whether the money was intended to meet public or private objects, it was invariably spent wastefully.

There was neither limit nor intelligence in his borrowing. He took money wherever it was to be had, and, with oriental largeness of spirit, never haggled about the rate of interest, with the result that harpies robbed him right and left. French financial groups in particular were ever ready to supply the spendthrift with funds. In 1868 the *Société Générale pour le développement du Commerce et de l'Industrie* lent him nearly twelve millions sterling. Two years later, the Banque Franco-Égyptienne advanced seven millions on the security of the family estates of the Khedive—the so-called Daira loan. In that year, even the Sultan, though never notable as a purist in money matters, deemed it expedient to protest to the Powers against the conclusion of any financial arrangements at variance with the conditions laid down in his firmans or prejudicial to the country's revenues. When Ismail's credit was gone, he resorted to other means of raising money. Treasury *bons* were issued at various times, on which 10, 12, even 15 per cent. interest was paid. In 1871, the *Monkabalah* Law was passed, under which persons subject to assessment for property tax could, by making six annual payments in advance, obtain relief in perpetuity from one-half of this tax. This discreditable device brought the Khedive five million pounds; but it was a bad bargain for his Treasury. When, by firmans of 1872, he obtained the power to contract loans on his own account, the last check upon his rake's progress disappeared. Thus it came about that, by 1876, Ismail had increased the public debt to over ninety million pounds, of which amount only a small fraction represented works of permanent public utility[1]. Every year of his reign, he had added to the debt a pound a head for every inhabitant of his impoverished country, the taxation of which had, in the meantime, increased by one-half.

It was directly owing to Ismail's monetary embarrassments that

---

[1] Lord Milner estimates the proportion at one-tenth at the most. See *England in Egypt*, p. 229.

Great Britain at this time acquired in Egypt a commercial interest carrying important political implications. Among the Khedive's few valuable assets were his shares in the Suez Canal Company. In the middle of November, 1875, it was reported to Lord Derby, the Foreign Secretary, that Ismail had to raise by the end of the month a sum of between three and four million pounds, so as to meet the interest due on the public debt, and that, in his straits, he was negotiating with a French financial group for the sale of these shares. Negotiations had, in fact, been opened with two such groups, not as yet for the sale of the shares outright, but for their mortgage, and, several days earlier, the Khedive had made a conditional offer to one of them, which retained the option until the 19th. That the transaction had not already been completed was due in part to the action of the rival group, at the head of which was F. de Lesseps, who was urging his Government to acquire the shares and so bring the Canal entirely into French hands, but also to the Khedive's hesitancy before taking a decision of which he was only now coming to understand the political significance. De Freycinet has recorded that Ismail actually offered the shares to the French Government through the *Société Générale* at the price of 100 million francs, but that, though the Duc Décazes, then Foreign Minister, favoured purchase, the Cabinet wavered and disagreed[1].

Equal indecision was shown by Lord Derby and the Foreign Office—by the latter not for the first or the last time in matters of the kind[2]. For, five years earlier (December, 1870) the same proposal had been made to Lord Granville when Foreign Secretary, on the initiative of the Khedive, who advised Great Britain, as contributing nearly four-fifths of the Canal traffic, to acquire the entire enterprise, in the interest both of British commerce and of the waterway itself, which was then in an unsatisfactory position. At that time, de Lesseps himself was understood to be willing to sell out. The Foreign Office, however, decided to "give no opinion on the matter," and a fair chance of acquiring at a bargain price control of a great but undeveloped undertaking was allowed to pass by. For in that year the gross receipts of the Canal only amounted to a quarter of a million pounds, and the number of ships which paid dues was under 500.

[1] C. de Freycinet, *La Question d'Égypte*, p. 151.

[2] It will be remembered how, nearly thirty years later, the Foreign Office similarly refused the opportunity of joining in the Bagdad Railway scheme on a copartnership basis, with the result that the scheme passed into hands which ultimately grew unfriendly, and the enterprise consequently became an international danger.

The same unbusinesslike attitude was, hereupon, once more shown. The idea of purchasing the shares appears for a time to have actually shocked the Foreign Secretary and his advisers. Lord Derby heartily disliked it, and hoped that it would not be necessary: all he cared for was that the Khedive should by some means be prevented from withdrawing from the Company, where his influence was a useful check upon the arbitrary ways of de Lesseps[1]. While, however, Lord Derby remained obstructive, the Prime-Minister, with a keener appreciation both of the commercial and the political possibilities of the transaction, was eager for purchase, and he soon took the matter into his own hands. Nevertheless, he had to overcome strong opposition in the Cabinet before he gained his way (November 17th) and obtained *carte blanche* to see the business through. Already, the Khedive had promised to give the British Government an option, should he decide to sell; and, on the 23rd, to the chagrin of the French groups, the shares were purchased by the Cabinet for four million pounds, Disraeli obtaining the money from the Rothschild firm. Two days later, the contract was signed, and on the following day the shares were deposited in the British Consulate at Cairo[2]. Before the year was out, the Khedive wished to sell to so good a customer his contingent interest in the profits of the Canal; but the offer was declined.

Credit for the Suez Canal shares transaction has been variously claimed and assigned. There can be little doubt that Lord Derby received information that the shares were on the market from Frederick Greenwood, a public-spirited London journalist, though his service in the matter was officially ignored. For the actual purchase, the praise was wholly due to the Prime-Minister. His biographer suggests that Disraeli, owing to his relations with the Rothschilds, had probably heard independently that the shares might be in the market, and even that he had for some time been watching for an opportunity to buy[3]. There was later some criticism of his action in allowing these private bankers to make a substantial profit out of

---

[1] "I sincerely hope we may not be driven to the expedient. The acquisition would be a bad one financially, and the affair might involve us in disagreeable correspondence both with France and the Porte." Letter to Lord Lyons, November 19th, 1875 (Lord Newton, *Lord Lyons; a Record of British Diplomacy*, II. 87).

[2] The number of shares mentioned in the contract of purchase was 177,642; but later the actual number in the Khedive's possession was ascertained to be 1040 less, and the purchase money was reduced proportionately, viz. from £4,000,000 to £3,976,580, equal to about £22. 10s. per share of a nominal value of £16.

[3] See *Life of Beaconsfield*, V. 439, 440.

the transaction, instead of arranging that the Bank of England should provide the money until the House of Commons had passed the necessary vote; and the 2½ per cent., yielding the sum of £100,000, which the bankers charged for a very short accommodation, "a good deal startled" the Lords Commissioners of the Treasury[1]. What was, however, altogether creditable—and to a later generation, less squeamish in such matters of public duty, incredible—was the fact that no one in the secret used his knowledge for personal gain.

At that time, commerce, finance and statecraft had hardly begun to think in millions with the facility which came later, and the transaction created everywhere a considerable sensation. At home, the purchase was unquestionably popular, and in the House of Commons Gladstone vainly endeavoured to whip up serious opposition to it. Abroad, except in France, where there was much resentment, the bold *coup* was similarly applauded. The King of the Belgians (Leopold II) professed to regard it as "the greatest event of modern politics." Queen Victoria rejoiced because "it was a blow at Bismarck"; but a blow which France shared with him fell lightly on that statesman, who warmly congratulated the British Government on having done "the right thing at the right moment," and professed to regard the purchase as a new guarantee of European Peace. Just before, Bismarck had told the British Ambassador in Berlin that England might have Egypt itself if she liked; Germany would not object[2].

An immediate consequence of the transaction was the appointment of three British Directors to the Canal Company's Board; subsequently, one-third of its membership was assigned to this country. Political effects followed. Before long, Great Britain clearly took the lead in Egypt, and in 1882 French influence experienced its Quebec at Alexandria.

The earliest indication that the British Government now regarded Egyptian questions from a new angle of vision was shown by the despatch to Cairo of Stephen Cave, an expert of authority, for the purpose of investigating the character and proportions of the financial incubus which lay on the country. A vague intimation that some large plan was forming in Disraeli's mind, and also of the manner in which he hoped to carry it out, is contained in a letter written to Lord Derby apropos of the Cave Mission. "We want a

---

[1] Sir Stafford Northcote to Disraeli, December 24th, 1875. *Life of Beaconsfield*, v. 441.   [2] Lord Odo Russell to Lord Derby, November 11th, 1875.

calm, conciliatory spirit to deal with Egypt," he wrote, "not to oppose their first impressions and suggestions, but to correct and change them in due time" (November 26th, 1875). Cave visited Egypt towards the end of the year, and reported in the following March. He found that, what with the heavy indebtedness and the *Monkabalah* Law, the state of the national finances was critical, yet that, given certain reforms and alleviations of interest, the position was not hopeless. The principal remedies proposed by him were the unification of the debt, the limitation of the budget to a maximum figure, the assignment of one-half of the revenue to the service of the debt, and the institution of an office of financial control.

In view of the Cave Mission, the Duc Décazes, not quite certain of his ground, and anxious lest his country's influence should be diminished, urged on Lord Derby the importance of a close understanding between the French and British Governments, and suggested as an earnest of cooperation the creation of a joint commission for the control of Egyptian finance, to be exercised by the two countries, with or without Italy. In reply, the Foreign Secretary, who dreaded the thought of intervention anywhere—so much so that Lord Salisbury said that he would have shrunk from annexing the Isle of Man—offered a general opposition to any measure that would entail "interference with the independence of Egypt," and added that the British Government "could not view with indifference any attempt to gain administrative control over Egypt by another Power."

Then, in April, the Khedive raised a signal of financial distress. His own and his country's credit being pledged up to the hilt, so that borrowing was now no longer possible, Ismail decided to resort to the last device of the insolvent gambler, and suspended payment of his debts, as his Suzerain, the Sultan, had done six months before. On April 8th a Decree was published prolonging for three months the Treasury Bills falling due in that month and May. Deeply concerned for the interests of the bondholders, and apprehensive lest a policy of more definite repudiation should follow, France pressed Great Britain more urgently than before to join her in asserting complete control over Egyptian finance. Yielding to the same pressure, the Khedive, by a Decree of May 2nd (probably drawn up in Paris), instituted the *Caisse de la Dette publique*. Four of the Great Powers were invited to nominate Commissioners, viz. Great Britain, France, Austria-Hungary, and Italy; and the last three exercised the option in favour of M. de Blignières, Baron von Kremer, and M. Baravelli, respectively. The British Foreign Office delayed action until the following year, when Sir Evelyn Baring (later Lord Cromer) was appointed.

The *Caisse* proved merely a half-way house to the more direct and rigorous form of control upon which the French Government had set its mind, and, following on an Anglo-French Financial Mission consisting of Mr Goschen and M. Joubert, a Commission of Control was instituted by Khedivial Decree of November 18th. Of this Commission de Lesseps was President; Sir C. Rivers Wilson, a British Treasury Official, was Vice-president and Controller of State revenues, while de Blignières was Controller of Treasury accounts and disbursements. The other members were Sir Evelyn Baring, Baron von Kremer, M. Baravelli, and Riaz Pasha. When, at the end of 1877, the country seemed on the threshold of bankruptcy and the spectre of repudiation again alarmed the bondholders, the British and French Governments carried their demand for a full and searching enquiry into the entire financial situation by Commission, and free from restriction or reserve of any kind.

The Commission was duly appointed (March, 1878) and its result was a bold scheme of financial and political reforms. The financial measures recommended for the Khedive's spontaneous and prompt acceptance included the restitution to the State of the Daira lands, which had been bought with public money, the employment of their revenues in the liquidation of the outstanding debt, and the suspension of the Dual Control. Equally important were the political reforms; for the Commission proposed to introduce the principle of Ministerial responsibility, and to give to Egypt a Constitutional *status* and, in a modified form, representative government. Less from conviction than under compulsion, the Khedive accepted the recommendations without demur. The enlightened influence of Nubar Pasha weighed heavily on the side of reform. While hostile to the principle of international interference in administration, even to the extent of the Anglo-French Financial Control, and eager that Egypt should govern herself alone, Nubar recognised the need for temporary outside assistance, and, as a measure of necessity, he particularly favoured the appointment of an Englishman as Minister of Finance. His unreserved approval of the Commission's recommendations did much to convince the Khedive of the uselessness of any further dallying with half-measures.

By Decree of August 29th, the now Constitutional ruler charged Nubar with the formation of a Cabinet, which he described as "*le point de départ d'un changement radical de système.*" In this Cabinet, the portfolio of Finance was offered to Sir Rivers Wilson and that of Public Works to de Blignières: all the other Ministers were natives. The immediate business of the new Administration was to carry out the reform scheme. It was the wish of Lord Salisbury, who had succeeded Lord Derby as Foreign Secretary in March, that the functions of the Control established in November, 1876, should be suspended so long as England and France were represented in the Cabinet, but should be revived in case either of them should be dismissed without prior agreement with his Government; and to this France agreed.

In the political reforms, a piece of machinery excellent in design and material had been created; but how would it work? Lord Salisbury was concerned not to lessen native responsibility, for which he regarded European cooperation as no adequate substitute. Hence, he reminded the Khedive that, though he had surrendered his personal power and a Constitutional *régime* had been introduced, his responsibility continued as before, and warned him that the new system would be made or marred by his personal bearing towards it. Instead of taking this admonition to heart, Ismail began a course of intrigue against his own Ministers, even using for his purposes the disaffected elements in the Army. After five months, he took the first step towards throwing off the irksome Constitutional fetters by dismissing Nubar (February 2nd, 1879). Had he dared, he would have rid himself of all his European advisers at the same time and returned at once to the comfortable old despotism.

Faced by the threatened collapse of their laborious handiwork, the Powers through their mandataries, the British and French Governments, served on the Khedive an ultimatum in which, without demanding the reinstatement of Nubar, they insisted on the conditions necessary to ensure the execution of the financial reforms. To this end, the two European Ministers were to have an absolute veto upon expenditure of all kinds. France was still concerned, as ever, for the bondholders. Lord Salisbury heartily disliked this responsibility, and, while not indifferent to the interests of creditors, insisted on regarding the financial question as a whole[1]. A compromise was agreed to, as a result of which the Khedive's eldest son, Prince Tewfik, was to be the President of a new Ministry, the two Europeans

---

[1] "It may be quite tolerable and even agreeable to the French Government," he wrote to Lord Lyons (April 10th, 1879), "to go into partnership with the bondholders, or rather to act as sheriff's officers for them. But to us it is a new and very embarrassing sensation. Egypt can never prosper so long as some 25 per cent.

continuing in office. Nevertheless, in April, in another hot fit of revolt, Ismail dismissed the Council, including Wilson and de Blignières, and made Cherif Pasha Prime-Minister. The first act of the incoming reactionary Ministers was to reject the European financial scheme and to produce one of their own.

In this situation, the two Governments gave the Khedive to understand that they intended to adopt just such measures as they might deem necessary in order to protect their interests and promote the welfare of the people of Egypt. Already, Waddington, the French Foreign Minister, was urging upon his British colleague the summary removal of a wily and obstinate Viceroy, who would neither reform his country's administration himself nor allow others to do it for him. To so strong a measure Lord Salisbury for a time demurred; but, in the end, he came round to the French view. In all the Chanceries of Europe agreement prevailed that Ismail had wilfully thrown away a fair chance of vindicating his position, and that no further indulgence of his whims and perversity was admissible. Accordingly, after futile attempts had been made by the British and French Representatives in Cairo to procure his abdication, the Sultan was induced, by strong though covert pressure, to decree his deposition. This he did by telegraph on June 26th, appointing Tewfik, a better man though a weaker, his successor by right of primogeniture[1]. Great Britain and France, thereupon, reestablished the offices of Controllers-General without protest.

of her revenue goes in paying interest on her debt. We have no wish to part company with France, still less do we mean that France should acquire in Egypt any special ascendancy; but, subject to these two considerations, I should be glad to be free of the companionship of the bondholders" (Lord Newton, *Lord Lyons*, II. 175). "In France finance, and even private finance, is politics," Lord Beaconsfield wrote to Lord Salisbury on June 6th, 1879 (*Life of Beaconsfield*, VI. 444); but he, likewise, did not want, and he believed the country would not approve, "a mere bondholders' policy" (June 24th, 1879, *ibid.* p. 445).

[1] Lord Salisbury's assurance to Waddington on June 26th, that "the Turkish move reported to-day does not proceed in any way from our suggestion," and that all the Government had done was to urge the Sultan not to interfere with what was being done in Cairo, is hardly an adequate statement of what actually occurred. On June 22nd, the Foreign Office instructed Sir Henry Layard to "inform the Sultan that there are grounds for thinking that some communication from the Porte is encouraging the Khedive to resist the advice which has been tendered to him by the Western Powers; that the misdeeds of the Khedive have been the fatal impediment to *the advance of any money by European capitalists to the Porte*, and that the Sultan is more interested than anyone else in a speedy and peaceful transfer of the Government of Egypt into other hands." The Sultan had, in fact, telegraphed to the Khedive that the question of his abdication was a matter for the Porte, and that the Powers had no right to make a proposal to him of a menacing character. On the 23rd, the Sultan was to be told that France and Great Britain had gone too

That the deposition of Ismail was a desirable, and in the circumstances unavoidable, act can hardly be doubted. Nevertheless, it contributed to bring about untoward consequences. The setting-up of a new ruler by external influence unquestionably heightened the existing Egyptian resentment against foreigners and strengthened nationalist sentiment; it may even have laid the train which, fired by the rebel leader Arabi, led to the explosion of 1881–2.

In the following year was passed the Law of Liquidation (July 17th, 1880), by which Egypt made what is known to bankruptcy law as an arrangement with creditors. This implied insolvency; but, instead of being declared a defaulter, the debtor was given his discharge on payment of a reasonable composition upon his liabilities. The rate of interest on the debt was reduced; but, in return, a limit was placed on national expenditure, with a view to ensuring the future punctual honouring of the bonds. The laws establishing the *Caisse de la Dette* and limiting expenditure became the sheet-anchor of so much sound finance as was possible in a country which had been so long and so pitilessly bled by prodigal rulers and greedy usurers. Both of these measures were forced on the Egyptian Government from without, and the Powers which instituted them claimed the right to enforce them, and therewith to direct the entire financial administration. From international control of finance to control of domestic and foreign policy in general was a logical, and an inevitable, step.

VI. The British Occupation of Egypt, 1879–1883

Egyptians in the mass had witnessed the abrupt removal of Ismail with comparative unconcern: like the rise and fall of the Nile, such was the will of Allah, and it was well. Different was the attitude of those sections of the population which represented what passed for public opinion. These, too, had little reason for lamenting the disappearance of a Khedive who had imposed upon their country an intolerable burden of debt and taxation. Nevertheless, they resented

far to recede, and that, "if owing to encouragement from Constantinople the Khedive resists the will of the Five Powers, it will probably result in Egypt being severed from the Turkish empire altogether.... You should use all the means of influence at your command." On the 25th, Layard was empowered to ask whether the British Government would be satisfied if the Sultan at once deposed the Khedive, withdrew the firman of 1873 altering the Succession, and appointed Tewfik. Lord Salisbury replied that it would be necessary to consult France. The deposition followed next day.

the instrumentality by which Ismail had been supplanted, for none of them was credulous enough to suppose that the Sultan cared so much for sound finance and good government in the Khediviate as to have deposed Ismail of his own accord. An act in itself defensible was viewed with suspicion insomuch as it afforded additional evidence of the growing subjection of Egypt and its Government to outside dictation.

The influence of the foreign population had long been resented, owing to the gross abuses which prevailed under the system of Capitulations. In no part of the Ottoman empire had the exercise of exterritoriality and the grant of concessions to foreign residents been carried so far as it had in Egypt, where, in 1876, the number of settled Europeans was estimated at 100,000. There were no fewer than seventeen Consular Tribunals, and in most of them the merest travesty of justice was administered. Europeans were systematically acquitted of crimes and offences which there was no difficulty in proving, while it was difficult for natives to come by their rights when the aggressors were aliens. Moreover, these exotic jurisdictions had gradually been extended in directions never intended originally.

Apart from the often illicit protection given to them by their national Courts, foreigners enjoyed other privileges detrimental to the interests of the native population; and, in particular, their immunity from certain kinds of taxation was a great grievance. Many foreigners, again, had benefited unduly by commercial privileges freely granted by the prodigal ex-Khedive under the pressure of financial difficulties, regardless of the country's permanent interests. Something had been done by the Powers towards correcting the more flagrant abuses incidental to a system of divided jurisdiction by a law of February, 1876, creating Mixed Tribunals. Owing to the opposition of France, however, the operation of these Courts was restricted to civil cases, and within a large sphere of jurisprudence there was still one law for the native and another for the foreigner.

A further grievance was the large and increasing number of foreigners in the public services, from the higher posts in which the natives were practically excluded. In the early 'eighties, on the testimony of a French statesman, "all the Government departments were run by French agents[1]." Egypt, according to this witness, was "France's adopted daughter," and, like many adopted daughters, she was loved chiefly for the sake of her fortune. The most efficient of

[1] Deschanel, P., *Gambetta* (1919), p. 303.

alien Governments can never be an altogether satisfactory substitute for the least efficient of native Administrations. It may be true that the native ruling class was, in the main, incapable and largely corrupt; but, at least, it was Egyptian and racy of the soil, and, when tried by native standards, its incompetence and venality cannot be said to have excited violent disgust. The personal quality of even the imported officials, however, was very unequal, and many of them were neither efficient nor upright; while, at the same time, their maintenance proved a heavy burden on the Treasury.

This intrusion of so large a foreign community, which for the most part had settled in Egypt for its own, and not the country's, good, was a source of profound offence to all sections of the native population, but most of all to the patriotic educated classes, little susceptible though they were to the cruder forms of prejudice and bigotry, and altogether free from taint of fanaticism. European statesmen had long talked of the possibility of the political internationalisation of Egypt. Here was an internationalisation of a far more objectionable kind progressing by leaps and bounds.

The Army had grievances of its own, of which low and uncertain pay and favouritism were those which rankled deepest. Early in 1879, when, in consequence of the large reduction in the native force insisted on in the interest of economy, 2500 officers were suddenly put on halfpay without receiving the arrears due to them, a military riot occurred at Cairo (February 18th). It was directed generally against the Government, but particularly against Nubar Pasha and Sir Rivers Wilson, both of whom were roughly treated by a large body of armed officers, while the rioters took possession of the Ministry of Finance as the assumed source and origin of their misfortune. On that occasion, the Khedive adopted prompt measures and, with the help of loyal troops, soon succeeded in quelling the riot. Nevertheless, the incident was alarming as a symptom of deep-seated unrest; and the British Representative in Cairo, in reporting upon it to the Foreign Secretary, spoke of an uneasy feeling of discontent as prevailing among the natives, owing to their jealousy of the large influx of highly-paid European officials.

The precedent thus established by the soldiery was of evil augury. Soon, a more systematic agitation began against foreigners, of the kind which has occurred so often among Oriental peoples upon whom Western ideas and institutions have been forced prematurely. Secret meetings of malcontents were held; rumours of intended pogroms against the Christians became current; and the leaders of the movement were said to be in confidential communication with the direct agents of the Khedive. It was a misfortune that, at a time so critical, the responsible Government lacked initiative, energy, and resolution. For this, the Powers were not free from responsibility. Their repeated interferences and invasions of the Khedive's powers, however excellent the intentions underlying them, had weakened the Administration, which, in proportion as it forfeited public respect and confidence, also lost authority and the ability to compel obedience.

In the Army, in particular, disaffection deepened, for the Khedive was able neither to pacify nor suppress the mutineers, who had found an able spokesman in Ahmed Arabi, a colonel of Fellah origin. The first dangerous mistake was committed by Tewfik, when, early in 1881, he dismissed the Minister of War at the bidding of the malcontent officers. Before the end of the year, the whole Ministry had succumbed to the same influence; and, in February, 1882, Arabi himself became War Minister. In September, the Sultan had wished to despatch a force of occupation to his unsettled province, and the British Government were willing; but, as France objected, the despatch of a Turkish Commissioner was suggested as an alternative. With characteristic inconsequence, the Sultan's Ministers sent two Delegates, armed with different Instructions, and each being expected to act and report independently of the other.

The British Government were as firmly opposed to active intervention as ever, and Lord Granville, the Foreign Secretary, wrote at that time that the only event which could justify even a temporary departure from this reserve would be "the existence of anarchy or some attack on the Canal." Influences, however, were at work, which were soon to force his hands. In France, Gambetta took office in November at the head of a Ministry most of whose members were but understudies of himself, who with the Presidency of the Council combined the control of Foreign Affairs. Jules Ferry, his predecessor, had leaned towards Germany more than the French nation approved. Gambetta came in as a strong advocate of a close understanding with both Great Britain and Russia. It was not that he loved either country —as to Russia he had declared only three years before that an alliance with an absolutist Tsardom was "unthinkable"—but he saw in such a double understanding the only safeguard against the Bismarckian policy of coalitions. "Let us keep the alliance with those two Powers as a reserve for the future," he had, just before he took office, said to de Freycinet; "leaning on London and St Petersburg, we shall be invincible." He was not less desirous than Ferry had been to cooperate with Great Britain in Egypt; but the cooperation favoured by him was to consist of active measures which should exclude the possibility of participation in it by any other Power, since he held that in such a relationship not more than two were good company. Thiers had warned him on one occasion: "Whatever you do, never let go of Egypt"; and Gambetta held on so long as he was able[1]. Convinced that intervention would become inevitable, he was also prepared to find an opportunity for it.

The calculating spirit and quickwittedness of French diplomacy were well shown in the steps taken by Gambetta to achieve this end. He was shrewd enough to see the advantage of assuming the lead, and this Lord Granville made easy for him. Before he had been a month in office (December 14th), he suggested, through Lord Lyons, that the moment was opportune for an intimate understanding between the two Powers, and suggested a frank exchange of views on the subject. For, while it was obviously their interest to give Tewfik all practicable support, the eventuality of the breakdown of his Government had to be reckoned with. Granville was, at first, unwilling to bind himself to hypothetical proceedings, and accordingly fell back upon the well-known diplomatic formula "liberty of action." Undiscouraged, Gambetta returned to the charge, and this time his impetuous will overcame opposition. As a result of conversations in the last week of the month, the terms of a Joint Note to the Khedive, whose authority was becoming ominously feebler, were agreed upon, and the Note was communicated on January 8th. It assured him that the two Powers would support him in his endeavours to cope with the difficulties of his situation, and invited him, in somewhat didactic terms, to draw from the assurance confidence and strength.

Whether the Joint Note was called for or not by the circumstances of the moment, from the standpoint of Great Britain it was very untimely; for her partner had quite recently outraged nationalist feeling by wanton aggression in another part of the Ottoman empire. Intended to encourage Tewfik and exert a salutary influence on public opinion, it actually intensified the anti-foreign movement, since, by seeming to suggest more active interference, it confirmed the apprehensions of thoughtful Egyptians that their country was about to share the experience of Tunis. Granville made a strong point of

---

[1] Deschanel, P., *Gambetta*, p. 304.

the fact that he had not committed his Government to any definite measures, or to any measures at all. This restricted view of the significance of the Note was not accepted by Gambetta, who took its meaning to be that whither France went Great Britain would be prepared to follow. Reduced to the lowest terms, the Note was a pledge of conditional joint intervention.

About this time, Bismarck, in response to the cooler temper of the French Cabinet since the fall of Jules Ferry, showed again special concern to strengthen friendly relations with the British Government, and with this idea in view he sent his son, Count Herbert, on a special Mission to London. He seems to have thought that the Foreign Office was only half-informed of the guiding lines of German foreign policy, and to have attributed the responsibility for this state of things partly to the British Embassy in Berlin and, in a greater degree, to the German Embassy in London. Odo Russell had, certainly, shown a disposition, on occasion, to accept the conversational confidences and conscious indiscretions of the magnetic Chancellor as serious indications of policy, and to report them as such to the Foreign Secretary. Yet the fact remained that the two Governments seemed never to come nearer to a permanent understanding. Granville welcomed the overtures, and the assurance, which followed, of Bismarck's wish to give cordial support to British policy in Egypt made his path for a time easier. Replying, at the end of the month, to suggestions from Gambetta that the two Powers should assert Dual Control in a more definite fashion, he now stated the British position in language which admitted of no misinterpretation. "The British Government," he said, "had no ambitious designs in Egypt for itself, and would object to an exclusive influence being seized by any other Power."

Gambetta had fired his last shot. On February 1st the impetuous tribune fell, and in de Freycinet he was succeeded by a Foreign Minister in greater sympathy with the official British attitude. Up to this point, that attitude had been one of abstention from intervention except on the clearest proof of necessity, in which event there was to be collective action by the Powers, including Turkey. Herein, Granville was in complete accord with the Head of the Government. Five years earlier Gladstone had warned the nation in prophetic words against the danger of setting foot in the Khediviate, predicting that such action would lead the country step by step forward until it found itself saddled with the responsibility, not only of Egypt, but of a great North and Central African empire.

For three months longer, the struggle between the Khedive and the military junta continued without apparent change in the situation. Towards the end of May, 1882, British and French squadrons were despatched to Alexandria for the protection of the foreign population, of which a steady exodus had already begun. It was known, however, that while the French Government were professing loyalty to Great Britain, their agent in Cairo, de Blignières, was consorting with the military conspirators and the anti-British party, and endeavouring to create faith in France as the country's one and only true friend. In that month, de Freycinet himself urged the deposition of Tewfik in favour of Halim Pasha, his uncle, of whose goodwill France had previously made sure. Now, insurrection raised its head again, and Arabi, who had been removed from the Ministry, was reinstated in deference to military pressure. Early in the following June, the Porte sent Dervish Pasha to Egypt to confer with the Khedive and his advisers and to take stock of the situation generally. A little later, the two Powers proposed that a Conference of Ambassadors should be held in Constantinople, taking as the basis of its deliberations the maintenance of the rights of the Sultan and the Khedive, the observance of international engagements and the arrangements existing under them, whether with Great Britain and France alone or with all the Powers, the preservation of the liberties secured by the firmans of the Sultan, and the prudent development of Egyptian institutions. The other Powers agreed; but the Porte demanded a postponement of the proposals until it should have tried to settle the country in its own way. It was ominous that, at this time, batteries were being constructed at Alexandria in proximity to the anchorage of the British and French squadrons. Required to discontinue this work, Arabi, now to all intents a military dictator, refused.

It was now too late to check by commissioners and conferences the mischief which had so long been brewing. The threatened storm broke with startling suddenness on June 11th, when revolution flamed up in Alexandria, taking the form of the massacre of sixty Europeans and an orgy of looting, before the rioters were suppressed by the Khedive's troops.

The Constantinople Conference opened on June 23rd, by which time it was known that the Dervish Mission had proved a total failure; for the Egyptian Ministry was in Arabi's power and the Khedive's orders were only executed with his assent and cooperation. On that day, the Sultan made, through Reschid Pasha, his Private Secretary, a remarkable communication to Lord Dufferin (who had been transferred to Constantinople from Petrograd in the previous year). Suspicious of Great Britain's movements, he put to him the pointed questions: "What are the intentions of England in regard to the present? What are the views entertained by Her Majesty's Government with respect to Egypt as regards the future?" Lord Dufferin gave the assurance that his Government had but one desire, which was "the preservation in their full integrity of the Sultan's sovereign rights, as defined by the firmans and the maintenance of the order of things established under them." Great Britain's direct interests in the country, he said, were the freedom of the Suez Canal and an administration so satisfactory as to preclude any foreign Power from finding an excuse for intervention.

Encouraged by these assurances, Reschid Pasha now asserted that the Sultan was ready and willing to come to an understanding with Great Britain to the exclusion of France, "which he hated"; and he offered to hand over to the former "the exclusive control and administration of the whole of Egypt, reserving to himself only those modified rights of sovereignty which he now possesses." Lord Dufferin replied that "if the Sultan were to hand over Egypt to Great Britain in fee simple with the approbation of all Europe, he doubted whether the British Government would accept such a burden of responsibility[1]." Gladstone and Granville took it upon themselves to refuse the Sultan's tempting offer, to the disappointment of the Queen[2].

The Conference accepted the proposal of the British Ambassador that the pacification of the country should be entrusted to the Sultan's troops, subject to strict limitations in regard to their employment and the duration of their stay. The Sultan was willing to send troops, but not to bind himself by conditions in doing so; and, as he refused to give way on that point, the Conference dragged on for many days without positive result. In the meantime, the condition of the country grew steadily worse, with the result that the British Government were brought daily nearer to the contingency of active intervention. Gladstone and Granville were convinced of its necessity, and the rest of the Cabinet now came round to it, with the single exception of Mr Bright, who resigned office.

As the insurrectionaries in Alexandria had continued their defensive works with a view to commanding the harbour, the British

[1] Despatch of June 23rd, 1882.
[2] Lord Morley's *Life of Gladstone*, III. 80.

Admiral on July 3rd received orders to fire on and destroy the forts and batteries, unless operations were discontinued after due warning. Though invited to join in this action, the French and Italian Governments declined. On the 11th, British vessels bombarded and destroyed the forts, and on the following day native troops fired the town, and departed, leaving the mob to pillage it, whereupon a British force was landed to restore order. So soon as the bombardment began the French fleet steamed away in virtuous disgust. Yet another chance remained for France to reconsider her attitude, and carry out her own policy of joint action, when, on July 15th, the British Government invited her, with the other Powers, to cooperate in measures for ensuring the safety of the Suez Canal. De Freycinet was willing, and his predecessor eagerly pushed him on. When, on the 18th, the Government asked the Chamber for a credit of eight million francs, Gambetta lent his fervent support to the motion.

"Let not France be shorn of her heritage," he pleaded; "it is not for the sake of Egyptian nationality or the Egyptian national party that we ought to go to Egypt; it is for the sake of the French nation. What I dread more than anything is that you may hand over to England, for good and all, territories, rivers, and rights of way where your title to live and to trade is no less valid than hers."

The belief had, however, at this time gained possession of the French people that Bismarck was engaged in a plot for dragging it into a morass of foreign complications, and, though this apprehension did not prevent France from embarking on the Indo-Chinese and Madagascar enterprises, it now kept her out of Egypt. The Senate voted almost unanimously the money needed for the protection of the Suez Canal; but in the Chamber the Government obtained only seventy-five votes, and de Freycinet resigned (July 30th).

Thus it was that France, who had been the first to promise the Khedive help in time of need, and had so long tried to drive Great Britain into active intervention, left her ally to carry out alone the onerous task of pacification. Granville's judgment upon the episode and its issue was warranted: "We have done the right thing; we have shown our readiness to admit others, and we have not the inconvenience of a partner[1]." Just before this, Gladstone told the House of Commons: "We should not fully discharge our duty if we did not endeavour to convert the present interior state of Egypt from

[1] Letter to Sir A. Paget, July 28th, 1882.

anarchy and confusion to peace and order. We shall look, during the time that remains to us, to the cooperation of the Powers of civilised Europe, if it be in any case open to us. But if every chance of obtaining cooperation is exhausted the work will be undertaken by the single power of England" (July 22nd). Here was resolute language, of a kind understood and beloved of Englishmen, and the House readily voted the money needed for the equipment of an expeditionary force.

By this time, the Sultan had tardily signified his willingness to enter the Constantinople Conference, and was also willing to send troops to his disturbed province, subject to the stipulation that, simultaneously with their landing, the British force should withdraw. Granville declined to comply with this demand, but remained still prepared to welcome Turkish military cooperation on the conditions already laid down, including the issue of a proclamation disowning Arabi as a rebel and supporting Tewfik's Administration. A proclamation to that effect was issued, and the proposal to despatch Turkish troops went as far as the drafting of a convention; but prevarication and equivocation on the part of the Porte led to further delay. The Constantinople Conference had broken up on August 14th, and, when, a month later, a British expeditionary force, preparations for which had been in progress for some weeks, was landed at Alexandria under Sir Garnet Wolseley, the Convention still remained unsigned[1].

During the night of September 12th–13th, Wolseley, his plans having been worked out to the smallest detail as to both time and place, led his force of 13,000 men on the famous march, silent as the stars which were his guide, to Tel-el-Kebir. There, at dawn, he attacked and decimated the rebel army, the remnant dispersing, glad to return to their neglected farms and homesteads. Arabi saved himself by flight. With the surrender of 11,000 native troops near Cairo and the occupation of the capital by British cavalry the insurrection was at an end. Now the need and justification for Turkish intervention existed no longer. The Sultan might have finally rolled up the map of Egypt

---

[1] The contention advanced by some admirers of Lord Dufferin, in proof of his sagacity, that he delayed the progress of the negotiations with the Porte of set purpose, until he could be assured that they would lead to no result, is hardly complimentary to that statesman, whose sagacity rests on better evidence. Lord Dufferin resented this suggestion. He wrote to the Foreign Secretary at the time: "From first to last we have acted in perfect sincerity and good faith." He had attained the result which he personally deemed most desirable, but, as he said, "without resorting to a single dubious act or expression." There the matter may be left.

on the morrow of Tel-el-Kebir; for Turkish rule in that country had from that date ceased for ever.

The Arabi rebellion has been judged in various ways, and its leader has been the object both of unfair condemnation and of indiscriminate apology. Though of humble origin, Arabi was a man of considerable natural capacity. That he was, also, according to his lights, a patriot, as many a rebel has been before him, cannot be doubted. To suppose that the revolt which owed so much to his leadership was merely a sordid military conspiracy would be to belittle both its character and its proportions. The initial military *émeute* itself had been directed, not against the British, French, Greeks or any Christian foreigners, but against the Turks and the preference shown to officers of the Sultan in the Egyptian army, coupled with the perennial abuses of oriental military systems, poor pay, rare reckonings, and heavy arrears. While, however, the mutiny of the soldiery limited the character of the movement at the outset, this was but a single, and ultimately became the least significant, phase of a genuine national outburst of discontent.

In its larger aspects, the episode undoubtedly focussed a long-maturing resentment against the inordinate growth of foreign domination and the continual outside interference with native institutions, traditions and customs, which were converting the dependence of Egypt upon Turkey into a still more hateful subjection to Western intruders. Viewed as the expression of nationalist sentiments and aspirations, the revolt was as legitimate and unassailable in purpose as it was crude and indefensible in form. As, however, the movement broadened and thus came to draw more and more of its strength from appeals to prejudice and passion, the good elements were overwhelmed by the dubious and the bad; every manifestation of foreign influence passed under the same unsparing condemnation simply because it was foreign; and, finally, whatever stimulus to success was needed, beyond the forces of interested motive, political discontent, and nationalist jealousy, was supplied by religious fanaticism[1].

So it came to pass that the Arabi rising in the end represented the composite antagonism of the Egyptian people against extraneous influences of every kind which were pressing upon their country and

[1] In a despatch to the Foreign Secretary of June 19th, 1882, Lord Dufferin wrote of Arabi, that "from being the mere chief of a military faction he had acquired not only in Egypt but in the estimation of the Mussulman world of Constantinople and elsewhere the character and position of a champion of the rights of Islam against the aggression of the infidel Western Powers."

making of it something they did not wish it to be. Before that point had been reached, however, the movement had passed beyond Arabi's control; he no longer led, but was carried on by it; and the view is tenable that the directions into which it was ultimately diverted were not of his designing.

Arabi and his fellow-conspirators were duly tried by an Egyptian tribunal, the prosecuting counsel being French and the counsel for the accused English; and the trial lasted through October and November. There was no wish that Arabi should suffer Oriental justice, and, the charge against him being reduced to one of rebellion, he followed the advice given to him and pleaded guilty. The death penalty was pronounced, but only formally; for it was immediately afterwards commuted to exile with degradation from military rank. No less satisfaction was felt in England than in Egypt at finding the adage that "those who make revolutions à demi dig their own graves" for once falsified.

The eye of the Sultan was unceasingly turned towards the Egyptian vineyard, which British energy was steadily making more fruitful; for to the Turk sovereignty has ever meant tribute. In the midst of an unforeseen conjunction of difficulties, the Porte pressed the British Government to fix a definite day for the evacuation of the country. To enter into any undertaking of the kind was obviously impracticable; yet, in spite of the possible developments of a constantly changing situation, the hope and intention of the British Government, both in 1882 and for many years, was a speedy withdrawal, subject only to the fulfilment of a given purpose. This was simply to "secure that the order of things to be established shall be of a satisfactory character and possess the elements of stability and permanence[1]." Whatever may have been the wishes of irresponsible politicians, prepared to appropriate territory anywhere, and if against the will of the Powers so much the more readily, it is not true, as some French writers maintain, that Great Britain contemplated annexation from the beginning, as France did when she entered Syria in 1860[2].

In a situation which called for caution rather than great daring, for patience rather than hustling activity, and above all for an indomitable faith in the capacity of crooked things to work straight,

---

[1] Circular letter of Lord Granville to the Great Powers, January 1st, 1883.

[2] Thus C. de Freycinet, speaking of England's position in Egypt in 1882, writes: "À partir de ce moment elle ne pense plus à l'évacuation; elle oublie qu'il y a une Europe. Elle escompte l'avenir, comme si l'avenir tout entier lui appartenait." La question d'Égypte (1905), p. 326.

the peculiar temperament and gifts of Lord Granville at that time found appropriate scope. It was clearly impossible to allow France any opportunity of reentering Egypt by the door which she had first herself closed behind her in May, and then deliberately locked in July. Accordingly, a necessary safeguard was the cessation of the existing divided jurisdiction. In a despatch to the Powers of January 3rd, 1883, which may be regarded as the basis and justification of all further development of British policy in Egypt, Lord Granville laid down the objects which his Government intended to pursue in undertaking more direct responsibility for the country's welfare. He referred, in particular, to the need for reforms relating to taxation, justice, and local and national government, and foreshadowed the abolition of the Dual Control of Finance in favour of the appointment of a single European adviser. Sir A. Colvin, the British Controller at that time, hereupon resigned, and the Khedive abolished the two officers by decree. Granville, certainly, carried concession far by inviting France to nominate the new adviser; but, since she declined, Colvin was appointed. The French Government duly protested, and resumed "liberty of action." The sensitive pride of France had been wounded. Having renounced the relationship towards Great Britain of a partner, she assumed the *rôle* of sheer obstruction. For twenty years, she did little more in Egypt than block her rival's way and impede progress in every direction.

Lord Dufferin had been sent from Constantinople to Cairo at the end of 1882, commissioned to carry out the needed reforms. Two months later (February, 1883), he issued a monumental report on Egyptian reorganisation, a document of statesmanlike grasp as well as literary charm. Its keynote was "the metamorphic spirit of the age." This spirit, it said, had reached and influenced the Egyptians, even of the strata to which the oppressed fellah belonged, "nor, like his own Memnon, has he remained irresponsive to the beams of the new dawn." Lord Dufferin believed that the Egyptians were capable of self-government, and, convinced that "the valley of the Nile could not be administered with any prospect of success from London," drew the logical conclusion that it must be governed in Cairo by the Egyptians themselves, under just so much guidance as might be un-avoidable. He, therefore, urged the creation, "within prudent limits," of representative institutions, from communal bodies upwards, in sympathy with "those instincts of patriotism and freedom which it has been our boast to foster in every country where we have set our foot." The British Government, only too glad to do something positive towards meeting nationalist aspirations and conciliating Liberal opinion at home, approved of the recommendations, and they were promulgated in an Organic Decree of the following May, in which month Lord Dufferin returned to Constantinople.

So rapid was the transformation of the government of the country under the Occupation that, by the time of Lord Dufferin's departure, its status had become in effect, though not in form, a British protectorate. The Khedive and his Ministers were allowed to preserve the outward show of independence; yet already they were little more than marionettes, playing to strings that were not always even invisible. From Constantinople no interference was permitted, and, when the Sultan forbade the Khedive to make changes in the Administration without his consent, his Viceroy had to plead that he was no longer his own master. "*Le véritable Khédive de l'Égypte,*" he said, "*c'est Lord Dufferin. C'est de lui qu'émanent tous les ordres, et le Khédive n'en est que l'instrument de transmission.*" Sir Evelyn Baring was now appointed British Agent and Consul-General, and he settled down in Cairo to the work of his life in September, 1883.

VII. The Rebellion in the Soudan and the Gordon Mission, 1883–1885.

In January, 1883, there were discussions between the British military authorities and the Khedive's advisers regarding the possibility of a reduction, which Lord Dufferin had recommended, of the army of occupation. Any such pleasant hope was frustrated by a new outbreak of rebellion, this time in the Soudan provinces of the Khediviate. The Soudan had never been held by Egypt on a very secure tenure. Such sovereignty as had been exercised there dated from the time of Mehemet Ali; but from the first it had been illusory and precarious. In that region, vast and vague, the rulers of Egypt had for a century been conquering, yet had never wholly conquered. Under Ismail, however, the Suakin and Massowah districts were formally assigned to Egypt by the Sultan, who confirmed the Khedive as their hereditary ruler. In 1870, Sir Samuel Baker, who had already done valuable work of exploration in Central Africa, annexed to Egypt the Equatorial provinces, suppressing the slave-trade and opening up the Great Lakes to navigation. In 1874 he was succeeded as Governor-General by General Charles Gordon, who did much for the settlement of the

Soudan and the consolidation of Egypt's empire on the Upper Nile. He waged drastic war upon the slave-trade and rooted out the nefarious traffic within the territories under his rule; and then, in 1879, the year of Ismail's deposition, he resigned.

Roughly, the area of the Soudan nominally held by Egypt in 1883 extended 1650 miles from north to south (Assouan to the Equator), and from 1200 to 1400 miles from east to west (Massowah to the western limit of the Darfur province). It was a hopelessly impoverished country, in which pashas oppressed, tax-gatherers plundered, and the soldiery were prone to violence; discontent and disaffection being widespread in consequence. All the conditions existing there were singularly favourable to the success of any leader who might prove able to focus the resentments and vague aspirations of a wild and fanatical population; and such a leader appeared in the person of a Mahdi, or Messenger of God. This remarkable man, the Sheik Mohammad Ahmed of Dongola, after he had lived for a time as a recluse upon an island in the Nile, waiting for his call, made himself known in the late summer of 1881, claiming to be a Saviour foretold of the Prophets and commissioned to emancipate the faithful from alien rule and win the heathen world for Islam. The religious appeal of the Mahdi, enforced as it was by rude eloquence and fiery fanaticism, produced a powerful effect upon the ignorant tribesmen. From the first, the crusade was taken up with great enthusiasm, and for the next two years its progress was unbroken. Such resistance as the Egyptian garrisons in the disturbed area offered was feeble and half-hearted, and the Mahdi's victories swelled his hosts until there seemed a fear that Egypt itself would be overwhelmed.

In the spring of 1883, General Hicks, an English officer on the staff of the Egyptian Army, who had been appointed its Commander-in-Chief, undertook, with the approval of the Khedive and his advisers, to equip and lead an expedition for the reconquest of the revolted region. The idea was discouraged, though not forbidden, by the British Government, who believed that their responsibility in the matter might be met by simply holding aloof from what, they were convinced, was an impolitic and dangerous enterprise. Hicks had a good friend at Cairo in Lord Dufferin, who, nevertheless, urged him not to push his operations beyond the western bank of the White Nile, and to be satisfied with the reconquest of the province of Senaar. Although unquestionably acting in accordance with the wishes of the Khedive and the Egyptian Government, Hicks received very inadequate support from either in the necessary preparations[1]. When the expedition was already on its way, in the middle of April, Hicks had to complain to the Minister of War that he lacked both men and food, that the pay was in arrear, and that his river-boats were too few, out of repair, and without fuel. From modest beginnings his plans expanded. Having driven the rebels from Senaar, he determined to push on to Kordofan. Minor successes still encouraged him unduly, and, late in May, he reported to Lord Dufferin from Khartoum his belief that faith in the Mahdi was rapidly decreasing. By August, matters were badly amiss with the expedition; men, moral, money, transport—everything that was essential was lacking. Early in September, Hicks and his army of 10,000 nondescript troops, ill-fed, ill-found, ill-disciplined and ill-paid, quitted Khartoum, and on the 24th the Nile, for a westward march in the direction of Kordofan, intending to challenge the Mahdi at El Obeid. Owing to treachery, he was led into the desert, and on November 5th, when but two days' march from his objective, his army was surprised by a strong rebel force, and he and all his men perished.

In France, the Hicks disaster was ostentatiously welcomed, in the hope that it would expedite the end of the British occupation[2]. Its effect was precisely the reverse. While, on the one hand, it destroyed for the time the prestige of the Egyptian Government, discredited the native Army, and compromised British authority, it also frustrated the hope of reducing the force of occupation and banished to the land of dreams the idea of evacuation. For, if the presence of the British in Egypt now became more difficult than before, it also became more necessary. Moreover, a new danger had appeared in the person of Osman Digna, an ex-slavedealer, whom the Mahdi had appointed Emir in the Suakin district, and who had collected a large force with which he terrorised the surrounding population.

Already, the expediency of abandoning the Soudan and concentrating attention upon the defence of a nearer frontier had been urged upon the Egyptian Government by the British authorities. It was suggested that Kordofan and Darfur, with the region beyond, should be regarded as outside the Egyptian pale. To the renunciation of any part whatever of the territory the Khedive and his Ministers were vehemently opposed; but, owing to pressure, the decision to abandon

---

[1] Hicks wrote to Lord Dufferin on his return to Constantinople: "Your departure from Cairo has been a calamity to me."
[2] Letter of Lord Lyons to Lord Granville, November 23rd, 1883.

the Soudan from the latitude of Assouan or Wady Halfa was taken at the end of the year.

Lord Granville, at this time, formulated the relations between the two Governments in a despatch which showed how far Egypt had already forfeited independence.

"In important questions," he wrote to Sir Evelyn Baring, "where the administration and safety of Egypt are at stake, it is indispensable that Her Majesty's Government should, as long as the provisional occupation of the country by English troops continues, be assured that the advice which, after full consideration of the views of the Egyptian Government, they may feel it their duty to tender to the Khedive, should be followed. It should be made clear to the Egyptian Ministers and Governors of provinces that the responsibility which for the time rests on England obliges Her Majesty's Government to insist on the adoption of the policy which they recommend, and that it will be necessary that those Ministers and Governors who do not follow this course should cease to hold their offices" (January 4th, 1884).

On this Instruction being communicated to him, Cherif Pasha, who had been Prime-Minister since September, 1882, resigned in protest, and Nubar Pasha formed a Ministry pledged to the policy of withdrawing from the Soudan.

An endeavour was made by the British Government in June of this year to relieve the financial difficulties caused in part by the rebellion and the Alexandria indemnity claims. A proposal to release, for the purposes of the general administration, such part of the revenue as was not required for the service of the public debt was vigorously opposed by France, concerned as ever for the interests of the bondholders, though by way of purchasing her support Lord Granville had promised that the British Occupation should cease in 1888 at the discretion of the Powers. Two Conferences were in consequence needed before an arrangement was arrived at by the London Convention of March 18th, 1885; and then the promise of conditional evacuation no longer held good. French writers later admitted the shortsightedness of their Government's attitude[1].

The abandonment of the Soudan implied more than the negative decision to leave it alone; for there were Egyptian garrisons there,

---

[1] "*Nous avons eu le tort de ne pas profiter de cette occasion unique Plutôt que de réduire le revenu de la dette égyptienne d'un demi pour cent, nous avons repoussé le rare avantage politique qui nous était offert. L'absorbant souci de l'intérêt des créanciers, qui nous avait déjà fait commettre tant de fautes, nous a fait commettre cette dernière, et nous avons consolidé de nos mains l'édifice encore chancelant des Anglais dans la vallée du Nil.*" C. de Freycinet, La question d'Égypte, p. 436.

and these could not be left to their fate. A suggestion made to the Government that General Gordon, of earlier Soudan and later Chinese fame, might prove helpful in the work of evacuation led to overtures being made to him. The Cabinet was divided on the subject, the Prime-Minister, Lord Derby, and the Earl of Kimberley being at first opposed to the despatch of Gordon, while Lord Granville, Lord Northbrook, and the Marquis of Hartington favoured it. The decision to engage his services was taken on January 18th, 1884, at a meeting attended by Gordon, who appears to have left on the minds of Ministers the impression that the danger at Khartoum had been exaggerated, and that the withdrawal of the garrisons would not be a difficult matter. The Government's idea was that Gordon's Mission should be one of investigation, leaving them with a free hand as to the measures to be adopted on the strength of his report. So ran his Instructions of the same day; but there followed the very elastic proviso that he was to regard himself as authorised and bound to perform "such other duties as the Egyptian Government may desire to entrust to you and as may be communicated to you by Sir E. Baring." Inasmuch as the views of the British and the Egyptian Governments on the general question of the abandonment of the Soudan differed fundamentally, this proviso was, to say the least, hazardous.

Gordon left London on January 18th, optimistically confident of complete success, and convinced that the settlement of the Soudan would occupy but a few months at the most—an opinion which no one in Cairo shared. At that time, he agreed that the Soudan was for Egypt "a useless possession—ever was so and ever will be so," and he understood clearly that its evacuation had been "irrevocably decided on," and that his concern was simply with the garrisons, their safety and withdrawal, while the Soudanese in general were to be left as "God has placed them[1]." It was ominous, however, that, before he reached Cairo, he was speculating upon the division of the region into a series of sultanates, just as had been the case before the Egyptian conquest, and the union of these in some sort of confederation.

The supplementary Cairo Instructions went far beyond the British Government's first plan, for they spoke frankly of "establishing organised government in the different provinces of the Soudan." Gordon was still to be bound to the policy of evacuation; but he was to be free as to the measures which that policy might involve. He had already, at his own request, been nominated to his old office of

[1] Memorandum on his Mission written by Gordon, January 22nd, 1884.

Governor-General of the Soudan, and, while the appointment gave to him a more authoritative *status*, it is not unlikely that with it he became conscious of a greater independence.

He reached Khartoum without mishap early in February, by which time he seemed to have forgotten that he was engaged on a Mission defined by written Instructions; his judgment and movements became increasingly erratic; he was continually changing his mind—and naturally so, since by ignoring his Instructions he had lost his bearings. While in Cairo, he had met Zobeir Pasha, an old slave-trader, who had aforetime wielded great authority in the Soudan and whose services he wished to secure. He now entertained the idea of creating a sort of neutral State or zone between Egypt proper and that part of the Soudan to which the Mahdi's influence was to be restricted, and of placing Zobeir in charge of this area as Governor, with his seat at Khartoum. Sir Evelyn Baring, General Stewart, and Nubar Pasha all favoured the idea; but, on its being communicated to the British Cabinet, it met with strong disapproval, and, eventually, Zobeir found his way not to Khartoum but, for reasons of caution, to Gibraltar.

By the end of February, Gordon was avowing the policy of "smashing the Mahdi"—an operation which he believed would be "comparatively easy," as it was merely a question of more men and more money. He even proposed that Egypt should continue to maintain its position as suzerain Power responsible for the government of the Soudan and the appointment of the Governor-General and Mudirs. Already, the British Government, disconcerted by these and other suggestions at variance with their plans, had sent emphatic refusals to sanction military operations of any kind or to assist Gordon with troops. Nevertheless, so late as August 23rd, Gordon continued to call for the despatch of a British expedition to the Soudan; and one of his last messages, addressed both to the Khedive and the British Agent, was to the effect that, "if the Sultan would send 20,000 of his troops, the Soudan could be handed over to him."

In the meantime, the Mahdi was astir and collecting his followers for an attack upon the intruder who disputed his authority; and by the end of April fears were entertained in Egypt that Khartoum would soon be isolated and Gordon's chances of coming away would disappear. Sir Evelyn Baring was already preparing the Home Government for the contingency of a relief expedition. The Cabinet saw no reason for alarm, but, in the middle of May, convinced that Gordon was acting no longer as their servant but as his own master, instructed him to consider, and if possible adopt, "measures for his own removal and that of the Egyptians at Khartoum who have suffered for him and served him faithfully, including their wives and children, by whatever route he may think best[1]." By this time, withdrawal was impossible, and soon Khartoum was practically invested.

For several months, the Cabinet discussed the question of a relief expedition without being able to make up its mind, though the section represented by Lord Hartington and Lord Northbrook never wavered in the opinion that, whether Gordon had acted wilfully or not, the Government and the country owed him a responsibility which could not be honourably evaded. In July, a half-expedition was decided on. A rescue force was to be sent so far as Dongola for a start, on the understanding that it would proceed further on the way to Khartoum, unless Gordon had succeeded in withdrawing, as Gladstone persisted in believing that he would.

Of two routes considered, the desert route from Suakin (which was in British occupation) to Berber and the slower Nile route, the latter was chosen, though it involved a serious loss of time in preparations. Lord Wolseley organised and commanded the expedition, and he reached Cairo on September 9th and Wady Halfa on October 5th, when the Nile progress and campaign began. It was a great enterprise, skilfully planned and doggedly carried through; and the failure to achieve the ultimate aim detracts from neither the boldness of its conception nor the heroism of the troops. By Christmas, the main part of the expedition was at Korti, where the force was divided. Sir Herbert Stewart, with one column, marched across the desert in order to strike the Nile again at Metemma, while General Earle continued up the river towards Berber, with a view to its capture. Stewart met with a horde of Dervishes on January 17th, and in the ensuing engagement was mortally wounded; but he brought his force to the Nile, where four steamers awaited it. Sir Charles Wilson continued the advance by river towards Khartoum, learning on the way (January 27th) that the Mahdi had entered the city and Gordon had been killed two days before.

The news of the disaster created intense excitement in England and let loose floods of controversy which left permanent traces behind them. For his share in the failure of the relief expedition Gladstone had to face much blame and recrimination, while colleagues whose responsibility was at least equal to his escaped lightly; but, for an

[1] Lord Granville to Sir Evelyn Baring, May 17th, 1884.

incriminated Minister, he bore his afflictions very aggressively. In later private utterances, he admitted that the despatch of Gordon was a great mistake, but a mistake "greatly excusable," and reproached the "hero of heroes" for having claimed the right to turn "upside-down· and inside-out every idea and intention with which he left England" and for which he had obtained the Government's approval. Neither Gladstone nor his Cabinet sympathisers seemed ever to grasp fully the fact that for the despatch of Gordon, whether wise or not, the country did not blame them; its blame was concentrated upon their failure to stand firmly by the man of their own choice. Nor was Lord Granville more convincing in his plea that Gordon's venture was a "forlorn hope," that against forlorn hopes the gods themselves are powerless, hence that in war "there is no obligation in honour on the commander of an army to risk lives" in their behalf. The obvious answer was that Gordon was not sent on a military but an administrative Mission—a Mission which, in Gladstone's words, was one of "peace and liberation"—so that appeals to the hazards of warfare had no application to his case[1].

[1] There was a good deal of futile controversy over the question whether Gordon's work was or was not intended to be limited to reporting. If it was, there existed no valid reason for sending him into the centre of Africa at all. With his knowledge of the country and people, and the knowledge of the military position which others could have given him, he could have reported equally well in Cairo, if not in London. If the Government had wanted merely a Report, they should not have sent a commander who had been Governor-General of the Soudan, but his orderly, who could at least have been relied on to return home with a full note-book. The Cabinet adverted, further, to the fact that Gordon had gone beyond the letter of his Instructions of January 18th. But those Instructions were intended to be supplemented in Cairo, and were supplemented, and Gordon left London with the authority and the injunction to do exactly what the Khedive's advisers on the spot deemed expedient. Certainly, Gordon was a difficult subject to deal with and one impossible to keep in his place. He was so familiar with the exercise of authority, and had so little respect for the obedience required of and habitual to the conventional official, that strict fidelity to Instructions of any kind was the one thing that should not have been expected of him. He was both too strong and too head-strong a man to be bound to the letter of any order. But all this, too, his employers knew beforehand. How far he actually deviated from his final orders and how far he was justified in so doing are questions open to legitimate difference of opinion; but such questions do not affect the material issue.

It was Gladstone's opinion that Gordon never had any reasonable hope of setting up a Government in Khartoum, and that he should have withdrawn as soon as he recognised the impracticability of his self-imposed task. Undoubtedly, Gordon could have extricated his own person from danger with time to spare; but he was concerned for the lives of the garrisons; and they, at least, had not been sent into the interior of the Soudan on a "forlorn hope." It is true that the garrisons were not British; but a British Government had compelled the adoption of a policy which made the attempt at their safe withdrawal a moral duty. It was impossible for Great Britain, who had practically superseded the native Administration of Egypt, to pretend that that duty was no concern of hers.

Several years later, Gladstone wrote: "In the long and complicated Egyptian business we were for the most part, as I think, drawn on inevitably by a necessity of honour[1]." That was unquestionably the case with the rescue expedition to Khartoum. But no one blamed the Government for having undertaken that gallant yet fruitless exploit. The country's grievance was that the national honour had to wait so long for recognition, and that the failure of the Nile enterprise was, humanly speaking, a consequence of delay.

On the receipt of the news of Gordon's fate the Government, with a view to appeasing national feeling, announced that the expedition would be resumed in the autumn and would prosecute its task until the Mahdi's power had been broken. Such was their serious intention at the time, and preparatory measures were ordered accordingly, including the commencement of a railway from Suakin to Berber. Second thoughts, however, suggested a waiting policy, and, when Sir Evelyn Baring advised the entire suspension of operations, in view of the fact that the main object of the expedition had been defeated, both the Government and the country accepted this view. It was, therefore, decided to fix the southern administrative limit of the Egyptian empire at Wady Halfa, leaving the whole of the Soudan beyond, with the exception of the Red Sea littoral, in the possession of the rebels. Lord Salisbury, coming into power in June, 1885, although he had condemned the policy of evacuation while in Opposition, now warmly upheld the decision of the outgoing Ministry.

In the same year, the Mahdi died and the Khalifa Abdullah-el-Taishi succeeded to his authority, though the religious character of the Mahdist movement gradually disappeared. The Soudan remained in the Khalifa's hands for ten years, until the activities of a rival Power in the basin of the Upper Nile compelled the British Government to resort to counter-measures, with a view to reasserting the rights of the Khedive.

[1] Letter to Lord Granville, March 12th, 1888.

BOOK V

THE SECOND AND THIRD SALISBURY ADMINISTRATIONS AND AFTER, 1886–1907

SECRETARIES OF STATE FOR FOREIGN AFFAIRS

February,   1886: Earl of Rosebery.
August,   — : Earl of Iddesleigh.
January,   1887: Marquess of Salisbury.
August,   1892: Earl of Rosebery.
March,   1894: Earl of Kimberley.
June,   1895: Marquess of Salisbury.
November, 1900: Marquess of Lansdowne.
December, 1905: Sir Edward Grey, Bart. (afterwards Viscount Grey of Fallodon).

UNDER-SECRETARIES OF STATE FOR FOREIGN AFFAIRS

February,   1886: James (afterwards Viscount) Bryce (*Parliamentary*).
August,   — : Right Hon. Sir James Fergusson, Bart. (*Parliamentary*).
April,   1889: Sir Philip W. Currie (afterwards Lord Currie) (*Permanent*).
—   — : Sir Thomas H. Sanderson (afterwards Lord Sanderson) (*Assistant*).
September, 1891: James William Lowther (afterwards Lord Ullswater) (*Parliamentary*).
August,   1892: Sir Edward Grey (afterwards Viscount Grey of Fallodon) (*Parliamentary*).
January,   1894: Sir Thomas H. Sanderson (afterwards Lord Sanderson) (*Assistant*).
—   — : Sir H. Percy Anderson (*Assistant*).
—   — : Hon. Francis L. Bertie (afterwards Viscount Bertie of Thames) (*Assistant*).
June,   1895: Right Hon. George N. Curzon (afterwards Earl Curzon of Kedleston).
July,   1896: Hon. Francis H. (afterwards Sir F. H.) Villiers (*Assistant*).
—   1898: Sir Martin Le M. H. Gosselin (*Assistant*).
October,   — : Right Hon. St John Fremantle Brodrick (afterwards Viscount Midleton) (*Parliamentary*).
November, 1900: Viscount Cranborne (afterwards Marquess of Salisbury) (*Parliamentary*).
August,   1902: Francis A. (afterwards Sir F. A.) Campbell (*Assistant*).
February,   1903: Hon. Charles Hardinge (afterwards Lord Hardinge of Penshurst) (*Assistant*).
October,   1903: Henry Algernon George Earl Percy (*Parliamentary*).
May,   1904: Sir Eldon Gorst (*Assistant*).
December, 1905: Lord Edward George Petty Fitzmaurice (afterwards Lord Fitzmaurice) (*Parliamentary*).
February,   1906: Right Hon. Sir Charles Hardinge (afterwards Lord Hardinge of Penshurst) (*Permanent*).
—   1906: Hon. Sir Eric Barrington (*Assistant*).
May,   1907: Louis (afterwards Sir L.) Mallet (*Assistant*).
July,   — : Walter L. F. G. (afterwards Sir W.) Langley (*Assistant*).

CHAPTER III

IMPERIAL POLICY IN THE OLD AND THE NEW WORLD, 1885–1899

I. FRONTIER DISPUTES IN CENTRAL ASIA

A. *The Afghan Boundary Delimitation*, 1884–1895

THE attempts, made in 1873, to delimit the Afghan Frontier on the northern side had resulted in the acceptance of the Oxus as indicating broadly the limit of the Ameer's sphere of influence. In the absence of clearly defined boundaries, however, the danger of renewed friction increased with every further Russian advance. Since the settlement of Afghanistan in 1881, Abdur Rahman had remained faithful to his pledges, and, in order to appease the growing alarm entertained in his country, the guarantee of aid in repelling unprovoked aggression was formally renewed in 1883. For Russia was steadily asserting her influence over southern Turkestan, and in the winter of 1880–1 the Téké Turkomans had been finally subjugated. There was little to be said in favour of the unruly Tartar khanates; yet, while their absorption was a gain for orderly government in that region, for Afghanistan it meant the nearer approach of an unwelcome neighbour. Then, early in 1884, Merv, which had so long and so often been declared to lie outside the range of Russia's interest or desire, was occupied, and, in the autumn of that year, Sarakhs, on the Perso-Afghan frontier, was also appropriated.

Lord Granville's remark to the Russian Ambassador in London, that the news of the occupation of Merv "had not been received by us with indifference," did not improve the situation, nor did the transmission to Petrograd of a long historical essay recounting all the promises and undertakings which the Russian Government had given on the subject since 1873. In view of past occurrences, there was much justifiable apprehension as to what would be Russia's next objective; and some alarmists professed to believe that the fate of Herat itself already hung in the balance. More and more, the conviction took root that there could be no certainty of any check to the Russian advance, until it struck against the hard granite of a legal compact between civilised Governments which understood that the written pledge of the one was the security and defence of the other.

In order to bring about such an understanding, however, it was necessary to determine exactly where Afghanistan ended and the Russian empire, actual or potential, began. The position of Great Britain was that she was responsible, whether she wished it or not, for the defence of a kingdom whose northern frontier was undefined and unknown, and, in any event, was many hundreds of miles distant from the confines of India, and whose ruler and people were, to say the least, uncertain allies. It was not the least valuable of the services of Lord Ripon to India that, convinced of its being high time that British responsibilities were accurately defined, and that it was wiser to stake the security of the Indian empire upon a formal agreement with a European Power than upon an unstable alliance with a despotic Oriental ruler, he, in the last year of his viceroyalty, instituted a joint British and Russian Boundary Commission with this end in view.

The completion of the Commission's work fell within the term of his successor, Lord Dufferin, whose appointment to the vice-royalty, in the late summer of 1884, was received with universal approval. He took over the office towards the end of the year, looking forward to a tranquil and uneventful administration and prepared to regard such an experience as "the greatest success and triumph" to which he could aspire. He went to India as a convinced supporter of what was known as "Lord Ripon's policy." That policy having been deliberately adopted, he was for continuing and "making the best of it"; nor was he convinced that it would not succeed "if but given a fair and patient trial[1]." He did not believe that Russia entertained aggressive designs against the Indian empire; and, though there were still about him ageing officials of the alarmist type who were honestly convinced that only the appearance of a Muscovite Napoleon was needed to precipitate a Central Asian catastrophe, he gave the Russians credit for commonsense and, within limits, for good-faith. Having, as Ambassador in Petrograd, studied Russia at close quarters, he regarded normal standards as applicable to her, and his exceptional knowledge of Eastern questions, combined with his wide outlook and freedom from narrow prejudices, enabled him to bring to the problems confronting him a judgment not only dispassionate but singularly just. To him, the weakest points of the "buffer" policy were that the frontier for whose integrity we were responsible was too long, distant, and vulnerable to admit of any real protection, and that the Afghans were so little interested in the outlying territories that they might not

[1] Letter to Lord Randolph Churchill, July 30th, 1885.

be willing to fight with any heart for their retention. He, nevertheless, cordially favoured the settlement of the Frontier question by means of a convention.

The proceedings of the Boundary Commission began inauspiciously. The principal Commissioners, Major-General Sir Peter Lumsden[1] for Great Britain and General Zelenoi for Russia, were to have been on the spot in the late autumn of 1884. Lumsden, with his party, was up to time, but only to hear that his Russian colleague was ill and could not be expected before February. Pending the arrival of Zelenoi, a strong Russian force had been trying to forestall the issue by pushing to the south of Sarakhs and occupying as much of the disputed area as possible, while the Afghans had done their best to frustrate this design. The Russians were bent on appropriating the fertile Penjdeh district, which hitherto had been regarded as lying within the Afghan sphere, and had given notice that any counterclaim would be contested. In November, they had advanced close to the town of Penjdeh and were in contact with the Afghan outposts. They were also asserting a claim to the Zulfikar Pass, which the Indian military authorities had likewise determined to retain for Afghanistan. So acute was the situation becoming that, early in March (1885), the Queen appealed to the Tsar, as in 1875, to use his personal influence to avert a conflict, and the Indian Government received orders from London to have an army corps in readiness to occupy and defend Herat, should a rupture ensue. A crisis was reached and war threatened when, on March 30th, the Russian and Afghan forces came into collision, and the latter were driven out of Penjdeh with a loss of 500 lives. Rashness and provocation were alleged on both sides, and probably with justice; yet, from the first, the Russian military command had shown an overbearing spirit, though the Government at Petrograd tried to minimise its indiscretions, as due to disregard of orders.

Happily for the prospects of peace, the Ameer was out of the country at the time, having gone on a visit to the Viceroy to Rawal Pindi, in the north of the Punjab. While he remained at that distance, and in tranquillising surroundings, it was not difficult for an urbane Viceroy to impose upon him restraint in a trying position. Abdur Rahman was persuaded not to take the episode tragically, and, on Lord Dufferin's suggestion, he agreed to abandon Penjdeh, on condition that the Zulfikar Pass remained to Afghanistan.

The Government at home likewise kept calm throughout the

[1] He was appointed August 25th, 1884.

crisis. While declaring his determination to "have right done," and seeking a vote of credit as a measure of precaution, Gladstone set his face sternly against the party which had again appealed to angry passions; and with a reference to arbitration of the question of responsibility for the Penjdeh incident—a British proposal which Russia accepted unwillingly—the war clouds began to disperse, so that by May 2nd the sky was again clear. On Lord Granville's proposal, it had been agreed that Penjdeh should be regarded as neutral ground, to be occupied by neither side, until an agreement by negotiation in London should have determined the question of title. A general understanding was reached on May 22nd, and the way was now open for the arrangement of details on the spot.

For the anxieties of the British Government at that critical time there was compensation in the praiseworthy attitude of the Ameer. Not only did Abdur Rahman show a restraint and moderation which greatly eased the task of his ally; but, while at Rawal Pindi, he gave, both publicly and privately, pledges of good-faith and attachment to the British Government and Crown, the sincerity of which admitted of no doubt. He, nevertheless, made it clear that the presence of British Agents in his kingdom remained undesired by him. Lord Dufferin showed all his wonted tact in the handling of the "strange strong creature," as he called his guest the Ameer. By treating him throughout the palaver as a royal personage he made the gratified Ameer feel like one. Abdur Rahman, as jealous of his position and rights as any of his predecessors had been, was superlatively pleased when, just before his departure, the Viceroy, with whom was a royal Prince, received the Ameer at a special durbar, not as a *protégé* but as an ally, with all the honour due to an independent Sovereign. Equally gratifying were the evidences of loyalty which the Penjdeh episode called forth on every hand in India. Native Princes freely volunteered military and financial help, and the tone of the Press and public opinion left no doubt that the Russian menace had for the time drawn the native races more closely together. However little they may at heart have liked British rule, they could not deny that it was at least honest and fairly unselfish, and they had no wish for a change.

No sooner had Lord Granville removed the frontier question out of the danger zone than the Gladstone Government came to an end; and during the greater part of the subsequent negotiations an untried statesman was at the India Office, in the person of Lord Randolph Churchill (June, 1885—February, 1886). This was one of Lord Salisbury's experimental appointments, variously viewed by his own party, but amply justified by the event. Wisely preserving silence until he had carefully taken his bearings, the new Secretary of State during his brief term of office showed a sagacity, a restraint in his decisions, and a grasp of affairs for which few people had given him credit. He was himself in sympathy with Lord Lytton's plan for breaking up Afghanistan, and, if he could have followed his personal bent, he would probably have been equally prepared to break up Russia's Asiatic empire into the bargain, as the only effective solution of the Central Asian problem; but as a statesman he recognised that such ideas were not practical politics. It was a fortunate check upon an excess of temperament, and upon a disposition to defer unduly to the military view, that on all important questions Lord Randolph never failed to seek Lord Salisbury's sage counsels.

Before Lord Salisbury's short-lived first Administration came to an end in November, the Penjdeh dispute had been settled on the lines already agreed upon (September 10th), Penjdeh being assigned to Russia and Zulfikar and the Pass to Afghanistan. Then, Gladstone returned to office, but only for a few months; for in the following July he was defeated on the question of Home Rule. Lord Salisbury now formed his second Cabinet, in which he succeeded the Earl of Iddesleigh (on his death in January, 1887) at the Foreign Office, Viscount Cross holding the Secretaryship for India. The details of the frontier delimitation remained still to be decided on the spot, and, owing to the difficulties encountered, frequent disagreements and consequent interruptions retarded the progress of the work, since constant reference, now to London, now to Petrograd, was necessary. So impossible did an understanding seem to be at one time, that the British Representative, Colonel Sir W. Ridgeway, proposed to confine the attention of the Commission to the collection of geographical and statistical data, leaving the boundary-line to be settled by negotiation in Europe, a proposal to which the Russian Government demurred. By the autumn of 1886, the delimitation of the Frontier had almost reached the Oxus, and negotiations *in situ* were discontinued, the remainder of the task being left to the home Governments. The final Protocol, delimiting the Frontier between the Hari-Rud and the Oxus, was signed in July, 1887. Abdur Rahman remained constant to his British allies until his death in 1901.

Several supplementary frontier demarcations were effected during the last decade of the century. In particular, the north-eastern frontier of Afghanistan was defined in the Pamirs region by agreement between the British and Russian Governments (March 11th, 1895), which undertook to use their friendly influence with the two Ameers of the territories affected.

Relieved from the menace of a Russian invasion of India, the military party, instead of standing at ease and letting well alone, turned their attention to forward movements in other directions. The Boundary Agreement had settled the limits of Afghanistan to the north; now, it was desired to restrict the Ameer's influence in the east by transferring the Border tribes there from his nominal control to the real control of the Indian Government. The object was in part attained, but at the expense of a series of little frontier Wars which for many years exercised a disturbing influence on Indian opinion and proved a serious tax upon the country's resources. A return made to the House of Commons in January, 1900, at the instance of Mr (now Lord) Morley, of the Wars and military operations on or beyond the borders of British India in which the Indian Government had been engaged since 1849, enumerated 110 Wars or expeditions during the fifty years following that date, of which 64 took place in the twenty years from 1878 to 1898. A frontier War which was deliberately sought by the military party, and caused much difference of opinion both in India and at home, was that which led to the annexation of Chitral. Relations had been established with Chitral during the viceroyalty of Lord Lytton; but disturbances in the Gilgit district led to the withdrawal of the British Agency there in 1880, and it was not reestablished until 1889, from which time the Indian Government subsidised the ruler of Chitral and supplied him with munitions of war on a moderate scale, in view of suspected Russian aggression in the Pamirs. Finally, in order to put an end to the repeated attacks on Chitral by neighbouring chiefs, and to establish lasting internal order in the State itself, the Indian Government first occupied this outlying territory in 1895, and then annexed it to the empire. In the same year, the boundary of Chitral in the direction of Afghanistan was delimited by an Agreement with the Ameer. Among Indian statesmen, and even military strategists, opinion was divided as to whether, on the whole, the effect of these frontier wars was so much to pacify as to unsettle, since they created among the free tribes a constant fear of aggression.

B. *Annexation of Upper Burma*, 1878–1886.

Lord Dufferin had hoped that the most characteristic achievement of his viceroyalty might be tranquillity. The hope was vain, for in "the unchanging East" change is ceaseless, and it was the peculiarity of India in especial, as he said, that "the bottom was always falling out of the bucket." Before the Afghan Boundary Question had been settled, trouble arose on another frontier of the Indian empire. Burma, lying to the east, had never been a good neighbour, and for a long time had been a very bad one. Already, there had been two Burmese Wars, as a result of which the Kings of Ava had forfeited to India their provinces on the Sea of Bengal, since known as British (Lower) Burma. Burma might have settled down to friendlier relationships had it been left alone. French influence was, however, active in the kingdom, and, thus encouraged, its attitude became more and more one of studied provocation. This had particularly been the case since the accession in 1878 of the savage ruler Thebaw, whose short reign had proved one of tyrannical misgovernment, violence and cruelty. He had begun it by the murder of such members of the royal family as were displeasing to him, and one of his last acts as King was the massacre of several hundred prisoners in Mandalay gaol. Under him, neither life nor property was secure, and he seemed to take a particular pleasure in overriding the rights of British subjects resident in his country. So hostile did he become, and so capricious was his temper, that the British Representative in his capital was recalled for safety's sake and was not replaced.

In the meantime, France steadily followed her policy of "pacific penetration," in the hope that Burma would in due time pass under her formal Protection, though her Governments were left in no uncertainty whether any attempt to impose French dominion upon States lying on the flanks of the Indian empire would be regarded by Great Britain as a hostile act. Burma responded readily to the French advances. Special Embassies were repeatedly sent to France from 1872 onward, and in 1874 the French Agent in Mandalay concluded with the Burmese Government a Treaty so objectionable that, on the request of the British Government, it was not ratified. When one of these Missions arrived in Paris in August, 1883, the British Ambassador on several occasions reminded the French Foreign Minister of Great Britain's special interest in Burma and urged that any agreement which might be concluded should be restricted to purely commercial questions. Ferry made light of the negotiations which were proceeding and gave satisfactory assurances. Nevertheless, the innocent negotiations resulted in the ratification of an earlier uncompleted Treaty which proposed to establish direct diplomatic relations between the two countries. Challenged on this point, Ferry now admitted that "the Burmese desired to throw themselves into the arms of France," but added that France had no wish to afford them this solace, and that nothing in the nature of an alliance, military or political, was contemplated. By Conventions in 1883 and 1885, however, the Burmese Government conferred special commercial and other privileges on French subjects.

In a report presented by him to the Chamber of Deputies in July, 1885, on behalf of the Commission to which the latest Treaty had been referred, de Lanessan advocated a bold extension of French operations in the Indo-Chinese peninsula. While speaking euphemistically of a "*tentative pacifique*," and professing to disown political aims, he made it clear that not merely commercial but political expansion must be the ultimate objective, and that this expansion ought to be at the cost of Burma and Siam, neither of which he could regard as a "regularly organised kingdom." He particularly mentioned the Great Lake, with the region adjacent, and the kingdom of Luang Prabang, both of which Siam was to be required to "disgorge"[1].

These openly avowed aims attracted the attention both of the India and the Foreign Office, and, on August 28th, Lord Randolph Churchill begged Lord Salisbury to warn the French Government that the undue pushing of French commercial ambitions in Burma would "necessitate such prompt and decided measures as may most effectually satisfy the paramount rights of India in the Indo-Chinese peninsula[2]"—words indicating that the annexation of the Ava kingdom was already thought of. Discussing the question in the following month with Lord Salisbury, Waddington suggested that negotiations should be opened with a view to the division of the Indo-Chinese peninsula into spheres of influence; whereupon, the counter-proposal was made that two Powers should adopt a self-denying ordinance,

[1] De Lanessan subsequently became Governor of French Indo-China; and the French treatment of Siam under his influence was, in the words of a British Foreign Secretary, "in exact fulfilment of the programme of undisguised aggression and encroachment laid down in his published work on French colonial policy." (Despatch of Lord Rosebery to the Marquis of Dufferin at Paris, September 5th, 1893.)

[2] W. L. S. Churchill, *Lord Randolph Churchill*, I. 522.

binding them not to acquire Siamese territory. To this suggestion Waddington gave no answer[1].

The conclusion of the Franco-Burmese Treaty, the knowledge of French designs, coupled with a more than usually audacious attempt made by King Thebaw to confiscate the property of a British trading company in order to transfer its rights to French rivals, and his peremptory refusal to refer the subject of dispute to arbitration, brought matters to a crisis. Thebaw had, in fact, become of late just as ostentatiously pro-French as he was ostentatiously anti-British, and it was felt that the time had come for a final settlement of accounts. In October, the Indian Government served on the King an ultimatum requiring him to receive at Mandalay a British Envoy, who should cooperate in adjusting outstanding differences, to consent to the presence of a permanent Resident at the Court of Ava, and to accept the advice of the Indian Government in his foreign affairs. A force of 10,000 troops, one-third of them British, was despatched to Rangoon, in order to give weight to this document. When the Burmese Government refused to comply with any one of the demands, this force invaded the country, early in November, by way of the Irrawaddy, and Mandalay was occupied within seven days. The Burmese army was unable to offer serious opposition, and the King surrendered himself as prisoner and was promptly deported to India.

The future political status of the kingdom had to be determined in difficult circumstances, since the collapse of the Government had been the signal for an outbreak of anarchy. Three courses were open. Thebaw might be deposed, a regent being put in his place, and the Burmese left to themselves, subject to due safeguards; or the kingdom might be converted into a vassal-State; or, finally, there remained the alternative of annexation to India. Lord Dufferin and the Secretary of State favoured this last drastic solution of the difficulty, though the Viceroy's Council discouraged it as likely to excite the hostility of China. Perhaps no more laconic proclamation of the kind was ever published than that of January 1st, 1886, in which, in fifty words, Lord Dufferin declared the territories hitherto governed by King Thebaw to be his no longer, but to have passed to the British Crown.

The work of settlement proved arduous. The weak rule of a half-insane King had everywhere encouraged lawlessness and a spirit of rebellion; raiding, robbery and local faction long continued rampant; and the fact that the small population was scattered over a wide area

[1] Despatch of Lord Salisbury to Lord Lyons, September 28th, 1885.

—for the annexed territory, with its 4,000,000 inhabitants, was larger than France—made difficult the enforcement of measures of control. As the Burmese refused to cooperate in the reorganisation of their own country, native troops and police from India, supported by a British force, had to undertake the task, and, for two years, a state of war continued, with sporadic rebellion either in the interior or on the frontiers for the greater part of two decades.

The annexation of Upper Burma necessitated various political adjustments with China, and also with France in relation to her Indo-Chinese empire. China claimed ancient, though shadowy, rights of suzerainty in respect of the kingdom, as symbolised by the decennial Missions which Burma had been wont to send to the Peking Court, there to present articles of native produce. These rights had long been waived, yet the possibility of their revival at any time existed, with the risk, in the absence of a clear understanding beforehand, of disturbance to the friendly relations with Great Britain. The result of an exchange of views in Peking was the conclusion of the Convention of July 24th, 1886, by which China, with truly Oriental amplitude of phrase, agreed that "in all matters whatsoever appertaining to the authority and rule which England is now exercising in Burma, England shall be free to do whatever she deems fit and proper"; while, on the other hand, Great Britain agreed that the decennial Missions should continue to be sent by Burma to Peking, according to immemorial custom, the members of such Missions to be of Burmese race[1]. The Convention also provided for the demarcation of the frontier between China and Burma; but the arrangements on this head were modified by agreements concluded in 1894 and 1897.

C. *Disputes with France concerning Siam*, 1889–1904

Great Britain had long taken a friendly interest in Siam, with which she had been in treaty relations since 1855. Lying between Burma and the Indo-Chinese possessions of France, its preservation as a strong independent State had become of paramount importance for the Indian empire. In April, 1889, the French Government proposed that the kingdom should be neutralised and its independence

[1] This loosely-drawn Foreign Office Convention states neither where or to whom Burma sent these Missions in the past, nor where or to whom they were to be sent in the future, leaving it to be assumed that Peking and the Chinese ruler are implied. Further, while the preamble of the Convention speaks in one place of "the United Kingdom of Great Britain and Ireland" and in another place of "Great Britain" only, as the Power with which China treated, the succeeding Articles speak nowhere of either Great Britain or Ireland, but only of "England."

formally recognised by the two Powers, which should regard it as a permanent barrier between the British and the French Asiatic empires. To that end, a general demarcation of the frontiers between the French possessions and Siam and Burma, respectively, was suggested   Lord Salisbury favoured the idea, but unfortunately failed to take action. France again raised the question in February, 1892, when she claimed influence so far as the Mekong river, in virtue of her Protectorate over Annam. To this claim the British Foreign Secretary strongly demurred, as being entirely new and without foundation.

Before the next exchange of views, in the following December, when Lord Rosebery was at the Foreign Office, the British Government had provisionally agreed with Siam as to the future frontier between that country and Burma. A feature of the settlement was the recognition by Great Britain of Siam's exclusive jurisdiction over Kyaing Chaing, one of the Burmese Shan States, lying on both sides of the Mekong, while British influence was held to extend to the river at one point only, owing to the acceptance of British protection by the State of Kyaing Tong. As part of the same adjustment, Great Britain was to cede to China her rights in Kiang Hung, which, together with Kyaing Chaing, was to form a " buffer " territory between Burma and the French possessions. Although France had made the first suggestion of an all-round settlement of boundaries, she took offence at this agreement on the ground that it had been concluded without consultation with her. She, also, advanced the contention that Siam had no title to any territory on the left bank of the Mekong, and claimed this territory for herself as Suzerain of Annam. This claim was soon afterwards supported by a formal charge of aggression against Siam, and a demand that the territory occupied by it on the Annam side of the river should be abandoned. Rejecting Siam's proposal of arbitration, France, without either warning or offer of conditions of peace, occupied a Siamese town on the Mekong, and war followed (May, 1893).

Great Britain could not remain an indifferent observer of a dispute affecting the future of a country whose independence was of vital importance to India, and whose trade was for the most part in British hands; and when, in April, it seemed clear that France intended to resort to force, British vessels of war were sent to Bangkok. From the first, Siam was involved in a hopeless struggle, and without the moral support of the British Government the kingdom might have been swept into the Indo-Chinese net in which France had already landed

Cochin-China, Annam, Cambodia and Tongking. As it was, more Siamese territory was seized, French gunboats steamed up the Mekong, and, in the middle of July, a drastic ultimatum was served on the Bangkok Government demanding, among other things, the cession of the entire left bank of the river and the payment of three million francs by way of compensation for injury done to French subjects and property. As these demands were not complied with, a blockade of the Siamese coast was declared, and the French commander called upon all neutral vessels to leave Bangkok within three days.

This officer had already shown resentment at the presence of a British flotilla, and he expected that it would now duly depart. A strong hand at the Foreign Office decided otherwise. Lord Rosebery was there for the second time, and was proving himself a power not to be trifled with. With a graceful erudition and a happy gift of oratory, more common in a pre-Reform than a modern statesman, he combined a breadth of political outlook and a warm sympathy with the policy of imperial expansion which drew him naturally to Foreign Affairs. No Foreign Minister of his day showed greater staunchness and tenacity in contending for his country's just rights; yet, in negotiation, none better understood that genuine success consists in furthering the larger interests by the sacrifice of the smaller. Learning that one of the British ships was about to leave Bangkok, Lord Rosebery telegraphed the order to remain (July 30th), and informed the French Government of what he had done. While holding that the action of France had throughout been of an aggressive and provocative character, the Foreign Secretary, nevertheless, did his best to induce the Siamese Government to give all reasonable satisfaction, with the result that the ultimatum was accepted in a modified form and the blockade was raised by the beginning of August.

By the Treaty of Peace and an accompanying Convention which were concluded on October 3rd, 1893, Siam conceded to France important rights, and renounced in her favour any claim to territory on the left bank of the Mekong and the islands in the river. It was due to the moderating pressure firmly exercised by Lord Rosebery that a far more drastic claim was withdrawn; for, at one stage of the negotiations, France had demanded the cession of territory 100,000 square miles in extent, equal to nearly one-third of the kingdom. As a result of the settlement, the trans-Mekong Burmese territory of Kyaing Chaing remained in British hands.

In the adjustment of the other territorial questions to which the

Franco-Siamese War gave rise France had to deal with Great Britain, and three years passed before an understanding was arrived at. The French Government clung tenaciously to the claim that all the territory lying on the left bank of the Mekong belonged to France, and that British influence began only on the west bank of the river. Lord Rosebery firmly opposed this claim, not only as being inconsistent with British rights acquired in virtue of the annexation of Burma, through which the Upper Mekong ran, but because its admission would have made the Indian and French Indo-Chinese empires conterminous, contrary to the principles of British policy in Asia. Accordingly, his efforts were in the first instance directed towards the creation of an intervening neutral or "buffer" zone. He was prepared to make great sacrifices for the sake of such an arrangement. While all that was to have been asked of France in the way of territory was a stretch of barren country which she had not long owned and had never explored, he offered to throw into the neutral zone the organised State of Kyaing Chaing, with its capital, whole villages of Kyaing Tong, and the control of the Mekong. But, if France did not agree, he was determined that Great Britain should keep her Mekong possessions and exercise to the full her rights in respect of them. France, however, set up the unreasonable claim that each Power should cede an exactly equal amount of territory, irrespective of intrinsic or strategic value. Lord Rosebery lost patience over the petty "acre for acre" principle of bargaining, as unworthy of great States.

In the end, an arrangement for the creation of a neutral zone 50 miles broad was adopted, its limits to be determined by a joint commission. Even then, France, pursuing her imperialistic designs with determined pertinacity, refused to regard the arrangement as final; and she gave the British Government no rest until she had gained her way. Lord Rosebery resisted to the last; but in 1895 Lord Salisbury, in virtue of one of the "graceful concessions" by which he from time to time purchased the temporary goodwill of Great Britain's neighbours and rivals, yielded to France all that she demanded without equivalent advantage. This was effected by the Declaration of January 15th, 1896, which fixed the Mekong as the boundary between the British and French possessions from the mouth of the Nam Huck northwards so far as the Chinese frontier. Simultaneously, the last remnant of exterritorial rights possessed by Great Britain in Tunis was abandoned.

For Siam, the most important provisions of the agreement were those which arbitrarily divided the most valuable part of the country into British and French spheres of influence. In a published despatch, Lord Salisbury gave the assurance that the selection of one part of Siam for this treatment was not to be regarded as throwing doubt upon the title and rights of the Siamese rulers to the remainder of their kingdom; but this disclaimer did not lessen the objection that the two Powers had asserted a lien upon so much of Siam as seemed to them of value. The only justification advanced on behalf of Great Britain for this invasion of the rights of a small nation was contained in the plea that the territory in question affected "our interests as a commercial nation," and that it might one day be the site of lines of communication which would be of great importance to neighbouring portions of the British Empire.

II. The European Partition of Africa; Heligoland and Madagascar, 1850–1904

During the last quarter of the nineteenth century the exploration of Africa reached a heroic climax, and the partition of the Continent among the several European claimants seemed to have entered its final stage. By the close of the century, the vast expanses of this Continent, with the exception of the relatively small area which remained under native sovereignty, had passed beneath the jurisdiction of seven States (here named in the order of extent of territory): France, Great Britain, Germany, Belgium, Portugal, Italy and Spain.

In wealth of resources and in value for the purpose of colonisation, the territory acquired by Great Britain as a result of the final arrangement was, perhaps, the most important addition ever made to the empire. It is difficult in these days of revived imperialism to appreciate the fact that, two generations ago, the official British attitude towards African colonisation was one of weariness and positive disfavour. In 1850, the Privy Council, in approving the annexation of the Orange River, did it unwillingly and urged upon the Queen that there should be no more appropriations of territory, however small, in South Africa. In 1865, a Committee of the House of Commons unanimously affirmed that in West Africa, likewise, "all further extension of territory or assumption of government, or new treaties offering protection to native tribes, would be inexpedient." When, two years later, Sir Philip Wodehouse as Governor of Cape Colony urged the declaration of British sovereignty over the region between that colony and the Portuguese colony of Angola, the Colonial Secretary, the Duke of Buckingham and Chandos, refused compliance, though some of the small islands in the neighbourhood of Angra Pequena were annexed. Basutoland was added in 1868; but in the same year a petition for the annexation of Namaqua and Damara Lands, on the south-west coast, sent to London by the German Missionary Society which had long worked there, was rejected, though the North German Government supported it.

One effect of this marked indisposition in the middle of the century to extend British rule in South Africa was that freer scope was offered for the roaming instincts of the discontented Dutch settlers at the Cape, who trekked northward at that time. Crossing the Orange River, they founded the Orange River State and the republic of the Transvaal, so introducing a strongly separatist spirit into the life of the white population of the south. The first of these Dutch common-wealths pursued a career of steady progress; while the career of the second was marked by vicissitudes which from the first menaced its stability and ultimately encouraged British designs upon its independence, as recognised by the Sand River Convention of January 16th, 1852.

Since the passing of the Canadian Confederation Act in 1867 the idea of Union had made headway in South Africa; and Lord Carnarvon, who had carried the Canadian Act and again became Colonial Secretary in 1874, did his utmost to induce the Cape Government to take the lead in the matter, but without immediate success. The internal difficulties experienced by the South African republic and its strained relations with the adjacent native populations, and particularly with the Zulus, seemed to convince Lord Carnarvon that it would welcome the relief and protection which would be afforded by his scheme of federation; and, should the Transvaal be brought in, he assumed that the Orange Free State would be willing to join later. In a "private and very confidential" letter (September 20th, 1876) to Lord Beacons-field, who, in contrast with the close attention which he gave to foreign affairs, allowed his colleague at the Colonial Office a large measure of freedom, Lord Carnarvon spoke of his intention, subject to the Prime-Minister's acquiescence, to send out at once Sir Theophilus Shepstone with "a secret despatch empowering him to take over the Transvaal Government and country and to become the first English Governor," if on his arrival circumstances rendered this step "in any way possible." He added that he was preparing legislation to enable other States and Colonies to come into a South African Union voluntarily.

Lord Beaconsfield was not convinced of the wisdom of the policy proposed; but he made no objection. Shepstone went out, therefore, not to explore the ground in a cautious way, but to carry out a predetermined policy and to discover reasons justifying it. Led away by the opinions of a small and unrepresentative minority of the population, he arbitrarily declared the Transvaal to be annexed to the British Crown (April 12th, 1877), not even consulting the *Volksraad* on the subject. A Constitution was promised; but in the event it was delayed for two years. In the meantime, protests rained upon the British Government from every section of the population, and delegates were sent to England to plead before the bar of public opinion the cause of a hardy little people whose appreciation of the blessings of European civilisation may have been unduly limited, yet whose passionate love of freedom was deserving of all admiration. The only result was that, at the end of 1879, the Transvaal, after enjoying independence for a quarter of a century, was reduced to the humiliating status of a Crown colony. The answer of the Boers was a solemn compact binding them not to rest until freedom had been regained. The country was, by this time, seething with disaffection and repressed revolt.

The Shepstone Mission was not the only miscalculation made by the British Government in South Africa at that time. A still worse one was the decision which sent Sir Bartle Frere thither in furtherance of the same design of a premature union. Frere went out as Governor of Cape Colony and High Commissioner for South Africa, which he was expected to organise on federal lines; and Lord Carnarvon indulged the hope that within two years he would become "the first Governor-General of the South African Dominion." A man of outstanding ability, Frere was yet entirely unsuited to his new sphere of duty. He had served with distinction in administrative positions in India, where a man who is not a great success is apt to be regarded as a great failure; and his mind ran on "forward movements," scientific frontiers, tribal subjugations, and imperialistic expansion as a policy in itself. He was honestly convinced that British rule was as good for the native States in South Africa as it was in India, and that, even if not welcomed, it was nevertheless an act of kindness to impose it on them. Zululand was the first native State to disappear. A frontier dispute between it and the Transvaal had been referred to arbitration, and the award was in favour of the Zulus and their warlike King, Cetewayo. Instead of allowing the award to take effect at once, Frere endeavoured to attach to it conditions inconsistent with the independence of Cetewayo's dominion. In addition to making amends for injuries done by his people in a raid into British territory—a demand which Cetewayo was willing to meet—he was required to abolish his military system, to agree to British control of his external relations, and to accept a British Resident. This was the rough and arbitrary method of Indian frontier statecraft, translated into surroundings where its application was doubly impolitic and dangerous.

The British Cabinet had begun early to entertain apprehensions that Frere, whose masterful and impulsive ways were well known, might resort to measures which would lead to serious trouble. Lord Beaconsfield, in particular, was chagrined at the turn which events at the Cape had taken. He had kept the peace in Europe, while his colleague at the Colonial Office had stirred up tumult at the other end of the world. In accepting the policy of confederation for South Africa, he had never contemplated confederation by the sword, and his resentment at so untoward a development found incisive expression. Early in 1878, Lord Carnarvon gave place to Sir Michael Hicks Beach, who urged Frere to exercise forbearance and reasonable compromise in his dealings with the Zulus. Frere's answer was to call for reinforcements, and these were sent, though with misgiving. An ultimatum offered to Cetewayo being disregarded, Lord Chelmsford invaded the King's country (January 12th, 1879), with the result that British arms quickly sustained an irritating and undeserved reverse as Isandhlwana (January 22nd). The reverse was quickly retrieved; but Lord Chelmsford's unfortunate conduct of the ensuing campaign was responsible for further mishaps of the same kind. The most tragic was that of June 1st, which involved the death of the Prince Imperial of France, who had gallantly pressed his services upon the British military authorities as a volunteer combatant.

Great excitement, mingled with indignation, was caused at home by the disaster of Isandhlwana, which was held to be due on the one hand to Frere's wilfulness and on the other to the incompetency of the military commander; yet, in accordance with an honoured tradition of the English public service, both men were allowed to remain at their posts. A majority of the Cabinet favoured the recall of Frere; but he only experienced a mild private rebuke, duly counterbalanced by warm public praise of his ability. The Prime-Minister defended the Government's action against the attacks of the Opposition, but only for form's sake; for it was his private opinion that the wilful Governor "ought to be impeached," and he strongly resented Frere's apparent inability to understand that he had done wrong[1].

In view of the prevalent public dissatisfaction, which was reflected by diminishing Ministerial majorities in parliamentary divisions, it was decided to send out Sir Garnet Wolseley as both High Commissioner and Commander-in-Chief for Natal, the Transvaal, and the adjacent territories, the authority of Sir Bartle Frere being limited to Cape Colony. The Queen protested vigorously against the humiliation thus inflicted on "poor Sir Bartle Frere"; but, while refusing to approve the new appointments, she accepted them. Before Wolseley took charge of affairs, however, Lord Chelmsford had inflicted signal defeat on Cetewayo (July 4th), so ending a campaign which, while it excited enthusiasm in no quarter at home, evoked on the part of a large section of the nation strong disapproval. A little later, Cetewayo was captured, his army disbanded, and his kingdom, provisionally divided into a number of chieftaincies, placed under British Protection.

The Beaconsfield Cabinet fell in April, 1880, and Gladstone came into office. He had assigned to the annexation of the Transvaal and the Zulu War a prominent place in his indictment of the outgoing Ministry. Of the former act he said that, even if the Transvaal were as valuable as it was valueless, he would repudiate the annexation, since it had been effected by dishonourable means; while, in deploring the Zulu War, he spoke of the ten thousand natives who had been "slain for the only offence of attempting to defend their independence and their homes." It was natural, therefore, that the Boers of the Transvaal should look to the champion of the rights of small nationalities for the speedy restoration of their treasured freedom. Frere was recalled after a short interval; but, relying upon official assurances that the new Government was proving increasingly popular, that the Boers were settling down, and that any disturbance of the existing status would be harmful, the Cabinet gave no sign of an intention to relinquish British sovereignty in the Transvaal, the hope being entertained that, with confederation and the grant of a liberal system of self-government, disaffection would die out.

---

[1] Letter of June 28th, 1879, quoted in *Life of Beaconsfield*, VI. 438. Beaconsfield, who had an inborn contempt for failure, was equally severe on Lord Chelmsford, whom he declined to receive except officially, on his return to England, though pressed to do so by the Queen, and to whom he denied credit for the culminating victory of Ulundi. (See letter to the Queen, August 30th, 1879, *ibid*. VI. 459.)

This hope received a rude shock, when, in December, the flag of revolt was again raised and the South African Republic proclaimed at Paardeberg by the Boer leaders, Kruger, Pretorius and Joubert. Hastening to the relief of the British garrisons with an inadequate force, General Sir George Colley was defeated in an attack on the Boer position at Laings Nek, near the Natal frontier (January 28th, 1881); and, in a minor engagement at Majuba Hill a month later (February 26th–27th), he was again defeated and himself killed. Negotiations for a settlement had been in progress between the Boer and the British authorities for some time, and, before learning of the Majuba Hill incident, the Boer leaders had sent word of their acceptance of the overtures made to them. In view of this fact and of the British commander's rashness in challenging the action which had proved fatal to him, the Cabinet refused to listen to the cries for vengeance, and agreed to continue the negotiations already opened, trusting to the healing influence of an act of real magnanimity.

By the Pretoria Convention of August 3rd, 1881, the independence of the Transvaal State was recognised, subject to British suzerainty, which involved the control of its foreign relations, including the conclusion of treaties. This arrangement was modified by the London Convention of February 27th, 1884, under which the old title of South African Republic was restored, and, while the control of treaties, except with the Orange Free State, was continued, the claim to formal suzerainty was left unmentioned.

The so-called surrender to the Boers in 1881 was for many years a subject of warm controversy. The military party and the aggressive imperialists condemned it as a cowardly betrayal of the national honour, while at the other extreme was an equally convinced body of opinion, represented by the doctrine that in all circumstances of life justice must be done, though the heavens should fall. A middle party, while holding that what is morally wrong cannot be politically right, declined to draw from this sound premise the conclusion that what is morally right must always be politically wise and expedient; and, while this party spared the Government reproach, it viewed their action with anxiety. There can be little doubt that the unconditional Armistice which followed Majuba Hill—in itself an insignificant incident when viewed merely from a military standpoint—left the Boers, entrenched as most of them were behind unsurmountable ramparts of ignorance and narrowness, dangerously self-confident and arrogant, and that the misfortunes which befell them twenty years later were, in some measure, attributable to this cause.

The Transvaal did not settle down under the new order of things. The large and increasing cosmopolitan immigration which was drawn to the country by its mineral wealth and industry, particularly after the reef gold discoveries of 1886, led inevitably to an irreconcilable conflict with the Boer peasant population. President Kruger at that time exercised almost despotic powers. To much native shrewdness and keen business capacity this remarkable man unfortunately united in a dangerous degree the narrowness of vision, prejudice, and obstinacy characteristic of a pastoral community born in the freedom of nature and nurtured exclusively on the Old Testament. Regarding the "Uitlanders" as an alien and godless element in the life of a sacrosanct commonwealth, yet one whose intrusion was sure to prove transitory, he refused to listen to their claim to equal civil rights. This unreasonable attitude had an unhappy sequel on December 29th, 1895, in Dr Jameson's ill-conceived "raid" on Pretoria, with the object of seizing the government of the republic. Although this foolish and lawless enterprise, undertaken with the knowledge and goodwill of Cecil Rhodes, then Prime-Minister of the Cape, proved a fiasco, the provocative telegram of sympathy which the German Emperor addressed to President Kruger at the time had an unfortunate and far-reaching influence on general Anglo-German relations.

The federal movement and its *sequelae*, which so violently stirred the life of South Africa in the late 'seventies, recalled European attention to the fact that the partition of the great Continent had not yet been consummated. A new and stronger impulse to the general scramble for territory which now began was due to the action of King Leopold II of the Belgians in originating the International African Association of 1876 and its more important offshoot, the International Congo Association of 1878. At that time, Stanley and de Brazza were exploring the little known interior of Central Africa; though in 1881 no fewer than forty-five expeditions, of all kinds and national origins, were said to be operating simultaneously in various parts of the Continent. Stanley entered King Leopold's service in 1879 and by his explorations between that year and 1883 laid the foundations of the later Congo Free State, which remained the King's personal property until 1908, when it passed into the possession of the Belgian State and nation. Similarly, de Brazza, operating from the Ogowai and Gabun, brought a further vast tract of territory in the Congo basin under French influence, which, in 1882, was organised as the French Congo. Subsequently, King Leopold made sure of the support of France for his own dominion by promising her a right of preemption in the event of its changing hands.

The activity of these two States, and of Portugal in relation to the Congo mouth a little later, gave a strong impetus to the German Colonial movement which had been steadily growing for half a century; and Bismarck now began to respond to the pressure to which he had long been subjected from many sides in its favour. Unfortunately for Anglo-German relations, Germany, in beginning her career as a colonial Power, rushed in precisely where the British Government had feared, or at least delayed, to tread. Competition from that quarter had not hitherto been expected, owing to the repeated assurances given during a period of ten years by Lord Odo Russell, the British Ambassador in Berlin, that Bismarck desired no Colonies and that the German Parliament would refuse support to any enterprises of the kind[1].

[1] Lord Odo Russell reported on Bismarck's hostility to the acquisition of Colonies as early as 1873, and he repeated his assurance with special emphasis in a despatch of September 18th, 1880, ignoring, or making insufficient allowance for, the rapid growth of the Colonial movement in the meantime. Lord Granville wrote to Russell's successor at Berlin, Sir Edward Malet, on February 7th, 1885: "Until the receipt of a report from Lord Ampthill (Lord Odo Russell) of the 14th June last (1884) of conversations he had had with Prince Bismarck, and up to the interviews which I had about the same time with Count Herbert Bismarck, I was under the belief that the Chancellor was personally opposed to German colonisation. The reports of Lord Ampthill were continuously and strongly to that effect, and on the 15th March, 1884, his Excellency, referring to the agitation on the subject among the shipping and commercial classes in Germany, stated that it was wellknown that the Prince was absolutely opposed to their ardent desire for the acquisition of Colonies by Germany, and was determined to combat and oppose their growing influence."
The same Ambassador was equally mistaken in his depreciation of the German Naval movement. The loss of a German ship of war off Folkestone in May, 1878, led him to write to Lord Salisbury, the Foreign Secretary: "The loss of the *Grosse Kurfürst* has produced a deep impression throughout Germany and has been felt as a great national calamity. In the future this impression will tend to confirm the innate dislike of most Germans to the navy as a profession, and it will likewise confirm the German Admiralty in their resolve not to add any more large ironclads to the German Fleet" (June 6th, 1878). As a misjudgment of a national movement which had already taken firm root, this forecast could hardly be surpassed.
It is interesting to recall the very different estimate of the imperialistic forces then at work in Germany which was formed by another British diplomatist a few years earlier (1874). Writing to Lord Lyons, who accepted Lord Ampthill's word on German questions as gospel, Lord Lytton said (October 27th): "Odo's impressions that Bismarck does not want colonies rather surprise me. It seems to me a perfectly natural and quite inevitable ambition on the part of a Power so strong as Germany not to remain an inland State longer than it can help, but to get to the sea and to extend its seaboard in all possible directions. Is there any case on record of an inland State suddenly attaining to the military supremacy of Europe without endeavouring by means of its military strength and prestige to develop its maritime power? But you can't be a maritime Power without colonies. Lord Derby says that, though Germany may probably cherish such an ambition, she will have as much seaboard as she can practically want as long as she retains possession of the (Elbe) Duchies. But that is not a very convenient commercial seaboard, and I confess I can't help

Within five years, Germany had acquired in South-west Africa a large tract of territory which might at any time prior to 1882 have been claimed by Great Britain, had her Government been less undecided and short-sighted, together with the smaller Colonies of Togo and the Cameroons on the West Coast, a vast portion of East Africa, and a considerable insular dominion in the Pacific, including the north-eastern portion of New Guinea (renamed Kaiser Wilhelmsland), the New Britain (henceforth the Bismarck) Archipelago, and divers groups of small islands. Her acquisition of South-west Africa, the Cameroons, and North New Guinea led to friction and a sharp exchange of despatches with Great Britain, which claimed prior rights, though with no justification in the case of the first and the last of these territories[1].

On the other hand, the attempts of the German pioneers to snatch from British hands St Lucia Bay and Pondoland were frustrated. The hopes of the Boers were similarly disappointed by the annexation, between 1884 and 1887, of Bechuanaland, Tongaland, Zululand, Goshenland and Stellaland. Delagoa Bay, though coveted by both Great Britain and Germany, remained in Portugal's possession as the result of an arbitration award given by the President of the French Republic, in July, 1875, subject to her undertaking not to alienate it except to the former Power.

In the welter of conflicting claims and interests incidental to that time of strenuous imperialistic adventure, the Congo Conference of 1885 intervened as a mitigating and conciliatory influence. Its immediate cause was an abortive Treaty, of February 26th, 1884, by which Great Britain and Portugal had claimed to regulate the status and navigation of the Congo without consultation with other Powers. Lord Granville, who was responsible for the British share in the transaction, fully recognised that "there could be no advantage in concluding a treaty which would not be accepted by other Powers whose acceptance would

---

doubting the absence of all desire for more and better outlets to the sea, so long as her military power and prestige remain unbroken. Anyhow, there seems to be now a pretty general instinct throughout Europe, and even in America, that a policy of maritime and colonial development must be the natural result of Germany's present position; and such instincts, being those of self-preservation, are generally, I think, what Dizzy calls 'unerring' ones." Lord Newton, *Lord Lyons*, II. 60–1.

[1] As to the German annexation of Angra Pequena (South-west Africa) Lord Derby, the Colonial Secretary, wrote to Sir Hercules Robinson (December 4th, 1884), when the incident was closed, that the dispute related to "a strip of territory to which the Queen of England had no sufficient title, and which Great Britain had never thought it worth acquiring until it seemed to be wanted by our neighbour." See also, in the same sense, Sir H. H. Johnston, *The Colonization of Africa*, p. 253 and J. S. Keltie, *The Partition of Africa*, pp. 186, 191–2.

be indispensable before it could come into operation" (March 15th, 1883), and honestly did his best to secure equal navigation and trading rights for all nations. In the first draft of the Treaty, he had also proposed that the navigation of the river should be regulated by an international commission, and only when pressed by Portugal had he accepted the alternative of joint Anglo-Portuguese control. The fact remained, however, that the Treaty was a dual arrangement made over the heads of other States concerned; and on this account it caused general dissatisfaction, of which Germany made herself the mouthpiece. It was in vain that Granville invited Bismarck to nominate a German delegate to the Congo Commission, and justly pleaded that, "but for the persistent opposition of the British Government, unsupported by any other Power, Portugal would in all probability have long since established herself in the Congo district." Supported by France, Bismarck proposed an international Conference. This sat in Berlin from November 15th, 1884, to February 26th of the following year, most of the States of Europe, together with the United States of America, taking part. The result of the deliberations, in which Great Britain had a leading share, was the Congo Act of February 26th, 1885, which affirmed the principle of freedom of navigation and trade for all nations in the regions forming the basins of the Congo and the Niger, provided for the adoption of joint measures for the suppression of slavery and the slave-trade, and laid down rules relating to the future appropriation of territory on the African coast. The proposal of Great Britain and Germany that the principle of free navigation should apply to the other rivers of West Africa and to the Zambesi was opposed by France and Portugal.

The restless energies of Belgian, German and French adventurers stimulated British ambition and rivalry, and several colonial enterprises were set on foot in different parts of the African Continent by masterful pioneers of empire, impatient at the apathy and indecision of the imperial authorities at a time when the last claims to territory were being pegged out. In this way there was revived the Elizabethan institution of the Chartered Company, a method of Colonial development and administration which Bismarck, also, held more desirable than Governmental action, granting, in token of this preference, in 1885, its first charter to the German East Africa Company.

Of the modern English Chartered Companies the first to receive an administrative and trading concession was the National African Company (incorporated in 1882 and working from the West Coast), on its incorporation in 1886 as the Royal Niger Company. The Charter implied a recognition of the special position occupied in the Lower Niger region by British merchants who, up to the beginning of the 'eighties, had enjoyed a practical monopoly there. The parent Company had acquired special privileges in the Sokoto and Gando kingdoms and the petty States of the Lake Chad basin; but it gradually extended its influence higher up the Niger. Later French and German Companies, operating from different points, also made their influence felt; yet the Royal Niger Company had hitherto held its own.

On that coast, France had been specially active, pressing forward both from the north and from the west into territories which the rest of the Powers had to a large extent left alone. Since 1848, Algeria, coveted long before, had been hers by conquest and formal assumption of government, and the province served as a foothold facilitating further advance; Tunis to the east, Morocco to the west, and perhaps Tripoli, being regarded as the next objectives. A Protectorate was proclaimed in Tunis in 1881, notwithstanding the formal protest of the British Government, who, though unable to prevent this act of sheer aggression, gave France to understand that a repetition of it would not be tolerated in Tripoli. The ambition of France was to create a great empire, stretching from the Mediterranean to the Congo, and from her old colony of Senegal on the Atlantic to the Nile; and, though baulked in some places, so as to leave several notable missing links and loose ends, she eventually went far towards achieving this design. The frustration, at a later date, of her plan to establish herself in the valley of the Upper Nile[1], may have shattered a still bolder scheme with which French imperialists have been credited—namely, the creation, by the absorption of Abyssinia, of a French trans-Continental belt.

Nevertheless, the methods pursued by France, even more than her success, brought her more than once into conflict with Great Britain. Having as yet a comparatively short coastline in West Africa, she tried her utmost, in one place after another, to gain possession of the interior—a proceeding, which, wherever it was carried out, had the inevitable result of crippling the prosperity and discounting the prospects of her neighbours' Colonies. Great Britain, at various times, suffered from, and resented, this unfriendly policy. Thus, after France had annexed Dahomey in 1894, at the end of several years of warfare, her agents attempted to cut off the hinterland of Lagos, which would have thereby lost access to the Niger. This design was, indeed,

[1] See below, pp. 251 ff.

frustrated; but a heated exchange of despatches took place before the dispute was settled by a series of boundary conventions. In a letter to Lord Dufferin (March 30th, 1892) Lord Salisbury called attention to another defect of the French Colonial system. "Wherever," he wrote, "in West Africa Great Britain has undertaken the task of developing and civilising the interior, French trade profits equally with that of this country; but the tendency of French arrangements with the natives is to obtain exclusive commercial privileges for French commerce."

In East Africa, the British East African Association entered the field simultaneously with the German East African Company; and both operated for a time on the coast, under lease from the Sultan of Zanzibar, as well as in the interior. The British Company was re-incorporated as the Chartered Imperial British East Africa Company in 1888, when its concessions were enlarged. Two years later, Uganda passed into the British sphere of influence, and the Company, by Treaty with King Mwanga—the same who as heir apparent had caused the murder of Bishop Hannington in 1885—undertook the administration of the ill-governed country.

In the south of the Continent, the British South Africa Company, whose leading spirit was Cecil John Rhodes, the British empire-builder *par excellence* of the nineteenth century, was constituted under a Charter of October, 1889, for the purpose of developing and administering Matabeleland, with the tributary Mashonaland, which had passed under British Protection in the preceding year. Its field of operations, known later as Rhodesia, was indefinitely described in the Charter as the region lying to the north and west of the South African Republic and Bechuanaland, and to the west of the Portuguese dominions in East Africa; but its jurisdiction was, in 1891, extended to the territory under British influence north of the Zambesi and south of the territories of the Congo Free State and the German sphere, excluding as yet Nyasaland.

It was not long before the Company, and with it the British Government, came into conflict with Portugal. Though warned by Lord Salisbury in August, 1887—when her cartographers were busy annexing territory wholesale in that region by the simple expedient of recolouring the official maps—that the British Government could not "recognise Portuguese sovereignty in territories not occupied by her in sufficient strength to enable her to maintain order, protect foreigners, and control the natives," Portugal had, in the meantime,

14—2

persisted in advancing all sorts of unsubstantial claims to sovereignty in the Zambesi region. Not only had her Government declared that river to be the north-western boundary of the Portuguese sphere of influence in East Africa; but it had attempted to close the river against all but Portuguese vessels, and had advanced exclusive rights over the valley of Lake Nyasa, and even over Mashonaland. Portuguese troops and mercenaries, under the notorious Colonel Serpa Pinto, even invaded territory which had been formally placed under British Protection and settled by British subjects; and, when requested to recall them, their Government refused. Portugal claimed, in effect, a solid belt of territory stretching across the Continent and so isolating the British Colonies in the south.

Lord Salisbury, now again at the Foreign Office, resolutely contested these immoderate pretensions as lacking any practical basis and supported solely by what he sarcastically called "archaeological arguments." Before the Portuguese Government came to reason, however, it was necessary to threaten the suspension of diplomatic relations (January 10th, 1890) and to despatch to Lisbon a mild ultimatum. In the end, the attack on the freedom of the Zambesi was abandoned, while by the Anglo-Portuguese Convention of June 11th, 1891, the spheres of influence of the two Powers in East Africa and the Zambesi basin were delimited in such wise that, while Portugal received a portion of the territory in dispute, Nyasaland and Mashonaland remained British. Nyasaland, in the acquisition of which for the empire Sir H. H. Johnston, as Consul-General in Mozambique, played an energetic part, henceforth formed, with the Barotse kingdom, British Central Africa, of which Johnston became Commissioner.

The early history of all the Chartered Companies was one of administrative and financial difficulties and constant trouble with the native populations, taking the form of local or general revolts, which usually led to punitive expeditions. In the case of the British East Africa Company, trading and administration proved incompatible functions, as they did in that of several of the German Chartered Companies. The attempt to administer Uganda, in particular, failed completely, and in 1892 the Company was preparing to withdraw both from that country and Witu without notifying the native rulers or denouncing the Treaties which it had concluded with them.

Fearing lest Uganda should be lost to British rule and fall back into its former condition of anarchy, Lord Rosebery, ever jealous for the retention of the empire's territorial footholds, obtained a postponement of the Company's withdrawal; and in November, 1893, Sir Gerald Portal was sent from Zanzibar to investigate the position and propound a policy. It was clear that something like a moonlight flitting had been contemplated. Many of the agreements contracted by the Company with the natives had not been fulfilled; the Soudanese troops who had been introduced into the country had not been duly paid off; and works of development to which the Company had been committed had remained unexecuted. Inasmuch as the chiefs and tribes believed that in entering into contractual relations with the Company they had placed themselves under the direct Protection of the British Crown, and as the Treaties concluded by the Company had been approved by the Secretary of State, the Government felt bound in honour to assume the responsibility of facing the undischarged liabilities. Accordingly, Uganda was, in 1894, constituted a British Protectorate, and the British East Africa Company was henceforth restricted to trading operations.

In West Africa, the Royal Niger Company similarly incurred responsibilities beyond its power to meet, and, in 1900, the political rights and duties entrusted to it by Charter were revoked, the Company continuing only as a commercial enterprise. The territories which it had administered, together with Lagos and the Oil Rivers region, now passed under imperial jurisdiction as Northern and Southern Nigeria.

The career of the British South Africa Company was, for a long time, clouded by even greater political and financial difficulties. In 1893, and again in 1896, there was war between the Company and the Matabeles, entailing a deplorable loss of life. After Lobengula's power had been finally broken, rebellion continued endemic for several years, and many acts of dubious equity, prejudicial to the interests of the aborigines of Matabeleland and Mashonaland, brought upon this great imperialistic undertaking both criticism and reproach.

Italy's share in the partition of Africa proved smaller than that of the other participating Powers; but, by the end of the century, she had, with Great Britain's assistance, gained a foothold at three points. Her first acquisition, definitely secured in 1882, was the bay of Assab, on the Red Sea coast, which speedily enabled her to extend her influence on the littoral southwards so far as Bab-el-Mandeb, thus creating the dependency of Eritrea. In February, 1885, she occupied Massowah, where her presence alleviated the pressure of Mahdiism in the Eastern Soudan at a critical time. From the coast, Italy essayed to extend her influence into the interior, and by the Treaty of Uccialli (1889), concluded with King Menelek of Shoa (who had proclaimed himself Negus in 1887), she believed herself to have acquired a recognised Protectorate over Abyssinia. But the claim was not admitted on the other side; and in an attempt to assert themselves by force of arms, the Italians suffered a crushing defeat at Adowah (March, 1896). A Peace was, however, concluded with Menelek in the same year (October) which abrogated the Treaty of Uccialli and recognised the absolute independence of Ethiopia. In pursuance of an Anglo-French Agreement with Abyssinia in 1904 (April), a Convention was signed in the following year between Great Britain, France and Italy; and in 1906 (July) the three European Powers concluded a further agreement mutually guaranteeing the maintenance of the integrity of Abyssinia and organising their trade there. The Agreement was for twelve years and subsequent shorter periods. (Germany concluded a less important Treaty of Commerce with Abyssinia.) In addition, however, to her Red Sea coast Colony, Italy obtained in 1887 a large part of the Somali coast lying south of the British sphere, as dating from 1884. (Her largest African dependency, Tripoli, was added in 1911–12.)

The appearance of Germany as a Colonial Power in East Africa in 1885 had far-reaching effects for the later development of that part of the Continent. Hitherto, the Sultan of Zanzibar had not only exercised sovereignty over that island and its satellites, Pemba and Mafia, but had claimed jurisdiction on the mainland over an undefined territory stretching far inland. Great Britain had long had important interests in Zanzibar; but it had been her unchanging policy both herself to refrain from interference with the Sultan's independence and to induce other Powers to do the same. In the hope of restraining the secret ambitions of France, she concluded with her, in 1862, a Treaty by which the ruler's independence was jointly recognised. On two later occasions, in 1878 and in 1881, the British Government was invited to exercise a Protectorate over the Sultan's dominions; but the invitation was refused. It followed, none the less, that any successful attempts to disturb the existing political status might impinge upon old and well-established British rights which had not hitherto been questioned.

British influence was still supreme in Zanzibar, and upon that influence it depended whether Germany's designs were likely to prosper or to come to grief. Warned by his experience in South-west and West Africa, and in New Guinea, Granville determined to offer to Bismarck, from the outset, a helping hand by suggesting a mutual understanding. So far did his desire to meet German wishes go that he divulged to the Chancellor (March 25th, 1885) the plan of a group of British capitalists (the nucleus of the British East Africa Company) originating with Mr (later Sir) William Mackinnon, for opening up territory between the coast and the Lakes, by virtue of concessions to be obtained from the Sultan, and invited an assurance that its operations would not conflict with the interests of Germany.

German enterprise therefore enjoyed for a time not only a fair field but abundant favour. Chiefly owing to the enterprise, often far more successful than ingenuous, of Dr Karl Peters, its originator, the German East African Company concluded Treaties with the chiefs of a number of native States in the interior, as well as with Witu, on the Tana, further north. By the first delimitation of the British and German spheres of influence in 1886, the Sultan's jurisdiction on the mainland was reduced to a narrow strip of coastal territory, and, two years later, he was persuaded to lease the administration of this to the two Companies, the British Company taking the northern, and the German the southern, portion. The high-handed proceedings of the German agents, however, excited the hostility of the natives; and, as the slave-traders, resentful at the measures then being taken to destroy their traffic, made common cause with the malcontents, a general rising occurred. A blockade of the coast was now instituted by the two Powers, with a view to preventing the export of slaves and the import of arms; and this lasted for nearly a year. By that time, the German Government had recognised that Peters, a man of violent character and dubious reputation, was a source of mischief, and his Company incapable of exercising administrative functions with efficiency and credit. In 1890, therefore, Germany's East African dependency was placed under imperial administration, and the Sultan was bought out of the leased territory on the mainland.

There can be little doubt that, had Peters been allowed to execute his bold plans, he would have carried German sway far north of Lake Victoria and into the valley of the Upper Nile. He did, indeed, acquire important rights both on the Tana and in Uganda—in the latter case, owing to the machinations of the French Roman Catholic missionaries, who did their utmost at a later date to prevent this territory from passing into British hands. While, however, he was on one of his expeditions, promiscuously concluding treaties, the British and German Governments were negotiating an all-round settlement, mainly concerned with East Africa, yet also adjusting frontiers and rounding off angular places in the colonial dominions of the two States both in the south-west and the south of the Continent. When, therefore, Peters returned to Lake Victoria in the autumn of 1890, it was to learn that on July 1st (nearly four months after Bismarck had ceased to be German Chancellor) a Treaty had been concluded by which the more ambitious of his plans were foiled.

In the negotiations which led to this agreement, Germany had begun by claiming as the natural hinterland of her East African dependency the whole of the territory so far as the Congo Free State —a demand which, if conceded, would have transferred to her a large part of Rhodesia and Nyasaland, already in British occupation. The British Government demurred; and, in the end, Germany renounced in favour of Great Britain all claims to the Somaliland coast, Witu, and Uganda, thus barring her own approach to the Upper Nile valley from the south-east, while, for the rest, her western boundary marched with Lakes Tanganyika and Nyasa, with the Congo State and British Central Africa, respectively, on their further shores. Germany, also, acknowledged a British Protectorate over Zanzibar and Pemba. A later West African agreement with Germany (November 15th, 1893) stipulated that her sphere of influence should not extend eastward beyond the basin of the Shari; Darfur, Kordofan, and Bahr-el-Ghazal being excluded from it.

In Germany's favour a rectification of boundaries in West and South-west Africa was agreed upon, involving in the latter case the cession to her of a strip of territory (the *"Caprivizipfel"*) giving access from her territories to the Zambesi. Her most important gain, however, was the island of Heligoland, lying in the estuary of the Elbe. In 1884, and again in 1885, Bismarck had raised the question of the cession of the island, in view of Germany's intention to construct a ship-canal between the North and Baltic Seas. Granville had not encouraged the overtures, however, and the matter had gone no further. He was of opinion that while the cession might ensure Germany's friendly cooperation in Egypt, it would be unpopular, and that Liberal Ministers were not the right people to make it[1]. It thus fell to Salisbury to meet the German Government's wish, though it

---

[1] See *Life and Letters of the Second Earl Granville*, II. 351, 362 and 425.

would appear that Chamberlain gave the effective impetus to the transaction[1].

The Anglo-German Convention of 1890 satisfied only reasonable men, and by no means all of these, in either country. The unreasonable on both sides wanted cessions without concessions; but the cautious were unsatisfied, more especially as Salisbury chose to ridicule the adverse arguments; and it was not the least curious feature of the confused and largely futile controversies which ensued that, while the transfer of Heligoland was widely regretted in England as disastrously prejudicial to her naval power, in Germany the value of its acquisition from the standpoint of naval defence received for a long time very grudging recognition. By an exchange of Declarations (August 5th, 1890) France recognised the British Protectorate over Zanzibar and Pemba, in return for concessions of far greater importance by Great Britain, who accepted the French Protectorate in Madagascar and acknowledged extensive claims by France in Central Africa. The kingdom of Sokoto fell, however, to the Royal Niger Company. Later, the Sultan of Zanzibar transferred the administration of his possessions on the mainland and the adjacent islands, exclusive of Zanzibar and Pemba, to the British Government, though without prejudice to his sovereignty; and, in 1896, the whole of the East African territories under British Protection, with the exception of Zanzibar, Pemba and Uganda, were merged for administrative purposes in one East African Protectorate.

A study of the political map of Africa, with special reference to the imperialistic efforts of the British, French, Belgian and German explorers and pioneers from 1880 onward, will show how naturally these efforts, though directed from different points, converged upon the Southern Soudan. As the Protector of Egypt and her Soudan provinces, Great Britain had a paramount interest in keeping intruders out of the valley of the Upper Nile. This object was attained by a series of Conventions, completed only in 1899, the negotiation of which required in most cases generous compensatory concessions. The earliest was concluded with Germany, the latest with France[2].

By various Treaties and Conventions concluded with neighbouring Powers during the period surveyed, an enormous addition had been made to the British empire and concurrently to its political, financial and defensive liabilities. Lord Rosebery, who took a prominent part

[1] See *Die Grosse Politik der Europäischen Kabinette*, 1871–1914, VI. 408.
[2] See pp. 250–7.

in furthering this policy of imperial expansion, estimated, in 1896, that in the course of twelve years territory to the extent of over two and a half million square miles—an area equal to two-thirds of Europe— had passed under British rule; and he warned his countrymen that their popularity with the rest of the world had not been increased in consequence.

Lord Salisbury observed, on one occasion, that Africa seemed to have been created in order to plague the lives of British Foreign Secretaries. Of the territorial disputes which for many years clouded the relations between Great Britain and France from 1882 onwards, none, with the single exception of Egypt, gave rise to greater anxiety than that which was caused by the attempts of successive French Governments to assert exclusive sovereignty over Madagascar. Any claims of France to political rights in this island were of the most shadowy kind, for the French were the latest of European nations to obtain any sort of footing there[1]. From the beginning of the nineteenth century, a close and ever strengthening tie was formed between Great Britain and the Hovas and their rulers, first owing to the help given to them by the flourishing Mauritius colony, and still more by the efforts of the missionaries, who carried to the island many of the arts and crafts of civilisation, with rational methods of agriculture, reduced the language to writing, brought in printed books, established schools and hospitals, and in great measure Christianised the population.

When this work had been done, France stepped in, and, reviving early political claims, which long ago had been formally renounced, gave the Hovas no rest until they had surrendered their independence as the penalty of defeat in war. In 1879, disputes on the subject of land tenure occurred between French settlers and the Hova Government, which dared to adhere to its own interpretation of Malagasy customary law. In order to bring matters to an issue, the French Government in 1882 claimed a Protectorate over the north-west of the island, in virtue of agreements said to have been concluded in 1841 with certain rebel chiefs, who had professed to cede rights which were not theirs to dispose of. The claim was the more remarkable,

---

[1] " L'histoire, la tradition, et beaucoup l'imagination, avaient créé entre Madagascar et nous de tels liens qu'aucun homme d'État ne pouvait les négliger." C. de Freycinet (on the War with Madagascar in 1885), Souvenirs, 1878-1893, p. 268.

since the British and French Governments were pledged to act in concert in all matters relating to Madagascar, and since, in 1868, they had joined with America in recognising the undivided sovereignty of the reigning Queen.

Worse was to follow; for the French Government next claimed rights over the whole island, and when this claim was challenged resorted to violent measures. In June, 1883, an ultimatum not having met with compliance, Tamatave was first bombarded and then occupied; whereupon the French naval commander, Admiral Pierre, proceeded to assert the rights of the conqueror as against both the Hovas and the British settlers. He insulted the British flag, ordered the British Consul, T. C. Pakenham, though dangerously ill, to leave Tamatave within twenty-four hours—an order only frustrated by his death—and threw into prison and confined for eight weeks Mr Shaw, a missionary of many years' standing, on the grotesque charge of having tampered with French troops and attempted to poison their food. Redress for these and other indignities offered to British subjects was demanded and given, and acceptance was the easier in consideration of the plea, which appears to have been well founded, that Admiral Pierre, who likewise died soon afterwards, was insane.

In the following year, the attack upon the rights of the Hovas was resumed on the old pretext, and there followed further overbearing treatment of British traders, whose interests suffered greatly. Bravely though they struggled, the Hovas never had a serious chance of successful resistance; yet, even when beaten, they continued for a long time to reject the French offer of peace on the basis of a Protectorate. In March of that year, the Ferry Cabinet fell, discredited by a military defeat in Tonkin, and for a time imperialism was unpopular in France. The incoming Minister, de Freycinet, took office with a programme devised to "delimit the field of our ambitions and in consequence the extent of our sacrifices"; and he accordingly proposed to moderate the French claims. At the end of the year, a Treaty was concluded by which the Malagasy Queen gave to France control of her foreign concerns, placed the Malagasies under French Protection abroad, and agreed to the institution of a French Resident at her capital, Antananarivo. Though the word was not used, the arrangement practically amounted to a Protectorate.

The British Government attached great importance to de Freycinet's assurance (December 27th) that this agreement "made no change in the Treaties already existing between the Hova Government and other States," and that it never entered into the thoughts of the French Government to impede the free development of the private interests of other nations in Madagascar. This assurance was repeated in a more specific manner in 1890, when Great Britain formally recognised the French Protectorate. The Declarations exchanged on that occasion (August 5th) stated explicitly that the Protectorate would "not affect any rights or immunities enjoyed by British subjects in that island." These rights, conferred by a Treaty with Madagascar of June 27th, 1865, included exterritorial jurisdiction, trading rights over the whole island (with the exception of three towns venerated as sacred), equal rights as to the acquisition of land, most-favoured-nation treatment, and a stipulation that the import and export duties should not exceed 10 per cent. *ad valorem.*

The first attack was made upon the Capitulations in 1892. Salisbury offered to accept French jurisdiction over British subjects in return for a reciprocal concession by France in Zanzibar (May 16th); but France wanted something for nothing, and contended that the acceptance of her Protectorate "with its consequences" implied the renunciation of every privilege which restricted French influence. For three years, no progress was made on this question; but, in the meantime, France continued the work of armed penetration and conquest. During 1894 and 1895 ensued more expeditions, ultimatums and blockadings. Tamatave was occupied, evacuated, and occupied again, until at last the Hova opposition was broken down, and by Treaties of October 1st, 1895, and January 18th, 1896, first the Government, and then the Queen of the island, formally accepted French rule.

Madagascar was still only a Protectorate, however, and, not having been annexed, it did not form an integral part of the French dominions. Hence, all the existing Malagasy Treaties and Conventions were legally valid. The French Government recognised this, and, in November, 1895, gave the assurance that, though Madagascar had passed under French influence, "no external difficulties would or could arise," since the Government would "respect the engagements which they had contracted with certain foreign Powers," adding: "France has always been faithful to her word[1]." As to the obligations which the Hovas had contracted, it was said that France would observe "with complete loyalty" the rules of international law applicable in such a case.

In the following year, the effect of the change of status was felt

[1] M. Berthelot in the Chamber of Deputies, November 27th, 1895.

when, in accordance with the principles which have governed French Colonial policy everywhere and at all times, preferential treatment was accorded to French trade with the island. Salisbury declined to waive the right to equal treatment which had been guaranteed to British subjects by the Treaty of 1865. In an acute and unanswerable argument from international law, developed in a despatch of April 25th, 1896, he contended that this Treaty was still in full and undiminished force, and he refused to admit "that a war which was avowedly undertaken to maintain the protectorate under which British rights were unassailable can be used to justify an arrangement by which these rights are abrogated."

France could not gainsay this claim, but she could evade it; and this was now done by converting protection into annexation. A month after the date of Lord Salisbury's despatch, a Bill with this object was introduced in the Chamber, and it took effect on August 6th. An *annexe* to the Law decreed the exemption of French goods from import duties in Madagascar and the isles. M. Hanotaux, then Foreign Minister, admitted that the Law was intended to meet the difficulty created by the existence of separate Treaties between Madagascar and Great Britain and the United States. The position was now left, in his words, "clear and decided," but it was by no means left satisfactory. Being masters of the situation, the French authorities in the island spared no pains to harm British enterprise, both commercial and evangelistic. Ignoring the conventional minimum of 10 per cent. *ad valorem*, they imposed import duties so high as to exclude all goods except those of French origin, which were admitted free; they restricted the coasting trade to vessels flying the French flag; they gave preference to French subjects in the matter of land tenure; and, in official publications, the natives were bidden to buy only French goods in token of loyalty to their new masters. In short, the traditional French Colonial policy of exclusive trading was enforced in the most virulent forms. In one district, the French administrator warned the native traders against buying from or selling to any "foreigners," and enjoined them to trade only with French merchants, on pain of imprisonment in irons. When the British Foreign Secretary brought this charge to the knowledge of the French Government, a declaration of its baselessness was produced from the Governor-General; but the British Ambassador in Paris was able to prove that this official had himself issued a printed Instruction to the provincial administrators which practically bore out the accusation.

It was in vain that Salisbury, in despatch after despatch sent to Paris, recalled the undertaking upon the strength of which Great Britain had agreed to recognise the French Protectorate, viz. that "the rights and immunities enjoyed by British subjects" should not be affected, and lodged his Government's resolute "protest against action which in their opinion is inconsistent with the international rights of this country and with the assurances given by the Government of the Republic." The French Foreign Minister deemed it a sufficient answer to this imputation of bad faith to remind Lord Salisbury that French customs, legislation and tariffs applied equally to the mother-country and to the Colonies, and to forward for his information copies of the laws and decrees by which British rights were annulled.

The new *régime* was eventually accepted by the British Government in the Anglo-French Convention of April, 1904, under which all protest against the preferential customs arrangements was withdrawn. In the meantime, the trade with Madagascar was more and more passing into French hands. In 1896, only one-half of the value of Madagascar's external trade fell to France, while twelve years later the proportion had increased to four-fifths.

III. TERRITORIAL SETTLEMENTS WITH THE UNITED STATES

A. *The Venezuela Boundary Dispute*, 1887–1899

During the later decades of the century the Monroe doctrine gained new prominence, and attempts were made by successive United States Governments to give to it an interpretation going far beyond that which had hitherto been tacitly accepted. In a Message of 1870, urging the annexation of San Domingo, President Grant formally asserted that "hereafter no territory on this Continent shall be regarded as subject of transfer to a European Power," and even predicted that the time was not far distant when, "in the natural course of events, the European political connexion with this Continent will cease." That declaration has since remained a mere expression of opinion; yet a later President, Roosevelt, could claim with truth that the Monroe doctrine had "not been allowed to be fossilised, but had been adapted to meet the growing and changeful needs of America" (August 11th, 1905).

It was a fact of happy augury that, concurrently with this tendency to attach new and far-going implications to a political maxim which has never yet received the force of international law, there has been an increasing disposition to resort to Arbitration for the settlement of the Boundary and other disputes which have occurred from time to time between American and European States. The long-standing frontier dispute between Great Britain and Venezuela relating to the western boundary of British Guiana was settled in this way in 1899. This dispute was practically as old as the British tenure of the colony, and for more than half a century it had been a source of constant friction with Venezuela. In 1848, Sir Robert Schomburgk was sent out to survey the colony; and the boundary adjacent to the Orinoco as defined by him, and known as the Schomburgk line, was thereafter accepted by the British Government. On the other hand, the Venezuelan Government had claimed the Essequibo river, lying further to the east, as the true and natural frontier between the two territories. The fact would appear to be undisputed that, in the absence of a clear understanding, each side tried at different times to encroach on the other.

In 1886, towards the close of Gladstone's third Administration, a Treaty was drawn up providing for the submission of the dispute to Arbitration by a third State or by several States, as might be arranged; but, before this agreement could be completed, a new Ministry came into power and declined to proceed with the arbitration proposal, falling back on the Schomburgk line. Annoyed by the British attitude, the Government of Venezuela had unwisely avenged itself by the illegal and violent treatment of British subjects trading in the country; and for an indefensible act of the kind committed in 1883 it was compelled to give compensation, though this was obtained only in 1887 as the result of an ultimatum. In that year, diplomatic relations between the two countries were suspended.

Already, the American Government, at the instance of Venezuela, had made repeated friendly representations on the subject in London, and in December, 1886, Mr Bayard, Secretary of State, tendered a formal offer of mediation, which Lord Salisbury declined. The refusal, however, had an important result; for it determined the American Government not to allow the question to fall again into the background. At its instigation, Venezuela provisionally resumed diplomatic relations with Great Britain in 1890; but, as further direct negotiations between the two States still proved unsuccessful, the American Ambassador in London in January, 1895, again sounded the British Foreign Secretary (now the Earl of Kimberley) as to whether his Government would accept Mediation. The result was an offer to the United States to arbitrate in regard to all territory outside the Schomburgk line and the submission, by arrangement, of a Memorandum on the subject to the American Government.

To this Memorandum, Secretary Olney made an elaborate and, for a friendly Power, highly contentious rejoinder (July 20th), emphasising the American standpoint and the solidarity of the republican States of the American Continent. He alleged that records published by the British Government as official showed that, between the years 1884 and 1886, Great Britain had claimed an extended dominion over a region of 33,000 square miles, and pointed out that this was a virtual challenge to the Monroe Doctrine, since it implied the "forcible assumption by a European Power of political control over an American State." Charging Great Britain with basing her titl to possession upon her strength and the inability of a weak State like Venezuela to enforce its rights, he suggested that this attitude was not to be defended or reconciled with "that love of justice and fair play so eminently characteristic of the English race," and added that it was quite impossible that the United States could assent to it. The British Government were, therefore, asked to state definitely whether they would consent or decline to submit the Boundary question in its entirety to impartial Arbitration; and it was stated that a refusal would be "calculated greatly to embarrass the future relations between this country and Great Britain."

Seldom had a British Government been subjected to such plain speaking on its duty to its neighbours as was contained in this document, whose importance was increased by the fact that a joint resolution of Congress had quite recently urged the determination of the dispute by friendly Arbitration. The Olney despatch was communicated in August to Lord Salisbury, who had succeeded to the Foreign Office in the previous month. In his reply (November 26th) he entered into an academic discussion of the Monroe doctrine, pointing out that the interpretation given by the despatch went beyond the intentions of its author in 1823, and disputing its relevancy, even in this extended application, to the question at issue. Nor was he prepared to admit the acceptance of the doctrine in any form by the British Government, since international law must be founded on the general consent of nations, and the doctrine had not hitherto been recognised by other countries. The entire tone of the reply was in so marked a contrast to the conciliatory attitude shown of late by Lord Salisbury in his negotiations on frontier questions with other Powers far less near than the United States to Great Britain in all national affinities, as to suggest the influence of minds less flexible and prescient than his own.

In his next Message to Congress (December 17th, 1895), President Cleveland openly accused Great Britain of taking possession of "the territory of one of our neighbouring republics," once more cited the Monroe doctrine against her, and claimed for the United States the right to decide the disputed boundary. In the following month a Commission was appointed under the authority of Congress to investigate and report on the true divisional line; but, before its work began, the Secretary of State invited the cooperation of the disputant Governments. Lord Salisbury at once concurred, and gave the British Ambassador in Washington full power to discuss the question at issue with the authorities there. The outcome was a proposal by the British Government (May 22nd) for the appointment of a more authoritative Commission, to consist of four members, two appointed by each country, to ascertain the historical facts of the question. The finding of a majority of the Commission was to be binding on both Governments, and on the basis of its report the Governments of Great Britain and Venezuela were to endeavour to agree upon a boundary-line. Failing agreement, the whole question was to be referred to a Tribunal of three members, one nominated by Great Britain, one by Venezuela, and the third co-opted by these two, who should fix the boundary-line finally. It was proposed, however, that the Tribunal should not have power to assign to either Great Britain or Venezuela territory which was *bonâ fide* occupied by subjects of the other State on January 1st, 1887, though it might make recommendations regarding such territory.

Against these reservations the American Government strongly protested as being intended to operate to the advantage of the British claim, and as ruling out of Court the discussion of rights which had been disputed for decades by Venezuela. "Venezuela is not to be stripped of her rightful possessions," wrote Secretary Olney on June 12th, "because the British Government has erroneously encouraged its subjects to believe that such possessions were British." Recognising that the time had come for finality in the matter, Lord Salisbury wisely withdrew his reservations in their uncompromising form, and agreed to the dispute being submitted to unconditional Arbitration, provided America were prepared to stand in Venezuela's place for that purpose. There was still some stickling for "national honour"; but the Foreign Office was now sensible of the indignity as well as danger of an unseemly wrangle over a few square miles of territory. The urgency of a definite settlement had also been emphasised by a further irritating incident—the arrest by the Venezuelan authorities in June of a British official, while engaged within the Schomburgk line, an act speedily repudiated by the Central Government.

In his speech at the opening of Congress on December 7th, 1896, President Cleveland was able to say that the Venezuelan Boundary Question had ceased to be a matter of difference between Great Britain and the United States. The result of further negotiations was a Treaty of February 2nd, 1897, by which the disputing States agreed to submit the question to Arbitration, to be exercised by a Tribunal consisting of five jurists: two on the part of, and nominated by, Great Britain, two on the part of Venezuela (one nominated by that State and the other by the United States of America), and the fifth to be chosen by the other four, or, failing such choice, by the King of Sweden and Norway. All questions, including the final decision, were to be determined by the vote of the majority of all the Arbitrators. The Tribunal met in Paris in December, 1898, the British members being Lord Russell of Killowen, and Sir R. H. (afterwards Lord) Collins; America was represented by Chief-Justice M. W. Fuller and Justice D. J. Brewer; and these four arbitrators coopted the Russian jurisconsult Professor F. de Martens. The award, as made on October 3rd, 1899, gave the larger part of the disputed area to the British colony[1].

B. *The Behring Sea Fishery and Alaska Disputes*, 1893–1899

In 1893 a dispute between Great Britain (representing Canada) and the United States relating to the Behring Sea seal fisheries was similarly settled by arbitration. In this case, each of the Powers concerned appointed two members of a tribunal of seven, while the others were appointed by disinterested European States. The American claim to regard the Behring Sea as *terra clausa* to foreign fishing was disallowed, and the principle of the three miles limit of exclusion was held to apply.

Before the Venezuela Boundary Commission had completed its work, Lord Salisbury proposed (July 1st, 1899) that the same Arbitration Convention should be applied in the adjustment of the dispute

---

[1] The precedent set in the Venezuela dispute was followed in the case of a dispute between French Guiana and Brazil in 1900, and in another between British Guiana and Brazil in 1904.

with the United States respecting the frontier between the south-eastern portion of Alaska—a vast, but sparsely populated, territory purchased by the United States from Russia in 1867—and British Columbia, since 1871 part of the Dominion of Canada. The difference was of long standing; but it had only become important 'owing to the opening of the Yukon gold region in 1897, inasmuch as the ownership of the principal sea entrance to the mining region was involved. The American Government, while not recognising the applicability of the Venezuelan procedure to the case of Alaska, nevertheless accepted the principle of settlement by Arbitration[1].

C. *The Panama Canal Treaties*, 1899–1901

While the Venezuela Boundary dispute was in process of adjust-ment, the British and American Governments were also engaged in a controversy relating to the Panama Canal scheme, which had been left uncompleted by a French Company in 1891. American opinion had approved the dictum of President Hayes, uttered in 1880 when de Lesseps was agitating his great scheme: "The policy of this country is a Canal under American control." As yet, however, the way was blocked by the Clayton-Bulwer Treaty of April 19th, 1850 (so called because it was concluded on behalf of the American and British Governments respectively by Secretary of State J. M. Clayton and Sir Henry Lytton Bulwer (afterwards Lord Dalling and Bulwer), then British Ambassador in Washington). By this Treaty, the two Powers renounced exclusive control over any waterway which might be con-structed between the Atlantic and Pacific Oceans in connexion with the river St Juan de Nicaragua, and agreed never to erect or maintain fortifications commanding it, or to occupy, colonise, or exercise dominion over, Nicaragua, Costa Rica, the Mosquito Coast, or any part of Central America, or to acquire any special rights or advantages in regard to commerce or navigation through the Canal. In the critical Article VIII, they finally agreed to extend their protection to any other practicable communications across the Central American isthmus, subject to the condition that only such charges and con-ditions of traffic thereupon should be imposed as the two Governments should approve as just and equitable, and that any such canal or railway should be open to the subjects and citizens of Great Britain and the United States on equal terms.

[1] Cf. p. 297.

15—2

So long as this Convention continued in force, it was open to neither Power to take independent action in constructing a canal or obtaining the exclusive control over a canal which construction would confer; and, from the beginning of the 'eighties there was an increasing desire in America to find a way out of the inconvenient contract. When de Lesseps abandoned his ill-fated venture, the American Government and nation determined to complete the unfinished work; and, during the next few years several Commissions of Enquiry were instituted, and negotiations were also opened with the Central American States affected. The result was that, in 1899, a Bill was laid before Congress empowering the President to acquire from the republics of Costa Rica and Nicaragua the control of such territory as might be necessary to the construction of the canal, and to make provision for its defence and that of its harbours when completed. Although Great Britain would have been within her legal rights in following an obstructive policy, her Government wisely met the American aspirations in a broad and generous spirit. By the Pauncefote-Hay Treaty of November 18th, 1901, all obstacles in the way of the construction of a canal by the American Government and the exercise by that Government of the rights incidental to such construction were removed, subject to the maintenance of the general principle of neutralisation, as affirmed by Article VIII of the Convention of 1850.

The Treaty was concluded towards the close of the third and last Government of Lord Salisbury, when the Marquis of Lansdowne had taken his place as Foreign Secretary. Several years earlier, the British and American Governments had concluded a General Treaty of Arbitration (February 18th, 1897), intended to operate in the first instance for five years; but it failed to pass the American Senate, and the first agreement of this kind with America did not take effect till 1908, after ten such Treaties had been concluded with European States between the years 1903 and 1905.

IV. FOREIGN ENCROACHMENTS IN CHINA, 1885-1898

The later years of the nineteenth century witnessed a complete change in the relations of the Chinese empire to the Western Powers. By the Treaty of Tientsin, 1858, China had partially opened her doors to the foreigner and his commerce, and had even promised toleration to the Christian religion. Supplementary Conventions followed from time to time, enlarging the sphere of intercourse with the outside world; yet every new concession was made grudgingly, and more or less on compulsion.

As the European Power having the greatest political and commercial interests in Central Asia, Great Britain exercised a predominant influence at Tientsin until far into the last quarter of the century, and her efforts were steadily directed towards the maintenance of the empire's integrity and independence. An entirely new situation arose when France, Russia and Japan began to advance territorial claims at China's expense. No country has shown greater skill and resource in converting shadowy claims into concrete rights than France; and the Treaties and Conventions concluded in the early 'eighties, by which she acquired a formal Protectorate over Annam, with its dependencies of Cochin China, Cambodia and Tongking, might all be traced to, more or less, vague agreements, going back many years and hitherto allowed to remain dormant.

The French republic was then on the threshold of a new epoch of Colonial enterprise, intended to efface the humiliations of 1870 and 1871, and minister to the nation's reawakened craving for glory. So long as these enterprises seemed to prosper, the most popular man in France was Jules Ferry, the Foreign Minister who initiated them. War with China, however, ensued; and a small defeat in Tongking, in March 1885, in which a French General was wounded, drove Paris, ever unstable as the waves of the sea, into a furious panic. Ferry fell, and his successor, de Freycinet, taking office as the liquidator of a Foreign Policy which for the time had become discredited, hastily concluded a Peace, by which China recognised full French domination in Tongking. Two provisions of the Treaty, in the traditional spirit of French Colonial policy, aroused British opposition. One was to the effect that, if China should decide to construct railways, she should employ French industry and *personnel*. Lord Granville objected to this stipulation as securing to France special advantages and hence conflicting with the "most favoured nation treatment" principle; but his apprehensions were removed by the addition of the rider: "It is understood that this clause shall not be regarded as constituting an exclusive privilege in favour of France." The opinion of plain men was that, if the rider had any meaning or value, it followed that the original provision had none, but that, if the French Government assented to it with a reservation, the Foreign Office must have allowed itself to be hoodwinked. France, subsequently, wished to bind China to impose lower import duties on goods entering by her land frontier from French territory; but to this proposal Lord Salisbury refused to agree.

While France was pressing China in the south, Japan and Russia were maturing designs against her dependencies of Corea and Manchuria in the north-east. In April, 1885, fearing that Russia contemplated the seizure of a position on the Corean coast, Great Britain suddenly occupied Port Hamilton, without prior communication with either the suzerain State or its vassal. Though described as a temporary measure, the act was an open violation of international law and comity; and the British Foreign Office, when challenged by the Chinese Government, could offer no defence except that, if Great Britain had not occupied the port, another Power would probably have done so. China made no further protest, and was preparing to enter into an agreement sanctioning the occupation as a temporary arrangement, subject to the protection of her suzerain rights, when an unexpected development occurred. This consisted in a formal warning by Russia to the Tsung-li-Yamen that, if the British occupation of Port Hamilton was permitted, she would, in her turn, seize some other foothold in Corea. In view of this threat, and of the probability that Japan would follow Russia's example, the Chinese Government declined to sign the intended agreement, and pressed for immediate evacuation, the Corean Government following suit, and refusing to consider a British offer to take a lease of the port as a coaling-station.

Lord Granville, making the best of a bad case, continued negotiations without success until June, when it fell to Lord Salisbury to straighten out what had by this time become a very awkward tangle. Meanwhile, a naval investigation of the port from the strategical standpoint had established the convenient fact that its occupation was undesirable, inasmuch as, unless converted into a first-class fortress, it would actually be a source of weakness to the squadron cruising in Chinese waters. Moreover, the occupation was proving expensive, and the vessels stationed there were needed for service elsewhere. In view of this report and of a promise by China that the port should not be occupied by any other Power, the British flag was hauled down in February, 1887, and Port Hamilton and the islands were abandoned as quietly as they had been occupied two years before.

Seven years later (June, 1894—March, 1895) the Corean War between Japan and China supervened; and the world awoke to the fact that with the rise of the island kingdom of the Pacific a new and powerful factor had entered into the politics of the Far East. For

China, the War was a sequence of disasters and humiliations, since, alike on land and on sea, the Japanese swept away all opposition. After Corea had been occupied, the victors turned their attention to Chinese territory and captured, in quick succession, Port Arthur, Kiaochow, Talienwan and Wei-Hai-Wei. Thus, before long, a little known State, smaller in area than France or Germany, and with a population of some forty millions, had reduced to impotence a vast empire twenty-five times its size, whose people were numbered by the hundred million. By the Treaty of Shimonoseki (April 15th, 1895) China was required to cede the Liao Tung peninsula, including Port Arthur, Formosa and the Pescadores Islands. Under the pressure of Russia, Germany and France, however, the victorious State was later compelled to forgo any foothold on the mainland. This it did in consequence of a strong Identical Note, which was served upon the Japanese Foreign Minister by the three Allied Powers on April 23rd[1]. Great Britain declined an invitation to join in inflicting this humiliation upon Japan, whom she had been the first of European Powers to welcome into the family of nations. Russia received from China, as a thank-offering for her help in time of need, important railway concessions in Manchuria.

The Corean War, following on that with France, and many indications that Russia likewise contemplated aggressive designs, did much to revive in China the old antipathy against foreigners, which had seemed to have died down. In 1891, there had been anti-foreign riots in many parts of the Yangtse region, in which several Englishmen were killed and much property, chiefly French, was destroyed. The Government duly punished the aggressors, and, in June of that year, an imperial Decree ordered the Viceroys and Governors to furnish protection to the missionary establishments and to discourage the growing readiness to credit the idle stories which were always current to their prejudice. Nevertheless, increasing vigilance and pressure were needed on the part of the Treaty Governments to secure the due observance of the various guarantees, concessions and capitulations on the strength of which their subjects had carried on the policy of commercial and industrial exploitation.

The first indication that a serious storm was near was the murder of two German missionaries in the province of Shantung in August, 1897. Germany promptly demanded redress, and occupied the harbour

---

[1] In its original form, the German Note contained a veiled threat of armed action, if Japan refused to comply, and the Minister insisted upon the omission of this.

of Kiaochow as a pledge. The Chinese Government was required to punish the murderers, to dismiss the provincial Governor on the ground of neglect of duty, to restore a German church which the rioters had destroyed, to pay an indemnity of 200,000 taels of silver, together with the costs of occupying Kiaochow, and to lease that port to the German empire for 99 years.

However convenient for Germany a pretext for the occupation of this Chinese territory may have been, the fact remains that occupation had been decided on at least two years before. In the spring of 1895, the German Emperor had sounded the Tsar as to his willingness to assist him in obtaining a naval foothold in China, and his overtures had been received favourably, though no particular part of the coast was named at the time[1]. In the following year, Admiral von Tirpitz, on his appointment to the command of the China station, received an express commission to "seek out a place on the Chinese coast where Germany could construct a military and economic base[2]." Three points were suggested as worthy of special attention—Amoy, Samsa Bay and the Chusan Islands. The acquisition of Kiaochow had been considered, but unfavourably, on the ground that the port lay too far north. Now, Tirpitz harked back to it. Having first come to an understanding with the Tsar, the German Emperor in November gave instructions for the occupation of the port, with the adjacent territory, and China formally leased it to Germany by the Treaty of January 5th, 1898.

The seizure of Kiaochow was the signal for an unseemly scramble for Chinese territory on the part of four of the other Great Powers of Europe. Several years earlier, the Chinese Government had offered to Russia the use of that port for her warships; but advantage was not taken of the offer. Count Muravieff, the Foreign Minister, now wished to seize at once Port Arthur or Talienwan, and to convert it into a permanent naval base, in spite of the fact that Russia had concluded a defensive alliance with China, which carried the recognition of her territorial integrity. The Ministers of War and Marine warmly supported the proposal, and, though other Ministers opposed it, the Tsar acquiesced against his better judgment, and both points were occupied in December, 1897, and formally acquired by forced agreement on March 15th following. Having ejected Japan from the

---

[1] See *Memoirs of Prince Hohenlohe* (English translation), II. 463, and Otto Hammann, *Der neue Kurs*, pp. 115–117.
[2] See his *Erinnerungen* (1919), pp. 61–78.

Gulf of Petchili two years before, Russia now took the forbidden booty, and with it the risks involved. In a letter of March 28th, William II complimented the Tsar upon his achievement and greeted him as "the master of Peking." Lord Salisbury judged more correctly, when he predicted that Port Arthur would prove an unprofitable investment for Russia. A proposal made at that time in England that an international conference should be called to deliberate on the affairs of China was discouraged by the German Emperor, as likely to prove a check upon Russia's freedom of action.

A little later, Great Britain obtained a lease of Wei-Hai-Wei, with the islands in the Bay, in the province of Shantung (July 1st, 1898), to be held so long as Russia retained Port Arthur; and she also acquired an extension of the Hong-Kong territory. In the following year, Great Britain concluded an agreement with Russia, by which Manchuria was recognised as the Russian, and the Yangtse valley as the British, sphere of influence. France obtained the assurance that Kwang-Chow-Wan should be reserved as her special sphere of influence, and Italy, too, put in a claim; but, by this time, China's patience was exhausted, and she refused assent. By these provocative appropriations of territory Chinese exasperation was heated to the flash-point. The agitation against foreigners grew in proportions and intensity, and eventually took the form of the Boxer outbreak, which, two years later, overspread and convulsed the northern part of the empire.

V. Unfulfilled Provisions of the Treaty of Berlin

A. *The Armenian Question*, 1894–1904

At the close of the War with Russia in 1877–8, Turkey gave an undertaking, first, to that Power in the San Stefano Treaty, then, to Great Britain in the Cyprus Convention, and finally to the Great Powers collectively in the Treaty of Berlin, that she would put an end to the misgovernment and terror from which her Armenian subjects had immemorially suffered. Nevertheless, the repeated attempts made to secure the fulfilment by the Porte of its pledge—as by the Powers jointly in 1880, by Lord Granville in 1883, and by Lord Rosebery in 1886—only produced further promises, which there was no intention of keeping; and, in the meantime, the condition of the Armenians became worse.

The undertaking given to Russia included a guarantee of security against the Kurds and Circassians in particular; yet the provincial

Governors and minor officials in the Armenian vilayets continued to encourage and incite the Kurdish irregular troops—the Bashi-Bazouks of Asiatic Turkey—to systematic massacre and pillage. In July, 1894, news reached Constantinople of an alleged Armenian revolt in the Sassoon district of the vilayet of Bitlis, and additional troops of this dangerous type were moved into the region. Sir Philip Currie, the British Ambassador, protested against their employment, and warned the Sultan's Ministers of the risk which was being run; but his words were ignored. The result was a repetition, on a larger scale, of the Bulgarian Atrocities of 1876. In due time, the so-called revolt was reported to have been suppressed; but nothing was said of the means employed, and, once again, it was due to investigation at the hand of foreign Powers that the awful facts were disclosed. The slaying, rapine and destruction of property now lasted with little intermission for over two years.

In London, the Earl of Kimberley (Foreign Secretary in Lord Rosebery's short-lived Government) and, in Constantinople, Sir Philip Currie were unremitting in their endeavours to check the excesses, and to bring the criminals to justice; but, even when their pressure caused an enquiry to be instituted, the Porte at first unblushingly described it as one into the conduct of the Armenians, and not into that of the licentious soldiery responsible for the massacres. Convinced that there was far greater likelihood of the truth being ascertained by means of an Ottoman enquiry assisted by Europeans, than by a European thwarted by the Ottoman authorities, the Ambassadors in Constantinople required that Consular Delegates should be attached to the Commission. The evidence taken in the course of the investigation, which lasted from January until the end of July, 1895, formed a record of iniquity hardly equalled before in the history of Turkish misrule. "Not merely massacres, but horrors unutterable, unspeakable, unimaginable by the mind of man[1]"—such was Lord Rosebery's description of the crimes now brought to light. The principal English investigator, Mr H. S. Shipley, reported that it was the conviction of the Delegates, "arrived at from the evidence brought before us, that the Armenians were massacred without distinction of age or sex, and indeed, for a period of some three weeks, it is not too much to say that they were absolutely hunted like wild beasts, being killed wherever they were found[2]." It was clear that whatever violence

[1] Speech at Newton Abbot, May 15th, 1896.
[2] *Memorandum on the Joint Report of the Consular Delegates to the Sassoon Commission of July* 29th, 1895, communicated to Lord Salisbury, October 16th, 1895.

had been shown at the outset by the Armenians had been a reply to unprovoked attacks deliberately made on them by the Kurds, with a view to justifying subsequent reprisals, and that in these reprisals the aggressors were encouraged by the local authorities and had the support of the Mussulman population.

Nevertheless, in a conversation with the Earl of Kimberley, Rustem Pasha, the Ambassador of the Porte in London, ignoring the Treaty of Berlin and the Cyprus Convention, coolly enquired upon what grounds the British Government based their claim to interfere in the internal affairs of Turkey (March 28th, 1895). On May 11th, a modest programme of reforms, which had been agreed upon by the British, French and Russian Ambassadors and approved by their Governments—the Tsar refusing, however, to be a party to any kind of coercion—was communicated to the Porte. What happened was just what had invariably occurred before in similar circumstances. The Porte protested, temporised and finally made counter-proposals of a more or less worthless kind—all for the purpose of evading action of any kind.

There was an outcry on the part of generous humanitarians in England, when the Government took no measures independently with a view to compelling the Porte to make amends for the present and give hostages for the future. Lord Rosebery, however, held that to have done so would have exposed Great Britain to the very real risk of having to face the opposition of the other Powers, and particularly Russia. Unable to see eye to eye on this question with Gladstone, who advocated a policy of resolute action, and deeming his position untenable in view of the state of parties both in the House of Commons and the country, Lord Rosebery resigned office in June. His Government had done all that was possible by moral means to move the Porte to action. Nevertheless, the fact remained, that the special obligation towards the Armenians which Great Britain had undertaken under the Cyprus Convention still remained unfulfilled.

The change of Government, inasmuch as it brought back Lord Salisbury to the Foreign Office, encouraged the belief in Constantinople that there would be an immediate relaxation of pressure on the part of the Powers. The Sultan's Ministers miscalculated. One of the first acts of the new Foreign Secretary was to impress on the Turkish Ambassador the danger to the Ottoman empire of further prevarication. He stated that he had been "much struck, on coming back to office, to find how much ground Turkey had lost in English opinion," and that "a settled conviction was growing that nothing was to be hoped from it in the way of improvement and reform, and that all that could be done was to finish with it" (July 10th). After a month had passed, his patience was exhausted, and he came to the conclusion that, since the Powers could not withdraw from their position without loss of credit, energetic measures should be taken to secure the acceptance of the reforms. Although Russia still opposed the use of force, whether by all the Powers together or by any one of them alone, it was due to Lord Salisbury's insistence that the Porte in October produced a scheme of reforms of its own. The reforms were to apply in the six vilayets chiefly inhabited by Armenians and, in principle, in other parts of Asiatic Turkey where Christians predominated.

Nevertheless, the year 1896 brought a repetition of the excesses against the Armenians. Each month and week added its contribution to the tale of rapine, pillage, extortion and murder, now local, now on a larger scale. Constantinople was the scene of the worst of these orgies of crime. Following an attack upon the Ottoman Bank, made by a small band of Armenian reformers for the purpose of calling attention to the desperate plight of their countrymen, a general massacre of Armenians took place between the 26th and 30th of August. There were scores of arrests, and it was characteristic that, when the trials took place, the Armenians met with drastic treatment, but the Moslems with a clemency which in many cases amounted to a condonation of guilt. Many of the former were sentenced to death, but not one Moslem shared that fate; and the periods of imprisonment imposed were on the average twenty times longer for the Armenians than for the dominant race.

The massacres were followed by the expulsion from the capital of thousands of Armenians, of whom the majority found their way into Asia, where a worse fate awaited them. For the Constantinople *émeute* led to immediate and violent repercussions in the provinces, and particularly in Asia Minor, where the misdoings of the political bank-raiders were exaggerated and avenged with terrible cruelty upon thousands of their innocent countrymen. The worst of all the massacres were perpetuated in September in the Eghin district, where murder, plundering and houseburning continued for a day and a night. It was estimated by Consular investigators that at least 1000 people were murdered, and almost as many houses destroyed.

Up to that time, the Porte had done little or nothing towards carrying out its own scheme of reforms. In a despatch to the British

Embassies of October 20th, marked by unaccustomed urgency of tone, and recalling the generous spirit of the early days of 1875, before he seemed to succumb for a time to the influence of Disraeli, Lord Salisbury bespoke the cooperation of the Powers in a joint endeavour to obtain the introduction into the Turkish administration of such reforms as would ensure better government and put an end to its record of cruelty and crime. In protecting the Turkish empire from dissolution, he said, the Powers had been inspired by "the hope that the many evils by which Ottoman rule was accompanied would be removed or mitigated by the reforming efforts of the Government. Not only has this hope been entirely disappointed, but it has become evident that, unless these great evils can be abated, the forbearance of the Powers of Europe will be unable to protract the existence of a dominion which by its own vices is crumbling into ruin." He proposed, therefore, that the Powers should come to a unanimous agreement as to the reforms needed, and should insist on their execution, "up to the measure of such force" as they had at command. France, Germany, Austria-Hungary and Italy were sympathetic, and Russia, though at first opposed to the use of coercion, acquiesced by the end of November.

There was more admonition and expostulation; but little came of it. Further murders and massacres were committed in the following year; and in July, 1897, Sir Philip Currie reported that the Porte was as reluctant as ever to move by the introduction of reforms, the punishment of known criminals, or the enforcement of punishments actually awarded. Turkish misrule had, in fact, taken a new lease of life. Seven years later (July, 1904), Sir N. O'Conor, the British Ambassador of that day, was still complaining to the Grand-Vizier that "the present radical vice of gross misgovernment continued to render the life of every Armenian unendurable."

B. *Crete and the Graeco-Turkish War*, 1878–1898

One of the tragedies of the Eastern Question has lain in the fact that imperious political readjustments have so often been made piecemeal, in the vain hope of eluding difficulties and rendering more tolerable to the Ottoman empire the disturbance incidental to inevitable changes. Meanwhile, misgovernment has continued as before, while unbearable conditions have seemed to receive the sanction of the Powers which had made themselves responsible for the welfare of the oppressed populations, and yet nothing has been gained in the end by procrastination. At any time since the middle of the nineteenth century, it might have seemed that Crete was ripe for severance from an empire in which it was absorbed by force, and to which it had never been attached in sentiment; yet, twenty years after Delyanni had vainly appealed to the Congress of Berlin to sanction annexation to the Hellenic kingdom on historical and ethnical grounds, the island still remained one of the most sullen and disaffected parts of the Sultan's dominion.

The application to Crete of the Organic Statute of 1868, modified according to existing needs, had been a condition of its retention by the Sultan in 1878; and, in October of that year, a Constitution, known as the Pact of Halepa, was issued, creating *inter alia* a Governor-General, with an 'Adjoint' belonging to the Orthodox Greek faith, and a representative Assembly. In the territories under Turkish rule, however, the best of laws never made an alien Administration popular, and, when revolt broke out again in 1889, the Pact of Halepa was annulled, in token that the Cretans still held their political liberties by arbitrary favour only.

The refusal of the Porte to grant reforms demanded by the Cretan Assembly at the end of 1895 led to a renewal of revolt and to conflicts with the Turkish troops, which resorted to drastic reprisals. In the following August, the Ambassadors in Constantinople drew up a scheme under which the island was to have political autonomy and a Christian Governor; this the Porte accepted, and a law was promulgated accordingly. The concession, however, failed to arrest the discontent of the Christians, while it proved a source of offence to the Moslems.

All this time, the Greek Government was looking on expectantly, prepared to intervene on however slight a pretext. The justification was afforded in February, 1897, when Athens was thrown into excitement by reports of Mussulman attacks upon the Christians at Canea. Arms and ammunition found their way to Crete freely and mysteriously, and many of the leaders of the Cretan revolutionary cause resident on the mainland crossed over to the island. The Great Powers were already represented by a strong naval force in Cretan waters, and they refused the Sultan's request that he might send additional troops, fearing the effect upon the excited population.

Whatever might have been its attitude if calm counsels had been possible, the hands of the Greek Cabinet were now forced by public opinion. On February 11th, Prince George of Greece sailed over to Crete with a flotilla of torpedo boats, and four days later Colonel Vassos, bearing the King's orders to occupy the island and eject the Turkish garrisons, landed with 1500 men near Canea. These hostile acts amounted to a declaration of war, and the Porte appealed to the Powers to intervene. The German Emperor called for the immediate blockading of the Greek coast, as in 1886, until the illicit expedition should have been withdrawn, and other Powers favoured this course. The British Government, conscious of a strong current of national opinion favourable to the Greek cause, were unwilling to commit themselves until the future status of Crete had been determined; and, as to this, they advocated the conversion of the island into an autonomous province of the empire.

Immediately on landing, Colonel Vassos had issued a proclamation announcing his occupation of the island in his King's name. This was a defiant challenge which the Powers could not ignore. Some of them were in favour of serving on the Greek Government an ultimatum demanding the immediate recall of the expedition; but, on the proposal of France, who supported Great Britain and Italy in their wish to let Greece down lightly, the milder procedure of *sommation* was adopted. Called upon to withdraw, and reminded that its action was a violation of the Treaty of Berlin (March 2nd), the Greek Government refused, influenced doubtless by the recollection that two successive rulers of Bulgaria had been allowed to override the Treaty no less arbitrarily. Lord Salisbury had, in the meantime, accepted the blockade proposal, though stipulating for its limited operation; and on March 21st this measure was applied, but restricted to the island. As, however, the Hellenic Government showed no disposition to withdraw, the blockade was, at the end of the month, extended to the mainland.

All the Powers still acted together; yet not all of them were able to give cordial support to the work of coercion. Lord Salisbury, who throughout took the lead in the concert of the Powers, saw clearly that the mere dragooning of Greece, however she might have merited such treatment, would not solve the Cretan problem. Accordingly, his energies were directed towards obtaining the withdrawal from the island of the Turkish and Greek troops equally, with a view to the speedy reorganisation of the administration under a new Governor. To the grant of autonomous administration the Porte offered no resistance; but it claimed that a Turkish subject holding the Orthodox Greek faith should be chosen as Governor. For Greece, however, no solution of the Cretan question was satisfactory which failed to place the administration of the island in her hands either as mandatory of the Powers or (as she demanded) by means of annexation.

The guerilla war begun by the Greeks in Crete proved the prelude to a bolder military enterprise. The outburst of national ardour which had driven the King and Government into aggressive measures revived, in intense form, the old animosities and resentments of the Greeks against the Turks at their doors; and, in March, the Powers were faced with the imminence of an invasion of Macedonia. On April 6th, the Ambassadors in Constantinople presented to the Porte and the Greek Ministry simultaneously a joint Declaration, to the effect that, in the event of a conflict, their Governments would hold the aggressor entirely responsible and that, however a struggle so begun might end, they would not allow him to derive from it the slightest advantage.

Incited by repeated provocative acts of Greek troops, who had crossed the frontier at several points, the Porte suspended diplomatic relations with the Hellenic Government on April 18th, and war broke out. In a number of minor frontier operations the Greeks at first seemed to carry all before them. As the campaign developed, however, the superiority of their adversaries, alike in fighting quality and in numbers, told with fatal effect. Isolated victories continued to be won, but, again and again, positions were occupied only to be relinquished immediately afterwards in panic and flight. The land campaign was practically fought and decided on Greek soil, while on the water Greece, owing to sheer supineness, achieved no result of value, though all the conditions and chances were in her favour.

A sequence of defeats brought about the dismissal of the Delyanni Cabinet (April 28th) and the appointment to office of the Opposition leader Ralli. Already it was clear how the campaign would end. The Allies had been prepared to propose terms of peace as soon as the belligerents had taken each other's measure; and, so early as April 23rd, Lord Salisbury sounded the other Cabinets as to the expediency of deciding upon the form and conditions of intervention. On the eve of his dismissal, Delyanni had been ready to cease hostilities on honourable terms; after later reverses in Thessaly, the incoming Ministry welcomed mediation by the Powers on whatever terms they might propose. As a condition of an armistice Turkey demanded that the old frontier should be restored, which would have meant the retrocession to her of Thessaly. Lord Salisbury refused to consider the proposal, being determined that no liberated Christian populations should be put back under Turkish rule. With the signing of the Armistice on May 19th–20th the War came to an end.

In the ensuing peace negotiations the greatest difficulty was caused by the frontier question, though the Porte also pressed for a larger indemnity than the Powers were prepared to sanction. Upon the frontier question Lord Salisbury was immovable, and on June 30th he told the Turkish Government that, while willing to discuss any territorial adjustments in Thessaly which could be shown to be required for strategical reasons, the British Government "could not consent to any rectification of the frontier between Greece and Turkey which would involve as a consequence any considerable number of Greeks being replaced under the rule of the Turkish Government." Hereupon, the Porte resorted to its habitual policy of evasion and obstruction; and it was only after the Powers had issued a stern warning of their determination to bring to an end the futile negotiations, which had "no other result than that of delaying the conclusion of a peace in which all Europe is interested" (July 8th), that it capitulated. The definitive Treaty of Peace was signed on December 4th, 1897. By it, the frontier between the two States was rectified by the cession to Turkey of several minor districts, and the indemnity was fixed at £T4,000,000. In order to enable Greece to pay this sum and set her finances in order, Great Britain joined France and Russia (March 29th, 1898) in guaranteeing a loan to her of £6,800,000, repayable within a maximum period of 60 years.

During the Cretan controversy and the Graeco-Turkish War, Germany, while at one with the other Powers in desiring to shield Greece from the worst consequences of her indiscretion, showed on the whole a friendly disposition towards Turkey. Baron von Marschall, the German Ambassador in Constantinople, had already entered on a policy of deference to the Sultan, which ultimately won for Germany a dominating influence at the Porte and secured to her concessions and privileges of great political and material value.

The withdrawal of Greece and her preoccupation with the campaign on the mainland relieved the tension in Crete, though, owing to want of unity amongst the Allies, the settlement of the island was still long protracted. The decision to put in operation the scheme of autonomous government which was drawn up in August, 1896, required the election of a Governor, and, for more than a year, the claims of different aspirants and nominees were considered with a dwindling prospect of agreement, the island being in the meantime administered in commission by the Admirals. In March, 1898, owing to the rejection of her advice that it should be administered for a time by two Powers at their pleasure, Germany withdrew from the Concert, bidding the other Powers dispose of Crete as they would, since she took no further interest in it. Austria-Hungary soon followed this example.

The Cretan Question had, in fact, begun to tire all the Powers, though none of them seemed willing to recognise that the deadlock which had occurred was due to their own indecision and divided counsels. In June a Provisional Government was instituted, in spite of Turkey's indignant protest, providing for the administration of the coast-towns by the Admirals and of the interior by the Cretan Assembly and Executive. Then, at the beginning of September, another Mussulman outbreak occurred at Canea, as a result of which a number of British soldiers and sailors were killed or wounded, many hundreds of native Christians massacred, and the town fired, by the mob. The consequence was a decision to enforce the immediate withdrawal of all Turkish troops and officials from the island and to disarm the Moslem population. As the Porte refused to recall its soldiers, and the Turkish Governor declined to move in the absence of Instructions from Constantinople, the Allied troops ejected them by force on November 5th.

By this time, the need of a regular Government had become clear to the four acting Powers; and, with a view to bringing about a condition of things promising stability and permanence, Prince George of Greece was offered the position of High Commissioner (*Harmostes*), which he accepted on November 26th, the Porte agreeing. With the promise of the Powers to provide a loan of £160,000 and the immediate advance of one-fourth of this sum to enable the High Commissioner to set up house, the new Government assumed office under favourable auspices, and the Regent's formal installation took place on December 21st. Several days later, the Admirals sailed away.

VI. RECONQUEST OF THE SOUDAN AND THE FASHODA DISPUTE, 1885-1899

The longer the British occupation of Egypt lasted, the more impatient became the demand of the Sultan and of France for its termination. While, however, Great Britain had never ceased to regard her presence in the country as temporary, it was obvious to the rest of the world that no Government with a sense of responsibility could give a promise of evacuation, to take place unconditionally on a fixed date. The British Cabinet, nevertheless, offered to discuss with the Porte the conditions of eventual withdrawal and any practicable measures to be adopted in the meantime for reducing the sphere of intervention. With this object in view, Lord Salisbury sent Sir Henry Drummond Wolff on a Special Mission to Constantinople in August, 1885. The result was the conclusion of a Convention (October 24th), providing that a Turkish and a British High Commissioner should be despatched to Egypt, there to cooperate with the Khedive in the reorganisation of the Army and the reform of the general administration. So soon as the High Commissioners were convinced that the time had arrived when withdrawal would be safe and expedient, they were to report to that effect to their Governments, which would confer as to the conclusion of a Supplementary Convention on the subject. The proposals, necessarily, were not very explicit, but they were honestly meant; and Great Britain had never before gone so far in her wish to satisfy the Porte and remove the suspicions of France.

Wolff went to Egypt as the British High Commissioner, and Mukhtar Pasha was appointed on behalf of Turkey. For a twelvemonth, they observed, investigated, and conferred, discovering no new and solving no old problems; and then they reported. They failed to agree as to the best way of reorganising the Army; they had little fault to find with the civil administration; and, while they condemned the Capitulations, they devised no plan for abolishing them. The critical question, however, was the withdrawal of the British force; and, in the hope of reaching a conclusion on this head, Lord Salisbury sent Wolff to Constantinople on a second Mission in January, 1887.

In a memorable letter of Instructions addressed to the Special Envoy (January 15th), the Foreign Minister repeated the desire of his Government to satisfy the Sultan, yet warned him, in the spirit of Lord Granville's pledges in the past, that they could not "fix even a distant date for evacuation until they are able to make provision for securing beyond that date the external and internal peace of Egypt." He accepted the principle of the "neutralisation of Egypt," but subject to conditions "designed to maintain the security and maintenance of the whole arrangement." Hence, he laid it down as a basic principle that "the British Government must retain the right to guard and uphold the condition of things which will have been brought about by the military action and large sacrifices of this country....England, if she spontaneously and willingly evacuates the country, must retain a treaty right of intervention if at any time either internal peace or external security should be seriously threatened."

In the succeeding negotiations, after much humouring, Turkey concluded a Convention (May 22nd, 1887) providing for evacuation at the end of three years on the conditions stated. Two years after the British force had been withdrawn, the British supervision of the Army was to end, and Egypt was thereafter to enjoy territorial immunity (*sûreté territoriale*)—an indefinite status preferred by the Sultan to neutralisation. On the ratification of the Convention, the Powers were to be invited to recognise and guarantee the inviolability of Egyptian territory. Provision was made for a joint Anglo-Turkish military occupation of a temporary character in certain contingencies. It was part of the arrangement that the Contracting States should endeavour to induce the Powers to agree to the abolition of exterritorial jurisdiction. Owing to the pressure and threats of France, who objected to a British right of reentry in any circumstances, the Sultan did not ratify the Convention, though it was understood that he was willing to do so. When, later, he invited the Foreign Office to resume negotiations in London, Lord Salisbury, annoyed as much by Turkey's cowardice as by French intrigue, refused. Once more France had blundered. Wishing to expel Great Britain from Egypt, she had merely strengthened and made more permanent her position there.

British relations with France had seldom been so strained as during the period which intervened between the two Egyptian Conventions; and both Lord Salisbury and Lord Rosebery complained bitterly of the hard life which our neighbour led them. After six months of contention, Lord Rosebery came to the conclusion that France was making mischief of set purpose. "Our relations with France," he wrote to Lord Lyons (August 10th, 1886), "are really more troublesome than with any other Power[1]."

At that time de Freycinet was President of the Cabinet and Foreign Minister; and, having been guilty of the mistake of allowing Great Britain to enter Egypt alone, he was bent on retrieving his reputation by compelling her withdrawal. This would have been a brilliant achievement, had it succeeded. In September, 1886, he sent M. Herbette as Ambassador to Berlin, in proof of his wish to establish a permanent *entente* with Germany; and, in the following month, the

[1] Lord Newton, *Lord Lyons: a record of British Diplomacy*, ii. 374.

Ambassador made a formal proposal to Count Herbert Bismarck, then Foreign Secretary of State, that, in the interest of such an *entente*, Prince Bismarck should join hands in compelling Great Britain to evacuate Egypt. He gave the assurance that "the English were abominated in France more than the Germans had ever been," and that an anti-English policy would be "immensely popular" with his countrymen. Count Bismarck received the proposal unsympathetically, and the Chancellor himself rejected it summarily when M. Herbette repeated it to him in November[1].

The Anglo-French tension had become still greater by the time Lord Salisbury was back at the Foreign Office. At the beginning of 1887, France was in disfavour with half Europe—with Great Britain, Germany, Austria-Hungary and Italy; even Russia looked coldly on her. Great Britain, in particular, she was troubling about questions of right and title in all parts of the world—in Egypt, on the Somali coast, in Newfoundland and in the New Hebrides. His patience at last exhausted, Lord Salisbury wrote to Lord Lyons, apropos of the relief which might accompany the military interlude which General Boulanger, Minister of War in the Goblet Cabinet, was believed to be planning, "It is very difficult to prevent oneself from wishing for another Franco-German War, to put an end to this incessant vexation[2]." A distempered France never returns to a normal condition until she has upset a Government; but, in the course of 1887, she upset three before settling down.

Bismarck put temptation in Lord Salisbury's way at this time, when he again made overtures for an alliance. It was a leading principle of his foreign policy to prevent the formation of coalitions capable of menacing Germany or, if that were impossible, to create a counterpoise in any given case. Russia and France were moving steadily towards the *entente* which was to issue in a military alliance, and, on the French side of the Vosges, patriotic emotions had been dangerously stimulated by the pinchbeck hero who was now nearing the height of his evanescent fame. "The French undoubtedly shrink from war," Lord Lyons wrote in April from Paris to the Foreign Secretary; "but they do not shrink from it as much as they did ten years ago." They shrank still less as the Boulanger spell grew upon them, and the apprehension of war which was repeatedly expressed in Bismarck's parliamentary speeches of that year was very real. In a private letter

---

[1] *Die Grosse Politik der Europäischen Kabinette,* 1871–1914, VI. 137–52.
[2] Letter to Lord Lyons, February 5th, 1887, Lord Newton, *Lord Lyons,* II. 386.

to Lord Salisbury, written on November 22nd[1] and ostensibly intended to disclaim on Germany's part any disposition to favour Russia at the expense of Austria-Hungary, he spoke of the latter Power and Great Britain as being, like Germany, "saturated States," and hence well suited to form with her a triple alliance, whose object could only be the maintenance of the *status quo*. While he did not admit that in the event of a simultaneous attack by France and Russia Germany's position would be a desperate one, he recognised that even victory in such a case would be a national misfortune; if threatened, therefore, by war on both fronts without allies, Germany would do her utmost to avert that calamity by conciliating Russia—her own traditional ally and Great Britain's traditional enemy.

This line of reasoning was not to be mistaken. Proceeding from the premiss that Great Britain and Russia were still divided by irreconcilable interests, he concluded that, if required to choose between a defensive agreement with Germany and a definite *rapprochement* of Germany and Russia, the British Government would be compelled to throw in their lot with the Triple Alliance. Lord Salisbury did not respond to these advances in the way desired by Bismarck; but he had already agreed that Great Britain should join Austria-Hungary and Italy in an *accord à trois* for the purpose of maintaining the *status quo* in European Turkey and the Mediterranean, Germany being a co-guarantor, though not a signatory, of the agreement, which took effect in December. In January, 1889, Bismarck made a formal proposal of an alliance with Great Britain, to meet the eventuality of an attack on either Power by France during a short term of years. His idea was that it should be published to the world, and he believed that the mere knowledge of its existence would ensure the maintenance of peace[2]. After conference with his colleagues Lord Salisbury replied that the time for such a departure from British tradition as a defensive alliance would imply was inopportune; all he could do for the time being was to leave the proposal "on the table, without saying yes or no[3]." A year and a half later, when Bismarck was out of office, Salisbury gave a further earnest of his desire to live on terms of cordial accord with Germany by concluding with her the Zanzibar-Heligoland Convention (July 1st, 1890)[4].

[1] This letter first appeared (in translation) in Otto Hammann's *Zur Vorgeschichte des Weltkrieges* (1918), pp. 154–159. See also *Die Grosse Politik der Europäischen Kabinette*, 1871–1914, IV. 376–80, 386–8, for the letter and Lord Salisbury's reply.

[2] Despatch of Bismarck to the German Ambassador in London, January 11th, 1889, in *Die Grosse Politik der Europäischen Kabinette*, 1871–1914, IV. 400–3.

[3] *Ibid.* p. 405.   [4] Cf. *ante*, p. 216.

The *impasse* in Egypt continued without interruption. On the return of Gladstone to power (August, 1892), the French Cabinet hopefully renewed the request that the British Government would name the date for withdrawing, but without success. Far from encouraging any expectation on the subject in that quarter, Lord Rosebery, the new Foreign Secretary, did much to strengthen the British hold upon the country. In January, 1893, Lord Cromer had to complain that the Khedive Abbas, who had succeeded Tewfik a year before, had arbitrarily and of his own motion dismissed the ailing Prime-Minister, Mustapha Pasha Fehmi, intending to substitute for him Fakhry Pasha, who was not less hostile to Great Britain than Mustapha was friendly, together with two other Ministers. Lord Rosebery at once put down his foot upon this claim to independence. Nine years earlier, Lord Granville had plainly stated the rule governing the relations between the British and Egyptian Governments; and, taking his stand upon his predecessor's despatch of January 4th, 1884, the new Foreign Secretary pointed out the logical consequence of the Khedive's claim to be master in a house which had ceased to be his castle, when he said, "Our soldiers would be mere sentinels to protect a policy, possibly injurious, of which we should be no more than idle spectators, and the British flag would become the cloak for an administration possibly no better—conceivably even worse—than that which we had intervened to supersede" (February 16th).

In the end, a compromise was found by which the Khedive dropped the Anglophobe Fakhry in favour of Riaz Pasha; it being understood that in making a new appointment he did so with the express consent of the British Government, though he was warned as to the grave consequences of "direct action" in future. It had been suspected from the first that French prompting was behind the Khedive in the matter, and the suspicion was confirmed when France formally protested against Lord Cromer's successful intervention as "high-handed."

By this time, events were in motion which threw back the question of withdrawal indefinitely, and, in effect, removed it out of the range of practical politics. These events were the reconquest of the Soudan and the unsuccessful attempt made by France to establish herself in the valley of the Upper Nile. Although, from the beginning of 1884, the Soudan had been nominally abandoned, and the garrisons for the most part withdrawn, the sovereignty over that region, which had been vested in the Khedives by imperial firmans, had not been renounced, and the hope of the eventual reoccupation of the southern provinces in a military and administrative sense had never been relinquished. Experience proved that a policy of abandonment, in the full meaning of the word, was impracticable. The tribes of the interior had been left to themselves, to wage war or make peace with the Mahdi as they would; but the abstention by the Egyptian Government from further interference in the Soudan did not prevent continual attempts by the rebel armies to transgress the new defensive frontier of Egypt and capture the Red Sea coast.

Never, in fact, had there been a moment when British and Egyptian troops had not been engaged in repelling or restraining aggression beyond the forbidden limits—now within attacking distance of Wady Halfa, now at Suakin, recovered from Osman Digna by the British in 1885 and since that year in their occupation. The policy pursued was that of harassing the rebels on every favourable occasion, in the hope of wearing out resistance and convincing them that they were fighting a losing cause. In the meantime, the rebellion was proving as exhausting for the Khalifa's followers as for Egypt; and, early in 1887, Colonel Kitchener, who in the previous year had become Governor of the Red Sea territories, was able to report to Sir Evelyn Baring that Mahdiism was dying out in the Soudan, and that the people in general wished for peace, tranquillity, and the renewal of trade. At the request of the Egyptian authorities, the British Government sanctioned the reopening of commercial relations with the Upper Nile region; but for several years they continued to discourage any idea of attempting the reoccupation of the forsaken territories.

It was not until 1896 that measures to this end were systematically organised. The Egyptian Army had now been strengthened in numbers and improved in quality. Its past inferiority had been chiefly due to inefficient training and lack of discipline, so that, in the crises of actual warfare, the men who were expected to fight either ran away or lay down and let themselves be killed. Under the old conditions of recruiting, however, a trustworthy Army was impossible, for the men formed part of what was practically an impressed force. No sooner had the military administration passed under British control, than the native soldier found himself welltrained, wellclothed, fed and armed, fairly wellpaid, and humanely treated, and he responded readily to the call of officers who treated him with respect. The result was that the new Army was as superior to the Khalifa's undisciplined hosts as the old Army had been inferior to the seasoned British troops.

Hostile movements of the Dervishes along the valley of the Nile beyond Wady Halfa, and the menace they offered to the country lying to the east of the river, determined the British Government to undertake the recovery of the Soudan as far as Dongola; and the expeditionary force moved forward in March, 1896. The bulk of the troops were Egyptian, though British regulars were attached for the sake of the moral help afforded by their presence; a British battalion also occupied Wady Halfa at the base, while Suakin was held at that time by Indian troops. Fighting the whole way and inflicting heavy loss upon the rebels, the victorious army in September occupied Dongola, which was retained.

During 1897, a railway was built by Egyptian troops from Wady Halfa in the direction of Berber, being intended as the base for a further advance, which was to clear the country as far as the coast. In April of the following year, after inflicting a crushing defeat upon the Dervishes under Osman Digna at Atbara, the Anglo-Egyptian Army occupied Berber; and, five months later, Kitchener crowned the work of reconquest by the victory of Omdurman (September 2nd), and the occupation of Khartoum (September 4th), where the British and Egyptian flags were significantly hoisted side by side. While at Khartoum, he heard of the presence of a French expedition further south.

French statesmen and writers, at a later date, advanced the theory that the abandonment and reconquest of the Soudan were part of a calculated plan for establishing British supremacy on the Upper Nile. There is no justification for ascribing so far-sighted a design to British statecraft, which at every stage of the Egyptian occupation had shown a notable incapacity to anticipate events or even to formulate a consistent policy. Unquestionably, the time came when the British Government, counting the cost of the efforts and liabilities which the occupation had occasioned, became increasingly dissatisfied with a position entailing upon Great Britain the duties of a handy man together with the obligations of a paying guest. But the decision to ask for territorial compensation—whether this decision was justifiable or not—was an afterthought. France, however, at least had no cause to complain of it, since it was due to her opposition that the Egyptian Government had not been allowed to provide money to meet the expense of reconquering the Soudan, with the result that the British Treasury had to advance the necessary sum.

British action in the valley of the Upper Nile, at this time, was powerfully influenced by developments which were taking place beyond the limits of Egypt's traditional sphere of influence. The extension of British dominion in Central Africa, both direct and through Chartered Company enterprise, led to the conclusion, between the years 1890 and 1894, of Agreements with Germany, Italy and the Congo Free State, by which the spheres of influence of all four States in that region were defined, the effect being to exclude the possibility of their invasion of the Upper Nile valley. A Central African Agreement was, also, concluded with France in 1890; but its effect was confined to determining Anglo-French claims eastward as far as Lake Chad. As to the rest, France preferred to retain a free hand.

It has been the systematic policy of France, when neighbours equally energetic have anticipated her in the acquisition of desirable portions of the Dark Continent, to endeavour to cut off their hinterlands, and so to gain control of the rivers upon which the prosperity of the lower territories largely depended. Colonisation by this dubious method was attempted to the prejudice of Great Britain in the case of Lagos, Gambia and the Gold Coast, to that of Spain in the case of Morocco, and to that of Italy in the case of Tripoli. In 1897, it was attempted by the same Power in relation to Egypt. No longer able, owing to her own want of decision and foresight, to enter the Nile region by the front door, France tried to enter from the rear; and she did this as part of a deliberate design of obtaining control of the Nile, the very source of Egypt's life.

On the question of title to territory in that region successive French Governments followed no consistent policy. Down to 1894, the view was taken that only the Sultan and the Khedive possessed rights of sovereignty in the abandoned Soudan provinces. This view, from the standpoint of international law, led to the inference that the several Conventions by which Great Britain had sought to assure for herself an exclusive position there were merely private compacts, affecting only the Governments by which they were made, and binding no others, least of all the Sultan and his vassal. From the same point of view, Great Britain's assignment to the Congo State, by the Convention of 1894, of a part of the Upper Nile basin, to be held in trust and in due time retroceded, was equally irregular; since, possessing no title to this territory herself, she was not in a position to transfer it to a third party.

It was the conclusion of this Convention that led the French Government to depart from its original and strong position as the advocate of the Sultan's rights. Its publication created consternation in French Colonial and political circles, and interpellations on the subject took place in the Chamber (June 7th, 1894). In reply to these, M. Hanotaux, the Foreign Minister, repeated the old contention, that the Sultan alone possessed the right of disposing of the Soudan, and declared the Convention to be in conflict with the principles, doctrines, and even the text, of the Treaty of Berlin, inasmuch as it violated, or at least menaced, the integrity of the Ottoman empire. He, also, addressed a formal protest to the British Government and the Minister of the Congo State.

Instead of maintaining this firm foothold, France now decided that her interests in Central Africa might be better advanced by seizing territory on her own account. Accordingly, she concluded with the Congo State an Agreement (August 14th, 1894) by which the latter undertook not to occupy certain portions of the territory which Great Britain had ceded to it west of the Nile; and this action she followed up by occupying them herself. According to her own contention, France had no legal claim to this region, and would be bound to renounce it if ever the Sultan or the Khedive in his name decided to claim it. In the meantime, she had taken her place, side by side with Great Britain, as an avowed rival in the disputed area.

A situation already not merely delicate but opening the door to serious misunderstanding was now deliberately aggravated by France, in spite of warning given in the most emphatic language known to the vocabulary of friendly diplomacy. Some time prior to the conclusion of the Convention of August 14th, the French Government commissioned two enterprising officers, Colonel Monteil and Captain (later Colonel) Marchand, to undertake an expedition into Central Africa as far as the Upper Nile valley, starting from the West Coast. Like the Diver in the poem, Marchand plunged into the depths of the dark unknown, and outside France no one was aware when or where he would return to the surface. He reappeared, four years later, at Fashoda, 300 miles south of Khartoum. While the utmost secrecy had been maintained as to the movements of the expedition, its object was admitted later to be to explore the "contingent possessions" of France in that region and to obtain recognition for her "provisional authority."

Early in 1895, disquieting rumours as to this expedition and its purposes reached England; and a question on the subject was asked in the House of Commons. In his reply (March 28th) Sir Edward Grey, the Under-Secretary for Foreign Affairs, after recalling the Conventions with Germany and Italy, to which, he said, objection had nowhere been raised, and the exceptional position of Great Britain as the protector of the interests of Egypt, gave the diplomatic assurance that the Foreign Office had no reason to suppose that a French expedition had been instructed or was intending to enter the Nile Valley, yet added that "the advance of a French expedition under secret Instructions right from the other side of Africa, into a territory over which our claims have been known for so long, would not be merely an inconsistent and unexpected act, but it must be perfectly well known to the French Government that it would be an unfriendly act and would be so viewed by England[1]." In that speech, Sir Edward Grey claimed that "the British sphere of influence covered the whole Nile waterway."

In spite of this plain and grave warning, for which at a later date Lord Rosebery avowed he was "personally and Ministerially responsible," France actually took the unfriendly step in question. In the meantime, her Government was not slow to respond to an unusually frank challenge. Besides making representations in London through the French Ambassador, the Foreign Minister replied to interpellations on the subject in the Chamber. "The position taken by France is this," M. Hanotaux said (April 5th): "the regions in question are under the sovereignty of the Sultan; they have a legitimate master, the Khedive." He added the belief, however, that, when the time came for determining the destinies of those regions, Great Britain and France, while duly respecting the rights of the Sultan and the Khedive, would be able to "find formulas suited to reconcile their interests and satisfy their common aspirations as regards civilisation and progress." One of these formulas he suggested would be, "To each according to his works." It was the first direct and official suggestion by France that she contemplated a time when a policy of partition would be applied to the Upper Nile valley, and that in this France expected to have her share.

The question, hereupon, rested for a time; but, in order that no uncertainty might exist as to the position, the British Government returned to the subject at the end of 1897, in the course of some

---

[1] Speaking of this declaration three years later, Lord Rosebery said, "The word 'unfriendly,' which socially amongst us has, perhaps, no particular meaning, or perhaps too common a meaning, is amongst diplomatists a word of exceptional weight and gravity, and when that word is used to denote an act committed by one Government against another the situation is grave" (October 12th, 1898).

negotiations relating to French claims in relation to the northern and eastern shores of Lake Chad. Lord Salisbury informed Hanotaux that the Government did not object to these claims; but he let it be understood that they did "not admit that any European Power other than Great Britain had a right to occupy any part of the valley of the Nile." As to this question, he adhered entirely to the language employed by Sir Edward Grey in 1895. In his reply (December 24th), Hanotaux recalled his protest against Sir Edward Grey's declaration and suggested that the settlement of the Niger question should be independent of any other. In the following year, the two Powers came to an arrangement determining their claims within the region extending from the Senegal to the Bahr-el-Ghazal (June 14th, 1898). Hanotaux wrote later that this agreement was intended by France to be anticipatory of the more important issue which would arise so soon as the Marchand expedition arrived at its destination—an admission that this expedition was undertaken for the deliberate purpose of forcing the hand of Great Britain upon the question of sovereignty in the Upper Nile basin[1].

According to the French official version, the Monteil-Marchand expedition, as originally planned, was countermanded on the conclusion of the Convention with the Congo State; but no change was made in that part of the project which was obnoxious to England, for Colonel Marchand was directed to make his way to Fashoda on the Upper Nile, as arranged. After a march of 2800 miles in the face of many difficulties and privations, Marchand and his companions, with their body-guard of Senegalese troops, reached Fashoda early in July, 1898, and there hoisted the French flag. At the beginning of September, Kitchener had completed his task of reconquering the Soudan by the reduction of Omdurman. Hearing of the arrival of six white men at Fashoda, he hastened forward and reached the spot on the 18th. The situation was a delicate and critical one, but the two soldiers proved themselves to be also statesmen, remembering that, the sooner the difficult question of title was translated into the atmosphere of

---

[1] "*La convention conclue, la voie était libre pour la question du Nil, la question Marchand....C'était l'idée suivie depuis le début par le Quai d'Orsay: traiter avant la rencontre, désormais trop facile à prévoir, dans le Bahr-el-Ghazal.*" G. Hanotaux, *Le partage de l'Afrique*, p. 124. Compare also the same writer: "*La rivalité de la France et de l'Angleterre en Égypte fut certainement une des causes initiales de l'incident de Fashoda* (ib. p. 70)....*Or, l'idée maîtresse de la diplomatie française en 1894 fut que cette question du Nil, nœud de toutes des questions pendantes, pouvait devenir, précisément, le nœud d'un arrangement général*" (p. 89). Hanotaux also speaks of the Fashoda "mission" as a direct reply to the Dongola expedition.

diplomacy, the greater would be the likelihood of a settlement which would leave no ill-will. There was no angry wrangling and pulling down of flags; having complimented Marchand on his gallant march, Kitchener regretted that it had ended at the wrong place, and informed him that it was his duty to claim possession of Fashoda for the Egyptian and British Governments. Marchand hinted, indeed, at the possibility of his having to die at his post and his readiness to do so if necessary; but Kitchener confined himself to carrying out his Instructions. These were to hoist the Egyptian and British flags, and, having done this, to hand to Marchand a written protest against "any occupation of any part of the Nile Valley by France," as being an infringement of Egyptian and British rights, and to instal an Egyptian garrison on the spot. Having done this, he parted from his rival, as he had met him, on terms of perfect amity.

The excitement caused in France by the episode was intense, and it needed little effort on the part of the Paris Press to convince the nation that its rights and honour had been wantonly outraged. On the other hand, nothing was lacking in resolute decision on the part either of Lord Salisbury in London or the British Ambassador in Paris, though it was recognised that the alternative to surrender by France was war[1]. Happily, French logic on that occasion gave timely assistance to French diplomacy. If the abandonment of her earlier standpoint had placed France in an inconsistent position, the return to it enabled her to extricate herself gracefully from an awkward predicament. No Power had more persistently emphasised the inviolability of the Egyptian dominions than France. As, therefore, the authority of the Khedive was now being reasserted in the Soudan, to claim the Fashoda district or any part of it would have been to

[1] "*C'était bien de guerre qu'il agissait. Durant cette période ('depuis le mois de Septembre 1898 jusqu'au mois de Mars, 1899') nous avons été à deux doigts des hostilités*" (C. de Freycinet, *La question d'Égypte*, p. 413). In his *Memoirs*, published by the London *Daily Telegraph* during the later months of 1920, Count Witte states that the French Government at this time appealed to Russia for support and received the advice not to allow the question to lead to a rupture. He also states that M. Delcassé visited Petrograd for the purpose of devising "a means whereby England might be held in check," and urged the Russian Government to push on with the construction of the Orenburg-Tashkend railway, since it would prove valuable as a menace to India should the need arise. As the opportunity of obtaining money for this contemplated work was too good to be lost, Russia agreed, and a loan was promised for the purpose. It was disappointment at Russia's coolness in the Fashoda affair, together with the feeble stand she made in the later Japanese War, which convinced Delcassé and other French statesmen that as an ally Russia left much to be desired, and that the policy of irritating Great Britain was both a mistaken and a dangerous one. The *entente cordiale* of 1904 was a direct result of this change of attitude.

dispute lawful authority and to challenge her own position. It was true that Hanotaux had seemed to forsake this position in April, 1895; but he did it in exceptional circumstances. There was, therefore, no question of any unconsidered trifles of territory in the Upper Nile region waiting for a claimant, and France could withdraw her flag without loss of honour.

Such was now the reasoning of Delcassé, Foreign Secretary since June; and on the strength of it he was able to make the surrender which saved the peace[1]. Wishing to protect the national *amour propre* to the utmost, he even fell back on the plea that the Marchand expedition was not official and its gallant leader merely an "emissary of civilisation." That unkind disclaimer had been anticipated by Marchand, who, when challenged by Kitchener, declared that he had occupied Fashoda by his Government's Instructions; while his superior, the French Colonial Governor Liotard, also made a public announcement at variance with the Minister's statement[2].

France having given way, every effort was made to appease her natural disappointment and to make good her loss in other ways. In accordance with his usual grand style in concessions, Salisbury met the French generously both on the Niger and the Congo. He proposed, as the basis of negotiations, that the British and French spheres of influence should be regarded as extending east and west, respectively, of a line agreed upon. The acceptance by France of that formula, however, would have implied her recognition of British or Brito-Egyptian dominion in regions which, for argument's sake, she was still prepared to contend belonged to the Sultan and the Khedive, and which, therefore, Great Britain at present held only on sufferance.

Delcassé proposed as an alternative a non-committal arrangement binding the two Powers to accept this line as merely defining the region beyond which, to the west and east respectively, they undertook to

---

[1] On September 9th, two months after Marchand had reached Fashoda, Lord Salisbury had instructed the Ambassador in Paris to inform Delcassé that "all the territories which were subject to the Khalifa passed by right of conquest to the Egyptian and British Governments." Delcassé made a half-hearted attempt to challenge the British claim (September 18th); whereupon Sir E. Monson warned him in friendly though firm language that the British Government "would not consent to a compromise" in the matter. In view of this emphatic reassertion of the Declaration of 1895, the latter action of France is inexplicable, except on the view that her Government was convinced that, having given way to her in other colonial disputes, Great Britain was certain to give way in this.

[2] In his work, *Le Partage de l'Afrique*, Hanotaux, who shared responsibility for this episode, speaks throughout of the Marchand "Mission" and nowhere suggests that it was not official.

acquire neither territory nor influence; and this proposal was adopted. The resulting Convention (March 21st, 1899) thus settled no question of sovereignty—which was, indeed, impossible—but simply restricted the area of rivalry and possible dispute between the two Powers, leaving them free to act as they would, on their own responsibility, within the spheres of influence claimed by them. Its greatest merit was that it satisfied France, by securing to her an enlarged sphere of operations and consolidating her interests in Central Africa. By mutual consent, the Egyptian Question in general was in no way introduced into the negotiations; so that France was still able to claim that Egypt was as much the vassal State of the Sultan as before, and Great Britain a stranger and sojourner in the land.

While the settlement with France was in progress, the British Government concluded an agreement with the Khedive (January 19th, 1899) with a view to regularising the situation created by the fact that the reconquest of the Soudan had been a joint enterprise. The agreement defined the Soudan as comprising all territories south of the 22nd parallel of latitude which had been evacuated by Egyptian troops since 1882, or which, having before the Rebellion been administered by the Khedive, had been temporarily lost to Egypt and had been reconquered by the British and Egyptian Governments in concert, or might hereafter be so reconquered. It was provided that the British and Egyptian flags should be used together both on land and water throughout the Soudan, except in the town of Suakin, where the Egyptian flag alone should be used, and that the supreme civil and military command of the region should be vested in an Administrator bearing the title Governor-General—the title used by the Khedives prior to the issue of the firman of May 27th, 1866— and appointed by the Khedive on the recommendation of the British Government, whose assent should, also, be necessary to his removal. Exterritoriality and, in consequence, mixed tribunals were barred in any part of the Soudan except the town of Suakin—a reservation annulled six months later.

The agreement was a formal assertion of an Anglo-Egyptian *condominium* in the Soudan, though not of the full British Protectorate loudly demanded by many imperialist voices at home. In effect, the Khedive professed to confer upon the future British Administrators of that region the position and powers which he had himself held and exercised there as the Sultan's vassal. The circumstance that this arrangement, to which the Sultan was not invited to be a party, was a direct infringement of the firmans under which the Khedive's delegated powers and his obligations to his Suzerain were defined, served to remind the world of how far Great Britain had travelled since she entered Egypt in 1882 with the positive intention of early and complete withdrawal[1]. Challenged on this point by Lord Kimberley in the House of Lords, Lord Salisbury asserted (February 6th, 1899) that Great Britain occupied the Soudan territories by two titles: the first, because they belonged to Egypt, and the second, right of conquest—the latter a title which he regarded as the simpler of the two and the easier to understand. The case for a *condominium*, so stated, carried conviction to most English minds; but it left unsolved some awkward questions of international law[2].

The renewed friction with France, from 1895 onwards, again turned the thoughts of some British statesmen to Germany. Early in 1898, Joseph Chamberlain, the Colonial Secretary, discussed with Count Hatzfeldt, the German Ambassador, the possibility of close cooperation between the two Powers in world-politics. What character this cooperation was intended to take is not known, though there is little doubt that both the purpose and the form contemplated were overstated for their own ends by those who took up the threads of the negotiations in Berlin. A fact which caused the matter to be treated there "dilatorily," in Bismarck's way, was the German Emperor's discovery that a short time before conciliatory advances had been made by Great Britain to Russia. This came to his knowledge, when he attempted to use Chamberlain's overtures as a means of regaining his lost position in the confidence of the Tsar and his advisers. Where Governments were thus working at cross purposes, no wholesome result was possible; and the Alliance negotiations were broken off before they had entered a practical stage.

---

[1] The firman of August 7th, 1879, forbade the alienation of any powers and privileges confided to the Khedive in virtue of the Sultan's sovereignty, or of any territory forming part of the Khediviate and its possessions. The Upper Nile territories were placed under the Khedive's Administration by firmans of 1873 and 1875.

[2] That from time to time there was lack of continuity in the policy followed by the Foreign Office on this question is shown by the fact that the Earl of Kimberley in 1895 informed Baron de Courcel, the French Ambassador, that the British Government "did not ignore the claims of Egypt, and that, if Egypt should hereafter be able to reoccupy the territories in the Soudan formerly under her rule, we should recognise her right to their possession." (Letter to Lord Dufferin, April, 1895.) Confronted by Sir Edward Grey's claim that the British sphere of influence covered "the whole Nile waterway," he gave the French Ambassador the assurance that such a claim "could not be regarded as a *prise en possession*."

Later in the year, however, a Colonial Treaty was concluded between the two Governments. In the anticipation that Portugal might be disposed to sell some of her possessions, it was agreed that, given the opportunity, Germany should be free to acquire the southern part of Angola and the northern part of Mozambique, while Great Britain was to be able to acquire northern Angola, southern Mozambique, Madeira, the Azores and the Cape Verde Islands. The Convention proved inoperative, though it alarmed Portugal; and, in the following year, the ancient Anglo-Portuguese Treaty of Alliance was confirmed by the Treaty of Windsor.

VII. The First Hague Peace Conference, 1899

It has been shown that encouraging progress was made during the last decade of the century in the application of the principle of Arbitration to the territorial and boundary disputes, usually due to antagonism between old rights and new claims, which were incidental to an epoch of transition and readjustment. Great Britain was one of the first States to welcome this method of settling international differences. In a different connexion, a precedent of historical interest had been set by the Alabama Arbitration of 1871–2; three years later, Great Britain and Portugal submitted the question of the ownership of Delagoa Bay to the decision of the French President; and from that time International Arbitration and adjudication by outside umpires were no longer uncommon in the event of differences between sovereign States.

An important impetus was given to the cause of International Arbitration by the Peace Conference which was held at the Hague in 1899 on the proposal of Tsar Nicholas II of Russia, who, in the previous year, had invoked the cooperation of all Governments in the work of ensuring for the world permanent peace. The invitation (dated August 12th) to take part in such a conference contained an earnest appeal for "the maintenance of universal peace and a possible reduction of the excessive armaments," as representing "an ideal towards which the efforts of all Governments should be directed." Count Witte has since claimed that the idea of the Conference was not in its genesis directly due to idealistic motives, and, further, that it originated with Count Muravieff, the Russian Foreign Minister, and himself. It grew, he says, out of a proposal made to the Tsar that he should approach Austria-Hungary with a view to the postponement of the renewal of her artillery, which was intended in 1898, on the understanding that Russia would do likewise. A partial arrangement of the kind being disapproved by the Minister of War, Kuropatkin, as a confession of weakness, the Tsar decided to raise the question of the limitation of armaments on a wider basis. Whatever its origin, his invitation was received with general satisfaction. The British Government at once returned an unconditional assurance of their sympathy and approval, and, in a later and less formal despatch to Petrograd (October 24th) Lord Salisbury, deploring the burden of armaments and the feeling of social unrest and discontent to which it gave rise, wrote: "Her Majesty's Government will gladly cooperate in the proposed effort to provide a remedy for this evil; and, if in any degree it succeeds they feel that the Sovereign to whose suggestion it is due will have richly earned the gratitude of the world at large."

The First International Peace Conference was held at The Hague and lasted from May 18th to June 29th, 1899. Twenty-eight States, including all the European Powers, the United States, and Japan, took part. The British Government appointed Sir Julian Pauncefote and Sir Henry Howard as their First and Second Plenipotentiaries respectively. It was not a hopeful augury that the Russian Delegates failed to carry their Government's proposals for an international accord, to cover a term of five years, stipulating for no increase of the peace strength of the Armies of the Powers beyond the existing numbers, fixing, if practicable, the peace strength of those Armies, exclusive of colonial troops, and maintaining the military budgets at the present figure during the same term. Strong opposition to these proposals was offered by the German Military Delegate, while the British Naval Expert (Sir John Fisher) criticised them from the standpoint of the naval Powers. The result was that the primary object for which the Tsar had called the Powers together was defeated; and all the Conference did to advance the question of Disarmament was to adopt an abstract resolution in favour of the restriction of military budgets as being "desirable for the increase of the material and moral welfare of mankind."

Irreconcilable differences of opinion amongst the Naval and Military Experts also made it impossible to go far in the direction of humanising warfare and curtailing the liberty of belligerent Powers. The American and other Delegates wished to obtain a clear expression of opinion on the subject of the immunity of private property at sea; but the British Delegates, following their Instructions, declined to associate themselves even with the discussion of the subject. The one tangible and hopeful result of the Conference was the formulation of a scheme of International Arbitration by the creation of a permanent Arbitration Tribunal at The Hague. Progress on this question was achieved in the face of great difficulties, which made impossible measures of a drastic character. The least of these difficulties was the existence of an infinite variety of opinion; the greatest was the jealousy by the various States for their sovereign rights. The result was a permissive scheme, excellent in workmanship and altogether laudable and promising as a first step, but no more. The General Act of the Conference (July 29th, 1899) was signed by twenty-six participating Powers.

There was singular appropriateness in the fact that it fell to Lord Salisbury to cooperate, as Foreign Secretary in his third and last Administration, in this attempt to strengthen confidence between Governments and to diminish the risks of international friction. For no statesman of his day had done more than he to promote the pacific adjustment of territorial differences and to smooth foreign relations generally. He formed three of the six Administrations in power between June, 1885, and the end of the century, and he held the office of Foreign Secretary in his own Cabinets for over fourteen years. It was well for the country that he thus exercised direct control over its Foreign Relations, for he knew by experience that slight failures in External Policy may be of incalculably greater moment for a country than the most brilliant successes.

As a leading member of the Disraeli Government of 1874–1880, he had been a party to a foreign policy marked by more or less unintelligent activity; as the head of three Administrations he adhered from the first to the line of safety and followed a policy which may be described as one of intelligent inaction. Henceforth, the country was agitated by no further courses of "spirited Foreign Policy." He came to entertain all the dislike of intervention which he was wont to ascribe to Lord Derby; and to the last he never abandoned the idea of withdrawing from Egypt. His policy in Europe in particular, whether in the East or the Mediterranean, was, as he repeatedly said, that of "maintaining things as they are." Without implying anything derogatory of the great Minister under whom he first served, it may be said that he carried Conservative Foreign Policy back into the accepted national traditions; it had taken a more or less exotic turn— in his hands it became again more consistently British. His caution was strikingly shown in his attitude towards coalitions and alliances. Tempted more than once, by a statesman whose confidence was supposed to be the highest form of flattery, to consider offers of the kind, he listened politely, and as politely declined, yet weakening no friendship because of his preference for the old national attitude of "splendid isolation."

No Conservative and few Liberal statesmen of modern times have brought to the treatment of Foreign Affairs so much of the "international mind" as Lord Salisbury. His ability to see two sides of a question—the result of a philosophic detachment of mind which was often mistaken for indifference—enabled him to solve many long-standing territorial misunderstandings with other Powers, and by so doing to counteract to some extent the view of British egoism which had long been fostered in Continental Chanceries. In some of these transactions, he departed almost defiantly from the national adage that charity should begin at home; for he was large-minded and incapable of pettiness.

But magnanimity in bargaining, however admirable in principle, only justifies itself in practice when there exists some sort of reciprocity. On three notable occasions, Lord Salisbury was accused, with some appearance of justification, of having concluded arrangements of a one-sided character. In two of these cases, however, he could fairly plead that he had to do with a bargainer who invariably wanted much for little or nothing, and that, in the Mekong and Madagascar episodes, the only possible hope of a settlement was to allow France to fix her own terms. The truth seems to be that in territorial negotiations, of which more fell to him than to any other statesman of his generation, he aimed at broad adjustments, to which, perhaps, as he would have admitted, exception might be taken in points of detail, yet which represented a fair balance as between conflicting claims not capable of exact equation. If, however, he declined to contend about points which mattered little, so that the undiscerning often regarded as weakness a deference to other nations which was really a sign of strength—when essential issues were involved, as the Zambesi and Fashoda episodes proved, he was as unyielding as adamant.

It is often said, with a dogmatism intended to discourage dispute, that Foreign Affairs, and in particular territorial interests, are naturally safer in the hands of Conservative than of Liberal Governments. A study of the line of our Foreign Secretaries and their works, from Clarendon onwards, should be sufficient to prove how far such a generalisation is from the truth. It will rather establish the fact that success in the conduct of Foreign Politics is less a question of party and party principles than of personality and, in a secondary degree, of circumstances. If it is possible, without exaggeration of his services, to rank Lord Salisbury as one of the greatest British Foreign Ministers of the century, the explanation must be sought, not in his party associations or in the fact that he represented a certain body of political doctrine— for, in truth, he renounced more than one of his party's most cherished axioms of Foreign Policy—but in his consummate gifts and aptitudes as a statesman and in the unique opportunities for their exercise which fell to him during the last two decades of an unusually full and active political life. After the death of Lord Beaconsfield, whose over- shadowing personality and dominating will seemed to arrest for a time his colleague's natural development, Salisbury's true self emerged, and he rapidly came to the front rank of European statesmen. After Bismarck's fall, his primacy in world politics was unchallenged: not since Clarendon had a British statesman spoken in the councils of the Powers with a voice which, while carrying equal weight, in- spired, also, equal confidence and respect.

Not only so; but it may be said with perfect truth, to his credit, that the preeminence to which he attained came by none of the arts and wiles and shifts of the diplomatist, by no tricks of shallow skill, no resort to petty intrigue, no paltering with high principles, or appeal to popularity, but was the tribute paid by international statecraft to a character in which strength and decision were conjoined with moderation, dignity, and lofty candour. The high estimate of his personality which he justified abroad was not the least valuable of the services rendered by him to a country whose political influence and prestige have been so largely based in the past, and will be in- creasingly dependent in the future, upon its reputation for justice and fair-dealing.

CHAPTER IV

THE BOER WAR AND THE INTERNATIONAL SITUATION, 1899–1902

I. The Jameson Raid and the South African War, 1895–1902

THE storm which broke over South Africa in the autumn of 1899 had been brooding for some years. The relations between the Boers of the small Transvaal Republic and the alien population, mostly British, who flowed in increasing numbers into the rich gold-fields which their enterprise had opened up, had grown more and more strained. A great British city had sprung up at Johannesburg; but President Kruger was too narrow-minded and masterful to concede to the *Uitlanders*, as the non-Boer settlers were called, the equality of treatment and the civic rights to which they, not unreasonably, laid claim, though he was ready enough to take heavy toll from the wealth which their industry produced. The British Government vainly pressed him to make some concessions; and, in 1895, when discontent had grown dangerously acute, Cecil Rhodes, who was then Prime-Minister of the Cape Colony and who had set his heart on creating a real South African Union by drawing Britons and Boers together in friendly cooperation, in an evil hour countenanced a plot for wresting by force from the Transvaal the recognition, obstinately denied by it, of the position to which the Uitlanders held themselves to have established their title by the large contribution they had made to the prosperity of a poor and backward State. Preparations followed for an insurrectionary movement in Johannesburg, to be supported by a military force secretly collected on the Transvaal border. The preparations miscarried; but Dr Jameson, an intimate friend and confidant of Rhodes, took the bit between his teeth and, on December 29th, 1895, attempted a raid into Transvaal territory, which promptly ended in failure and the surrender of its leader on January 2nd, 1896. President Kruger, who had been warily lying in watch for the movement to develop, arrested the ringleaders in Johannesburg—mostly men of considerable wealth and influence in the Uitlander community; and, though their sentences were ultimately commuted or remitted, they were sentenced to heavy penalties, and some of them even to death. The sensation created by the raid itself was suddenly intensified by the still greater sensation produced by a telegram from the Emperor William II to President Kruger, congratulating him on having "succeeded without appealing for help from friendly Powers" in repelling by his own might and with his own people "the armed hordes which had burst as disturbers of the peace" into his land[1]. To this telegram, which was regarded by the British people, if not as a menace of war, as at least a provocative attempt on the part of a foreign Power to interfere in a matter of purely British concern, the British Government replied by mobilising a flying squadron. The German Government, hereupon, prudently sought to attenuate the meaning of the Emperor's telegram, though it had been given great prominence in the German Official Gazette and was at first described to the present writer by the then head of the German Foreign Office, Baron Marschall von Biberstein, as "an action of State for which the Imperial Government took full responsibility"; and Anglo-German relations gradually resumed their normal character. The consequences, however, of the raid itself remained in South Africa. It had been an indefensible gamble, which not only went far to wreck Cecil Rhodes' own life-work in South Africa, but seriously hampered the British Government in their subsequent attempts to secure some tolerable settlement of the Uitlander grievances. President Kruger's attitude became more uncompromising than ever, and he demanded even the withdrawal of the London Convention of 1884 as, "amongst other things," injurious to the dignity of an independent republic. The British Government refused to waive the suzerain rights which it claimed under that Convention for the British Crown; and, when, at last, in response to a petition signed by 21,000 Uitlanders in the spring of 1899, Chamberlain induced President Kruger to meet Sir Alfred (now Lord) Milner, H.M.'s High Commissioner in South Africa, in conference at Bloemfontein on May 31st, there were few signs of any possible accommodation.

Nevertheless, the negotiations dragged on for over four months until, on October 9th, 1899, President Kruger finally broke them off by an ultimatum which was in fact a declaration of war, and President Steyn announced that the Orange Free State stood by the Transvaal. Even then, scarcely a single Englishman or Boer anticipated the con-

---

[1] In his (wholly untrustworthy) *Memoirs* the ex-Kaiser has sought to minimise his responsibility for the telegram, which he professes to have signed with reluctance. The present writer was informed, on excellent German authority, a short time after the despatch of the telegram that the Emperor had been persuaded with difficulty to tone down his original draft, some of the terms of which were considered by both the Chancellor and the Foreign Secretary to be needlessly provocative. (See letter to the Editor of *The Times*, Nov. 14, 1922.)

sequences that were to flow from that challenge. Both sides alike under-estimated the stubbornness of their adversaries. While most Englishmen believed that President Kruger was merely 'bluffing,' he had set his face against any settlement that would curtail his arbitrary power; and the Boers, remembering Majuba, not only despised the military power of Great Britain, but were convinced that they had friends amongst the Great Powers of Europe who would not stand by and allow the independence of the Boer Republics to be destroyed. Both sides thus entered blindly on a struggle which lasted for more than two years and a half, and placed a severe strain upon the resources of the British empire, but resulted finally in the annexation of both the Transvaal and the Orange Free State and the full recognition of British Supremacy in South Africa.

There is no need for us to dwell at any length on the military aspects of the War, except to recall its chief stages; since they frequently reacted, more or less directly, upon the international situation outside South Africa. The first stage covers the invasion of British territory by the Boers and the severe reverses inflicted by them upon the first expeditionary force sent out from England at Modder River, Stormberg, Magersfontein and Colenso; and it closes with the Relief of Ladysmith on February 28th, 1900. The second stage covers the successful advance of the British army, largely reinforced from home, under Lord Roberts as Commander-in-Chief and Lord Kitchener as Chief of the Staff—beginning with the surrender of Kronje at Paardeberg, and ending, after the occupation of the two Boer capitals, with the formal annexation of the Transvaal on October 25th. The third and longest, and the last, stage was that of the desperate guerilla warfare organised by the Boer Generals after President Kruger had fled to Europe, which was only slowly worn down, and not without frequent reverses, by the mobile British columns into which Lord Kitchener divided his forces, operating along chains of blockhouses, and driving the non-combatant Boer population into concentration camps, so as to deprive the Boer commandos of the supplies they drew from every farmhouse. These operations were carried on over a vast area, equal in size to France and Germany put together; but they were at last successful. On March 23rd, 1902, Representatives of the Boer Governments came into Pretoria to negotiate, and, on May 15th, sixty Delegates, almost all fighting-men from the commandos, and the members of the Transvaal and Free State Governments assembled at Vereeniging, to decide, in the light of those negotiations, between the two alternatives of surrender or dying in the last ditch. After prolonged debates, in which many stalwarts were still for resuming the hopeless struggle, a Commission, consisting of Louis Botha, De Wet, De la Rey, Smuts and Hertzog, proceeded to confer with the British Commander-in-Chief and the High Commissioner at Pretoria. They returned with a draft Treaty, to which they had themselves subscribed, but which was to be submitted to the Boer Convention for acceptance or rejection by the evening of May 31st. Again, heated discussions ensued; but the motion setting forth the inexorable necessity of surrender was at last adopted by fifty-four votes to six; and the Boer Commissioners travelled back to Pretoria in time to sign the Treaty only an hour before the expiry of the term of grace. The Boers surrendered and acknowledged the authority of His Majesty King Edward VII as their lawful Sovereign, while on the other hand the Imperial Government promised them a grant of £3,000,000 towards reconstruction, the liberation and return of all prisoners of war, the personal freedom of all burghers who made their submission and the restoration of their property, except in certain specified cases of transgression against the usages of warfare, together with the use, whenever necessary, of the Dutch language in schools and Courts of Justice. The Boers had to acknowledge defeat; but under the terms thus secured to them the sacrifice of national independence was, as General Smuts had himself said with prophetic vision at Vereeniging, "to lead our nation, under God's will, through defeat, through abasement, yea, and even through the valley of the shadow of death, to the glory of a nobler future, to the light of a brighter day."

II. The International Situation at the Outbreak of War, 1899

Invaluable as were the lessons of the long struggle—though only imperfectly taken to heart at the time—both for our military organisation and for the defensive coordination of the vast resources of the empire, the South African War plays a still more important part in history as a decisive turning point in British Foreign Policy.

Since the Napoleonic Wars, Great Britain had kept rigidly aloof from the entanglements of a permanent alliance with any Continental Power. The Alliance with France, Turkey and Piedmont during the Crimean War was purely a war alliance, of which the scope and duration were limited to the defeat of Russia in the Near East. Under the Cyprus Convention of 1878 with Turkey, Great Britain did, it is true, undertake permanent responsibilities for the defence of Asiatic Turkey against Russia; but, though Great Britain remained in occupation of Cyprus, the Convention became otherwise a dead-letter, when the Sultan repudiated in practice the corresponding obligation which he had incurred of amending Turkish misrule in his Asiatic dominions. Not till the South African War were British statesmen brought face to face with the full consequences of the profound change which had taken place in the values of international relationships since the Franco-German War of 1870. The Continent of Europe was divided into great armed camps, and their relative strength was evenly enough balanced to give pause to the greatest even of the Continental Powers before challenging any one of the others to mortal combat. On the other hand, the rapid development of trade and industry by scientific processes and on a scale hitherto quite unknown, the improved means and rapidity of communication by land and sea, the opening-up of new regions of the earth, the need of new markets for the vast output of European countries, and, in some cases, the pressure of increasing population, combined to induce these Powers to seek a less perilous outlet for their energies in the larger field of overseas expansion. Of that field, Great Britain had, almost without dispute, secured for herself the lion's share, since Trafalgar had ended in her favour the duel for sea-power with France which had filled the eighteenth century. Now, old and new rivalries were springing up again, and the world-wide interests and responsibilities of a world-wide empire laid her open to attack on many new land frontiers: Russia concentrated her action on Asia, advancing, as it seemed, with the irresistible momentum of a glacier upon Persia and towards India, as well as to the warmer waters of the Pacific Ocean. France, elbowed by us in 1882 out of her former position of preeminent influence in Egypt, but firmly established in Tunis, and from her older base in Algeria pressing on Morocco in the west and across the Sahara to the south into Central Africa, threatened to squeeze the British Colonies in West Africa back into the Atlantic, and at the same time carved out for herself in Eastern Asia a large empire in Indo-China, which was impinging from the south on the vast but inert mass of the Chinese empire almost as heavily as was Russia from the north. Italy burnt her fingers in Abyssinia, but kept a foothold on the East African coast and an eye on Tripoli in Northern Africa. The sovereignty of the vast Congo State conferred upon King Leopold II was converting even Belgium into a Colonial Power. Germany, though a very late comer, was only the more determined to secure for herself "a place in the sun," where-ever she could still get one, by hook or by crook, whether in Africa or in Asia or in the remote Pacific. Even the United States had so far departed from the Washington tradition as to retain a hold upon the Philippines as well as upon Cuba after the Spanish-American War, and the emergence of Japan as an Asiatic Power prepared to compete with the Western Powers, on terms not far removed from equality, formed another entirely new factor of incalculable importance. Great Britain, as the corner-stone of a far-flung empire loosely built up out of dominions and dependencies and colonies scattered over the whole face of the globe, came into contact—and contact meant at least potential conflict—with all these forces. They were necessarily rival, if not antagonistic, forces, and she seemed merely to have focussed upon herself the eyes of a jealous world in the splendid pageants of empire held in London on the occasion of Queen Victoria's two Jubilees in 1887 and 1897. To the masters of armed legions on the European Continent the military weakness of the British empire was more apparent than its still undisputed sea-power; for, while compulsory universal service had converted most of the Continental nations literally into nations in arms, Great Britain was still content to rely on voluntary recruitment for a small army, unlikely, it was assumed, to be ever required for any other purpose than the defence of the home shores or occasional oversea expeditions against uncivilised or semi-civilised peoples still unfitted to meet any well armed and disciplined European force.

This great transformation scene, by which the old conflict of rival European forces had been projected across the seas to the remotest Continents, had been watched at home in England only "as through a glass darkly," until it was suddenly and vividly illuminated by the South African War. Before the first three months of the War were over, the dangers of isolation made themselves as acutely felt as the unexpected strain to which a small Boer "nation in arms" subjected our military forces. The struggle was to last more than two and a half years, and, before the final victory was achieved, the British empire had to make its first effort to coordinate its scattered resources for a common effort, and to seek in permanent alliances an external safe-guard against the growing perils of that "splendid isolation" in which only a few years earlier one of the shrewdest of British statesmen had gloried.

When hostilities began in South Africa in October, 1899, Great Britain was, at least technically, to use a diplomatic phrase, on terms of peace and amity with all Foreign Powers. Of all the smaller European Powers only one had any direct interests in South Africa, namely, Portugal, whose South African possessions bordered in the north on German East Africa and British Central Africa and, after marching with the eastern frontier of the Transvaal, touched the British Protectorates of Swaziland and Tongaland in the south. From Delagoa Bay and Lorenzo Marquez on Portuguese territory started the only railway that gave the Boers direct access to the sea, independently of the great trunk lines under British control to Natal and the Cape. The Portuguese, who knew the value of Delagoa Bay, had refused both British and Boer overtures for the acquisition of territorial or other rights, and, during the critical days that followed the Jameson raid and the German Emperor's telegram to President Kruger at the end of 1895, the Portuguese Government had stoutly refused permission for a German naval detachment to land there and be conveyed to Pretoria for the alleged protection of German interests. Friction had frequently occurred between Great Britain and Portugal over Colonial questions, and much apprehension had been caused in Lisbon by an Agreement concluded in 1898 between the British and the German Governments and kept a profound secret, but dealing, it was shrewdly suspected, with the distribution between them of the Portuguese colonies, in the event of Portugal being driven to part with them. Nevertheless, Portugal prided herself upon being England's most ancient ally in Europe, and history having, also, taught her how largely she relied on British sea-power for her safety, neutrality was for her a matter of necessity as much as of choice.

Of the other small Powers, who all remained neutral, Holland alone deserves special mention, since, in the absence of political interests in South Africa, she was bound to the Boer republics by exceptionally close ties of race and sentiment. The Boers were of Dutch stock and spoke a Dutch dialect, and the people of Holland had always followed the destinies of their South African kinsmen with sympathy and pride. Hundreds of Hollanders, not a few of them of considerable influence and ability—such as, for instance, Dr Leyds, who, as State Secretary, was in charge of the Transvaal Foreign Affairs—had been imported into the service of the Boer republics. Holland was the centre of Boer propaganda in Europe, and the Netherlands Government often served, quite honourably, both before and during the War, as a friendly intermediary for communications between other Continental Governments and the Boer republics. Once only, towards the very end of the War, the Dutch Government made a tentative suggestion of its own in the hope of hastening peace, namely, that the British Government should grant safeconducts to the members of the Boer Governments then in Europe for returning to South Africa, in order to consult with their colleagues and come back armed with full powers to make peace. The British Government refused. But there was no disposition in this country to resent even this manifestation, however ill-timed, of the natural sympathies of the Dutch for their Boer kinsmen.

Among the Great Powers, France and Russia, our relations with whom had been most frequently and seriously strained, had no direct interests in South Africa. Neither had Austria-Hungary or Italy, who, as Mediterranean Powers, were alike concerned to maintain their traditional friendship with us, any such interests. The brief storm raised in the United States concerning Venezuela at the end of 1895[1] had quickly subsided, and much older prejudices and jealousies had been softened by the friendly attitude of Great Britain throughout the Spanish-American War.

Germany was the only Great Power who had direct interests in South Africa. It was in the scramble for Africa, when a large part of it could still be described as a "Dark Continent," that she had first displayed her determination to possess colonies of her own beyond the seas, and besides Tongaland and the Cameroons on the West Coast and German East Africa on the East Coast, she had acquired German South-West Africa, marching with British Bechuanaland and Cape Colony. British public opinion had recovered in a great measure from the first shock of amazement and indignation produced by William II's telegram to President Kruger at the time of the Jameson raid, and the German Emperor had gained the confidence of Cecil Rhodes when he visited Berlin in March, 1899, by promising all facilities for carrying the Trans-African Telegraph through German East Africa from Rhodesia to Uganda. But Germany's claim to make her voice heard in any emergency that might affect the balance of power in South Africa had not been forgotten, and, though she professed to have advised President Kruger to come to terms with Sir Alfred Milner, few Englishmen believed that the Boer republics would have rushed into a conflict, had they not been encouraged to imagine that they could rely on something more than platonic assurances of German goodwill. Nor was it to Africa that Germany had confined her disquieting activities. Even in British official circles most friendly to Germany, there was an undercurrent of alarm at the ubiquitous restlessness of German policy, ever since the young Emperor had dismissed

[1] See *ante*, pp. 222–6.

Bismarck and taken the control of Foreign Affairs into his own hands. The Imperial Chancellor, Prince Hohenlohe, was known to be too old, and his position too insecure, to exert much influence over William II; and his Foreign Secretary, Count (afterwards Prince) von Bülow, brilliant, versatile, cynical, was chiefly intent on qualifying for the succession to the Chancellorship by adapting his views to those of his Sovereign lord and master. In the Far East, under the pressure of Franco-Russian encroachments upon the Chinese empire, Great Britain and Germany had at times been drawn closer together; but the British Government had found it well to acquiesce in Germany's occupation of Kiaochow and in her far-reaching claims, based on that occupation, to a virtual monopoly of economic enterprise in the Province of Shantung. In the Near East, German diplomacy successfully paralysed the European Concert at Constantinople, whenever the British Government pressed for retribution for the Armenian Massacres or urged administrative reforms anywhere in Turkey; and Germany's purpose was made plain, when the spectacular demonstrations of the German Emperor's friendship for the Sultan Abdul Hamid during the Graeco-Turkish War of 1897 and the imperial progress to Constantinople and Jerusalem in 1898, were rewarded by the Turkish Concession for the construction of the Bagdad Railway with all its obvious implications. German attempts to manœuvre Great Britain into heading a sort of European diplomatic crusade against the United States during the Spanish-American War had failed egregiously; but, at the moment when hostilities broke out in South Africa, negotiations between the German, British and American Governments concerning the Samoan Islands had just reached a very critical stage.

To none of the Great Powers could Great Britain, therefore, look for more than strict, and not always very friendly, neutrality; and she had to reckon not only with the policy of foreign Governments, but with the indirect pressure exercised upon them by public opinion, which was, in most countries and for many reasons, extremely hostile to the British. Ill-informed, for the most part, as to the origin of the South African conflict, foreign nations were apt to see in it merely an heroic, because unequal, fight put up by the two sturdy little Boer republics against the aggressive power of the mighty British empire. The sympathy which in these circumstances not unnaturally went out to the weaker side was, in most cases, stimulated by popular prejudice against Great Britain and by special causes of resentment, sometimes real, sometimes artificially fomented. In France, still very sore from the Fashoda incident, intense bitterness was provoked by the very great sympathy, often expressed in unmeasured terms, with which the wrongs of the unfortunate Dreyfus had met in this country at a time when the French people were reft in twain over his case; and, while these manifestations of sympathy were put down to sheer hypocrisy and malice by the majority of Frenchmen, who had been taught to regard Dreyfus as a traitor, many of those who believed in his innocence resented any claim on the part of foreigners to sit in judgment on a French domestic quarrel. Frenchmen as well as Russians—in so far as there was in those days any Russian public opinion among the masses—united in regarding Great Britain as a Power whose insatiable imperialism clashed everywhere with the interests of their own country, and they idealised the Boers as the latest victims of British greed. In Austria-Hungary, the personal friendliness of the old Emperor Francis Joseph and of many Hungarian magnates failed to exempt the German-speaking element in the Dual Monarchy from the fever of Anglophobia imported from Germany. Even in Belgium, where the Flemish population was drawn towards the Boers by racial kinship, and the French-speaking population took its cue largely from France, King Leopold II knew how to exploit against the British the national susceptibilities aroused by the attacks already directed from Great Britain at his misrule of the Congo State. Only in Italy, in Greece and in Norway, the memory of the warm sympathy and support which the British people had extended to them in their struggles for national unity and independence, withstood in a great measure the inflowing tide of pro-Boer sentiment. How powerful these memories still were in Italy, was shown when General Ricciotti Garibaldi, with all the prestige of his father's name, offered to raise an Italian contingent to join the British in South Africa, and Visconti-Venosta, then Italian Minister for Foreign Affairs, recalled in Parliament the great debt of gratitude which the Italian *Risorgimento* owed to Great Britain. In the United States, the hostility of Irish and German Americans did not seriously disturb the new atmosphere of goodwill created by Great Britain's attitude during the Spanish-American War, and the straight hint given by Captain Chichester to the German Admiral in Manila Bay, that, if he attempted to interfere with the American squadron, he would have to reckon with the White Ensign of the British Navy as well as with the Stars and Stripes, was still fresh in the minds of most Americans. The United States had no political interests in South Africa, and the material interests of the few, but not uninfluential, American citizens connected with the mining industry in the Transvaal enlisted their sympathies wholly on the British side. Before the War was over, Theodore Roosevelt, who was known to be a friend of England and a sincere believer in the closest possible relations between the two countries, succeeded to the Presidency, on the assassination of McKinley in September, 1901.

Nowhere was public opinion more solidly and profoundly anti-British than in Germany. For the reactionary Prussian *Junkers*, who were still the ruling military and official caste, Great Britain only concealed under the thin disguise of a Constitutional monarchy those hateful principles of democratic government which paved the way to Revolution. In the eyes of the more modern German middle-classes, bent on industrial and commercial expansion, Great Britain was Germany's chief and most objectionable rival, and, in those of the new Pan-German school for whom, in William II's own words, the future of the German Empire lay on the sea, the British empire was the adversary that blocked Germany's path on every ocean highway. Though one of the cardinal principles of Bismarck's foreign policy was never to quarrel with England, the old Chancellor had himself been at pains to create a strong anti-British current of feeling through his organs in the German Press, when a battle royal was raging between him and the Empress Frederick about the engagement of one of her daughters to Prince Alexander of Battenberg, sometime Prince of Bulgaria, which he and the old Emperor regarded, not only as a *mésalliance* for a Prussian Princess, but as a scheme for embroiling Germany with Russia. The need for his campaign against "English petticoat government" passed away when the fatal disease declared itself which carried off the Emperor Frederick in the prime of life, within three months after the old Emperor's death. But the evil seed which Bismarck had sown, not only amongst the German people but in the mind of the youthful Prince who became German Emperor under the title of William II at the early age of 29, fell on receptive soil. The German people were being gradually trained under their young Sovereign's ambitious inspiration to look upon "world-dominion" as their rightful goal, and the British empire as the chief obstacle to its attainment, especially when he gave them the new watchword that "Germany must grasp the trident in her fist." No other foreign Government had the Press so thoroughly under its control, and, when the South African War broke out, it was attuned to hatred. The German people saw in Great Britain's hour of difficulty the hour of their own opportunity. So also did the German Government, though it read Germany's opportunity in a different sense from that in which a large number of Germans read it, who believed that now was their chance for settling once and for all their long account with British arrogance. There were some cooler heads in Berlin who preferred to exploit the South African War, not merely for extorting graceful concessions from Great Britain in the Samoan and other pending questions, but for luring her into the network of alliances which Bismarck had woven round the German empire for the consolidation and preservation of his life's work. Only through German disclosures after the Great War has it become known that Bismarck's mind had already moved in this direction as soon as he ceased to be haunted by the fear that, if the Crown-prince Frederick ever came to the throne, British influence at the German Court would try to make Germany's foreign policy subserve British rather than German interests. In reply to enquiries made by Lord Salisbury from the German Ambassador in London as to the anti-British bias imputed to Prince William (afterwards William II), the old Chancellor took, in November, 1887, the, for him unprecedented, step of addressing to the British Prime-Minister a long private letter, in which Prince William was stated to have concurred, denying the charge in very dignified terms, and then proceeding to review at considerable length the whole European situation, with the purpose, implied rather than explicit, of suggesting that the close association of interests between Germany and Great Britain might be suitably translated into the still closer association of an actual alliance. The British Prime-Minister's reply was extremely friendly, but evaded the question of an alliance, and the subject was not revived until the German Government had reason to hope that the South African War would make Salisbury, who was now again Prime-Minister, more amenable to pressure. For Germany, the advantages of an alliance with Great Britain had become in the meantime still more obvious, as in the intervening years Bismarck's "Reinsurance" Treaty with Russia had been dropped, when William II assumed control of German Foreign Policy, and the intimacy between France and Russia had developed into a definite Alliance.

British Ministers had also, in the meantime, been awakened to the drawbacks of a policy of "splendid isolation," and the South African War drove home the lesson which they had been gradually learning. Salisbury's long experience of Foreign Affairs enabled him to see more clearly than any of his colleagues how ill-organised and equipped the British empire was, with all its vast resources—but with all its equally vast responsibilities—to meet the crucial strain to which it might at any moment be subjected by the growing ambitions of rival Powers, all armed to the teeth. His mind, however, more massive than flexible, was slow to break loose from the traditions of a lifetime, and he still preferred to trust to the old methods of meeting emergencies as they arose rather than to venture into the perhaps smoother but deeper waters of a permanent alliance with any Power. While he distrusted profoundly the instability of French Ministries and the tortuousness of Russian diplomacy, he had felt, so long at least as Bismarck was at the helm, that he knew pretty well what course Germany was steering. But that sense of relative confidence, already impaired from the moment when William II threw the old pilot overboard, had been greatly shaken during his interview with the young German Emperor at Cowes, immediately after he had returned to office as Prime-Minister in 1895. Of what actually happened at that interview no official record has been made public in this country, if indeed Salisbury ever kept one. According to recent revelations in Germany and to the statement drawn up by the Emperor himself at the time for the information of the Chancellor, which his successor, Prince Bülow, allowed the writer to peruse, Salisbury disclosed a scheme for the partition of Turkey between the European Powers, and more especially between Great Britain and Germany, which William II indignantly rejected. When the substance of that statement was communicated to Salisbury, the only reply made by him was that it showed the importance of having a third party present at any conversation with the German Emperor. The chief interest attaching now to that interview is that, whatever was its precise nature, Salisbury's attitude gave deep offence to William II, who never forgave him, while it left behind in Salisbury's mind an almost invincible distrust of the German Emperor, which strengthened, so far as Germany was concerned, his instinctive aversion from any permanent form of alliance. In Chamberlain, however, Salisbury had a very powerful colleague, whose mind was cast in a different mould and trained in a different school. The outbreak of hostilities in South Africa brought home in an acute form to Chamberlain's practical and positive mind the dangers with which the British empire was confronted, not in South Africa only. He saw that, as a result of her "splendid isolation,"

Great Britain might not merely have at any moment to resist alone and unaided an attack on any one of the many vulnerable points of her empire, but would, at all events, be constantly subjected to heavy blackmail in matters which were not worth going to war over. For he regarded as nothing less than blackmail the demands sprung with increasing frequency upon Great Britain from Berlin, of which he resented the form even more than the substance. But when he compared these exactions and the hectoring tone in which they were driven home with the formidable menace of the pressure steadily exercised by France and Russia on the British position in West Africa and in Asia, respectively, he came to the conclusion that, whereas there appeared to be a profound and irreconcilable antagonism between British interests and those of France and Russia, there was no such contrast between those of Great Britain and Germany as to prevent a square deal in lieu of intolerable wrangles over piecemeal agreements.

III. ANGLO-GERMAN NEGOTIATIONS, 1898–1901

Thus it came about that, during the first two years of the South African War, while popular opinion was nowhere more universally and aggressively hostile to Great Britain than in Germany, and nowhere was such hostility more frequently reflected than there in the public utterances of responsible statesmen, negotiations were intermittently carried on, and at times with every promise of success, between London and Berlin, for a formal alliance, which might have changed the whole course of recent history.

No authoritative account of these negotiations has been published in this country, but their course can be accurately traced from illuminating publications in Germany since the Great War, and especially from the *Reminiscences* of Freiherr von Eckardstein, the German diplomatist who, for the greater part of that time in charge of the Embassy in London, acted as the principal channel for the communications that passed between the two Governments[1]. He not only gives a full account of the many vicissitudes through which the negotiations passed, but also the text of his confidential Instructions from, and reports to, Baron von Holstein, the "*éminence grise*" of the German Foreign Office who, almost unknown to the outside public and very rarely accessible even to the foreign diplomatists in Berlin, controlled and directed German policy with practically unchallenged authority for many years after the fall of the old Chancellor, of whom

[1] Cf. *ante*, p. 147 note 2.

he had been one of the most trusted disciples and servants. Numerous letters from Chamberlain and other personages in London—many of them reproduced in facsimile—furnish equally strong evidence of the anxiety of the British Government to promote the proposed alliance. A curious feature of the negotiations is that while they were on the one hand conducted in London, for the most part, not so much with Lord Salisbury, even when he was himself still Secretary of State for Foreign Affairs as well as Prime-Minister, as with other members of his Cabinet and notably with Chamberlain and his chief Liberal-Unionist colleagues, the Foreign Office in Berlin, on the other hand, abstained so carefully from keeping the German Emperor acquainted with the details of their progress that his impulsiveness sometimes prompted him to hasty action on his own account which could not conduce to their success.

Before war broke out, it had been arranged that the Emperor, accompanied by Count von Bülow, should pay, in the late autumn, a visit to England in response to an invitation from Queen Victoria. Once the War had begun, it was impossible for the visit to take place, until the Samoan Question had been got out of the way. For neither was the German Emperor inclined to face the unpopularity of such a visit, unless Great Britain did something tangible to allay the violent anti-British feeling in Germany, nor could the British Government incur the risk of dangerous complications with Germany at so critical a juncture. On November 14th, 1898, an Anglo-German Convention was signed which ended the *condominium* in Samoa. In return for a few unimportant concessions elsewhere in the Pacific, Great Britain waived her claims to any of the islands, which were divided by subsequent agreement between Germany and the United States. The former acquired in complete sovereignty the two principal groups, including Sawaii and Upolu, the latter Tutuila and some smaller islands. On November 20th, 1899, William II arrived at Windsor, and during his stay there he and his Secretary of State had long conversations with Chamberlain, in which an exchange of views as to the possibility and desirability of an alliance encouraged the Colonial Secretary to advocate it publicly and warmly. Fresh from Windsor and in complete agreement, as he believed, with Count von Bülow and his imperial master, he delivered on November 30th, 1899, a great speech at Leicester, in which he stated that "every farseeing English statesman had long desired that we should not remain permanently isolated on the Continent of Europe, and that, from the moment that aspiration was formed, it must have appeared to everybody that the most natural alliance is between ourselves and the great German Empire." He paid an eloquent tribute to the fine qualities of the Germans, a people of the same stock as ourselves; and such an alliance, he declared, would be based both on interest and on sentiment. That he spoke in equally warm terms of America and expressed his desire to see the United States form with Great Britain and Germany a "new triple alliance" for the Peace of the World, was due not only to his own intense faith in the closest possible relations between the two great English-speaking nations but to the wish expressed to him by Count von Bülow himself that in any public utterance advocating an understanding between Germany and Great Britain the United States should be also included.

Chamberlain's speech at once provoked in the German Press a storm of indignation at the suggestion that Great Britain could be a fit and worthy ally for the German empire. Neither Count von Bülow nor his organs made the slightest attempt to check this outburst, and, to the astonishment and disgust of British Ministers, he hastened to cast the Windsor conversations to the winds in a speech in the *Reichstag* on December 11th in which he ostentatiously ignored the overtures made in full agreement with him only a few days earlier by Chamberlain for a "new triple alliance," and laid all his stress on the existing Triple Alliance between Germany, Austria-Hungary and Italy and on the maintenance of friendly relations with Russia. As regards Great Britain, he did not confine himself to the frigid assurance that "we are entirely prepared to live in peace and friendship with that Power on the basis of complete reciprocity and mutual consideration," but went on, in a tone of almost undisguised menace: "It is exactly because our international position is now favourable that we must utilise it to make ourselves secure for the future." To that end, Germany's Navy above all needed strengthening. "For without might, without a strong army, without a strong navy we cannot become a world power. In the coming century the German nation will be either hammer or anvil."

With extraordinary hardihood, Count von Bülow nevertheless persisted in sending Chamberlain, through confidential channels, private communications pleading the difficulties of the internal situation in Germany, and conveying assurances that he still held fast to the policy agreed upon during the imperial visit to England, and that a time would yet come when he would be in a position to uphold it fully and openly, without thereby provoking dangerous opposition in the *Reichstag* and in the country. He even took credit to himself for an official order issued in Berlin, forbidding any German officer to take service with the Boers during the War. But it was clear to British Ministers that, if Count von Bülow had ever meant what he said at Windsor, the news of the military reverses inflicted upon the British arms in South Africa had made him change his mind; and, in a private letter dated December 28th, Chamberlain conveyed to Berlin, through the same channels through which these empty excuses for a palpable breach of faith had reached him, a plain statement that, in the circumstances, all further negotiations for an alliance must be dropped for the present, and that it must be left for the future to show, when the South African War was over, whether or not they could ever be usefully resumed.

At this juncture, too, an incident occurred in South African waters which threatened to strain Anglo-German relations still more severely. News reached Berlin, in the last days of 1899, that British cruisers had stopped German mail-steamers on the high seas under suspicion of carrying contraband of war, and had taken them to Durban to be searched. The German Government put forth in London so forcible a protest that Salisbury[1] was constrained to express his surprise at so abrupt and offensive a communication from the Representative of a Power with whom Her Majesty's Government believed themselves to be on friendly terms. Two of the steamers, the *Herzog* and the *General*, were, however, speedily released, as the suspicions which led to their seizure were at once shown to be unfounded. The detention of the *Bundesrat* was more prolonged; but though there were many circumstances that seemed to justify the action of the naval commanders on the spot, the search proved fruitless. The British Government had given assurances that the matter would be dealt with as expeditiously as possible, and expressed regret for the inconvenience caused to steamers carrying mails. But indignation ran very high in Germany, and Admiral von Tirpitz, bent on exploiting the incident in support of the new German Navy Bill about to be laid before the *Reichstag*, urged on the Emperor, with whom he enjoyed great favour, the advantages of some more demonstrative action. At his suggestion, William II decided to send an Admiral over to London with a message to Lord Salisbury which would have virtually amounted to an ultimatum. Salisbury, warned

[1] *Parliamentary Paper, Africa*, No. 1 (1900).

in time, was just able to forestall so provocative a step by informing the German Representative in London that, the Admiralty having just learnt that no contraband of war had been found on board the *Bundesrat*, orders would be sent for the ship to be immediately released; and he promised that not only would suitable compensation be paid to the German shipping company, but that German steamers would not be again molested on mere suspicion.

There was, nevertheless, still the flavour of a retrospective ultimatum in Count von Bülow's arrogant recital of the various demands made by Germany and accepted by Great Britain, when, on January 19th, he announced to the *Reichstag* that the incident had been settled to the satisfaction of the German Government. It served Admiral von Tirpitz's purpose. A Navy Bill was introduced on February 3rd, doubling the strength of the German Navy as adopted only two years previously in the Navy Bill of 1898, and the preamble emphasised its significance. "Germany," it ran, "must have a fleet of such strength that war with the mightiest naval power would involve risks threatening that power's supremacy." William II's phrase that "Germany must grasp the trident in her fist" was being translated into practice.

The German Government was not yet prepared to risk an open conflict with England, unless she could rely on the support of other Powers. Almost as soon as hostilities began in South Africa, communications passed between Petrograd, Paris and Berlin as to the expediency of diplomatic intervention in order to stop the South African War. They were abortive. William II hastened to take credit to himself with the British Government by conveying private assurances that he had defeated Russian and French attempts to win Germany over to a policy of intervention[1]. In any case, the chief consideration that restrained Germany may safely be inferred from the statement in the German answer to Russia that "German policy could not entertain a suggestion for intervention in the Boer War as

---

[1] There is evidence to show that Count Muravieff mooted the question in a conversation with Delcassé in Paris shortly after the outbreak of hostilities in South Africa, and that the Russian Embassy in Berlin formally approached the German Government in February, 1900, and returned to the subject again in November, 1901. The present writer, on the other hand, has been assured that the original suggestion was made in one of the many private letters with which the German Emperor constantly importuned the Tsar, in the shape of an appeal to the Russian Sovereign to follow up the generous initiative he had taken in inviting the Powers to the Peace Conference of the Hague by an opportune word of friendly remonstrance in London against the danger to the peace of the world involved in the South African War.

long as Germany had to reckon with the hostility of her French neighbour." This was a fairly plain invitation to Russia to secure the cooperation of France as the condition precedent to Germany's cooperation, and France was not willing. For Delcassé, who had joined the Waldeck-Rousseau Cabinet as Minister for Foreign Affairs in June 1898, had already conceived the desire, which he afterwards fulfilled, of bringing France and Great Britain together by a comprehensive settlement of all the principal questions that divided them.

The German Government, meanwhile, had taken more note than had the German public of the resolute effort by which the British people, not only at home but in every part of the empire, were retrieving the military situation in South Africa. With the large reinforcements sent out from home under Lord Roberts and Lord Kitchener, and contingents from Canada and Australia which offered a signal demonstration of the British empire's unity and of the extent of its resources in times of stress, Roberts had driven the Boers out of British territory and occupied the capitals of the two republics, before the German Navy Bill was finally adopted in the *Reichstag* on June 12th. The wave of anti-British agitation which had borne it to acceptance was allowed to subside for the time. Events, moreover, were happening in the Far East which were to bring home once more to the German Government the value of friendly relations with Great Britain, whose naval supremacy could certainly not yet be effectively challenged. In the summer of 1900, the Boxer troubles gave the German Emperor a welcome chance of showing the "mailed fist" in Northern China, and a large expeditionary corps was despatched from Germany to join with the other international forces in the restoration of order. But the German Government was quite conscious that, whatever might be happening in South Africa, Germany was dependent upon British naval stations and upon the goodwill of Great Britain for the transport of her troops to and from China, and also for their safety when there. Moreover, anxious though Germany was to stand well with Russia, she could not view without apprehension the way in which that Power was exploiting the situation in China for its own ends. Negotiations between Berlin and London had drawn the two Governments together before the actual conclusion of an Anglo-German Agreement with regard to China in October, 1900, which was at once regarded as a notable sign of *rapprochement*, especially when Count von Bülow, who had just succeeded Prince Hohenlohe as Chancellor, himself followed it up by giving proof of a much more conciliatory disposition, even in a matter relating to South Africa.

While the Boers were not yet at all prepared to give in, they were coming to perceive that there was little hope for them without foreign help; on a last quest for it, President Kruger had sailed for Europe from Lorenzo Marquez on September 11th on the Netherlands cruiser *Gelderland*, which the Queen of Holland placed at his disposal, after obtaining from the British Government an assurance that he would not be molested. When he landed at Marseilles and proceeded to Paris, he was greeted with great popular demonstrations and received in audience by the President of the French Republic. He intended to visit Berlin and reached Cologne. Here he was also acclaimed as a hero by enthusiastic crowds, when he was abruptly warned by the authorities that his presence was not desirable in Germany, and that, in any case, he would not be received by the Emperor. The warm sympathy of the Dutch people and his reception by the Queen of the Netherlands at the Hague were but a poor compensation for the unexpected rebuff from Berlin.

The ground was thus prepared for the resumption of conversations about an alliance, and, early in 1901, Baron von Eckardstein was able to inform his Government that the Colonial Secretary and his friends in the British Cabinet had been at last driven, by the renewal of Russian pressure in the Far East and French in Morocco, to recognise that the time had come for Great Britain to choose between joining the Triple Alliance or coming to terms, even should these prove very costly, with France and Russia. They had acknowledged their preference for an understanding with Germany, and would do everything in their power to promote it. Just then Queen Victoria's last illness brought over the German Emperor to his royal grandmother's death-bed, and the warmth of feeling which he showed during the funeral ceremonies, in which he played a singularly conspicuous part, created a notable revulsion of British opinion in his favour, both in Court and Government circles and amongst the British public generally. In the course of his conversations with British Ministers, including Lord Lansdowne, to whom Lord Salisbury, while retaining the Premiership, had transferred the Foreign Office in November, 1900, the word "alliance" was not used; but the international situation was discussed in so conciliatory a spirit and with so complete an agreement on both sides that actual negotiations for an alliance could be at once resumed. They did not, however, on this occasion have in view either the "new triple alliance" discussed between Bülow and Chamberlain in November, 1899, or an exclusively Anglo-German alliance; but they extended to the accession of Great Britain to the existing Continental Triple Alliance, in which Germany was the predominant partner; and the Germans themselves added the suggestion, which alone was ultimately to bear fruit, though in quite a different shape from that which they then had in mind, that Japan might be brought into this great defensive league. The new treaties were to include some provision showing that they were not in any way directed against the United States, and they were only to be kept secret until public opinion had been sufficiently prepared to allow them to be laid before the legislatures of the different Contracting Parties without encountering a storm of ill-informed opposition. Rapid progress was being made, when one of the Emperor's sudden bursts of ill-temper created a serious hitch. King Edward might even then have asked the question which he put some years later to Baron von Eckardstein, "If only I knew who really rules in Berlin!" Omnipotent as the Emperor was and omniscient as he conceived himself to be in the conduct of Foreign Affairs, Count von Bülow and the German Foreign Office, who rightly dreaded his wild and often very precipitate irruptions into the domain of diplomacy, considered themselves justified in carrying on negotiations in London to which the Emperor had assented in principle, without keeping him too closely informed as to the various stages of their progress. The form in which China was to pay the compensation claimed by Foreign Powers for losses caused by the Boxer disturbances gave rise to differences of opinion between London and Berlin, which, however, were not of sufficient importance to affect the much larger issues under discussion. The Emperor had always taken a keen personal interest in the Chinese imbroglio, and, irritated by what he regarded as the dilatoriness and illwill of the British Government, suddenly mounted his high horse, used very abusive language about British Ministers and finally wrote a rude letter to King Edward, in which he described British Ministers as "unmitigated noodles." The incident in itself was as trivial as the question which gave rise to it; but it made British Ministers ask themselves once more what reliance could be placed upon an understanding with a country whose all-powerful Sovereign was liable to such fits of utter irresponsibility. The negotiations flagged, but received a fresh stimulus from the renewed French activities in Morocco and the far more ruthless activities of Russia in Manchuria.

But, when the British Government invited Germany to act upon the Anglo-German Agreement of the preceding year and to join in a protest at Petrograd against the high-handed action of the Russian Generals in Manchuria, the German Government replied that the Anglo-German Agreement did not apply to Manchuria, but only to the eighteen provinces of China proper within the Great Wall—an interpretation of the Agreement which once more justified Lord Salisbury's distrust of German good faith; and, while an acute controversy arose between the two Governments over this point, a fierce conflict of public opinion broke out again in both countries as to the South African War.

The occupation of the two Boer capitals had not broken the stubborn resistance of the elusive Boer commandos, which not only managed to escape pursuit in spite of the much larger forces which the British had steadily brought into the field, but often inflicted very unpleasant surprises upon them. Anti-British feeling revived all over the Continent, and nowhere more fiercely than in Germany, when the military measures adopted by Lord Kitchener to deprive the combatant Boers of their supplies by massing the non-combatant population into concentration camps provoked malevolent criticism even in England. A "stop-the-war" campaign which some of the responsible leaders of the Opposition themselves encouraged found a ready echo abroad, and German newspapers indulged in the most venomous attacks upon the conduct of the British troops who were accused of inhuman cruelty. The German Government was known to have, in the reports from the German Military Attachés accompanying the British Army, ample material for enlightening the German Press which it controlled, as to the truth in those matters, and for calling a halt to its organised campaign of vituperation and calumny. It did nothing, and, in a speech at Edinburgh on October 25th, Chamberlain protested that, severe as might be the military measures taken in South Africa, they were much less severe than those taken in the course of warlike operations by other nations now intent upon vilifying the British Army, and he referred, amongst other instances, to the doings of the Germans in France during the War of 1870. The rebuke was stern but not unmerited. At first, the German Press showed singular reticence and generally refrained from comments. Count von Bülow himself made no reference whatever to Chamberlain's speech in a conversation with the present writer, who, as Director of the Foreign Department of The Times, had been privately invited by the German Foreign Office to Berlin for a discussion on the whole question of Anglo-German relations in view of the proposed alliance[1]. The Chancellor was chiefly concerned to establish in an exhaustive review of Anglo-German relations a large credit balance for Germany and to prove, in particular, the German case in regard to Manchuria. He professed to deplore the violent anti-British feeling, of which he did not deny the existence, in Germany, and ended with an emphatic assurance that, so long as he was Chancellor, he would not allow it to deflect him by a hair's breadth from his policy of unswerving friendship towards Great Britain. Nevertheless, before many more days had passed, the German Press was suddenly given its head and fell furiously on Chamberlain for daring to institute comparisons between British mercenary troops and Germany's incomparable army. In the interval, the German Government had been given to understand that Great Britain was not prepared, in the circumstances, to proceed further with the alliance negotiations or to acquiesce in the German interpretation of the China agreement. So there was no longer any need for restraining German Anglophobia, and, when the *Reichstag* reassembled at the beginning of 1902, the Chancellor himself, distorting the language actually used by Chamberlain, delivered what purported to be a reply to him only less offensive in form than the phraseology already used in his accredited organs. The German Army, he said, stood on too high a pinnacle to be reached by any detractors, and, like Frederick the Great, he could only warn any Foreign Minister who ventured to attack it, that he was "biting on granite."

Thus came to an end the long drawn negotiations for an alliance, fitfully carried on for nearly two years between Berlin and London in an atmosphere charged all the time with the passionate jealousy of Great Britain which the South African War had brought to the surface in Germany. It had been a curious chapter of secret diplomacy—as unreal indeed as it was secret—but it had had its uses. Outwardly, there was no striking change in the official relations between the British and German Governments, and, as the South African War gradually approached its appointed close, German public opinion relapsed into more or less sullen indifference, and its occasional ebullitions came to be regarded in this country as customary exhibitions of German boorishness which British public opinion could afford to treat with something like amused contempt. The worst

[1] See *The Times*, September 11th and 13th, 1920. (Letters to the Editor.)

indecencies of the German Press could moreover always be matched in the French and in that of many other continental countries, whilst very few people in England understood how much closer than in other countries were the relations between the Government and the Press in Germany, controlled, as they were, by a special department in the German Foreign Office, which submitted every day voluminous excerpts not only to the Chancellor, but to the Emperor himself who duly returned them with his own marginal comments in blue pencil. British Ministers, however, had once and for all satisfied themselves that, if security could no longer be found for the British empire in the old policy of "splendid isolation," it was least of all to be sought in an alliance with the German empire. The first result was the conclusion, within the next few months, of an alliance between Great Britain and Japan which, though advocated only a short time previously by the German Government, was promptly denounced as the treacherous betrayal of the sacred interests of a common white civilisation to an aggressive yellow race. Shortly afterwards, on his farewell visit to Windsor, Baron von Eckardstein, who had resigned in disgust at the bad faith and folly of his own Government, overheard the word "Morocco," recurring too frequently not to sound ominous in his ears in the course of an intimate conversation between Chamberlain and Paul Cambon, the French Ambassador in London. Chamberlain had warned the Germans more than once during his negotiations with them as to the inevitable consequences of their failure, and the British Government was already feeling its way towards the entente, first with France and then with Russia, which was to shape the Foreign Policy of Great Britain during the next decade, in prevision of the day when, in fulfilment of Count von Bülow's sinister speech in December, 1899, Germany would feel herself strong enough to play the part of hammer on the anvil of the world.

IV. THE ANGLO-JAPANESE ALLIANCE, 1898–1902

The grave events of which Northern China was the scene in the second year of the South African War had the effect, on the one hand, of producing a certain temporary and superficial community of interests between Great Britain and Germany and, on the other, of demonstrating a far more real and enduring community of interests between Great Britain and Japan.

In the Far East, Germany and Great Britain had been drawn

together only by the menace of Russia's growing ascendancy in Peking. The establishment of a large sphere of Russian interests behind the strategical base, created by the leasing of Port Arthur from China, and the construction of the Manchurian railway, linking it up with the great Siberian trunk line were held to threaten both the older sphere of British interests in the Yang-Tsze valley and the more recent German sphere of interests in the Shantung peninsula, created by the occupation and leasing of Kiaochow. Japan had been drawn for the first time towards Great Britain, when, before the Chinese-Japanese War, Lord Rosebery recognised her long contested right to emancipate herself gradually from the many servitudes imposed upon her by the Western Powers when they compelled her to emerge from her long seclusion and throw her ports open to intercourse with the outside world. She was again drawn, still more closely, towards Great Britain at the close of the Chinese-Japanese War, when the British Government refused to join with Russia, France and Germany in coercing her into a revision of the Treaty of Shimonoseki and the retrocession to China of the hard-won fruits of her victories in the Liaotang peninsula. Japan, therefore, welcomed the British occupation and leasing of Wei-Hai-Wei as a reply to the Russian occupation and leasing of Port Arthur in 1898, and, according to Count Hayashi, Chamberlain, already at that time, assured Baron Kato, then Japanese Minister in London, that Great Britain was quite disposed to enter into an alliance. When, in September, 1899, the United States, alarmed by the creation by foreign Powers of spheres of interest, which, in the case of Russia especially, tended steadily to expand and to be converted into spheres of monopoly, invited all the Powers concerned to make joint Declarations that they would observe the principle of equal economic opportunity for all nations, Great Britain and Japan again found themselves in complete agreement in expressing their immediate and unequivocal adherence to that principle. Throughout the Boxer disturbances there was closer agreement between Great Britain and Japan than between any other two Powers and more friendly and more intimate relations prevailed between British and Japanese, and, it may be added, American troops on the spot, than between them and any of the other foreign contingents.

The appointment of Prince Tuan, himself a professed Boxer, to the Presidency of the Tsungli-Yamen or Chinese Board of Foreign Affairs showed that the Chinese Court was either powerless or unwilling to repress the Boxer movement, or to ensure even the safety of the foreign Representatives in Peking. On June 10th, 1900, Sujiyama, a member of the Japanese Legation, was murdered in the streets of the capital, and, nine days later, the German Minister, Baron von Ketteler, had the same fate. It was clear that the relief of the Peking Legations and the restoration of order in Northern China could only be effected by a considerable force, to be supplied as far as possible by all the Powers whose interests and dignity were in this case equally affected. But to have awaited the arrival of contingents from each of the several countries concerned would have meant dangerous and possibly disastrous delays. Russia, who was bent upon playing her own game and was already overrunning the whole of Manchuria, would have been only too willing to take over the whole affair on her own account. But to this the other Powers were quite unprepared to consent, and she could not openly separate her cause from theirs. She had 30,000 men in Manchuria alone, and, making a virtue of necessity, she supplied a contingent to cooperate with those of the other Powers, but on lines which she kept more or less distinct. Of the other Powers, Japan, owing to her geographical proximity, was in a position to give earliest assistance, and was ready to do so. British forces were hurried up from Hongkong and from India, and French troops from Tongking and Americans from the Philippines. Austria-Hungary and Italy were represented only by small detachments, to show the flag. Germany was determined to play a conspicuous part; but she was a long way off. A large expeditionary force was at last despatched under Field-marshal Count von Waldersee, for whom the Emperor ultimately, by a characteristic device, secured the supreme command, however nominal in some cases, over the international forces in Northern China. It only reached Tsientsin after the Peking Legations had been relieved, on August 13th, by other allied contingents, among whom the British and Japanese were the first to penetrate to the hard-pressed British Legation, the chief European place of refuge and centre of resistance.

The appearance of unity between the Powers became still more difficult to preserve when the main object of the operations had been attained and negotiations were reopened with the Dowager Empress, who had fled to Siyanfu. The German forces, though too late to join in the relief of the Legations, were at pains to act up to the injunctions given to them before they started by the Emperor, William II, that they should inspire such terror in the Chinese as would make them tremble for generations to come; and they carried out a series of punitive expeditions west and south-west of Peking which gave the unfortunate population a foretaste of German methods of frightful-ness. The Russians completed the conquest of Manchuria to the borders of Korea on the one hand and the treaty-port of Niu-Chwang on the other. Meanwhile, negotiations between Germany and Great Britain resulted, on October 16th, 1900, in an agreement upholding the principle of the open door in China (Article I), disclaiming territorial designs upon China on the part of the Contracting Powers (Article II), and declaring (Article III) that

In case of another Power making use of the complications in China in order to obtain under any form whatever territorial advantages, the two contracting parties reserve to themselves the right to come to a preliminary understanding as to the eventual steps to be taken for the protection of their own interests in China.

Of greater value than the actual provisions of the Convention was the visible demonstration it furnished of an understanding between the two Governments at a time when the relations between Great Britain and Germany were subjected to a severe strain by the South African War. Germany had given hostages to fortune by sending to Northern China a large expeditionary force dependent for its communica-tions and its safety upon the goodwill of Great Britain, who was in possession of all the chief coaling stations between German and Far Eastern waters, and still undisputed mistress of the seas. In these circumstances, the Convention served actually to bind Germany over to abstention from any interference in South Africa, while the Ger-man Government construed it as a recognition of the community and equality of German and British rights in China, and notably in the Yang-Tsze valley, which the British had hitherto regarded as their own particular sphere. Japan was the first Power to adhere, on October 29th, to the principles embodied in the Convention, and France, Austria-Hungary, Italy and the United States followed suit, while Russia accompanied her acceptance of the principles with the sarcastic comment "that the Convention had not perceptibly modified the situation in China," or "infringed in any way the *status quo* established in China by existing Treaties." The trouble was to discover what were the existing Treaties which Russia had in mind; for she had followed up her occupation of Manchuria by a series of Treaties with the Chinese of which the terms and scope were kept secret, or, when they leaked out, were neither affirmed nor denied in Petrograd. In Peking, the Russian Representative stood ostentatiously aloof from those of the other Powers, and finally separated himself from them when they pressed for the punishment of a number of Chinese officials concerned in the worst Boxer excesses. While seeking by such means to ingratiate herself with the Chinese, Russia continued to press them to sign a Manchurian agreement which was intended to confirm her in the possession of the provinces which she had occupied under cover of the Boxer troubles. Nor did she cease to press her demands upon China when, on September 17th, 1901, the Peace Commission of the eleven Powers at last signed at Peking with the Chinese Plenipotentiaries the final Protocol for the resumption of friendly relations.

Throughout this critical period Great Britain and Japan had acted in close accord diplomatically in resisting and encouraging China to resist Russian pressure; and herein they had the general support of the United States. For Japan especially, much more than the future of Manchuria was at stake. She perceived that Manchuria would only be a starting-point for the Russian penetration of Korea, whose independence, in the eyes of all Japanese statesmen, was an absolutely vital interest for Japan. She had gone to war with China in 1894 in order to put an end to Chinese suzerainty over Korea, and there had been ever since an acute struggle between Russia and Japan at Seoul for ascendancy over the Korean Court. British statesmen were equally convinced that, so long as Russia remained in possession of Manchuria, she would completely dominate the Chinese Court at Peking, to the detriment of British influence and interests. In the diplomatic contest at Peking the German Representative had, in most cases, cooperated with the British, Japanese and American, rather than with the Russian Representative, and he had insisted stoutly and successfully on the despatch of a Chinese Prince to Berlin to do penance before the Emperor for the murder of Baron von Ketteler.

During the negotiations for an alliance between Germany and Great Britain, the German Government had been the first to suggest that Japan should be drawn into it as an ally whose military support in the Far East would be of immense value to Great Britain in the event of a conflict with Russia. Baron von Eckardstein himself, in March, 1901, broached the question with the Japanese Minister in London, Count Hayashi, who had long been anxious to bring about an alliance between his country and Great Britain. Count Hayashi was quick to take the hint, and, having obtained authority from Tokio to sound the British Government, he made the first overtures to Lord Lansdowne on April 17th, 1901. The British Secretary of State gave him every encouragement, and, with the approval of Lord Salisbury and of King Edward himself, cordial conversations followed, in which the idea of a formal alliance was accepted on both sides in principle, so that only an agreement as to the actual terms remained for discussion. It was not, however, till October 16th that these negotiations entered upon a formal and final stage. By that time, fresh difficulties were hampering the progress of the Anglo-German negotiations. When the Germans found British Ministers eager to respond to the suggestion that Japan should be brought into the alliance, they began to fear that Great Britain might conclude an alliance with Japan before concluding one with Germany and would then possibly feel less anxious to bind herself to the latter. They therefore suggested that not till after the conclusion of the Anglo-German alliance should Japan be invited by Great Britain to join it. This point was left in abeyance, and a far more serious obstacle to an Anglo-German understanding arose when the British Government, invoking the Anglo-German Agreement of 1900, requested the German Government to support its protest at Petrograd against Russian action in regard to Manchuria. Germany maintained that China, as referred to in Article III of the Convention, meant only the eighteen provinces of China proper and did not include Manchuria, which was merely a Chinese dependency outside the Great Wall. Both sides insisted on their own interpretation, Germany being determined not to jeopardise her friendship with Russia by supporting the British interpretation against her. The Anglo-German negotiations broke down altogether as other circumstances revived the antagonism between the two countries; so that, when Count Hayashi bluntly asked Lord Lansdowne what were his plans with regard to including Germany in the alliance, the Secretary of State replied that he thought the best way was for Japan and Great Britain to carry on their own negotiations and to defer inviting Germany to join till later, if necessary. The question of including her in the alliance was never again revived.

But, just at this stage, the British Government learnt with some surprise and alarm that Prince Ito, the foremost of all the Japanese "Elder Statesmen," had arrived in Europe from Japan on his way to Petrograd. It was under Prince Ito's own Administration that Count Hayashi had made the first overtures for an alliance with Great Britain, and he was known to have expressed complete agreement with his successor, Count Katsura, when the latter proposed to pursue the same policy. Count Hayashi, who was left in complete ignorance of the purpose of Prince Ito's Mission to Europe, found himself in a position of great embarrassment, as there was no doubt that the Elder Statesman intended to sound the Russian Government as to the possibility of a direct understanding between Japan and Russia. Prince Ito was not alone among Japanese statesmen in believing that a Russian alliance might be preferable to one with Great Britain, since the conclusion of the former could, they thought, alone avert an actual conflict between Japan and Russia, while that of the latter would merely place Japan in a much stronger position for hazarding such a conflict if Russia made it inevitable. The Japanese Government felt, however, that the negotiations with Great Britain had advanced too far by the time Prince Ito reached Europe for him to be left a free hand at Petrograd; and, though he proceeded to the Russian capital, and had several conferences with Russian Ministers, nothing came of them. Whatever views he may have entertained, they had not prevailed in the Council of Elder Statesmen held before the Throne at Tokio on December 7th, which decided unanimously in favour of the Anglo-Japanese alliance; and, after communications had passed between London and Tokio with regard to a few relatively unimportant modifications in the original draft, the Anglo-Japanese Agreement was actually signed by Lord Lansdowne and Count Hayashi on January 30th, 1902.

Article I of the Agreement declared:

"The High Contracting Parties, having mutually recognised the independence of China and Korea, declare themselves to be entirely uninfluenced by any aggressive tendencies in either country. Having in view, however, their special interests, of which those of Great Britain relate principally to China, while Japan, in addition to the interests which she possesses in China, is interested in a peculiar degree politically, as well as commercially and industrially, in Korea, the High Contracting Parties recognise that it will be admissible for either of them to take such measures as may be indispensable in order to safeguard those interests, if threatened either by the aggressive action of any other Power, or by disturbances arising in China or Korea, and necessitating the intervention of either of the High Contracting Parties for the protection of the lives and property of its subject."

Under Article II

Great Britain and Japan undertook that if, in defence of their respective interests as above described, either of them should become involved in war with another Power, the other ally would maintain a strict neutrality and use his efforts to prevent others from joining in hostilities against his ally.

Article III provided that,

should any other Power or Powers join in hostilities against that ally, the other was to come to his assistance and conduct war in common and make peace in mutual agreement with him.

Under Article IV both parties agreed that

neither of them should without consulting the other enter into separate arrangements with another Power to the prejudice of the interests above described.

And, under Article V, that

the two Governments should communicate with one another fully and frankly whenever, in the opinion of either, the above-mentioned interests were in jeopardy.

Article VI stipulated that

the agreement should remain in force for five years from the date of its signature, when it was to come at once into effect, and afterwards until the expiration of one year from the date on which either Power should have denounced it; but in no case was it to expire while either ally was actually engaged in war, the alliance continuing *ipso facto* until peace was concluded.

Though merely called an "Agreement," this instrument was in fact a formal treaty of defensive alliance, the first under which Great Britain had in modern times contracted obligations of such a nature for a term of years. No less remarkable was the fact that this Alliance was concluded with an Asiatic Power which, less than fifty years earlier, was still shut off by its own laws from all intercourse with the outside world, and which had only recently emerged from its seclusion and passed from medieval into modern civilisation under actual coercion by the Western Powers. The effects were far-reaching. The Anglo-Japanese Alliance did not avert the conflict between Russia and Japan which the inordinate ambitions of the former Power, steadily encouraged from Berlin, had already rendered inevitable; but the knowledge that Great Britain would stand by Japan if any other Power joined with Russia, confined the War to a duel between the two protagonists. If it helped Japan to achieve by force of arms a position of great ascendancy in the Far East, not altogether free from danger, as regards the integrity and independence of a distracted and enfeebled China, it placed Great Britain in a position to exercise a restraining influence over Japanese statesmen, and the very defeat which it enabled Japan to inflict upon Russia served to open the eyes of Russian statesmen to the real trend of German policy and to render them more responsive than they had shown themselves before to British overtures—backed henceforth by the friendly advice of their French allies—for a settlement of Asiatic differences.

CHAPTER V

CONTINENTAL AGREEMENTS, 1902–1907

I. Great Britain and Germany, 1902–1905

ON the termination of hostilities in South Africa it appeared as if something of the old friendliness between Great Britain and Germany might be restored. In September, 1902, Lord Roberts and the Secretary for War, Mr Brodrick (afterwards Viscount Midleton), accepted an invitation to the German autumn manœuvres. In October, the Kaiser declined to receive the Boer Generals, who had come to Europe to collect funds for their stricken fellow-countrymen, unless they were presented by the British Ambassador—a condition which they declined to accept[1]. In November, the Kaiser paid a family visit to Sandringham for King Edward's birthday, and the Prime-Minister, Lord Lansdowne and Mr Chamberlain were invited to meet him. Two days later, at the Guildhall banquet, Mr Balfour referred scornfully to the "fantastic imaginings" of the newspapers with regard to the visit; but it was speedily followed by armed cooperation against a recalcitrant South American State.

Venezuela had long enjoyed unenviable notoriety for the frequency of its revolutions; and the civil turmoil inevitably involved the subjects of Foreign Powers. At the opening of the new century, the country was in the grip of President Castro, who showed as little consideration for the Great Powers as for the rebels who challenged his rule. The series of incidents which were to goad Great Britain to action opened in February, 1901, with the seizure of four vessels which had taken refuge in a storm on an island off the coast of Trinidad[2]. "Very serious notice should be taken," wrote the Governor to Lord Lansdowne, "otherwise neither life nor property will be safe in those parts of the island nearest the mainland." Other outrages quickly followed on Venezuelan soil. While Downing Street was addressing futile protests to Caracas, the Government of Venezuela retaliated with a complaint which recalled the Alabama controversy. At the end of 1901 the *Ban-Righ*, a British vessel, was bought by Columbia;

[1] The Kaiser was anxious to receive them, but yielded to urgent advice from England. See Eckardstein, *Lebenserinnerungen*, II. 405–10.
[2] See Venezuela, No. 1, 1903.

and Venezuela urged the British authorities to detain her, suspecting that she would be employed to carry arms to the rebels. Lord Cranborne, the Under Secretary for Foreign Affairs, cogently replied that, since the Columbian Minister had declared the vessel to have been bought for his Government, and, since Columbia was not at war with Venezuela or any other State, it would constitute an act of war against Columbia to prevent her sailing. Accordingly, she sailed from a British port under a British flag to Antwerp, where she was laden with arms and ammunition. On reaching Martinique, she took on board a Venezuelan rebel, was handed over to the Columbian Government, and was proclaimed a pirate by Venezuela. After being employed for a few weeks in acts of hostility against Venezuela, during which she was observed to fly the British flag, she arrived in a damaged condition at Trinidad, under Columbian colours, on March 23rd, 1902. For her depredations President Castro held the British Government responsible, stubbornly refusing to discuss British grievances till he had received satisfaction. Meanwhile, a British schooner was boarded and destroyed by a Venezuelan gunboat, and another vessel was confiscated on suspicion of carrying arms, her crew being put ashore in a destitute condition.

On July 29th, Lord Lansdowne instructed the British Minister at Caracas to warn the Government that, unless it assured him that similar incidents would not recur and promptly paid compensation, the British Government would take such steps as might be necessary to secure reparation. Castro replied that claims could not be discussed till the *Ban-Righ* question was settled, and repeated his old complaint that the Trinidad authorities had shown favour to the rebels. On receiving this reply, Lord Lansdowne requested the Admiralty to suggest "the most effectual and convenient manner of putting pressure on the Venezuelan Government." The Admiralty replied that the North American and West Indies fleet could blockade selected ports in November, when the unhealthy season would be over. Convinced that Castro's obstinacy would yield to force alone, Lord Lansdowne welcomed support from other victims of Venezuelan misrule. He informed the German Ambassador, who broached the subject in conversation, that we intended to obtain satisfaction for the claims of British subjects, and that we should be quite ready to confer with the German Government with a view to joint action. The Ambassador replied that a joint naval demonstration might perhaps be undertaken; and, on October 22nd, a Foreign Office

Memorandum to the German Government officially invited co-operation. On November 11th, Count Wolff-Metternich replied that Germany would support the warning to Venezuela, and agreed to our suggestion that the first step should be to seize the Venezuelan gunboats. Each Power should uphold the demands of the other.

On the same day the Foreign Secretary telegraphed a final warning to Caracas, and instructed the British Ambassador at Washington to inform the Secretary of State of the British grievances and of the steps in contemplation[1]. John Hay replied that, though he regretted that European Powers should employ force against Central or South America, the United States could not object to their obtaining redress for injuries, provided that they aimed at no acquisition of territory. When, at the eleventh hour, Italy announced her desire to cooperate, Lord Lansdowne replied that there was no time for fixing the conditions of her conjunction, but that she might send a ship to join in the blockade. France, on the other hand, informed the British Government that the seizure of the customs, part of which had been earmarked for French creditors, would prejudice French interests; to which the Foreign Secretary replied that French interests should not suffer.

To the warning of November 11th Castro rejoined, as usual, that, far from there existing grievances on the part of Great Britain against Venezuela, the latter had serious grounds of complaint in the case of the *Ban-Righ* and the partisanship of Trinidad. This parrot-like response swept away the last hesitation, and on December 7th the British and German Ministers at Caracas presented ultimata. Even now the incorrigible Castro merely repeated his reply of November 14th, adding that the Treasury was empty. When the warships in the harbour of La Guayra were seized and the coast blockaded, he retaliated by arresting British and German subjects in Caracas, but quickly liberated them on the intervention of the Minister of the United States. In a flaming Manifesto the President denounced the attack as barbarous and cowardly; but, on December 11th, he invited the United States Minister to propose that Great Britain and Germany should submit their claims arising out of the insurrection to arbitration. Since the offer only applied to a portion of the Allied claims, the coercion continued. Lord Lansdowne, however, accepted arbitration in principle, and expressed the hope that President

---

[1] The American side of the Venezuelan incident is told in J. B. Bishop, *Theodore Roosevelt*, vol. I. ch. 20, and Thayer, *Life of John Hay*, II. 284-90.

Roosevelt himself would act as arbitrator. The President was not unwilling, and Castro agreed to the choice. The American Secretary of State, however, dissuaded the President from acceptance, and proposed a reference to the Hague Tribunal, which was adopted by all the parties concerned.

The blockade continued till February 13th, when Venezuela signed a Treaty recognising the British claims in principle, and undertook to pay at once those arising from the seizure and plundering of British vessels. Secondary demands were to be referred to a mixed Commission consisting of a British and a Venezuelan Representative, with an Umpire appointed by President Roosevelt. The Hague Tribunal was to decide whether the claims of the blockading Powers should have priority, as they demanded, or whether all the claimants should be on the same footing. Venezuela undertook to assign 30 per cent. of the customs of her two chief ports, and new arrangements were made for meeting the bondholders' interest. The Tribunal met in October to settle the question of priority, and the British contention was accepted.

Though the British and German Governments cooperated harmoniously throughout the winter, their association was viewed by large sections of British opinion with profound distaste, and Ministers took pains to minimise their commitments. There was no alliance, declared Lord Cranborne; and Lord Balfour of Burleigh spoke of "a mere casual cooperation for a specific purpose and a limited time." The hostility shown was noted in Germany with surprise and resentment. "We have acted in full agreement and perfect loyalty," declared the Chancellor in the *Reichstag*[1]. "All the more curious is the hostility of a portion of the British Press, which is only explicable by a certain embitterment resulting from the violent attacks of the Continental Press during the Boer War. I am glad to say that no change has occurred in the relations between the monarchs and the Cabinets, who meet in the old friendly manner." The end of the partnership, however, left the relations of the two countries less satisfactory. "The suggestion for common action," writes Count Bernstorff, at that time Secretary to the German Embassy, "came from England; but we should have been wiser not to listen to it[2]."

American opinion, though deeply suspicious of German designs since a German squadron had been sent to Manila during the War of 1898, had not become seriously incensed against the action of Great

---

[1] Bülow, *Reden*, vol. I. January 19th, 1903.   [2] *My Three Years in America*, p. 13.

Britain. Our avowed sympathy with the United States in the Spanish-American War, followed by the voluntary surrender in 1901 of our rights under the Clayton-Bulwer Treaty, had healed the smart of the crisis of 1896, and made it possible for controversies, whether old or new, to be settled in an amicable spirit. When the blockade of Venezuela was over, the discussion of the treaties relating to the Alaska Boundary was resumed[1]. The discovery of gold in Klondike necessitated an exact delimitation; but negotiations, which began in 1898, proved fruitless, owing to the claim put forward by Lord Herschell, the British Commissioner. A proposal by Lord Salisbury in 1899 to refer the controversy to arbitration was declined by the United States, mindful of the unfavourable award in the case of the Seal Fisheries. The question slumbered till 1903, when Roosevelt warned the British Cabinet that, if the negotiations again fell through, he would establish the Boundary as the United States claimed it, adding that, while ready to discuss the minor issues, he would not agree to Arbitration on the large sections of Alaska demanded by Canada, and that the Canadian claim to deep water was indefensible. The British Government appointed Lord Alverstone, who, while the two Canadian Commissioners maintained their full claims, was compelled by the evidence to accept the main contentions of the three American Delegates. The adoption of the American standpoint by the Lord Chief Justice in October, 1903, confirmed the belief in British goodwill, and, in the President's words, removed the last obstacle to absolute agreement between the two peoples.

In the following year, Hay concluded Treaties of Arbitration with Great Britain and other Powers, referring to the Hague Tribunal matters not affecting territory, honour or vital interests, after the Contracting Parties had concluded an agreement defining the dispute. The Senate, however, jealous of its power, substituted the word "treaty" for "agreement," thus retaining in its hands the power to permit or forbid arbitration. This denoted a step backwards, since no dispute could be referred without a special treaty; and the President naturally vetoed the amendment. The failure of his last effort for peace wrung from the Secretary of State a cry of distress. A treaty entering the Senate, he complained, was like a bull entering the arena. No one could say when the fatal blow would fall; but it was certain that it would never leave the arena alive. His efforts, however, were

[1] See Thayer, *Life of John Hay*, II. 203–13; Bishop, *Theodore Roosevelt*, vol. I. ch. 23.

not thrown away; for the relations both of the Governments and the peoples became more and more friendly. Early in 1907, the British Cabinet paid the United States the compliment of sending James Bryce to Washington; and the hoary dispute relating to the status of American fishermen in the waters of Newfoundland and Nova Scotia was, shortly after, referred to the Hague.

The Venezuelan adventure was scarcely concluded, when the British Government was confronted with a problem of far greater importance to Anglo-German relations. Despite British predominance in Constantinople for a generation after the Crimean War, only a few short railways were built in Asia Minor; and it was not till 1888, when Constantinople was linked up with Central Europe, that the project of a trunk line through Asiatic Turkey took practical shape[1]. In return for a loan, a German group, headed by the *Deutsche Bank*, obtained a Concession for 99 years to administer the line of 57 miles from Haidar-Pasha (opposite the capital) to Ismid, and to continue it to Angora, with a substantial kilometric guarantee and preferential right of extension. Angora was reached in 1892; and in 1893, in return for another loan, a concession was granted from Eski-Shehr (midway between Haidar-Pasha and Angora) to Konia, which was reached in 1896. By 1899 Germany had won the complete confidence of the Sultan, and the Anatolian Railways Company secured in principle a Concession to the Persian Gulf.

Some London financiers had been associated with the German concessionaires in 1888, and in 1899 Chamberlain remarked to the Kaiser, on his visit to London, that he would like to see Great Britain cooperating with German enterprise in Hither Asia. But, while French financiers took shares in 1899, German efforts to secure British assistance were unavailing. The attempt was renewed in February, 1901, when, however, G. von Siemens, Director of the *Deutsche Bank*, returned empty-handed from a journey to London. On January 1st, 1902, the Company received a Concession for 99 years to build a railway from Konia to the Gulf, with a kilometric guarantee of 12,000 francs, and 4500 francs for working expenses. As the security was not yet specified and no terminus was selected, this document was merely a preliminary outline. The final Convention was signed on March 5th, 1903, extending the line from Konia to Basra, *via* Adana, M'osul and Bagdad, with branches to

---

[1] The story of the project and of Anglo-German negotiations was related by an official of the Foreign Office in *The Quarterly Review*, October, 1917.

Aleppo, Urfa, Khanikin and other cities north and south of the main line, and with preferential rights to build lines to the coast between Mersina and Tripolis in Syria. The Concession included conditional permission to work all minerals within twenty kilometres each side of the railway, to construct ports at Bagdad and Basra, and to navigate the rivers in the service of the railway.

It was a magnificent gift, which required British goodwill to turn it to full account. On April 8th, in answer to a complaint from Mr Gibson Bowles that the Government were hanging on to the skirts of German financiers, the Prime-Minister (Mr Balfour) admitted that the matter was under consideration. Germany had suggested that British capital and control should be equal to that of any other Power; that Great Britain should sanction the increase of the Turkish customs; that the Indian mails should be carried by the railway, and that we should employ our good offices to secure a terminus at or near Koweit. Whether or not we cooperated, he argued, the railway would be built. German and French financiers were in agreement, and we had to consider whether it was desirable that the shortest route to India should be entirely in foreign hands; whether the terminus should be at Koweit, within our own sphere of influence; and, finally, whether British trade would benefit if British capital were represented. "I think that this great international artery," he concluded, "should be in the hands of three Powers rather than of two or one. It is to our interest that countries which we cannot absorb should not be absorbed by others." This announcement, which clearly indicated the leanings of the Prime-Minister, stimulated the campaign against cooperation; and on April 23rd he informed the House that the invitation had been declined. The Cabinet had desired the whole line, including the portion already constructed, to be international, with equal rates, equal powers of control, construction and management for Germany, Great Britain and France. The German proposals did not offer sufficient security for the maintenance of these principles, and we were therefore unable to meet their wishes in regard to the Indian mails, a terminus at Koweit, or the appropriation of an increase of the customs duties to the kilometric guarantee.

It was quite true that the German proposals did not afford the "absolute equality" which we demanded; but it was hardly to be expected that the nation which had planned the great enterprise and taken its risks would accept a position which gave the majority of shares—carrying with them the power of control—to Great Britain and France. The Cabinet was well aware of the unpopularity of the Venezuela partnership, and knew that their followers would scrutinise with a jealous eye any renewal of the association. In asking so high a price for cooperation it virtually declined the invitation. It was a momentous decision, and has been judged in very different ways. It was greeted by Unionist opinion with relief, as an escape from the embrace of a Power whose ambitions were beginning to cause apprehension; and we may add that it prevented the completion of the Bagdad Railway by 1914. On the other hand, it was regretted by so stalwart a champion of an Anglo-German understanding as Sir Frank Lascelles, the British Ambassador at Berlin, as a needless widening of the gulf that had already opened between the two nations.

The Bagdad discussions were quickly followed by the revival of a troublesome controversy. The grant by Canada in 1897 of a preference of 33⅓ per cent. on imports from the Mother-country had led to formal protests from Belgium and Germany against the breach of most-favoured-nation treatment. Lord Salisbury had replied by giving the year's notice required to terminate the Treaties and suggested a new agreement, allowing the self-governing Colonies to make their own arrangements for inter-imperial trade. According to German law, the general or higher Tariff automatically came into force on the termination of a commercial treaty; but in 1898 the German Government, in order to afford time for negotiations, continued most-favoured-nation treatment for a year to every part of the British empire except Canada[1]. This provisional arrangement was renewed in 1899, 1900 and 1901, the law of the last named year prolonging the provisorium till the end of 1903.

On March 18th, 1903, Lord Lansdowne enquired what action Germany intended to take after December 31st. Baron Richthofen, the Foreign Secretary, replied that he hoped to prolong most-favoured-nation treatment to Great Britain, but that, if Germany were differentiated against in important parts of the empire, and if, in particular, South Africa followed the example of Canada, he was doubtful whether public opinion would sanction it. At this point, a new element of discord was introduced by the insertion of a clause in the Canadian Tariff imposing a surtax of 10 per cent. on the goods of any country which discriminated against imports from Canada. In explaining this

[1] See *Correspondence with the Governments of Belgium and Germany*, 1903. Cd. 1630.

decision Lord Lansdowne pointed out that it was only taken after the failure of every effort to secure fair treatment of Canadian produce, and would be revoked if Germany restored most-favoured-nation terms. Should the German Government persist in their attitude, and extend to the products of other British Colonies, and even to those of the United Kingdom, the discrimination which they had enforced against Canada, a very serious issue would inevitably be raised, involving the fiscal relations of the two countries.

Each country had a grievance against the other, and on June 27th the German Foreign Secretary set forth his case in a lengthy despatch. The maintenance of the lower Tariff after the denunciation of the Treaty of 1865, he argued, revealed a special desire to meet the wishes of Great Britain, and the application of the General Tariff to Canada, far from inflicting a penalty, was merely the automatic consequence of the expiration of the Treaty. If the British Colonies were free to determine their own customs policy, other countries must be allowed to treat them as separate customs entities. The responsibility for the initiation and aggravation of the conflict could not be laid on Germany; but the Government was ready for an exchange of ideas, and would leave it to Great Britain to make suitable proposals. To this apologia Lord Lansdowne despatched a spirited rejoinder. Canada had not increased the duties on German goods or treated Germany differently from other countries. She had been made to suffer because she refused to extend to Germany, as to all other foreign Powers, a special concession made to the Mother-country. If it were true that the Colonies were independent customs units, which foreign Powers were at liberty to treat as such, it followed that no responsibility could attach to Great Britain in consequence of their acts. Having thus given vent to his indignation at the threat to punish the Mother-country for the generosity of one of her children, the Foreign Secretary concluded by promising to approach any discussion of the difference in a most conciliatory spirit. Since, however, the British market was too valuable to risk for considerations of logic or pride, and since German trade with Canada continued to increase despite the preference, no more was heard of retaliation. The controversy, none the less, had added to the store of ill-will which was steadily accumulating between the two nations.

The main cause of Anglo-German tension in the years following the Boer War was neither Venezuela, nor the Bagdad Railway, nor Canadian Preference, nor commercial rivalry, but the resolve of

Germany to build a formidable Fleet. British anger at the Kruger telegram of 1896, declares Reventlow, converted Germany to the idea of a Fleet[1]. In 1898, a small programme of construction to be carried out by 1904 was accepted by the *Reichstag*, and the German Navy League was founded. Little interest, however, was aroused till the Boer War, when the Kaiser utilised the excitement created by the stoppage of German vessels on the east coast of Africa to secure acceptance of an enlarged programme to be completed by 1917. The decision of 1900 brought Germany into what German publicists describe as the danger-zone; and in his political apologia, *Imperial Germany*, Bülow claims credit for careful steering. When Bebel quoted in the *Reichstag* articles by naval officers arguing that the fleet must be strong enough to defeat England, the Chancellor dismissed them as rubbish to which no sensible German paid attention. Even when the programme of 1900 was completed, he pointed out, the German Navy would only stand fourth or fifth on the list; and it harboured no aggressive designs[2]. In July, 1904, King Edward visited his nephew at Kiel. Among the guests was Count Seckendorff, formerly Chamberlain of the Empress Frederick, and a friend of both King Edward and Bülow. Finding that the King considered the Chancellor hostile to Great Britain, Seckendorff informed the latter, who promptly forwarded a copy of the newly published volume of his speeches with the passages relating to England marked. In an interview sought by a British journalist in November[3], the Chancellor continued his efforts to dissipate the suspicion of his policy and character. He consented to see Mr Bashford, so he explained to the *Reichstag* on December 5th, because in recent months certain British publicists had sown tares in the garden of Anglo-German relations. The fleet was purely defensive.

I cannot imagine that the thought of a war can be seriously entertained by sensible people. So I do not take the enmities of a section of the English Press too tragically. I hope the destinies of both countries will always be guided by cool heads who know that England and Germany, not only now but for ever, are best served by the preservation of the present peaceful relations.

The rumour that he was personally hostile to England he dismissed as unintelligible[4].

[1] *Deutschland's Auswärtige Politik*, p. 96. [2] *Reden*, January 22nd, 1903.
[3] Published in the *Kölnische Zeitung* and *The Nineteenth Century*, and reprinted in Bülow, *Reden*, II. 393–400.
[4] Hammann (*Zur Vorgeschichte des Weltkrieges*, pp. 144–5) relates that Bülow desired Germany's navy to consist mainly of defensive units, as advocated by Admiral Galster, but that Tirpitz insisted on capital ships.

Official assurances failed to dispel the anxiety of the British Government, which was fostered, not only by the Navy Law of 1900, but by provocative utterances of the Kaiser, who styled himself Admiral of the Atlantic, and of certain of his subjects. It was owing to the danger anticipated from a new quarter that it was decided, in 1903, to construct a first-class naval base at Rosyth; that the Cawdor programme of four battleships annually was sanctioned, and that Sir John Fisher, on his appointment as First Sea Lord in 1904, proceeded drastically to overhaul the distribution and composition of the British Fleet. Our relations with France and the United States had by this time become cordial; the Russian Fleet sailed away to its doom at Tsushima, and the Japanese Alliance safeguarded our interests in the Far East. The North Pacific and South Atlantic squadrons were accordingly abolished, the Mediterranean and China Fleets were almost denuded of battleships, and the Channel Fleet was strengthened. An Atlantic Fleet, resting on Gibraltar, was planned, and a home fleet was due to appear in the North Sea in 1906. Obsolete ships were scrapped; and, in October, 1905, the *Dreadnought*, the largest and most heavily armed vessel in the world, was laid down.

Long before Great Britain had begun to suspect the ulterior designs of the German Navy, fleetless Germany had felt alarm at the irresistible strength of our Fleet; and her apprehensions were strengthened by occasional indiscretions in the British Press. In 1897, an article in *The Saturday Review* contended that, if Germany could be swept away to-morrow, every Englishman would be the richer. This mischievous nonsense attracted no attention in England; but it was diligently exploited to whip up enthusiasm for a Fleet. In 1904, an article in *The Army and Navy Gazette*, suggesting that Great Britain should veto any further increase of the German warships, was accepted in Germany as the authentic voice of the Admiralty. Early in 1905 a still more threatening note was struck by a member of the Ministry. In explaining to his constituents the object and result of the policy of concentrating our Fleet in home waters, Mr Arthur Lee, Civil Lord of the Admiralty, urged his hearers to turn their face from France and the Mediterranean to the North Sea. If war were declared, it would be possible to strike the first blow before the other party read the news in the papers. The speaker in vain complained that he was misreported and misunderstood. The Kaiser complained to the British Ambassador[1], and large sections of German opinion began to believe that their country was threatened by a

See Baron Greindl's despatch of February 18th, *Belgische Aktenstücke*, p. 3.

sudden attack. The construction of the *Dreadnought* intensified the feeling of danger and impotence.

" I was besieged by a demand for a large increase to meet British threats," writes Tirpitz[1]. "Even the Kaiser favoured propaganda by the Navy League and wished me to reduce the life of our big ships, which was longer than elsewhere. I resisted this and offered my resignation. My Bill of March, 1906, added the six large cruisers which had been refused in 1900, and obtained money to widen the Kiel Canal, through which Dreadnoughts could not pass."

The naval rivalry entered on a new and more dangerous stage, and each Admiralty attributed aggressive designs to the other.

A speech by the Prime-Minister on May 4th, 1905, explaining the views of the newly-founded Committee of Imperial Defence, contributed in some degree to tranquillise opinion. The Army and Navy, explained Mr Balfour, should be concentrated so far as possible; but experts had decided that, even if the Regular Army were abroad and our organised fleets at a distance, an invasion would not be attempted with less than 70,000 men, and could not reach London. In the following month Lord Roberts issued an appeal to make rifle-shooting "a national pursuit." Failing Conscription, he argued, the security of the State depended on the ability of the nation thus to take up arms in self-defence. He appealed for £100,000 to promote rifle clubs; but the slender response showed that the German danger was not yet taken seriously by the people at large.

II. GREAT BRITAIN AND FRANCE, 1902–1904

While our relations with Berlin were drifting from bad to worse, London and Paris made up their quarrel. Delcassé had informed his first visitor at the Quai d'Orsay of his intention to restore cordial relations[2]; and the decision to evacuate Fashoda cleared the ground for a new orientation. His views were shared by M. Paul Cambon, whom he transferred from Constantinople to London shortly after the Fashoda crisis, and whose first task here was to delimit boundaries in North Africa. "The work," he declared before leaving London in 1921[3], "went quickly and smoothly, for Lord Salisbury knew his own mind. . . . Then I suggested that there were several other matters which might be settled in an equally friendly spirit. He shook his head and smiled. 'I have the greatest confidence in M. Delcassé,' he

---

[1] *Memoirs*, vol. i. ch. 15.
[2] Stephane Lauzanne, *The Fortnightly Review*, February, 1918.
[3] See the interview in *The Times*, December 22nd, 1920.

said, 'and also in your present Government. But in a few months' time they will probably be overturned, and their successors will do exactly the contrary. No, we must wait a bit.'"

To the soreness created by Fashoda and the Dreyfus case a new irritant was added by the Boer War; but the advocates of reconciliation abated neither hope nor effort. Work of enduring importance was accomplished by Sir Thomas Barclay, who by long residence had won for himself a distinct place in the life of the French capital, and to whom it occurred that it would be of service to the good cause if the British Chambers of Commerce were invited to meet in Paris in 1900. The meeting was a great success, and English visitors flocked to the Exhibition. Though Kruger's visit took place shortly after, the seed had been sown, and the gross caricatures of Queen Victoria in the French illustrated papers disappeared. No decisive advance, however, was possible while Lord Salisbury's influence was supreme and the Boer War in progress, and Delcassé remarked impatiently to Sir Thomas Barclay that it was hopeless to try to conciliate England. Salisbury withdrew into private life on July 12th, 1902, full of years and honours, and Lord Lansdowne now obtained a free hand. "I told him of my talk with Lord Salisbury," records M. Paul Cambon, "and suggested the subjects on which I should have liked to negotiate an agreement. He asked me whether he might make a note of them, but I said he need not trouble, as I would write him a letter. Next evening, at a dinner-party at Buckingham Palace, I was placed next King Edward, who said, 'Lansdowne has shewn me your letter. It is excellent. You must go on. I have told the Prince of Wales about it. You can discuss it also with him.' After dinner, the Prince spoke to me eagerly of the letter, and said what a good thing it would be if we could have a general agreement. He wanted to know when it would be concluded. I told him we could not go quite so fast as he might wish." The Ambassador's conversations with Chamberlain and Lord Lansdowne in 1902 indeed brought about no agreement.

In the spring of 1903 King Edward set forth in his yacht on the first foreign tour of his reign, and, after visiting Lisbon and Rome he reached Paris on May 1st, for the first time for more than three years[1]. "The visit was his own idea," testifies Cambon.

One day Lord Lansdowne told me that on the way back from the Mediterranean the King wished to stay in Paris. I asked whether it would be an official visit, and said that, however unofficial it might be, the President

[1] The King's journeys are chronicled by J. A. Farrer, *England under Edward VII*.

would at least have to ask him to dinner. Lord Lansdowne thought it would be quite an informal affair, and shewed some apprehension as to how he would be received. I informed my Government, and Lord Monson was not a little astonished by an enquiry from the Quai d'Orsay as to how the King would wish to be received. He telegraphed to the King, who answered that he desired his reception to be as official as possible, and that the more honours that were paid to him the better. So I went to Paris to help in arranging matters. Before Lord Monson started to meet the King, I suggested that he should advise him to make a little speech at the first opportunity and to say how much he always felt at home in Paris. When he arrived at the Bois de Boulogne station, the crowd was enormous and respectful, but a trifle cold; but after he had made his speech at the British Chamber of Commerce the whole atmosphere changed. He won the hearts of the Parisians in a day. Without King Edward the Entente might never have been made[1].

The President of the Republic was equally anxious for cordial relations and equally willing to run risks. "I had misgivings about the expediency of a visit," confesses Sir Thomas Barclay, "for, though the Entente had been ardently and successfully championed throughout provincial France, the fierce passions, which in Paris had developed into an over-sensitive patriotism, had not calmed down. When the President sent for me, I suggested that the visit should wait until next year. 'Impossible,' replied M. Loubet; 'the King wishes it. I know the danger; but I shall send for the leaders and tell them he is not responsible for the acts of his Ministers, and that he has been always a friend of France[2].'"

The speech, which won the heart of France, struck a personal note rare in royal utterances. "It is scarcely necessary to tell you with what sincere pleasure I find myself once more in Paris, to which, as you know, I have paid very frequent visits with ever-increasing pleasure, and for which I feel an attachment fortified by so many happy and ineffaceable memories. The days of hostility between the two countries are, I am certain, happily at an end. I know of no two countries whose prosperity is more interdependent. There may have been misunderstandings and causes of dissension in the past; but that is all happily over and forgotten. The friendship of the two countries is my constant preoccupation, and I count on you all, who enjoy French hospitality in their magnificent city, to aid me to reach this goal." The visit terminated the acute stage of the estrangement between the two countries. "A new Triple Alliance is in process of

[1] See *The Times*, December 22nd, 1920.
[2] Barclay, *Anglo-French Reminiscences*, pp. 219–220.

formation," reported Eckardstein from Paris to the German Chancellor[1]. King Edward's share in the momentous transformation which followed has, no doubt, been exaggerated by foreign observers, ignorant of the working of British institutions. "The King," writes Lord Sanderson, "did much to promote an atmosphere of goodwill; but he did not start the notion nor take any active part in the details[2]." "His visit gave a great impetus to the movement," records Lord Lansdowne in his official survey of the influences which were to produce the agreements of 1904. But even these guarded tributes secure him honourable mention among the architects of the *entente cordiale*.

Three months later, President Loubet returned the King's visit, and was lodged at St James's Palace—the first French Chief of the State to cross the Channel since Napoleon III. "I hope," declared the royal host with a warmth unusual on such occasions, "that the welcome you have received today has convinced you of the true friendship, indeed I will say the affection, which my country feels for France. I shall never forget the reception that was recently given to me, and the sentiments which I now express are those which I have always entertained. I hope our countries will always retain the most intimate relations and the deepest friendship." The toast of the Lord Mayor at the Guildhall was no less cordial. "Now we have shaken hands in the firm intention of letting no cloud obscure the path we have marked out, is it too much to hope that our statesmen will find means of removing for ever the horrible possibility of a war between the two peoples who have so many common interests, and whose hopes and aspirations are the same?" The reference of the Lord Mayor to removing the possibility of war was inspired by an Arbitration Convention at that moment in course of negotiation. The first documentary symbol of the *rapprochement* was due to Sir Thomas Barclay and Baron d'Estournelles de Constant. On July 16th a formula approved by the French Cabinet was presented at Downing Street:

" Differences of a juridical order, particularly those relating to difficulties of interpretation of existing conventions, shall—provided they affect neither the vital interests nor the honour of the Contracting Powers and cannot be solved through diplomatic channels—be submitted to the permanent Court of Arbitration in accordance with Article 16 of the Hague Convention."

[1] Eckardstein, *Erinnerungen*, II. 425.
[2] Memorandum on M. Cambon's interview in *The Times*, December 22nd, 1920.

The formula was approved by the Cabinet, and the Treaty was signed on October 14th.

In welcoming M. Delcassé, who had accompanied President Loubet to London in July, Lord Lansdowne observed: "And now we are going to talk." A long and fruitful interview took place; and the conversations, which lasted eight months, were carried on by the two Foreign Ministers and M. Paul Cambon, with assistance from Sir Eldon Gorst, then Financial Adviser to the Egyptian Government. Success was rendered less difficult by the very magnitude of the field of controversy. However impossible it might appear to settle particular issues in isolation, sacrifices might be tolerable as items in a balanced settlement. The diplomatic artists worked in large perspective, convinced that the removal of inflammable material would be more than worth the renunciation of this or that ancient claim or glittering ambition.

"The immediate origin of the Entente," records Lord Cromer, "is to be found mainly in the local situation in Egypt. Egyptian finance was then in a flourishing condition; but, owing to the international fetters imposed in circumstances which had wholly ceased to exist, the country was unable to derive any real profit from the surplus funds. The position had, in fact, become intolerable. It was determined to make an effort to improve it. A high Egyptian official, Tigrane Pasha, was sent to Paris to feel the pulse of the French Government. Responsible Frenchmen had simultaneously come to the conclusion that it was practically impossible for the British Government to redeem the pledge to evacuate Egypt. The British advances were therefore met in a friendly spirit. The Fashoda incident convinced France that Great Britain would remain in Egypt as long as she wished; but the humiliation was gradually softened by the discovery that the occupation was beneficial to the material interests of France. It was equally desirable for both countries that the situation should be cleared up. France could not evict her rival, but she could still inconvenience her[1]."

Not less eager to clear her path in Morocco than Great Britain was to secure a free hand in the valley of the Nile, France, by the conquest of Algeria, came to take a special interest in the tranquillity

---

[1] "The actual determining cause of the Entente," adds Lord Sanderson, "was Lord Cromer's anxiety for an arrangement with France which would let him place Egyptian finances on a more satisfactory footing, and pave the way for abolishing the Capitulations. The proposals relating to Egyptian finance formed a sort of nucleus from which the further agreements developed themselves."

of its neighbour. The frontier was roughly fixed by Treaty in 1845, and, in 1877, Muley Hassan petitioned for a permanent military mission to aid the reorganisation of his country. The wall of obstruction was breaking down, and in 1880 the Powers, on the initiative of Great Britain, met in Conference at Madrid. The insidious practice of extending Consular protection to natives, which furnished a pretext for interference, was restricted, and all the Signatory Powers of the October Treaty obtained most-favoured-nation treatment. The occupation of Tunis on the east and Senegal on the south made many Frenchmen desire to round off their West African dominions by incorporation of the whole or part of Morocco; and the surrender of Fashodâ created the demand for a substitute. Pacific penetration began; and, in 1900, M. Delcassé secured the benevolent neutrality of Italy by the recognition of her claims to Tripoli.

If Egypt and Morocco thus provided the elements of a bargain satisfactory to both parties it seemed that the principle of barter might prove equally acceptable in other parts of the world. Great Britain was anxious to sweep away the grievance of "the French Shore" of Newfoundland; and France entertained some minor ambitions in West Africa which it was in our power to satisfy. While the other differences presented less difficulty, the outbreak of the Japanese War increased the necessity for a comprehensive settlement. The King's Speech, delivered on February 2nd, 1904, registered the new spirit of cordiality. "Apart from its intrinsic value, the Arbitration Agreement affords a happy illustration of the friendly feelings prevailing between the two countries." The note of confidence and satisfaction was echoed by the Liberal leaders. "The country feels deep gratitude to the King," declared Lord Spencer, "for the impulse and support he has given to this friendly feeling"; and Campbell-Bannerman echoed the sentiment in the Lower House. "I do not think you will find, either here or in France," rejoined Lord Lansdowne modestly, "that too much credit is taken to themselves by the diplomatists for this happy condition of things. I believe it to be due mainly to a deep-seated conviction on the part of the two countries that there is no real divergence between our interests, and that the greatest of our common interests is peace." Two months later, on April 8th, a Convention relating to Newfoundland and West Africa, accompanied by four Declarations, concerning respectively Egypt and Morocco, Siam, Madagascar and the New Hebrides, was signed[1].

[1] See France, No. 1 (1904) and No. 2 (1904).

The most important of the agreements which collectively form the Treaty of 1904 was the following Declaration respecting Egypt and Morocco.

I. His Britannic Majesty's Government declare that they have no intention of altering the political status of Egypt. The Government of the French Republic declare that they will not obstruct the action of Great Britain in that country by asking that a limit of time be fixed for the British occupation or in any other matter, and that they assent to the annexed Khedivial Decree containing the guarantees considered necessary for the protection of the interests of the Egyptian bond-holders. The post of Director of Antiquities shall continue to be entrusted to a French savant, and French schools shall continue to enjoy the same liberty as in the past.

II. The Government of the French Republic declare that they have no intention of altering the political status of Morocco. His Britannic Majesty's Government recognises that it appertains to France, more particularly as a Power whose dominions are conterminous for a great distance with those of Morocco, to preserve order in that country, and to provide assistance for the purpose of all administrative, economic, financial and military reforms which it may require. They declare that they will not obstruct the action taken by France for this purpose, provided that such action shall leave intact the rights which Great Britain enjoys in Morocco in virtue of treaties, convention or usage.

III. The British Government will respect the rights which France, in virtue of treaties, conventions and usage, enjoys in Egypt.

IV. The two Governments, being equally attached to the principle of commercial liberty both in Egypt and Morocco, declare that they will not countenance any inequality either in the imposition of customs duties or other taxes or of railway transport charges. This engagement shall be binding for thirty years. Unless this stipulation is expressly denounced one year in advance, the period shall be extended for five years at a time.

V. The British Government will use their influence in order that the French officials in the Egyptian service may not be placed under less advantageous conditions than the British officials in the same service. The French Government will do the same for British officials in the Moorish service.

VI. In order to ensure free passage of the Suez Canal, the British Government declare that they adhere to the stipulations of the Treaty of 1888, and agree to their being put in force.

VII. In order to secure the free passage of the Straits of Gibraltar, the two Governments agree not to permit the erection of any fortifications or strategic works on the coast of Morocco between, but not including, Melilla, and the heights which command the right bank of the river Sebu. This condition does not apply to the places at present in the occupation of Spain.

VIII. The two Governments, inspired by their sincere feeling of friendship for Spain, take into special consideration the interests which that country derives from her geographical position and her territorial possessions on the Moorish coast. In regard to these interests the French Government will come to an understanding with the Spanish Government, which shall be communicated to the British Government.

IX. The two Governments agree to afford one another their diplomatic support, in order to obtain the execution of the present declaration.

A Khedivial Decree, in 68 Articles, annexed to the Declaration, laid down regulations for the administration and repayment of the Egyptian debt. "If accepted by the other Powers concerned," wrote Lord Lansdowne, "it will give the Egyptian Government a free hand in the disposal of its own resources, so long as the punctual payment of interest on the debt is assured. The *Caisse de la Dette* will remain; but its functions will be strictly limited to receiving certain assigned revenues on behalf of the bondholders, and insuring the due payment of the coupon." The surplus of 5½ millions in its possession was to be transferred to the Government. Financial liberty for Egypt was balanced by the settlement of the juridical position of the Suez Canal in time of war in accordance with the wishes of France.

Lord Lansdowne's despatch defines with equal precision the manner in which the British Government regarded the aspirations of France in Morocco:

In spite of well-meant efforts to assist the Sultan, but little progress has been effected. Without the intervention of a strong and civilised Power there appears to be no probability of a real improvement. It seems not unnatural that in these circumstances France should regard it as falling to her lot to assume the task of attempting the regeneration of the country. Though in no wise desiring to annex the Sultan's dominions or to subvert his authority, France seeks to extend her influence in Morocco, and is ready to submit to sacrifices and to incur responsibilities with the object of putting an end to the condition of anarchy which prevails upon the borders of Algeria. His Majesty's Government are not prepared to assume such responsibilities or to make such sacrifices, and they have therefore readily admitted that, if any European Power is to have a predominant influence in Morocco, that Power is France.

Next to Egypt, no part of the world had given rise to so much ill-feeling between the two countries as Newfoundland; and the settlement of the Fishery dispute was the second outstanding achievement of 1904. The controversy dated from the Treaty of Utrecht, which, while recognising that the island should thenceforth belong to Great Britain, gave to the French "the right to catch and dry fish" on part of the coast henceforth known as "the French Shore." By the Treaty of 1783, a new stretch of coast was substituted, in order to prevent the frequent quarrels of the fishermen, and Great Britain undertook to prevent British subjects from interrupting the French by their competition, and to remove fixed British settlements on "the new French Shore." The friction arising from divergent interpretations of these Treaties increased with the economic development of the island and the grant of self-government. Frequent attempts were made to settle the differences, and in 1857 and 1885 Conventions were signed, though, owing to the opposition of the colony, they were never ratified. The failure of the second of these efforts was followed by a renewed assertion of French rights in their extreme form; and Newfoundland retaliated with a Bait Act, forbidding the sale of bait to French fishing boats except on "the French Shore." The French, thus restricted, turned in some cases from cod to lobster fishing, which the British Government argued was not included in the Treaty rights, and which thus introduced a new element of discord.

"It was obviously our duty," wrote Lord Lansdowne, "to find some means of terminating this dispute, which has involved a constant risk of collisions between the two Governments. Such collisions have, in fact, only been averted by the tact, moderation and good temper exhibited by the naval officers of both Powers. The existence of these French rights over two-fifths of the coast has meant the obstruction of all useful developments."

By the First Article of the Convention signed on April 8th France renounced her privileges under the Treaty of Utrecht and its successors. By the Second, she retained the right of catching all kinds of fish in territorial waters on "the French Shore" during the fishing season. French fishermen might enter any harbour on "the French Shore" and obtain bait or shelter on the same conditions as the inhabitants, but subject to the regulations now in force, or hereafter determined for the improvement of the fisheries. The policing of the fishing on "the French Shore" and the prevention of illicit liquor traffic were to form the subject of a separate agreement. Article III provided for compensation to the fishermen obliged to abandon their establishments on "the French Shore." Thus the main cause of friction, the right of landing on "the French Shore," was at length removed.

The French negotiators contended that the surrender of an ancient privilege required territorial compensation; and the British Government, recognising the strength of the argument, made three concessions in West Africa. The frontier fixed in 1898 between the

British colony of the Gambia and Senegambia was slightly modified, in order to give France access to the navigable portion of the river. The Los Islands, commanding Konakry, the capital of French Guinea, were ceded, with the stipulation that the rights of British fishermen there should be maintained for thirty years. Of far greater importance was the revision of the 1898 boundary between British and French Nigeria, which compelled French convoys from the Niger to Lake Chad to follow a circuitous and waterless route or to pass through British territory. France thus obtained 14,000 square miles and uninterrupted access from her territories on the Niger to those on Lake Chad. It was further agreed that on the Lake itself the frontier line should, if necessary, be modified so as to assure to France communication through open water at all seasons between her possessions on the north-west and the south-east.

A third document contained a Declaration concerning Siam, Madagascar and the New Hebrides. As to Siam, the two Powers confirmed the Agreement of 1896, in which they undertook to refrain from armed intervention or the acquisition of special privileges in the basin of the Menam. France now recognised all Siamese possessions on the west of this neutral zone and of the Gulf of Siam, including the Malay Peninsula and the adjacent islands, as henceforth under British influence; while Great Britain recognised all Siamese territory on the east and south-east of the zone as henceforth under French influence. As regards Madagascar, the British Government abandoned the protest which had been maintained against the Tariff introduced after the annexation of the island. Finally, the difficulties in the New Hebrides arising from disputes as to land-title and the absence of jurisdiction over the natives were to be referred to a Commission.

At the close of his covering despatch, Lord Lansdowne argued that, desirable as were these Agreements on their intrinsic merits, they should be regarded not merely as a series of separate transactions, but as forming part of a comprehensive scheme for the improvement of the relations between the two countries. The antipathies and suspicions of the past had given place to friendship:

And it may, perhaps, be permitted to the Government to hope that, in thus basing the composition of long-standing differences upon mutual concessions, and in the frank recognition of each other's legitimate wants and aspirations, they may have afforded a precedent which will contribute something to the maintenance of international goodwill and the preservation of the general peace.

The Treaty was accepted in the spirit which had inspired its authors. Lord Spencer having hailed it as a great achievement, Lord Lansdowne declared that its reception had been all that he could have expected or desired. In a memorable debate on the second reading of the Anglo-French Convention Bill (necessitated by the monetary indemnity for French private rights in Newfoundland and by cessions of territory) the House of Commons found an opportunity for expressing its not less hearty satisfaction; and the tribute of the Under-Secretary to his Chief was warmly cheered: "It is due to Lord Lansdowne to say that the result would never have been obtained at all but for his patient perseverance and sympathetic tact, with which he has insisted through these long months on subordinating all minor considerations to the great object he had at heart." Earl Percy proceeded to summarise the provisions of the Treaty, pointing out the value of our gains in Newfoundland and the slenderness of our sacrifices in West Africa. Egypt gained virtual control of her own finances and of the surplus hitherto locked up, with power to pay off her debt in the most economical manner. Above all, she could enter on capital expenditure without charging it to annual revenue. The mixed administration of the Port of Alexandria and of the railways and telegraphs would disappear, and the functions of the *Caisse de la Dette* would be limited to securing the punctual payment of interest. The regularisation of our position as a Signatory of the Suez Canal Convention had always been the aim of Lord Salisbury. While we had purchased a free hand in Egypt, we had given up nothing in Morocco, where indeed we should be substantial gainers. Our trade would increase, as it had increased in Tunis, and our strategic position would be strengthened by the veto on the fortification of the Straits of Gibraltar. In Madagascar we merely recognised a *fait accompli*, and in Siam we reaffirmed the agreement of 1896.

"The distinctive feature," he concluded, "is that the parties pledge themselves not merely to abstain from poaching on each other's preserves but to do all in their power to further one another's interests. We promise to give one another, as friends, advantages which are ordinarily given only to allies; and it is as the pledges of friendship rather than as the terms of a compromise between jealous and exacting litigants that we ask the House to assent to these concessions. I hope the agreement will prove a working model for the adjustment in other parts of differences between ourselves and rival nations."

Sir Edward Grey and Campbell-Bannerman followed with a

benediction from the Front Opposition bench. In a speech to the Liberal League Lord Rosebery declared that no more one-sided agreement was ever concluded between two Powers at peace, and that he hoped that the country which held Gibraltar might never have cause to regret having handed over Morocco to a great military Power. Lord Cromer, on the other hand, records that the day of the signature of the Treaty was the happiest of his life.

England gained by the removal of financial restrictions and obtaining a practically valid sanction to a position which was previously to some extent irregular. France also gained. The large French interests at stake in Egypt are secured by specific engagements, and are still more amply secured by the traditional character of British predominance.

The Governments of Germany, Austria and Italy subsequently adhered to the Khedivial Decree, and "the Egyptian Question" ceased to be an international problem. The French Yellow-book, issued on May 26th, expounded our partner's view of the bargain. Both Governments, declared M. Delcassé, recognised that great moral and material interests demanded an amicable settlement. In Newfoundland, France had only abandoned privileges which were difficult to maintain and in no way necessary, while the essential right of fishing in territorial waters was preserved, and the right of fishing for and purchasing bait along the whole extent of "the French Shore" was explicitly recognised. In West Africa, the British concessions were of considerable importance.

"Under our influence," the French Minister continued, "Morocco would be a source of strength for our North African Empire. If subject to a foreign Power, our North African possessions would be permanently menaced and paralysed. The moment had arrived to decide who was to exercise preponderant influence. The present state can only last on condition that it is sustained and improved. On the importance of securing from England the promise not to hamper us it is superfluous to insist."

The sacrifice in Egypt was small. No change was to be made in the political status, and all necessary guarantees for French financial interests had been obtained.

M. Delcassé's unreserved satisfaction with his handiwork was shared by few of his countrymen. M. Hanotaux, who had directed the Foreign Policy of France from 1894 to 1898 with firmness, if not always with success, denounced the long list of his concessions since 1898. "On the Nile, in China, Siam, Muscat, Constantinople, Egypt, Newfoundland, Tripoli, it is only retreat." The Foreign Minister should have profited by the unique opportunity of the Boer War to solve both the Egyptian and the Moroccan problems[1]. "It is a retreat in good order," commented René Millet, ex-Governor of Algeria. "The error of twenty-five years ago perhaps rendered it inevitable; but why celebrate it as a diplomatic triumph? We are not yet in Morocco, while England is in Egypt. We exchange rights for hopes. To hold Morocco we lack just a trifle—the consent of the Sultan." Moreover, though Italy had been satisfied, Germany had been deliberately set aside. "It is impossible for France to undertake anything without knowing the inner mind of Germany. Of all pretensions the maddest would be to wish to isolate her. One does not isolate a strong Government—one exposes oneself to its resentment." The veteran Freycinet, on the other hand, though lamenting the final surrender of French aspirations in Egypt, declared the *entente* worth the price[2].

The Treaty was far more sharply criticised in the Palais Bourbon than at St Stephen's. England, declared M. Deschanel, had nowhere made a real sacrifice; for she retained in Morocco all that mattered to her—liberty of commerce.

One sees a powerful school of diplomacy, resting on long tradition, admirably informed and served, which yields nothing essential, which manages to create new guarantees even in what it appears to surrender, which always keeps the marrow and throws away the bone. Tendencies were driving British policy towards us. We should have obtained better conditions if we had arranged our affairs one by one.

All speakers, however, approved the policy of accord with England; and, on November 12th, the Chamber by a vote of 443 to 105 sanctioned the Convention concerning Newfoundland and West Africa, though M. Delcassé was forced to accept a motion pledging him to further negotiations with regard to the Newfoundland fishermen[3]. The Senatorial Committee of Foreign Affairs reported that, though not beyond reproach, it was useful to the country, and the Senate ratified it by a majority of 215 to 37.

The process of cleaning the slate, so auspiciously begun in 1904, was completed at leisure. The friction between French and British traders and missionaries who had settled in the New Hebrides in the course of the nineteenth century led, in 1887, to an Anglo-French

[1] Preface to R. Millet, *Notre politique extérieure*.
[2] *La Question d'Égypte*, ch. 4.
[3] In 1905 445 fishermen received compensation from the British Government; but the regulations to be issued by the two Governments relating to the marine police on "the French Shore" gave rise to prolonged discussion.

Convention, which provided for supervision by a mixed commission of naval officers. The remedy proved inadequate, and annexation or partition was demanded by different schools of politicians, not only in the islands, but in France, Great Britain and Australia. On October 20th, 1906, a Convention was signed in London declaring the New Hebrides "a region of joint influence," each Power exercising jurisdiction over its own nationals. A British and French High Commissioner were appointed, with authority over the native chiefs, while order continued to be maintained by the Naval Commission and police forces of equal strength. A mixed Tribunal was created with three Judges, the President of the Court being chosen by the King of Spain.

A further question was settled, which had troubled the relations of the two Powers since 1896. A French railway company, formed to construct a line from Jibuti to Addis Abeba, obtained assistance from the French Government in 1902; but a British group had secured a majority of the shares. In 1902 the frontier between Abyssinia and the Sudan was delimited, and the Negus bound himself not to construct any work on the Blue Nile or the Sobat which could interfere with its flow, and authorised the passage of the Cape to Cairo Railway through his territory. British influence was supreme, and in April, 1905, Menelek contemptuously refused the French Company permission to continue the railway to the capital. The British financiers urged that the line should be neutralised or built with funds advanced by the Bank of Abyssinia, that is, with English money. On July 6th, 1906, Great Britain, France and Italy signed an Accord recognising the interests and the *status quo* in Abyssinia. Great Britain received assurances as to the flow of the Nile, Italy was authorised to continue her railways in Eritrea, and the construction and exploitation of the whole line from Jibuti to the capital remained in the hands of the French Company, with an English, Italian and Abyssinian representative on the Board.

A year later, a Franco-Siamese Treaty secured for France the territory bordering on Cambodia in return for the abolition of exterritoriality. The goodwill displayed by Great Britain in this matter was rewarded when France smiled on the doubling of British possessions in the Malay peninsula. Finally, in June, 1907, Great Britain and France concluded an arrangement with Spain guaranteeing their respective possessions in the Mediterranean and the Atlantic, and thus securing an additional pledge for the safety of the road to India.

III. GREAT BRITAIN AND RUSSIA, 1900–1905

While British and French statesmen were joyfully burying the hatchet, the antagonism between Great Britain and Russia remained a source of acute anxiety. The Anglo-German Treaty of 1900 and the Anglo-Japanese Alliance of 1902 proclaimed, as from the housetops, our suspicion of her aims in the Far East; and our responsibility for the defence of India led us to watch her activities in the Middle East with even more jealous eyes. A conterminous frontier and the weakness of Persia furnished Russia with constant opportunities of exerting political and economic pressure; and in the closing years of the nineteenth century the rivalry of the two Powers at Teheran was unconcealed. Though the Imperial Bank of Persia represented British interests in the capital, Russian influence predominated; and the Shah's need·of money enabled our competitor to rivet her yoke more firmly on the neck of a decadent State.

The position was closely analysed by Lord Curzon, in a lengthy despatch dated September 21st, 1899, the first year of his Viceroyalty, in response to a request from the Cabinet for the views of the Government of India[1]: "The political interests of Great Britain are mainly, but no longer exclusively, Indian. Ever since the first visit of the late Shah to Europe, Persia has been drawn increasingly into the vortex of European politics. She is one of those countries which must inevitably have attracted the attention of Europe, partly from increasing infirmity, but still more from the opportunities suggested by their latent though neglected sources of strength. Closely pressing upon Persia and Afghanistan is the ever-growing momentum of a Power whose interests in Asia are not always in accord with our own, while the Gulf is beginning to attract the interest of other and sometimes rival nations. For the present, our ambitions are limited to prevent the interest we have built up from being undermined. We have no desire to disturb the political *status quo* as long as it can be maintained; but we press for an early decision and for early action, since, unless we bestir ourselves, there is good reason for fearing that the already trembling balance may be disturbed to our disadvantage. The advance of Russia across the deserts that form the natural barrier between West and East Persia could not be regarded without uneasiness by the Government of India; for Russian pledges to respect the interests and independence of Persia are quite insufficient to save Persian or British interests from erosive agencies."

[1] Persia, No. 1 (1908).

At the moment when this weighty despatch reached London, the attention of the Cabinet was monopolised by the Boer War. It was a time rather for graceful concessions than for valiant resistance to future dangers, and Russian influence in Persia increased apace. Fresh advances from the Russian Bank brought the total loan up to four millions; Russian concessionaires were allowed to build roads from Tabriz to Teheran and to Kazvin, and in 1902 a Russo-Persian Commercial Treaty threatened the Indian tea-trade. Not content with dominating the north, Russia pushed forth her tentacles in the east and south. Though Seistan adjoined the Indian frontier, she despatched a Consul in 1900 to fish there in troubled waters, and the Russian Bank opened branches in the province. To counterwork her influence, Lord Curzon built a railway from Quetta to Nushki, thence across the plains to the frontier, and finally to Nasratabad, the chief town of Seistan, opening post and telegraph offices *en route* and establishing a Consul at the terminus. Though there was little trade in this remote province, Russian intrigues were thus held in check.

Even more vital to the safety of India and the prestige of the empire was the maintenance of our position in the Persian Gulf, where Russian emissaries—officers, "explorers," doctors "studying plague"—were beginning to swarm. In February, 1900, a small Russian gunboat anchored off Bunder Abbas. The Commander asked for coal, and three hundred tons were ordered from Bombay. When it arrived, he declared that he could not take it all on board, and proposed to land a portion. It occurred to the Governor, however, that it would need Russian guards, who might stay; and, when a British cruiser arrived, he plucked up courage to refuse permission. Thus the attempt was foiled to create a nucleus store from which a coaling station might develop. During the next three years, Russian warships toured the Gulf; but no further attempts were made to acquire a footing. Consulates were, nevertheless, established at Basra, Bushire and Bunder Abbas, though no Russian nationals were to be found there and little trade, despite the visits of four ships a year belonging to a subsidised Company formed at Odessa in 1901.

The termination of the Boer War had restored to Great Britain her freedom of action; and, on May 15th, 1903, Lord Lansdowne made the most momentous declaration of British policy since Sir Edward Grey's pronouncement in 1895. "Firstly, we should protect and promote British trade in the Gulf. Secondly, we should not exclude the legitimate trade of others. Thirdly, we should regard the establishment of a naval base or a fortified port in the Gulf by any other Power as a very grave menace to British interests, and we should certainly resist it by all the means at our disposal." The announcement, he added, was made in no minatory spirit, because he knew of no such proposal. This emphatic warning was reinforced by Lord Curzon's demonstration in the Gulf in November, 1903. It was the first visit of a Viceroy during his term of office, and no such assemblage of warships had ever been seen on its quiet waters. After touching at Muscat, an independent Arab State under British influence, the squadron entered the Gulf, and a Durbar was held on board the *Argonaut* at Shargah, where the Chiefs of the Arab coast in treaty relations with us were addressed by the Viceroy in a speech of sonorous eloquence[1]. He reminded his hearers of the steps by which the British Government became, with their own consent, their overlords and protectors and the guardians of intertribal peace.

Why should Great Britain continue to exercise these powers? The history of your States and of your families, and the present condition of the Gulf, are the answer. We were here before any other Power, in modern times, had shown its face in these waters. We found strife, and we have created order. It was our commerce as well as your security that was threatened and called for protection. At every port along these coasts the subjects of the King of England still reside and trade. We saved you from extinction at the hands of your neighbours. We opened these seas to the ships of all nations, and enabled their flags to fly in peace. We have not seized nor held your territory. We have not destroyed your independence, but preserved it.... The peace of these waters must still be maintained; your independence will continue to be upheld; and the influence of the British Government must remain supreme. The Sovereign of the British Empire lives so far away that none of you has ever seen or will ever see his face; but his orders are carried out everywhere throughout his vast dominions, and it is as his representative in India, who is responsible to him for your welfare, that I am here today to exchange greetings with you, to renew old assurances, and to wish you prosperity in the future.

British prestige was enhanced by the journey, which proclaimed, not only to those who saw the squadron and heard the voice of the Viceroy, but to listeners far away in Teheran, Petrograd and Berlin, the determination of Great Britain to defend her position in the Gulf from challenge or attack.

The struggle against Russian encroachments was waged, not only in Manchuria and Persia, but on the lofty plateaus of Tibet, where

[1] Reprinted in *Lord Curzon in India*, pp. 500–503. Cf. Lovat Fraser, *India under Lord Curzon*, pp. 78–115.

the priestly hierarchy which governed the country under the shadowy suzerainty of China had done its utmost to close the gates against approach from the south. Warren Hastings sent envoys to Tibet; but their work bore no lasting fruit. A hundred years later a Mission to Lhasa was organised in 1886 but countermanded; and the Tibetans took advantage of the collapse of the project to invade Sikkim in 1887. They were expelled in the following year, but received no punishment for their offence. In 1890, the senior of the two Chinese Ambans who represent the Suzerain at Lhasa journeyed to Calcutta, and signed a Treaty fixing the boundary between Tibet and Sikkim (over which China recognised a British Protectorate), reserving for a joint Commission questions of trade, pasturage and communication. The Tibetans refused to recognise the boundary, and a second Agreement, signed in 1893, proved equally worthless[1]. A mart was established at Yatung; but the Tibetans built a wall to prevent their own traders from approaching it, levied an unauthorised duty on Indian goods, and overthrew the boundary pillars erected by British and Chinese Representatives. In March, 1899, Lord Curzon described the situation to the Secretary of State. "We seem to be moving in a vicious circle. If we apply to Tibet, we either receive no reply or are referred to the Chinese Resident. If we apply to the latter, he excuses his failure by his inability to put any pressure on Tibet." Lord Salisbury was consulted and advised that, since the Tibetans argued that China had no authority to act for them, the Government of India should try to negotiate directly with Lhasa. The advice was followed; but a letter from the Viceroy to the Dalai Lama in 1900 was returned unopened, no one having dared to forward it to the capital. In the following year the Viceroy wrote again, adding that discourtesy would be followed by steps to enforce the Treaty. The letter was delivered to the Dalai Lama, who returned it unopened, on the ground that he could not correspond with foreign Governments without the consent of the Ambans.

The exasperation provoked by this studied insolence was intensified by the simultaneous reception at Petrograd, in September, 1900, of a mysterious emissary named Dorjieff, a Siberian Buddhist, who had resided for many years at Lhasa, where he had gained influence as tutor to the Dalai Lama. A year later, he reappeared in Russia as the head of a Mission, the political character of which was

[1] See *Papers relating to Tibet*, 1904, Cd. 1920, Cd. 2054 and 2370; and 1910 Cd. 5240; and Younghusband, *India and Tibet*.

emphasised by the Russian Press. "Tibet has heard of the taking of Peking," wrote the *Novoye Vremya*, "and perhaps also of the valiant resistance of the Boers. A *rapprochement* with Russia must seem to the Lama the most natural step, as Russia is the only Power able to counteract the intrigues of Great Britain, who has so long been trying to obtain admission and only awaits the opportunity to force an entrance." The Foreign Minister, naturally, told the British Ambassador a very different story. "The conclusion of certain Russian papers that Tibetans have any diplomatic or political mission is ridiculous and unfounded. Dorjieff comes to Russia occasionally to collect for his Order from Russian Buddhists, and has no official character whatever." After the Mission had been received by the Tsar, de Witte and Lamsdorff himself, and announced in the official journal as "Envoys Extraordinary of the Dalai Lama," the British Ambassador again visited the Foreign Secretary, who reiterated that the Mission had no political character. The Dalai Lama, he explained, was a Buddhist Pontiff, and the mission was of the kind which the Pope was accustomed to send to Catholics in other lands. Lord Lansdowne, hereupon, instructed the Ambassador to tell Lamsdorff that his assurances had been received with satisfaction, and to add that the British Government could not regard with indifference any proceedings that might have a tendency to alter or disturb the existing status of Tibet.

Dorjieff's journeys had taught Tibet to look to Russia for protection and Russia to regard Tibet as a pawn in her world-wide game against Great Britain. Lord Curzon's patience was wearing thin, and on July 28th, 1901, he proposed coercion if a third attempt to communicate with the Dalai Lama broke down; but the Boer War was still in progress, and Lord George Hamilton deprecated strong measures. When, however, the third attempt proved equally fruitless, the Viceroy suggested that the Political Officer for Sikkim should set up pillars where the Tibetans had encroached, and that, if these pillars were overthrown, we should occupy the Chumbi valley.

The time seems to us to have arrived when we should decline any longer to allow our boundary to be transgressed, our trade to be strangled, and the rights secured to us by treaty defied. It is the most extraordinary anachronism of the twentieth century that there should exist within less than three hundred miles of the borders of British India a State and a Government with whom political relations do not exist and with whom it is impossible even to exchange a written communication.

The approval of the Cabinet having been secured, the Political Officer proceeded, in the summer of 1902, to the north of Sikkim and ordered the Tibetans inside the frontier to withdraw; and on January 18th, 1903, the Government of India proposed an expedition to Lhasa, where we should meet Chinese Representatives, and negotiate a treaty, to be signed both by the Chinese and the Tibetans, a British Representative being hereupon installed in the capital. The suggestion leaked out; and, before the Cabinet had time to consider the proposal of the Indian Government, a Memorandum was presented by Count Benckendorff. "A British military expedition to Tibet has been reported. Such an expedition would produce a situation of considerable gravity, and might oblige Russia to take measures to protect her interests in those regions." The British Foreign Secretary replied that this Note was unusual and almost minatory, and that the rumour was baseless. "Russia," retorted the Ambassador, "has no designs at Tibet, and I presume you have not." A week later, Lord Lansdowne informed him that he learned from apparently trustworthy sources, of Russia having lately concluded an agreement for a Protectorate over Tibet and intending to appoint Agents, or Consular Officers at Lhasa. "I believe there is no foundation for the report," replied the Ambassador, "but I will enquire." "As we are much more closely interested in Tibet than Russia," rejoined the Foreign Secretary, "if Russia displays activity, we must reply by a greater display. We are simply trying to get the Tibetans to fulfil the Treaty of 1890, and it is no use trying through China."

Sparks had already begun to fly; and, on February 27th, the Secretary of State for India, Lord George Hamilton, sent a cautious reply to the despatch of January 8th. The Cabinet recognised the importance of the problem, and feared that Tibet under Russian influence might press Nepal into her orbit. But it could not sanction armed intervention, which might lead to permanent occupation or a Protectorate. The Russian Ambassador informed Lord Lansdowne that no Russian Agents were in Tibet; that there was no intention to send any; and that Count Lamsdorff was astounded to find we could believe it. Russia, on the other hand, was not indifferent to any serious disturbance of the *status quo*. Lord Lansdowne explained in reply that, where an uncivilised country adjoined a civilised, a certain local predominance was inevitable, but that this did not involve designs on its independence.

Now that the diplomatic situation had been to some extent

simplified, the Indian Government proposed that Chinese and Tibetan Representatives should negotiate at Khamba Jong, the first village across the frontier, with a British Representative, who should be accompanied by an armed escort of two hundred men, with reserves in Sikkim, which would enable him to reach Lhasa if the negotiators should not arrive. The Cabinet sanctioned the parley at Khamba Jong, but vetoed an advance to Lhasa. On June 3rd, the Viceroy informed the Senior Amban that Colonel Younghusband had been selected as the British Commissioner, and would accompany the Political Officer at Sikkim to Khamba Jong in July. But, though the rendezvous had been chosen with China's consent and accepted by the Dalai Lama, the Chinese Delegates were of a rank too low to negotiate, while the Tibetan Delegates, after the first meeting, refused to hold further conversations or to convey messages to Lhasa. Lord Lansdowne at once informed Benckendorff that the Mission would advance to Gyantse, owing to the outrageous conduct of the Tibetans, but that we had no intention to annex or permanently occupy Tibetan territory. The Russian Ambassador having observed that the project involved a grave disturbance of the Central Asian situation, Lord Lansdowne retorted that he was greatly surprised at the excitement of Russia, who would not herself have shown such forbearance and who had never hesitated to encroach on her neighbours—witness Manchuria and Persia. "May I say that you advanced reluctantly," rejoined the Ambassador, "with the sole object to obtain satisfaction for affronts?" The Foreign Secretary replied that he might, and added that the Mission had been ordered not to fight unless attacked. Since the Ambassador continued to express at intervals the hope that we should not alter our policy, Lord Lansdowne informed him in writing, on June 2nd, 1904, that, "so long as no other Power tried to intervene in the affairs of Tibet, Great Britain would not annex it, or proclaim a Protectorate, or control its internal administration." To critics at home who enquired why we could not leave Tibet in peace, the Foreign Secretary replied[1] that we merely wanted a neighbourly agreement, demarcating the frontier and granting facilities for trade. Since the Tibetans believed that they were backed by Russia, a final settlement was necessary. Almost at the same moment, the Viceroy restated the principles of British policy in his Budget speech of March 30th, employing a simile which was to become famous.

[1] In the debate on the Address, February 2nd, 1904, and on February 26th, in a debate raised by Lord Reay.

India is like a fortress with the vast moat of the sea on two of her faces, and with mountains for her walls on the remainder. But beyond those walls extends a glacis of varying breadth and dimensions. We do not want to occupy it; but we cannot afford to see it occupied by our foes. He would be a short-sighted commander who merely manned his ramparts in India and did not look out beyond[1].

In December, 1904, the Mission entered the Chumbi valley, and Gyantse was reached on April 11th, 1905. The camp was attacked; but, when reinforcements arrived under General Macdonald, the fort was taken. On July 8th, the Cabinet at length sanctioned the march to the capital, and the Mission reached the Forbidden City on August 3rd, to find that the Dalai Lama had fled. Meanwhile, the terms to be imposed on Tibet were being anxiously discussed between Simla and Whitehall[2]. In a despatch, of June 30th, the Government of India urged the establishment of a permanent Mission, preferably at Lhasa, to watch trade interests and guard against foreign influence, the retention of the Chumbi valley, and the construction of a road to facilitate trade. The terms should include trade-marts at Gyantse, Shigatse and Lhasa (if a Resident was to be settled there), an indemnity, the razing of the forts, and a veto on the manufacture and import of arms. If an Agent at Lhasa were not desired, he should reside at Gyantse, with the right of proceeding to the capital for discussion with the Amban or the Dalai Lama's officials. We should also inform Tibet that, unless she abstained from intercourse with any other European Power, we should appoint an Agent at the capital. Finally, we should obtain both from Tibet and China a formal recognition of our exclusive political influence in Tibet, and an engagement that they would not admit the Representative of any other Power, or cede territory, or enter into relations with any other Power, without our consent. While the despatch was on its way, Mr Brodrick, who had succeeded Lord George Hamilton as Secretary of State, telegraphed the policy of the Cabinet on July 6th. A Political Resident at Lhasa or with access to Lhasa was disallowed. The indemnity should not be beyond the power of Tibet to pay, and might be spread over three years. The Chumbi valley was to be occupied till the indemnity was paid or till trade-marts had been opened for three years, "whichever is the latest." A despatch, amplifying the telegram, was sent on August 5th.

[1] *Lord Curzon in India*, p. 408.
[2] Lord Curzon had returned home after his first term on April 30th, leaving Lord Ampthill as Acting Viceroy.

Colonel Younghusband was in a difficult position; for, though he was in possession of a draft Convention sent him by the Indian Government and had been informed of the Cabinet telegram, the despatch in which the policy was explained only reached him after the Treaty was signed. Moreover, the military orders to leave Lhasa in the early autumn compelled him, as he believed, to purchase a Treaty, willingly and promptly signed, at the cost of some departure from his Instructions. Tibet undertook to observe the Treaty of 1890, to erect boundary pillars, to open marts at three places, to maintain an agent at each in order to forward communications, to keep open the roads leading to them, and to raze all forts on the routes to the capital. The Ninth (and last) Article was designed to terminate the Russian menace. Tibet engaged that, without the previous consent of the British Government, no portion of Tibetan territory should be ceded, sold, leased, mortgaged or otherwise given for occupation to any Foreign Power; no such Power should be permitted to intervene in Tibetan affairs; no Representatives or Agents of any Foreign Power should be admitted; no concessions for railways, roads, telegraphs, mining or other rights should be granted to any Foreign Power or the subject of any Foreign Power; but, if they were, similar or equivalent concessions should be granted to Great Britain; and finally, no Tibetan revenues should be pledged or assigned to any Foreign Power or the subject of any Foreign Power.

Having thus secured all his political and economic demands, Colonel Younghusband accepted the request that the indemnity, which had been fixed at £500,000, should be paid at the rate of one lakh annually for seventy-five years—a change which involved the occupation of the Chumbi valley during a similar period. With this important modification, the Treaty was signed on September 7th in the presence of the Amban, who undertook to sign when permission had been obtained from Peking. Seals were affixed by the Acting Regent, the Council, the three great monasteries and the National Assembly. On the same day, a separate Agreement was signed empowering the British Trade Agent at Gyantse to visit Lhasa to discuss trade affairs.

A week later, a telegram arrived stating that the Secretary of State had asked the Government of India whether the period for the payment of the indemnity could not be reduced; but the Mission took its departure without further negotiation. In subsequent Memoranda and later, in his book *India and Tibet*, its leader stoutly defended his conduct. If he had refused the Tibetan proposal, the Regent might have fled and the Convention been lost. In any case, Tibet would have been left to nourish angry feelings. She had accepted everything else, and General Macdonald had advised that the return journey should begin not later than September 15th. He had, therefore, departed after signing the Treaty, as he had promised to do. If he had immediately asked for an alteration, he would have forfeited the confidence of the Tibetans, without persuading them to accept the change; whereas he had left the country much friendlier in feeling than when he entered it.

The real object of the Mission, the establishment of goodwill, had been secured. Lord Curzon was now back in India, and the Government of India, in a despatch to the Secretary of State, approved his conduct in not trying to amend the newly-signed Treaty. He had established more friendly relations than could have been expected, and he ought not to be condemned for one error of judgment, however serious. The circumstances demanded generous condonation. Mr Brodrick, however, refused to be mollified. As regards the indemnity, he declared, the Convention was signed in defiance of express Instructions that it was to be a sum payable in three years. "We cannot accept the situation created for us by our Representative's disobedience to orders." When the Convention came to be ratified, it must, therefore, be amended in this sense. Tibet was also to be informed that the Special Agreement allowing the Trade Agent to proceed to Lhasa was regarded as needless and therefore was to be cancelled. The British Cabinet had given repeated assurances to Russia that no lengthy occupation of territory and no intervention in internal affairs was sought; and the Cabinet alone could decide matters of policy.

Despite the wrath of the Secretary of State, the twofold object of the Mission appeared to have been attained. In the first place, the monks had learned that the British arm was long enough to reach the Forbidden City, and on the outstanding questions of boundary, trade and communications, our demands had been accepted. Secondly, in Mr Brodrick's words, the risk of Tibet having political relations with other States had been removed. The settlement was ratified by the Suzerain Power on April 27th, 1906, Great Britain undertaking not to annex territory nor to interfere in internal affairs, while China promised to prevent any other Power from doing so, and agreed to be responsible for the indemnity and to pay it in three years.

After the Russian menace on the northern section of the glacis had been warded off, there remained the danger on the north-west[1]. In setting up Abdur Rahman in 1880 we transformed Afghanistan into a buffer State. For practical purposes the country was closed; but, though the Ameer throttled trade, intrigued with the hill tribes and resented our refusal to receive a Representative at St James', he never made serious advances to Russia. The agreement with Abdur Rahman was purely personal; but his son, Habibulla, who succeeded in 1901, argued that the engagements still existed and therefore needed no renewal. He did not, however, draw the subsidy and declined invitations to India. The Japanese victories had a disturbing effect in Cabul, where the Ameer boasted that he was as powerful as the Mikado. Early in 1904, the Government of India suggested the despatch of Sir Louis Dane, the Foreign Secretary, to discuss the situation, and Habibulla agreed to receive him. He reached the capital on December 12th, expecting to stay two weeks; but the fortnight lengthened into three months. Though he was courteously treated at personal interviews, and the Ameer and his chiefs for the first time ate with infidels, the negotiations were chiefly conducted by letter, and the official correspondence was frankly insolent. All Cabul knew that the Ameer had declined to visit India, and that India had come to visit him. While the Government of India desired a fresh engagement on the old lines, the Ameer wished to continue the arrangements concluded with his father, thus transforming an individual into a dynastic pact. His terms were virtually accepted, and though Sir Louis Dane claimed success, the Treaty was considered in some quarters to have lowered British prestige.

That the Cabinet was by no means reassured, was proved by a pointed warning in the Prime-Minister's speech of May 11th, 1905, on Imperial Defence. Russia, he declared, was making steady progress towards Afghanistan, and railways were under construction which could only be strategic. War was improbable; but these factors altered the position. India could not be taken by surprise and assault. A war on the North-west Frontier would be chiefly a problem of transport and supply. We must, therefore, allow nothing to be done to facilitate transport. Any attempt to make a railway in Afghanistan in connexion with the Russian strategic railways should be regarded as an act of direct aggression against us. "I have, however," he said, "not the smallest ground to believe that Russia intends to build such a railway. If ever attempted, it would be the heaviest conceivable

[1] See Lovat Fraser, *India under Curzon*, pp. 63–77.

blow at our Indian Empire. As long as we say resolutely that railways in Afghanistan should only be made in time of war, we can make India absolutely secure. But if, through blindness or cowardice, we permit the slow absorption of the country, if strategic railways are allowed to creep close to our frontier, we shall have to maintain a much larger army."

Friction in Persia, Tibet and Afghanistan had increased the traditional tension between Great Britain and Russia; and the outbreak of war in the Far East opened a period of dangerous strain. Since the Dual Alliance did not extend to Asia, France was not compelled to join her Ally; but in time of war benevolent neutrality may at any moment stiffen into belligerency. British opinion openly favoured Japan; but the Cabinet observed strict neutrality, and, on February 12th, Lord Lansdowne denied the foolish rumour that Japan had been permitted to use Wei-Hai-Wei as a base. A struggle which required ships no less than soldiers was certain to raise the question of the Straits. In 1896, a plan was approved by the Tsar for seizing the Bosphorus and settling, once for all, the question of free passage for the Black Sea fleet; and the audacious project was only dropped owing to the combined opposition of Witte and Pobiedonostseff[1]. Russia's aspiration for the free disposal of her naval forces remained; and, in the autumn of 1902, she obtained permission for four destroyers to pass the Straits. On January 6th, 1903, Sir Nicholas O'Conor presented a formal protest to the Porte, and announced that we should not hesitate to use the precedent for British ships in case of war. During the opening months of the Japanese conflict the Black Sea fleet remained tranquil; but trouble began in July, when the *Smolensk* and the *Petersburg*, two cruisers of the Volunteer fleet, which had been founded at the time of the Penjdeh crisis, and which was permitted to pass the Straits under a commercial flag, assumed the character of warships, and stopped British and German ships in the Red Sea[2]. The P. & O. *Malacca* was searched, despite the assurance that she carried ammunition for the British fleet at Hong-Kong and a general cargo for Yokohama. The Russian captain demanded to see the latter, and, since it could not be reached without endangering the stability of the vessel, a prize crew was placed on board and the ship ordered back to Suez, whence she was to sail to Libau to a

[1] See Dillon, *The Eclipse of Russia*, pp. 231–44.
[2] The juridical character of the Volunteer fleet is explained in Sutherland Edwards, *Sir William White*, ch. 20.

Russian Prize-Court. Almost at the same time, the *Ardova*, a British ship carrying explosives from the Government of the United States to Manila, and the *Formosa* were seized.

Russian ships of war were justified in searching neutrals for contraband, but converted cruisers had no such right. The British Ambassador lodged an emphatic protest, demanding the release of the *Malacca* on the ground that the status of the *Petersburg* was irregular, and that the ammunition was for the British navy and bore the British Government mark. The reply was conciliatory. The *Malacca* was not to go to a Prize-Court, and no such incident should occur again; but, "as a matter of form," her cargo would be examined at a neutral port. Since this appeared to maintain the claim of volunteer cruisers to be ships of war, the Mediterranean squadron was sent to Alexandria, and a cruiser was ordered to Suez to anchor close to the *Ardova*. At the same moment the *Knight Commander*, bound from New York to Yokohama with an American-owned cargo, was sunk by the Vladivostock squadron on suspicion of contraband, and because the ship could not spare a prize crew to take her to port. When announcing this outrage, the Prime-Minister and Foreign Secretary added that Russia had given orders that seizures by the volunteer ships should not be recognised, and had withdrawn these from the Red Sea. A strong protest had been made against the sinking of the *Knight Commander*, and the release of the crew had been demanded. On August 8th, the Prime-Minister announced that the *Malacca* had been released after a purely formal examination, and that the ships of the Volunteer fleet would no longer act as cruisers. Three days later, Lord Lansdowne declared that we could not admit Russia's claim to settle what was contraband or to destroy a neutral vessel with contraband on board, but added that the destruction of neutrals was not likely to recur. In making the same announcement in the House of Commons, Mr Balfour added that ports should not be used as bases nor should neutrals supply coal—a gentle hint to both France and Germany, whose efforts to assist Russia were unremitting. Despite Russian assurances, the *Smolensk* and the *Petersburg* resumed their activity off the Cape, and, on August 21st, the *Comedian* was boarded near Port Elizabeth. The shock was diminished by the Prime-Minister's announcement that, at Russia's request, British cruisers had been sent to bid the vessels stop their activity, as they had not received orders. They were found at Zanzibar, and no British vessel was interfered with during the remainder of the War.

The Baltic fleet was now ordered to the Far East. Emerging from the Belt, Admiral Rojdestvensky mistook some Norwegian vessels for Japanese destroyers, and fired several shots without reaching them. On the afternoon of October 21st the *Kamchatka* fell behind on account of engine trouble. Towards evening, she met and fired on a Swedish vessel and others unknown, and informed the Admiral by wireless that she was attacked on all sides by torpedo-boats. The Admiral, therefore, signalled to the fleet to redouble its vigilance. Just after midnight a green rocket was fired, and the anxious watchers on the flagship, believing that they saw a suspicious vessel, gave orders to fire. The *Gamecock* fleet of about thirty steam-trawlers from Hull was on the Dogger Bank that night, with about fourteen trawlers of another fleet, and it was by them that the rocket had been fired as a fishing signal. All carried their regulation lights, and some had powerful lamps on deck to facilitate the cleaning of the fish. Five warships passed north-west of them, followed by four to the south-west of them and partly moving actually among them, which fired shell and quick-firers. Some of the trawlers were only 350 yards away. One was sunk (with two men killed and all the crew wounded but one); another, though also hit, sent a boat to the sinking vessel and rescued the wounded. Two others were sunk, and the hospital ship was damaged. The firing lasted nearly half an hour. A steamer, thought to be Russian, was seen at dawn. The trawlers at once returned to Hull, which they reached on the following evening.

Lord Rosebery spoke for the nation in denouncing the "unspeakable outrage," and public anger rose to fever pitch. A deputation of the fishermen visited the Foreign Office, and Benckendorff was hooted in his carriage. Preliminary orders for mutual support were sent to the Home fleet at Cromarty, to the Channel fleet at Gibraltar, and to the Mediterranean fleet at Pola, while four battleships were ordered to Portland and submarines were despatched to Dover. The offence, however, was generally ascribed to drink or nerves, and the two Governments kept their heads. The Tsar sent a message that, in the absence of news, he could only explain the incident as a regrettable misunderstanding, adding that he sincerely regretted the loss of life, and that he would afford complete satisfaction to the sufferers so soon as the mystery was solved. The favourable impression produced by this message, however, was weakened by an impenitent report from Rojdestvensky, telegraphed from Vigo.

The incident, he declared, was provoked by two torpedo-boats which advanced to attack without lights. The *Kamchatka*, a transport, signalled that she was attacked on all sides and Russian searchlights revealed several vessels like fishing steamers, which the Russian gunners endeavoured to spare. Fire ceased when the torpedo-boats were out of sight. The vessel referred to in the English Press as remaining till the morning must have been one of these torpedo-boats searching for its companion. The "small steam vessels" which were hit were not assisted, as they were suspected of complicity owing to their persistence in cutting the warships' line of advance, while some showed no lights. If fishermen were there, he expressed sincere regret for the unfortunate victims of circumstances in which no warships, even in time of peace, could have acted otherwise.

The Cabinet met on October 28th, and on the same evening the Prime-Minister addressed a meeting at Southampton. In Rojdestvensky's story, he declared, there was much romance. The Russians were out of their course, and they knew that the Dogger Bank was frequented by fishermen. To suggest that torpedo-boats were waiting there implied that we were furnishing a base. In scathing terms he denounced the Admiral's claim to fire on neutral ships, adding that a fleet animated by such sentiments deserved to be hunted out of existence. Happily, the Russian Government had expressed its regret; the Tsar had promised liberal compensation; the officers and material witnesses would stop at Vigo; an enquiry would be held by an International Commission; the guilty would be tried and punished, and Russia would issue Instructions to prevent a recurrence of the offence. In a word, the Russian Government had shown an enlightened desire that truth and justice should prevail.

Though certain Conservative organs pronounced the speech a weak compromise, public opinion was profoundly relieved, and the Opposition leaders commended the moderation of the Government. The departure of the Russian fleet from Vigo, leaving only four officers of inferior rank, revived the smouldering fires for a moment; but with the signature of a Convention at Petrograd on November 25th the crisis was over. The settlement had been facilitated by the mediation of M. Delcassé. The Commission was to consist of a British, a Russian, a French and an American naval officer, a fifth to be coopted, or, if necessary, to be appointed by the Emperor Francis Joseph; and the decision was to be by majority. The Commission met at Paris on December 22nd, under the chairmanship of Admiral Fournier, and by February 25th, 1905, the work was done[1]. The report implicitly,

[1] See *Memoir of Sir Edward Fry* (British Legal Assessor), pp. 180–91.

if not explicitly, dismissed the Russian case. The trawlers had committed no hostile act; the *Kamchatka* had been deceived, for no Japanese torpedo-boats were in the vicinity, and the firing was therefore unjustifiable. There were, however, extenuating circumstances. The Admiral did his best to prevent the trawlers, when recognised as such, being fired on, and the uncertainty as to the danger explained the decision not to aid the injured crews. The majority added an expression of their regret that the Admiral did not inform the authorities as he passed the Straits of Dover that the trawlers needed aid. These findings, concluded the Commissioners, did not throw any discredit on the valour or humanity of the Russian fleet. It was a discreet Report, conveying censure in a form which it was possible for a Great Power to accept.

The sailing of the Russian fleet involved a danger of war not only with Russia but with Germany, whose sympathies with Russia were unconcealed. The Central Powers informed the Tsar that he might safely leave his western frontier undefended; and Germany supplied the coal without which the Baltic squadron could never have reached its destination. On August 25th, Lord Lansdowne warned the German Ambassador that if Japan were to become involved in war with Germany, Great Britain would, at her request, recognise the *casus foederis*[1]. The Kaiser naturally complained to Petrograd of the threat, and proposed a scheme for meeting the common danger. "It is not impossible," he telegraphed to the Tsar on September 27th, "that the Japanese and the British Governments may launch joint protests against our coaling your ships, coupled with a summons to stop. The result of such a threat of war would be the inability of your fleet to proceed for want of fuel. This new danger would have to be faced by Russia and Germany together, who would both have to remind your ally France of her obligations.... In this way a powerful combination of the three Continental Powers would be formed, and the Anglo-Saxon group would think twice before attacking it." "I agree fully with your complaints about England's behaviour concerning the coaling of our ships by German steamers," replied the Tsar. "Whereas she understands the rules of keeping neutrality in her own fashion, it is certainly high time to put a stop to this. The only way, as you say, would be that Germany, Russia and France should at once unite upon arrangements to abolish English and Japanese arrogance and

[1] This was revealed by the German Government in the *Norddeutsche Allgemeine Zeitung* in September, 1917.

insolence. Would you like to frame the outlines of such a treaty?" The Kaiser and Bülow promptly forwarded the following draft for the Tsar's approval.

Their Majesties, in order to localise the War, have laid down the following articles of a defensive alliance.

I. If one [of the Allies] is attacked by a European Power, its Ally will help. The two allies, in case of need, will also act in concert so as to remind France of her obligations under the Franco-Russian treaty.

II. No separate peace shall be concluded.

III. The promise of help includes the case where acts, such as the delivery of coal to a belligerent, should give rise after the War to complaints by a third Power as to pretended violations of the rights of neutrals[1].

The Tsar approved the draft but desired, before signing it, that France should see it—a proposal to which the Kaiser was utterly opposed.

On December 3rd it was announced that a German ship had been stopped under the Foreign Enlistment Act from coaling at Cardiff, because its cargo was believed to be destined for the Russian fleet; and the Kaiser at once renewed his pressure at Petrograd. "It is far from my intention to hurry you in your answer about our treaty; but you will, I am sure, be fully alive to the fact that I must now have absolutely positive guarantees whether you intend leaving me unaided in case England and Japan should declare war against me on account of the coaling of the Russian fleet. Should you be unable to guarantee me that in such a war you will loyally fight shoulder to shoulder with me, then I regret I must immediately forbid German steamers to continue to coal your fleet." Instead of signing the treaty, the Tsar forwarded Admiral Rojdestvensky's complaint that two Hamburg-American coaling ships had not received orders to follow the fleet beyond Madagascar; and the Kaiser replied that he could give no Instructions, and had told Ballin that he must act on his own responsibility and at his own risk. The project of a treaty now slumbered for several months.

Early in 1905, after the fall of Port Arthur, President Roosevelt, unofficially but in vain, advised Russia to make peace; but on May 31st, after the crowning victory of Tsushima, Japan secretly asked the President to invite the belligerents to negotiate. The Tsar agreed in principle; and, on June 8th, Roosevelt telegraphed an identic

[1] The story of Björko is summarised by Fay, "The Kaiser's Secret Negotiations with the Tsar, 1904–1905," *American Historical Review*, October, 1918.

invitation, offering to arrange time and place. As France and Germany were already urging Russia to make peace, the President suggested that Lord Lansdowne should exert pressure on Japan. The Foreign Secretary declined; and, when the belligerents met at Portsmouth, he was not in a position to second the President's heroic efforts to avoid a rupture. "The English Government has been foolishly reluctant to advise Japan to be reasonable," he wrote on August 23rd; and on September 11th, when the Treaty was signed, he told Whitelaw Reid that the Kaiser had stood by him "like a trump[1]." But, although the British Government declined to press its victorious Ally, it had taken a step which contributed to make her accept somewhat less than she had demanded. Though the Treaty of 1902 was concluded for five years, a new Compact, of wider scope, was signed in London, on August 12th, 1905, for ten years. The objects of the two Powers, the Preamble declared, were (i) the maintenance of peace in Eastern Asia and India; (ii) the preservation of the common interests of all Powers in China by insuring the independence and integrity of the Chinese empire and the principle of equal opportunities for the commerce and industry of all nations; (iii) the maintenance of the territorial rights and the defence of the special interests of the signatories in Eastern Asia and India. These interests were set forth in Articles III and IV: "Japan, possessing paramount political, military and economic interests in Korea, Great Britain recognises her right to take such measures of guidance, control and protection in Korea as she may deem necessary, provided that they are not contrary to the principle of equal opportunities for the commerce and industry of all nations. Great Britain having a special interest in all that concerns the security of the Indian frontier, Japan recognises her right to take such measures in the proximity of that frontier as she may find necessary for safeguarding her Indian possessions." Article II provided that, if either party should be involved in war in defence of its territorial rights or special interests by reason of unprovoked attack or aggressive action, wherever arising, the other should come to its assistance. The new Treaty, in addition to handing over Korea to Japan, introduced two principles of vital moment to Great Britain. In the first place, the scope of the agreement was extended to embrace India, thus correcting what was generally regarded as the inequality of advantage under the Pact of 1902. In the second, each was to come to the assistance of the other, if attacked

[1] Bishop, *Theodore Roosevelt*, vol. I. chs. 31–2.

by a single Power—a stipulation which not only increased our liabilities, but involved for us the obligation, in certain circumstances, to intervene in a struggle between our Ally and the United States.

Lord Lansdowne instructed Sir Charles Hardinge to communicate to the Russian Government the text of the new Compact, "which has a purely pacific purpose and tends to protect rights and interests of incontestible security." Lamsdorff observed that everyone, from the Tsar downwards, regarded the Treaty as directed against Russia. The Ambassador rejoined that only the mention of India could have justified such a notion, and that the Treaty was purely defensive. These assurances exercised no effect on the Tsar, who, on July 24th, had signed at Björko the Treaty with Germany which had been discussed in the previous autumn.

I. If any European State shall attack either Power the other would aid with all its forces.

II. Neither would conclude a separate peace.

III. The Treaty should come into force on the conclusion of peace with Japan, and might only be cancelled at a year's notice.

IV. Russia would make its terms known to France and invite her to sign it as an ally.

The Kaiser returned home delighted with his handiwork. "The Alliance," he asserted, "will be of great use to Russia, as it will restore quiet in the minds of the people and confidence in the maintenance of peace in Europe, and encourage financial circles in foreign countries to place funds in enterprises to open up Russia. In times to come, even Japan may feel inclined to join it. This would cool down English self-assertion and impertinence. July 24th is a corner-stone in European politics and turns over a new leaf in the history of the world." But, while the Kaiser was dreaming of the Dual and Triple Alliance leagued against perfidious Albion, the unwary Tsar, on the other hand, was oppressed by his guilty secret. On his return from Björko he appeared to Lamsdorff to be embarrassed; and, when he at length produced the Treaty, the Foreign Minister was appalled. No action, however, was taken till the return of Witte from America; and the opposition of the two Ministers was strengthened by the reply of the Russian Ambassador at Paris, who, on being ordered to sound the French Government, replied that it was useless, since France would never join a German league nor recognise the settlement of 1871. The Tsar now plucked up courage to write to the Kaiser that it was impossible to carry out the Pact; and the Russian Ambassador in

Berlin was instructed to add that it must remain inoperative till Russia, Germany and France could agree, since the adhesion of France was at present impossible. The Treaty of Björko, treacherously extorted and quickly denounced, was the prelude to a new orientation of Russian policy.

IV. THE CONFERENCE OF ALGECIRAS, 1904-1906

After receiving the imprimatur of Great Britain on her work in Morocco, France turned with new zeal to the task of reform in that country[1]. At the close of 1904 M. Delcassé drew up his Instructions for Saint-René Taillandier, who was selected for the Mission to Fez. On reaching the Moorish capital in February, 1905, the Envoy reported the Sultan as saying that, while most of the suggested changes were practicable, some were very difficult to accept and must be discussed with the Maghzen. But, before the discussions were concluded, a third party intervened, and the problem of Moroccan reform brought Europe within sight of war.

The attitude of official Germany towards the Anglo-French Treaty had at first been friendly. "We have no cause to imagine that it has a point against any other Power," declared the Chancellor. "As to Morocco, we have commercial interests which we must and shall protect. We have, however, no ground to fear that they will be overlooked or infringed." It was natural that the Pan-Germans should grumble at the Chancellor's self-effacement; but the Kaiser informed King Edward, on his visit to Kiel in June, that he had no objection to the Treaty, and that Morocco had never interested him[2]. The despatch of the French Envoy to Fez with a comprehensive programme of reforms was the signal for a change of front at Berlin. Holstein suggested that the Kaiser should visit Tangier, and the Chancellor approved the plan[3]. The *Norddeutsche Allgemeine Zeitung* issued a warning that the French negotiations at Fez did not square with the avowed policy of maintaining the *status quo*; and the object of the coming demonstration was explained by the Chancellor in the *Reichstag* on March 29th. "No one who has no aggressive aim in view can find cause for apprehension. We have economic interests; and in Morocco, as in China, it is our interest to keep the open door.

---

[1] See *Affaires du Maroc*, 1901-1905; Tardieu, *La Conférence d'Algéciras*; and Morel, *Morocco in Diplomacy*.
[2] Eckardstein, *Erinnerungen*, III. 88.
[3] Hammann, *Zur Vorgeschichte des Weltkrieges*, ch. 8.

We merely ask that our economic interests are not endangered." On March 31st, the Kaiser landed from his yacht at Tangier and addressed the German colony[1]:

I am happy to salute the devoted pioneers of German industry and commerce who aid me in my task of maintaining the interests of the Fatherland in a free country. The Empire has great and growing interests in Morocco. Commerce can only progress if all the Powers are considered to have equal rights under the sovereignty of the Sultan and compatible with the independence of the country. My visit is the recognition of this independence.

The theme was developed in a speech to the Sultan's uncle and Plenipotentiary.

My visit is to show my resolve to do all in my power to safeguard German interests in Morocco. Considering the Sultan as absolutely free, I wish to discuss with him the means to secure these interests. As for the reforms which he contemplates, it seems to me that he should proceed with great caution and consider the religious sentiments of the people, so that public order is not troubled.

The reason for this dramatic change in Germany's attitude commonly given in France and Great Britain was that the Kaiser took advantage of the collapse of Russia in the Far East to coerce her Ally. The motive was frankly avowed by the Pan-German Press, but it was not the main one. The French Press spoke openly of setting up a second Tunis, and Germany believed that, unless she entered an emphatic protest, Morocco would be swallowed up before her eyes. Moreover, the apprehensions aroused by French ambitions were confirmed by the discovery of Secret Treaties.

A Treaty had been signed by Lord Lansdowne and M. Paul Cambon on April 8th, 1904, at the same time as the documents published to the world. The Mediterranean coast from Melilla to the Sebu river, whenever the Sultan ceased to exercise authority over it, was to come within the sphere of influence of Spain and be administered by her, she, on her part, pledging herself to commercial liberty and undertaking to abstain from fortifying the straits or from alienating any part of the territory. When Spain adhered to the Anglo-French Declaration in the following September, and declared herself " firmly attached to the integrity of the Moorish empire under the sovereignty of the Sultan," a similar Franco-Spanish Convention was signed, which frankly contemplated partition[2]:

[1] He yielded with reluctance to the Chancellor's desire for a political demonstration. Schön, *Memoirs of an Ambassador*, pp. 19–23.

[2] See Morocco, No. 4 (1911).

In case the continuance of the political *status* of Morocco should become impossible, or if, owing to the weakness of the Government or to its continued inability to uphold law and order, or to any other cause the existence of which is acknowledged by both parties, the *status quo* can no longer be maintained, Spain may freely exercise her right of action in the territory which henceforward constitutes her sphere of influence.

Each Power promised to inform the other if obliged to undertake military action, and French and Spanish rights in their respective spheres were to be respected. The Pact was communicated to Lord Lansdowne with the request to keep it secret. The two Secret Treaties were not published till 1911; but they were quickly known at Berlin[1]. Germany's case was that, if she did not act, she would one day wake up to find Morocco closed to her commerce.

The root of the trouble lay in the fact that M. Delcassé had not purchased Germany's assent in advance. The goodwill of Italy had been bought by recognition of her claims to Tripoli, that of Great Britain by assent to her position in Egypt, that of Spain by the hypothetical reversion of the northern littoral. Germany, it is true, was not a Mediterranean Power; but her commerce was rapidly developing and her pride was morbidly sensitive. "With incredible blindness," wrote M. René Millet, "the Government took precautions with everybody except the only one of its neighbours whom it had serious cause to fear[2]." M. Delcassé, echoed M. Hanotaux, offered Germany a pretext for conflict, and chose the moment when Russia was locked in deadly conflict in the Far East[3]. In England, Mr Gibson Bowles had foretold that Germany would send in her bill. It is regrettable that the British Cabinet did not perceive—or at any rate did not help France to perceive—the wisdom of securing German consent by a *solatium*. Though the Secret Treaties of 1904 reserved no share for Great Britain in the contingent partition of Morocco, and though it has been argued[4] that it was reasonable for the contracting parties to make alternative arrangements in the event of Morocco collapsing from internal weakness, our share in a transaction which suggested double-dealing involves the British Government in partial responsibility for the crises of 1905 and 1911.

[1] Valentin, *Deutschlands Aussenpolitik*, p. 54.
[2] *Notre Politique extérieure*, p. 224.
[3] *Ib*. Introduction.
[4] Gilbert Murray, *The Foreign Policy of Sir Edward Grey*, pp. 55–6. When the secret clauses were revealed, the criticism was renewed. Baron d'Estournelles de Constant condemned them as a double game, and statesmen so far apart as Ribot and Jaurès denounced the contradiction between public professions and private aims.

Despite the provocation to which it was a reply, the Tangier demonstration was a colossal blunder; for its first effect was to strengthen the *entente cordiale*, and to turn a limited obligation into a general defensive understanding against aggression or dictation. It was promptly announced that a British squadron would visit Brest, that a French squadron would return the visit at Portsmouth, and that King Edward would stop at Paris in May on his way to join the Queen at Marseilles. Yet, though France was angered by the peremptory tones of the Tangier manifesto, there was a widespread conviction that the Foreign Minister had led France into danger. On April 19th he was attacked in the Chamber not only by Jaurès and de Pressensé, but by M. Deschanel and other Imperialists. M. Rouvier offered a lukewarm defence of his colleague, whose policy he detested, and the days of the Minister were numbered.

The French Envoy had been busily engaged at Fez since February, and on April 11th he reported that the Sultan consented to his troops being organised on French models at Tangier, Rabat, Casablanca and Ujda. But the atmosphere rapidly changed when a German Envoy, Count Tattenbach, reached Fez on May 13th, and on May 28th Abdul Aziz rejected the French proposals. A day or two later, a British Mission reached the capital, but was unable to reverse the decision. Abdul Aziz explained that he could only accept the French proposals if ratified by the Powers; and on May 30th he invited the Signatories of the Treaty of 1880 to meet at Tangier.

Though Germany alone among the Powers desired a conference, the peace of Europe hung on France's reply to the invitation. In this emergency, the Kaiser turned to President Roosevelt, and on April 5th, Speck presented a Memorandum, in which his master declared that he must insist on a conference[1]. He believed that the attitude of Great Britain would depend on that of the United States, and asked the President to tell the British Government that he thought a conference should be held. Roosevelt, who was away hunting bears, began to be alarmed. "I am sincerely anxious to bring about a better state of feeling between England and Germany," he wrote to Mr Taft on April 20th. "Each nation is working itself up to a condition of desperate hatred of the other—each from fear the other is going to attack." On returning to Washington at the end of May, he found the French and German Ambassadors apprehensive of war. "Durand was bitter about Germany, and so far as he represented the

[1] Bishop, *Theodore Roosevelt*, vol. i. chs. 26–7.

British Government it would appear they were anxious to see Germany humiliated by France's refusal of a conference and quite willing to face war. I desired to do anything I could for France because I thought her in the right." On June 5th, Mr Whitelaw Reid, the American Ambassador in London, telegraphed that Lord Lansdowne regarded the proposal for a conference as unfortunate and as, possibly, designed to embarrass France.

Strengthened by the support of Great Britain and Russia and by the assurance of Austria that she would side with the majority, M. Delcassé held out stubbornly against a Conference. But the game he was playing appeared to his colleagues to be fraught with danger. Prince Henckel von Donnersmarck visited Paris—where he was a familiar figure at the end of the Second Empire—and had interviews with the Premier and some of his colleagues. The air was thick with rumours of a German ultimatum and talk of the unpreparedness of the Army. The decisive Cabinet was held on June 6th. President Loubet remained faithful to the Foreign Minister; but all his colleagues, unwilling either to bluff or to fight, were hostile. M. Delcassé argued that France could not take part in a conference without humiliation, and asserted that Great Britain was ready to back her up to the very end, and would mobilise the fleet and land 100,000 men in Schleswig-Holstein. The Premier replied that the acceptance of the British offer would mean war, and that it was necessary to accept the conference. His colleagues supported him; and the Foreign Minister, after warning them that their pusillanimity would encourage German insolence, withdrew and resigned[1].

"The British offer," on the strength of which M. Delcassé was prepared to risk a war, existed only in his imagination. In the middle of May, the French Ambassador complained to Lord Lansdowne of the general attitude of the German Government, which was seeking in all parts of the world to sow discord between France and Great Britain[2]. He stated that M. Delcassé regarded the situation not as profoundly dangerous, but as sufficiently serious to occasion him much preoccupation. Lord Lansdowne replied that the moral seemed to be that each Government should continue to treat the other with the most absolute mutual confidence, should keep it fully informed of everything which came to their knowledge, and should, so far as

[1] The story was told by Stephane Lauzanne in *Le Matin*, October 6th, 7th, 8th, 1905. Mévil, *De la paix de Francfort à la Conférence d'Algéciras*, chs. 4 and 5, contains Delcassé's apologia.

[2] This paragraph is based on information kindly supplied by the Foreign Office.

possible, discuss in advance any contingencies by which they might in the course of events find themselves confronted. In a conversation with Sir Frank Lascelles on June 10th, Prince Bülow, speaking in the strictest confidence, said that information had reached him that Great Britain had made an offer to France to enter into an offensive and defensive Alliance with her against Germany. France had refused; but the fact that the offer had been made was a proof of unfriendliness against Germany. Sir Frank could only say that he was astonished to hear that such an offer had been made, and was strongly inclined to doubt the accuracy of the news. Prince Bülow said that the information was not official, but that it came from a source which made it impossible for him to doubt its accuracy. Hereupon, Lord Lansdowne sent for the German Ambassador and told him that he could scarcely believe that the assertion as to an alleged offensive and defensive Alliance was seriously made or that the story was worth contradicting. If, however, the Ambassador thought a contradiction would serve a useful purpose, he was glad to assure him that no offensive and defensive Alliance had ever been offered or even discussed on either side. According to Hammann, he added that he must leave it open whether public opinion, which saw in the theatrical Tangier journey an unfriendly act against Great Britain as well as against France, might not force the Government to aid France if she were attacked[1]. Such a warning against aggression was very different from a solemn engagement to engage in hostilities; and the "offer" is rightly characterised by M. Poincaré as a formula of entente even less definite than the Franco-Russian Pact of 1891. How little weight was attached to it in Downing Street, is revealed by the fact that in his retrospect of August 3rd, 1914, Sir Edward Grey made no reference to the incident. M. Delcassé's mistaken interpretation of the British official attitude was doubtless due to the *obiter dicta* of certain highly-placed personages, who expressed their individual convictions as to what was likely to occur[2].

On the fall of M. Delcassé, M. Rouvier took over the Foreign Office, and on July 8th he and the German Ambassador made a joint Declaration defining the conditions on which France accepted the conference, while the Ambassador formally declared that Germany did not contest the Anglo-French Agreement of 1904. On July 12th, the British

---

[1] Hammann, *Der missverstandene Bismarck*, p. 120.
[2] On his way from Biarritz to London King Edward told French Ministers that in case of need Great Britain would intervene on their side. Eckardstein, III. 105.

Government also agreed to the conference. The Premier expressed his hope that, in Count Radolin's words, there would be "*ni vainqueur ni vaincu*"; and the accord signed by M. Rouvier and the Ambassador on September 28th seemed to put this aspiration into words. The organisation of the police, except on the Algerian frontier, was to be international. A State-bank was to supply credits for the police, the troops and public works. Morocco was not to alienate any public service to the profit of particular interests, and the principle of adjudication without distinction of nationality was to be adopted for public works. The Conference was to be held at Algeciras, and both Missions were to return from Fez.

At this moment the Balfour Government was tottering to its fall; but in a speech on October 20th Sir Edward Grey declared that the accession to power of a Liberal Government would involve no change in our Foreign Policy, since the Liberals would accept the three cardinal features now distinguishing it—friendship with the United States, the Japanese Alliance and friendship with France. The roots of estrangement from Russia lay solely in the past, and both Governments should encourage mutual confidence. Our relations with Germany were more delicate.

If there is a desire for the improvement of relations—the relations of the Governments are quite correct—between the Press and public opinion, it will meet with no obstacle here, provided it be clearly understood that nothing we do is in any way to impair our existing good relations with France. In other words, it must be a condition of any improvement that the relations of Germany with France on all matters which come under the French Agreement should be fair and good also.

The speech aroused wide attention, for it was known that Sir Edward might succeed Lord Lansdowne at any moment. On the resignation of Mr Balfour on December 4th, Sir Henry Campbell-Bannerman formed a Liberal Ministry, and explained its policy at a meeting at the Albert Hall on December 22nd[1]. The references to Foreign Affairs were brief, but clear.

I wish emphatically to reaffirm my adhesion to the policy of the *Entente cordiale*. Even more important than any actual amicable instrument is the real friendship developed between the two peoples; and one of the objects of our policy will be to maintain that spirit of friendship unimpaired. As regards Russia, we have nothing but good feelings towards that great people. In the case of Germany, also, I see no cause whatever of estrangement in any of the interests of either people, and we welcome the unofficial

[1] This speech is reprinted in his *Speeches*, p. 179.

demonstrations of friendship which have lately been passing between the two countries. With other European Powers our relations are most friendly. Our relations with Japan are sufficiently known to the world by the recent Treaty; and with the United States we are bound by the closest ties of race, tradition and fellowship. This is a most pleasing outlook, which I trust will not be marred by any events that can occur. Our general foreign policy will be opposed to aggression and to adventure, and will be animated by a desire to be on the best terms with all nationalities.

The new Ministry was well received abroad. Baron Richthofen expressed to Baron Greindl, the Belgian Minister, his satisfaction at the change, which, he declared, had produced a certain *détente*. Sir Henry Campbell-Bannerman, he added, had a reputation for sincerity and loyalty which inspired confidence. The love of the new Premier for France was well known in Paris.

A few days after this reassuring survey, the Military Correspondent of *The Times* wrote an article on the hostility of Germany to France, ending with a warning to Berlin that a war might unchain animosities in unexpected quarters. On the following day, December 28th, Major Huguet, the French Military Attaché, in discussing the article, remarked that the French Embassy was anxious because the new Foreign Secretary had not renewed the assurances given by Lord Lansdowne. The Ambassador was on leave, and the Algeciras Conference was to meet on January 16th. Colonel Repington asked why one of the staff of the Embassy did not make enquiry at the Foreign Office. Major Huguet replied that, in the absence of the Ambassador, it was impossible to gain information there; but, if Sir Edward would broach the subject at the next diplomatic reception, the Embassy would be greatly relieved. The French Navy, he added, was prepared, and reservists were coming to barracks to ask for orders; for Germany might probably attack through Belgium. Colonel Repington reported the conversation to the Foreign Secretary, who was engaged in his constituency, and who replied that he had not receded from anything Lord Lansdowne had said[1].

Meanwhile, the Ambassador, who had returned from his holiday, visited the Foreign Secretary on January 10th, 1906, and, after informing him[2] that the French Government considered the danger to be real, asked whether Great Britain would think she had so much at stake as to be willing to join in resisting an unprovoked attack. If this were even a possible attitude, conversations would be desirable

[1] Repington, *The First World War*, vol. I. ch. I.
[2] See Lord Haldane, *Before the War*, pp. 29–30.

between the General Staffs as to the form of cooperation in the northern portion of France. The French Army was not so large as that of Germany. Could we, then, reconsider our military organisation, so that, if we ever thought it necessary, we could rapidly despatch, say, 100,000 men, not to invade Belgium, which no one thought of doing, but to guard the French frontier of Belgium, in case the German Army sought to enter France that way? If the German attack were made further south, where the fortresses rendered the defensive position strong, the French Army, set free from the difficulty of mustering in full strength opposite the Belgian boundary, would be able to guard the southern frontier.

The Foreign Secretary replied that he could promise nothing to any foreign Power, unless it was subsequently to receive the whole-hearted support of public opinion here if the occasion arose[1].

I said, in my opinion, if war was forced upon France on the question of Morocco, public opinion in this country would have rallied to the material support of France. I gave no promise, but I expressed that opinion during the crisis to the French Ambassador and the German Ambassador. I made no promise, and I used no threats. That position was accepted by the French Government; but they said to me at the time, and I think very reasonably: "If you think it possible that the public opinion of Great Britain, should a sudden crisis arise, justifies you in giving to France the armed support which you cannot promise in advance, you will not be able to give that support, even if you wish it, when the time comes, unless some conversations have already taken place between naval and military experts." There was force in that. I agreed to it, and authorised those conversations to take place, but on the distinct understanding that nothing which passed between military or naval experts should bind either Government or restrict in any way their freedom to make a decision as to whether or not they would give that support when the time arose. I had to take the responsibility of doing that without the Cabinet. It could not be summoned. An answer had to be given. I consulted Sir Henry Campbell-Bannerman, the Prime-Minister; I consulted Lord Haldane, who was then Secretary of State for War; and the present Prime-Minister (Mr Asquith), who was then Chancellor of the Exchequer. That was the most I could do, and they authorised that on the distinct understanding that it left the hands of the Government free whenever the crisis arose.

The War Minister visited Campbell-Bannerman on January 14th, and obtained leave for Sir Neville Lyttelton and General Grierson to concert cooperation. The Premier, adds Colonel Repington, was very firm and clear that we should be prepared for all emergencies, but that the conversations should not bind the Governments. On

[1] See his speech of August 3rd, 1914.

January 17th Grierson began his talks with Huguet, and they signed a declaration that the conversations should not bind either Government.

"I summoned the heads of the British General Staff," adds Lord Haldane, "and saw Colonel Huguet. I became aware at once that there was a new army problem. It was how to mobilise and concentrate opposite the Belgian frontier a force calculated as adequate (with the assistance of Russian pressure in the East) to make up for the inadequacy of the French armies for their great task of defending the entire French frontier from Dunkirk to Belfort, or even further south if Italy should join the Triple Alliance in an attack."

The conversations thus begun continued without interruption till 1914[1].

Almost at the same moment that military conversations began with French experts, Colonel Barnardiston, our Military Attaché in Brussels, initiated similar discussions with General Ducarne, Chief of the Belgian General Staff. According to the latter's Report to the Belgian Minister of War, dated April 10th, 1906, the Colonel spoke of the preoccupation of the British General Staff with the possibilities

---

[1] "I only told Buckle," records Colonel Repington (*The First World War*, vol. I. ch. I). But what was known to the Editor of *The Times* was unknown to the majority of the Cabinet. "The fact that conversations between military and naval experts took place," declared the Foreign Secretary in 1914, "was later on—I think much later on, because that crisis passed and the thing ceased to be of importance—brought to the knowledge of the Cabinet." The neglect to consult the Cabinet was a grave offence against the theory and practice of Ministerial solidarity. "Sir Edward's phraseology," writes Lord Loreburn, "rather conveys that his selection of confidants was casual; but Mr Asquith and Lord Haldane were with him Vice-Presidents of the Liberal League. There was no difficulty whatever in summoning the Cabinet during the election to consider so grave a matter. A good many Members were in London or within an hour of it, while those whom he consulted were at a distance. And there are railways and post offices in Great Britain. The weekly meetings of the Cabinet were regular in December, and were held on January 3rd and January 31st. From February 1st they were again regular. The Cabinet might have been told within a very short time of the conversations between the military experts and of the statement made to the two Ambassadors. The reason apparently given for not informing the Cabinet as soon as it did meet (January 31st) is 'that the crisis passed and the thing ceased to be of importance.' On the contrary: events have unhappily proved that it was of the utmost importance. It was the first recorded communication pointing to our making war on behalf of France if she should come to blows with Germany. The thing of which Sir Edward made light proved to be the parting of the ways in our relations with France. Enmity had already given place to goodwill; but we had not yet espoused the quarrel of France or held out the prospect of fighting by her side. In the beginning of 1906 her statesmen learned that even this was possible. The concealment from the Cabinet was protracted and must have been deliberate. Parliament knew nothing of it till August 3rd, 1914. Some of those who were in close confidential communication with the Prime Minister at that time will not believe that he understood the scope and significance of what was in fact done, unless some evidence is given" (*How the War Came*, pp. 80–81).

of war, declared that we should send about 100,000 men, who would disembark between Dunkirk and Calais, and asked whether Belgium could defend herself during the ten days required for their transport. The General replied that Namur and Liége were safe against a surprise attack, and that the Belgian Army of 100,000 men would be ready to take the field in four days. After expressing his satisfaction at the information, the Colonel declared that the conversation was absolutely confidential; that it was in no way binding on his Government; that his Minister and the British General Staff were the only persons aware of the matter; and that he did not know whether his Sovereign had been consulted. In succeeding interviews British assistance and Belgian cooperation were discussed in detail. A marginal note on the dossier stated that "the entry of the English into Belgium would only take place after the violation of her neutrality by Germany." No convention was suggested on either side, and these conversations, unlike those with France, were purely unofficial[1].

At the Conference of Algeciras, which was attended by twelve States in addition to Morocco and opened on January 16th, Great Britain was represented by Sir Arthur Nicolson; and King Edward remarked to M. Cambon, "Tell us what you wish on each point, and we will support you without restriction or reserves." The two main questions of the Police and a State-bank were reached early in

---

[1] See *Collected Diplomatic Documents relating to the Outbreak of War*, pp. 350–67. When General Ducarne's report was published in the *Norddeutsche Allgemeine Zeitung* on October 3rd, 1914, the Foreign Office addressed a Circular Telegram to British Ministers abroad, denying the existence of an Anglo-Belgian agreement. "In view of the solemn guarantee to protect the neutrality of Belgium against violation from any side, some academic discussions may have taken place as to what assistance the British army might be able to afford, should one of her neighbours violate that neutrality." When Bethmann-Hollweg in 1915, on the strength of this document, charged Great Britain and Belgium with conspiring against Germany, Sir Edward published a reply in *The Times* of August 26th. "The conversation of which most use has been made was never reported to the Foreign Office, nor, as far as records show, to the War Office. But it bears on its face that the entry of the British into Belgium would take place only after the violation of Belgian territory by Germany, and that it did not commit the British Government." "We were among the guarantors of Belgian neutrality," echoes Lord Haldane, "and it was of course conceivable that, if she called on us to do so, we might have to defend her. It would be part of the duty of our Military Attaché to remember this, and, if opportunity offered, to ascertain in informal conversation the view of the Belgian General Staff as to what form of help they would be likely to ask for. This he doubtless did. But even so, the conversation must have been very informal, for in the account by the Chief of the Belgian Staff there are errors about the composition of the possible British force which indicate that either he took no notes or that Colonel Barnardiston had not thought it an occasion which required him to obtain details from London." Lord Haldane himself only learned of the conversations from the German publication in 1914 (*Before the War*, pp. 181–2).

February[1]. France's demand for the Police mandate and her revised offer to share it with Spain were rejected by Germany, who first proposed that the Sultan should select officers from the minor Powers, and later that she should choose from "foreign" nations. These suggestions were in turn rejected by France and Spain, and at the same moment discussions on the State-bank reached a deadlock. A rupture was generally expected; but pacific influences were at work behind the scenes. In urging France to accept the Conference, President Roosevelt had promised her fair play; and, in the middle of February, he intervened on her behalf in secret negotiations with the Kaiser[2]. A Franco-Spanish mandate under a Swiss Inspector-General was at last accepted, at the end of March. The main difficulty having been overcome, the delegates were anxious to be gone. "They are throwing concessions at each other's heads," wrote Sir Donald Mackenzie Wallace in his diary on March 29th; and on April 7th the Act was signed. Though both sides pretended to be satisfied with the results of the wrestling-match, the Conference of Algeciras proved not more than a breathing-space between the rounds. Its main result was the tightening of the bonds between Great Britain and France; for the maintenance of the Balance of Power involved that we should throw our weight now into this scale, now into that, but always against any Power aspiring—or believed by us to be aspiring —to a European dictatorship. The process which Germans describe as encirclement, and Englishmen as insurance, had begun[3].

V. THE SECOND HAGUE CONFERENCE, 1906–1908

The *détente* following the Algeciras Conference was employed by the newly-installed British Cabinet to strive for a reduction of armaments. On April 3rd, 1906, Benckendorff informed Sir Edward Grey that, in convoking the Second Hague Conference for July, Russia desired to secure improvements in the working of the Court and additions to the Rules of War by land and sea, but did not propose to discuss the Limitation of Armaments. The Foreign Secretary

---

[1] See *Protocoles et Comptes Rendus de la Conférence d'Algéciras*; Tardieu, *La Conférence d'Algéciras*; Morocco, No. 1 (1906). I have here been able to use a MSS. Diary of Sir D. Mackenzie Wallace, who represented *The Times* during the Conference.
[2] Bishop, *Theodore Roosevelt*, 1. 489–505.
[3] In *La France conquise*, published in 1906, M. Flourens, the ex-Foreign Minister, bitterly complained that King Edward reigned in London and governed in Paris; but his was a voice crying in the wilderness.

replied that, as he gathered, Russia did not desire to exclude discussion of the subject, and that it was the wish of the British Government to see it included[1]. The Conference was postponed till the following year; but, as evidence of our good faith, it was announced in July that one of the four battleships of the Cawdor programme would be omitted, with corresponding reduction in destroyers and submarines. If any expectation existed that this step might evoke a response from Berlin, it was quickly disappointed; and the Kaiser observed to Sir Frank Lascelles that, if disarmament were to be brought up at the Conference, he should decline to be represented[2]. Every State must decide for itself what forces it required. In August, King Edward visited Cronberg, where the Kaiser remarked to Sir Charles Hardinge that the approaching Hague Conference was great nonsense. That his attitude was not dictated by hostility to Great Britain was shown by his cordiality to the British War Minister at the September manœuvres.

" I was invited," writes Lord Haldane[3], " to examine for myself the organisation of the German War Office, which I wished to study for the purposes of reform at home, and this I did in some detail, in company with Colonel Ellison, an expert adviser. The authorities explained to us the general nature of the organisation for rapid mobilisation developed under Moltke and subsequently carried further. Of course, I neither tried to obtain nor did obtain any information not available to the general public there. I was everywhere cordially welcomed....I do not think that my impression was wrong that even the responsible heads of the Army were then looking almost entirely to peaceful penetration."

The Morocco crisis had proved too much for Bülow's strength, and it was not till November 14th, 1906, that he reappeared in the *Reichstag* and surveyed the European situation.

We have no idea of disturbing the Franco-English friendship....Good relations between Germany and Russia have not damaged the Franco-Russian Alliance, and good relations between Germany and England are not incompatible with the Entente, if it pursues peaceful aims. The Entente without good relations of its members to Germany would be a danger to peace. A policy aiming at encircling Germany, forming a ring of Powers in order to isolate her, would indeed be dangerous....We have no idea of building a fleet as strong as the English, and we shall never break the peace. Time and patience are needed. The barometer has moved from Rain and Wind to Changeable. To point to Fair, both sides must avoid irritations.

---

[1] *Correspondence concerning the Second Peace Conference*, 1908, Cd. 3857.
[2] Sir E. T. Cook, *How Britain strove for Peace*.
[3] *Before the War*, pp. 23–26.

Undeterred by the hostility of the Kaiser to a discussion of armaments, the British Prime-Minister, in the first number of *The Nation*, published on March 7th, 1907, in an article entitled "The Hague Conference and the Limitation of Armaments," made an impressive appeal to Europe. "The disposition shown by certain Powers, of whom Great Britain is one, to raise the question of the limitation of armaments at the approaching Conference has evoked some objections. I wish to indicate my reasons for holding them to be baseless. The first Conference was convened for this very question. The hope was not fulfilled, but I never heard it suggested that the discussion left behind it any injurious consequences. It was desirable in 1898; and to day the burden has enormously increased. I know of no special circumstances which would make the discussion a matter of international misgiving. Since 1899 the points of disagreement between the Powers have become not more but less acute; they are confined to a far smaller field; the sentiment of peace has become incomparably stronger and more constant; and the idea of arbitration has attained a practical potency and a moral authority undreamt of in 1898. We have already given earnest of our sincerity by considerable reductions in our naval and military expenditure, as well as by the understanding that we are prepared to go further if we find a similar disposition in other quarters. Our delegates will not therefore go to the Conference empty-handed. It has, however, been suggested that our example will count for nothing, because our preponderant naval position will remain unimpaired. I do not believe it. The sea power of this country implies no challenge to any State or group of States.... Our known adhesion to these two dominant principles— the independence of nationalities and the freedom of trade—entitles us, of itself, to claim that, if our fleets be invulnerable, they carry with them no menace across the waters of the world, but a message of the most cordial goodwill, based on the belief in the community of interests between the nations." The article was discussed throughout Europe, and the writer's sincerity was confirmed by a Navy programme of three capital ships and a promise to drop one of them, if other Powers would do the same. The offer was communicated officially to seven Powers; but, on April 30th, Bülow, to whom the invitation was virtually addressed, announced in the *Reichstag* that the German Government could not participate in a discussion which they believed to be unpractical, if not actually dangerous. Russia and Austria, also, expressed a wish to postpone the question.

On April 7th Benckendorff reported that Great Britain, the United States and Spain desired a discussion on Armaments at the Hague; and, on June 12th, the Foreign Secretary signed elaborate Instructions to Sir Edward Fry, who was accompanied by Sir E. Satow, Lord Reay, and Sir H. Howard, British Minister at the Hague, with General Elles and Captain Ottley, Director of Naval Intelligence, as experts[1]:

The Government, in accepting the invitation, reserves the right of suggesting the discussion of other questions. Foremost among them is that of expenditure upon armaments.... They felt it was better to have a discussion, even if it did not lead to a satisfactory conclusion. Discussion without results would at any rate have kept the door open for continuing negotiations on the subject; whereas to put the question aside would seem like an admission that it was hopeless and had receded since the First Conference, of which it was the prime object. But, after the apparently final declaration of the German Government, that under no circumstances would they take part in such a discussion, it is doubtful how far it would be expedient to proceed with it. The position of Germany both as a military and as a naval Power is such that it is difficult to regard as serious any discussion in which she does not take part. The Government would be most reluctant that anything should take place at the Conference, summoned as it is in the interests of peace, that would be of a nature to cause friction or ill-feeling. You will therefore consult with the United States and Spanish Delegates and consider what line to take. Should it be decided that the subject shall be discussed and a practical proposal be invited, the Government would agree that the Great Powers should communicate in advance their programmes of naval construction.... The Government are aware that this would not necessarily lead directly to any reduction in expenditure; but they are hopeful that the mere fact of communication would provide opportunities for negotiation that do not now exist and would tend to alleviate the burden or retard its increase.

A discussion was initiated by Sir Edward Fry on August 17th, at the fourth Plenary Meeting of the Conference[2]. He began by quoting Muravieff's Circular of 1898, and pronounced its true and eloquent words to be more opportune than ever. The charges of Europe, the United States and Japan had risen from 251 to 320 millions.

Such is the expenditure which might serve better objects; such is the burden under which our peoples groan; such is the Christian peace of the civilised world in the twentieth century. I know you will agree with me that the realisation of the wish expressed in 1899 would be a great blessing for the whole of humanity. Is this hope capable of realisation? I cannot

[1] Count Wolff-Metternich in vain advised his chiefs not to decline discussion.
[2] *Protocols of the Eleven Plenary Meetings*, 1908, pp. 27–31, Cd. 4081.

give a categorical reply. I can only say that my Government is a convinced adherent of these lofty aspirations, and that it charges me to invite you to cooperate in realising this noble object.... Today, the sentiment of solidarity of the human race is more than ever spread. It is this sentiment which has rendered possible this Conference, and it is in its name that I beg you not to separate without asking the Governments to devote themselves very seriously to the question.... The British Government, recognising that several Governments desire to restrict their military expenses, and that this can be realised by the independent action of each Power, would be ready to communicate yearly to the Powers who would do the same the programme of new ships of war and the expenditure this would entail.... In conclusion, I propose the following resolution: "The Conference confirms the resolution adopted in 1899[1], and, seeing that the charges have considerably increased in almost all countries since that year, the Conference declares that it is highly desirable to see all Governments resume the serious study of this question."

This eloquent appeal was supported by the spokesmen of the United States, France and Spain; and the session of the Conference was closed by a brief address from the President. In 1899, declared M. Nelidoff, the discussions had been so lively that they threatened to wreck the Conference. The Russian Government had therefore not put it on the programme, since it was no topic for fruitful discussion, and decided not to take part in debating it. It would be best to reaffirm the *vœu* of 1899. The resolution was put to the meeting, and the President declared that the unanimity of the applause rendered a vote unnecessary.

While the British Government had thus to watch the frustration of their hopes, in another field they were themselves the obstacle to a change eagerly desired in many parts of the world and not without its champions in this country. One of the grounds on which large Navies, and above all a large German Navy, were demanded was the necessity of defending commerce in time of war; from which it seemed logically to follow that, if this danger were removed, one of the excuses for naval armaments would disappear. The case for abolition was cogently stated by the Lord Chancellor (Lord Loreburn); but the Admiralty declined to dispense with a powerful weapon in their armoury, and the Foreign Secretary explained to Sir Edward Fry, that the surrender could only be contemplated in return for concessions of equal value.

It is probable that a proposal will be brought forward to sanction the principle of the immunity of enemies' merchantships and private property

---

[1] "That the limitation of military charges which weigh on the world is highly desirable for increasing the material and moral well-being of humanity."

from capture at sea in time of war. If carried to its logical conclusion, the principle must entail the abolition of the right of commercial blockade. During recent years the proportion between the British Army and the great Continental Armies has come to be such that the British Army, if operating alone, could not be regarded as a means of offence against the mainland of a Great Continental Power. For her ability to bring pressure to bear upon her enemies in war Great Britain has therefore to rely on the Navy alone. The Government cannot agree to any resolution which would diminish the effective means which the navy has of bringing pressure to bear upon an enemy. You should, however, raise no objection to the discussion, nor need you necessarily take the initiative in opposing a resolution. If, at some future date, the great Continental Armies were to be diminished, and if such a change could be brought about by immunity from capture and was dependent upon it, the Government might feel that the risks they would run would be outweighed by the general gain and relief. But, at present, they cannot accept a resolution which might so limit the prospective liability of war as to remove some of the considerations which now restrain public opinion from contemplating it and might, after the outbreak of war, tend to prolong it.

When the United States proposed the abolition of the capture of private property, except when running a blockade, Germany and other Powers supported the proposal with reserves; but though it was carried in the Committee[1], the project failed, owing to the opposition of Great Britain and other leading Sea Powers.

The Conventions incorporated in the Final Act represented but a slender harvest for the labours of four months[2]. The machinery established in 1899 for the pacific regulation of disputes was amended. The Drago doctrine that force should not be employed for the recovery of debts was adopted; but it was not to apply, if the debtor State refused Arbitration or repudiated an Arbitral decision. A formal Declaration of War was to precede hostilities. Neutral territory was declared inviolable, and the rights of neutrals defined. Belligerent merchantmen at sea or in enemy ports when hostilities broke out were to be immune from capture. The British proposal to forbid the conversion at sea of merchantmen into warships was whittled down to a definition designed to exclude privateering. In like manner, the British proposal to forbid floating mines, thus limiting them to the territorial waters of the belligerent and to the defence of fortified places, was opposed by Russia, Germany and Austria; but Germany proposed to forbid floating mines altogether for four years. The Convention finally forbade unanchored automatic control mines which do

[1] Committee Four, on Juridical Questions of Naval War.
[2] Final Act, 1908, Cd. 1175.

not become innocuous after one hour, and anchored mines which do not become innocuous on breaking loose. The British Delegation, while accepting the instalment, stated that "an act will not be regarded as lawful merely because the Convention permits it." Naval bombardment of places undefended or defended only by mines was forbidden; but military works might be destroyed after notice. The Geneva Convention was extended to naval war. Fishing-boats, scientific and mission vessels, and mails (except to or from a blockaded port) were excluded from capture.

Among the reforms in the laws of naval war approved at the Hague, however, none compared in importance with the creation of a Prize-Court. Germany desired a special tribunal to be created after the outbreak of hostilities, consisting of an admiral and a civilian representing each belligerent, with a coopted member, which would hear appeals from belligerent Prize-Courts. Great Britain, on the other hand, argued for a permanent Court, to which every Signatory whose mercantile shipping exceeded 800,000 tons should appoint a jurist, but to which only neutrals might appeal. A compromise was reached, allowing appeals from neutrals or private persons and, in certain cases, from belligerents. The Court was to sit at the Hague, and to consist of fifteen judges, eight permanently representing the Great Powers of Europe, the rest supplied by the Minor States in rotation. This Convention was not to be ratified till June, 1909, a year later than the rest; for an international Court required an international code. Early in 1908, Great Britain issued invitations to a Conference in London for discussing the unsettled points of maritime law on which the Court would have to adjudicate.

"The results are less than might have been looked for," reported Sir Edward Fry to the Foreign Secretary at the close of the Conference, "but perhaps as great as could reasonably be expected." The bitter disappointment of idealists was freely expressed when Parliament met in January, 1908. Mr Asquith spoke of the Prize-Court as a very solid and fruitful achievement; but Mr Balfour complained that to create a Court before determining the law it should administer was to put the cart before the horse. To no one was the slender harvest a source of keener regret than to Sir H. Campbell-Bannerman. Though the President had laid the foundation stone of Carnegie's Palace of Peace, few members of the Second Conference left the Hague without heightened forebodings for the security of a lightly-poised civilisation.

VI. The Entente with Russia, 1905-1907

During the long-drawn discussions at Algeciras the Anglo-French Entente, to adopt the expressive phrase of M. Tardieu, passed from the static to the dynamic stage; but the Conference also witnessed the beginning of a wider association. While Great Britain and Russia scowled at one another across Europe and Asia, the new friendship might be strained at any moment; and it was to the termination of the ancient feud that the statesmen of both countries now directed their attention.

On his way home from Portsmouth (U.S.) in 1905, Count de Witte broke his journey in Paris, whither the First Secretary of the Russian Embassy in London brought an invitation from King Edward to pay him a visit[1].

I could not accept it without my monarch's express permission, which I failed to obtain. At the same time, our Ambassador in Paris submitted to me a project of an agreement with Great Britain, substantially identical with the one later concluded. I asked Poklevski-Koziell to inform the King that, should I assume power, I would use all my influence to establish friendly relations with Great Britain. I added, however, that I was decidedly opposed to the idea of concluding the Treaty sketched to me by Izvolsky, because it was best for us not to tie ourselves down.

On reaching home, he discovered that in his absence his master had actually tied Russia down; and he promptly proceeded to cut the knot. Soon after the repudiation of the Pact of Björko the Tsar began to discuss the questions at issue with Sir Charles Hardinge, the British Ambassador. Sir Edward Grey entered warmly into the plan of a *rapprochement*; and the Conference of Algeciras provided a welcome opportunity for cooperation and common counsel. Our Delegate, Sir Arthur Nicolson, was already converted, and his conversations with M. Cassini, the Russian Delegate, were assisted by Sir Donald Mackenzie Wallace, Foreign Editor of *The Times*, a leading British authority on Russia and a *persona grata* at the Russian Court.

British opinion had sympathised with the reform movement of 1905; and the opening of the Duma in May, 1906, was anticipated with disinterested satisfaction. The governing classes in Russia, however, could hold the Duma at bay so long as they could obtain money from abroad, and a large loan was needed to tide the country over the financial crisis of the Japanese War. When Count de Witte became Prime-Minister on October 20th, 1905, he at once began negotiations

[1] Witte, *Memoirs*, pp. 432-3.

for an international loan, and the contract was signed in Paris on April 3rd, 1906[1]. British finance participated for the first time since the Crimean War in such an operation, and the warnings uttered not only in London but in Paris and Petrograd rendered its participation all the more significant. "Opposition organs," wrote the Petrograd Correspondent of *The Times* on April 9th, "continue their campaign against a foreign loan before the Duma meets. They fear that the Government, having secured a large sum, will try to terrorise the Duma." Their apprehensions were only too wellfounded. The Duma opened on May 9th, only to be dissolved on July 22nd. The news reached London on the eve of the meeting of the Inter-Parliamentary Union; and Campbell-Bannerman added to his inaugural address a resonant warning to the Russian Government and a message of hope to the Russian people. "*La Douma est morte. Vive la Douma!*"

The discussions between the two Governments proceeded without regard to the internal politics of Russia. The Secretary of State for India was as anxious for a settlement as Sir Edward Grey, and rendered effective help.

"It would have been unreasonable," writes Lord Morley, "to expect the Government of India to approach the proposal of a change of policy at once with a friendly mind. Russia had for most of a century been the disturber of peace in Central Asia. There was, therefore, nothing to surprise us in the frowns of incredulity, suspicion and dislike with which the idea of an Anglo-Russian Agreement, dealing with Afghanistan, Persia and Tibet, was greeted at Simla. The duty of the India Office, and it did not prove too easy, was to moderate these apprehensions, while conveying the arguments to the Foreign Office."

"Suppose you were coming to some sort of understanding with Russia," he wrote to Lord Minto, "and suppose we hold the upper hand in the negotiation, what would be the terms that you would exact from Russia as essential to the bargain? I mean, what, from military, strategic and political points of view, are the things that she is to undertake to do or not to do?"

The Viceroy replied that if we were to conclude an *entente*, we should bargain elsewhere than in Central Asia; to which the Secretary of State rejoined that an *entente* omitting Central Asia would be a sorry trophy[2]. The views of the Viceroy and the Commander-in-Chief were maturely considered in Whitehall; while Sir Arthur Nicolson, who was sent to Petrograd in the early summer, quickly won the confidence of his hosts. In May, 1907, *The Times* hinted that an agreement was on the point of being signed.

[1] Witte, *Memoirs*, ch. 11.   [2] *Recollections*, II. 177–8.

"It does not exist," replied the Foreign Secretary on May 24th, "but I must add that there is a growing tendency in both countries to occupy themselves in a friendly manner with questions of common interest as they arise. This tendency has recently led the two Governments to cooperate on more than one occasion. It is a tendency which we shall be happy to encourage, and which, if it continues, will naturally involve the progressive settlement of questions and the strengthening of friendly relations between them."

On August 31st, 1907, Sir Arthur Nicolson and M. Izvolsky signed a Convention at Petrograd[1]. While the Anglo-French Treaty of 1904 included the world in its embrace, the Anglo-Russian Treaty was confined to Persia, Afghanistan and Tibet, for it was in the Middle East alone that friction remained. Lord Salisbury's famous declaration that in the Near East we had put our money on the wrong horse had terminated the tension in Europe; while the Anglo-Japanese Alliance and the defeat of Russia by Japan removed all apprehensions regarding the Far East. Thus the Pact of 1907, though more limited in scope than that of 1904, achieved a similar result by cleaning off the slate the causes of antagonism between the two historic rivals.

The first of the three Agreements concerned Persia:

The Governments of Great Britain and Russia, having mutually engaged to respect the integrity and independence of Persia, and sincerely desiring the preservation of order throughout that country and its peaceful development, as well as the permanent establishment of equal advantages for the trade and industry of all other nations; considering that each of them has, for geographical and economic reasons, a special interest in the maintenance of peace and order in certain provinces of Persia adjoining, or in the neighbourhood of, the Russian frontier on the one hand, and the frontiers of Afghanistan and Baluchistan on the other hand; and being desirous of avoiding all cause of conflict between their respective interests in the above-mentioned provinces; have agreed on the following terms:

I. Great Britain engages not to seek any concessions of a political or commercial nature beyond a line from Kasr-i-Shirin, passing through Bagdad and including Ispahan and Yezd, and ending at a point on the Persian frontier at the intersection of the Russian and Afghan frontiers, and not to oppose demands for similar concessions in this region supported by the Russian Government.

II. Russia engages not to seek concessions beyond a line from the Afghan frontier, through and including Gazik, Birjand, Kerman and ending at Bunder Abbas, and not to oppose demands for concessions in this region supported by the British Government.

---

[1] See the White Paper, *The Anglo-Russian Convention*.

III. Russia and Great Britain engage not to oppose, without previous arrangement, any concessions to British or Russian subjects in the regions between the lines mentioned in Articles I and II. All concessions existing at present in the regions indicated in Articles I and II are maintained.

A letter from Sir Edward Grey to Sir A. Nicolson, dated August 29th, explained why the Persian Gulf formed no part of the Convention:

The arrangement respecting Persia is limited to the regions of that country touching the respective frontiers of Great Britain and Russia in Asia, and the Persian Gulf is not part of those regions, and is only partly in Persian territory. It has not therefore been considered appropriate to introduce into the Convention a positive declaration respecting special interests possessed by Great Britain in the Gulf, the result of British action in those waters for more than a hundred years. His Majesty's Government have reason to believe that this question will not give rise to difficulties between the two Governments, should developments arise which make further discussion affecting British interests in the Gulf necessary. For the Russian Government have, in the course of the negotiations leading up to the conclusion of this arrangement, explicitly stated that they do not deny the special interests of Great Britain in the Persian Gulf—a statement of which His Majesty's Government have formally taken note. In order to make it quite clear that the present arrangement is not intended to affect the position in the Gulf, and does not imply any change of policy respecting it on the part of Great Britain, His Majesty's Government think it desirable to draw attention to previous declarations of British policy, and to reaffirm generally previous statements as to British interests in the Persian Gulf and the importance of maintaining them. His Majesty's Government will continue to direct all their efforts to the preservation of the *status quo* in the Gulf and the maintenance of British trade; in doing so, they have no desire to exclude the legitimate trade of any other Power.

The second agreement concerned Afghanistan:

The High Contracting Parties, in order to ensure perfect security on their respective frontiers in Central Asia and to maintain in these regions a solid and lasting peace, have concluded the following Convention:

I. The British Government declare that they have no intention of changing the political status of Afghanistan. They further engage to exercise their influence only in a pacific sense, and they will not themselves take, nor encourage Afghanistan to take, any measures threatening Russia. The Russian Government, on their part, declare that they recognise Afghanistan as outside the sphere of Russian influence, and they engage that all their political relations with Afghanistan shall be conducted through the intermediary of the British Government. They further engage not to send any Agents into the country.

II. The British Government having declared in the Treaty signed at Kabul on March 21st, 1905, that they recognise the agreement and the engagements concluded with the late Amir Abdurrahman, and that they have no intention of interfering in the internal government of Afghan territory, Great Britain engages neither to annex nor to occupy in contravention of that Treaty any portion of Afghanistan or to interfere in the internal administration of the country, provided that the Amir fulfils his engagements under the above-mentioned Treaty.

III. The Russian and Afghan authorities, specially designated for the purpose or in the frontier provinces, may establish direct relations with each other for the settlement of local questions of a non-political character.

IV. The British and Russian Governments affirm their adherence to the principle of equality of commercial opportunity in Afghanistan, and they agree that any facilities which may have been, or shall be hereafter, obtained for British and British-Indian trade and traders, shall be equally enjoyed by Russian trade and traders. Should the progress of trade necessitate Commercial Agents, the two Governments will agree as to what measures shall be taken, due regard, of course, being had to the Amir's sovereign rights.

V. The present arrangements will only come into force when the British Government shall have notified to the Russian Government the consent of the Amir to the terms stipulated above.

The third agreement related to Tibet.

The Governments of Great Britain and Russia, recognising the suzerain rights of China in Tibet, and considering the fact that Great Britain, by reason of her geographical frontier, has a special interest in the maintenance of the *status quo* in the external relations of Tibet, have made the following arrangement:

I. The two High Contracting Parties engage to respect the territorial integrity of Tibet and to abstain from all interference in its internal administration.

II. In conformity with the admitted principle of the suzerainty of China over Tibet, Great Britain and Russia engage not to enter into negotiations with Tibet except through the intermediary of the Chinese Government. This engagement does not exclude the direct relations between British Commercial Agents and the Tibetan authorities provided for in the Conventions of 1904 and 1906. It is clearly understood that Buddhists, subjects of Great Britain or of Russia, may enter into direct relations on strictly religious matters with the Dalai Lama and other representatives of Buddhism in Tibet. The Governments of Great Britain and Russia engage not to allow these relations to infringe the stipulations of the present arrangement.

III. The British and Russian Governments respectively engage not to send Representatives to Lhasa.

IV. The High Contracting Parties engage neither to seek nor to obtain any concessions for railways, roads and telegraphs, and mines or other rights in Tibet.

V. The two Governments agree that no part of the revenues of Tibet shall be pledged or assigned to Great Britain or Russia or to any of their subjects.

In an Annex Great Britain reaffirmed the Declaration appended to the ratification of the Convention of September 7th, 1904, to the effect that the occupation of the Chumbi valley should cease after the payment of three annual instalments of indemnity, provided that the trade-marts had been effectively opened for three years, and that in the meantime the Tibetan authorities had faithfully complied with the terms of the Convention. If the occupation had, for any reason, not been terminated at the time anticipated in the above Declaration, the British and Russian Governments would enter on a friendly exchange of views. At the suggestion of the British Government, identic Notes were exchanged, by which the Governments undertook to forbid the entry of any scientific mission into Tibet for three years except by mutual consent, and to invite China to accept a similar obligation. On September 10th, the Viceroy wrote to inform the Ameer of the Convention; and on September 29th Habibulla replied that he was away, but would consider the matter on his return.

In Russia the Treaty was received with mixed feelings. To Witte it appeared a triumph of British diplomacy, making it impossible for Russia to annex Persia. The British Parliament had risen before the signature of the Treaty, and the expert analysis had to be deferred till the new session. The attack was opened on February 6th, 1908, by Lord Curzon, who found little to praise in what he described as the most important Treaty concluded in the last half-century by a British Government. The conception was right, but its execution was faulty. The Persian Clauses amounted to surrender. The Russian sphere included Ispahan, where there was scarcely any Russian trade, and Yezd, where there were no Russian interests. The Preamble declared that each Power possessed a special interest in peace and order in the territories adjoining or in the neighbourhood of their frontiers; but these cities were hundreds of miles away from Russia. Eleven of the twelve cities of 30,000 inhabitants, and seven of the eleven trade routes by which commerce entered the country, were included in the Russian zone. Every argument for bringing Russia to Ispahan and Yezd applied to bringing our own sphere up to these points. In the south, where we were supreme, we were to have no more rights than Russia, Germany or the latest comer. The British sphere contained only Kerman and a single trade route. It was half the size of the Russian zone, empty, and mainly desert. Our interests in Persia were not merely strategical, but also political and commercial. Everything had been sacrificed to Seistan. Why did not Russia state her position concerning the Gulf in her own words, and why did we not include the Persian shore in the agreement? If we had made great and needless sacrifices in Persia, we had gained nothing in Afghanistan, and had not even secured the Ameer's consent to the Treaty. We pledged ourselves not to threaten or encourage Afghanistan to threaten Russia. Why did not Russia give a similar pledge? Russia had forts and troops on the northern frontier, and there was not a word about their withdrawal. Her recognition of Afghanistan as outside her sphere merely repeated an engagement eleven times renewed since 1869. The Tibetan Clauses were an absolute surrender, and the promise to consult Russia as to the evacuation of the Chumbi valley was almost a humiliation. The criticisms of Lord Lansdowne, another ex-Viceroy, were in refreshing contrast to this shrill denunciation. The neutral zone in Persia, he foretold, would be virtually Russian, since the Russian Government was willing to spend money freely, and we were not. Our position in the Gulf should have been explicitly recognised in an exchange of notes. The value of the Treaty would depend on Russia's conduct in such matters as the Buddhist pilgrims to Lhasa and the Russian Agents in Afghanistan; but he had confidence in her loyalty. While Lord Curzon spoke of her as of an enemy still to be watched, the Leader of the Opposition was clearly prepared to regard her as a friend.

The official reply by Lord Fitzmaurice, the experienced Under-Secretary for Foreign Affairs, was mainly devoted to Persia. Perhaps the British zone was more important from the strategical than from the commercial point of view; but in 1903 a Departmental Committee unanimously agreed that a triangle of territory, including Seistan, Kerman and Bunder Abbas, was essential to British security. This line, which would prevent Russia from building a railway to Bunder Abbas or eastward, had now been followed. Lord Curzon had complained that Russia had secured the Bagdad-Khanikin-Teheran route; but she would have broken off negotiations had we refused it. The Imperial Bank in Teheran had approved the Treaty. It was right to exclude the Gulf, which was partly Turkish, and as to which our policy had been defined in 1903. As regards Afghanistan, Russia had for the first time renounced in a treaty all claim to interfere; and, since we had no desire to intervene in Tibet, we had surrendered nothing in that quarter. The official defence was reinforced by the Earl (now Marquess) of Crewe, who justified the allotment of the lion's share of Persia to Russia by the logic of facts. She had constructed three fine roads from her frontier; she had built the Trans-Caspian railway and a line in Caucasia to Julfa on the border of Persia. The Cossack Brigade was officered by Russians, and her trade was extending in the south. As regards the Gulf, M. Izvolsky had handed to our Ambassador a statement that Russia did not deny our special interests. The weightiest defence of the Treaty, however, came from the veteran Lord Sanderson, who had entered the Foreign Office under Palmerston and had risen to the post of Permanent Under-Secretary. It would have been impossible, he argued, to secure more than had been won; and our trophies were of real value. Positive and permanent engagements had been given concerning Persia and Afghanistan in place of the rather fluid assurances which were all that Russia had previously been willing to offer. The zones of influence in Persia were not exclusive, for both Powers promised equal opportunities for trade to all nations, and all existing concessions were maintained. It was impossible to define British interests in the Gulf, real though they were, and he did not envy the draftsman who attempted to set them forth in the precise language required in a treaty. Dealing with the argument that the British frontier was nearer Tibet than the Russian, he reminded his hearers that Russia was quite near enough to exert influence; and it was therefore desirable to neutralise the country.

In the House of Commons, Earl Percy opened the attack with the complaint that the Treaty sacrificed British interests and, unlike the Pact of 1904, failed to remove all the causes of friction. While Lord Curzon's hostility to Russia reappeared in the speech of the ex-Under-Secretary, Mr Balfour followed the moderate line of Lord Lansdowne. The exclusion of Russian influence from Seistan was a real addition to the security of India; but the price was higher than necessary. The Agreement as a whole, though not a great diplomatic success, brought substantial advantages. To these criticisms, and to the more formidable attack in the Upper House, the Foreign Secretary made a spirited reply. Conditions in Persia, he argued, rendered some agreement necessary if we were to avoid friction. The governing consideration was not commercial, but strategical. It was the strategical position which made the Agreement essential; and the key to the strategical problem was Seistan. The traditional anxiety lest Russia should push into Seistan and reach the Indian Ocean was at an end. Lord Curzon argued that the Agreement threw away a hundred years of diplomacy and trade; but he seemed to have forgotten the facts. In the last twenty years Russian influence had extended to the south, and subsidised steamers sailed the Gulf. Consuls were stationed in Ispahan, Bushire, Bunder Abbas, and even in Seistan, into which she had pushed the telegraph line. The Customs were under a foreign control favourable to Russia. And behind all there was the shadow of the Russian forces. "In this Agreement we have given up nothing that was not lost before. All that we have sacrificed in Persia are some possibilities—exceedingly remote—of trading. In Tibet and Afghanistan we have sacrificed nothing at all." At the conclusion of his speech Sir Edward turned to answer Liberal and Labour critics who feared that the mere fact of a Treaty would strengthen the Russian autocracy and lead to new loans.

I have received many resolutions protesting against an agreement with Russia during the Constitutional crisis; but interference merely irritates. Our relations with Russia have improved greatly in the last two or three years; but without some agreement they must have grown worse. There comes a turning-point in the relations between nations, and if you pass it by you may not have it again.

In 1907, as in 1904, the Government and their expert advisers secured as much, and at as low a price, as the situation permitted; but the later balance-sheet, if regarded purely as a business transaction, was the least successful. The character of the bargain was determined when Lord Kitchener, the Commander-in-Chief in India, on being asked how much of Persia he could defend, replied that he could only be responsible for the south-east. For this reason, we confined our zone to Seistan, the larger part of the province of Kerman, and Persian Mekran, and insisted on a neutral zone against the wishes of Izvolsky. It was of the utmost importance that henceforth Russia could no longer threaten the approaches to India; but we tacitly surrendered our preferential position not only in the south, but in the Gulf, where it had been unchallenged for a century. No answer was given by the spokesmen for the Government to the criticism that Russia's recognition of our position in the Gulf was not explicitly stated in her own words and over her own signature.

In defending the Afghan Clauses, the Secretary of State for India anticipated the Ameer's assent, which was the necessary condition of the stipulations coming into force; but his confidence proved to be misplaced. The Ameer had visited India in the early months of 1907; and though political discussion was barred on the ground that the Dane Treaty rendered it needless, the journey improved the relations of Simla and Cabul. This new friendliness, however, was rudely interrupted by the news of the Treaty. He had handed over the control of external relations; but he had never surrendered the right to be consulted. The argument that consultation would have involved interminable delay and held up the whole Treaty, though sound enough in the meridian of Greenwich, appeared less convincing at Cabul. Though Great Britain and Russia regarded the Afghan Articles as operative, they had no binding force, and the Ameer remained a bad neighbour.

The Tibet Clauses were naturally judged with severity by the sponsors of the expedition to Lhasa, who argued that its results had been completely surrendered. This criticism left the Government indifferent, since the Liberal leaders had never approved the Tibetan policy of their predecessors; and on January 2nd, 1908, Mr Morley proposed the evacuation of the Chumbi valley immediately after the third instalment of the indemnity was paid, without waiting till the elaborate commercial negotiations, held over from 1904, had been concluded at Calcutta. Sir Edward Grey approved, but informed China that we should expect in return that our wishes in the negotiations would be met. The final cheque was paid on January 27th, 1908, and orders were at once despatched for the evacuation. On April 20th the trade regulations were signed by Great Britain, Tibet and China. When, in 1910, the Dalai Lama was deposed by China and fled to India, he was told that we could not interfere. China was at the same time informed that we could not allow any change in Tibet to affect the integrity of Nepal, Sikkim and Bhutan, with the last named of which we had recently signed a Treaty giving us control of foreign relations; and it was hinted that no Chinese troops should be stationed near the frontier. But with the payment of the indemnity and the evacuation of the Chumbi valley, Tibet passed out of the range of British politics. The Russian danger was at an end, and the strengthening of China's grip over her distant province was no concern of ours.

If the Anglo-Russian Convention was open to criticism as a business transaction, its political success was to prove beyond cavil. Lord Lansdowne had truly observed that a final judgment of the Treaty was impossible till we knew how Russia would conduct herself; and Russia was in a position which made the goodwill and confidence of the British Government a necessity. She had undergone a spectacular humiliation in the Far East, and she could only regain her position as a Great Power by adding British friendship to the French Alliance. Great Britain, for her part, having definitely sided with France, required the assurance of Russian support in face of the growing danger from Germany. Thus the removal of local friction was followed, as had been the case with France, by diplomatic cooperation in various fields. The Anglo-French Entente and the Dual Alliance broadened into the Triple Entente, which confronted the Triple Alliance on the European chess-board. Though we were allied to no Power except Portugal and Japan, and in theory retained perfect liberty of action, we had now half unwittingly, but not the less irrevocably, thrown in our lot with France and Russia. It was this novel system of attachments which was to govern our policy in the coming years, and to determine its course in Persia, the Balkans and Morocco.

VII. The Congo, 1891-1907[1]

In addition to revising our relations with the Great Powers, the British Government was called upon during the opening years of the century to grapple with two difficult and thankless tasks—the rescue of the Congo natives from the misrule of King Leopold II, and the mitigation of the tragic lot of the Christians in Macedonia. In both cases we were under Treaty responsibilities; but the old strain of idealism in British policy, inherited from Canning, Russell and Gladstone, was the driving force.

The Congo Free State had commenced its career with the sympathy of the world; but it changed its character when its vast wealth in rubber and ivory was revealed. In 1891, a Secret Decree reserved to the State the monopoly of rubber and ivory in "vacant lands," which were interpreted to include all except those on which the natives lived and "effectively cultivated." State agents were instructed to supervise their collection, and natives were commanded to sell their produce to the State. The Government hereby asserted its claim to almost the whole country, and transformed itself into a

---

[1] The Despatches and Consular Reports, on which this section is based, fill a long series of Blue-books. The most recent and impartial book on the subject is A. B. Keith, *The Belgian Congo and the Berlin Act* (1919).

monopolist trading concern. Extensive districts were leased to Companies, with exclusive right to the produce of the soil; but the State retained a financial interest in the success of the concessionaires. Another Secret Decree, of 1896, created the *Domaine de la Couronne*, a territory of over 100,000 square miles containing the richest rubber districts, which was regarded as the personal property of the King. In 1898 the example and advice of Leopold induced the French Government to parcel out the French Congo among concessionaire companies, in which Belgian capitalists held a large number of shares; and Paris was thus bound to Brussels by the ties of common interest.

It was impossible to keep secret the sinister transformation in the Free State, for British traders and missionaries were scattered over the country. In 1896, the Aborigines Protection Society called the attention of the Government to the plight of the natives, and its Secretary, Mr Fox Bourne, published an arresting volume on the natives of the Congo. A preface was contributed by Sir Charles Dilke, who in 1897 vainly suggested in Parliament that the Government should convene an international conference on the African natives. These champions of oppressed races were joined by Mr E. D. Morel, who was soon to become the soul of the struggle against the system of King Leopold[1]. He had entered the office of the Elder Dempster Line at Liverpool in 1890, and the business of the firm often took him to Brussels and Antwerp, where his suspicions were aroused. When his chief declined to take the matter up, he resigned his post and threw himself into the task of reform. The movement arose from humanitarian motives alone; but the infringement of the Treaty rights of British traders was no less flagrant than the exploitation of the natives. John Holt, the head of one of the firms injuriously affected, brought the matter before the Liverpool Chamber of Commerce. The example of Liverpool was followed, and nine Chambers sent a joint Memorial to the Government in 1901, protesting against trade monopolies in the Congo basin as contrary to the Berlin Act. A British Consul was appointed to reside permanently in the Free State; but his time was too much taken up with the complaints of British subjects to allow him to travel in the interior.

In 1903, the British Government was compelled by accumulating evidence and by the restiveness of public opinion to define its attitude. The year opened with the testimony of an experienced observer.

[1] See Cocks, *E. D. Morel*, pp. 59–169.

"I have visited the Belgian stations of Kiro and Lado," wrote Lord Cromer to Lord Lansdowne, "in the course of a voyage south of Khartum. In the Sudan there are numerous villages and the people run along the banks, making signs for the steamer to stop. They flock into the settlements to work. The contrast when once Congolese territory is entered is remarkable. For eighty miles from the frontier to Gondokoro, the left bank is Belgian, the right under the Sudan or Uganda Government. Whereas there were numerous huts and villages on the eastern bank and the islands, on the Belgian side not a sign of a village existed. I do not think any one of our party saw a single human being in Belgian territory except the Belgian officers and their families. The reason is obvious. The Belgians are disliked. The people fly from them, and no wonder, for I am informed that the soldiers are allowed full liberty to plunder and that payments are rarely made for supplies. The British officers wander practically alone over most part of the country. I understand that no Belgian officer can move outside the settlements without a strong guard. The Government, so far as I can judge, is conducted almost exclusively on commercial principles."

On May 20th, 1903, the first debate took place in the House of Commons, when Mr (now Sir) Herbert Samuel moved "That the Government of the Congo Free State having at its inception guaranteed to the Powers that its native subjects should be governed with humanity, and that no trading monopoly or privilege should be permitted within its dominions, this House requests the Government to confer with the other Powers, signatories of the Berlin Act, by virtue of which the Congo Free State exists, in order that measures may be adopted to abate the evils." The motion was accepted by the Prime-Minister and carried without a division. Before the Government proceeded to carry out the commands of the House, the British Minister at Brussels asked the Belgian Government to supply the documents relating to the Commission for the Protection of Natives instituted in 1896. The Commission had been ordered to suppress cannibalism, human sacrifices, the slave-trade and other abominations; but, as its members dwelt far apart and seldom met, its result was small.

After considering the documents furnished by the Belgian Government and all other material at his disposal, Lord Lansdowne drew up a weighty despatch, dated August 8th, 1903, which was forwarded to our diplomatic Representatives abroad.

The attention of H.M. Government has in recent years been repeatedly called to alleged cases of ill-treatment of natives and to the existence of trade monopolies, by philanthropic societies, commercial bodies, the Press and despatches from British Consuls.

In the debate it was alleged that the object of the Administration was not so much the care and government of the natives as the collection of revenue; that this object was pursued by a system of forced labour differing only in name from slavery; that the demands on each village were exacted with a strictness which constantly degenerated into great cruelty; and that the men composing the armed force of the State were in many cases recruited from the most warlike and savage tribes, who not unfrequently terrorised their own officers and maltreated the natives. It is reported that no efforts are made to fit the native by training for industrial pursuits; that the method of obtaining men for labour or military service is often but little different from that formerly employed to obtain slaves, and that constant compulsion has to be exercised to exact the collection of the amount of forest produce allotted to each village. H.M. Government do not know precisely to what extent these accusations may be true, but they have been so repeatedly made, and have received such wide credence, that it is no longer possible to ignore them; and the question has now arisen whether the Congo State can be considered to have fulfilled the special pledges given under the Berlin Act to watch over the preservation of the native tribes and to care for their moral and material advancement....In these circumstances H.M. Government are of opinion that it is incumbent on the parties to the Berlin Act to confer together and to consider whether the obligations undertaken by the Congo State in regard to the natives have been fulfilled; and, if not, whether the Signatory Powers are not bound to make such representations as may secure the due observance of the provisions. H.M. Government also wish to bring to the notice of the Powers the question which has arisen in regard to rights to trade in the basin of the Congo; and in particular whether the system of making grants of vast areas is permissible under the Act. This important question might perhaps constitute, in whole or part, the subject of a reference to the Tribunal at the Hague.

None of the Powers except Turkey responded to this impressive appeal; while the reply of the Congo Government denied that the Berlin Act had been broken and added that, as no evidence accompanied the charges, it did not propose to take action. Evidence, however, was soon forthcoming which even the Congo State was unable to ignore. The Foreign Secretary had instructed Consul Casement to visit the interior of the Congo during the summer, and his Report was dated December 11th, 1903. Returning to districts which he had known in 1887, he noticed a great reduction in the number of inhabitants, only part of which was due to sleeping-sickness. While fully recognising the energy of the Government in opening up the country by railways and steamers, he described the operation and results of commercial exploitation. It was a calm and unemotional record of things seen; and Lord Lansdowne, in forwarding it to Brussels in February, 1904, described it as a grave indictment, showing that in extensive regions the treaty pledges were not fulfilled. The Report was also circulated to all the Signatories of the Berlin Act, with a request for a reply to the despatch of August 8th, 1903. The publication of Casement's Report strengthened the hands of the British friends of the natives; and in April the Congo Reform Association was founded, with Mr E. D, Morel as Honorary Secretary. The Congo Government declared that the Consul had only made a hasty visit; but it consented to investigate the charges, and for that purpose asked for a copy of the complete report, including the names of the witnesses. Lord Lansdowne promised to furnish it in return for an undertaking that the witnesses should not suffer, and suggested that the enquiry would carry more weight if at any rate some of its members were unconnected with the Congo. The Congo Government finally announced that the Commission would consist of a Belgian official, a Boma judge and a Swiss jurist. It added that, though it was impossible to guarantee witnesses against hostility, any such manifestations would be punished.

Meanwhile, on June 9th, 1904, the House of Commons debated the matter a second time. Sir Charles Dilke opened the attack, urging that the Government should take stronger action than writing despatches. Sir John Gorst described the Congo problem as the one subject on which they were all agreed. Sir Edward Grey argued that the Congo State must become responsible to the Belgian Parliament, and expressed a wish for a conference to revise the Berlin Act. Lord Edmond Fitzmaurice pleaded for Consular Courts, and even hinted that Boma might be occupied. In replying for the Government, Earl Percy scouted as simply ridiculous the idea that we were actuated by any selfish motive, though we were quite aware that these philanthropic crusades did not contribute to our popularity abroad. He refused to adopt the suggestion of claiming exterritorial jurisdiction. We had a right to it, but it would not benefit the natives. We did not claim any special responsibility or right to intervention. Wishing the protest to be international, we had first appealed to the other Signatories of the Berlin Act, and we had also communicated the Casement Report to the United States.

Lord Lansdowne's efforts were now directed to making the Commission effective. The Commissioners, he observed to the Congo Government, were good names and would doubtless be impartial. He hoped that the enquiry would not be hurried, that missionaries would be allowed to give evidence, that the sessions would be held in public, and that a British Representative would be allowed to watch their proceedings. The Congo Government rejoined by publishing the Instructions to the Commission to "devote all their efforts to eliciting the whole truth"; but it declined the request for public sittings. Lord Lansdowne tartly retorted that the Congo Government must not be surprised if this decision destroyed in advance the moral authority of the Commission. The British Government handed over the names, places and dates suppressed in the published copy of the Casement Report; and the Commission reached the Congo State in October, ascending the river so far as Stanleyville and leaving the country in February, 1905. Lord Lansdowne's persistency was ultimately rewarded by the permission to hold public sittings and to send a British Consul to watch; but the Consul was only in time to attend the closing sittings. The Report was published in November, without the evidence for which the British Government pressed; but copies were obtained from the British and American missionaries of their own evidence and of that of the natives, which was published by the Congo Reform Association.

In enclosing a copy of the Report on November 7th, 1905, the British Minister at Brussels expressed his satisfaction at the result of the enquiry. Sir Edward Grey, who succeeded Lord Lansdowne at the Foreign Office in November, and fully shared his detestation of the Congo scandals, forwarded his observations on the Report in a long despatch, dated January 9th, 1906. The Commission, he declared, had confirmed the statements of Consul Casement on the condition of the natives; but he was surprised at the verdict that a tax on labour was beneficial to natives and essential to the development of the country. Compulsory service was admissible for a period when the interests of the citizens were directly concerned; but in the Congo the "tax" was for the commercial benefit of the State or the Company, not for that of the natives—"a form of servitude differing in essence but little from actual slavery." The Report urged the Companies to surrender all administrative power; but it should equally have condemned the association of trade and administration by the State. The despatch concluded with the hope that the Committee which had been appointed after the publication of the Report would introduce without delay that large measure of reform which it had shown to be absolutely indispensable for the welfare of the natives.

While the Committee on reform was sitting at Brussels, impatience and indignation were steadily increasing in Great Britain. A citizens' protest meeting was summoned by the Lord Mayor of Liverpool in January, 1906, and his example was followed by most of the great cities. To Sir Edward's enquiry when the Committee would report, the Secretary of the Congo State replied that it would meet for the last time on February 29th. When the question was repeated, he was informed that it would be needless to publish the recommendations, since the Congo Government was already drafting decrees to give effect to them. On June 3rd King Leopold signed twenty-four Decrees, presumably embodying the recommendations of the Reforms Commission in relation to land, taxation, justice, police and other branches of the administration, and accompanied them by a provocative Declaration, which aroused the anger of British reformers.

I sanction the measures you propose to me. Our duty is to neglect nothing which may develop the property of the Congo, ameliorate the lot of the natives, and put in good order a country which Belgium may one day possess. You must correct the false juridical notions whenever you meet them. All the responsibilities and all the expenses were left to me. The Congo was a personal work; and there is no more legitimate or respectable right than that of an author to the fruits of his labour. Not one of the Powers was called on to share in my efforts, and therefore not one of them has the right to intervene. They have recognised the independence of the Congo. The Berlin Act made provisions for the Conventional Basin of the Congo, applying equally to all the States; and they alone restrict sovereign rights. My rights over the Congo cannot be shared; they are the fruits of my labour and my expenditure. If I watch over them, it is from patriotism. The creation of the State has been pacific, legitimately accomplished with the assent of the natives, and without cooperation from foreign States.

The Decrees were regarded by the British reformers as wholly inadequate; and the British Consul and Vice-Consuls in the Congo were instructed to watch how they were carried out. Their Reports proved the persistence of the old evils. The people were overworked and underfed, taxation was crushing, and the rubber was being wantonly used up. It was obvious alike to British and to Belgian critics that there was no chance of improvement while the State remained the private property of the King, and reformers proceeded to urge that Belgium should enter on her inheritance without further delay. By a will drawn up in 1889, the King had bequeathed the State to his country; and in 1890, in return for a loan without interest, the State of Belgium obtained the option of annexation after ten years. It was not, however, till the Free State had become a crying scandal that the country began to claim its inheritance. In 1907, the Belgian Premier announced that negotiations with the Congo State with a view to annexation would begin. The first stage of the long campaign had been won by the British reformers, aided by a little band of Belgian comrades.

VIII. MACEDONIA, 1901–1907

The endeavours of the British Government to secure tolerable conditions in Macedonia were not less arduous and not less disinterested than their efforts in the Congo basin, and met with equally little success. For the misrule of the Turk not only produced chronic exasperation among its victims, but encouraged the neighbouring Christian States to peg out claims for the future by armed propaganda and organised massacre. Early in 1901, Lord Lansdowne, in reply to complaints from Athens, instructed the British Ministers at Sofia and Constantinople to call attention to the activities of Bulgarian bands[1]. The Bulgarian Government replied that it had no control over the Revolutionary Committee in Macedonia, while the Porte rejoined that it had in vain urged Bulgaria to control the movements of the bands. The year passed in fruitless protests and recriminations, Greece complaining of Bulgaria and Servia of Albanian outrages in the vilayet of Kossovo, while the Sultan looked idly on, and the British Foreign Secretary watched the boiling cauldron of Balkan politics with growing impatience and disgust.

In June, 1902, Turkey invited the Powers to press Bulgaria to dissolve the Macedonian Committee; but Russia and Austria, who had covenanted in 1897 to cooperate in the Balkans, informed Abdul Hamid that the first move lay with him. The Sultan, therefore, promised a Commission to propose reforms; but the two Powers warned him that, unless grievances were redressed, an insurrection in Macedonia and Albania in the spring was probable, and might involve European intervention. The Turkish plan, announced in December, promised reforms in administration, justice and education, to be carried out by an Inspector-General. Hilmi Pasha, who was appointed to the post, had a creditable record in the Yemen; but Sir Nicolas O'Conor, like other experienced observers on the Bosphorus, described the scheme as palpably insufficient. Lord Lansdowne's sole desire was

[1] The despatches and consular reports fill a long series of Blue-books. The best books on Macedonia are Brailsford, *Macedonia*; *The Balkan Question*, edited by L. Villari, and Sir C. Eliot, *Turkey in Europe*.

the reform of Macedonia, and he cared little who received the credit. On January 16th, 1903, he informed the Austrian Ambassador that he was watching Austro-Russian efforts with close attention. The British Government recognised that these two Powers were specially interested in the problem and in a specially advantageous position for dealing with it; but the Ambassador would understand the immense importance we attached to the question. Three days later, he outlined a far-reaching programme of reform in a despatch to Sir Nicolas O'Conor. "In our opinion the condition of the population in Macedonia has become almost intolerable. The appointment of one or more Christians on the Commission of Enquiry at Constantinople and on the Committee of Inspection in Macedonia would be valuable; but enquiry is not enough. We need the appointment of European Inspectors in the Departments of Justice and Finance, and European officers to reorganise the Gendarmerie and Police. Without arrangements for payment of salaries no reforms are possible."

On February 17th the Austrian and Russian Ambassadors handed to the Foreign Secretary an outline of the reform scheme drawn up by Counts Lamsdorff and Goluchowsky, and asked him to support it. The Inspector-General was to be irremovable for a term of years except by agreement with the Powers. Foreign experts were to reorganise the Police and Gendarmerie, the latter to consist of Christians and Mussulmans. Amnesty was to be granted to all accused or condemned for political offences in the three vilayets in connexion with recent disturbances. A Budget was to be drawn up for each vilayet, and local revenues, checked by the Ottoman Bank, were to be assigned in the first place to the needs of the local administration. Finally, the collection of tithe was no longer to be farmed out. The Foreign Secretary accepted the scheme in principle and undertook to recommend it to the Sultan; but he significantly reserved the right to recommend alterations after closer examination. Sir Nicolas O'Conor, accordingly, informed the Grand-Vizier that Great Britain supported the programme and hoped that it would be carried out without delay. Similar representations having been made by the other Powers, the Sultan accepted the scheme, and undertook to apply it not only to Macedonia but to the three other European vilayets of Turkey. To ensure that Turkey should have no pretext for inaction, Count Lamsdorff had visited Sofia and Belgrade and persuaded the several Governments to suppress revolutionary agitations.

Despite the Sultan's acceptance of the reform scheme and the readiness of Bulgaria to hold her hand, the Balkan sky remained dark with clouds. Sarafoff, the leader of the militant Macedonian Bulgars, announced his refusal to lay down his arms, adding that the Christians of Macedonia were prepared to sell their lives dearly and to make Europe shudder. These gloomy prognostications were promptly realised. On March 30th a bridge was blown up shortly before the arrival of the Orient Express, and the Russian Consul at Mitrovitza was shot by an Albanian, while Albanian tribesmen attacked Turkish troops in Old Serbia. The Russian and Austrian Ambassadors sharply ordered the Sultan to repress Albanian lawlessness and to carry out the reforms, and invited Great Britain to support their representations. At this moment, however, an attack on a bank at Salonica by Bulgarians enabled the Grand-Vizier to renew his complaints of Bulgarian bands and to threaten hostilities. Bulgaria, in turn, urged the Powers to warn Turkey not to concentrate troops on her frontier but to push on with the reforms. Lord Lansdowne, however, declined to take action, as Turkey denied aggressive intentions.

Turkey required her troops elsewhere; for in July the anticipated explosion occurred in Macedonia. "The insurrection is so formidable," reported Sir Nicolas O'Conor on August 10th, "that Turkey will need all her forces for its repression; and the insurgents' acts will probably provoke reprisals, which will compel European intervention, as is their aim. I suggest that Military Attachés should accompany the troops." The insurgents stood no chance against the regulars, and on August 31st Bulgaria appealed to the Powers. Austria and Russia proposed a warning from the Powers to Turkey and Bulgaria, that neither could count on support if they resisted the Austro-Russian programme; but Lord Lansdowne replied that the time had come for the stronger measures which he had from the first held himself free to propose. No Mussulman could now secure the confidence of the population as Inspector-General, and Military Attachés should accompany the troops. Turkey should be informed that the February programme was the minimum, that its execution was lamentably inadequate, and that far prompter and more effective measures were needed. The Powers should join in these representations; and, if Bulgaria was told that such action was being taken, this might calm her. Without waiting for joint action, Lord Lansdowne warned Sofia against aggressive action, and reminded the Porte of the inevitable effect of the "quite inexcusable" acts of the Turkish armies on European opinion.

The rebellion was over by the end of September; and the Foreign Secretary now forwarded suggestions to Vienna, where Counts Lamsdorff and Goluchowski were engaged on a fresh scheme of reform. A Christian Governor, unconnected with the Balkans or the Great Powers, or a Mussulman, assisted by European Assessors, selected by Austria and Russia, was to be appointed, and European officers, in adequate numbers, were to reorganise the Gendarmerie. Turkey was to withdraw her troops from the Bulgarian frontier, and Austria and Russia would guarantee that Bulgaria would not send troops or allow bands across the frontier. The Austrian and Russian Governments thanked the British Minister for his suggestions, adding that they were in accord with decisions reached at Mürzsteg before they were received. Lord Lansdowne replied that he hoped they would not be content with promises, and that the withdrawal of irregulars, the appointment of European officers to accompany the troops, and the organisation of relief need not wait. When the Turkish Ambassador urged him to forbid relief through private channels, since it would encourage agitators, he sharply replied that he was shocked beyond measure that the Turkish Government wished to deny such assistance to the thousands rendered homeless mainly by the conduct of Turkish troops, and expected the Turkish authorities to render every facility for supplying it.

On October 24th the Austrian and Russian Ambassadors brought the Mürzsteg programme to Downing Street.

1. Civil Agents of Austria and Russia were to accompany the Inspector-General, call his attention to the needs of Christians and the misdoings of the local authorities, watch the introduction of reforms and the pacification of the country, and report to their respective Governments.

2. A foreign General, with foreign officers, should be appointed to the gendarmerie, dividing up the country for supervision, instruction and organisation.

3. After the pacification of the country, Turkey should modify the boundaries of the administrative units, with a view to the more regular grouping of the nationalities.

4. The administrative and judicial institutions should be reorganised, and Christians be admitted to the public service.

5. Mixed Committees, with an equal number of Christians and Mohammedans, should enquire into the crimes committed during the recent troubles.

6. Turkey should pay for the repatriation of Christian refugees, and the rebuilding of houses, churches and schools destroyed by Turks. The

money should be distributed by Committees on which Christian notables would sit, under the supervision of Austrian and Russian Consuls.

7. A year's taxes should be remitted to Christians in the burnt villages.

8. Turkey should undertake to introduce the reforms of the February and the Mürzsteg programmes without delay.

9. The irregulars should be disbanded.

Five days later, the Austrian Ambassador called to ask for the Foreign Secretary's comments and impressions. Lord Lansdowne replied that it would be better to dispense with Hilmi Pasha, and that the reorganisation of the Administration and Judiciary should not be deferred till after pacification. He regretted the absence of any reference to finance, which lay at the root of all Macedonian reforms. Count Mensdorff explained that finance had been dealt with in the February programme; and the interview closed with a promise that the British Government would support the scheme, reserving the right to make further recommendations. At the same moment Lord Lansdowne instructed Sir N. O'Conor to tell the Porte, if it asked for the British view, that the new programme was an improvement on that of February, and to advise its acceptance in principle and the discussion of its details in a conciliatory spirit. The Porte turned a deaf ear to this appeal, declaring that the Assessors were needless, that the Gendarmerie required no foreign General, that the foreign officers must not interfere with the troops, that the February programme was being carried out, and that nothing more was necessary. But, after a peremptory warning from Austria and Russia, supported by Germany, the Mürzsteg programme was accepted by the Sultan in principle.

An Austrian and a Russian Assessor were appointed, and General di Giorgis was selected for the Gendarmerie, with headquarters at Salonica. Colonel Fairholme, Military Attaché at Vienna, was chosen as the British Staff Officer for the Gendarmerie, and Lord Lansdowne insisted that he should be paid by Great Britain and wear British uniform. An attempt to prevent the appointment of subordinate officers brought a sharp rebuke from Downing Street, and, after a warning from Petrograd and Vienna, Turkey consented to twenty-five officers, of whom Great Britain chose five. Macedonia was divided into zones, Great Britain undertaking Drama. Germany undertook no zone, but supplied a Director for the Gendarmerie school at Salonica. An agreement between Turkey and Bulgaria in April removed the fear of another rising. The Civil Agents reported the presentation of hundreds of petitions, and, by the summer, thirty-eight foreign officers were at work. The experienced British Consul, Mr R. W. Graves, reported from Salonica a temporary improvement, but added that it would not last unless finance and the judiciary were reformed. Lord Lansdowne, in acknowledging and approving the reports of the Civil Agents, expressed a hope that Russia and Austria would prepare and press a scheme for regular budgets, control over expenditure and adequate salaries for the Judiciary. At the end of the year, the Sultan, after repeated refusals, consented to accept twenty-three more officers for the Gendarmerie, on condition that no further increase should be demanded.

Lord Lansdowne, whose heart was in his work, never believed in the adequacy of the Austro-Russian programmes, and on January 11th, 1905, he outlined bolder measures in a despatch. Disquieting reports of murders and of armed bands crossing the frontiers pointed to an outbreak in the spring. The Turkish forces in or near Macedonia numbered 130,000 and were increasing, while Bulgaria was completing her military preparations. No part of the reform scheme had been carried out except the organisation of the Gendarmerie, in which the European officers were still too few. The first demand to be pressed was the immediate reduction of the troops in and near Macedonia to the number required for internal order, while Bulgaria was to make a corresponding reduction and prevent the organisation of bands. The second was for the appointment of a Commission of Delegates, nominated by the Powers and under the presidency of the Inspector-General, possessing administrative and executive powers. Financial reforms should include the commutation of the tithes, and provide for a fixed payment to the Porte by each vilayet, the balance remaining for local purposes. The Inspector-General, assisted by the Commission, might command the troops. This scheme should include some districts, especially the vilayet of Adrianople, to which the Mürzsteg programme did not apply, but which the Porte held to be included in the February programme of 1903.

Meanwhile, Russia and Austria presented a financial reform scheme according to which all Macedonian revenues should pass through the local branches of the Ottoman Bank, which should control its expenditure under the supervision of the Inspector-General and the Civil Agents. Moreover, if the money was earmarked for Macedonian reforms and compensation to the Christian victims of 1903, the two Powers were willing to agree to the raising of the customs from eight to ten per cent. Turkey's reply was a rival scheme of financial reform without foreign control; but Lord Lansdowne refused to accept either the one or the other. Before he consented to the raising of the customs, he must ask why the deficit could not be diminished by reducing the troops and must obtain a guarantee that the proceeds would go, not to the Ottoman Bank, which was unequal to the task, but to some competent authority which would apply them to the Macedonian reforms. Russia and Austria consented that the other Powers should send Delegates to cooperate with their Civil Agents in the supervision of finance. The appointment of Financial Delegates now became the official policy of the Powers, and, in August, the six Ambassadors urged Turkey to allow them to exercise their functions in cooperation with the Civil Agents. When she refused, the Powers announced that their Delegates would proceed to join the Civil Agents at Uskub. In view of Turkish recalcitrance, Lord Lansdowne suggested a naval demonstration and urged that it should be utilised for a purpose beyond that of merely securing assent to the Financial Commission. A Collective Note accordingly demanded the extension of the mandates of the Inspector-General, the Civil Agents and the Gendarmerie for two years longer, the recognition of the four Financial Delegates, and the acceptance of the Règlement of the Financial Commission, which was to consist of the Inspector-General, the Austrian and Russian Civil Agents, and a Delegate from each of the four other Powers, with headquarters at Salonica. After a demonstration at Mitylene by ships of all the Powers, except Germany, and the occupation of the custom-house and telegraph office, the Sultan yielded to necessity. At this very time, however, Lord Lansdowne left the Foreign Office, having placed Great Britain at the head of the European Concert and secured at least partial control of the finances of Macedonia, in which he had always discerned the true key to reform.

Sir Edward Grey, finding the Concert "exhausted by the effort it had made," was reluctantly compelled for a time to play a watching game. But, while the Macedonian question slumbered, a new cause of conflict arose through an attempt by the Turks to extend their authority on the Egyptian frontier[1]. Under the firman issued on the accession of the Khedive Abbas in 1892, the administration of the Sinai Peninsula was recognised as belonging to Egypt; for a telegram from Lord Cromer, defining the frontier by a line from El Arish to the head of the Gulf of Akaba was, without objection from the Porte,

[1] *Correspondence respecting the Turco-Egyptian Frontier*, 1906, Cd. 3006.

annexed to the firman and formed part of it. In 1905, owing to the lawlessness of the nomads, a British official was sent to report, and was subsequently appointed Commandant and Inspector of the Peninsula. He was provided with a small force and proceeded to construct a rest-house, barracks and a mosque at Nekhl. The task of the Mission was purely administrative; but the Turks, suspecting interference with the Hedjaz railway and intrigues with the Yemen rebels, occupied Tabah, a post within the line of 1892. On January 12th, 1906, the Sultan complained to Sir N. O'Conor that a British officer and Egyptian troops were camped close to Akaba and had announced their intention to erect guard-houses there and at other points within the Turkish territory, and asked for their withdrawal. A similar complaint was made to the Khedive, who denied the charge of trespass and suggested a discussion between a Turkish and an Egyptian Commissioner. The Porte haughtily replied that no question of frontier was involved, since Egypt formed part of Turkey. Turkish troops now occupied other posts within the line of 1892, and it was discovered that boundary-posts at the Mediterranean end of the peninsula had been overthrown. On March 31st, Mukhtar Pasha, the Turkish Commissioner in Egypt, formally claimed Tabah as within the Akaba district, and demanded that the boundary-line should be drawn from El Rafeh to Suez and from Suez to Akaba. The Khedive appealed to the firman of 1892, and again offered a Delimitation Commission. Lord Cromer, already rendered anxious by the Pan-Islamic ferment in Egypt, now perceived that he was confronted with a deliberate attempt to carry the Turkish frontier and strategic railways to the Canal. On May 2nd the British Ambassador informed the Grand-Vizier that the Turkish troops must evacuate Tabah within ten days, or the position would become grave. The French, Russian and German Ambassadors advised the Sultan to yield, and part of the Mediterranean fleet was sent to Phalerum. At the eleventh hour the Sultan yielded, and consented to a joint Commission on the frontier line. The posts were replaced, and the frontier line fixed in 1892 was confirmed; but the brief crisis left its mark in the increase of the British troops in Egypt.

Meanwhile, Turkey passively obstructed the working of the reform machinery in Macedonia, and the Financial Commission complained that the funds for the deficits on the Macedonian budget were not forthcoming. The brightest feature in the landscape was the *Gendarmerie*; but the condition of the hapless country went from bad to worse. Hideous lists were sent home every month by British Consuls, tabulating the savage outrages committed by the rival bands. The Government at Sofia seemed to Sir Edward to be doing its best, and the Greeks now won the unenviable distinction of being the chief offenders. On January 9th, 1907, Sir Edward informed the Austrian and Russian Ambassadors that something would have to be done in the year that was opening. The most urgent needs, he proceeded, were the enlargement of the powers of the Financial Commission, and the entrusting of the foreign officers in the Gendarmerie with some form of executive authority. At this moment, General Giorgis visited Constantinople, and discussed with Sir Nicolas O'Conor the lessons of his three years' work. Despite obstruction from civil and military authorities, he declared, the corps had been radically reformed. He did not desire to raise the question of executive powers for the officers, which Lord Lansdowne had vainly endeavoured to secure in 1904. Sir Nicolas therefore contented himself with urging the Sultan to accept the demands which the General proceeded to make.

The British Representative on the Financial Commission, H. P. (afterwards Sir H. P.) Harvey, reported hopefully on its work, and paid a tribute to Hilmi Pasha's courtesy and helpfulness; and in April, 1907, Sir Edward Grey, in view of the recurring deficits, agreed to the raising of the customs duties by three per cent., to take effect in July. At the same moment, he informed Benckendorff that, though the administration was improved, the Powers must in his opinion make a much more serious effort to stop the bands.

The Greek bands are at the root of the whole problem. The Greek Government must be sharply warned, as they are helped by Greek officers, recruited in Greek territory, and supported by money from outside. It is too bad that the efforts of the Powers to improve things in Macedonia, which would have been successful but for the bands, should be destroyed and defied in this way.

The attitude of the Foreign Secretary was explained to a deputation from the Balkan Committee on July 9th, which complained of what appeared to be a policy of drift. The reforms, he declared, had had considerable success, and the Financial Commission and the increased customs funds could not but do good. But the intervention of the Powers had set up the expectation of partition, and the bands were busy pegging out claims. The plan of a Governor of Macedonia appointed by the Powers, suggested by Lord Lansdowne in 1903 and approved by the deputation, could not be proposed by us alone, and would offend certain Powers. We were not the whole conscience of Europe. We should concentrate on the suppression of the bands and on judicial reform. We would do our utmost to maintain the Concert and render it effective; but Powers nearer the centre of disturbance possessed a special interest. The emphatic refusal to take the initiative chilled the deputation, and conveyed a misleading impression of the deep interest which Sir Edward Grey felt in the problem.

In consequence of British pressure, the Austrian and Russian Governments addressed a joint Note on September 30th to Greece, Bulgaria and Servia. The bands, it was suggested, were now fighting each other, partly owing to a misunderstanding of Article III of the Mürzsteg programme. The Committees apparently thought that, if they enlarged the area of their nationality, it would serve as the basis for delimitation. The Austrian and Russian Governments now stated that changes in the delimitation of national limits might be recommended to Turkey after the disappearance of the bands. Article III had been wrongly interpreted as conveying the intention to divide the country into national spheres. Only relatively unimportant changes, to facilitate the work of local authorities, were contemplated. Any delimitation would ignore the regrouping of nationalities brought about by the activities of the bands. This being so, the Greek, Bulgarian and Servian Governments must try to stop the bands receiving support. The Austro-Russian Note was supported by the Ministers of the other Powers; but not one of the Balkan States admitted Article III to be a cause of the trouble. Bulgaria rejoined that she had never wished to partition or annex Macedonia. Servia pointed out that Bulgarian bands began in the summer of 1903 before the Mürzsteg programme, and that the first Servian band was only formed in 1904 to defend Servian villages against Bulgarian attacks. The Sultan, moreover, was as stubborn as ever, and it was only after weeks of pressure and menace that he gave way and renewed all the mandates till 1914.

BOOK VI
BEFORE AND IN THE WORLD WAR, 1907–1919

SECRETARIES OF STATE FOR FOREIGN AFFAIRS

———   Sir Edward Grey, Bart. (afterwards Viscount Grey of Fallodon).
December,   1916: Right Hon. Arthur James (afterwards Earl of) Balfour.
July,   1918: Right Hon. Lord Robert Cecil (*Assistant Secretary of State till January 1919*).
October,   1919: Earl (afterwards Marquis) Curzon of Kedleston.

UNDER-SECRETARIES OF STATE FOR FOREIGN AFFAIRS

May,   1907: Louis (afterwards Right Hon. Sir Louis) Mallet (*Assistant*).
July,   — : Walter L. F. G. (afterwards Sir Walter) Langley (*Assistant*).
October,   1908: Thomas (afterwards Right Hon. Thomas) McKinnon Wood (*Parliamentary*).
November, 1910: Right Hon. Sir Arthur Nicolson, Bart. (afterwards Lord Carnock) (*Permanent*).
October,   1911: Francis (afterwards Right Hon. Francis) Dyke Acland (*Parliamentary*).
January,   1912: Sir Eyre Crowe (*Assistant*).
October,   1913: Sir Ralph S. Paget (afterwards Right Hon.) (*Assistant*).
February,   1915: Hon. Neil J. A. Primrose (*Parliamentary*).
May,   — : Right Hon. Lord Robert Cecil (*Parliamentary, afterwards Assistant Secretary of State*).
June,   1916: Lord Hardinge of Penshurst.
November,   — : Sir Ronald W. Graham (*Assistant*).
January,   1917: Commander the Right Hon. Frederick Leverton Harris (*Assistant*).
October,   — : Sir Arthur Steel-Maitland, Bart. (*Additional Parliamentary*).
July,   1918: Right Hon. Sir Laming Worthington Evans, Bart. (*Parliamentary*).
October,   — : Sir William G. Tyrrell (*Assistant*).
July,   1919: Colonel Sir Hamar Greenwood, Bart. (*Additional Parliamentary*).

CHAPTER VI

TRIPLE ALLIANCE AND TRIPLE *ENTENTE*, 1907–1914

I. The German Danger, 1907–1908

THE signature of the Anglo-Russian Convention was not immediately followed by a diplomatic partnership, and nobody interpreted it as precluding friendly relations with Germany. The invitation to the Kaiser to visit Windsor in the autumn of 1907, and his decision to spend a brief holiday in the mild air of the Solent, filled the friends of peace in both countries with satisfaction. The *Norddeutsche Allgemeine Zeitung* pronounced the visit a fitting complement to the meeting of the Sovereigns at Wilhelmshöhe in the summer; and *The Times* hailed the imperial guest as "a personality whose many characteristic qualities are universally admired, and nowhere more than here." At the Guildhall banquet, the Prime-Minister announced that "a most cordial welcome is assured to him"; and Sir John Fisher, in replying for the Navy, assured his countrymen that there was no ground for the nightmare of invasions, and that they might sleep quiet in their beds.

On November 11th the *Hohenzollern* steamed into Portsmouth harbour; and in reply to an address by the Mayor of Windsor the Emperor remarked, "It seems like coming home again; I am always glad to be here." His party included Freiherr von Schön, the Foreign Secretary, and von Einem, the War Minister. At the banquet on November 12th, he testified to his profound respect for his Grandmother, and recalled the happy memories of his childhood. "I am so glad to be here again," he wrote to his friend, Bishop Boyd Carpenter, "and am most touched and grateful for all the kindness shewn me by everybody[1]." The climax of the visit was the ceremony at the Guildhall.

"When I addressed Sir Joseph Savory from this place sixteen years ago, I said that my aim was above all the maintenance of peace. History, I venture to hope, will do me the justice that I have pursued this aim unswervingly ever since. The main prop and base for the peace of the world is the maintenance of good relations between our two countries, and I shall further strengthen them as far as lies in my power. Blood is thicker than water. The German nation's wishes coincide with mine."

[1] W. Boyd Carpenter, *Further Pages of My Life*, pp. 163–194.

"Sir Edward Grey, who sat next me," records Baron von Schön, the German Foreign Secretary, "was visibly moved, and we promised with a warm handshake to do our utmost in the sense of the Kaiser's speech."

On arriving at Windsor, Schön had declared to an interviewer that there was no intention to discuss concrete political questions. The Emperor, however, was temperamentally incapable of excluding high politics from his conversation. No project was nearer his heart than the Bagdad Railway; and, finding the British War Minister among the guests, he broached the subject of British cooperation.

"The first evening of my visit," relates Lord Haldane, "the Emperor took me aside and said he was sorry that there was a good deal of friction over the Bagdad Railway, and that he did not know what we wanted as a basis for cooperation[1]. I said that I could not answer for the Foreign Office, but that, speaking as War Minister, one thing I knew we wanted was a 'gate' to protect India from troops coming down the new railway. He asked me what I meant by a 'gate,' and I said that meant the control of the section which would come near to the Persian Gulf. 'I will give you the gate,' replied the Emperor. Next morning, about 7.30 o'clock, a helmeted guardsman knocked loudly at the door and came into my bedroom, and said that he had a message from the Emperor. It was that he did mean what he had said the night before. I at once got up and caught a train for London. There I saw the Foreign Secretary, who, after taking time to think things over, gave me a Memorandum he had drawn up. The substance of it was that the British Government would be very glad to discuss the Emperor's suggestion, but that it would be necessary, before making a settlement, to bring into the discussion France and Russia, whose interests also were involved. I was requested to sound the Emperor further[2].

After telling King Edward of what was happening, I had another conversation in Windsor Castle with the Emperor, who said that he feared that the bringing in of Russia, not to speak of France, would cause difficulty; but he asked me to come that night to his apartments, to a meeting to which he would summon the Ministers he had brought with him. He took the Memorandum which I had brought from London, a copy of which I had made for him in my own handwriting, so as to present it as the informal document it was intended to be. Just before dinner, Baron von Schön spoke to me, and told me that he had heard from the Emperor what had happened, and that the Emperor was wrong in thinking that the attempt to bring in Russia would lead to difficulty, because he, Baron von Schön, when he was Ambassador to Russia, had already discussed the

[1] *Before the War*, pp. 48–52.
[2] Sir Edward Grey informed the Russian Government of the conversations and received the thanks of Izvolsky. Siebert, *Diplomatische Aktenstücke zur Geschichte der Ententepolitik*, pp. 319–20.

general question with its Government, and had virtually come to an understanding. At the meeting that night we could therefore go on to negotiate. I attended the Emperor in his State rooms at the Castle at one o'clock in the morning, and sat smoking with him and his Ministers for over two hours. His Foreign Minister, and Count Metternich and the War Minister, von Einem, were present.... Count Metternich did not like what I suggested, that there should be a conference in Berlin on the subject between England, France, Russia and Germany. In the end, but not until after much keen argument, the idea was accepted; and the Emperor directed Schön to go next morning to London and make an official proposal to Sir Edward Grey. This was carried out, and the preliminary details were discussed between him and Sir Edward at the Foreign Office.

Some weeks afterwards difficulties were raised from Berlin. Germany said that she was ready to discuss with the British Government the question of the terminal portion of the railway; but she did not desire to bring the other two Powers into that discussion, because the conference would probably fail and accentuate the differences between her arld the other Powers. The matter thus came to an end. It was, I think, a great pity.... I came to the conclusion afterwards that it was probably owing to the views of Prince Bülow that the proposal had come to an untimely end. Whether he did not wish for an expanded entente; whether the feeling was strong in Germany that the Bagdad Railway had become a specially German concern and should not be shared; or what other reason he may have had, I do not know; but it was from Berlin, after the Emperor's return, that the negotiations were finally blocked."

The veto of Prince Bülow on a Four Power conference in Berlin ended the brief period during which reconciliation was in the air[1]. For a few weeks Anglo-German relations had breathed a cordiality which they had not known since the Kruger telegram, and which they were never to know again. Under the mellowing influence of a warm popular welcome, the Emperor's instinctive dislike for British ideas and institutions momentarily yielded to a revival of family associations and a desire to resume the political intimacy of the early years of his reign. If the British refusal of cooperation in 1903 was an error, the German refusal of British conditions in 1907 was a calamity.

The King's Speech at the opening of the Session of 1908 began with a warmly-phrased reference to the Kaiser's visit, and Schön's proposal for a pact guaranteeing the *status quo* in the North Sea was accepted; but the sky was quickly filled with driving clouds.

[1] Schön defends the veto on the ground that Germany would have been one against three; that the interests of France and Russia were smaller; and that Sir Edward perhaps desired a certain recognition of the new grouping of the Powers. *Memoirs*, pp. 62–3.

"It was in the last weeks of February," writes Colonel Repington[1], "that I learnt that the Kaiser had addressed a letter to Lord Tweedmouth on naval policy. This letter appeared to me an insidious attempt to influence, in German interests, a British First Lord, and at a most critical juncture, namely, just before the estimates were coming on in Parliament. ...It seemed to me a public duty to expose this proceeding in order to prevent its recurrence; and this seemed all the more necessary, considering the weakening of our Government at a moment when firmness was absolutely indispensable."

Accordingly *The Times* published a brief letter from its Military Correspondent on March 6th with the title "Under which King?" The Kaiser had addressed a letter to Lord Tweedmouth on British and German naval policy, and a reply had been despatched. Both letter and reply should be laid before Parliament without delay. The letter was accompanied by a shrill leader, suggesting that the Emperor had tried to cut down British shipbuilding, in order to steal a march on our naval supremacy.

"It was a purely private and personal communication," declared the Prime-Minister on March 6th, "conceived in an entirely friendly spirit. The answer was equally private and informal, and neither the letter nor the answer was communicated to the Cabinet. Before the letter arrived, the Cabinet had come to a formal decision with regard to the Navy estimates." A little further information was supplied on March 9th by Lord Tweedmouth. "The letter came by the ordinary post. It was private and personal, very friendly in its tone and quite informal. I shewed it to Sir Edward Grey, who agreed that it should be treated as a private and not an official one; and on February 20th I replied in a friendly and informal manner." Lord Lansdowne followed with a few sensible words. The letter appeared to be very much what a Sovereign and a British Minister would say in conversation without its being thought improper; and the Opposition would not press for publication. Such communications, however, were irregular, and should only be made in cases of real necessity. Lord Rosebery concluded the brief debate with a few sentences which were warmly appreciated in Berlin.

My only apprehension is that we may be making ourselves quite ridiculous by the fuss which has been made. We have seen a whole world of absolutely insane inferences drawn. There is a section of the Press in both countries which seeks to create bad blood. Those sections take up

---

[1] *Vestigia*, ch. 21. Schön, to whom the Kaiser showed it, saw no reason for vetoing the despatch of the letter. *Memoirs*, p. 101.

every trivial incident—this is a trivial incident—to excite morbid suspicions between the two nations which is gradually developing into a danger to European peace. There is no earthly reason that I know why our friendship with France should necessarily entail a hostile attitude to Germany.

Prince Bülow dealt with his own critics in a similar manner.

I cannot publish the letter because it is private. I wish I could. It could be signed by any of us, by any sincere friend of good relations. Every Sovereign has a right to address other statesmen. It is a gross libel to suggest that it is an attempt to influence the Minister in the interest of Germany, or a secret interference in the domestic affairs of Great Britain.

In view of the excitement worked up by the Press, the Cabinet would have been wise to ask the Kaiser's permission to reveal the correspondence. The letter, like many other of his pronouncements, was susceptible of two interpretations. To one class of mind it seems a Machiavellian attempt to overtake the British lead in capital ships by allaying suspicion of German designs. To another, it appears as an effort, tactless indeed, but made in good faith, to improve the relations between the two peoples[1].

The Navy Estimates for 1908–9, providing for only two Dreadnoughts, although in March the German programme was enlarged, testified to the conciliatory spirit of the British Cabinet. The promotion of Mr Asquith to the Premiership in 1908 brought Mr Lloyd George to the Exchequer, and Mr Churchill into the Cabinet; and for the next three years these two men led a crusade for social reform and a reduction of armaments. At a meeting under the auspices of the Peace Society at the Queen's Hall on July 28th, the Chancellor of the Exchequer stated the German case for armaments.

"Men have not got the imagination to project themselves into the position of the other party. Look at the position of Germany. Her Army is to her what our Navy is to us—her sole defence against invasion. She has not got a two-Power standard. She is between two Powers who, in combination, could pour in a vastly greater number of troops than she has.... I want our friends who think, because Germany is a little frightened, she really means mischief to us, to remember that she is frightened for a reason which would frighten us under the same circumstances. Why should there not be an Anglo-German Entente? We have done it with France, we have done it with Russia, we have done it with the United States."

A week or two later, on August 15th, Mr Churchill sounded a similar note.

---

[1] The letter was published in *The Morning Post*, October 30th, 1914, and is reprinted in Repington's *Vestigia*.

"There is no collision of primary interests between Great Britain and Germany in any quarter of the globe, no real cause of difference. They have nothing to fight about, no prize to fight for, and no place to fight in. We honour that strong, patient, industrious German people, who have been for so many centuries divided, a prey to European intrigue. We wish them well from the bottom of our hearts."

The aspirations, if not the confidence, of the Left wing were shared by the Right; and the Cabinet determined to utilise King Edward's visit to the Kaiser at Cronberg, on his way to Marienbad, for opening negotiations[1]. Sir Charles Hardinge explained the causes of British anxiety, and urged that a friendly discussion of armaments should take place between the Governments. The Kaiser renewed the assurance of his friendliness, but impulsively declared that no pressure from a foreign Government could be tolerated, and that he would rather go to war than submit to it. The personal aspects of the visit were pleasant enough. "Uncle Bertie was all sunshine at Cronberg and in very good humour," reported the Kaiser to the Tsar on August 18th. "He intends visiting Berlin officially with Aunt Alix next year."

King Edward proceeded from Cronberg to Ischl to congratulate Francis Joseph on his diamond jubilee. "It was not an official visit," writes the biographer of Aehrenthal; "but the King tried to give it that character. In the course of a walk with the Emperor, he brought up the topic of the German Fleet, explained the resentment it aroused in England, and asked his host to persuade Germany to limit her shipbuilding. Francis Joseph refused. The parting was friendly; but the conversation was a landmark[2]." The King had no other purpose than to diminish the tension which was beginning to threaten peace, and Sir Edward Grey could truthfully aver that we had carefully avoided anything likely to make mischief between Germany and Austria. But the Emperor remarked that his guest had gone away dissatisfied, and to suspicious eyes his action came to appear as another link in the chain of his machinations against the Central Powers.

The Chancellor of the Exchequer left home soon after the King to study the German system of Old Age Pensions and, incidentally, to discuss the problem of armaments. Bethmann-Hollweg, the

---

[1] Cook, *How Britain strove for Peace.* The Kaiser reported the interview in two telegrams to the Chancellor, printed by Hammann, *Bilder aus der letzten Kaiserzeit,* pp. 141–144.

[2] Molden, *Graf Aehrenthal,* p. 56.

Minister of the Interior, travelled to Berlin to do him honour, and Mr Lloyd George returned home impressed with the wealth, the energy and the friendliness of the German people. The German Chancellor professed himself equally eager to dissipate the cloud of mistrust. "That the present mutual suspicion has lost little of its strength is a deep grief to Prince Bülow," wrote Sidney Whitman in *The Standard*[1] after a visit to Norderney. "He regards it as a sort of popular madness. As to our fear of an attack by sea, he says the apprehension would be more excusable for Germany." A few days later, the Chancellor opened the fifteenth Inter-Parliamentary Conference, which was held in the *Reichstag* building, with a few words of welcome. "Taught by history, which for three hundred years has not spared her the hardest experiences, Germany must and will be strong enough to defend her independence. She does not and will not misuse her strength." At a garden-party at the Chancellor's palace Lord Weardale thanked the Prince for his interview with Sidney Whitman, and added that ninety-nine out of every hundred Englishmen desired the very best relations. The Chancellor replied in English, on behalf of the Kaiser and the German people, that their only aim was to have the very best relations, and expressing the hope that his visitors had convinced themselves of this good feeling.

While the relations of the two countries were being eagerly discussed by Ministers and the Press, the publication of an undated and anonymous interview with the Kaiser in *The Daily Telegraph*, on October 28th, let loose a hurricane[2]. Its dominant theme was his friendship for Great Britain, as evinced both openly and secretly during the Boer War, and steadily maintained, though neither shared by his own people nor recognised by the object of his affections. While *The Daily Telegraph* informed its readers that the interview was the work of a retired diplomatist, the *Norddeutsche Allgemeine Zeitung* issued a statement that the Emperor had received from an English gentleman the manuscript of an article collating a series of conversations at various times and with various personages, with a request to sanction its publication in the interests of good relations. The Emperor forwarded it to Bülow at Norderney, who sent it to

[1] September 14th, 1908.
[2] The Kaiser read the interview before it appeared and corrected one or two words so that his meaning should be made clearer. It is reprinted in the Appendix to D. J. Hill, *Impressions of the Kaiser*. The most authoritative accounts of the incident are given by Spickernagel, *Fürst Bülow*, ch. 5; Schön, *Memoirs*, pp. 102–8; Hammann, *Um den Kaiser*, ch. 6; and William II, *Memoirs*, ch. 4.

the Foreign Office at Berlin for revision. As the Foreign Office raised no objection, it was published. The interview, like the letter to Lord Tweedmouth, however well-intentioned, increased the *malaise* which it was intended to dispel. When the Kaiser confessed that his subjects as a whole were unfriendly to England, he was generally believed; but when he affirmed his own undeviating goodwill, he failed to carry conviction. Moreover, the rashness of his language deepened the impression already prevalent throughout Europe that his personality was an explosive element in world-politics.

While Cabinet Ministers expressed their confidence in the goodwill of Germany, a growing number of observers came to regard a collision as probable, if not inevitable. On July 20th, 1908, Lord Cromer warned the Government in the House of Lords that "their main duty was to make provision betimes for the European conflict which might not improbably be forced upon us before many years." Powerful French voices struck the same note. During his cure at Marienbad in the same year King Edward received a visit from Clemenceau, the French Premier, who spoke of another war as probable. If war broke out between Germany and England, the German armies would invade France by way of Belgium, and seek in France an indemnity for losses at sea. To destroy the German Fleet would not save Paris. A hundred thousand men in Belgium would not be of much use; but two hundred and fifty thousand or five hundred thousand would change the course of the struggle. Our Territorial Army was a plaything, and the position of France would be one of extreme danger until Great Britain had a National Army. "If France were smashed for want of timely help, England would have to incur vastly greater obligations than any now requisite, or would have to bend her neck to the victor."

On November 23rd, Lord Roberts delivered a weighty speech in the House of Lords, which succeeded in making compulsory service a living issue.

"Hitherto," he began, "I have failed to wake people up to my warnings against a danger that is all too obvious. If you, who ought to realise that our naval supremacy is being disputed, neglect to place this country in such a state of defence as would make even the most powerful nation hesitate to attack it, I cannot help feeling that a terrible awakening may be in store for us at no very distant period....The Navy is not enough. The Territorial Army is too small and too untrained to cope with highly trained troops....There lies in front of us one of the strangest spectacles ever witnessed. Within a few hours' steaming of our coasts, there is a people numbering over sixty millions, our most active rivals in commerce and the greatest military Power in the world, adding to an overwhelming military strength a naval force which she is resolutely and rapidly increasing; while we are taking no military precautions in response. Germany cannot justly be blamed for the situation; rather, she should be praised and her example followed, for her people, by their industry, their perseverance, their sound system of education, and the military training which every able-bodied man receives, have made her a great nation. Words cannot express the responsibility which lies on the members of the Legislature. We are trustees for the future of the Empire. It is my absolute belief that, without a military organisation more adequate to the certain perils of the future, our Empire will fall from us and our power will pass away."

Lord Crewe replied, for the Government, that Lord Roberts's scheme would cost twenty millions a year, and that, as the people believed the Fleet to offer practical immunity, it would dissipate belief in the necessity of a supreme Navy. It was true that we needed a considerable force, so that the enemy would require large numbers for the attempt; but we were not prepared to revolutionise our theory and practice not only of military but of naval defence. It was impossible to accept the motion[1], because it could not be dissociated from the speech, with its demand for a million men, and because it suggested that the Army, not the Navy, was the real defence against invasion. Lord Lansdowne, while admitting Lord Roberts's contention that circumstances had changed since 1905 to our disadvantage, also declined to accept his remedy; but the motion was carried by 72 to 32. While the official leaders of both parties thus clung to the voluntary system, the debate left an abiding impression; and the principle of compulsory service was accepted by an ever-growing number of Conservatives within and without the Legislature[2].

---

[1] "That the defence of these islands necessitates the immediate provision of an army so strong in numbers and so efficient in quality that the most formidable nation would hesitate to attempt a landing on these shores."

[2] While Lord Roberts was proclaiming his fears and propounding his remedies, Sir John Fisher secretly proposed to avert the menace by very different means. As far back as 1905, on his appointment to office, the First Sea Lord in a written Memorandum predicted an Anglo-German war in August, 1914; and on March 14th, 1908, he wrote to King Edward, "that we have eventually to fight Germany is just as sure as anything can be." "Early in 1908," he writes, "I had a long secret conversation with the King, in which I urged that we should 'Copenhagen' the German fleet at Kiel à la Nelson, and I lamented that we possessed neither a Pitt nor a Bismarck to give the order." The criminal design of seizing the Fleet of a foreign Power in time of peace, without even Canning's excuse in 1807, was never communicated to Ministers; for the reception of the plan by those to whom it was confided did not encourage its author to enlarge the circle of initiates. *Memoirs*, pp. 18–19, 64, 183.

The tension was recognised and deplored by no one more than by the German Ambassador in London, Count Wolff-Metternich, who complained in 1908 that the provocative methods by which the German Fleet was boomed were affecting British nerves. It was now clear that there was only one path back to confidence and cordiality; and this the Kaiser and Bülow stubbornly refused to take. "I am asked why we oppose limitations," declared the Chancellor in the *Reichstag* on December 10th, 1908.

"The technical difficulties are very great.... Besides we are in the middle of Europe, in the most strategically unfavourable position on the world map.... Our position would be bad indeed, and peace would be imperilled if we reduced our armaments below the level demanded by our position in Europe. Finally, the growth of our fleet is determined by a law, the sole object of which is to assure the defence of our coasts and our commerce."

When he added that no definite proposals for the limitation of armaments had reached the German Government, his statement was only formally true; and the British Government replied that no definite proposals had been made at the Hague in 1907 or at Cronberg in 1908, because Germany had refused to engage in discussions. Meanwhile, the construction of a mighty Fleet was pressed steadily forward, to the noisy accompaniment of the Pan-German orchestra.

II. MACEDONIAN REFORM, 1907–1908

While the German challenge to our naval security constituted the main anxiety of the Government, the problem of Macedonian reforms continued to demand unremitting attention, and at the end of 1907 Sir Edward Grey boldly resumed the initiative[1].

"The situation has become so unsatisfactory," he declared in a Memorandum of December 18th, "as to claim the immediate attention of the Powers.... The gradual extermination of the Christian inhabitants is being tolerated in Macedonia, where the Ottoman authorities have displayed an utter incapacity to maintain public tranquillity. The experience of the last four years would tend to shew that, by its very constitution, the gendarmerie is not capable of remedying the chief evil from which Macedonia is suffering —the absence of public security. It is quite unfitted by numbers and organisation to cope with the bands, and H.M. Government are profoundly convinced that the time has now arrived when General de Giorgis and the foreign Staff Officers should be entrusted with a full measure of executive control, and when the force under his command should be properly qualified for effective action by a substantial increase in numbers and an adequate equipment. In these circumstances they would strongly urge

[1] See *Turkey*, No. 1 and *Turkey*, No. 2, 1908.

that the Powers should represent to the Sublime Porte that the heavy charges on the Macedonian Budget for the maintenance of Turkish troops are out of all proportion to the services which they render in the maintenance of public security, and that the only effective means of suppressing the bands lies in the increase upon a large scale of the gendarmerie, the formation of mobile columns of gendarmes, and in granting executive power to the officers in command. The savings effected by the reduction of the troops would provide funds for their increase and adequate equipment."

This vigorous call fell on deaf ears; for none of the other Powers cared for the sufferings of the Macedonian peasant. Well might Lord Newton exclaim that Great Britain was the only sentimental country in the world!

While pleas for inaction were trickling in to Downing Street, a deadly blow was struck at the waning prestige of the Concert. On January 27th, 1908, Baron Aehrenthal, the masterful diplomat who succeeded the pliant Goluchowski at the Ballplatz in 1906, announced that he had obtained from the Sultan permission to survey the route for a railway through the *sanjak* of Novibazar, connecting the Bosnian system with the Turkish terminus at Mitrovitza[1]. Article XXV of the Treaty of Berlin empowered Austria to construct military and commercial roads through the *sanjak*; and, though railways were not specifically mentioned, nobody argued that the Austrian Minister was exceeding his Treaty rights. On March 24th, Prince Bülow spoke with sympathy of the Austrian project, "though we neither gave nor were asked our advice." "I was informed of the intention," echoed Tittoni in the Italian Chamber, "but I could not dispute the right. There is no danger to the Concert or to peace if all the Powers regard railways as an item in the reforms of Macedonia." Very different was the reception of the news in Russia. Izvolsky complained that it was a gross violation of the spirit of the Mürzsteg Agreement; and the cooperation in the Balkans inaugurated in 1897 came suddenly to an end. The wound was far too deep to be healed by Aehrenthal's subsequent acceptance of the project of a railway from the Danube at the junction of Servia and Roumania to San Giovanni di Medua in northern Albania.

Sir Edward Grey's references to Austria's action were polite, but unambiguous.

"Our attitude towards these railway projects," he declared on February 28th, "is one of benevolent neutrality. But this latest project has undoubtedly

[1] See Molden, *Graf Aehrenthal*, pp. 32–8.

been the occasion of very marked comment. That this special moment should be chosen for promoting a large railway scheme which requires the Sultan's consent was sure to excite apprehension lest individual Powers should be turning their attention to objects specially adapted to their interests. Any impression of that kind must produce a most unfortunate effect on public opinion in the Balkans, at Constantinople and on the Concert itself. I should regret exceedingly that any such impression should gain ground, because I wish to see the Concert maintained for Macedonian reforms....Moreover, in discussing the Macedonian question you are never far from the Turkish question, which has more than once led to a European war. As long as the Concert exists you have a certain guarantee that the question will not lead to war. Once they lose touch with one another, you cannot tell what misunderstandings may creep in and how far they may go. Has then the launching of a railway scheme really affected the Concert adversely? I trust not; but I do feel that it is incumbent on the Powers, after all that has passed, to make it clear that there is no ground for such an apprehension."

The Foreign Secretary proceeded to repeat the demands, the acceptance of which by the Powers he had been privately endeavouring to secure throughout the winter, and added that it might be necessary to go further.

"If a Turkish Governor were appointed for a fixed term of years—a man whose character and capacity were accepted and recognised by the Powers—and if he had a free hand and his position were secure, I believe that the whole Macedonian question might be solved. Under secure and effective administration the Financial Commission and the gendarmerie would have the fullest use made of them, and the country, I am convinced, would be swept of bands and pacified. I am not putting that forward as a definite proposal to which we ourselves are pledged. We have no *amour propre* in the matter. We are perfectly ready to abandon any proposal of our own, if any of the Powers will come forward with any other proposal likely to be as effective or more effective and which recommends itself more to the Concert as a whole. For I am convinced that the Macedonian problem can be settled if the Concert will only seriously take it in hand. Tinkering at the Mürzsteg programme will not improve the situation. Anything less than a real remedy can be little better than a farce. We are rapidly arriving at that point when the Concert must either justify itself or stultify itself. Macedonia, if it continues to be neglected, must sooner or later provoke a catastrophe."

Sir Edward Grey had recovered the unfaltering accents of Lord Lansdowne.

Aehrenthal complained to the British Ambassador that, according to this argument, Austria was prevented from doing anything to promote her interests in the Balkans, lest she should thereby encourage

Turkish resistance to reform. The Austrian Press, led by the *Fremden-blatt*, roundly declared that an independent Governor was impossible without coercing Turkey; and comment in the other capitals was no more encouraging. Undeterred by the hostile reception of his speech, Sir Edward Grey embodied its substance in a vigorous despatch to the Great Powers. The Government, he declared, had received the replies on his Gendarmerie proposal with great regret; and no alternative scheme had been proposed.

" If the note on judicial reforms is not presented, and if it is understood that the Powers have dropped this project without putting forward any other proposal of reform, the effect will be most deplorable. The situation is not beyond remedy; but it cannot be remedied by half-measures. Were a Governor of Macedonia to be appointed who would be given a free hand and be irremovable for a term of years except with the consent of the Powers, and were an adequate force of gendarmerie and of European officers placed at his disposal, the Government are convinced that the country might be cleared of bands and pacified in a short time. The Governor would be a Turkish subject, and might be a Christian or a Mussulman. The Government believe that, if all the Powers make it known that they are equally in earnest and resolved, they can secure the acceptance of any proposal which does not involve a disintegration of Ottoman territory. If the Powers are not prepared to assume this attitude, the Concert, as an instrument for securing reforms, has ceased to exist."

The prompt response of the Russian Government, which since the *sanjak coup* was now free to pursue its own line, manifested a welcome advance towards the British standpoint. While still unable to accept the proposed reduction of Turkish troops, it supported the increase of the numbers and powers of the Gendarmerie. If the appointment of a Governor for Macedonia had no chance of being adopted unanimously by the Powers or accepted by the Sultan, the same object could be attained by making the Inspector-General irremoveable for a term of years. At the same time, judicial reform should be seriously pressed. Sir Edward, delighted by the reply, virtually accepted the proposal that the Inspector-General should be raised to the rank of Vizier, confirmed for a term of years and superseded only with the consent of the Powers. There seemed at last to be some prospect of advance. If further progress was to be made it could only come from the growing intimacy of Great Britain and Russia; and it was to foster the spirit of confidence and cooperation that King Edward accepted the invitation to visit the Tsar at Reval in June.

The first visit ever paid by a British Sovereign to Russia aroused unusual interest both at home and abroad. Radical and Labour circles in England deplored the step at a time when the struggle between the Tsar and his people was at its height, and Nicholas dared not welcome his guest in his own capital. Grim stories of "Stolypin's necktie," of prisons crowded with untried prisoners, of a torture-chamber at Riga, of exiles rotting in Siberia, had filtered through to the West. The Conservative Press, on the other hand, pointedly recalled the King's journey to Paris in 1903. The visit was sharply challenged by the Labour party in the debate on the Foreign Office vote on June 4th, and warmly defended by Sir Edward Grey on grounds of high policy. The King's visits abroad, he began, had been uniformly beneficial. No negotiations were on foot for any new treaty or convention with Russia, and none would be initiated during the visit. But it would emphasise the fact that the relations between the two countries were of a friendly character. The Convention of 1907 and the Reval visit were parts of the same policy. "I am for a loyal understanding between the countries, working together where their interests touch. I stand by that, and if the House rejects it or makes it impossible I fall with it. That is a policy of peace. The other policy urged on us leads in the direction of war." The visit, moreover, was long overdue, and could not be postponed without marked discourtesy. We might as well tear up the Convention, and to continue the discussion of Macedonian reforms would be fruitless. The internal condition of Russia was irrelevant to the issue, and we had no Treaty rights to justify interference. "You think you are simply advocating a breach between two Governments," concluded the Foreign Secretary. "You are advocating something which in the long run is bound to make bad blood between the two peoples." If it was too late to cancel the visit, replied Keir Hardie on behalf of the Labour party, let it be of a private character. "For the King to pay an official visit is to condone the atrocities for which the Tsar's Government and the Tsar personally must be held responsible." Mr Balfour supported the official policy, which was approved by 225 to 59; but the large number of abstentions in a crowded House was symptomatic of a widespread repugnance to intimate relations with the Russian Government.

King Edward was perplexed and annoyed at the outburst of resentment.

"The visit," writes Sir Sidney Lee, "followed his cruises round the other northern capitals, and he regarded as overdue the personal civility to the

Tsar, who was nephew to his wife, and to whom he was deeply attached. The unrest in Russia was no concern of his, and only awoke in him sympathy with the ruler whose life it oppressed. He was hardly conscious of the deep-seated feeling which the alleged tyranny of the Russian Government had excited in many quarters in England[1]."

On June 10th, the King and Queen, accompanied by Sir John Fisher, Sir John French and Sir Charles Hardinge, reached Reval.

"I am confident," declared the Tsar, "that this meeting will strengthen the numerous and powerful ties which unite our Houses, and will have a happy result of bringing our countries closer together, and of maintaining the peace of the world. During the past year several questions of great importance for Russia and Great Britain have been settled satisfactorily. I am certain that Your Majesty appreciates as much as myself the value of these agreements, for, despite their limited scope, they can only aid in spreading between our countries the sentiments of goodwill and mutual confidence."

"I can cordially subscribe to the words of Your Majesty on the Convention recently concluded," replied the King. "I believe it will serve to strengthen the ties which unite our peoples, and I am certain it will lead to a satisfactory settlement of some important matters in the future. I am convinced that it will also greatly aid to maintain the peace of the world."

Izvolsky and Sir Charles Hardinge also issued a *communiqué* stating that they were in complete agreement on all points. "The two Ministers have convinced themselves anew of the desire of Russia and Great Britain to maintain the best relations with all the other Powers, and to give none of them reasons for disquietude as to the object of the special agreements between the two countries or of their general policy."

These soothing assurances merely stimulated speculation, and far-reaching designs were confidently attributed to the actors in the drama. In Germany and Austria, fantastic legends were current. "The assumption at the time," wrote Reventlow in 1915, "and later proved correct, was that the monarchs arranged to launch a war of annihilation against Germany and Austria, in association with France and the Balkan States, as soon as Russia had reorganised her army. The Russian experts calculated that this would require from six to eight years." Prince Bülow displayed his anxiety by pointed enquiries; and Izvolsky assured him that "no open or secret Anglo-Russian Conventions existed which could be directed against German interests." That apprehension was felt in still higher quarters, as was revealed by a speech of the Kaiser to his officers during an inspection

[1] *Dictionary of National Biography, Edward VII.*

at Döberitz. "It seems they wish to encircle and provoke us. We shall be able to support it. The German has never fought better than when he has had to defend him on all sides." A few days later he was greeted at the Hamburg regatta with unusual enthusiasm and by *Die Wacht am Rhein*. "When I asked myself what this outburst meant," he declared, "our old German song burst forth. Then I knew. Gentlemen, I thank you and I have understood you."

Germany was mistaken in attributing to the chief actors at Reval designs against her security or welfare; but she was justified in the belief that the visit had tightened the bonds between the two Powers. In a letter to Benckendorff, written on June 18th, Izvolsky reported that the general impression of the visit was extremely favourable[1], and that the King had openly expressed his satisfaction, referring with special pleasure to the happy trend in Russia's domestic affairs and Stolypin's activities. He had had long conversations with Hardinge on the European situation. The latter did not think that Anglo-German relations would grow worse just at present; but, if Germany continued to build at her present pace, in seven or eight years an extremely disquieting situation would arise. Then, doubtless, Russia would be the arbiter. It was, therefore, the wish of Great Britain, in the interest of peace and the Balance of Power, that she should be as strong as possible by land and sea. Sir Charles Hardinge spoke warmly of the result of the Convention of 1907, and declared the Cabinet to be resolved on cooperation in Persia. Macedonian reforms were fully discussed, and the British proposals were reduced to dimensions which Izvolsky hoped would be accepted by the Powers.

Nowhere was the Reval visit more anxiously canvassed than in certain secret conventicles both within and without the dominions of the Sultan. Young Turk exiles in Western Europe had long planned and plotted for a republic and a Constitution, and a network of committees was formed in European and Asiatic Turkey, with their headquarters at Salonika[2]. Fearing discovery, the Committee of Union and Progress planned a rising for September; but the meeting at Reval determined it to forestall by immediate action the intervention which it appeared to foreshadow. On July 3rd, Niazi Bey raised the flag of revolt at his native village of Resna, and, on July 23rd, the Constitution of 1876 was proclaimed. On the following day, Abdul Hamid, confronted by the Young Turk ultimatum, "Sur-

---

[1] Siebert, *Diplomatische Aktenstüche*, pp. 777–9.
[2] See Moore, *The Orient Express*, ch. 21: "The Young Turks."

render, or we march on Stambul," granted the Constitution. The revolution was hailed with delight throughout the Ottoman dominions, and the murdering bands disappeared as if by magic.

Opinion in this country greeted the revolution with enthusiastic and almost unanimous approval, though a few of the older Gladstonians grumbled that nothing good could come out of Turkey. The sentiment of relief was shared to the full by the British Diplomatic and Consular Representatives and by the Foreign Secretary himself[1]. Sir Edward Grey instructed our Chargé d'affaires to congratulate the new Grand-Vizier, Kiamil Pasha, the Grand Old Man of Turkey, on his accession to office and the promulgation of a Constitution.

"His Highness should be assured that the warmest sympathy has been called forth by this event in England, in which country the welfare of Turkey is earnestly desired by means of a regeneration of the Administration....As far as H.M.'s Government are concerned, the Macedonian question and others of a similar character will entirely disappear, once good government throughout the Turkish dominions is established. You may assure his Highness that any changes or genuine efforts on such lines will not be embarrassed by us, but will receive our fullest sympathy."

On the same day, Petrograd was informed of the opinion of the British Government that "any representations for the creation of a mobile force should be suspended." Izvolsky agreed that it was "essential that Great Britain and Russia should avoid placing themselves in antagonism to a Mussulman movement productive of genuine reforms, and that a fair chance of showing what good it could bring about should be afforded to that movement." Thus ended the five years' wearisome struggle, waged almost single-handed by Lord Lansdowne and Sir Edward Grey, for the relief of the suffering peasantry of Macedonia. In the course of the summer the whole machinery of control—the Gendarmerie, the Financial Commission and the Civil Agents—was scrapped. If it was in some measure an act of necessity, it was, in scarcely less degree, an act of faith.

The disinterested sympathy of Great Britain was warmly appreciated at Constantinople.

"A deputation visited the British Embassy at Pera to-day," reported Mr G. H. Barclay, "and said that they entertained the most friendly feelings to England as the country which was the champion of liberty. Englishmen have been the recipients of many expressions of friendliness from Turks, who feel that their aspirations to Constitutional liberty cannot lack the moral support of Great Britain."

[1] *Turkey*, No. 1, 1909. *Correspondence respecting the Constitutional Movement in Turkey.*

The new Ambassador, Sir Gerald Lowther, in presenting his credentials to the Sultan on August 7th, informed him that his wise action in granting the Constitution had made an excellent impression in England.

"In reply, he twice assured me that he was firmly resolved to act in future in accordance with the principles of the Constitution, and stated that he depended on H.M.'s Government giving him material and moral support. Along the entire route from Yildiz to the Sublime Porte and from there to the Embassy, a distance of about four miles, large crowds made me an enthusiastic and spontaneous demonstration."

In a cordial interview with the Turkish Ambassador on July 31st, Sir Edward Grey asserted that our quarrels had never been with the Turkish people, but only with that particular form of government which the Turks themselves had now overthrown.

III. THE BOSNIAN CRISIS, 1908–1909

While this country was still ringing with praises of the Young Turk revolution and of the almost miraculous restoration of tranquillity in the bloodstained valleys of Macedonia, the harmony of the European Chanceries was rudely disturbed by a proclamation of the Emperor Francis Joseph, announcing the formal incorporation of Bosnia and Herzegovina in his dominions, on the ground that annexation was the essential preliminary to the grant of a Constitution[1]. Aehrenthal had secured the concession for the *sanjak* Railway without consulting Russia; but he never dreamed of annexing Bosnia without a previous understanding. The *sanjak* controversy left Izvolsky angry and suspicious; but the mood passed, and in April, 1908, he expressed his desire that the *entente* of the two Powers should be renewed. In a Memorandum, dated June 19th, he accepted the *sanjak* Railway and announced his readiness, should the maintenance of the *status quo* prove impossible, to discuss changes, among them the annexation by Austria of Bosnia, Herzegovina and the *sanjak*, in return for the opening of the Straits to Russian warships. The intimation that Austria might annex Bosnia was a delightful surprise to Aehrenthal; and, once assured of Russia's conditional assent, he determined to carry out the project with the least possible delay. The statesmen met at Buchlau, Berchtold's castle in Bohemia, on September 15th. It was agreed that Aehrenthal should give his colleague notice before

[1] See the Austrian Red-book, *Diplomatische Aktenstücke betreffend Bosnien und die Hercegovina*; Friedjung, *Das Zeitalter des Imperialiances*, II. 165–284; Molden, *Graf Aehrenthal*, pp. 39–110; Conrad von Hötzendorff, *Aus meiner Dienstzeit*, vol. I.

taking action; but they afterwards differed as to the date when such action was expected[1]. The German and Italian Ministers were informed of the impending annexation, but not of its exact date. After completing his cure at Carlsbad, the Russian Minister crossed the Alps, intending to discuss coming events with Italy, France and Great Britain. The Austrian Minister, on the contrary, returned to Vienna resolved to act, and arranged with Ferdinand that he should simultaneously proclaim Bulgaria's independence of the Sultan. On October 1st, the Austrian Ambassadors to France and Italy, Great Britain and Germany, were despatched from Budapest with autograph letters from their Sovereign which they were ordered to deliver on October 5th. When he reached Paris on October 3rd, Izvolsky found a letter awaiting him from Aehrenthal, announcing that annexation would take place on October 7th. Since, however, President Fallières was to be away on October 5th, the audience of Count Khevenhüller was fixed for October 3rd; and on that day the letter of Francis Joseph was presented. "This letter," commented the President, "announces the annexation of Bosnia. What of the independence of Bulgaria?" "It is all arranged," was the prompt, but indiscreet, reply. "Bulgaria will anticipate us by a day."

When Count Mensdorff presented the Emperor's autograph letter, King Edward made no attempt to conceal his displeasure, and the Ambassador afterwards complained that he had been "turned out[2]." Lord Redesdale, who was staying at Balmoral when the news arrived, has described the anger of his royal friend. The King's autograph reply expressed his regret at the action taken by Austria, and reminded the Emperor of the Pact of 1871. The monarch's indignation was shared by the Press, *The Times* leading the hue and cry with resonant denunciations. In a speech to his constituents on October 7th, Sir Edward Grey declared that any modification of the Treaty of Berlin must be approved by another European Congress, just as Russia's repudiation of the Black Sea Clauses of 1856 had to be ratified at the London Conference of 1871, in which Austria had taken part, and which decreed that "no Power can free itself from the engagements undertaken by treaty nor modify its stipulations without consent of the Contracting Parties." "We cannot recognise the right of any State to alter any international treaty without consent, and we cannot

---

[1] Izvolsky's story was told in *The Fortnightly Review*, September, 1909. Aehrenthal's reply appeared in the November issue.
[2] *Man hat mich fortgejagt.*

recognise the result of any such action till the other Powers, Turkey included, have been consulted." The actual change involved in the proceedings of Austria and Bulgaria was not great; but the manner was irregular and abrupt, and the incident was particularly deplorable at a time when Turkey was setting her house in order. "Our relations with the Government of Turkey have changed from friction and remonstrance to very deep sympathy.... Hatred, strife and oppression have been swept away, and have been replaced by fair-play, peace and goodwill. Never in history has there been, I think, a change more sudden and so beneficent." The British Government wished the Young Turks to have a fair chance. Any slighting of the new régime must give a military direction to a movement entirely peaceful, and plunge Macedonia and Armenia back into the deplorable state from which they had recently emerged. Turkey might rest assured that, in any revision of the Treaty of Berlin which freed Austria or Bulgaria from their obligations, her status and interests would receive full consideration. The British, French and Russian Ambassadors at Constantinople were instructed to tell the Porte that all changes in the Treaty of Berlin required the assent of all its Signatories; and a British squadron was sent to the Aegean as a symbol of sympathy and support.

On October 12th, Lord Lansdowne asked the Government for information, adding that there was a feeling of the utmost dismay in the country. Lord Fitzmaurice replied that no definite arrangements for a Conference had yet been made, and expressed a hope that the aggrieved States would indulge in no hasty action. On the following day, however, an official *communiqué* announced that the British and Russian Ministers had agreed to demand a Conference. Izvolsky had thus secured the first item of his programme; but the second and far more important of his demands—compensation for Russia—had been refused. The Russian Minister had agreed in advance to the annexation of Bosnia and Herzegovina in return for Austrian support for the opening of the Straits. The British statesman, on the other hand, had known nothing of the conspiracy against the Treaty of Berlin; and, after denouncing its breach by Austria, he could hardly support the proposal for a further encroachment on Turkish sovereignty. On the day of Izvolsky's arrival, *The Times* had roughly warned Russia "not to join in the undignified scramble, which would alienate Turkey and forfeit the goodwill of Powers with which she was on the best of possible terms." The Foreign Secretary made it plain to his visitor that the question of the Straits must not be raised at the Conference; but he accompanied his decision with a written assurance, approved by the Cabinet, that he sympathised with the object and that the veto was only temporary.

On October 16th, a Foreign Office *communiqué* summarised the result of the week's discussions. A Conference was necessary, but it should be limited to questions arising out of the violation of the Treaty of Berlin. Its primary object would be to provide compensation for Turkey, and means might perhaps be found to meet the reasonable wishes of the smaller Balkan States, though not at Turkey's expense. "There is no intention of submitting the question of the Straits to the Conference. It is a question in which Russia and Turkey are primarily concerned, and there is no desire on Russia's part in any sense hostile to Turkey or to seek for it as compensation; for Russia enters the Conference as one of the disinterested Powers." On the same day a semi-official Anglo-French-Russian programme for the projected Conference was issued in Paris, and Pichon expressed the hope that Europe would assert her moral unity. Of such unity, however, there were few signs. Miliukoff expressed the opinion of his countrymen when he complained that a Conference would be useless, unless it secured compensation for the Slavs. On October 13th, Bülow informed the British Government that Austria was opposed to a Conference and that Germany must support her; but, on October 22nd, Aehrenthal explained to the Delegations that Austria had no objection to a meeting, if the programme was settled in accordance with her views, and the annexation sanctioned but not discussed.

At the Guildhall on November 9th, the Prime-Minister appeared in the *rôle* of "honest broker." It was a matter of indifference to Great Britain in what way a settlement was reached. "We shall urge on all parties moderation and restraint. We are entirely disinterested in the Near East. We ask nothing for ourselves. Our sole objects are to maintain the public law of Europe, to secure a fair chance for the new régime in Turkey, and to promote the adjustment of conflicting interests." Ten days later, the Foreign Secretary reiterated the policy of the Government, and once again paid a generous tribute to the Young Turks. "A few months ago, I should have summed up the relations of Europe and Turkey by the word Despair. It has been one of the most wonderful and beneficent changes in history." We had no territorial ambitions, he added, no past injuries to rankle, no scores to pay off. On November 23rd, Mensdorff reported a conversation with the Foreign Secretary which revealed an approximation to the Austrian standpoint; for, though a discussion of the annexation at the Conference could not be ruled out, an understanding might be reached before it began. He added that, if Austria reached an agreement with Turkey, Russia and Italy, Great Britain, Germany and France might accept it.

If the annexation came as a shock to Great Britain, it was a staggering blow to Montenegro and Servia, who at once began to make military preparations. "My country," lamented Milovanovich, the Servian Foreign Minister, to a Vienna journalist, "feels it almost like physical pain, so that the very soul of the people cries out." Since the accession of Peter Karageorgevich in 1903 the hope of ultimately detaching the Jugoslav provinces from the Habsburg empire by Russian aid had taken root in the country. Milovanovich, well aware that the annexation could not be reversed, set forth on a round of visits to the Chanceries to ask for a corridor to the Adriatic as a consolation prize.

"Yesterday afternoon," he reported from London on October 16th[1], "I was first received by Hardinge, with whom I remained for half an hour. I then accompanied him to Grey, with whom we conferred more than an hour. Both listened to me very attentively, and exhibited a very lively and sympathetic interest. As regards territorial compensation, they are doubtful of success, as Austria positively refuses assent. Are we to hold a Conference, observed Grey, with the prospect that Austria stands by the annexation and at the same time retains the Sanjak? I replied that they need not fear to leave this question open, for Austria would not dare to permit the present tension to continue for long. We must stick to this demand to the end, and so long as Great Britain did not abandon us, the prospect of success still remained. Great Britain's attitude will likewise encourage Turkey, who is not inclined to yield anything further. 'We must,' I exclaimed, 'prepare for the war which is inevitable in the near future, if they refuse us this compensation.' In reply, Grey and Hardinge promised that they would persist in supporting our territorial compensation demand so long as Russia should give it her support. The entire Press sympathises greatly with Servia."

An even warmer welcome awaited Prince George and Pasitch at Petrograd. "The Tsar," reported the latter, "expressed great sympathy for Servia, but advised a quiet line of conduct, as our cause was just but our preparations were weak."

[1] Bogitshevich, *Causes of the War*, p. 110.

Autumn passed into winter with Europe in turmoil, though no State cared or dared to challenge Austria to ordeal by battle[1]. The hysterics of Belgrade aroused the contemptuous anger of Vienna, and the fiery Chief of the Staff, Conrad von Hötzendorff, urged summary chastisement. When the new year dawned, the idea of a conference was already fading away. Austria declined to attend without a preliminary agreement and unless a discussion of the annexation were ruled out; and, if her actions were to be condoned in advance, it seemed futile to bring the Powers together in solemn conclave. There were, however, three urgent problems to be liquidated—the relations of Austria to Turkey, the relations of Bulgaria to Turkey, and the relations of Servia to Austria; and all three were solved without bloodshed before Easter.

Aehrenthal had argued that the withdrawal of the garrisons from the *sanjak* formed an adequate compensation to Turkey for the loss of her shadowy rights over Bosnia and Herzegovina; but the Turkish boycott of Austrian goods and the desire to diminish the number of his opponents finally persuaded him to add a financial *solatium*. The news that Austria would pay two-and-a-half millions for the loss of Crown property in the annexed provinces was hailed by Sir Edward Grey as "the first blue sky." British sympathy with the Turkish reformers, he added, was unabated, and the wisdom of Kiamil received the tribute that it deserved. The relief was increased when Bulgaria's offence against Turkish sovereignty was purged by a covenant to pay five millions for her share of the Oriental railways; and the transaction was arranged by Russia's redeeming the Turkish indemnity of 1878 by a similar amount.

In Aehrenthal's opinion, the Suzerain's acceptance of the annexation ought to carry the assent of less directly interested States; but this view was not shared by Servia. The Powers, however, endeavoured to build a bridge for her retreat[2]. Sir Edward Grey promised the Russian Government diplomatic aid in securing compensation for Servia and Montenegro, adding that Servia's claims must in the interest of peace be reduced to a minimum. "The British Government," telegraphed Benckendorff on February 24th, "quite realises the danger of the situation. Despite the earnest wish to help Servia, it is aware that without war it is impossible to procure more than

---

[1] In private, Izvolsky freely vented his anger. "Aehrenthal is not a gentleman," he cried. Szilassy, *Der Untergang der Donaumonarchie*, p. 194.
[2] See Siebert, *Diplomatische Aktenstücke*, ch. 1.

economic concessions." This cautious realism was shared by the French Government; and the pressure of London and Paris was reflected in Izvolsky's advice to Belgrade. Servia replied that she demanded from Austria no territorial, political or economic compensations. If, however, the Powers were to deal with the questions arising from the new situation, she would explain her standpoint before their tribunal. She was ready to cancel her military preparations, if Austria would do the same, or if the Powers would guarantee her against attack. This reply satisfied Izvolsky, subject to the omission of the reference to military preparations and other minor changes; and Sir Edward Grey promptly approved his alterations, which Belgrade was advised to incorporate in her forthcoming Circular Note to the Powers.

Meanwhile, on March 5th, the situation was complicated by a Note from Aehrenthal requiring from Servia a direct assurance of a change of attitude, and a recognition of the annexation. "No Serbian Government could accept this," telegraphed Izvolsky to Benckendorff; and Sir Edward Grey agreed that Servia could not recognise the annexation before the Powers. The Servian reply to the *démarche* of the Powers, when it came on March 10th, was less satisfactory than had been expected.

"Servia, considering that her juridical relation to Austria remains normal, has no desire to provoke a war nor to modify her legal relations, continuing to fulfil, on the basis of reciprocity, her duties as a good neighbour. Assuming the Bosnian question to be a European question, and that it belongs to the Signatories of the Treaty of Berlin to settle the question and to decide the new version of Article XXV, Servia, confiding in the wisdom and equity of the Powers, remits her cause to them without reserve, and claims no territorial, political or economic compensation."

Aehrenthal replied that this was not an answer to his Note of March 5th, though it indicated improvement. Sir Edward Grey confided to Mensdorff that the Note to the Powers was approved by none of them. Servia, he added, could have replied that she would recognise any modification of the Berlin Treaty sanctioned by the Powers, would maintain neighbourly relations with Austria, would not encourage disturbances on Austrian territory, and was ready to discuss a commercial treaty. Sir F. Cartwright informed Aehrenthal that the British Government disapproved the reply, and that our Minister in Belgrade was instructed to support Russian attempts to persuade Servia to yield, and to present a formula like that suggested to Mensdorff. Aehrenthal replied that such a formula was insufficient without a reference to disarmament. The Ambassador, accordingly, asked him to suggest a formula, and on March 19th it was ready: "Servia recognises that her rights have not been infringed. She abandons the attitude of protest and engages to change the direction of her policy towards Austria and to live on neighbourly terms. In conformity with her pacific declarations, she will reduce her army to the standard of the spring of 1908." Having persuaded Aehrenthal to accept some minor changes, Cartwright undertook to propose that the Powers should assure Austria in writing that they would sanction the Constantinople Protocol at the forthcoming Conference.

With Aehrenthal and Cartwright in agreement, the solution of the crisis seemed within grasp; but it was not to end without a final alarm. On March 17th, the German Ambassador informed Izvolsky that Bülow was ready to suggest that Aehrenthal should acquaint the Powers with Turkey's sanction of the annexation; and, if Russia approved, Germany, perhaps in association with Russia, would propose to the Powers to recognise it in an exchange of Notes, thus fulfilling Russia's wish for a European sanction. Izvolsky thanked Pourtalès for his friendly communication, but remarked that it appeared to negative a Conference, to deliver Servia into Austrian hands, and to relieve Austria of the necessity of solving the other problems. He promptly telegraphed the news to London and Paris, adding that he might accept the offer in principle, with a guarantee for the meeting of the Conference. Sir Edward Grey replied that the proposal was obviously inspired by Vienna; that the Conference was by implication shelved; that, if Russia was willing to dispense with a Conference, Great Britain would content herself with an exchange of Notes; and that Russia ought to postpone her reply till the latest Austro-Servian crisis was ended.

On March 23rd, after six days had elapsed without a response to the German proposal, Bülow applied what he asserted to be gentle pressure, but what was regarded throughout the world as something closely resembling an ultimatum[1].

"The German Government is glad to note that the Russian Government recognises the friendly spirit of Germany's step, and that the Powers seem

[1] Schön declares the story of an ultimatum to be a legend. "It was not an ultimatum but a proposal for mediation," echoes Jagow, "which Izvolsky welcomed as an escape from a *cul-de-sac*. His assistant, Tcharikoff, observed that Germany had rendered Russia a great service," p. 17. Kiderlen-Wächter, however, then Acting Foreign Minister, boasted to Take Jonescu that he alone framed the ultimatum. "I knew Russia was not ready for war. Schön would never have dared to do it." Take Jonescu, *Personal Impressions*, p. 58.

inclined to accept the proposal. It is ready to suggest to the Vienna Cabinet to invite the Powers, while notifying them of the Austro-Turkish Agreement, to assent formally to the cancelling of Article XXV of the Berlin Treaty. Before doing so, however, it wishes to be sure that the Russian Cabinet is ready to accept the Austrian proposal and to give its unconditional consent. It expects a precise answer, Yes or No, and any ambiguous reply would be regarded as a refusal. We should then withdraw and allow things to take their course. The responsibility for subsequent events would rest exclusively on Izvolsky[1]."

After consulting the Tsar, Izvolsky replied that, if Austria invited the Powers to assent to the cancelling of Article XXV, the Russian Government would declare its formal and unconditional acceptance. In reporting the incident to London and Paris, Izvolsky explained that refusal was impossible, since it would have involved an Austrian invasion of Servia.

Bülow promptly instructed his Ambassadors to invite Rome, Paris and London to follow the example of Petrograd. Italy at once accepted. France replied that she would accept, but hoped that Austria would postpone her request till the Austro-Servian conflict was ended. Downing Street was more intractable. Sir Arthur Nicolson had informed Pourtalès of its being by no means certain that the British Government would follow the Russian lead, and he complained to Izvolsky that he had yielded without consulting his friends. On March 25th, Wolff-Metternich expressed the hope that Sir Edward Grey would follow the example of Russia. The Foreign Secretary was angered by the threat from Petrograd, and scented a similar menace in the enquiry. He replied that the Servian question must be settled by discussion, refused to give the required assurance, and handed to the Ambassador a Memorandum embodying this reply. Wolff-Metternich rejoined that his answer created a very serious situation, and that Great Britain alone stood out. Sir Edward replied that he was not aware that all the Powers had assented, and that the recognition of annexation must follow, not precede, an Austro-Servian settlement. The Foreign Secretary went calmly on with his search for a formula. He had accepted the Cartwright-Aehrenthal formula with modifications, which Aehrenthal rejected; and Aehrenthal in turn made some trifling changes. On March 27th, he approved the Note in its final form, and announced that when Servia had despatched it and Austria had accepted it, he would

---

[1] This important despatch is printed in Hammann, *Bilder aus der letzten Kaiserzeit*, pp. 155–156.

recognise the abrogation of Article XXV, if invited to do so. If Servia refused, he would none the less assent, if all the Signatories would do the.same. This undertaking was conditional on the execution of Aehrenthal's verbal assurances that he would accept modifications of Article XXIX of the Treaty of Berlin concerning Montenegro. On March 31st, the Servian Minister brought to the Ballplatz his country's formal surrender. The Triple Entente now complied with a request to accept the abrogation of Article XXV, Austria for her part surrendering the right to police Montenegrin waters.

The course pursued by the British Government in the Bosnian crisis was sharply challenged by Sir Charles Dilke on the Foreign Office vote[1]. The title of Great Britain and Russia to remonstrate, he argued, was singularly weak. The Treaty of Berlin had been violated over and over again, by Turkey no less than by the Powers. The nominal reservation of Turkish sovereignty should not be taken too seriously in the case of Bosnia, any more than those of Cyprus and the Sudan; and the annexation of Eastern Roumelia by Bulgaria had won our approval and support. Nobody imagined that Austria was entrusted with a purely temporary occupation of the provinces, which she had actually taken over on the proposal of Great Britain herself. Moreover, we were not sufficiently interested to make it wise for us to play a leading part in the game, or to allow Russia to force us too far in the direction of an interference certain to encounter resistance and doomed to failure. Sir Edward Grey rejoined that the best way to keep peace was to stand by public engagements. We held to the Declaration of 1871, and we should have raised the same protest against any other Power. Austria's action had been against the public law of Europe, and struck a damaging blow at the prestige of Turkey. Our intervention had been far from fruitless. Was it certain that, if we had taken a less decided line, the compensation for Turkey would have been so peacefully arranged? Partly as the result of our action, patience, restraint and commonsense had prevailed and a peaceful settlement was secured. After this debate Anglo-Austrian relations gradually resumed their traditional friendliness. A meeting between the monarchs at Ischl was frustrated by Aehrenthal; but during King Edward's last visit to Marienbad in August, 1909, courteous telegraphic greetings were exchanged.

The close association of British and Russian policy throughout the Bosnian crisis had not diminished the hostility of Radical and Labour

[1] July 22nd, 1909.

circles to the Tsarist autocracy; and the Chairman of the Labour Party seized the opportunity to protest against the Tsar's approaching visit to Cowes. "It is a policy repulsive to multitudes of our people," declared Mr Henderson. "Thirteen months ago we were told that the visit to Reval would exercise a salutary influence on official Russia. There is no sign of any such improvement. We are not interfering in Russia's internal affairs; we are concerned with the attitude of our own Government." The Foreign Secretary replied that his critic placed the Government in an impossible position.

"He reads out certain statements about the internal condition of a foreign country in regard to which we have no treaty rights or obligations, and he challenges the Government to disprove them. It is not our business to know what passes in other countries, and even if we do know we cannot discuss it. I am asked to prove that the visit to Reval had a beneficial effect on internal affairs in Russia. If it were the case, I would not say so. I do not accept the figures. All I have seen goes to show that his account is not true or fair. I ask the House to drop dealing with the internal affairs of foreign countries; but if they insist, they should bring out the whole of the case. We have lately had an unofficial visit of members of the Duma. The Tsar who is going to pay us a visit will be remembered in history as the Sovereign who granted Constitutional Government. On behalf of the Government we welcome him as the head of a great State with whom and with whose people we desire to be on friendly terms. What the two Governments have done is beginning to have a most beneficial influence on the feelings of the two peoples. I am sure the House will not by an act of marked discourtesy undo the good work which has been done."

The confidence of the Foreign Secretary was justified; for, whenever the Left wing of the ministerial majority became restive at the conduct of Foreign Affairs, the Opposition rallied to his support.

IV. PERSIA, 1906–1911

The growing intimacy between the British and Russian Governments aroused disapprobation in certain circles—not only on account of "the Terror," as it was styled by Prince Kropotkin in a widely-read booklet, but because it appeared to range Great Britain against the cause of Persian nationalism. Sir Edward Grey was by no means without sympathy for the aspirations of Persia; but the governing principle of his Persian policy was the necessity of retaining the friendship of Russia, on which he relied in an increasing degree as the tension with Germany grew.

The history of Persia since the accession of Mozaffer-ed-Din in 1890 is one of increasing degradation, which in turn led to the awakening of national self-consciousness[1]. The Shah squandered his country's slender resources in costly journeys to Europe, and the gradual mortgaging of the country to Russia gave rise to great indignation. In 1906 about 13,000 citizens of Teheran took "bast" in the grounds of the British Legation in support of the demand for a Mejliss or Parliament, which the Shah reluctantly granted. From the beginning, the Russian colony in Persia looked askance at the Constitutional movement, while the sympathies of the British Representative were openly avowed. When Mohammed Ali, who succeeded his father soon after the grant of a Constitution, struggled against the financial reforms of the Mejliss and the abolition of sinecures, Mr Spring-Rice bluntly told him that he was surrounded by evil influences, and that he must come to an amicable arrangement with the reformers.

While the Mejliss was hewing its way through the jungle of corruption, news of the Anglo-Russian Convention reached the capital. The Treaty was viewed with apprehension by the Persian Nationalists, whose feelings were depicted in a cartoon in *Punch*, in which the British lion and the Russian bear are mauling a Persian cat. The lion remarks, "You can play with his head, and I can play with his tail, and we can both stroke the small of his back." The cat moans: "I don't remember having been consulted about this." Though Teheran had not been consulted, Sir Edward Grey instructed Mr Spring-Rice to propose to his Russian colleague an identic communication in the following terms.

"Desiring to avoid any cause of conflict between their respective interests in regions, on the one hand, contiguous with or in the neighbourhood of the Russian frontier, and, on the other, of the frontier of Beluchistan and Afghanistan, the Governments of Great Britain and Russia have signed a friendly Agreement. The two Governments mutually agree to the strict independence and integrity of Persia, and testify that they sincerely desire, not only the permanent establishment of equal advantages for the industry and commerce of all nations, but also the pacific development of that country. Each binds itself to seek no concession in regions conterminous with or in the neighbourhood of the frontier of the other. The above-mentioned regions are clearly defined, in order that future misunderstandings may be avoided, and to avoid a state of things which might

---

[1] This section is based on the Blue-books, which are very numerous. Cf. Professor E. G. Browne, *The Persian Revolution*; and David Fraser, *Persia and Turkey in Revolt*.

embarrass the Persian Government. The two States, in signing the Agreement, steadfastly kept the fundamental principle in view that the independence and integrity of Persia should be respected absolutely. The sole object of the arrangement is the avoidance of any cause of misunderstanding between the contracting Powers. The Shah's Government will be convinced that the Agreement cannot fail to promote the prosperity, security and ulterior development of Persia in the most efficacious manner."

The Memorandum, with a few minor changes, was presented by the British and Russian Ministers on September 11th[1].

In addition to the official communication, the British Minister wrote a reassuring letter to the Persian Foreign Minister on September 5th[2].

"Information has reached me that it is rumoured in Persia that an Agreement has been concluded between England and Russia which will result in the intervention of these two Powers in Persia, and the partition of that country between them. Your Excellency is well aware that the negotiations between Russia and England are of a wholly different character.... They have no sort of intention of attacking Persia's independence, which it is their object in concluding this Agreement to ensure for ever. Not only do they not seek a pretext for intervention; but their aim in these friendly negotiations is not to permit one another to intervene in Persia on the pretext of safeguarding their own interests. The two Powers hope that in the future Persia will be for ever delivered from the fear of foreign intervention, and will enjoy complete freedom to manage her affairs in her own way."

For some time the two Powers loyally fulfilled their pledges; but the Shah smarted at the loss of his authority, and feared the activity of the *Anjumans*, or political secret societies. "There is now in Persia an intense feeling of patriotism," reported Mr Spring-Rice on September 13th, 1907. The first conflict arose in December, when, in reply to a demand by the Mejliss for the dismissal of his reactionary advisers, the Shah arrested his Ministers. The news was brought to the British Legation by a servant of the Premier, Nasr-ul-Mulk. The Oriental Secretary of the British Legation, Mr H. L. Churchill, galloped to the palace to save their lives; and the Shah, professing that they were never in danger, liberated his prisoners. The timid Nasr-ul-Mulk hurried off on the following morning towards Europe, shepherded by guards from the British Legation; but the Shah's nerve failed him, and after five days, during which the Parliament

---

[1] Published as a White Paper, Persia, No. 1, 1912.

[2] Abridged. The letter was published on September 14th in a Teheran newspaper and may be read in Browne, pp. 90–2. It does not appear in the Blue-books, and remained unknown to Sir Edward Grey till 1911.

House was defended by National Volunteers, he promised to dismiss his counsellors. The British and Russian Ministers asked him to declare that he had no hostile designs against the Constitution; and the monarch obediently replied that he had none. The failure of the *coup* was hailed with satisfaction both in London and Petrograd. "At the New Year's reception," reported Sir Arthur Nicolson, "I told the Tsar that the British Government were much gratified by the cordial cooperation during the crisis; to which the Tsar rejoined, 'I too'."

The brief crisis intensified the enmity between the Shah and the reformers, and shortly afterwards a bomb was thrown at his motor-car. The Constitutionalists affirmed that the outrage was staged by the reactionaries; and, on June 1st, 1908, the Mejliss secured the eviction of six more reactionary courtiers. Next day the Russian Minister and the British Chargé d'affaires visited the Foreign Minister, to warn him of the consequences if anything happened to the Shah. "His life is in danger," declared Hartwig, the Russian Minister, "the Nationalists wish to depose him. This we cannot allow. If it occurs, Russia will intervene with British approval." The warning having been endorsed by the British Chargé d'affaires, the Foreign Minister reported the conversation to the President of the Mejliss. Early on the following morning, the Shah, guarded by Colonel Liakhoff and the Cossack brigade, fled to his country palace. Russian sympathies, at both Petrograd and Teheran, were now openly on the side of the Shah, and it was commonly believed that on this occasion it was the hand of Hartwig which had pulled the strings. But Sir Edward Grey declined to accept the Russian proposal of a joint declaration to maintain the dynasty. "Tell Izvolsky," he telegraphed to Sir A. Nicolson, "that I strongly deprecate any action which might have the appearance of intervening in internal affairs. I am convinced the best course is to limit our action; otherwise we may become burdened with the responsibility of maintaining an unpopular Government." A few days later, the Parliament House and the chief Mosque were bombarded by Liakhoff, who was appointed Military Governor of Teheran. In reply to his critics, Sir Edward Grey observed that Liakhoff was in the Persian service, and that Russia was not responsible for his actions. When Sir A. Nicolson suggested that these officers should be withdrawn for a time, Izvolsky answered that this would be hazardous; but he added that Liakhoff had acted without the knowledge and approval of the Russian Government.

The Mejliss had committed errors, for it was necessarily inexperienced; but it had begun to reform the finances, and had produced the first budget that Persia had ever seen. "A large proportion, probably a majority of the members," declares Professor Browne, "were animated by patriotic and public spirit." Even Mr Donald Fraser, who thinks the Mejliss on the whole a failure, admits that the Constitutional movement had attracted all the best men. The newspapers, which had sprung up to the number of about one hundred, disappeared. The Constitutional leaders who were not caught took "bast" at the British Legation, which was promptly invested by the Government troops. When the Shah telegraphed to King Edward to protest against his Representative inviting the rebels to take "bast," the King denied the accusation and peremptorily ordered the withdrawal of the troops.

On September 1st an Anglo-Russian Note urged the Shah to convene the Mejliss in November; but he replied that it was impossible till order was restored in Tabriz. A week or two later, he promised a Constitution, though he had no intention of again putting his neck under the yoke.

"Anglo-Russian exhortations were useless," writes Mr Fraser, "because the Russian Minister gave one counsel to the Shah in public and a totally different one in private. Jointly and publicly the two Representatives urged conciliation, singly and secretly Hartwig advised obstruction. In December, 1907, the Shah acted alone; in June, 1908, he succeeded because he had Russian support. The real victor was Hartwig, the vanquished were the British. He could not conceal his satisfaction, and his manners became insufferably patronising. It was with his cognisance that the Legation was picketed, and British prestige fell to zero."

Hartwig's performances were too much for Izvolsky, who recalled him to Petrograd, though he retained the title of Minister till another post became vacant, and his family remained in the Legation. His place was taken by M. Sablin as Chargé d'affaires, who worked loyally with Sir George Barclay, the new British Minister. At this dark moment in the fortunes of Persia, the Persia Committee was founded by British friends of the reformers, led by Professor E. G. Browne and Mr H. F. B. Lynch.

Though the Shah was triumphant in Teheran, the Constitutionalists held their ground in Tabriz, the second city in the country. Neither side showed much fight; but, early in February, 1909, after seven months, the city was completely isolated. Russian troops were held in readiness at Julfa, on the frontier, and Petrograd desired to meet the Shah's wish for a loan.

"I should prefer to stand aloof," answered Sir Edward Grey on February 3rd, "and let the chaos go on till the strongest wins. But, if Russia differs, I will cooperate. If a Constitution is granted, tranquillity will be restored over the whole country. The Shah should therefore be urged to fulfil his promises by a certain date. We should not consent to a loan till an elected Mejliss has approved it; for at the present time it would be a demonstration against the Constitutionalists."

The two statesmen continued to differ. Izvolsky complained to Sir A. Nicolson that he could not understand our objection to providing a fund for starting a workable Government, or our insistence on the consent of the Mejliss, for Persia was now penniless. "If Russia likes to advance her half of the loan now," rejoined Sir Edward, "we will give ours when the whole loan is sanctioned."

As the spring advanced, the British Government became alarmed for the safety of the Europeans in Tabriz, and on March 26th Russian troops marched in from Julfa and raised the siege. By a curious irony, the complete triumph of the Royalist cause had been frustrated at the eleventh hour by the action of Russia; and Sir Edward Grey resolved to profit by the situation. At his suggestion, the British and Russian Ministers urged the Shah to dismiss his reactionary advisers, restore the Constitution, appoint a new Cabinet, proclaim an amnesty, and fix dates for the elections and the opening of a new Mejliss. When these steps had been taken, Russia might lend £100,000 and Great Britain might follow suit later. The Shah obediently fixed the date of the elections and accepted a Cabinet constructed with Anglo-Russian advice, whereupon Sir Edward announced that if the Nationalists were not satisfied with this surrender he could make no further efforts on their behalf. They had, however, no confidence in their ruler, and hardly was the ink of the new proclamation dry when the Baktiari chiefs began to march north. During the siege of Tabriz the Nationalists in Ispahan, aided by Baktiari chiefs, had overthrown the hated Governor, expelled the garrison, and convened a local assembly. Resht now followed suit in the north. The Royalist Governor was killed, and the Sipahdar, who had changed sides, assumed nominal control, though the moving spirit was the Armenian soldier, Ephrem. The advance on the capital from north and south proceeded simultaneously, the Sipahdar marching to Kazvin, ninety miles from Teheran. "Intervention must be avoided," telegraphed Sir Edward to Sir George Barclay, "but efforts should be made to persuade Sardar Assad to abandon his advance, and you should explain to him the reforms proposed by the two Governments." The warnings produced no effect, and the Russians began to become restless. "I told Benckendorff today," telegraphed Sir Edward to Petrograd on June 30th, "that the less interference the better. If a Russian force occupied Teheran, all Persians would consider that the Shah depended on Russian support alone, and all the rest of the country would disown his Government and break it up. Any great disaster can, I think, be prevented by the Persian Cossacks." Russia accordingly despatched troops to Kazvin, with orders not to enter the capital unless foreigners were in danger.

Sardar Assad, the Baktiari leader, and the Sipahdar met outside the capital, and after a skirmish entered Teheran on July 13th. The Shah sought refuge in the Russian Legation, the Sipahdar became Minister of War, and the valiant Ephrem was appointed Chief of Police. The Nationalist leaders and the members of the Mejliss met to depose the Shah, and chose his son, a lad of twelve, under a Regency. The ex-Shah left for Odessa, his pension being fixed at £16,000, which was to lapse if the British and Russian Representatives in Persia were convinced that he was intriguing against the Government. The new Mejliss opened in November, and the newspapers reappeared. The Government found a guide, philosopher and friend in Sir George Barclay, who was loyally supported by Sablin.

When the Shah had been happily overthrown, Sir Edward Grey turned his attention to the Russian troops, of which 4000 were in Teheran, 1700 in Kazvin, and a smaller number in Ardebil. He had repeatedly warned Benckendorff and Izvolsky not to make Russia unpopular in Persia or at Westminster by what looked like a permanent occupation, and he renewed his advice when the Russian Foreign Minister accompanied the Tsar to Cowes[1]. Izvolsky replied that he was anxious to withdraw them, but that it was difficult to remove the troops from Tabriz till security was guaranteed, or from Kazvin while the situation at Teheran was so uncertain. The Tabriz force, however, was shortly halved; but the garrison remained at Kazvin, though Sir George Barclay reported the road to the coast safe and the capital quiet. The British Government had taken no similar steps in the south. In March, gunboats were sent to Bushire and Bunder Abbas to protect foreigners in the event of disturbances, and, in July, after an attack on the British Representative, the Consular Guard at Shiraz was reinforced. British trade, however, suffered from the increasing anarchy. After waiting with exemplary and un-

[1] Siebert, *Diplomatische Aktenstücke*, pp. 169–70.

rewarded patience for the restored Government to assert itself, Sir Edward sent an ultimatum to Teheran on October 14th, 1910, on the state of the southern roads. Unless within three months order was restored on the road from Bushire to Ispahan, Great Britain would police it. The threat, however, was never carried out, and we loyally supported the Swedish gendarmerie, to whom the task of restoring order was committed by the Persian Government.

The root of Persia's maladies lay in finance; and on December 25th, 1910, President Taft was asked to select a Treasurer-General, with four assistants, for three years. Neither the British nor the Russian Government raised any objection, though the latter disapproved the step, and on May 12th, 1911, Mr Shuster entered Teheran[1]. The Regent, Nasr-ul-Mulk, an Oxford graduate, now returned from Europe, and the Russian troops were at length withdrawn from Kazvin. It seemed as if at last a brighter day was to dawn. Mr Shuster perceived from the outset that he must take a firm line against native and foreign enemies of reform, and, on June 13th, he obtained full powers over finance from the Mejliss. "Shuster has apparently created a great impression on the Persians," reported Sir George Barclay, "and the unanimity with which all parties have given him the full powers for which he has asked proves that they repose the utmost confidence in him. He has let it be widely known that if he finds obstacles placed in his way by any person or persons, he will denounce them to the Mejliss, and if he cannot remove their obstruction he will return."

Mr Shuster had, on his voyage across the Altantic, read the Bluebooks and the writings of Professor Browne, and he knew that he would have to meet the hostility of Russia. The first round of the match was not long delayed. For collecting the revenue a Treasury *Gendarmerie* was required; and in Major Stokes, now near the end of his four years' service as Military Attaché, he found the man whom he needed. Sir George Barclay, on being consulted, replied that the Major would have to resign his commission in the Indian army. Sir Edward Grey referred the matter to Petrograd before replying, and Sir George Buchanan reported the result.

The Acting-Minister (Neratoff) did not object to the gendarmerie; but it must be under one officer, preferably the subject of a smaller Power....I pointed out that it might be very difficult to secure the right man, and that Stokes seemed eminently qualified; to which Neratoff rejoined, "A Swede would do."

[1] Mr Shuster has told his own story in *The Strangling of Persia* (1912).

Sir Edward, accordingly, telegraphed to Teheran on July 13th, "Would a Swedish officer do to command the Treasury gendarmerie?" Mr Shuster replied that Stokes was the best man, and that a Swede would have to spend a year or more before he could be any real use. Sir Edward Grey was convinced, and, on July 21st, he telegraphed to Teheran: "Before Stokes accepts command, he must resign his commission in the Indian army." The Russian partner in the firm took a very different view of the matter. "Benckendorff," reported Sir Edward Grey to Sir George Buchanan, "spoke with great anxiety lest Stokes might take part in military operations, when perhaps Russian officers might be on the other side. I agreed that it was undesirable he should do so." The Foreign Secretary informed Teheran that Major Stokes had been appointed without consulting Great Britain; that his employment in the North might involve political difficulties, and that he could not deprecate Russian objections to it. Sir George Buchanan reported that the Russian Press was now thoroughly excited. "We cannot prevent Stokes serving Persia," replied Sir Edward Grey, "but Russia is entitled to object to his employ in the North." The Foreign Secretary had now completely adopted the Russian standpoint. "Warn Persia to drop Stokes unless they intend not to employ him in the North," he telegraphed to Teheran. A few days later, the Persian Government was informed that we could not accept Stokes' resignation of his rank in the Indian army.

While the Stokes crisis was running its course, a formidable danger threatened the Constitutional régime in Persia. In January, 1911, Sir Francis Bertie, the British Ambassador at Paris, was informed by his Persian colleague that the ex-Shah had been there, and that he would probably attempt to regain the Throne. Sir Edward promptly warned Sazonoff, but no precautions were taken, and on July 18th the ex-Shah landed in North Persia from a Russian steamer. Sir Edward Grey was for once thoroughly roused. "I do not see how we or Russia can acquiesce in his return," he telegraphed to Sir G. Buchanan. "Ask if she will notify him that under no circumstances can his return be allowed. We will gladly join." Neratoff replied that there was now a new situation. The ex-Shah had burnt his boats and must pursue his enterprise to the bitter end. It was useless to make any communication to him, as he would take no notice. The British proposal of a joint veto was finally whittled down to a colourless communication. "As the ex-Shah has returned, contrary to advice repeatedly given by the British and Russian Governments to abstain from any intrigue in Persia, they recognise that he has forfeited his pension. Since, however, he is in Persian territory, they cannot interfere." On August 11th the Russian Minister declared that the ex-Shah would soon be in Teheran; but the situation was saved at the eleventh hour by Ephrem, who defeated the rebels forty miles from the capital.

No sooner was this danger over than a new crisis arose. The estates of a brother of the ex-Shah having been confiscated by the Government, Mr Shuster was ordered to transfer the property to the Treasury. On proceeding to seize the palace in Teheran, his agents were driven off by officers of the Russian Consulate and armed Cossacks. "I therefore told the Russian Minister," relates Mr Shuster, "that I should send next day to take possession, and my assistant did so with one hundred gendarmes. A lying report was sent to Petrograd by the Consul." At the same time, Russia protested against the despatch of Mr Lecoffre, a British subject, to Tabriz to inspect the finances, though he had long worked in Teheran, which was also in the Russian sphere of influence. Mr Shuster could no longer control his indignation, and in interviews taxed the Russian and British Governments with unfriendliness to reform. When *The Times* declared the charge unfounded, he drew up an Open Letter, which was printed in that journal on November 10th and 11th. Russia's opportunity had now come. The Russian Minister demanded the withdrawal of the Treasury gendarmes from the park of the ex-Shah's brother and an apology for the "insult" to the Consul. Sir Edward Grey advised Teheran to tender the required apology, for these incidents had convinced him that Mr Shuster must go. He informed Petrograd that he would not oppose a demand for his dismissal, adding that he had given him endless trouble by his appointment of British subjects. On November 18th, the Russian Legation announced the rupture of diplomatic relations, since the demands had not been accepted. The Persian Cabinet now ordered Mr Shuster to withdraw his gendarmes, and the Foreign Minister apologised to the Russian Minister "for the affront to the Consular officers."

The drama in Teheran was witnessed with indignation by the British friends of Persian reform. It had been the policy of Russia, cried Mr Dillon, to make the government of Persia impossible, so as to have an excuse to come in; and Great Britain had condoned every step she had taken. Russian actions made the regeneration of Persia almost impossible, echoed Lord Ronaldshay from the Conservative benches. Persia ought to have a fair chance. The Foreign Secretary opened his reply by reminding his hearers of the Anglo-Russian Convention.

"Its object was to prevent the two nations mining and countermining against each other, and to end the constant friction; and it has done so. Both have loyally observed the bond. If it were upset, we should have large problems in place of these small problems. I am quite certain that Mr Shuster set about his task with ability and good intentions. He had no political axe to grind, and he was quite innocent of any political intrigue. But he took no account of the peculiar political considerations which underlie the Anglo-Russian Agreement....How can I, with the best intentions in the world, promote a settlement when there is an official publicly making attacks on the Russian Government? The independence of Persia must take account of the interests of her neighbours, and her hostility to Russia is unjustified by facts. If the Russian officers in Teheran had intervened on behalf of the ex-Shah, he would never have been turned out. But the Persian Government, having got rid of the Shah, determined to get rid of Russian influence in Persia. That was a perfectly hopeless policy to adopt....Having got rid of the Shah, Persia ought at once to have assumed a friendly spirit towards Russia, and, had they done so, I believe things would have worked well. Without the Anglo-Russian Agreement the independence of Persia would have been infinitely more threatened than today, and the relations of England and Russia imperilled."

On November 29th, two days after this debate, Russia launched a second ultimatum, demanding within forty-eight hours the dismissal of Mr Shuster and Mr Lecoffre; a pledge to engage no foreigners without the consent of the Russian and British Legations; and payment for the troops now on the march. Mr Shuster was consulted and advised submission. The Cabinet yielded; but the Mejliss, helpless though it was, unanimously refused, and was dissolved. The eight months of Mr Shuster's Mission were at an end; and when he drove northwards to the Caspian Persia lost the best friend she possessed. "I am very glad that M. Neratoff approves my speech," wrote Sir Edward Grey on December 1st. "But I am much concerned at the new development in Persia. There are apparently to be new demands. If Russia were compelled to apply force to secure acceptance of the three new demands, it would be a great pity." Next day, Benckendorff visited the Foreign Office, and found the Foreign Secretary in very serious mood[1]. He regretted the new demands, especially that for compensation. If cooperation in Persia

[1] Siebert, *Diplomatische Aktenstücke*, pp. 239–44.

ceased, he argued, it would mean the breach of the *entente* and a new orientation of British policy, which would occur on the day when he informed Parliament that complete agreement no longer existed. In that case he must resign, as he could not strike out the new line of policy which would become inevitable. The Ambassador reported that he had never seen the Foreign Secretary so disturbed, a verdict that was confirmed by the French Ambassador. "To maintain the Entente in England," added Benckendorff, "we must assure him that we will observe the Convention; otherwise it is certain that he will resign."

When the debate was resumed on December 14th, the situation was easier, and the Foreign Secretary defined his attitude to the new demands. He could not object to the dismissal of Mr Shuster. "I quite admit his ability and his good intentions; but you.cannot have the spirit of the Anglo-Russian Agreement upset and two great nations embroiled by the action of any individual." Nor could he object to the demand that the British and Russian Legations should be consulted in the appointment of foreign advisers. The demand for the indemnity, on the other hand, would doubtless be withdrawn. His own Persian policy was summarised in six points which he had presented to Russia:

1. A Government that will conform to the principles of 1907.
2. The exclusion of the ex-Shah.
3. The selection of a financial adviser acceptable to both Powers
4. A loan to restore order.
5. An indemnity not to be pressed.
6. Russian troops to withdraw when Russian demands are complied with and order restored in the North.

Sir Edward Grey's Persian policy from beginning to end was non-intervention and friendship with Russia; and, if the two objects clashed, the former had to yield. "If the Persian question was mismanaged," he argued, "the Persian question might disappear, and bigger issues would arise." It was this conviction which governed his action in the Shuster crisis, and it was this subordination of purely Persian interests to the demands of the European situation which divided him from his critics.

"The Foreign Secretary," complained Mr Ponsonby bitterly, "always seemed to consider what Russia thought and to disregard the feelings of Persia. I, too, am for observing the spirit of the Convention of 1907; but Russia has broken it. Sir Edward does not sufficiently take into account

that Persia is trying to work out her own salvation. We are playing second
fiddle to Russia. We complain of Agadir, but not of Fez, Tripoli or
Kazvin."

As a matter of fact he did complain of Kazvin; but Petrograd was
never afraid of British protests. "The English," wrote Sazonoff in a
revealing letter to the Russian Minister in Teheran on October 8th,
1910, "pursuing as they do vital aims in Europe, will if necessary
sacrifice certain interests in Asia in order to maintain the Convention
with us. These circumstances we can naturally turn to our own
advantage, for instance in our Persian policy[1]." When Mr Shuster
had gone, Anglo-Russian harmony was not again disturbed, for Persia
ceased to struggle against the chains which bound her to her two
formidable guardians.

V. The Congo Again, 1907–1913

Among the lesser, though not less difficult, tasks of the Cabinet
was the campaign for reform in the Congo Free State[2]. British opinion
had demanded its cession to Belgium; but the *Fondation de la
Couronne* was maintained with all its privileges intact and its profits
secured to the Royal Family, and the acquired rights of third parties
were likewise preserved.

The Draft Treaty of November 18th, 1907, aroused astonishment
within and without Belgium. "My Government are fully aware of
the great anxiety felt with regard to the treatment of natives": so
ran the King's Speech at Westminster on January 29th, 1908. "Their
sole desire is to see the Government of that State humanely administered in accordance with the spirit of the Berlin Act, and I trust
that the negotiations between the Sovereign of the Congo State and
the Belgian Government will secure that object." The Lord Mayor
presided at a meeting at the Queen's Hall on February 21st, which
resolved that no annexation could be recognised which did not restore
to the natives their rights in land and trade. On February 24th, the
House of Lords gave free vent to the indignation of British reformers,
and Lord Cromer declared that he had never seen or heard of anything comparable to these abuses. The gravity of the situation was
fully recognised by Lord Fitzmaurice, who announced the appointment of a third Vice-Consul, and expressed approval of an International River Commission. Of much greater importance was the fact

---

[1] Siebert, p. 206.
[2] This section is based on the Blue-books, which continue to be very numerous.

that the Ministers of the United States and the United Kingdom were now cooperating in Brussels. "The Government," he concluded, "view the present situation with anxiety. These debates cannot go on for ever with no result. We could not accept any arrangement which did not secure the vindication of treaty rights and the claims of humanity." "The position," echoed Lord Lansdowne from the Opposition benches, "is intolerable. We all favour a transfer; but it must be complete....I hope this debate will convince the Government and people of Belgium that the Government and people of Great Britain are determined that an end shall be put to a condition of things they have long regarded with feelings of abhorrence and shame."

Two days later, the House of Commons gave vent to similar indignation. Mr Leif Jones, who opened the discussion, reminded his hearers that this was the ninth debate on the subject in five years. The Consular reports were terrible. The natives spent about twenty days in the month collecting rubber. The population dwindled, and the resources of the country—rubber, stock, food—were decreasing. It was the murder of a race. Belgium, replied the Foreign Secretary, had no responsibility for these horrors, and she would feel as strongly as ourselves when she knew the facts.

"I do not believe Belgium will accept responsibility without full control. Given real Parliamentary control, the results we desire will follow. We cannot intervene officially in the present discussion. When the Belgian Government proposes its scheme, we can speak. I welcome more than I can say the cooperation of the United States. The American Consul-general's Report confirms that the State has morally forfeited every right to international recognition."

These vigorous speeches were hotly resented by King Leopold, who bade us mind our own business.

On March 27th, the Foreign Secretary submitted views for the friendly consideration of the Belgian Government.

"We have every confidence in the earnest desire of the Belgian Government to introduce far-reaching reforms, and are anxious to abstain from interference; but we must in fairness say that the existing administration has not fulfilled the Treaties, and therefore requires changes, including the relief of natives from excessive taxation, the grant to them of sufficient land to obtain the food they require and sufficient produce to buy and sell, and the possibility for traders to acquire land for factories, so as to establish direct trade relations with the inhabitants. We are surprised at the intention to maintain the rights of the *Concessionaire* Companies, which cover three-fifths of the State, and thereby to prevent freedom of trade and the amelioration of the lot of the natives. We therefore advise the introduction of a currency as a proper standard of value, the abolition of compulsory labour without pay, and a large increase of the land allotted to natives."

The Belgian Government replied that it was no less anxious to improve the lot of the natives. A currency would be introduced as soon as possible, taxation reduced, labour remunerated, and natives established on land which would belong to them. New arrangements would be made with the *Concessionaire* Companies, and the Government promised an immediate amelioration in the moral and material conditions of the natives and the extension, as rapidly as possible, of economic freedom. Sir Edward promptly expressed his liveliest satisfaction at these assurances. Throughout the negotiations, he added, the most friendly sentiments had been entertained towards the Belgian Government and people.

The Foreign Secretary was soon to learn that he had been a little too sanguine in differentiating so sharply between the King and the Belgian Government; for, with the exception of *Le Peuple*, the official organ of the Socialists, one Catholic and one Liberal paper, the Belgian Press was hostile to the British reform movement, arguing that Belgium was her own mistress. Though the clauses in the Treaty maintaining the *Fondation de la Couronne* were annulled, the King was amply compensated for its surrender; and Belgium agreed to respect the concessions included in the *Fondation* granted to Companies in which the Congo State had large holdings. On November 14th, 1908, the Congo State ceased to exist, and its administration was vested in the newly-created Ministry of the Colonies. The transfer was promptly recognised by Germany and France; but a further struggle was necessary before the British Government would relax its frown.

When the decisive step had been taken, the Foreign Secretary stated his attitude in a firm despatch dated November 1st. He reiterated the right of Great Britain to guarantees that the new Administration should not repeat the fatal errors of the old, and demanded that the grievances should be remedied within a reasonable time. A despatch from the Government of the United States, dated January 11th, 1909, reiterated the British demands. King Leopold, however, was still on the Throne, and the passive resistance of the two Powers was treated with indifference. A Blue-book, presented to Parliament in January, 1909, containing the Consular Reports of 1908, revealed the continuance of illegal methods and the cutting down of rubber trees. The Belgian reply to the British despatch of November 1st, 1908, dated March 15th, 1909, renewed conciliatory assurances, pointed out that in four months little could be done, and asked for sympathy and confidence. On June 11th, Sir Edward Grey replied that he was anxious to recognise annexation, but that he must first be satisfied that the abuses of taxation and forced labour had ceased.

On the occasion of the Whitsuntide adjournment, the British reformers loudly expressed their disappointment. We had been overcautious, declared Sir Charles Dilke, and the position was the same as five years ago. No fear of European complications need affect our policy. Our difficulties were increased by annexation, echoed another angry member. We had been bluffed. Belgium did not care whether we recognised the annexation or not. We ought to send a gunboat to blockade the Congo, and occupy the custom-house at Boma. The impatience of his critics had the usual effect of cooling instead of heating the blood of the Foreign Secretary. "If this question is rashly handled," he replied, "it might grow into a European question compared to which those we have recently had to deal with (Bosnia) might be child's play. We are now drawing up a reply to the Belgian reply, which was satisfactory in principle but vague in details." Two months later, on the Foreign Office vote on July 22nd, the critics returned to the charge. Sir Charles Dilke detected signs of weakening in the British attitude, caused by an undue terror of the risks. The Belgians treated us with lofty scorn in their debates and despatches, and they had suggested that annexation released them from international obligations. Sir George White asked what had brought about our change of attitude. There was no weakening, replied the Foreign Secretary. Indeed, the Belgian Government had complained that the strong language published by our Government was impairing good relations.

"Sir Arthur Hardinge, on my orders, said it was our habit to publish facts, and that criticism of things before the annexation should not harm our relations. We only desired the Government should have a fair start. I said to the Belgian Minister that the Government was not responsible for the Congo Reform Association, but that it represented very deep feeling which would remain till reform was accomplished. We do not forego our rights to take action; but we say the Belgian Government should have more time to make their intentions clear. Their Colonial Minister is now in the Congo, and they and we must wait for his proposals. To have stepped in now and said we would wait no longer would be generally regarded as premature. But, till the system of forced labour ends, we cannot recognise annexation. There are British subjects with their treaty rights to trade in the Congo; and a most serious *impasse* would arise if some question concerning them cropped up. To defer recognition is a serious embarrassment to Belgium and to ourselves. I am most anxious to see the question settled not only on humanitarian grounds, but to preserve friendly relations."

On the return of the Colonial Minister from Africa the Belgian Government, on March 22nd, 1910, issued a Decree abolishing forced labour and restoring the right to the natives of collecting and selling the produce of the soil in three zones, to be opened successively in July, 1910, 1911 and 1912. At last, the end seemed in sight. A Consular Report in October recorded improvement. "Missionaries and traders say the natives are better treated since the Reform Decrees came into force on July 1st. The former régime is undergoing a radical change. Taxes are often paid in money, and natives may sell their produce. I cannot see why forced labour should not be abolished everywhere in 1911—were it not for the budget." The British Minister at Brussels gently suggested the shortening of the three stages before complete freedom of trade was attained, but received the reply that the previous system could not be abolished at a blow. Early in 1911, Sir Edward Grey announced that, where the old system was discarded, the improvement was so rapid that we would recognise annexation as soon as the whole area was opened to trade. The death of King Leopold II at the end of 1910 removed an obstacle, and in the same year the abolition of the *Concessionaire* system in the French Congo revealed that the old régime was passing away.

In forwarding a Report on the year 1911, Consul Lamont emphasised "the very different standard of policy from the commercialism hitherto encouraged." Systematic brutality had disappeared; but there were still dangers from the quasi-commercial character of the administration; many of the old officials were still in control, and contract labour on the plantations was largely "impressed." In February, 1912, the Belgian Government expressed the hope that Great Britain would at last recognise annexation, as in July Free Trade would prevail throughout the country. From another quarter, Sir Edward Grey was adjured not to hurry. The Baptist Missionary Society put forth a warning against recognition till the rights of natives to dispose freely of their labour and produce should have been guaranteed, the reforms made irrevocable, and the rights of missions secured. The Congo Reform Association added that, in regard to native rights in the land, the position remained as insecure as ever. The Edicts of 1891–2 were unrepealed, and the natives only possessed land within the village boundaries, and could not develop their industries. Access to land was the main need, and it must be secured before recognition. Sir Edward proceeded to enquire at Brussels, and received the reply that, if the natives asked for land to cultivate for profit, they might obtain it without payment.

By May, 1913, the execrable system of King Leopold had vanished. The *Concessionaire* Companies had disappeared or lost their privileges. The tax on rubber had been abolished, and Free Trade prevailed over the greater part of the Congo, the fortunes of which were now in the hands of the Belgian nation. Mr Morel now announced that, "in view of the immense and steady improvement," the Congo Reform Association would no longer oppose recognition. With such a certificate from the chief guardian of native interests, Sir Edward hesitated no longer, and, on May 29th, he announced British recognition of the transfer of sovereignty effected five years earlier. A final meeting of the Congo Reform Association was held at the Westminster Palace Hotel, and the story of a long campaign ended with tributes to the Liverpool clerk who had rescued millions of African natives from a cruel and degrading servitude.

VI. The German Fleet, 1909–1911

British relations with Germany in the earlier stages of the Bosnian crisis were less strained than with Austria, since, as every one was aware, she had to stand by her Ally. The inevitable friction was eased by the official journey of the King and Queen to Berlin in February, 1909, the novel feature of which was the King's visit to the *Rathaus*, where he spoke gratefully of his "splendid reception" by the municipality. "He made a specially favourable impression on the City Fathers," testifies Mr Hill, the American Ambassador. "His simplicity, his good humour, and his straightforwardness were remarked upon. Socially, the visit was a pleasant event; but, politically, it may be doubted if it was of the slightest value[1]." Controversial topics were studiously avoided.

"Hardinge tells me," reported the Russian Chargé in London to Izvolsky, "that the reception by the Kaiser and the people was very warm, and the few political conversations he had with Bülow and Schön were friendly. They were, however, quite general, and therefore the visit has not led to

[1] D. J. Hill, *Impressions of the Kaiser*, pp. 105–7.

any concrete results. The Fleet and Bagdad were not mentioned. Bülow blamed Aehrenthal's methods, and lamented Germany's obligation to support her Ally even when she could not agree. He expressed pleasure at the Morocco Agreement and emphasised German peacefulness. England is satisfied that Germany is pacific."

The Report was confirmed by the Russian Ambassador at Berlin, who learned from Schön that there was no word of politics between the Kaiser and the King, and that the conversation of Bülow and Hardinge dealt mainly with the Balkans[1]. The King's Speech on the opening of Parliament declared that he was much impressed and gratified by the warmth of his reception by all classes of the community.

"In its extremely harmonious course," echoed the Chancellor, "it was a happy event. The warm welcome they received here and the King's words of sincere love of peace and friendship—repeated in the King's Speech and in the debate on the Address—have shewn once again to both peoples how much cause they have to respect each other and to cooperate in peaceful work. Germany is England's best customer, and England is ours."

A few days before German pressure at Petrograd ended the Bosnian crisis, British nerves received an unexpected shock. The Navy Law of 1908, reducing the life of capital ships from 25 to 20 years, conformed to the general practice and excited no alarm in Whitehall; but, in the autumn, the Admiralty learned that the German naval programme of 1909–10 was being anticipated. The Admiralty's proposal for meeting the new German Navy Bill was, accordingly, to lay down six Dreadnoughts in 1909–10, and a similar number in the two succeeding years. A battle raged within and without the Cabinet, Mr Lloyd George and Mr Churchill fighting for four capital ships; but Mr McKenna emerged victorious, for his defeat would have involved the resignation of the Foreign Secretary. The Estimates were indeed for four, but it was added that the Government "might find it necessary to make preparations for the rapid construction of four more large armoured ships." Thus, the Admiralty, in the guise of a compromise, obtained power to build two more than they originally proposed. Mysterious whispers of coming trouble had filled the lobbies during the opening weeks of the session; but few were prepared for the dramatic scene when the First Lord of the Admiralty rose on March 16th, 1909. For the first time, the Estimates were defended by selecting Germany as the standard by

Siebert, *Diplomatische Aktenstücke*, pp. 723–7.

which to measure our requirements; and British and German Dreadnoughts were balanced against each other down the vista of the
coming years. Germany might have 13 in 1911 to our 16; and, if
she again accelerated her programme, she might have 17 to our 16
in April, 1912, and would, in any case, have 17 in the autumn of
1912. The Government, therefore, asked for power to build four
extra ships if the suspected acceleration took place, thus providing us
with 20 to 17 in March, 1912. Mr Balfour made his hearers' flesh
creep by suggesting that our rival might possess 25 ships in 1912.
The Prime-Minister, while rejecting the exaggerations of the Leader
of the Opposition, confessed that 17 ships in April, 1912, were a
possibility, and 13 a certainty.

"The effect produced by these speeches on the House of Commons,"
writes a witness of the scene, "was simply overwhelming[1]. When Mr
Asquith sat down, no one rose to speak, and the vote would have been put
from the Chair without further discussion, had not a well-known "crank"
caught the Speaker's eye. Mr McKenna had indeed secured the safe
passage of his Estimates, including the four contingent Dreadnoughts; but
he had proved almost too much, and had created a first-class naval scare."

A wave of panic swept over the country. Men began to speak openly
of war as possible and even probable, and the legend of stealthy
acceleration seemed proof positive of a fell design to wrest the trident
from Britannia's hands. A few days later, the Prime-Minister felt it
his duty to pour oil on the troubled waters, and rebuked the Opposition for "an artificial and manufactured anxiety"; but the panic was
due far more to the figures and foreboding of himself and his lieutenant than to the dirges of unofficial critics.

When the dragon's teeth had been sown, Sir Edward Grey
accepted the explanations and assurances—"some vouchsafed before
March 16th, but more precisely after it"—that there had been no
acceleration in the date for the completion of the German vessels.
But the public continued to believe that Germany had tried to steal
a march on her rival. The political result of the crisis was deplorable;
but the British Navy profited by the panic, for six of the eight vessels
of our 1909–10 programme were super-Dreadnoughts, with 13·5 inch
instead of 12 inch guns. This smart stroke delayed the construction of the German vessels that had already been laid down, and,
when the danger-point of the spring of 1912 was reached, Germany
possessed, not the thirteen monsters which Mr Asquith had foretold

[1] Roch, *Mr Lloyd George and the War*, p. 28.

as a certainty, but nine. Mr McKenna, on the other hand, followed up his eight Dreadnoughts by five in each of the two succeeding years, thus completing in his three years of office the programme of eighteen which he had originally proposed.

On the day on which Bülow was disclaiming acceleration, Mr Arthur (now Lord) Lee moved a Vote of Censure on the Government for not at once laying down eight Dreadnoughts. In a weighty speech, the Foreign Secretary replied that he was not sure that the four extra ships would be required, and that, in any case, they need not be ordered before July, as they could not be completed any sooner. But he made no attempt to disguise the serious nature of the problem.

"A new situation in this country is created by the German programme, whether it is carried out quickly or slowly. When it is completed, Germany will have a fleet of 33 Dreadnoughts—the most powerful the world has ever seen. That imposes on us the necessity, of which we are now at the beginning—except so far as we have Dreadnoughts already—of rebuilding the whole of our fleet."

Passing to the political aspect of the problem, he spoke calmly and hopefully. Algeciras was a period of tension; but, since then, diplomatic relations had proceeded perfectly smoothly, and the new Agreement between Germany and France had removed the fear that the Morocco barrier might be reerected. "As regards our future, I see a wide space in which both of us may walk in peace and amity. Two things would produce conflict. One is an attempt by us to isolate Germany. The other is the isolation of England attempted by any Great Continental Power so as to dominate and dictate the policy of the Continent." There was no reason to apprehend either the one or the other. The naval rivalry was the only obstacle to confidence. There had been frank and informal discussions. We had told Germany that the Navy was to us what the Army was to her.

"The German view of their programme is that it is made for their own needs and has no reference to ours; that, if we build fifty or a hundred, they will not build more, and, if we cease building, they will not build less. Our view is that our expenditure is and must be dependent upon the German, though the German is not dependent upon ours. It is essential that we should keep a position of superiority....If I was asked to name the one thing which would most reassure Europe with regard to the prospects of peace, I think it would be that the naval expenditure in Germany would be diminished and that ours was following suit."

The speech concluded with the sensible suggestion that future panics should be obviated by the Admiralties exchanging information and providing facilities for inspection by Naval Attachés; but the proposal was declined by the German Government.

Despite a bitter outcry from Mr Churchill, in a published letter to his constituents on April 15th, denying the existence of danger in view of "our tremendous margins of safety," it was announced in July that the four contingent Dreadnoughts would be laid down; and the decision was received almost without protest. In vain did the Chancellor of the Exchequer, with his heart in his Land Values Budget, protest against the prevailing excitement.

"I predict that, even if the Budget goes through, another concerted effort will be made to rouse a fresh naval and military panic, so as to rush the Government into the criminal extravagance of unnecessary armaments by land and sea. There will be the usual crop of rumours about German plans and preparations. We know how little foundation existed for the last scare. In the light of established facts the fright which shook Britain and convulsed the Colonies looks rather foolish[1]."

The protest was unavailing. "Armaments are increasing," declared Lord Rosebery in an impressive speech at a banquet to Colonial journalists on July 9th; "this calm before the storm is terrifying." The rejection by the House of Lords of the Declaration of London, which had been drawn up during the winter by naval experts to assist the projected Appeal Prize-Court at the Hague, was due to the growing apprehension in Conservative circles that Great Britain might before long find herself at war, and should not surrender any belligerent rights.

Though Bethmann-Hollweg was powerless to alter the course of the ship when he succeeded Bülow in July, 1909, a more accommodating spirit entered the Wilhelmstrasse. The new Chancellor was convinced of the goodwill of the British Government, and determined on a frank interchange of views. He declares that he found no obstacle in the highest quarter.

"As we could not dissolve the Franco-Russian partnership, we could only obviate its danger by an understanding with England. Not only did the Kaiser agree with this view, but he repeatedly indicated it to me as the only possible policy. In the opening days of August I began discussions on the fleet with Sir E. Goschen. I found him rather sceptical, and never at any time zealous for a *rapprochement*. At any rate, he was much cooler than his predecessor, who was a convinced champion of an understanding. The negotiations led to no result, as the London Cabinet hardly showed interest in their success, and no formula was found to satisfy the Admiralties[2].

---

[1] *The Nation*, October 30th, 1909.
[2] *Betrachtungen zum Weltkriege*, vol. I. ch. 2.

" The Chancellor sent for the British Ambassador," relates Sir E. Cook, "to whom he said that he perceived that the naval question was regarded by Great Britain as the chief obstacle to really cordial relations between the two countries; that the German Government were now ready to make proposals for a naval arrangement, but that discussion on that subject could profitably be undertaken only as part of a general understanding based on a conviction that neither country had hostile or aggressive designs against the other[1]. The British Government were naturally much gratified by the Chancellor's messages, and met his overtures cordially. The naval question was the dominant one for them; but they were ready to consider with the utmost sympathy any proposals for a general understanding so long as these were not inconsistent with Britain's existing obligations to other foreign Powers. The naval proposals made by Bethmann-Hollweg were somewhat vague. There could be no question, it was explained, of any departure from the German Navy Law as a whole, since any such would meet with insuperable opposition in the *Reichstag*; but the German Government were willing to discuss the question of 'retarding the rate' of building new ships. Precise explanation of this formula was not forthcoming. What was understood to be meant was that the total number of ships to be completed by 1918 would not be reduced, but that the number of capital ships might be reduced in the earlier years and equivalently raised in the later. There was, it will be seen, to be no ultimate reduction of expenditure, and no definite reduction of the total German programme.

The basis of naval negotiation suggested by the Chancellor was thus undefined, slender, shadowy. The *quid pro quo* which he required for it was positive and substantial. Great Britain was to be a party to an agreement declaring that (1) neither country had any idea of aggression, and that neither in fact would attack the other; and (2) that, in the event of an attack made on either Power by a third Power or group of Powers, the Power not attacked should stand aside. To the first condition there was and could be no objection; to the second the objection from the British point of view was serious. If Great Britain accepted the German condition, it became practically certain, owing to the general position of the European Powers, that she would be bound to stand aside from any Continental struggle. In any such struggle Germany could arrange without difficulty that the formal inception of hostilities should rest with Austria. If Austria and Russia were at war, Germany was pledged to support Austria; while, as soon as Russia was attacked by two Powers, France was bound to come to her assistance. The giving of the pledge proposed by the German Government would, therefore, prevent Great Britain from supporting France, no matter what the reasons of the conflict or its results might be. Thus French trust and goodwill would be forfeited, since Great Britain could be of no assistance to France, should Germany determine to press to the ultimate issue of war any demands she might choose to make. It could not be overlooked by Ministers acting as trustees for their country's future that the period of forced British neutrality, involved in the Chan-

---

[1] *How Britain strove for Peace.*

cellor's proposals, might be used by Germany strenuously to consolidate her supremacy in Continental Europe. Great Britain would be a paralysed spectator until Germany were free to devote undivided strength to reducing her. Moreover, the German proposal involved, in the second place, a repudiation in certain events of Great Britain's treaty obligations to Belgium. Suppose Germany in a war with France were to invade Belgium, Great Britain would have been prevented by this proposed agreement with Germany from vindicating Belgium's neutrality. It is not surprising, therefore, that in the autumn of 1909 the British Government declined the German Government's proposal. Politically, it was open to the gravest objections, and on the naval side it offered no substantial reduction of expenditure."

In May, 1910, the Kaiser came to London for King Edward's funeral, and his manifest sympathy was warmly appreciated. Negotiations were resumed in the summer, the course of which was subsequently described by Sir Edward Cook.

"Speaking in Parliament in July, 1910, Mr Asquith said: 'We have approached the German Government. They have found themselves unable to do anything. They cannot, without an Act of Parliament, repeal their Naval Law. They tell us, and no doubt with great truth, they would not have the support of public opinion in Germany to a modified programme.' The German Chancellor replied to this speech that the German Government had not opposed a *non possumus* to the British approaches; they could not agree to reduce naval construction, but they were ready to discuss temporary retardation. The precise meaning of this proposal was, again, not defined; but the British Government at once responded to the overtures, and in August, abandoning their previous contention that any naval agreement must be based upon a reduction of the existing German naval programme, they intimated their readiness (1) to discuss the suggestion of 'temporary retardation'; (2) to negotiate a naval agreement on the basis that the existing German programme should not be increased, and that information should be exchanged with regard to the actual progress of ship-building in each country; (3) with regard to a political understanding, to give assurances that in any agreement between themselves and any other Power there was nothing directed against Germany, and that they themselves had no hostile intentions respecting her.

The reply of the German Government was received in October and negotiations continued till the spring of 1911.

(1) With regard to 'temporary retardation,' this proposal, upon which the German Chancellor had relied to justify his denial of a *non possumus* attitude, was withdrawn in May, 1911—a withdrawal which was strange, since the reason given (namely, the importance of feeding the shipbuilding industry with a definite quantity of Government orders) would have been equally cogent against the offer when first made.

(2) With regard to the negotiation of a naval agreement on the basis of no increase in the German programme and of exchange of information,

the German Government agreed to discuss the latter subject. Negotiations continued for many months, and the final British Memorandum, accepting the German conditions on all essential points, was communicated at the end of January, 1911. As for the basis of no increase in the German programme, the German Government in October, 1910, asked what equivalent engagement would be made by Great Britain. The British Government were considering their reply, when the German Emperor informed the British Ambassador that he would on no account ever consent to any agreement binding Germany not to enlarge her naval programme. The discrepancy thus apparent between the attitude of the Emperor and the Chancellor respectively was not cleared up; but in May, 1911, the German Government intimated their readiness to examine any proposals for a mutual reduction of expenditure on armaments not involving a departure from the requirements of the Navy Law. The withdrawal at the same time of the offer of temporary retardation did not inspire confidence; and the professed readiness of the German Government to negotiate a naval agreement on a fresh basis had been preceded by a very uncompromising official declaration in the *Reichstag*.

On March 13th, 1911, Sir Edward Grey made a speech in Parliament indicating between the lines the course of negotiations with Germany, defining the limits within which alone those negotiations could hopefully proceed, and declaring it to be a paradox that while sentiments of friendship were sincere armaments should increase. This speech met with a favourable reception in the German Press; but, on the subject coming up in the *Reichstag*, the Chancellor took occasion to apply cold water. 'I consider,' he said, 'any control as absolutely impracticable, and every attempt in that direction would lead to nothing but continual mutual distrust and perpetual friction. Who would be content to weaken his means of defence without the absolute certainty that his neighbour was not secretly exceeding the proportion allowed to him in the disarmament agreement? No, gentlemen, anyone who seriously considers the question of universal disarmament must inevitably come to the conclusion that it is insoluble so long as men are men and States are States.'

(3) While Germany was thus alternately coming forward and drawing back on the naval side of the negotiations with England, the German Government continued to attach great importance to a political understanding. They laid emphasis on this point in their reply of October, 1910; and when negotiations were resumed after the General Election in this country, the British Government assented to the German view that some wider agreement of a political nature should be a condition precedent to a naval arrangement, and submitted suggestions as a basis for discussing such a political agreement. An arrangement, as foreshadowed by the Imperial Chancellor, embodying a general political formula, might be considered more comprehensive, far-reaching, and intimate than any Arrangement, short of actual alliance, that England had concluded with any other Power; and such an arrangement, therefore, might cause misunderstanding in France and Russia. The British Agreements with France

and with Russia were not based on a general political formula; they were settlements of specific questions; and the settlements had transformed relations of friction and pinpricks into friendship. There was nothing exclusive in those friendships, and the British Government had seen with satisfaction the settlement of some questions between France and Germany, and between Russia and Germany. Why should not something of the same kind be attempted between England and Germany? The reply of the German Government (May, 1911) to these suggestions seemed not unfavourable, though the withdrawal of the previous naval offer was discouraging. The German Government declared that the British suggestions might form a suitable basis for an agreement, though they repeated their preference for a general political formula."

The underlying difference between the standpoint of the two nations was revealed in Sir Edward Grey's ready welcome to President Taft's arbitration proposals.

"He has sketched a step in advance more momentous than any practical statesman in his position has ventured to make before, for he is willing to refer questions of national honour. Suppose two of the greatest nations made it clear that by such an agreement they would under no circumstances go to war again. It would probably lead to an agreement to join each other if a third Power refused arbitration. Great risks would require, not only the signature of both Governments, but the deliberate sanction of Parliament. The great nations are in increasing bondage to their armies and navies."

The speech created world-wide interest, but was regarded in Germany as purely Utopian.

While the diplomatic barometer thus remained unsteady, the Cabinet quietly continued to prepare the country to meet a possible attack. In January, 1911, at the instigation of Mr (now Lord) Haldane, whose reorganisation of the Army was then almost complete, the Prime-Minister appointed a Standing Sub-Committee of the Committee of Imperial Defence for "the coordination of Departmental Action on the outbreak of war[1]." A "War-Book" was compiled, in which each Department had its own chapter arranged on an identical plan in sections, each dealing severally with a phase of the transition from peace to war. By constant revision these details were carried to a high degree of precision. All necessary papers, Orders in Council and Proclamations were printed or set up in type; and so far was the system carried that the King never moved without those which required his immediate signature. A further precaution was taken, in 1912, in the decision to supply Cromarty and Scapa Flow with

[1] See Sir J. Corbett, *Naval Operations*, I. 18–22.

defences, Rosyth having become inadequate for the reception and defence of the Fleet.

Despite the failure to abate the naval rivalry, the Anglo-German tension seemed to be growing less acute. "Our relations are decidedly better," proclaimed Professor Schiemann in March, 1911. "The supposed plan of annihilating the German fleet may be regarded as non-existent." The Anglo-German Friendship Committee, founded in 1905, was merged in the Anglo-German Friendship Society at a meeting in the Mansion House on May 15th, 1911. Its chief promoters were its Chairman, Sir Frank Lascelles, for thirteen years British Ambassador at Berlin, and its President, Lord Avebury. Among its Vice-Presidents were a host of civil and ecclesiastical dignitaries, Generals and Admirals. A similar society was founded in Germany, largely owing to the efforts of Professor Sieper of Munich, with the ex-Ambassador, T. von Holleben, as President. In May the Kaiser accepted King George's invitation to attend the unveiling of the Memorial to Queen Victoria, and was received with the usual cordiality. "I observed with my own eyes," reported Count Lalaing, the Belgian Minister, "that the welcome of the public became warmer from day to day. The death of King Edward seems to have brought about a slight *détente* in Anglo-German relations[1]." Shortly afterwards, the Crown Prince attended the coronation of George V, and paid a round of visits to the nobility. But at this moment a rash resolve in the Foreign Office at Berlin sundered the two nations once again, and plunged Europe into a crisis even more acute than that of 1908.

VII. THE AGADIR CRISIS, 1907–1911

The Conference of Algeciras was followed by improvement neither in the relations between France and Germany nor in the internal conditions of Morocco[2]. In 1907, France entrenched herself at Ujda on the Algerian frontier and at Casablanca on the Atlantic; and, in 1908, a dispute about deserters from the Foreign Legion brought the countries to the verge of war. The controversy was

[1] May 22nd, 1911. Schwertfeger, *Zur Europäischen Politik*, III. 245–6.

[2] See *Affaires du Maroc*, 1906–1912, 4 vols.; Caillaux, *Agadir*; Tardieu, *La Conférence d'Algéciras* (edition of 1909); and *Le Mystère d'Agadir*; Louis Maurice (Bompard), *La Politique Marocaine de l'Allemagne*; Morel, *Morocco in Diplomacy*; *Un Livre Noir*, vol. I. The speeches of the Chancellor and the German Foreign Secretary are translated in the White Papers, Morocco, Nos. 1, 2, 3, 1911. Cf. Hammann, *Bilder aus der letzten Kaiserzeit*, 83–94 and 156–159.

referred to the Hague Tribunal; and early in 1909 an Agreement was signed by which Germany recognised "the special political interests" of France, and France undertook "not to obstruct German commercial and industrial interests." This economic partnership, which created high hopes in both countries, led to endless friction. Meanwhile, Morocco drifted towards anarchy; and, in April, 1911, the French Government announced an expedition to Fez, on the ground that the Sultan was powerless to defend himself or the European residents against insurgent tribes, and in spite of reiterated warnings from Berlin that the occupation of the capital would reopen the whole Moroccan problem.

While Germany and Spain regarded the march to Fez as the death-knell of the Algeciras Settlement, and the latter proceeded to occupy the zone assigned to her by the Secret Treaty of 1904, Sir Edward Grey accepted the assurances of Paris without question. On May 2nd, in answer to an enquiry whether he had been consulted concerning the military measures in Morocco and whether he approved the attack on its independence, he announced that France had informed the British Government, like the others, of the measures to succour the Europeans there. Her action, he added, did not aim at changing the political status of Morocco, and he saw no objection to it. He made the same reply to an enquiry by the German Ambassador. It was not only the right but the duty of France to succour the Europeans, and French intervention would be of benefit to the world[1]. Not content with thus publicly approving the action of France, he instructed the British Ambassador at Madrid to call the attention of the Government to the danger of Spanish action in Morocco, and invited it to announce that, if order continued in El-Kasr, the troops would be withdrawn to Larache, since France had declared that her troops would quit Fez as soon as possible.

Kiderlen-Wächter's wish, according to his friend Reventlow, had long been to wipe Morocco off the slate. He considered that Bülow's policy had been a failure, and he determined to meet French wishes in Morocco in return for colonial compensation. The expedition to Fez provided the opportunity for which he had waited, and he seized it with both hands. On July 1st, the German Ambassador at Paris informed the French Foreign Minister, de Selves, that the *Panther* had been sent to Agadir. In presenting the Note, he added that the Act of Algeciras was dead, and that Germany desired to eliminate

[1] Siebert, *Diplomatische Aktenstücke*, p. 417.

the Morocco question by friendly discussion. A despatch was communicated to all the Signatories of the Act of Algeciras.

"Some German firms established in the south of Morocco, notably at Agadir and in the vicinity, have been alarmed by a certain ferment among the local tribes, due, it seems, to recent occurrences in other parts of the country. These firms have applied to the Imperial Government for protection for their lives and property. At their request, the Government have decided to send a warship to Agadir to lend help in case of need to their subjects and *protégés* as well as to the considerable German interests in that territory. As soon as the state of affairs has resumed its normal tranquillity the ship will leave."

The news of the *Panther's* spring was received with even greater indignation and surprise in Downing Street than at the Quai d'Orsay; for the British Government was resolved, at all costs, to prevent Germany from securing a naval base in Morocco[1], and appears to have known little of the repeated warnings from Berlin when the troops set forth for Fez. "You are violating the Act of Algeciras," observed Sir Arthur Nicolson, who in the absence of the Foreign Secretary received the Ambassador. "That has already lost its validity," was the prompt reply. In communicating the *Aide-mémoire* to the British Government, Count Wolff-Metternich was furnished with an explanatory Memorandum.

"Though our information as to the position of the Europeans at Fez did not tally with that of the French, no objection was raised to the advance. A situation had meanwhile gradually arisen which rendered the Algeciras Act illusory. Whilst, for instance, a limited cooperation in the establishment of police under international control was granted to France and Spain in the open ports, similar institutions were now growing up under the direction of French officers at the most important points of the interior. It might appear questionable whether it would be possible to return to the *status quo* of 1906. We were therefore prepared, if it became necessary, to seek, in conjunction with France, some means, which would be compatible with the interests of the other Signatory Powers, of arriving at a definite understanding on the Morocco question. Direct negotiations could hardly meet with insuperable difficulties in view of the good relations between us and France."

Sir Edward Grey regarded the voyage of the *Panther* as an unprovoked attack on the *status quo*.

"The official communication," he declared on November 27th, "was accompanied by an explanation given to us at the same time, which seemed to me much more important than the actual communication of the sending

---

[1] Sir Francis Bertie, the British Ambassador in Paris, believed that Germany intended to seize a port. *Un Livre Noir*, I. 104.

of the ship....It made it clear that the German Government regarded a return to the *status quo* in Morocco as doubtful, if not impossible, and that what they contemplated was a definite solution of the Moroccan question between Germany, France, and Spain. The whole question, or at least the kernel of the question, after that communication was received, was: What was the definite solution of the Moroccan question which Germany contemplated? Was it to be the partition of Morocco? The communication was made to the Foreign Office on the Saturday. On the next Monday, July 3rd, I asked the German Ambassador to come and see me. I informed him I had seen the Prime-Minister, and that we considered the situation created by the despatch of the *Panther* to Agadir as so important that it must be discussed in a meeting of the Cabinet. The next day, I asked the German Ambassador to come and see me again, and said that I must tell him that our attitude could not be a disinterested one with regard to Morocco. We must take into consideration our Treaty obligations to France and our own interests in Morocco. We were of opinion that a new situation had been created by the despatch of a German ship to Agadir. Future developments might affect British interests more directly than they had hitherto been affected, and, therefore, we could not recognise any new arrangements that might be come to without us. I made it quite clear to the Ambassador that this communication, and the exact words which I used, were those of his Majesty's Government sitting in Cabinet."

The Ambassador replied that his Government had absolutely no wish to exclude England from the new arrangement of things, or to prevent any possible safeguarding of British interests in Morocco.

The Foreign Secretary made a simultaneous declaration to the French Ambassador.

"The British Government deems a discussion necessary between France, Germany, Spain and England. But before it opens the British Government must know what the French Government desires. For instance, the solution might be a return to the *status quo*, Germany retiring from Agadir, Spain from El-Kasr and Larache, and France from Fez and the interior. Or there might be a new arrangement consolidating the position of France, securing the assent of Germany by certain compensations. In that case, Great Britain would have to see what conditions were required in her own interests."

The Ambassador replied that the French had already left Fez, that the French Military Mission, dating from before Algeciras, did not constitute occupation, and that the posts in the interior were merely to supply the troops. Next day, the French Premier telegraphed that his Ministry would examine the solution to be proposed by Great Britain and ask her support for it in the discussions to which Germany invited them. "I must, however, make clear at once to the British

Government the impossibility of compensations in Morocco. Since Germany asks us to talk, she must tell us her wishes." After thus sounding France, the Prime-Minister stated the attitude of Great Britain, in reply to Mr Balfour on July 6th. Recent events were the subject of negotiation between the Powers most interested, and he wished it clearly to be understood that the Government considered that a new situation had arisen in Morocco, in which it was possible that future developments might affect British interests more directly than had been the case. He was confident that diplomatic discussion would find a solution, and in the part we should take in it we should have due regard to the promotion of those interests and to the fulfilment of our treaty obligations to France, which were well known to the House.

On July 9th, Kiderlen-Wächter and Jules Cambon began the conversations, which were to continue for four months. The German Foreign Minister declared himself ready to renounce territorial claims in Morocco, and asked for compensation in the Congo. It would be impossible, he added, to admit a third party to the discussions without inviting all the Signatories of the Treaty of Algeciras. The Ambassador did not demur, but remarked that France must keep her friends and allies informed. While these conversations were proceeding in Berlin, the British Government were waiting for news. Sir Edward Grey regarded his communication of July 4th as a request for information; but it had not been couched in an interrogatory form. "The declaration that Agadir created a new situation," declared the German Chancellor on December 5th, "did not appear to us an enquiry necessitating an answer." Both parties were, no doubt, to blame—Sir Edward Grey in not definitely asking for explanations, the German Government in failing to volunteer a reassuring statement. In the absence of direct communication suspicion was inevitable.

"After July 4th," declared the Foreign Secretary on November 27th, "there was a period of silence. The German Ambassador was not instructed to make any comment to me with regard to my communication, and we received no information from the German Government as to what their aims or desires were, or as to what they had in mind when they spoke of a definite solution of the Moroccan problem. Some information reached us from other quarters, leading us to apprehend that the settlement contemplated by the German Government might be a partition of Morocco, arrived at by negotiations to which it was not intended we should be a party. It is obvious, if the Moroccan question was to be reopened and a new settlement made, unless we were consulted,...the strategic and economic conditions stipulated for between ourselves, France and Spain in 1904 might be upset. On July 12th, the British Ambassador in Berlin had occasion to see the German Foreign Secretary on some minor matters, and took the opportunity to say that there had been at one time some mention of a conversation *à trois* between Germany, France and Spain, the inference being that we were to be excluded from it. The German Foreign Secretary told our Ambassador to inform us that there never had been any idea of such a conversation; and, except for this negative communication, we had no further information from the German Government of their views. A little later, it appeared in the Press—and indeed it was the case—that the German Government had made demands with regard to the French Congo of an extent to which it was obvious to everybody who thought of it that neither the French Government nor the French Chamber could agree. That at once made me anxious as to the development of the situation."

Sir Edward Grey here speaks as if he had been unaware that the French Government were in agreement with the German in excluding other Powers from their conversations, on condition that France reserved her right to inform her friends and allies of their course. When Spain asked the German Government to be allowed to take part, she was informed that Spanish interests would not be affected and that the sole object of the discussions was to remove Franco-German friction. A partition of Morocco, again, which haunted his mind, was never suggested by the German Government; for the French Government had made it clear from the outset that it could not be considered. A more legitimate source of apprehension was the extent of the German demands in the Congo. On July 20th, the British Ambassador asked the French Foreign Minister as to his opinion of a conference in the event of a rupture of negotiations. The negotiations of France and Germany about French equatorial Africa, replied de Selves, would probably last for some time. If they failed, France would not object to Great Britain inviting a Conference of the Signatories of the Act of Algeciras. The cession of Moroccan territory to Germany, however, would be contrary to the pacts of 1904 and 1909. On the same day Jules Cambon reported a heated interview in which Kiderlen loudly complained of indiscretions in the French Press, and censured de Selves for saying to Schön that he could not take Germany's excessive demands seriously. "In such a grave affair I only utter serious words," added the Foreign Minister. "We must both observe discretion. If conversation is rendered impossible, we shall resume our liberty of action, and demand the integral application

of the Act of Algeciras, and if necessary we will go *jusqu'au bout.*"
"I understand your menace," rejoined the Ambassador with dignity,
"and your wish to go far, and we are equally willing."

The extent of the demands in the Congo filled Sir Edward Grey
with alarm. He was, moreover, afraid that the German Government
might suddenly yield to the widespread demand in the German Press
for a portion of Morocco.

"I therefore asked the German Ambassador to see me again on July 21st,"
he informed the House of Commons on November 27th. "I said to him,
I wished it to be understood that our silence, in the absence of any communication from the German Government, must not be interpreted as
meaning that we were not taking in the Moroccan question the interest
which had been indicated by our statement of the 4th of that month. I had
been made anxious by the news which appeared the day before as to the
demands which the German Government had made on the French Government—demands which were in effect not a rectification of the frontier, but
a cession of the French Congo, which it was obviously impossible for the
French Government to concede. I heard that negotiations were still proceeding, and I still hoped that they might lead to a satisfactory result; but
it must be understood that, if they were unsuccessful, a very embarrassing
situation would arise. I pointed out that the Germans were in the closed
port of Agadir; that according to native rumours they were landing and
negotiating with the tribes, so that, for all we knew, they might be acquiring
concessions there and that it might even be that the German flag had been
hoisted at Agadir, which was the most suitable port on that coast for a
naval base. The longer the Germans remained at Agadir the greater the
risk of a state of affairs which would make it more difficult for them to
withdraw and more necessary for us to take some steps to protect British
interests. The German Ambassador was still not in a position to make any
communication to me from the German Government."

The account of the conversation given by Kiderlen-Wächter on
November 17th, on the basis of the German Ambassador's Report,
fills in the outline of the picture.

"If the Franco-German negotiations failed," observed the Foreign
Secretary, "which in view of our demands appeared by no means unlikely,
the Agadir question, in which British interests were also involved, would
at once come into the foreground. Therefore, he believed that the time had
come when England also should take part in the negotiations."

The Ambassador refused to admit that our demands were inacceptable;
and he knew nothing of an intention to establish a naval base.

"We had not the slightest intention of injuring English rights and
interests, and he could not admit that this had been done by the despatch of
a warship. A European Power was justified in undertaking the protection
of her interests in a semi-barbaric country. Germany was bound by the

Act of 1906 and the Treaty of 1909, not by the Anglo-French Convention of 1904. After the occupation of the Shawia and the recent conquering march no one could seriously maintain that Moroccan territory had not been violated or that its Sultan was still independent. Owing to those events, we were now compelled to come to an understanding with France on the Morocco question. If France desired that we, like England, should step into the background in Morocco, she must offer some compensation, as England had offered compensation in Egypt. Sir Edward appeared to have two standards, one for France, another for Germany. If he attached so much importance to the inviolability of Morocco territory, he should apply first to France for explanations, as the occupations of the Shawia and the spreading of a French army over the interior constituted a far more active intervention."

Sir Edward Grey replied that

" he would in no way obstruct an extension of German colonies in the heart of Africa; but English interests might be most seriously affected by the Moroccan question itself. He had therefore honestly hoped for an understanding between France and Germany, as he had welcomed that of 1909. The situation would become less acute if an exchange of views took place between us before fresh events occurred at Agadir which would compel England to take up a definite attitude."

The two men had spoken plainly, though the interview was perfectly amicable. The Ambassador's telegraphic report reached Berlin the next day, and a reassuring message was at once despatched. It would have been well had Downing Street waited for that reply, and it would also have been well if the German Government had explained its views before instead of after the conversation. A few hours after the interview, a declaration of British policy introduced new elements of danger into a delicate situation.

" In the course of that day, July 21st," related the Foreign Secretary, " the Chancellor of the Exchequer told me that he had to make a speech on an occasion of importance at the Mansion House the same evening. He consulted the Prime-Minister and me as to what should be said. It was fourteen days since the last public statement about Morocco had been made here, and that had been only the very short statement made by the Prime-Minister in the House. We were anxious as to the way in which things were developing, and we all three felt that for a Cabinet Minister of first-rate importance to make a speech on a formal occasion and to say no word about Foreign Affairs after the interview would be misleading to public opinion here and everywhere."

" I am bound to say this," declared Mr Lloyd George, " that I believe it is essential in the higher interests not merely of this country but of the world, that Britain should at all hazards maintain her place and her prestige amongst the great Powers of the world. If a situation were to be forced on us in which peace could only be preserved by the surrender of the great and beneficent position Britain has won by centuries of heroism and achievements, by allowing Britain to be treated, where her interests were vitally affected, as if she were of no account in the Cabinet of Nations, then I say emphatically that peace at that price would be a humiliation intolerable for a great country like ours to endure."

The significance of the declaration was emphasised by a strident leader in *The Times*.

"Mr Lloyd George's clear, decisive and statesmanlike reference to the European situation created by the German demands in West Africa will be endorsed without distinction of party by all his countrymen. In making public the amazing character of these demands on Thursday last, we called attention to the extreme gravity of the claim which they imply. Europe has nothing to lose by revelations which shew the true pretensions of its greatest military Power, even though the diplomacy of that Power may prefer to move, as Dick Turpin preferred to move, in the dark. The purport of such demands as were outlined in Berlin last week is nothing less than a claim for absolute European predominance. Neither France nor Great Britain could have entertained them for a moment without confessing themselves overborne by German power. That is not the intention of our French neighbours, nor is it our own. Mr Lloyd George made that perfectly clear last night."

The date of the Chancellor's speech had long been fixed; and it was keenly resented by more than one of his colleagues that a step of such importance should have been taken on the spur of the moment without reference to the Cabinet. The Foreign Secretary, who must bear the chief responsibility, seems to have been unaware that he was launching a high explosive, and he defended his action in his historic speech of November 27th.

He claimed no preeminence, no predominance for us in international affairs. [The utterance] contained no menace, such as the saying of "Hands off!" to anyone anywhere. "It did not say that there was any particular demand or claim on the part of Germany that was inconsistent with British interests. Its purport and its point was that where British interests were affected, we must not be treated as if we were of no account. If the time ever comes when this cannot be said by a Minister speaking in the position the Chancellor of the Exchequer was in then, we shall have ceased to exist as a great nation."

It was precisely the same claim to be considered that the Kaiser had championed at Tangier in 1905, and it provoked the same explosion in Germany as the Tangier declaration had provoked in England[1]. The German people saw France and Germany engaged in discussing

---

[1] There were not wanting, however, German verdicts of a different character; for men so different as Tirpitz and Bernstein have blamed their Government for leaving Sir Edward Grey in the dark.

the Moroccan Question, and no French statesman had raised the alarm. Suddenly a contingent declaration of war was flung across the North Sea by the leader of the British Radicals. It was regarded in Germany as a wanton interference in a matter which concerned France and Germany alone, and as convincing evidence that Great Britain was as eager to thwart the colonial and commercial ambitions of Germany as she was to encourage those of France.

The reply of the German Government to Sir Edward Grey's queries in the interview of July 21st had been despatched before the text of the Chancellor's speech reached Berlin; but orders were at once sent to Count Wolff-Metternich, in presenting the reply, to complain of the Mansion House declaration.

"On July 24th, three days after the speech of the Chancellor of the Exchequer, the German Ambassador came to see me. He informed me that the German intention in sending a ship to Agadir had not changed. Not a man had been landed there. The German Government regretted the credence which was given to the insinuations as to the intentions of Germany that came from hostile quarters. Germany had never thought of creating a naval port on the coast of Morocco, and never would think of it. Such ideas were hallucinations. As to the negotiations with France, if the German demands were rather high, his Government were ready to make concessions in Morocco as well as in colonial matters; but the chauvinistic tone of the French Press and a part of the British Press menacing Germany with the interference of the friends of France, did not tend towards a settlement. I said that I was likely to be asked in Parliament what was happening at Agadir, and I should like to know whether I might say that the German Government had informed me that not a man had been landed. The Ambassador asked me to make no public statement with regard to this communication until he had had time to communicate with his Government. The next day, July 25th, he came to see me again, and told me that the information that he had given me on the previous day was confidential, and that the German Government could not consent to its being used in Parliament, in view of the speech of the Chancellor of the Exchequer. He then made to me in regard to that speech a communication which has now been published by the German Government, and which I need not read in full to the House, because it has been in the Press here already, except to say about it that that communication was a strong criticism upon the effect of the speech upon the Press rather than upon the substance of the speech itself. The communication, however, was exceedingly stiff in tone, and I felt it necessary to say at once that as the speech of the Chancellor of the Exchequer seemed to me to give no cause for complaint, the fact that it had created surprise in Germany was in itself a justification of the speech, for it could not have created surprise unless there had been some tendency to think that we might be disregarded. The speech had not claimed anything except that we were entitled to be considered as one of the great nations. It had claimed no preeminence, and it had not even indicated that there was a crisis. It dealt in general terms with remote contingencies. The German Government had said that it was not consistent with their dignity, after the speech of the Chancellor of the Exchequer, to give explanations as to what was taking place at Agadir. I said to the Ambassador that the tone of their communication made it inconsistent with our dignity to give explanations as to the speech of the Chancellor of the Exchequer. I said that it was not intended, by anything that had been said, or would be said here, to embroil the negotiations between Germany and France. On the contrary, we sincerely desired that they should succeed."

Further light was shed on these momentous conversations by the German Foreign Minister on November 17th.

"The Ambassador was instructed to point out that the speech had given rise to violent attacks against Germany by a large portion of the English and the whole of the French Press. It might remain an open question how far the Minister had intended to produce this effect. If England desired to express her wishes, it was open to her to convey them through the usual diplomatic channel. If, instead of doing so, the Government conveyed public declarations by one of its members which could be interpreted at least as a warning to us, and which were in fact interpreted by English and French papers as a warning bordering on a threat, the friendly understanding between Germany and France, which they professed to desire, would not be advanced thereby. If they had intended to complicate and embroil the political situation and to bring about a violent explosion, they would certainly have chosen no better means than the Chancellor's speech, which took so little into account the dignity of a Great Power which was claimed by him for England. We had never intended to dispose of English interests or rights. Threatening warnings would only have the effect of encouraging Germany to uphold her rights."

After the interview of July 25th the clouds quickly dispersed, and on July 26th Sir Edward Grey was authorised to communicate to the House the reassuring message of July 24th.

"On the 27th the German Ambassador came to me again and made another communication from his Government, in conversation, so that I took down the words. 'We trust that Sir Edward Grey, by our very open and candid communication, has gathered the conviction that our *pourparlers* with France at the moment do not touch British interests. We trust to the Minister's great loyalty, that he has so often shown, that he will find it possible to state this fact in Parliament, without, however, giving any details of our confidential communication. We acknowledge with pleasure that the Minister has stated that he desires an agreement between Germany and France, and feel quite convinced that this will prove most helpful to the progress of the negotiations. But, having in view the wish expressed by Sir Edward, we cannot quite see how he can, in the present state of the *pourparlers*, describe our demands as obviously impossible, without knowing what we on our side have the intention to offer to France in the political and colonial field. It is not possible in regard of the formal pledge of secrecy we have given to go into details; but, as the territories to be eventually exchanged are exclusively German and French, we do not believe that special English interests could be touched, and it seems advisable to leave it to the two Parties immediately concerned to form an estimation of the value of the objects to be eventually exchanged. Adverse criticism from the English side must obviously render the negotiations more difficult. On the other hand, a public statement that England would be pleased to see a successful conclusion of the Franco-German *pourparlers* would have a most beneficial influence on an auspicious result, for which we most earnestly hope. We most seriously wish to diminish any points of friction we have with France in the Colonial sphere, especially in Africa, and hope it may eventually be possible to make them disappear entirely. We could not look forward, even if this was done, to establishing intimate relations with France; but we believed that it would do away with a cause of frequently recurring tension. If the wishes of England are in the same direction, the best way to help to bring about this result would be by having a calming influence on public opinion in France, which just now, by half-truths and inaccurate statements, has been brought to considerable excitement.'

I at once expressed appreciation of the friendly tone in which the communication was couched. The Ambassador and myself then had some further conversation of a general and informal kind, in the course of which he expressed some regret at the way in which our public opinion had been misled to adverse conclusions as to German action. I asked what else could have been expected, when the German Government suddenly sent a ship to Morocco, to a closed port, which was said to be the most suitable place on the west coast of Morocco for a naval base. Of course, this action had mobilised British public opinion. I also pointed out that, after I had made to him on July 4th a declaration on behalf of the British Government, we had had no communication from the German Government until July 24th, and even then their denial of any intention to establish a naval base had been in a form which I could not use to allay the suspicions which had been roused here. I expressed the hope that this latest German communication might be taken as a new point of departure, and that we need not go back upon things which might lead to mutual recriminations. From that date onwards there were no further difficulties between the German Government and ourselves about the Moroccan negotiations."

On the same day, the Prime-Minister made a reassuring communication to the House:

"It is obvious that this Moroccan question has reached the point at which it will become increasingly difficult, embarrassing and anxious, unless a solution be found. Too close an analysis, at the present moment, of the causes and antecedents might provoke in more than one quarter recrimination and retorts which it is on every ground desirable to avoid. I propose simply to state to the House what is the actual situation today. Conversations are proceeding between France and Germany; we are not a party to those conversations; the subject-matter of them may not affect British interests. On that point, until we know the ultimate result, we cannot express a final opinion. But it is our desire that those conversations should issue in a settlement honourable and satisfactory to both the parties and of which His Majesty's Government can cordially say that it in no way prejudices British interests. We believe that to be quite possible. We earnestly and sincerely desire to see it accomplished. The question of Morocco itself bristles with difficulties; but, outside Morocco, in other parts of West Africa we should not think of attempting to interfere with territorial arrangements considered reasonable by those who are more directly interested. Any statements that we have so interfered to prejudice negotiations between France and Germany are mischievous inventions without the faintest foundation in fact. But we have thought it right from the beginning to make it quite clear that, failing a settlement such as I have indicated, we must become an active party in discussion of the situation. That would be our right as a signatory to the Treaty of Algeciras; it might be our obligation under the terms of our agreement of 1904 with France; it might be our duty in defence of British interests directly affected by further developments. There have been times when we were not sure how far this was fully understood. I am glad to say we are now quite satisfied that that is not the case. The statement which I made here at this table more than three weeks ago, and the speech since made elsewhere by my right hon. friend the Chancellor of the Exchequer, have, I hope and believe, made it perfectly clear that we claim, not any predominant or preeminent position, but that of one party interested in possible developments and in seeing a solution of the present difficulties. In our judgment, it would have been a grave mistake to let such a situation drift until an assertion of our interest in it might, owing to our previous silence, cause surprise and resentment at the moment when this assertion became most necessary and imperative. That, I trust, we have sufficiently guarded against by the statements already made. I repeat that we earnestly desire a successful issue of the conversations now in progress, and I would venture in the general interest to make a strong appeal to the House not, on the present occasion, to enter into further details or open up controversial ground."

The Mansion House speech, while inflaming German opinion, modified German demands. "Kiderlen demanded the Congo from the coast to the Sangha," writes Reventlow, "and he told Cambon, No haggling; take it or leave it! Then came the speech, and he drew back." "Yesterday's conversation was very different from the last," reported the French Ambassador on July 24th. The danger, however, was not yet over. "Opinion is excited," reported Cambon on August 20th. "If the negotiations fail, Germany will probably refuse a Conference and occupy the Sus. The internal situation affects the external. The elections approach, and the parties compete in patriotism. I hope our apprehensions may be groundless, but it would be levity not to see the possibility of conflict." The Ambassador's apprehensions were shared in Downing Street. "I am not quite satisfied about the negotiations," observed Sir Edward Grey to Benckendorff[1]. "This unnatural delay does not please me. Much will depend in Berlin on its view of Russia's attitude. What would you do in case of complications?" "There is the alliance," replied the Ambassador. "If there is war between Germany and France, England will have to take part. If Russia is involved, it would be no longer a Franco-German duel but universal war. I do not think the Kaiser desired war when this began, and I do not believe he wants war today. It seems impossible that he would decide on war for such a question, if he realises the fearful consequences." On August 23rd, the Defence Committee considered the contingency of sending troops to France; but no decision was reached, and the question was not discussed by the Cabinet.

Returning from his holiday on August 17th, the French Premier, Caillaux, took the helm from the hands of his inexperienced Foreign Minister, summoning the brothers Cambon from Berlin and London and Barrère from Rome to assist the Cabinet with their counsel. An appeal to Sir Edward Grey to renew his warning to Germany against the occupation of Agadir brought the response that if negotiations broke down he would propose a conference. On August 30th Jules Cambon left Paris for Berlin with two sets of Instructions, one for Morocco, the other for the Congo. The concessions in the latter were only to be discussed when France had definitely obtained the Protectorate of the former. On September 4th, when the conversations were renewed, Kiderlen-Wächter virtually accepted the Morocco proposals, but demanded larger compensation than was offered by France. The situation was reported to Sir Edward Grey, who remarked to Cambon that the Protectorate of Morocco was worth large concessions. The sky darkened again when, on September 8th, the German Foreign Secretary proposed a rival scheme for Morocco, which its author defended as merely designed to prevent the expulsion of German industry, but which was scouted by the Ambassador as an attempt by Germany, under cover of economic guarantees, to retain her position in Morocco. The critical stage reached in the negotiations became known, and a financial panic ensued. German stocks fell,

[1] Siebert, *Diplomatische Aktenstücke*, pp. 434–5.

there was a run on the banks, and the bankers declared that Germany was not financially prepared for war. The Kaiser and the Chancellor were throughout opposed to war; and, after this revelation of economic weakness Kiderlen-Wächter showed himself more accommodating. The Morocco Accord was signed on October 11th, and the covering letters on October 14th.

On the following day the Congo discussions were resumed, and the German negotiator remarked: "If you wish them to succeed, you must give us access to the Congo." The thorny question was on the verge of settlement when, on October 27th, he suddenly raised the question of the French preemption of the Congo. His tone suggested a rupture, and the Ambassador accompanied his report with the words, "We must not yield." The incident was promptly reported to London and Petrograd, with a request for communication of their views. Russia suggested that "any change of sovereignty in the Conventional basin must be discussed by all the Signatories of the Berlin Act." The formula was approved by Great Britain, and accepted by France and Germany. The Congo Treaty was signed on November 3rd, and the Joint Treaty on November 4th. The exhausting debate of four months, in which Kiderlen and Jules Cambon had had over one hundred interviews, was at an end, and the French Ambassador was satisfied with the result.

Nowhere was the feeling of relief caused by the settlement stronger than in London. "Tell M. Caillaux," said Mr Asquith, "that he returns from Berlin, like Lord Beaconsfield, bringing peace with honour." Sir Edward Grey expressed to the French Chargé d'affaires his great satisfaction. He noted the renewed guarantee of economic equality in Morocco; but in Article I Germany consented to French measures of reorganisation of control and financial guarantees on condition that such action did not infringe the economic equality of the two nations. He presumed this did not mean that Germans would have superior rights to British subjects. He also reiterated, in the presence of the Diplomatic Corps and the Municipal and Sanitary Institutions, the importance Great Britain attached to the preservation of the exceptional character belonging to Tangier. He was sure France would agree to placing the town and district under international control.

On November 27th, Sir Edward Grey reviewed the crisis and replied to his British and German critics. The Treaty was signed; but the sea was still rough.

"So much suspicion and gossip have collected that it is exciting men's minds and corroding their tempers to a greater extent than ever before. Some people take delight in suggesting how near we were to war. It is as if the world were indulging in a fit of political alcoholism. The German Foreign Minister now declared that there was never any intention of appropriating any port of Morocco. If, after my communication of July 4th, that intention had been confided to us as definitely as that, a good deal of misunderstanding would have been avoided. Captain Faber's speech had intensified the bitterness of feeling. Of course, there was considerable anxiety, not constant but intermittent, as to how the negotiations between France and Germany would find a solution. If either had broken off negotiations—and once or twice late in the summer it looked as if they must reach a deadlock—it is very difficult to see what the next move would have been. We knew France would not break them off abruptly. We did not believe Germany would, either; but there was a possibility, though I never thought a probability. If a deadlock arose we had in mind to propose a Conference. But when I had proposed it hypothetically in July, Germany, while not actually refusing, suggested it might not prove acceptable.... It was a period of tension, not as to what was going to happen in the next twenty-four hours, but anxiety as to what might take place."

The speech closed with a vigorous defence of the methods adopted.

"There is another foreign policy which would be simply disastrous—that we should give it to be understood that in no circumstances, however wantonly a friend of ours was attacked, would we give any assistance. That would be an attempt to revert to a policy of splendid isolation. It would deprive us of the possibility of having a friend in Europe, and it would result in the other nations of Europe, either by choice or necessity, being brought into the orbit of a single diplomacy from which we should be excluded. In a few years, we should be building warships not against a Two-Power standard but probably against the united navies of Europe. Such an attitude would not even gain us the friendship of Germany. One does not make new friendships worth having by deserting old ones. Is that policy necessarily a bar to good relations with Germany? I do not believe it is. They say in Germany that it is part of our policy always to stand in Germany's way and object to her expansion. It is unfortunate that the Morocco question has come up so often; but that is a special case, where we have a special Agreement. If Germany has friendly arrangements to negotiate in Africa with other Powers, we are not anxious to stand in their way. We cannot at this moment force the pace in improving relations. The Chancellor's speech is friendly, and, though the breeze is at present anything but favourable, in some ways one can see the horizon is already brightening. He said the Treaty also cleaned the slate in respect of German relations with England. Its effect must be to relax the tension and remove a great obstacle from the path of European diplomacy."

The debate which followed was highly critical of the Government. Mr Bonar Law, on behalf of the Opposition, pronounced the Government policy to be right, but censured the intervention of Mr Lloyd George on the ground that important declarations on Foreign Affairs should be made by the Prime-Minister or by the Foreign Secretary in Parliament. Mr Ramsay Macdonald condemned the Mansion House speech, as he had condemned it on July 27th. Mr Dillon denounced the French policy in Morocco, and denied the danger at Fez, which had been engineered as a plausible excuse for tearing up the Treaty of Algeciras. Mr Noel Buxton asked why Sir Edward Grey did not tell the German Ambassador on July 4th that an early response was desired, or ask the British Ambassador in Berlin to find out when it was expected. From several benches came expressions of regret that the references to Germany were not warmer. The most searching criticism came from Lord Courtney in the House of Lords on the following day. Our Foreign Office, he complained, had always paid less attention to the Act of Algeciras than to our obligation under the Treaty of 1904. We should have pointed out to our friends in France that interference with the integrity and independence of Morocco would provoke complaints from other signatories; but we had allowed the matter to drift and only woke up when the *Panther* anchored at Agadir.

The Chancellor replied in the *Reichstag* on December 5th. He would follow Sir Edward Grey's good example and avoid recriminations; but the tension could have been avoided if greater confidence had been placed in the German declarations and if the Chancellor of the Exchequer had not intervened. The root of all the trouble was the disposal of Morocco in 1904 by France and England without consideration for German interests. "From this arose the necessity for us to go to Algeciras, and then to Agadir, to safeguard our economic interests and to shew the world that we are firmly resolved not to allow ourselves to be elbowed aside." This was now at an end. "The English Ministers have unanimously expressed a desire for better relations with us, and I associate myself entirely with this desire. But it can only come if the British Government is prepared to give in her policy positive expression to her need for such relations."

Among the repercussions of the Agadir crisis was the seizure of Tripoli by Italy, who had long cast greedy eyes on the African coast[1]. In June, 1911, San Giuliano informed Aehrenthal that Italy might

[1] See Sir Thomas Barclay, *The Turco-Italian War and its Problems.*

have to annex the country, and when Jagow announced the voyage of the *Panther* he remarked: "Tripoli's hour is nigh." An ultimatum was issued on September 26th, and war was declared on September 29th. The complaints as to ill-treatment of her nationals and opposition to her trade were mere pretexts. British opinion was hostile; but no word of rebuke was heard from the Minister who had so sharply condemned the annexation of Bosnia. British interests were affected in two ways—first, by the change in ownership, and, secondly, by the proximity of Egypt to Tripoli. It was a relief to the British Government that the last piece of Turkish territory on the African coast should fall into the hands of a friendly Power; and Mr Maxse, in the *National Review*, welcomed the War as a means of preventing Germany from seizing Tobruk and establishing a naval base in the Mediterranean. The British occupation of the theoretically Turkish province of Egypt gave rise to no difficulties; for the Sultan did not ask leave to send troops across the Nile, nor did he request the service of Egyptian troops, as in the Crimea and in the War of 1877. Egypt was declared neutral, and the Italian Consuls remained at their posts. The only friction occurred when the opportunity was taken to clear up the question of the Egyptian frontier. Turkey and Italy had been informed in November, 1904, that Egypt included Sollum[1]; but, in notifying the blockade of Turkish Africa, Italy adopted the boundary claimed by Turkey. The Egyptian Government accordingly sent troops to Sollum, and the eastern frontier of Tripoli was thus definitely drawn to the west of the bay.

"Italy is unpopular," reported Benckendorff on November 6th, "but the Government will not endanger good relations." This passive attitude was sharply challenged on November 27th by Mr D. M. Mason, who moved "that this House protests against the unwarrantable seizure of Tripoli by Italy and desires to express its horror and detestation at the recent massacre of Arabs, and urges the Government to protest against this outrage on humanity." "His speech puts me in an absolutely impossible position," replied the Foreign Secretary. "He assumes that I have official information confirming his reports. I have not. I have no means of investigating all the statements. A neutral Government cannot collect and publish information about the War. We have adopted neutrality, and we could only depart from it under circumstances gravely concerning British interests." The Foreign Secretary was less pro-Italian than

[1] This fact was revealed by the Foreign Office, December 19th, 1911.

his critics imagined, and he had to think of the damage to British trade. He twice invited the Great Powers to address a joint warning to Italy not to tamper with the Dardanelles; but his appeal was in vain. Aehrenthal handed the second invitation to the Italian Ambassador, remarking: "This may amuse you; I shall not answer it[1]." Though the War involved Great Britain in no direct controversy with Turkey, its result was to accentuate the estrangement which had begun with the overthrow of Kiamil early in 1909, and had been intensified by the hideous massacre of Armenians in Adana and by the ruthless policy of Ottomanisation pursued by the Young Turks.

VIII. Lord Haldane's Mission, 1912

The spectacle of Great Britain standing in shining armour beside France produced its inevitable result beyond the Rhine. "I went to Berlin in the autumn," writes Tirpitz, "and represented to the Chancellor that we had suffered a diplomatic check, and must salve it by a Supplementary Naval Bill." The Kaiser agreed, and the Chancellor was instructed to work the Supplementary Bill into the Budget of 1912. But while Tirpitz was striving for an increase of the Fleet, wiser heads resolved on a fresh attempt to relieve the tension which had threatened the Peace of the World. At the beginning of December, the Kaiser approved a suggested sounding of British statesmen, and shortly before Christmas Count Wolff-Metternich had a promising discussion with Sir Edward Grey[2]. At the same time, a Memorandum was drawn up by Mr Lloyd George and Mr Churchill. Germany was to recognise British superiority at sea, not to increase her Navy programme, and possibly to reduce it. Great Britain, on her side, was not to impede German Colonial expansion. Both Powers were to declare that they would take no part in aggressive plans or in combinations against each other. With the approval of the Foreign Minister, this Memorandum was entrusted to Sir Ernest Cassel, who in January, 1912, was about to pay one of his periodical visits to Berlin, for presentation to the Kaiser[3]. Sir Ernest Cassel returned with an answer that all steps towards better relations would be welcome. The German Government assented to the Memorandum, with the important reservation that its standpoint in the Navy problem

[1] Seton-Watson, *Europe in the Melting-Pot*, p. 94.
[2] Bethmann-Hollweg, *Betrachtungen*, I. 48–50.
[3] Since 1908 Sir Ernest Cassel and Ballin had engaged in semi-official discussions on naval rivalry, reporting the results to their respective Governments. See Huldermann, *Albert Ballin*, ch. 8.

was the Navy Law plus the *Novelle* or Supplementary Law then ready for production. The Kaiser suggested a direct exchange of views between the Governments, and an early visit from Sir Edward Grey was proposed. Shortly afterwards, the German Government was informed of his readiness to come to Berlin, if the conclusion of an agreement appeared assured; but, meanwhile, Lord Haldane would be sent on a private Mission. Sir Edward Goschen travelled to London to make arrangements for the forthcoming visit; and Lord Haldane arrived in Berlin on February 8th.

On the day after Lord Haldane reached Berlin, the First Lord of the Admiralty delivered a speech at Glasgow which was scarcely calculated to facilitate the pacific efforts of his colleague.

"The purposes of British naval power are essentially defensive. We have no thoughts, and we have never had any thoughts, of aggression, and we attribute no such thoughts to other Great Powers. There is, however, this difference between British naval power and that of the great friendly empire of Germany. The British Navy is to us a necessity, and from some points of view the German Navy is to them more in the nature of a luxury. It is existence to us; and it is expansion to them. The whole fortunes of our race and empire, the whole treasure accumulated during so many centuries of sacrifice and achievement, would perish if our naval supremacy were to be impaired. It is the British Navy which makes Great Britain a Great Power. But Germany was a Great Power, respected and honoured all over the world, before she had a single ship. The Prime-Minister and his colleagues without exception are resolved to maintain the naval supremacy which this country enjoys; and the country was never more united in its resolve to see the supremacy of the Navy maintained. We learn that there are prospects of further naval increases among the Powers of the Continent. Whatever may happen abroad, there will be no whining here; no signals of distress will be hoisted, no cries for help or succour will go up....We should be the first Power to welcome any retardation or slackening of naval rivalry. We should meet it not by words but by deeds. But, if there are to be increases on the Continent, we shall have no difficulty in meeting them. We shall make it clear that other naval Powers, instead of over-taking us by additional efforts, will only be more outdistanced. I say, build your great dock, build it long and build it deep, and above all build it wide. We will provide you with no lack of great vessels to fill it; and you will know that your citizens are aiding the British Navy, which enables us to pursue our path through the world, seeking no quarrel and fearing none."

The reference to the "luxury fleet," though not inaccurate, was singularly tactless, and strengthened the suspicions with which Tirpitz and his friends regarded the olive-branch carried by Lord Haldane.

"My first interview," relates the Envoy, "was with the Imperial Chancellor[1]. We met in the British Embassy, and the conversation, which was quite informal, was a full and agreeable one. My impression, and I still retain it, was that he was then as sincerely desirous of avoiding war as I was myself. I told him of certain dangers quite frankly, and he listened and replied with what seemed to me to be a full understanding of our position. I said that the increasing action of Germany in piling up magnificent armaments was, of course, within the unfettered rights of the German people. But the policy had an inevitable consequence in the drawing together of other nations in the interests of their own security. This was what was happening. I told him frankly that we had made naval and military preparations, but only such as defence required, and as would be considered in Germany matter of routine. I went on to observe that our faces were set against aggression by any nation, and I told him, what seemed to relieve his mind, that we had no secret military treaties. But, I added, if France were attacked and an attempt made to occupy her territory, our neutrality must not be reckoned on by Germany. For one thing, it was obvious that our position as an island protected by the sea would be affected seriously, if Germany had possession of the Channel ports on the northern shores of France. Again, we were under treaty obligation to come to the aid of Belgium in case of invasion, just as we were bound to defend Portugal and Japan in certain eventualities. In the third place, owing to our dependence on freedom of sea-communications for food and raw materials, we could not sit still if Germany elected to develop her fleet to such an extent as to imperil our naval protection. She might build more ships, but we should in that case lay down two keels for each one she laid down. The Chancellor said that he did not take my observations at all in bad part; but I must understand that his Admirals and Generals were pretty difficult. I replied that the difficulty would be felt at least as much with the Admirals and Generals in my own country. ...I left the Chancellor with the sense that I had been talking with an honest man struggling somewhat with adversity.

Next day I was summoned to luncheon with the Emperor and Empress at the Schloss, and afterwards had a long interview with the Emperor and Admiral von Tirpitz in the Emperor's Cabinet room....My reception by the Emperor was very agreeable; that by Tirpitz seemed to me a little strained....The Emperor handed me a confidential copy of the draft of the proposed new Fleet Law, with an intimation that he had no objection to my communicating it privately to my colleagues. I was careful to abstain even from looking at it then, for I saw that, from its complexity and bulk, it would require careful study. So I simply put it in my pocket. But I repeated what I had said to the Chancellor, that the necessity for secure sea-communications rendered it vital for us to be able to protect ourselves on the seas. Germany was quite free to do as she pleased; but so were we, and we should probably lay down two keels for every one which she added to her programme. The initiative in slackening competition was

[1] Haldane, *Before the War*, pp. 57–70.

really not with us, but with Germany. Any agreement for settling our differences and introducing a new spirit into the relations of the two nations would be bones without flesh, if Germany began by fresh ship-building, and so forced us to do twice as much. Indeed, the world would laugh at such an agreement, and our people would think that we had been fooled. I did not myself take that view, because I thought that the mere fact of an agreement was valuable. But the Emperor would see that the public would attach very little importance to his action, unless the agreement largely modified what it believed to be his shipbuilding pro-gramme.

We then discussed the proposal of the German Admiralty for the new programme. Admiral von Tirpitz struggled for it. I insisted that funda-mental modification was essential, if better relations were to ensue. The tone was friendly; but I felt that I was up against the crucial part of my task. The Admiral wanted us to enter into some understanding about our own shipbuilding. He thought the Two-Power standard a hard one for Germany, and, indeed, Germany could not make any admission about it. The idea then occurred to us that, as we should never agree about it, we should avoid trying to define a standard proportion in any general agree-ment that we might come to, and, indeed, say nothing in it about ship-building; but that the Emperor should announce to the German public that the agreement on general questions, if we should have concluded one, had entirely modified his wish for the new Fleet Law, as originally con-ceived, and that it should be delayed, and future shipbuilding should at least be spread over a longer period. The Emperor thought such an agree-ment would certainly make a great difference, and he informed me that his Chancellor would propose to me a formula as a basis for it. I said that I would see the Chancellor and discuss a possible formula, as well as terri-torial and other questions with him, and would then return to London and report to the King (from whom I had brought him a special and friendly message) and to my colleagues the good disposition I had found, and leave the difficulties about shipbuilding and indeed all other matters to their judgment. For I had come to Berlin, not to make an active agree-ment, but only to explore the ground for one with the Emperor and his Ministers. I had been struck with the friendly disposition in Berlin, and a not less friendly disposition would be found in London.

At my final meeting with the German Chancellor, I pressed on him how important it was for public opinion and the Peace of the World that Germany should not force us into a shipbuilding competition with her— a competition in which it was certain that we should have to spare no effort to preserve our margin of safety by greater increases. He did not controvert my suggestion. I could see that personally he was of the same mind. But he said that the forces he had to contend with were almost insuperable. The question of a retardation of building under the proposed Fleet Law was not susceptible of being treated apart from that of the formula of which he and the Emperor had both spoken. He suggested that we might agree on the following formula:

I. The High Contracting Powers assure each other mutually of their desire for peace and friendship.

II. They will not, either of them, make any combination, or join in any combination, which is directed against the other. They expressly declare that they are not bound by any such combination.

III. If either of the High Contracting Parties become entangled in a war with one or more other Powers, the other of the High Contracting Parties will at least observe toward the Power so entangled a benevolent neutrality, and use its utmost endeavour for the localisation of the conflict.

IV. The duty of neutrality which arises from the preceding Article has no application in so far as it may not be reconcilable with existing agreements which the High Contracting Parties have already made. The making of new agreements which make it impossible for either of the Contracting Parties to observe neutrality toward the other beyond what is provided by the preceding limitations is excluded in conformity with the provisions contained in Article II.

Anxious as I was to agree with the Chancellor, who seemed as keen as I was to meet me with expressions which I might take back to England for friendly considerations, I was unable to hold out to him the least prospect that we could accept the draft formula which he had just proposed. Under Article III, for example, we should find ourselves, were it accepted, precluded from coming to the assistance of France should Germany attack her and aim at getting possession of such ports as Dunkirk, Calais, and Boulogne, a friendly occupation of which was so important for our island security. Difficulties might also arise which would hamper us in the discharge of our existing treaty obligations to Belgium, Portugal, and Japan. The most hopeful way out was to revise the draft fundamentally by confining its terms to an undertaking by each Power not to make any unprovoked attack upon the other, or join in any combination or design against the other for purposes of aggression, or become party to any plan or naval or military combination, alone or in conjunction with any other Power, directed to such an end. He and I then sat down and redrafted what he had prepared, on this basis, but without his committing himself to the view that it would be sufficient. We also had a satisfactory conversation about the Bagdad Railway and other things in Turkey connected with the Persian Gulf, and we discussed possibilities of the rearrangement of certain interests of both Powers in Africa. He said to me that he was not there to make any immediate bargain; but that we should look at the African question on both sides from a high point of view, and that, if we had any difficulties we should tell him, and he would see whether he could get round them for us. I replied that I, also, was not there to make a bargain, but only to explore the ground, and that I much appreciated the tone of his conversation with me, and the good feeling he had shewn....

I entertain no doubt that the German Chancellor was sincerely in earnest in what he said to me on these occasions, and in his desire to improve relations with us and keep the peace. So I think was the Emperor; but he was pulled at by his naval and military advisers, and by the powerful, if then small, chauvinist party in Germany. But still there was the possibility of an explosion; and, when I returned to London, although I was full of hope that relations between the two countries were going to be improved, and told my colleagues so, I also reported that there were three matters about which I was uneasy. The first was my strong impression that the new Fleet Law would be insisted on. The second was the possibility that Tirpitz might be made Chancellor in place of Bethmann-Hollweg. The third was the want of continuity in the supreme direction of German policy."

Lord Haldane's picture of the friendliness and frankness of the conversations is confirmed by the Memoirs of Bethmann-Hollweg, who adds one or two details[1].

"In private conversation Lord Haldane expressed himself as extraordinarily pleased with his impressions and hopeful as to the success of the line of action here begun. In the discussion of Colonial questions he made far-reaching offers in return for German concessions in the Bagdad Railway. In addition to the extension of German South-West Africa on the basis of an understanding as to Angola, he also threw out the possibility of the cession of Zanzibar and Pemba to Germany."

The naval discussion with the Kaiser and Tirpitz, adds the Chancellor, was, also, not unsatisfactory.

"Haldane admitted to me that we must have a *novelle* and a third squadron. The latter would compel England to keep a larger North Sea fleet, but that was a matter of indifference to her. His chief point was that she should not be compelled to reply to new German Dreadnoughts with double the number. He recognised that it would meet English wishes for the postponement of the three Dreadnoughts if they were laid down in 1913, 1916, 1919. He then asked if we could not drop all additions for the next three years. If we reached a political agreement, our relations would be so good that an addition at a later period would do no harm."

Tirpitz's narrative, as might be expected, is written in a spirit of undisguised hostility both to the Chancellor and to the guest[2].

"The audience (with the Kaiser) was preceded by a lunch at which the Chancellor was present. No politics were talked during the lunch; but the atmosphere was pretty tense. During the succeeding audience I really only played the part of a witness, as the Emperor led the conversation himself. Haldane began to open up to us the prospect of a big African empire, not only of Portuguese but of Belgian and French territories as well. The extravagance of this offer of colonial possessions which did not belong to the English suited the Emperor's temperament. It made a painful impression upon me, because the method was too crude and the design too obvious. I admired Haldane, when he claimed with simple modesty 'only'

[1] *Betrachtungen*, I. 50–4.
[2] *Memoirs*, vol. I. 218–224. The Kaiser shares Tirpitz's view of the visit, *ibid.* ch. 5.

the Cape to Cairo Railway. I began by declaring that I should welcome an understanding. He politely declined a 2 : 3 proportion—which Lloyd George in 1908 and later Churchill proposed—and maintained the Two-Power Standard. He next proposed a delay in the building of the three ships. I tried to make clear the difficulties which a further change in the Bill would involve, as we had already reduced our programme considerably out of regard for England. But, when he proposed we should retard the rate of our increase, and, 'in order to lubricate the negotiations,' should at least cancel the first of the three ships, I sacrificed the ship against my real principles and without any return. I would have sacrificed the whole Bill for a really solid agreement of neutrality, as I had told the Kaiser. After he had pocketed this concession, he cautiously touched on the question whether the Navy Bill itself must be carried out; but here the Kaiser intervened, and he withdrew his feeler. I felt certain that the real desires of the English were not directed against the bagatelle of the three supplementary ships, but against the Bill itself. Though the later negotiations came to nothing, I kept to the sacrifice of the ship so as to leave no doubt about our goodwill. As we left the Castle, Haldane expressed himself satisfied with the conversation. I had gathered:

1. That the real object was to cripple the development of our Fleet.
2. That the naval offer was not three to two but two keels to one.
3. That Bethmann's neutrality formula was not considered.
4. That our naval subjection was to be rewarded solely by reversions in Africa.

Haldane was not ready to sugar our subjection if we entered into vassalage. He offered us nothing, but skilfully sowed discord among us. If he had made a reasonable offer I was prepared to say, When we get the 2 : 3 proportion and a solid friendship, we will discuss the reduction of the Navy Bill."

The visit gave genuine pleasure to friends of peace in both countries. The Tsar privately expressed his satisfaction with the result of the mission. Lord Haldane's business in Berlin was defined by M. Jules Cambon as "a *détente*, not an *entente*," and it was welcomed as such by M. Poincaré; though military circles in France feared that a naval agreement would allow Germany to spend more on her Army. When Parliament met, on February 14th, the leaders of both parties expressed their goodwill to Germany and their desire for cordial relations.

"Last summer," observed Lord Lansdowne, "we were on the eve of a serious quarrel with the Power with which every right-thinking Englishman desires not only to live at peace but to cooperate. It is lamentable that such misunderstandings and apprehensions should exist, and it is the duty of all right-thinking persons to dispel them. If Lord Haldane has come back with an olive-branch in his buttonhole, we shall congratulate him on this side of the House as warmly as on his own."

In his first conversation with the German Ambassador after Lord Haldane's return, Sir Edward Grey declared himself "immensely impressed" with his colleague's report of his conversations with the Chancellor, and declared with the greatest emphasis his determination to carry on the work thus begun. He hoped it would be possible gradually to disperse the war-cloud. Everything depended on a detailed examination of the German suggestions[1]. But when the *Novelle* was studied by the Admiralty, it was discovered to involve a sensational increase in the size and striking power of the Fleet. If it became law, declared the Admiralty, Great Britain would have to spend eighteen millions a year more on her Navy.

"The British mistrust of the plans of the German naval authorities," writes Bethmann-Hollweg, "was as obvious as the apprehension in German naval circles that our naval armament might be paralysed. I was resolved to work for the utmost concessions in the Navy question if I could secure compensation in a political arrangement. But that was refused by England."

The negotiations began with the presentation and rejection of the neutrality formula which the Chancellor had outlined to Lord Haldane in Berlin.

Count Metternich upon this pressed for counter-proposals, which he stated would be without prejudice and not binding unless we were satisfied that our wishes were met on the naval question[2]. On this understanding, Sir Edward Grey, on March 14th, 1912, gave Count Metternich the following draft formula, which had been approved by the Cabinet:

"England will make no unprovoked attack upon Germany, and pursue no aggressive policy towards her.

Aggression upon Germany is not the subject, and forms no part of any treaty, understanding, or combination to which England is now a party, nor will she become a party to anything that has such an object."

Count Metternich thought this formula inadequate, and suggested two alternative additional clauses:

"England will therefore observe at least a benevolent neutrality, should war be forced upon Germany; or

England will therefore, as a matter of course, remain neutral if a war is forced upon Germany.

This," he added, "would not be binding unless our wishes were met with regard to the naval programme."

Sir Edward Grey considered that the British proposals were sufficient. He explained that, if Germany desired to crush France, England might not be able to sit still, though, if France were aggressive or attacked Germany, no support would be given by His Majesty's Government or approved by

---

[1] Bethmann-Hollweg, I. 54–5.

[2] This official account of the negotiations was issued by the Foreign Office in 1915.

England. "It is obvious that the real object of the German proposal was to obtain the neutrality of England in all eventualities, since, should a war break out, Germany would certainly contend that it had been forced upon her, and would claim that England should remain neutral."

Sir Edward Grey eventually proposed the following formula:

"The two Powers being mutually desirous of securing peace and friendship between them, England declares that she will neither make, nor join in, any unprovoked attack upon Germany. Aggression upon Germany is not the subject, and forms no part of any treaty, understanding, or combination to which England is now a party, nor will she become a party to anything that has such an object."

Sir Edward Grey, when he handed this formula to Count Metternich, said that the use of the word "neutrality" would convey the impression that more was meant than was warranted by the text; he suggested that the substance of what was required would be obtained and more accurately expressed by the words "will neither make, nor join in, any unprovoked attack."

Count Metternich thereupon received Instructions to make it quite clear that the Chancellor could recommend the Emperor to give up the essential parts of the *Novelle* (the Bill then pending for the increase of the German Navy) only if we could conclude an agreement guaranteeing neutrality of a far-reaching character and leaving no doubt as to any interpretation. He admitted that the Chancellor's wish amounted to a guarantee of absolute neutrality, failing which the *Novelle* must proceed.

Count Metternich stated that there was no chance of the withdrawal of the *Novelle*, but said that it might be modified; it would be disappointing to the Chancellor if we did not go beyond the formula we had suggested.

Sir Edward Grey said that he could understand that there would be disappointment if His Majesty's Government were to state that the carrying out of the *Novelle* would put an end to the negotiations and form an insurmountable obstacle to better relations. His Majesty's Government did not say this, and they hoped the formula which they had suggested might be considered in connexion with the discussion of territorial arrangements, even if it did not prove effective in preventing the increase of naval expenditure.

Sir Edward Grey added that, if some arrangement could be made between the two Governments, it would have a favourable though indirect effect upon naval expenditure as time went on; it would have, moreover, a favourable and direct effect upon public opinion in both countries.

A few days afterwards Count Metternich communicated to Sir Edward Grey the substance of a letter from the Chancellor, in which the latter said that, as the formula suggested by His Majesty's Government was from the German point of view insufficient, and as His Majesty's Government could not agree to the larger formula for which he had asked, the *Novelle* must proceed on the lines on which it had been presented to the Federal Council. The negotiations then came to an end, and with them the hope of a mutual reduction in the expenditure of the two countries.

The negotiations failed because each side suspected the other of entertaining unavowed designs.

"Grey only offered us neutrality in an unprovoked attack," complained the Chancellor, "and refused our addition 'if a war is forced on Germany,' so as not to endanger English relations with France and Russia. Why should such a strictly limited neutrality formula hurt the feelings of England's friends? It would merely have shewn them that they could not rely on her help in an anti-German policy. Ever since 1909, Grey had told me on every occasion of his primary obligation to the Dual Alliance; but in return for his neutrality formula I could not surrender the *Novelle*. England's effort of reconciliation was sincere; but perhaps we were wrong in under-estimating her intimacy with France and Russia."

The Chancellor offered his resignation; and his enemies were filled with satisfaction. "The neutrality discussions were a waste of breath," comments Reventlow with his usual acrimony. "England had no intention of promising it, or, if she did so, of keeping her promise." "The negotiations," echoes Tirpitz, "shewed that England was only concerned with extracting concessions in the construction of our Fleet, while giving nothing in return."

The termination of the neutrality negotiations was followed by the recall of Count Wolff-Metternich, who observed to Benckendorff that he bequeathed to his successor a better situation than had existed for a long time[1]. He was followed by Marschall von Bieberstein, the best horse in Germany's diplomatic stable. His seven years' tenure of the Foreign Office after the fall of Bismarck and his commanding position at Constantinople had given him the knowledge and habit of affairs, and his towering figure set off his qualities of mind and will. Though the author of the Kruger telegram had never been reckoned an Anglophil, he took his new task very seriously. "I have long wanted to be Ambassador to England," he remarked to his old friend Sir Edwin Pears, "because, as you know, for years I have considered it a misfortune to the world that our two countries are not really in harmony. I consider that I am here as a man with a mission, my mission being to bring about a real understanding between the two nations[2]."

The burning question, as he was well aware, was the Fleet.

"He immediately began to study seriously the preparations of the two Navies," writes Tirpitz, "without a knowledge of which it was impossible to undertake any real negotiations with England. He came to see me shortly before his departure, and we agreed as to our naval policy. His appearance

---

[1] Benckendorff to Sazonoff, May 18th. Siebert, p. 767.
[2] *Forty Years in Constantinople*, p. 330.

in London stopped for a time the German method of kow-towing to the English. He knew that the Briton becomes more respectful, the more resolutely his competitor maintains his own standpoint. He declared that Germany could not carry out her economic policy without possessing sea power that avoided the necessity of yielding to England at every turn. When he presented his credentials at Buckingham Palace in July, 1912, the King honoured him with an address in German. On this occasion he complained that he saw his reception, otherwise so favourable and promising, compromised by the English Press in consequence of another Navy scare speech by Churchill. If things went on in this strain, he felt he would be exerting himself in vain. Our Naval Attaché, an eye-witness, said the effect of this firm and dignified manner was very marked."

The Ambassador quickly learned to appreciate the high qualities of Sir Edward Grey; but the few weeks of his residence in London before his sudden death during a summer holiday were too short to achieve political results.

On the failure of the attempt to limit the naval rivalry, the British Government proceeded to consider its reply to the *Novelle*. In May, the Prime-Minister and Mr Churchill met Lord Kitchener, now Agent-General in Egypt, at Malta to discuss the problem of the Mediterranean[1]; and the decisions of the Cabinet were announced by the First Lord of the Admiralty in the House of Commons on July 22nd, on introducing a Supplementary Estimate. The speech opened with the first detailed account of the *Novelle* which had been given to the British nation. The main feature, he declared, was the increase not in capital ships, but in the striking force of all classes always available. The seventeen battleships in the active Battle-fleet were raised to twenty-five, the four battle cruisers to eight, the twelve small cruisers to eighteen. Out of 144 torpedo-boats ninety-nine would be ready instead of sixty-six. Four-fifths of the entire Navy would be in full permanent commission—a proportion unknown elsewhere. The personnel would increase by 15,000, which would make a total in 1920 of 100,000. Two battleships and two small cruisers were added to the programme. When completed in 1920 there would be forty-one battleships, twenty battle cruisers, forty small cruisers. The aspect and scale of this Fleet were extremely formidable. It aroused no opposition, and the only criticisms were of its inadequacy. "We ought to learn from our neighbours, whose policy marches unswervingly towards its goal across the lifetime of a whole generation." The increased fighting power of the German

[1] Arthur, *Life of Lord Kitchener*, II. 336–7.

fleet, added Mr Churchill, involved a considerable reorganisation of the British fleet to maintain the margin of safety. The full-commissioned battleships in home waters would be raised from sixteen to twenty-four. The Mediterranean was quite safe, for neither Austria nor Italy possessed a Dreadnought. The British and French fleets were superior to any possible combination. Mr Balfour, following the First Lord in debate, declared the speech calculated to cause even graver anxiety than that of the Foreign Secretary in 1909. The best hope for the preservation of peace lay in the system of alliances, which enabled one Power to restrain a colleague within its own group from precipitate action. Three days later, the Prime-Minister, in opening a debate on the Committee of Imperial Defence, made a reassuring statement. "We cultivate with great and growing cordiality our special friendships; but they are in no sense exclusive. Our relations with the great German empire are at this moment—and I feel sure are likely to remain—relations of amity and goodwill."

The concentration of our naval forces was facilitated by the fact that France had to face the prospect of dealing with the combined fleets of Austria and Italy, and therefore desired to focus her whole Battle-fleet in the Mediterranean[1]. This involved exposing the Atlantic and Channel coasts to attack; but it was anticipated that the British fleet would fill the vacuum. In the early autumn, accordingly, it was announced that the Third French Battle Squadron, based on Brest, was to join the First and Second in the Mediterranean; and, in the spring of 1913, the whole of the Atlantic defence flotillas were demobilised and the defence of the ports was handed over to the army. There only remained at the northern bases six old armoured cruisers, and the flotillas which were to cooperate in the defence of the Channel. These momentous changes appeared to necessitate a closer political understanding.

"The British and French General Staffs," writes M. Poincaré[2], "had examined a hypothetical programme of defence; but even if we were the victims of an unjustifiable attack, the British Government had entered into no engagement towards us. We could not abandon the safeguarding of the Channel and our Atlantic coasts without being assured that in case of danger discussions would take place on the attitude, and if necessary the practical measures, to be taken. Accordingly M. Cambon, with my approval, proposed to the British Ministry to record in an exchange of letters the mutual assurance that, if the peace of Europe was threatened,

[1] See Sir J. Corbett, *Naval Operations*, I. 7–9.
[2] Poincaré, *Les Origines de la Guerre*, pp. 79–81.

the two Governments would at once examine the situation. Mr Asquith and Sir Edward Grey accepted in principle this idea which I had submitted to the French Government; and on October 30th the British Cabinet adopted a text suggested by M. Cambon, declaring that if war appeared inevitable the two Governments would put into operation the military and naval conventions prepared by the Staffs."

Three weeks later, on October 22nd, the nature of the *entente* was defined in an exchange of letters between Sir Edward Grey and the French Ambassador.

"From time to time in recent years," wrote the Foreign Secretary, "the French and British naval and military experts have consulted together. It has always been understood that such consultation does not restrict the freedom of either Government to decide at any future time whether or not to assist the other by armed force. We have agreed that consultation between experts is not, and ought not, to be regarded as an engagement that commits either Government to action in a contingency that has not yet arisen and may never arise. The disposition, for instance, of the French and British Fleets respectively at the present moment is not based upon an engagement to cooperate in war. You have, however, pointed out that, if either Government had grave reason to expect an unprovoked attack by a third Power, it might become essential to know whether it could in that event depend upon the armed assistance of the other. I agree that, if either Government had grave reason to expect an unprovoked attack by a third Power, or something that threatened the general peace, it should immediately discuss with the other, whether both Governments should act together to prevent aggression and to preserve peace, and, if so, what measures they would be prepared to take in common."

To this communication the Ambassador replied by a letter in similar terms.

"The formula," comments M. Poincaré, "was purely hypothetical and involved no definite obligation of reciprocal aid. The situation was only very slightly modified. The Cabinet did not feel able to contract a positive engagement without the authority of Parliament. But, in default of an Alliance, the friendship of Great Britain gave to our foreign policy more authority, and during the crises which followed one another since 1905 we stood shoulder to shoulder with England, united with her at least as closely as with Russia. In Balkan affairs we consulted her first. For several years the two Governments consulted each other day by day, hour by hour, and not once did either take an isolated initiative."

The Grey-Cambon formula[1] left the British Government in theory with its hands free; but M. Poincaré's comments show that it understated the intimacy of the relationship which had grown up in eight years of diplomatic cooperation.

[1] It became known to the German Government in March, 1913.

" To make plans with one Power," writes Lord Loreburn, "for a common war against another Power, should necessity arise, is a serious matter; and whatever reservations may be expressed as to preserving freedom of action, the attitude of the one country towards the other will be indelibly affected by such an intimate cooperation. It does not create, but it portends, a future alliance, and indeed makes such a conclusion almost unavoidable[1]."

The freedom of the British Government continued to be solemnly reiterated at intervals by the Prime-Minister and the Foreign Secretary; but, from 1911 onwards, every Frenchman regarded Great Britain as bound in honour to come to the assistance of France if attacked by Germany. The problem was further complicated by the fact that France was allied to Russia, whom she was bound to aid if attacked. It was not deemed necessary to embody our relations to the great Slavonic Power in a written formula; yet the action of Russia might concern the fortunes of Great Britain very closely, since an attack on Russia would involve an attack on France. We were thus conditionally involved in the quarrels and ambitions of a distant Power over whose policy we exercised no control. "In effect," writes Lord Loreburn bluntly, "it left the peace of Great Britain at the mercy of the Russian Court." The statement is too sweeping to be literally accurate, for no British Government would have lifted a finger in support of unprovoked aggression. Yet it contains an element of truth; for wars usually arise from such a complex of claims and recriminations that both sides are able to maintain with a certain plausibility that they are the victims, not the authors, of the attack which sets the world aflame.

In April 1912, the discussions between British and Belgian experts, commenced in 1906, were revived. As a European War appeared to become more probable, the part which Belgium and the Scheldt might be forced to play became an object of increasing interest to her neighbours. Colonel Bridges, the British Military Attaché, conversed with General Jungbluth, head of the Belgian General Staff, on the technicalities of military cooperation; but, on receiving the General's Report, the Belgian Government took no steps to continue the conversations. No convention was concluded or even discussed. Indeed, when General Jungbluth was invited to attend the British manœuvres in 1912, the invitation was declined in order to afford no foundation for the rumour of an *entente*. But

---

[1] *How the War Came*, pp. 78–9.

though no common action was taken, both countries proceeded to prepare for the expected storm. Belgium introduced compulsory service in 1913, and elaborate surveys of Belgian roads and railways were undertaken by the British War Office.

IX. The Last Years of Peace, 1912–1914

"When the neutrality negotiations were on the eve of failure," writes Bethmann-Hollweg, "Grey told Wolff-Metternich that, even if no agreement were realised, he hoped that Lord Haldane's visit and the free exchange of views would form the foundation of more trustful intercourse." The hope was fulfilled when concrete problems were taken in hand. The Treaty of 1898, defining British and German spheres of influence in the Portuguese Colonies, was taken out of its pigeon-hole and reexamined; while the more difficult problem of the Bagdad Railway was attacked with a determination to reach an agreement. These negotiations, however, were only beginning when war broke out in the Balkans in October, 1912; and their story must be postponed till the date when this agitating interlude, which occupied the Chanceries of Europe for nearly a year, was at an end.

The year 1912 opened with dark clouds on the eastern horizon. The death of Count Aehrenthal, once the stormy petrel of European politics, was regretted; for he had championed the cause of peace since 1909 against the bellicose Chief of the Staff, Conrad von Hötzendorff, and his successor, Count Berchtold, was headstrong and incapable. A Military Convention between Servia and Bulgaria was signed in April, determining the conditions of mutual aid in the event of attack by Turkey, Roumania and Austria, or of an attack on Turkey. A Græco-Bulgarian Military Convention followed in September, and a verbal understanding was reached with Montenegro. In the same month, Austria enquired whether the Great Powers would join in "recommending to Turkey the adoption of a policy of progressive decentralisation, which would secure to the Christian nationalities their legitimate guarantees, and in urging the Balkan States to await peacefully the results of their policy." The Powers approved; but Berchtold seemed in no hurry to follow up his suggestion, and on October 8th Montenegro gave the signal for the Balkan War by attacking her ancient foe.

Though Turkey at once concluded peace with Italy, and though her population was nearly double that of her four enemies, her armies were rolled back by their impetuous onslaught, and within a month the campaign was decided. British opinion was almost unanimously on the side of the Christian States; but the Foreign Secretary watched the struggle with a critical eye[1]. When visiting Balmoral on the eve of war, Sazonoff found him opposed to the coercion of Turkey by the Powers.

"The action of England," he reported to the Tsar, "is now governed by a resolve not to arouse Moslem hostility, especially in India. Thence arises the apparent indifference to the fate of the Turkish Christians. Moreover, he does not wish to weaken the Kiamil Government, or to see him replaced by some pro-German Young Turk. Though anxious to cooperate in keeping the Balkans quiet, he often hesitates to accept plans for fear of their effect in Constantinople. We cannot reckon on English support if energetic coercion of the Porte seems necessary[2]."

This attitude of detachment was quickly modified by the outbreak of hostilities, as Benckendorff telegraphed with satisfaction in reporting a conversation on October 21st. Even if Turkey won, declared Sir Edward Grey, radical reforms must be secured by direct intervention of the Powers. If necessary, a nominal Turkish sovereignty might be preserved. The territorial *status quo* was desirable; but, in any case, there should be no Turkish gains. The Prime-Minister spoke for the country when he declared, at the Guildhall on November 9th, that the Powers would recognise accomplished facts, and would not oppose the territorial changes resulting from the victory of the allies.

The rapid triumph of the Balkan States raised difficulties for their champions. Sir Edward Grey expressed the hope that the Tchataldja lines would be held, adding that, if the Turks were ejected from their capital, it should be internationalised. His apprehensions, however, were quickly relieved; for the Bulgarian wave had spent its force. A far graver problem was raised by the victories of Servia and by her resolve to secure an outlet on the Adriatic. These possibilities of explosion threw a special responsibility on Great Britain, of which she showed herself fully conscious throughout the Conference of Ambassadors which sat in London from December onwards. The task of its Chairman, Sir Edward Grey, was to prevent Russia and Austria flying at each other's throats. Russia was compelled to accept the veto of Austria and Italy on Servia's occupation of Durazzo; and her disappointment was no less keen when the King of Montenegro,

---

[1] Fresh light is thrown on British policy during the Balkan wars by the French Yellow-books, *Les Affaires Balkaniques*, 1912–1914, 3 vols. 1922.
[2] Siebert, *Diplomatische Aktenstücke*, pp. 546–50.

whose forces had entered Scutari after a siege lasting throughout the winter, was commanded to withdraw, since the town was destined for the new State of Albania. All the more tenaciously did she insist on the inclusion of certain Albanian villages within the frontiers of Servia. Throughout these agitating controversies, the British and German Governments worked in perfect accord for the preservation of peace. "Sir Edward," writes Prince Lichnowsky, who had succeeded Marschall von Bieberstein and speedily learned to admire the character of the Foreign Secretary, "from the very beginning took up the position that England had no interest in Albania. He merely wished to mediate between the two groups as an 'honest broker.' He, therefore, by no means took sides with the Entente, and his authoritative influence contributed in no small measure to agreement. On all questions we took sides with Austria and Italy, while Sir Edward Grey hardly ever backed the French or Russian claims....Thus with his assistance it was possible to coax King Nicholas out of Scutari.... He conducted the negotiations calmly and tactfully. When a question threatened to become involved, he sketched a formula which was always accepted. His personality inspired equal confidence in all the participants[1]." A slightly different account is given by Jagow, the German Foreign Minister. "The credit of an attitude of mediation should not be denied to him. Certainly, he often advised yielding at Petrograd, as we did at Vienna, and found formulas of agreement; but he represented the Entente, because, like us, he neither could nor would abandon his associates. We, like England, played a mediatory part[2]." Sir Edward Grey's services to the calming of the waters were publicly acknowledged by the Foreign Minister in the *Reichstag* on February 7th, 1913. "We have now seen that we have not only points of contact with England of a sentimental nature. I am not a prophet; but I entertain the hope that on the ground of common interests, which in politics is the most fertile soil, we can continue to work with England, and perhaps to reap the fruits of our labours." Europe, added the Chancellor on April 7th, owed gratitude to the discussions of the Ambassadors for repeatedly dissolving antagonisms. The Kaiser, who also desired a pacific solution, was grateful for the diplomatic lightning-conductor erected in London.

It was fortunate for the peace of the world that the Conference

---

[1] *My Mission to London*, pp. 10–11.
[2] Jagow's reply to Lichnowsky appeared in *Norddeutsche Allgemeine Zeitung*, March 23rd, 1918. A translation was published in *Current History*, June, 1918.

had been established; for the conflict dragged on beyond all expectation. After a few weeks of war, Turkey had asked for a truce, which was refused by Greece, but granted by her allies. The Representatives of the belligerents met in London in December, and signed a Treaty which was promptly repudiated in Constantinople, where the Government was overthrown with brutal violence by Enver Bey on January 24th, 1913. During the second stage of the War, Adrianople fell to the combined attack of Bulgarians and Serbs, and Jannina to the Greeks, and in April the diplomats returned to London. But there was now almost open enmity between the victorious allies, Servia demanding a revision of the Partition Treaty of 1912, and receiving the support of Greece. The Treaty with Turkey was drafted on May 2nd; but the progress of the negotiations was so slow that, on May 28th, Sir Edward Grey intervened. "Those who are willing to sign the Preliminary Treaty without any alterations should do so immediately. Those who are not disposed to sign had better leave London, as it is useless for them to continue to engage in discussions of which the only result is indefinite delay." Two days later, the Treaty was signed by all the Delegates. European Turkey emerged with nothing beyond a foothold in Eastern Thrace; but her victors proceeded to quarrel over the spoil. On June 29th the Bulgarians treacherously attacked their late allies; but Servia and Greece were reinforced by the advance of a Roumanian army across the Danube, while the dashing Enver reoccupied Adrianople without a blow. The struggle was over so quickly that there was no time for the Powers to take collective action, and Peace was dictated by the victors in August at Bucharest.

The ten months of war had left a profound *malaise*, not only in the Balkans, but also on the broad arena of European politics. The overthrow of Turkey by a League formed under the auspices of the Tsar, and the aggrandisement of his *protégé* Servia, filled the Central Powers with alarm. The German Army was increased, and a capital levy of 50 millions was devoted to strengthening the frontier fortresses, improving the artillery, and augmenting the gold reserve at Spandau. The German military effort inevitably provoked a French response, and the Three Years' Service, which had been abolished in 1905, was restored. Austria, where Conrad von Hötzendorff had been restored to his position as Chief of the Staff after the death of Aehrenthal, was only restrained from action against Servia, when Bulgaria attacked her late allies, by the refusal of her own allies to cooperate. That opinion in Russia was no less inflamed than in Germany, Austria and France was proved when, in response to a request from Turkey for a German officer of high rank to reorganise her army, Liman von Sanders was appointed in November, 1913, to command the First Army Corps[1]. Sazonoff telegraphed to Benckendorff that a German Commander of an army corps in the Turkish capital was tantamount to a German garrison on the Bosphorus, and suggested that Great Britain and France should make a joint representation at the Porte and ask for compensations. Sir Edward Grey agreed that a German garrison at Constantinople could not be permitted, and proposed to try to persuade Germany to modify her plan. Meanwhile, he was willing to join France and Russia in asking the Porte if it was really intended to give Liman command of Turkish troops in the capital.

Sazonoff, hereupon, asked Sir Edward Grey to approve the following peremptory Note. "The German command would put the whole diplomatic corps in the power of Germany, and the General could take military measures in violation of the Sultan's sovereignty. If Germany obtains such a privileged position, the other Powers would have to consider their own interests." He objected to the threat, and suggested that the three Ambassadors should make a verbal communication to the Porte. "We have heard that a German General has received a very far-reaching command. We assume Turkey will do nothing to jeopardise the independence or security of the Straits and the capital. Other Powers are also interested, and we should be glad of information regarding the contract." A written Note by the Three Powers, he explained, would be a very serious step, while an enquiry was itself a warning. Sazonoff resented the British Foreign Secretary's attempt to pour water into his wine, and complained of his coolness "in a matter of such importance for us"; but he was compelled to adopt the milder course. "If we have changed," he complained to Benckendorff, "it is due to want of confidence in English support. This lack of cohesion and solidarity is a source of lively anxiety; for it constitutes an organic weakness of the Triple Entente, which always damages us in comparison with the solid block of the Triple Alliance." On December 13th, the three Ambassadors accordingly asked the Grand-Vizier for information, and on December 15th the official reply was received. "The General is Chief of the Mission, Member of the War Council, Inspector of Military Schools,

[1] See Siebert, *Diplomatische Aktenstücke*, ch. 17; and Liman von Sanders, *Fünf Jahre Turkei*, ch. 1.

and Commander of the First Corps. His command is purely technical. The Straits, the forts, and the maintenance of order in Constantinople are not in his jurisdiction." Sazonoff complained that the Turkish reply contained nothing new, and informed Sir Edward that he would now await a British initiative. But the Foreign Secretary, who observed to Lichnowsky that no event had made so profound an impression in Russia since he had been in office, refused to be driven into violent courses; for a conciliatory breeze was blowing from Berlin. A compromise was finally adopted, by which Liman resigned the command of the First Corps and was appointed Inspector-General of the Turkish Army; and at the New Year's reception the Tsar warmly thanked the German Ambassador for complying with his wishes.

Great Britain's support of Russia in the Liman incident emphasised anew the intimacy of their relations. In 1912 the training of the Turkish fleet had been entrusted to Admiral Limpus; and, in November, 1913, a contract was signed with the firm of Whitworth and Vickers for thirty years to reorganise the wharves and naval arsenal in the Golden Horn, and to construct a floating dock on the Gulf of Ismid as a naval base. It might well appear strange that the Power which had accepted the task of reforming the Turkish Navy should support Russia's protest against Turkey's invitation to Germany to reform her Army. But British policy in the Near East was to follow Russia, wherever possible. When, in 1913, the Turks had asked for British money and British advisers to reform the administration in Asia Minor, Sir Edward Grey consulted Russia, and in view of her objections declined the mandate, which was consequently entrusted to a Dutch and a Norwegian Commissioner.

The Liman incident had inspired Sazonoff to submit a Memorandum to the Tsar "on the necessity of a comprehensive programme of action, in order to assure for us a satisfactory solution of the question of the Straits in the event of being compelled at no distant period to defend our interests in the Bosphorus and Dardanelles[1]." The Tsar ordered the questions to be discussed by a Crown Council, which met on February 21st, 1914, and made detailed recommendations relating to transport by land and sea, the construction of new railways in the Caucasus and the strengthening of the Black Sea fleet. Its decisions were unknown to the public; but the tension was

---

[1] See Laloy, *Documents Secrets publiés par les Bolsheviks*, pp. 74–100; and *Das deutsche Weissbuch über die Schuld am Kriege*, pp. 169–81.

revealed in a sensational article in the *Kölnische Zeitung* of March 2nd by its Petrograd Correspondent. "The Russian danger is not imminent; but in 1917 the army reforms will be completed and troops are already being massed on her Western frontier.... Russian armaments are enormous, and she will turn her arms against Germany. Such a War would be acclaimed by the whole people." This forecast, which was believed—wrongly, according to Jagow—to have been inspired from Berlin, produced a panic on the Exchanges, and an article in the *Bourse Gazette* of March 13th, universally attributed to Sukhomlinoff, the War Minister, increased the excitement. "Russia wishes for peace, but is ready for war. The army is not only large, but excellently equipped. Russia has always fought on Russian soil and has always been victorious. Russia is no longer on the defensive. Russia is ready."

While the relations between the Dual Alliance and the Central Powers thus grew steadily worse, a welcome *détente* had occurred between Great Britain and Germany. Though Prince Henry, who was sent on a political Mission in the winter of 1912, was informed that our relations to France and Russia were as close as ever and that Germany must not reckon on our neutrality in any European War, even the Navy problem seemed for a moment about to enter on a new stage. "Churchill," writes Tirpitz, "who in 1912 still hoped through Haldane to arrange for two keels to one, accepted in 1913 the 3 : 2 proportion proposed by Lloyd George in 1908. Thus naval agreement was practically achieved, for we had no more Supplementary Bills up our sleeve." The problem, however, was too complex to be solved by a formula. "Churchill was annoyed that Tirpitz accepted it," writes Reventlow, "and therefore introduced reservations, such as that the British total was not to include ships far away or indeed in the Mediterranean or the Colonial ships; and he added that 16 : 10 would not suffice when the pre-Dreadnoughts were withdrawn. His proposal was obviously impracticable and dishonest." Mr Churchill's plan of a naval holiday—that no new ships should be laid down in either country for a year—was put forward in a speech but never brought to the notice of the German Government and never officially supported by the Foreign Secretary. "There are great technical difficulties," observed Bethmann-Hollweg, "and the English Government has not taken it up; so we must wait. But the fact and the manner of the offer constitute a great advance. It seems to me that the confidence begins to return which has long been lacking, to the detriment of both countries and the world." His optimism was shared by Mr Lloyd George, who, in an interview reported in *The Daily Chronicle* on January 1st, 1914, declared that this was the most favourable moment for twenty years to overhaul our expenditure on armaments, since our relations with Germany were infinitely more friendly than they had been for years. Prince Lichnowsky informed his Government that, though Great Britain would indubitably support France if attacked, she would under no circumstances attack or support an attack on Germany.

After the settlement of the Morocco crisis, Sir Edward Grey had declared that we had no desire to oppose German expansion in Central Africa, and the possibilities of Colonial cooperation were briefly discussed by Lord Haldane with Bethmann-Hollweg at Berlin. Negotiations were begun in London after his return[1], and the first task was to overhaul the Portuguese Agreement of 1898. When Lichnowsky reached London, he found that the conversations begun by Wolff-Metternich had been carried on by Baron Kühlmann. "Thanks to the accommodating spirit," he writes, "the new Agreement fully accorded with our wishes and interests." Angola, San Thomé and Principe, and northern Mozambique were earmarked for Germany, to whom the Agreement was far more favourable than that of 1898. The negotiations were, practically, completed when King George visited Berlin for the marriage of the Kaiser's daughter in May, 1913, and the Agreement was initialled in August.

Though the negotiations had proceeded smoothly, a hitch now arose. Sir Edward Grey would only sign if the Agreement of 1898 and the Windsor Treaty were published with it, though Germany might select any time for publication within one year from signature. The Wilhelmstrasse declined.

"We intended publication," writes Jagow, "but only at a suitable moment, when the danger of hostile criticism should be less acute, and if possible with the simultaneous announcement of the Bagdad Agreement, then near completion. Our hesitation was due to our wish not to stir up fresh trouble. We also had to consider German efforts to acquire economic interests in the Portuguese colonies, which would have been more difficult had the agreement been announced."

The real reason for Germany's reluctance was, doubtless, that it would be understood to negative the partition which public opinion

[1] See Lichnowsky, *My Mission to London*; Jagow's reply to Lichnowsky; Helfferich, *Die Vorgeschichte des Weltkrieges*; and "The Bagdad Railway" in *The Quarterly Review*, October, 1917.

regarded as the goal of the negotiations. The delay involved practical difficulties; and, in the spring of 1914, Mr L. Harcourt, the Colonial Secretary, told Lichnowsky that he wished to safeguard German interests, but was in doubt whether he should proceed on the terms of the old or those of the new Treaty. It was urgently desirable to clear up the situation. Lichnowsky's despatch reporting this conversation merely brought Instructions to leave matters alone. When, however, the German Ambassador visited Berlin at the end of June, the Chancellor assented to the signature and publication of the Treaty. It still, however, required repeated applications from Lichnowsky, supported by the Colonial Minister, Dr Solf, before sanction was finally obtained, at the end of July. By that time, however, the War was in sight, and the Treaty was never signed.

The discussions relating to Asiatic Turkey were more difficult and far-reaching. On assuming office in January, 1913, Jagow at once took up the question of the Bagdad Railway. After the failure of the Windsor negotiations in 1907, Sir Ernest Cassel and Gwinner, the Director of the Deutsche Bank, vainly attempted to reach an agreement; but the withdrawal of Russian opposition at the meeting between the Tsar and the Kaiser at Potsdam in November, 1910, rendered British acceptance of the scheme in some form a mere matter of time. On January 17th, 1911, Sir Edward Grey observed to Benckendorff that his position as a negotiator had been greatly weakened. Great Britain had no legal title to protest against German control of the proposed line from Bagdad to Khanikin; but such control would give Germany financial and political influence in Persia. "Germany is strengthened, England weakened. But I make no reproaches. I only ask Russia to keep exclusive control of the line in Persia. A Turkish army under German officers with the use of a railway to Teheran would be a danger. Germany must not have privileges in the Russian sphere which England did not get in 1907." A day or two later, King George urged the Ambassador to draw up the Pact with care. "Russian control of the Persian line would be a security for England, German control a danger." The King strongly favoured a junction of Russian and Indian lines, in which he saw a solution of many difficulties raised by the Bagdad railway. Sir Arthur Nicolson was even more alarmed than his chief or his Sovereign. If Russia allowed German control, he informed Benckendorff, Great Britain would alter her whole policy. "If no way out is found, it is the end of the British policy of the last six years." After these agitating conversations,

Benckendorff reported efforts to prevent the Foreign Secretary from resigning. "Our action in the railway question has shattered his conviction that Russia retains complete freedom in her sphere, and he thinks England should have been consulted." "The nervousness of the English is astonishing," replied Sazonoff. "They knew in October that the main theme of the coming negotiations would be the Khanikin-Teheran line. They are still going on, and nothing is settled. We have no idea of giving Germany control." These assurances exerted a tranquillising effect; and, when "The Potsdam Agreement" was finally reduced to writing on August 19th, 1911, Sazonoff sent a copy to Sir Edward to show there was no cause for alarm. Like many other projects, however, it was not carried out by 1914.

In the autumn of 1912, the British Government withdrew the demand to share in the Bagdad-Gulf section of the line and agreed to the increase of the Customs on condition: that the interests of Turkey and Great Britain in the Gulf region were defined; that Turkey recognised our right to light, buoy and police the Gulf; that the railway should not be built beyond Basra without our consent; that we reached an agreement in the navigation of the Shatt-el-Arab and the control of the port of Basra; that our rights to navigate the river were confirmed and extended; that differential treatment on all railways in Asiatic Turkey was forbidden; and that two British representatives should sit on the Bagdad Railway Board. It was on these lines that the final negotiations were conducted, when the Grand-Vizier, Hakki Pasha, visited London for the Peace negotiations after the First Balkan War. On May 21st, 1913, the Foreign Secretary informed the Russian and French Ambassadors that he could no longer oppose the line, and was about to conclude an agreement with Turkey and to concede the customs increase. The attempt to internationalise the section south of Bagdad had failed; but the line would not be continued beyond Basra without our leave, and two British Directors would watch over the interests of British trade. The negotiations proceeded smoothly. Turkey accepted our definition of the *status quo* in the Gulf, and we recognised the nominal suzerainty of the Sultan over Koweit, though we retained the control over the Sheik's foreign policy and a veto on the alienation of his territory. An International Riverain Commission, with a Turkish façade and British control, was to regulate the navigation of the Shatt-el-Arab. The Lynch Company was confirmed in its privileges on the Tigris, and a new Turkish Company was to be formed to take over the existing Turkish Company—half the capital to be Turkish and half British, the latter possessing a casting vote. Turkey might alienate 20 per cent. to Germany, in return for her surrender of her navigation rights under the concession of 1903 and her consent to a British share in the construction of the ports at Basra and Bagdad.

The German Government was informed of the Anglo-Turkish settlement, and Anglo-German discussions, which began immediately, resulted in a Convention initialled on June 15th, 1914.

In this, Great Britain undertook not to oppose the Bagdad Railway system, and Germany not to oppose British control of river navigation. The terminus was to be at Basra; two British directors were to sit on the Board; the construction and exploitation of the ports at Bagdad and Basra to be undertaken by a separate Company, in which British capital was to hold 40 per cent.; while the navigation of the Shatt-el-Arab was to be entrusted to a Company in which Great Britain should hold half the capital, Turkey being allowed to hand over 20 per cent. to German capital. Agreements were also concluded in regard to irrigation and oil. As to the former, Germany undertook to avoid competition with the plans of Sir W. Willcocks. In the Oil Company the British share was to be 50 per cent., the German and Dutch 25 per cent. each. The Anatolian Railway Company waived to the Smyrna-Aidin Company its right of objection to certain competing branches. Both parties undertook to prevent discrimination on the railways and rivers of Asiatic Turkey. Germany engaged not to support the establishment of any port or railway terminus on the Gulf without our consent, and recognised our special position on the Shatt-el-Arab. Our promise not to support a railway in direct competition with the Bagdad line did not exclude a line from Egypt to the Gulf or lines needed as feeders for river navigation.

On the occasion of the Foreign Office vote, June 29th, the Foreign Secretary announced the settlement. We had signed some Compacts with Turkey, and initialled others with Turkey and Germany, which we could not sign till Germany and Turkey had finished their own negotiations. It was a very complete settlement of many very troublesome questions. The most important result was that the Railway should not advance beyond Basra except by agreement with us. Equal rights and equal rates were to prevail, and two British directors were to see that the line, over which we had no control and in which we did not participate, was being worked fairly for commerce. Turkey recognised the *status quo* in the Gulf as we had understood it for many years—a real understanding, which would prevent either Turkey or ourselves from stirring up trouble. The British negotiators, testifies Helfferich, were stubborn; but the result was satisfactory.

Sir Edward Grey's most important concession, observes Lichnowsky, was the continuation of the Railway to Basra, the whole of Mesopotamia north of Basra being thus recognised as within the German sphere of influence. Friends of peace on both sides were thankful that the chief cause—except the Navy—of Anglo-German friction had at last been removed.

Our negotiations with Germany were watched by our friends with a certain element of suspicion. At the end of 1912, the French Ambassador was instructed to mention that the press rumours of a *rapprochement* with Germany were damaging the *entente*, and that M. Poincaré was to answer an interpellation. Sir Edward Grey replied that there was no foundation for the rumours, and that he was only discussing colonial and other subordinate questions in a friendly way. The French Premier accordingly read to the Chamber a reassuring statement which he had submitted to the Foreign Secretary and Mr Asquith.

"Since certain doubts have arisen in the public opinion of France as to the present orientation of British policy, Sir Edward Grey has informed the French Ambassador that nothing in British policy is altered, that no new relations with other Powers have been entered into, and that the close Entente with France exists in its full extent[1]."

When M. Poincaré, the newly elected President of the Republic, visited London in June, 1913, he was able to assure himself that all was well. "There is no doubt that the warmth of his reception exceeded that of Loubet and Fallières," reported Benckendorff. "Grey tells me he is extremely satisfied with the visit, which has greatly strengthened the Entente[2]." The feeling of insecurity, however, could not be wholly eradicated. "Goschen asked Cambon his view on a naval holiday," reported the Russian Minister at Berlin in February, 1914.

"Cambon replied that he could not approve, as all savings on the Navy would go to the Army and be used against France in a future collision. He looks very sadly at the continual rumours of an improvement in Anglo-German relations, as it suggests the possibility of a *rapprochement*. Though I do not wholly share these apprehensions, I cannot wholly forget that Germany and England, when they begin to settle their economic interests in Africa, may go on to more important negotiations which in the long run might lead to a political pact. I can see from here how the German Government is trying to meet the English[3]."

---

[1] Siebert, *Diplomatische Aktenstücke*, pp. 802–3.
[2] *Ibid.* pp. 804–5.   [3] *Ibid.* p. 775.

The Liman crisis, in which he deemed Sir Edward Grey in some degree to have left him in the lurch, intensified Sazonoff's desire to tighten the bonds of the Triple Entente. On his visit to Balmoral in 1912 he had told him of the new Franco-Russian Naval Convention, and asked if the British Fleet would not render a similar service in the north by drawing off the German Fleet from Russia's coasts.

"Recently we have often felt," he wrote to Benckendorff and Izvolsky on February 12th, 1914, "that an instrument is lacking to us which unifies the views and acts of the Powers, like the Ambassadors' Conference in London last year. Correspondence causes delay, which impedes the conduct of affairs....Perhaps Grey would not object to the Entente Powers establishing the community of their aims through their Representatives in London; for, while the Powers of the opposing group act, we only take counsel[1]."

The project was well received in London and Paris; but Sazonoff determined to utilise the forthcoming visit of King George and Sir Edward Grey to Paris to secure something more than a mere Standing Committee of Ambassadors. The transformation of the Triple Entente into a new Triple Alliance, he wrote to Izvolsky, seemed to him desirable.

"Such an Alliance, while absolutely safeguarding the international position of Russia, France and England, would threaten nobody, as they entertain no thought of conquest, and would be the best security for the maintenance of peace. Certain steps towards cooperation and closer definition of their mutual obligations have been taken between France and England. We must work in the same direction....Unfortunately, the domestic situation in Great Britain absorbs the attention of the Government and public opinion. The soil for international conventions is therefore very unfruitful, and we must proceed very cautiously. I share your view, however, that it would be well if Poincaré and Doumergue, taking advantage of the meeting with the King and his Minister, could point out confidentially that a closer relationship between Russia and England would be joyfully welcomed in France and would be equally desirable for all the members of the Entente. The conditions of such a political pact would of course be reserved for direct negotiations between Petrograd and London; but perhaps the French Government would propose to Grey to inform us of the Anglo-French political compact, which would serve as the foundation for a similar arrangement."

The King and Queen arrived in Paris on April 1st, and the importance of the occasion was emphasised by the presence of the Foreign Secretary, who had never left our shores during his long

---

[1] The Russian despatches relating to closer relations with Great Britain and the discussion of a Naval Convention are printed by Siebert, *Diplomatische Aktenstücke*, pp. 805–27.

tenure of office. While enthusiastically welcoming the guests, almost the whole of the French Press urged that the *entente cordiale*, which had stood the stress of ten years, should be transformed into an Alliance. According to arrangement, Doumergue pleaded for closer relations between Great Britain and Russia, and Izvolsky reported the result to Petrograd. An Alliance was impossible; but Sir Edward Grey was ready for an arrangement with Russia like that existing with France. A naval convention was possible, and the Anglo-French Agreements might be communicated. "Doumergue and Cambon told me they were astonished at Grey's clear and definite willingness for a close *rapprochement*."

On May 12th, Benckendorff reported a memorable interview with the Foreign Minister after his return from Paris.

"Sir Edward sent for me to express how profound were the impressions of his journey—impressions which were shared by the King and all who had taken part in the visit. These impressions had far surpassed his expectations, and he could not sufficiently congratulate himself on his reception by Poincaré and Doumergue, with whom entire agreement on current issues and the general situation was reached. The reception of Their Majesties, wherever they appeared, was unmistakable. The British Government had drawn the conclusion that the Entente had struck as deep root in France as in England. Grey spoke with a warmth that is not usual with him....He went on to say that I was doubtless aware of his conversation on Russia with Doumergue. He could not in that interview give more than his personal assent to the plan that Russia should be informed of all the military arrangements between England and France. He could now tell me that the Prime-Minister had no objection, but that the matter was of course too important to be settled without the assent of the Cabinet. I thanked him for his words, and said he doubtless knew your views on the necessity of a closer connexion between the members of the Entente, which would not exclude an Alliance. Sir Edward replied that an Alliance was impossible and added, 'You see we have even today no Alliance with France.'"

Four days later, the Ambassador reported the favourable result of the Cabinet discussion. Russia would be informed of the Grey-Cambon letters, and negotiations would then take place between the Russian and British Admiralties. The Russian Naval Attaché in London might be empowered to negotiate after obtaining his Instructions in Petrograd, whereas the arrival of high Russian officials would certainly become known. Benckendorff was fully satisfied.

"My sojourn in Paris," he wrote to his Chief, "has confirmed my view that an alliance or any public compact is impossible. The reception of the King and Queen was extraordinarily cordial—far more, I was told, than on previous English visits. If, nevertheless, the impossibility of a formal Alliance between England and France was recognised, all the more is that the case between England and Russia. I doubt if a stronger guarantee for common military operations is possible than the spirit of this Entente as it has revealed itself, strengthened by the existing military agreements. Looking back on its different phases, one cannot deny that at critical moments England has never hesitated to take her stand at the side of France. The same is true for Russia, whenever English and Russian interests were simultaneously affected, despite the difficulty of agreement on questions as they arise, and despite the fact that the Entente between Russia and England has not taken such root as that between France and England. A public Alliance would arouse such opposition—not in the Liberal party alone—that it is not worth while, and would add very little to the guarantees which England offers. Even the Englishman who is most deeply convinced that a conflict with Germany is sooner or later inevitable shrinks from binding his country by obligations the results of which he cannot foresee."

On May 23rd, the Foreign Secretary gave the Russian Ambassadors the Grey-Cambon letters, adding that there was no objection to a similar agreement with Russia, which would naturally deal with the Navies. The Russian Naval Attaché at once returned home for Instructions, and found his Government in high spirits. "Apart from its practical value," wrote Sazonoff to Benckendorff, "we attach special importance to the political aspect. We see in it an important step in associating England more closely with the Franco-Russian Alliance." After full discussion, the Russian Admiralty recommended that Great Britain should hold as large a part of the German Fleet as possible in the North Sea, and thereby render possible a Russian landing in Pomerania; that for this purpose she might send merchant ships to Russia and the Baltic ports before the beginning of hostilities; that Russian ships should be allowed to use British harbours in the eastern Mediterranean, as they were already allowed to use French harbours in the Western half; and that information as to signals, ciphers, etc., should be exchanged.

Captain Wolkoff returned to London with the Admiralty scheme; but Benckendorff wisely counselled him not to mention the plan of sending transports to the Baltic. After conversation with Prince Louis of Battenberg, the Naval Attaché reported that the British Government was in no hurry, and that the Prince would visit Russia in August for discussions with the Admiralty. By this time, however, the secret had leaked out. At the end of May, the *Berliner Tageblatt*, at the instance of the German Government, announced that Great Britain was making a naval convention with Russia[1]. When, on June 11th, Benckendorff informed the Foreign Office that Wolkoff had returned with powers to negotiate, Sir Edward lamented the indiscretions that had occurred, as he would be forced to answer a question in the House; and he sketched the reply which he proposed to make and which would veil the negotiations. Meanwhile, he sought to relieve the apprehensions of the Chancellor, who had instructed Lichnowsky to ask for explanations.

On June 24th, Prince Lichnowsky thanked the Foreign Secretary for his declarations, and communicated the Chancellor's belief that trustful cooperation was the key to peace. Sir Edward Grey replied that it was also his object to continue hand in hand with Germany and to remain in close touch in all new questions. He had not the slightest ground to doubt the pacific views of the Russian Government. Benckendorff was no Germanophobe, while the Tsar and Sazonoff always spoke to Sir George Buchanan in a peaceful sense. The French had not the slightest desire for war. There were no unpublished agreements between Great Britain and her friends, and he would never do anything to give the *entente* a point against Germany; but his relation to the two friends was very intimate and had lost nothing of its strength, and in all important questions they were in continual touch. On receiving Lichnowsky's report of this interview, Zimmermann, the Under-Secretary, wrote to the Chancellor that the Ambassador was once again talked over by Sir Edward Grey, and suggested that he should be shown the proofs of the negotiations in progress between England and Russia[2]. On July 11th, the Foreign Secretary replied to questions by Mr King and Sir W. Byles whether a naval convention with Russia had been or was being made.

"A year ago the Prime-Minister said that, if war broke out between the European Powers, no unpublished agreements existed which could limit the freedom of the Government or Parliament. No negotiations with any Power have been or are being or are likely to be undertaken which would make this less true. If any such convention were contemplated which would modify the Prime-Minister's declaration, it would have to be laid before Parliament."

This ambiguous phraseology was interpreted in different ways; but the inability to meet the question with a direct negative confirmed the suspicious in their fears.

[1] From 1909 till the outbreak of war an official in the Russian Embassy in London communicated to the German Government the confidential correspondence between London and Petrograd. See Valentin, *Deutschland's Aussenpolitik*, p. 145.
[2] Kautzkv, *Die deutschen Dokumente zum Kriegsausbruch*, I. 6–8.

The slow progress of the discussions annoyed Sazonoff, who reminded Benckendorff of the necessity for concluding the Convention as soon as possible. "I will do all I can to hasten the negotiations between Captain Wolkoff and the Admiralty," replied the Ambassador on July 2nd; "but I see no reason to believe that the Government has the least objection to carry out the Paris project. If it is not yet finished, it is because Prince Louis is to complete the negotiations in Petrograd. The exact date of this private visit, which is to be kept secret, is not fixed. Another cause of delay is the indiscretions. Perhaps Sir Edward wishes that the disquietude in Berlin should diminish before he goes further. As a matter of fact, he would find it difficult at the same moment to issue *démentis* and to negotiate—a *rôle* he would have to play towards Germany and also towards a large part of his own party and the English Press." Before, however, Sir Edward had time to solve his problem in casuistry, or Prince Louis to sign the Naval Convention in the Russian capital, the whole energies of the British Government were engaged in a desperate effort to maintain the Peace of the World.

X. The Outbreak of the War, 1914

The European atmosphere was already charged with electricity when Archduke Francis Ferdinand and his wife were murdered by Austrian Serbs at Serajevo on June 28th[1]. Count Berchtold resolved to seize the opportunity for the final reckoning with Servia for which he had been waiting; and, in answer to an autograph letter from Francis Joseph, William II promised his full support on July 5th. The Chancellor informed the Austrian Ambassador that it was not the German Emperor's business to express an opinion on the questions at issue between Austria and Servia, but that Francis Joseph could rely on his support in accordance with his treaty obligations and his old friendship. No Crown Council was held; but, before starting on his annual cruise in Northern Waters on July 6th, William II summoned Representatives of the War Office and the Admiralty to Potsdam and warned them of the danger of European complications. The contention that Vienna was the tool of Berlin was as baseless in 1914 as in 1908; but, by encouraging Austria to take action which was almost certain to plunge Europe into war, the German Government incurred a share in the guilt of the catastrophe scarcely less than that of Austria

---

[1] The most complete collection of official publications is that of J. B. Scott, *Diplomatic Documents relating to the Outbreak of the European War*, 2 vols., 1916.

herself. That William II regarded the Serbs as regicides and savages, and believed that the Tsar would view them in the same light, affords no excuse for the criminal levity with which he urged their prompt and exemplary punishment.

While Berchtold was preparing his thunderbolt and assuring himself of German support, Lichnowsky, who had just returned from a visit to Kiel and Berlin, warned Sir Edward Grey, on July 6th, that relations between Vienna and Belgrade were likely to become strained, and suggested that he should persuade Russia to advise Servia to submit to the Austrian demands[1]. The Foreign Secretary perceived that Austria could hardly refrain from strong measures, promised to remain in touch with Germany, and repeated that he had no evidence of anti-German sentiment in Petrograd. The conversation was resumed on July 9th. Sir Edward Grey was ready to urge Russia to moderation if Austria was compelled to adopt sharper measures against Servia; but much would depend on whether they would inflame Slav feeling to a degree rendering it impossible for Russia to remain passive. The Foreign Secretary, reported the Ambassador, was in good spirits and remarked that he had no reason for taking a pessimistic view of the situation. The ominous silence of Vienna prompted him to ask Lichnowsky, on July 20th, whether he had any news from that quarter. Austria, replied the Ambassador, would certainly take some steps; the situation was very uncomfortable, and it would be very desirable if Russia could mediate with Servia. The Foreign Secretary rejoined that Austria would doubtless do nothing till she had disclosed her case, founded presumably on what she discovered at the trial. This would make it easier for other Powers, among them Russia, to counsel moderation in Belgrade. In fact, the more Austria could keep her demands within reasonable limits, and the stronger the justification she could produce, the more chance there would be of smoothing over the situation. He hated the idea of a war between any of the Great Powers, and that any of them should be dragged into a war by Servia would be detestable. In reporting the conversation, Lichnowsky described the Minister as still taking an optimistic view of the crisis.

While the British and German Governments were expressing their desire to avoid a world-war, Vienna was preparing to render it virtually inevitable. After receiving the reply of the German Government

---

[1] Lichnowsky's despatches are printed in Kautzky, *Die deutschen Dokumente zum Kriegsausbruch*, 4 vols., 1919.

on July 6th, the Ministers of the Dual Monarchy met on July 7th to discuss the situation. Count Berchtold expressed his view that the moment had come to put an end to Servia's intrigues once for all. All present except Tisza, who argued that an attack on Servia involved a world war, agreed that in view of Servia's record a purely diplomatic success would be worthless, and that therefore such stringent demands be presented as to ensure a refusal. In a second Crown Council, held on July 19th, the text of the note to Servia was settled and it was agreed to present it on July 23rd. Tisza's assent was secured by a resolution that Austria should disclaim annexations. It was understood, however, that the strategic frontiers could be corrected and portions of the country be assigned to other States. On July 22nd, Sir Edward Grey, unwilling to wait longer without information, asked the Austrian Ambassador to see him on the following day; and the Ambassador explained the nature of the ultimatum, which was not to be officially communicated till July 24th.

"Count Mensdorff told me he supposed there would be a time-limit. I said I regretted this very much. It might inflame opinion in Russia, and it would make it difficult, if not impossible, to give more time, even if after a few days it appeared that by giving more time there would be a prospect of securing a peaceful settlement. I admitted that, if there was no time-limit, the proceedings might be unduly protracted; but I urged that a time-limit could always be introduced afterwards. If the demands were first made without a time-limit, Russian public opinion might be less excited. After a week it might have cooled down, and, if the Austrian case was very strong, the Russian Government might use their influence in favour of a satisfactory reply from Servia....I could not help dwelling on the dreadful consequences involved. It had been represented to me that it would be very desirable that those who had influence in Petrograd should use it on behalf of patience and moderation. I had replied that the amount of influence would depend upon how reasonable were the Austrian demands....Count Mensdorff said all would depend on Russia. I remarked that it required two to keep the peace, and I hoped very much that, if there were difficulties, Austria and Russia would be able in the first instance to discuss them directly with each other."

In reporting the conversation, Count Mensdorff notes that the Foreign Secretary was "as cool and unprejudiced as ever, friendly and not without sympathy for our side, but undoubtedly very anxious as to the possible consequences[1]." On the following day, July 24th, the Ambassador presented a copy of the ultimatum, which demanded

---

[1] Mensdorff's despatches are printed in the Austrian Red-book, 1920. A translation in three volumes has been published by Allen & Unwin.

the suppression of anti-Austrian propaganda and the cooperation of
Austrian Representatives in this task; and the Foreign Secretary
renewed his complaint that a time-limit had been adopted at this
stage. He had never known any State address to another a document
of so formidable a character. The merits of the dispute between
Austria and Servia were not the concern of the British Government.
He would exchange views with other Powers, and must await their
views as to what could be done. His first task was to send for the
French Ambassador. He told him that he was to see the German
Ambassador in the afternoon, and should say that, if Russia took the
view of the ultimatum which it seemed to him that any Power interested in Servia would take, he would be quite powerless to exert any
moderating influence. The only chance of mediation was that Germany, France, Italy and Great Britain, who had no direct interests
in Servia, should act jointly and simultaneously in Vienna and
Petrograd. M. Cambon replied that nothing could be said in Petrograd
till Russia had expressed some opinion or taken some action; that, in
two days, Austria would march into Servia, since the Servians could
not possibly accept the ultimatum; that Russia would be compelled
by public opinion to take action as soon as Austria attacked Servia;
and therefore that, so soon as the Austrian attack began, it would be
too late for mediation. The Minister rejoined that, if Austria entered
Servia and Russia mobilised, it might be possible for the four Powers
to urge both to halt, pending mediation; but German participation
would be essential to success. M. Cambon reiterated his opinion that,
after Austria had moved against Servia, it would be too late, and
argued that the best chance lay in gaining time by mediation in
Vienna, preferably on the initiative of Germany.

In the afternoon, the Foreign Secretary saw the German Ambassador, who brought a Circular Note denouncing the Serb intrigues
against the integrity of the Dual Monarchy, approving the Austrian
demands, and expressing the opinion that the matter concerned
Austria and Servia alone. Sir Edward Grey observed that, if the
ultimatum did not lead to trouble with Russia, he had no concern
with it. But he was very apprehensive of the view Russia would take,
and, in view of the extraordinary character of the Austrian Note and
the short time allowed, he felt quite helpless so far as Russia was
concerned. The only chance was that the Four other Great Powers
should mediate and gain time; and this was only possible if Germany
would propose and participate in such advice at Vienna. In reporting

the conversation, Lichnowsky added that the Minister was obviously anxious to do everything possible to avoid European complications. The Kaiser, on the other hand, wrote on the margin of the despatch that he would only take part in mediation at Austria's express wish, which was unlikely, "since in vital matters people consult nobody." Having thus proposed mediation to Paris and Berlin, Sir Edward Grey, on the same day, urged Servia to promise the fullest satisfaction if any of her officials should prove to have been accomplices in the Serajevo murder.

The efforts of the Foreign Secretary were bravely seconded by the German Ambassador, who, on July 25th, after reading the morning papers, telegraphed that the effect of the ultimatum was overwhelming; that Germany was considered morally responsible, since without her encouragement such a Note could never have been sent; and that, unless she took part in mediation, British confidence in her love of peace would be finally destroyed. In a second telegram, he urged support of Sir Edward Grey's proposal to postpone hostilities against Servia. A confidential telegram to Jagow added that the proposal for mediation by the four Powers was the only escape from a world war, and that, if France were drawn in, he did not believe that England could remain indifferent. The Ambassador's reading of the barometer was confirmed by a visit to the Foreign Office, where the Foreign Secretary hinted that Great Britain, though having entered into no binding arrangements, could not be indifferent to European complications. The Government, added Lichnowsky in reporting the conversation, would remain friendly and so far as possible impartial, so long as it believed in the sincerity of Germany's love of peace and desire to cooperate in preventing an explosion. Refusal of the proposal to mediate, or any step suggesting that Germany wished for war with Russia, would probably throw England on the side of France and Russia.

On July 26th, Sir Edward Grey telegraphed the proposal for mediation which he had discussed with the Ambassadors to the Governments of Paris, Berlin and Rome.

"Would the Minister of Foreign Affairs be disposed to instruct the Ambassador here to join with the Representatives of France, Italy, Germany and myself to meet in confidence immediately for the purpose of discovering an issue which would prevent complications? If so, Representatives at Belgrade, Vienna and Petrograd should request that all active military operations should be suspended pending results of conference."

France and Italy promptly accepted the proposal; but Jagow explained to Sir Edward Goschen that such a conference would practically amount to a Court of Arbitration and could only be summoned at the request of Austria and Russia, and that he must therefore decline, desirous though he was to cooperate for the maintenance of peace. He added that he had just heard of the intention of Petrograd to exchange views with Vienna, and that it would be best, before taking any steps, to await the result. Lichnowsky, on the contrary, informed Sir Edward Grey that his Government accepted in principle mediation by the four Powers, and conveyed the Chancellor's request to influence Petrograd to localise the War. The Foreign Secretary rejoined that the Servian reply, which he had just seen and which went further than could have been expected towards meeting the Austrian demands, was obviously due to Russian prompting, and it was therefore at Vienna that moderating influence was now required. If Austria marched into Servia, it would show that she was determined to crush her, regardless of consequences. The reply should at least be treated as a basis for discussion, and Germany should urge this course at Vienna. Lichnowsky reported that he found the Minister for the first time in low spirits. "He spoke very gravely and seemed very definitely to expect us to use our influence to settle the question. Everybody here is convinced that the key is in Berlin, and that, if Berlin wishes peace, it will hold back Austria." The Chancellor, who was not less anxious for Peace than Sir Edward Grey, telegraphed Lichnowsky's despatch to Vienna, adding that, having already declined the proposal for a Conference, it was impossible to reject the new suggestion.

Unfortunately for the Peace of the World, Vienna was resolved on a final reckoning with her troublesome neighbour, who made no secret of her desire to build up a Greater Servia and had been encouraged by Russia to find her "Promised Land" in the Habsburg dominions. "The integral acceptance of the ultimatum," reported Sir Maurice de Bunsen, "was neither expected nor desired....The country believed it had before it only the alternative of subduing Servia or of submitting sooner or later to mutilation at her hands." Mensdorff was instructed to inform Sir Edward Grey that Servia had not accepted the demands, that Austria must proceed to force, and that she counted on British sympathy in the struggle. Sir Edward Grey replied that he could not understand this reading of the answer. The Ambassador admitted that it might, on paper, seem satisfactory; but the cooperation of Austrian officers and police, which alone would guarantee the cessation of the subversive campaign, had been refused. The Foreign Secretary retorted that in Russia, where the Servian reply was expected to diminish the tension, it had now been increased by Austria's decision. The response of Belgrade involved the greatest humiliation he had ever known a country undergo, and it was very disappointing that Austria had treated it as a blank negative. He added that the Fleet, which had assembled for manœuvres, was not being dispersed, though there was no menace in the decision.

If Austria was determined, at any cost, to have the war with Servia of which she had been baulked in 1913, and which she regarded as essentially defensive, Russia was no less resolved to honour her reiterated promises of support to her *protégé*. In the Bosnian crisis, she had been too weak to draw the sword; but she had now recovered her breath, and, if she were to allow Servia to become an Austrian vassal, her prestige and authority in the Near East would be gone. Moreover, an influential party looked forward to a conflict of which Constantinople might be the prize. In the Central empires it was hoped, and in some quarters sincerely believed, that she would stand aside while Servia was receiving her chastisement; but there was no ground for such a supposition. After reading the Austrian ultimatum, which by a refinement of duplicity was issued immediately after the French President had concluded his visit to Petrograd and had taken ship, Sazonoff described it to Sir George Buchanan as provocative and immoral, and expressed the hope that the British Government would proclaim its solidarity with Russia and France. The Ambassador replied that he did not expect any unconditional engagement of armed support, since no direct British interests were involved, and a war for Servia would never be sanctioned by British opinion. Sazonoff rejoined that the general European Question was involved; that Great Britain would, sooner or later, be dragged in if war broke out; and that we should render it more probable if we did not from the outset make common cause with France and Russia.

Such was the situation when, on July 27th, the Foreign Secretary in a few pregnant sentences informed the House of Commons, whose attention had been focussed on the crisis in Ireland, of the gravity of the situation and of the steps he had taken to meet it. On learning the ultimatum, he had suggested cooperation with France, Germany and Italy to keep the peace.

"The cooperation of all four Powers is essential. In a crisis so grave as this the efforts of one Power alone to preserve the peace must be quite ineffective. The moment the dispute ceases to be between Austria and Servia, it can but end in the greatest catastrophe that has ever befallen Europe at one blow. No one can say what would be the limit of the issues that might be raised by such a conflict, and the consequences would be incalculable."

On the same day, the Cabinet for the first time discussed the momentous issues of British interests and obligations in the event of a European War. The Foreign Secretary had uttered no word since the beginning of the crisis to bind himself or his colleagues; but an important decision had been taken on the previous day by the Admiralty on its own responsibility. It had been decided in March that, instead of the usual summer manœuvres, a test mobilisation would be held in July. On July 16th, accordingly, 460 ships were assembled at Portland, and on July 23rd, at the conclusion of the exercises, Admiral Callaghan announced that he was beginning to disperse the Fleet, and that the process would be complete by July 27th. Desiring to allay anxiety, the Government at first took no steps to arrest the dispersal; but, at 4 o'clock on the afternoon of July 26th, when many minor vessels had already departed, the Admiral was instructed that no ships of the First Fleet were to leave till further orders, and that the ships of the Second Fleet were to remain at their home ports. This order was despatched on the initiative of Prince Louis of Battenberg, the First Sea Lord, with the approval of Mr Churchill. It was an elementary precaution, and, as the Foreign Secretary had explained to the Austrian Ambassador, there was no menace in it. The time had come, declared Sir Edward to his colleagues, to settle whether we should intervene or remain neutral in a European struggle. The Cabinet could naturally choose which it preferred; but, if it chose neutrality, he was not the man to carry out such a policy. The meeting ended without a decision, and without a clear indication on which side it would ultimately fall.

Cabinet discussions and sectional meetings continued throughout the week, Ministers being divided almost equally into interventionists and neutralists, though both sides were equally anxious for the success of the Foreign Secretary's efforts to avert the dread catastrophe. Though they had worked together for over eight crowded and anxious years, during which a European war had on several occasions seemed very near, they had never decided what part we should play in such a struggle. The negotiations which followed Lord Haldane's Mission of 1912 resulted in a significant refusal to tie our hands by a formula of rigid neutrality; but no advance was made, at that time or in the Grey-Cambon correspondence, towards deciding how we ought to employ our liberty. Meanwhile, the conversations between the military and naval experts had continued without interruption, though they remained unknown to Parliament. From the day of his accession to office, the Foreign Secretary had never doubted that it would be our duty and our interest to support France in arms if she were attacked by Germany; but neither the Cabinet nor the country had reached this definite conclusion, and he was in consequence handicapped, when the storm broke, by his inability to speak in decisive tones. Till August 2nd, when the Government reached its first decision, he replied to all appeals for support that we must keep our hands free. After the ineffective Cabinet discussion on July 27th, he explained his attitude to Benckendorff, who complained that in German and Austrian circles an impression prevailed that, in any event, we should stand aside. This impression, replied Sir Edward Grey, ought to be dispelled by the orders we had given for the First Fleet not to disperse; but that fact must not be taken to mean that anything more than diplomatic action was promised.

On July 28th, when Sir Maurice de Bunsen expressed the desire of the British Government that the four Powers should work for peace, Berchtold replied, "quietly but firmly," that no discussion could be accepted on the basis of the Servian Note; that war would be declared that day; that no temporary arrangement with Servia was worth concluding, as she had deceived Austria before; that she was not a civilised nation; and that the Peace of Europe would not be saved if the Great Powers backed her up. If Austria accepted mediation, Servia would feel encouraged to go on as in the past, and the question of war would quickly crop up again. When the Declaration of War was known at Petrograd, mobilisation was ordered in southern Russia, and Sazonoff telegraphed to Benckendorff that it put an end to the idea of direct communications between Petrograd and Vienna. Action by the London Cabinet with a view to suspension of military operations was now most urgent; for, unless they were stopped, mediation would only give Austria time to crush Servia.

The Austrian Declaration of War against Servia, though not less deeply resented in Whitehall than had been the ultimatum, wrought no change in British policy. The Foreign Secretary continued to make no promises of support which might inflame the martial ardour of Petrograd, and no promise of neutrality which might encourage hotheads in Vienna and Berlin. On July 29th, he informed M. Cambon that, if Germany and France became involved, we had not made up our minds what we should do. We were free from engagements, and we should have to decide what British interests required us to do.

"I thought it necessary to say that, because, although we were taking all precautions with the fleet and I was about to warn Lichnowsky not to count on our standing aside, it would not be fair that M. Cambon should suppose this meant that we had decided what to do in a contingency that I still hoped might not arise."

The Foreign Secretary next appealed to Berlin to suggest any method by which the Four Powers could prevent war. The whole idea of mediation, or mediating influence, was ready to be put into operation by any method Germany could suggest, should his own be unacceptable. Mediation, for instance, might be possible if Austria, while insisting that she must hold the occupied territory till she had received satisfaction, stated that she would not advance further pending the effort to mediate between her and Russia. If Germany would recommend this at Vienna, he would secure Russian assent. The conversation with Lichnowsky was continued later in the day, when Sir Edward Grey, after repeating that the Austrian Declaration of War rendered vain the direct conversations between Vienna and Petrograd which the Chancellor had favoured, added what the Ambassador afterwards described as "the famous warning."

"This afternoon," he telegraphed to Sir E. Goschen, "I said that I wished to say to him, in a quite private and friendly way, something that was on my mind. The situation was very grave. If Germany became involved and then France, the issue might be so great that it would involve all European interests; and I did not wish him to be misled by the friendly tone of our conversation into thinking that we should stand aside. He said he quite understood this; but he asked whether I meant that we should under certain circumstances intervene. I replied that I did not wish to say that, or to use anything that was like a threat or an attempt to apply pressure. ...But, if the issue did become such that we thought British interests required us to intervene, we must intervene at once and the decision would have to be very rapid....The Ambassador took no exception to what I had said; indeed, he told me that it accorded with what he had already given to Berlin as his view of the situation."

Lichnowsky's despatch, which Jagow confessed to the British Ambassador he read with regret but without surprise, did not reach

Berlin in time to influence the Crown Council held on the same evening at Potsdam, whither the Kaiser had returned from his northern cruise. No authoritative account of the meeting has been published; but, on returning from Potsdam, the Chancellor made to Sir Edward Goschen what the latter described as a strong bid for British neutrality. It was clear, he observed, that Great Britain would never stand by and allow France to be crushed; but that was not Germany's object. If British neutrality were certain, every assurance would be given to the British Government that Germany aimed at no territorial acquisition at the expense of France, should she prove victorious in a war. When questioned about the French Colonies, he said he could not give a similar undertaking. Germany would respect the integrity and neutrality of Holland, so long as her adversaries did the same. It depended on the action of France what operations Germany might be forced to enter upon in Belgium, but, when the War was over, Belgian integrity would be respected if she had not sided against Germany. His object had always been to bring about an understanding with England. He had in mind a general neutrality agreement; and an assurance of British neutrality in the conflict which the present crisis might possibly produce would enable him to look forward to its realisation.

Sir Edward Grey promptly replied, with a heat which he had not hitherto displayed, that the Government could not for a moment entertain the Chancellor's proposal of neutrality on such terms.

"Without having further territory taken from her in Europe," he telegraphed to Sir Edward Goschen, "France could be so crushed as to lose her position as a Great Power; and it would be a disgrace from which our good name would never recover to make this bargain at her expense. Nor could we bargain away our obligation or interest in the neutrality of Belgium. We must preserve our full freedom to act as circumstances seem to us to require. You should add, most earnestly, that the one way of maintaining the good relations between England and Germany is that they should continue to work together to preserve the peace of Europe. If we succeed in this object, they will be *ipso facto* improved. If the Peace of Europe can be preserved, my own endeavour will be to promote some arrangement, to which Germany could be a party, by which she could be assured that no aggressive or hostile policy would be pursued against her or her Allies by France and Russia and ourselves, jointly or separately. I have desired this and worked for it through the last Balkan crisis, and, Germany having a corresponding object, our relations sensibly improved. The idea has hitherto been too Utopian to form the subject of definite proposals; but, if this present crisis, so much more acute than any that

Europe has gone through for generations, be safely passed, I am hopeful that the relief and reaction may make possible some more definite *rapprochement* between the Powers."

The Kaiser and the Chancellor had rashly encouraged Berchtold to set the stone rolling; but after the Servian reply they attempted to apply the brake to the Austrian chariot. "The wishes of the Monarchy are in the main fulfilled," wrote the Kaiser to Jagow. "A capitulation of the most humiliating character is enshrined therein, and every ground for war disappears. But the piece of paper is only of value when it is translated into fact. The Serbs are Orientals, false and procrastinating. In order that these fair promises materialise, a *douce violence* must be applied. Austria could hold Belgrade as a guarantee. The Austrian Army must have a visible *satisfaction d'honneur*. That is the condition of my mediation." This proposal was despatched to Vienna on the evening of June 28th, anticipating a similar proposal of Sir Edward Grey. But information received a day later from the Ambassador at Petrograd caused the Chancellor to address a sharp warning to Vienna, which would have been of greater utility at an earlier date. "The refusal to exchange views with Petrograd would be a grave mistake. We are ready to fulfil our duty. As an Ally, we must, however, refuse to be drawn into a world-conflagration through Austria not respecting our advice. Tell Berchtold, with all emphasis and great seriousness."

Berchtold at once permitted the renewal of conversations at Petrograd, which he had refused two days previously, and added that neither the infraction of Servia's rights nor the acquisition of territory was contemplated. A Crown Council decided to send a courteous reply to the British offer of mediation, which Austria was willing to consider on condition that the operations in Servia were not interrupted thereby, and that Russia instantly ceased mobilisation and dismissed her reserves. The readiness for an eleventh hour compromise with which Austria has been sometimes credited was thus largely imaginary; for it was of the essence of the Anglo-German proposal that the campaign against Servia should stop, and no one could expect Russia to cease mobilisation and dismiss her reserves while the Austrian army continued to trample the Servians underfoot. When, however, Sir Edward Grey was informed by Lichnowsky that, as a result of German representations, conversations between Russia and Austria had been resumed, he expressed his gratification and instructed the British Ambassador to tell Sazonoff that he earnestly hoped he would encourage them. He did not, however, see how Russia could suspend military preparations, unless some limit were put by Austria to the advance of her troops into Servia. To meet the difficulty, he now instructed Sir Edward Goschen to sound the German Government as to a fresh proposal.

"It has occurred to me that Germany might sound Vienna, and I would sound Petrograd, whether it would be possible for the four disinterested Powers to offer to Austria that they would undertake to see that she obtained full satisfaction of her demands on Servia, provided that they did not impair Servian sovereignty and the integrity of Servian territory, which she has already declared her willingness to respect. Russia might be informed by the four Powers that they would undertake to prevent Austrian demands impairing Servian sovereignty and integrity. All Powers would of course suspend further military operations or preparations."

The Ambassador was ordered to repeat the promise and the warning which the Foreign Secretary had just given to Lichnowsky.

"I said that, if Germany could get any reasonable proposal put forward which made it clear that Germany and Austria were striving to preserve European peace, and that Russia and France would be unreasonable if they rejected it, I would support it at Petrograd and Paris, and would go the length of saying that, if Russia and France would not accept it, the Government would have nothing more to do with the consequences; but, otherwise, I told the Ambassador that, if France became involved, we should be drawn in."

Sir Edward Grey's conversation with Lichnowsky on the morning of July 31st took place, and his Instructions to Berlin were despatched, in ignorance of the fact that Russia, who had mobilised fifty-five divisions on July 29th in answer to Austria's twenty-two, had now mobilised her entire forces. According to Sukhomlinoff, the Russian War Minister, the Tsar signed the order for general mobilisation on the afternoon of July 29th; but, after a friendly telegram from the Kaiser, he ordered that mobilisation should only take place against Austria[1]. The War Minister, however, and the Chief of the Staff allowed general mobilisation to continue, while concealing this from the Tsar and denying it to the German Military Attaché. Their disobedience was not discovered at the time; for, in the afternoon of July 30th, Sazonoff, the War Minister and the Minister of Marine, on learning of the bombardment of Belgrade, agreed that general mobilisation was necessary. The Tsar's consent was obtained the same night, and in the early hours of July 31st the capital was

[1] The revelations at Sukhomlinoff's trial for embezzlement were summarised in *The Manchester Guardian*, September 22nd, 1917.

placarded with notices. A few hours later Austria also ordered general mobilisation.

The provocation involved in Austria's attack on Servia was grievous, and the guilt of the Austrian ultimatum was beyond comparison greater than that of the Russian mobilisation, because it was first in time and invited the response which it received. The World-war was, nevertheless, precipitated by the action of Russia, at a moment when conversations between Vienna and Petrograd were being resumed, when the Chancellor was at length endeavouring to restrain his ally, and when the Tsar and the Kaiser were in telegraphic communication. The proclamation from Berlin of *drohende Kriegsgefahr*, followed by an ultimatum demanding the cessation of Russia's general mobilisation within twelve hours, was hailed throughout Germany as the inevitable reply to the dread menace of invasion.

While Sir Edward Grey had been gallantly struggling to build a bridge between Vienna and Petrograd, France was convinced that nothing but a public assurance of British support for the Dual Alliance would arrest the avalanche; and, throughout the week, she made repeated but unavailing efforts to secure it. On July 30th, the French Ambassador reminded Sir Edward Grey of the letters of 1912. "He did not ask me to say directly that we would intervene, but he would like me to say what we should do if certain circumstances arose; for instance, if Germany demanded that France should cease her preparations or demand her neutrality." The Foreign Secretary promised a reply after the Cabinet meeting on the following day; and, meanwhile, the Prime-Minister announced in the House of Commons the postponement of the Irish Amending Bill. "The issues of peace and war are hanging in the balance. It is of vital importance in the interests of the whole world that this country, which has no interests of its own directly at stake, should present a united front and be able to speak and act with the authority of an undivided nation." On the following day *The Times*, which was still regarded abroad as reflecting the policy of the Foreign Office, began an active campaign for intervention. "The interest of self-preservation," it wrote, "compels us to be ready to strike with all our force for our own safety and that of our friends, the European equilibrium, and the more direct interest of preserving the independence of Belgium and the Channel." This view was shared by almost every Opposition organ, while the Ministerial Press was at this stage equally solid for neutrality.

On July 31st, after the Cabinet, the Foreign Secretary, according to promise, saw the French Ambassador, who referred to a telegram from his brother that it was the uncertainty as to our intervention which encouraged Berlin.

"I said it was quite wrong to suppose we had left Germany under the impression we would not intervene. I had refused overtures for neutrality, and this morning I told Lichnowsky we should be drawn in, if France and Germany were involved. That, of course, was not the same thing as taking an engagement to France. He then asked me for my reply to his question. I said we had come to the conclusion in the Cabinet today that we could not give any pledge at the present time. We could not pledge Parliament in advance. Up to the present we did not feel that any treaties or obligations were involved....He repeated his question: whether we would help France if Germany attacked her. I said we could not take any engagement."

A direct appeal from the President to the King repeated the familiar argument. If Germany were convinced that Great Britain would not intervene, war would seem to be inevitable; but, if she were convinced that Great Britain would take the field, there was the greatest chance of peace. The King replied, on August 1st, that he was still not without hope, and that he was using his best endeavours with the Emperors of Russia and Germany. "As to the attitude of my country, events are changing so rapidly that it is difficult to forecast future developments; but you may be assured that my Government will continue to discuss freely and frankly any point which might arise of interest to our two nations with M. Cambon." It was a polite, but perfectly definite, refusal to promise assistance, which reflected the mind neither of the King nor the Foreign Office, but represented the makeshift of a divided Cabinet.

When the news of the Russian mobilisation and the formal proclamation by Germany of *drohende Kriegsgefahr* reached London on July 31st, Sir Edward Grey telegraphed to the French and German Governments to ask whether they would engage to respect the neutrality of Belgium, and informed Belgium that he assumed she would herself uphold her neutrality to the utmost of her power. France at once gave the desired assurance, while the German Foreign Secretary ominously replied that a response would reveal the plan of campaign. Sir Edward Grey, accordingly, read to the German Ambassador a warning message unanimously adopted by the Cabinet.

"The reply of the German Government is a matter of very great regret, because the neutrality of Belgium does affect feeling in this country. If

Germany could see her way to give a positive reply as France has done, it would materially contribute to relieve anxiety and tension here; while, if there were a violation by one combatant while the other respected it, it would be extremely difficult to restrain public feeling."

At this point, the Ambassador naturally asked whether we would remain neutral if Germany promised not to violate the Belgian frontier.

" I replied that I could not say that. Our hands were still free. Our attitude would be largely determined by public opinion, and the neutrality of Belgium would appeal to it very strongly. I did not think we could give a promise of neutrality on that condition alone."

The Ambassador then asked whether the Foreign Secretary could not formulate conditions on which we would remain neutral, and even suggested that the integrity of France and her colonies might be guaranteed. "I said that I felt obliged to refuse definitely any promise to remain neutral on similar terms, and I could only say that we must keep our hands free." The Foreign Secretary was to incur sharp criticism when the Report of this conversation was published in the White-book; and he replied to his critics that the conditional offer to guarantee the integrity of France and her Colonies was unofficial and academic. The matter is of no great importance, since the Foreign Secretary was resolved to remain neutral only if the Dual Alliance rejected a reasonable proposal for keeping the peace.

King George's indefinite reply to the President, despatched on the morning of August 1st, was supplemented by the Foreign Secretary, who informed the French Ambassador after the morning Cabinet that he would propose to his colleagues that the Fleet should oppose the passage of the Straits of Dover or any demonstration on the French coast by the German Fleet, and would ask leave to declare in Parliament that we could not permit the violation of Belgian neutrality. The proposals were made to a Cabinet the same evening, and the discussion was resumed on the following morning, when the Foreign Secretary was empowered to promise conditional naval support.

" I am authorised to give the assurance that, if the German Fleet comes into the Channel or through the North Sea to undertake hostile operations against French coasts or shipping, the British Fleet will give all the protection in its power. This assurance is, of course, subject to the policy of the Government receiving the support of Parliament, and must not be taken as binding the Government to take any action until the above contingency of action by the German Fleet takes place."

In handing M. Cambon the Memorandum, the Foreign Secretary

pointed out that the Government could not bind themselves to declare war upon Germany if it broke out between France and Germany to-morrow; but it was essential to the French Government, whose Fleet had long been concentrated in the Mediterranean, to know how to make their dispositions with their north coast entirely undefended. In taking the momentous decision on August 2nd, to oppose a German naval attack on the French coasts, the Cabinet had before it a letter which was brought to Downing Street during the sitting.

"Dear Mr Asquith,

Lord Lansdowne and I feel it our duty to inform you that in our opinion, as well as in that of all the colleagues whom we have been able to consult, it would be fatal to the honour and security of the United Kingdom to hesitate in supporting France and Russia at the present juncture, and we offer our unhesitating support to the Government in any measures they may consider necessary for that object.

Yours very truly,

A. BONAR LAW[1]."

"This Cabinet Memorandum," writes Lord Loreburn, "fixes the date when we were irrevocably committed to war with Germany; for war between France and Germany was then certain, and was declared next day. It prohibited Germany from using her Fleet against French coasts or shipping, without a corresponding prohibition of the use of the French Fleet against German coasts or shipping."

Several Ministers assented with reluctance; and, when the Cabinet met again the same evening Mr Burns, who regarded it as a Declaration of War, reiterated his determination to resign. Lord Morley added that he, too, must go; and, though he accepted the Prime-Minister's appeal to defer a final decision till the morrow, he sent in his resignation on the following morning. Two other resignations were received from Cabinet Ministers, but were quickly withdrawn. No fresh decision as to policy was taken on August 3rd; but, after the Cabinet, orders were issued for the mobilisation of the Army.

Belgium had hitherto played a secondary part in the discussions of the British Cabinet; but she now advanced to the centre of the

---

[1] In his article "Retrospect and Reminiscence," in *The National Review*, August, 1918, Mr Maxse narrates the genesis of this historic letter. Fearing that the Cabinet might not support France, a number of Unionists, among them Mr Maxse himself, Mr Wickham Steed and Sir Henry Wilson, determined on August 1st to mobilise the Unionist leaders. A meeting was hastily summoned at Lansdowne House, and on the following morning Lord Lansdowne and Mr Chamberlain took a draft letter to Mr Bonar Law. An alternative draft by the latter was accepted, and was taken to Downing Street at midday in Lord Lansdowne's car.

stage. A sealed ultimatum, stating that the French had resolved to cross the Belgian frontier and demanding permission for the passage of German troops, had been sent to Brussels on July 29th, and was presented on the evening of August 2nd. The Belgian Cabinet refused, and on August 3rd King George received a telegram from the King of the Belgians. "Remembering the numerous proofs of your Majesty's friendship and that of your predecessor, the friendly attitude of England in 1870, and the proof of friendship you have just given us again, I make a supreme appeal to the diplomatic intervention of your Majesty's Government to safeguard the integrity of Belgium." Though only diplomatic intervention was requested, the reply despatched on the following morning offered to join France and Russia in resisting the attack which had already commenced[1].

Sir Edward Grey opened his speech on August 3rd by recognising that the Peace of Europe could not be maintained. He, like the Prime-Minister, had always promised, that, if such a crisis arose, the House would be free to decide, and that they would not spring a secret engagement on Parliament, nor tell it that, because they had entered into such an engagement, there was an obligation of honour on the country. The Triple *Entente* was a diplomatic group, not an alliance; the military conversations begun in 1906 in no way restricted the freedom of the Government; and his letter to M. Cambon on November 22nd, 1912, which he read to the House, recognised that the Government was uncommitted and pledged it to nothing more than discussion if peace were threatened. Thus, the Government was free, and, *a fortiori*, the House of Commons was free. We had merely to consider what the situation required of us. For many years we had had a friendship with France.

"But, how far that friendship entails obligation, let every man look into his own heart and his own feelings, and construe the extent of the obligation for himself. I construe it as I feel it; but I do not wish to urge upon anyone else more than their feelings dictate. The House, individually and collectively, may judge for itself. The French Fleet is now in the Mediterranean, and the Northern and Western coasts of France are absolutely undefended because of the feeling of confidence and friendship between the two countries. My own feeling is that, if a foreign fleet, engaged in a war which France had not sought, came down the Channel and bombarded

---

[1] The Guarantee of 1839, as Palmerston pointed out, gave a right, but did not impose an obligation, to defend Belgian neutrality. Gladstone's Treaties with France and Russia in 1870 were only necessary because that of 1839 did not automatically invoke action. See Sanger and Norton, *England's Guarantee to Belgium and Luxemburg*.

the undefended coast of France, we could not stand aside. France was entitled to know at once, whether in the event of attack on her unprotected northern and western coasts she could count on British support, and I therefore gave the promise yesterday to the French Ambassador. It was not a Declaration of War."

A still more serious consideration was the neutrality of Belgium. He had asked France and Germany whether they would engage to respect her neutrality. France agreed; but the German Foreign Minister said he could not reply before consulting the Emperor and the Chancellor, and he doubted whether they could answer at all. News had just arrived of a German ultimatum to Belgium.

" If true, and if she accepted, her independence would be gone, whatever might be offered in return. If her independence goes, that of Holland will follow. If France was beaten, if Belgium fell under the same dominating influence, and then Holland, and then Denmark, consider what would be at stake from the point of view of British interests. It may be said that we might stand aside, and intervene at the end to adjust things to our own point of view. If in a crisis like this we turn away from those obligations of honour and interest as regards the Belgian Treaty, I doubt whether, whatever material force we might have at the end, it would be of very much value in face of the respect we should have lost. And if we are engaged in war, we shall suffer but little more than if we stand aside. I do not believe for a moment that, even if we stood aside, we should be able to undo what had happened, to prevent the whole of the West of Europe —if that had been the result of the War—falling under the domination of a single Power, and I am quite sure that our moral position would be such as to have lost us all respect. Though the Fleet is mobilised and the Army is mobilising, we have taken no engagement yet to send an Expeditionary Force out of the country; but if, as seems not improbable, we are forced to take our stand on those issues, then, I believe, when the country realises what is at stake, we shall be supported, not only by the House of Commons, but by the determination, the courage and the endurance of the whole country."

Though the decision was in theory left to the House, it was clear that the Foreign Secretary's mind was made up, and his hearers felt that intervention was a matter of hours. Mr Bonar Law promised the support of the Opposition in the event of war; Mr Redmond assured the Government that they might withdraw their troops from Ireland, which would be defended by her armed sons; but Mr Ramsay Macdonald declared for neutrality on the ground that the speech had not persuaded him that the country was in danger. The House adjourned till the evening. When it met again, the Foreign Secretary announced that a German ultimatum had been presented to Belgium on the previous evening demanding passage through the country, and added that the Government would take the matter into grave consideration.

Early on August 4th, Sir Edward Grey despatched a protest against the ultimatum of Belgium. "H.M. Government are bound to protest against this violation of a Treaty to which Germany is a party in common with themselves, and must request an assurance that the demand made on Belgium will not be proceeded with, and that her neutrality will be respected by Germany. You should ask for an immediate reply." Before a reply could be received from Berlin, news arrived from the Belgian Legation that the frontier had been crossed. It was in vain that Jagow instructed Lichnowsky to repeat that under no circumstances would Germany annex Belgian territory, and to impress on Sir Edward Grey that the German army could not be exposed to a French attack across Belgium, "which was planned, according to absolutely unimpeachable information." It was too late for excuses, and German promises were now at a discount.

When the Cabinet met on the morning of August 4th, all doubts and hesitations had been swept away.

"On Saturday, August 1st," declared Mr Lloyd George in an interview in 1915, "a poll of the electors would have shewn 99 per cent. against embroiling their country in hostilities. A poll on the following Tuesday would have resulted in a vote of 99 per cent. in favour of war. The revolution in public sentiment was attributable entirely to an attack by Germany on a small and unprotected country which had done her no wrong; and what Britain was not prepared to do for interests political and commercial she readily risked to help the weak and helpless. I would not have been a party to a Declaration of War had Belgium not been invaded, and I think I can say the same for most if not all of my colleagues[1]."

The ascription of his own views to the great majority of his colleagues is unwarranted, but the *apologia* illustrates the changed atmosphere in which the ultimatum to Berlin was drawn up, approved and despatched.

"We hear that Germany has addressed a Note to the Belgian Minister for Foreign Affairs stating that the German Government will be compelled to carry out, if necessary by force of arms, the measures considered indispensable. We are also informed that Belgian territory has been violated at Gemmerich. In these circumstances, and in view of the fact that Germany declined to give the same assurance respecting Belgium as France gave last week in reply to our request made simultaneously at Berlin and Paris, we must repeat the request and ask that a satisfactory reply to it and to my telegram of this morning be received here by

[1] *Pearson's Magazine*, March, 1915.

12 o'clock tonight. If not, you are instructed to ask for your passports, and to say that His Majesty's Government feel bound to take all steps in their power to uphold the neutrality of Belgium and the observance of a Treaty to which Germany is as much a party as ourselves."

Sir Edward Goschen delivered the ultimatum to the Foreign Minister, who expressed his poignant regret at the crumbling of his entire policy, which had been to make friends with Great Britain, and through Great Britain to draw closer to France. The Ambassador then paid a farewell visit to the Chancellor.

" I found him very agitated. Just for a word, 'neutrality,' just for a scrap of paper, Great Britain was going to make war on a kindred nation who desired nothing better than to be friends with her! The policy to which he had devoted himself had tumbled down like a house of cards. What we had done was unthinkable. It was like striking a man from behind while he was fighting for his life against two assailants. The blow was all the greater in that he had been working with us to maintain peace between Austria and Russia. I said that this was part of the tragedy, which saw the two nations fall apart just at the moment when the relations between them had been more friendly and cordial than they had been for years."

No reply was expected or received; and when the listening Ministers in Downing Street heard Big Ben toll the hour of midnight, they knew that the British empire was launched on the greatest struggle in its history.

On the following day, the Prime-Minister informed the House that a state of War existed with Germany, and on August 6th he moved a credit of 100 millions. With the utmost reluctance and infinite regret, he declared, the Government had been compelled to declare War on what had been for generations a friendly Power. Every possible effort for peace had been made, but war had been forced on us. Germany had invited us to betray our friend and dishonour our obligations, in return for a promise given by a Power which was at that very moment announcing its intention to violate its own Treaty and inviting us to do the same. If we had dallied or temporised, we should have betrayed the interests of this country.

" If I am asked what we are fighting for, I reply in two sentences. In the first place, to fulfil a solemn international obligation—an obligation which, if it had been entered into between private persons, would have been regarded as an obligation, not only of law but of honour, which no self-respecting man could possibly have repudiated. Secondly, we are fighting to vindicate the principle that small nationalities are not to be crushed, in defiance of international goodfaith, by the arbitrary will of a strong and overmastering Power. I do not believe any great nation ever entered into a great controversy with a clearer conscience and a stronger conviction that it is fighting not for aggression nor for the maintenance of its own selfish interest, but in defence of principles vital to the civilisation of the world."

The action of the Government was approved by the great majority of its supporters and by the leaders of the Opposition in both Houses.

The Declaration of War was ratified by public opinion mainly owing to the anger evoked by the wanton attack on unoffending Belgium. But it was also the logical outcome, if not indeed, in Lord Esher's words, "the inevitable sequel," of our policy since 1906. Had we stood aside at Armageddon, the Central Powers would have won an easy victory, and at the conclusion of the contest we should have found ourselves alone in Europe. France and Russia would have scorned us as false friends, who, after years of diplomatic co-operation, deserted them in the crisis of their fate; and the German menace, intensified by the collapse of the Triple *entente*, would have compelled us to arm to the teeth on sea and land. It is more difficult to pronounce judgment on the steps taken by the Foreign Secretary to prevent the outbreak of war. Alone among European statesmen he laboured night and day to preserve peace; and during the twelve days he proposed schemes which would have preserved it, had the will to peace in Vienna, Berlin and Petrograd been equal to his own. "No one at the head of affairs quite meant war at that stage," Mr Lloyd George truly observed, on December 23rd, 1920: "it was something into which they glided or rather staggered and stumbled." But Sir Edward Grey had to deal with obstinate and angry men; and it has been argued that, when his offer of mediation by the four Powers had been rejected by Austria, he should have announced in unhesitating tones what action Great Britain was prepared to take. He might, for instance, have followed the precedent of 1870, and proclaimed our resolve, with the assent of a united Cabinet, to resist with all our strength the violation of Belgian neutrality. The combination of warnings to Berlin with the refusal of pledges to Paris and Petrograd was ineffective, for neither warnings nor refusals were taken very seriously. The chauvinists in Petrograd were encouraged by the prevalent conviction that we should be dragged in, and the chauvinism of Berlin and Vienna was stimulated by the possibility that we might stand out. "Unless Germany has lost her reason," remarked the Tsar in the critical week, "she would not dare to attack Russia, France and England." France shared his view, and President

Wilson has expressed his conviction that, had Germany been certain that we should intervene, she would have restrained her Ally and held her own hand. It has also been maintained that, had we informed France and Russia that we should decline to take part in a conflict arising out of the Austro-Servian quarrel, Petrograd would not have dared to pick up the glove which Vienna had thrown down. On such conjectures it is not possible to express a final judgment; and, in any case, it would have been impossible to announce either of these decisions, since the Cabinet was divided.

The inability to take action which might conceivably have prevented the War was the result of the lack of precision in our relations to France. A policy of limited liability is easy to define, but difficult to execute. Sir Edward Grey declared, on August 3rd, that every Member could construe the case for himself; but his whole speech breathed the conviction that we should be for ever disgraced, if we left France in the lurch. The assurances that we were unpledged were formally correct, but inaccurate in substance. "There was a moral obligation not to leave us unprotected," declares M. Paul Cambon, who was in a position to know. "We were tied to France inextricably," wrote an acute critic[1], "tied by countless invisible threads such as fastened down Gulliver while he slumbered in the land of little men." Mr Lloyd George himself afterwards came to feel that we had not been really free. "We had a compact with France," he declared on August 7th, 1918, "that if she were wantonly attacked we would go to her support." Mr Herbert Samuel at once interposed that there was no such compact or contract obliging us to fight; and the Prime-Minister, accepting the correction, confessed that the word "compact" was too strong. "In my judgment," he added, "it was an obligation of honour." And such will doubtless be the judgment of History. On the other hand, the time has not come for a judicial verdict on the whole policy of Continental commitments, unaccompanied as they were in this instance by an Army of Continental proportions or by a frank explanation to Parliament and the nation of their contingent liabilities. It is clear that, on the one hand, this policy increased the probability of war by involving us in the quarrels and ambitions of our friends, and that, on the other, it ensured that in the event of a German attack we should not be left to face the ordeal single-handed. The risk and the premium will have to be balanced against each other by the historical actuaries of the future.

[1] In *The Candid Review*, edited by Mr Gibson Bowles.

CHAPTER VII

EPILOGUE. THE WAR AND THE PEACE

I. THE WAR, 1914–1918

WITH the outbreak of hostilities the Foreign Policy of Great Britain became a branch of the military problem of winning the War. Its tasks were to consolidate existing alliances and understandings, to secure new partners in its action, and to prevent the Central Powers from obtaining allies. Great Britain, declared the Prime-Minister at the Guildhall on Lord Mayor's Day, 1914, would not sheathe the sword until Belgium had recovered all and more than all that she had sacrificed; until France was adequately secured against the menace of aggression; until the rights of the smaller nationalities were placed on an unassailable foundation, and until the military dominion of Prussia was finally destroyed. The *entente* started with a preponderance of human and material resources; but the very magnitude of the new Grand Alliance endangered unity of control, while the whole strength of the enemy was directed by a small group of masterful men in Berlin.

The first task of the Foreign Secretary was to call for the aid of our Ally in the Far East. On August 15th, Japan demanded the withdrawal of German warships from the waters of Japan and China, and the surrender of Kiaochow with a view to its eventual restoration to China. No reply was received, and she proceeded to reduce the fortress of Tsing-tau. Timely aid was also rendered in sweeping the German flag from the Pacific, in convoying troopships from different parts of the empire to the scene of action, and in supplying Russia with the munitions of which she stood in need. Her task was limited; and she did not at first sign the Pact of London, by which, on September 4th, Great Britain, France and Russia engaged not to conclude peace separately, and not to demand terms of peace without previous agreement.

The next urgent task was to prevent or postpone the entry of Turkey into the War on the side of the Central Powers[1]. On August 3rd, the Cabinet had taken over the two battleships which were being

---

[1] The British White-book on the rupture with Turkey has been reprinted by J. B. Scott, *Diplomatic Documents relating to the outbreak of the European War.*

built for Turkey in British yards; and the wisdom of the decision was confirmed by the admission of the *Goeben* and the *Breslau* to the Bosphorus. For several weeks, however, there seemed to be a chance of purchasing neutrality by a crescendo of promises. If Turkey remained neutral, we declared, and Egypt tranquil, we should not alter the status of the latter. The *entente* would uphold Turkish independence and integrity against all attacks, if she would observe scrupulous neutrality. When the Minister of Marine demanded the immediate abolition of the Capitulations, Sir Edward Grey promised, subject to the assent of France and Russia, to surrender our rights "as soon as a scheme satisfying modern conditions is set up." King George sent a personal message to the Sultan, expressing his deep regret at the necessity of seizing the ships, and promising to restore them after the War. The Sultan and the Grand-Vizier invariably replied with words of peace; but they were merely playing for time, for the die was already cast. On August 1st, Turkey had signed a Treaty promising support to the Central Powers if they were involved in war with Russia. Mobilisation proceeded, and German officers, sailors and money poured into Constantinople. On October 29th, Turkish torpedo-boats attacked Russian ships at Odessa, and the British, French and Russian Ambassadors at Constantinople promptly demanded their passports. Great Britain retaliated by the annexation of Cyprus, the proclamation of a Protectorate over Egypt, the deposition of the Khedive Abbas, whose hostility was unconcealed, and the selection of a son of the Khedive Ismail as Sultan of Egypt. Russia proceeded to work out a plan for the partition of the Turkish empire; and, on March 12th, 1915, her Allies assented in principle to the annexation of Constantinople and the Straits[1].

The loss of Turkey was balanced six months later by the gain of Italy. The unwillingness of Vienna to bid high for Italian neutrality was ultimately overcome by pressure from Berlin, and Francis Joseph consented to cede the Trentino and the west bank of the Isonzo, with concessions in Trieste and a free hand in Albania. The offer was sufficient for Giolitti; but the Salandra-Sonnino Ministry preferred the risks of war in return for the far higher price offered by the *entente*. In addition to the Austrian concessions, the Treaty of London, signed on April 26th, 1915, promised southern Tyrol up to the Brenner Pass, Gorizia, Trieste, Istria and northern Dalmatia[2].

[1] See Cocks, *The Secret Treaties*, ch. 1.
[2] *Ibid.* ch. 2.

The only excuse for a Treaty which handed over the German population of southern Tyrol and the Slavonic population of northern Dalmatia was the familiar plea of necessity. "The French and ourselves were fighting for our lives on the western front," bluntly testifies Mr Asquith, "and the Treaty represented the terms on which Italy was prepared to join forces." Though it increased the material strength of the Grand Alliance, it diminished its moral authority; and Servia learned within a week of the Pact which had disposed of Jugo-Slav territory behind her back.

The Turkish alliance could only be turned to full account by the Central Powers if Bulgaria joined their ranks; whereas, if Ferdinand sided with the *entente*, communications with Russia could be opened from the Mediterranean, Turkey isolated, Servia's flank secured, and Greece and Roumania encouraged to intervene. Bulgaria's price was Macedonia; but Servia refused to disgorge the province she had conquered in 1912, and the *entente* hesitated to compel her. No serious attempt to win Bulgaria was made till the Russian armies were hurled back in Poland and Galicia and the costly attack on the Dardanelles seemed likely to fail. In June, 1915, the Powers offered to guarantee her the possession of Macedonia, on condition that she should not occupy it till the peace, and that Servia received compensation in Bosnia, Herzegovina and on the Adriatic. This conditional acceptance of her demands did not tempt her calculating monarch, who was not only in political sympathy with the Central Powers, but had convinced himself that they were destined to win. At the end of August, he agreed to intervene on their side, and obtained permission to conquer Macedonia for himself. Sir Edward Grey promised the Servians "all the support in our power, in a manner that would be most welcome to them, without reserve or qualifications"; while Venizelos, regarding the Bulgarian attack on Servia as a *casus foederis*, urged Greece to fulfil her duty, and invited Great Britain to assist with 150,000 men. King Constantine, however, who was determined to maintain neutrality, dismissed his Minister, and a British offer to cede Cyprus, if he would intervene, was declined. British and French troops were hurried to Salonika; but an Austro-German attack from the north, synchronising with a Bulgarian invasion from the east, overran Servia without difficulty. Only military successes, explained the Foreign Secretary on October 14th in answer to angry critics, could have won Bulgaria; and the Central Powers had been able to offer her more than the *entente*. The intervention of Bulgaria opened a direct route from Berlin to Constantinople, and rendered the continuance of the Dardanelles adventure inadvisable. The troops were accordingly withdrawn; but large *entente* forces were kept at Salonika to hold the Bulgarian Army. The struggle against Turkey was facilitated by an Agreement with the Sherif of Mecca, who entered the War in return for recognition as King of the Hedjaz and for promises of a share in the spoils of victory.

In the War of 1914, as in the struggle with Napoleon, the exercise of sea-power involved Great Britain in dangerous friction with neutrals. Despite the indignation aroused by the attack on Belgium and the preponderant sympathy with the Allied cause, both the Government and the people of the United States desired at the outset to remain "above the battle"; for Europe was far away, Germany had many friends, and the Russian autocracy was detested. President Wilson invited the belligerents to observe the Declaration of London; and, when Great Britain made reservations, he announced his resolve to see the rights and duties of the United States settled in accordance with the accepted principles of International Law and treaty obligations. Great Britain's blockade of the North Sea on November 3rd, 1914, evoked a protest against searching ships for contraband. Sir Edward Grey's interim reply undertook that neutral commerce should not be interfered with further than was necessary, and repudiated a desire to interfere with genuine commerce, but affirmed the right to check trade in contraband. He challenged the complaints of a large decrease in American trade owing to British policy, and emphasised the suspicious increase of the export of copper to Scandinavia and Switzerland. It was necessary to bring a ship into port before it could be searched, as copper might be hidden in bales of cotton. In regard to food, Sir Edward Grey refused an unconditional undertaking, in consequence of the belligerent methods of Germany.

When, on February 4th, 1915, Germany announced that all vessels in the waters round Great Britain would be sunk, the United States proposed the cessation of attacks on merchantmen except for detention and search, in return for the free passage of food consigned to agents chosen by the United States for distributing it to civilians. The compromise was accepted in principle in Berlin, but rejected in London, where, on March 1st, the Prime-Minister issued his rejoinder to the German blockade which, he argued, substituted indiscriminate destruction for regulated capture.

"Her opponents are therefore driven to frame retaliatory measures to prevent commodities of any kind reaching or leaving Germany; but they will be enforced by Great Britain and France without risk to neutral ships or to neutral or non-combatant lives. The Governments will hold themselves free to take into port ships carrying goods of presumed enemy destination, ownership or origin. It is not intended to confiscate such vessels or cargoes, unless they would otherwise be liable to confiscation."

The British refusal to mitigate the blockade annoyed the President; but the loss of a hundred American lives in the *Lusitania* relieved the British Government of all fear of a break with Washington. Arrangements for rationing the European neutrals were made; but further encroachments on the Declaration of London became necessary. On August 21st, 1915, cotton was declared contraband, and on July 7th, 1916, the Declaration itself was denounced.

"As the struggle developed," explained the official Memorandum, "it became clear that the attempt made in time of peace to determine not only the principles of law, but even the forms under which they were to be applied, had not produced a wholly satisfactory result. These rules, while not in all respects improving the safeguards afforded to neutrals, do not provide belligerents with the most effective means of exercising their admitted rights....The successive modifications may probably have exposed the purpose of the Allies to misconstruction; they have therefore come to the conclusion that they must confine themselves simply to applying the historic and admitted rules of the law of nations."

Sir Edward Grey added that "the Freedom of the Sea" might be a very reasonable subject for discussion, definition and agreement between the nations after the War; "but not by itself alone, nor while there was no freedom and no security against war and against German methods on sea and land."

The crippling of Russia, the fiasco in the Dardanelles, the overthrow of Servia, and the failure of the attempts to pierce the German front in France, rendered 1915 a year of evil memory for the Allies; and 1916, though less disastrous, brought no relief from anxiety. The battle of Jutland was claimed as a victory by both sides; and Italy battered in vain against the Austrian defences. For months, the invaders strove to capture Verdun, and for months the defenders of French soil endeavoured to break the German line on the Somme. The deadlock, at length, compelled the Allies to pay the extravagant price which Bratiano had long demanded for the intervention of Roumania. Her Declaration of War on August 28th was hailed as a presage of victory; but her speedy collapse, and the addition of her corn and oil to the dwindling assets of the Central Powers, seemed to postpone the decision to an indefinite future.

The British Government, convinced that time was on the side of the Allies, would not allow the defeat of Roumania to disturb their equanimity or to weaken the will to victory. The struggle, declared the Prime-Minister on October 11th, could not be allowed to end in some patched-up, precarious compromise. "The ends of the Allies are not selfish nor vindictive; but they require adequate reparation for the past and adequate security for the future." An address by Sir Edward Grey to the Foreign Press Association on October 23rd struck the same note of determination.

"For years before this War we were living under the deepening shadow of Prussian militarism extending itself over the whole of Germany and then extending itself over the whole Continent. There must be no end to this War except a Peace which is going to ensure that the nations of Europe live in the future free from the shadow of the great anarchist. A neutral has asked me what neutrals can do. The best thing is to work up an opinion for such an agreement between nations as will prevent a war like this happening again. If they had been united in such an agreement, and prompt and resolute to insist in July, 1914, that the dispute must be referred to a conference or to the Hague, and that the Belgian Treaty must be observed, there would have been no war."

The reference of the Foreign Secretary to an Association of Nations made a deep impression on the German Chancellor, who believed that the time had come to invite the belligerents to discuss the possibility of peace, and who secured the assent of Austria, Turkey and Bulgaria to take action in this sense so soon as Bucharest fell. On December 12th, he transmitted a note to the Governments of France, Great Britain, Russia, Japan, Roumania and Servia. The latest events, he declared, proved that the resistance of the Central Powers was unbreakable; but they did not seek to crush or annihilate their adversaries, and they proposed negotiations.

"They feel sure that the propositions which they would bring forward would serve as a basis for the restoration of a lasting peace. If, notwithstanding this offer of peace and conciliation, the struggle should continue, the four Allied Powers are resolved to carry it on to the end, while solemnly disclaiming any responsibility before mankind and history [1]."

The French Premier, M. Briand, denounced the invitation as a manœuvre to divide the *entente*, the Russian Foreign Minister rejected it "with indignation," and Sonnino urged Italy not to separate

[1] See G. Lowes Dickinson, *Documents and Statements relating to Peace Proposals and War Aims*, pp. 1–2.

herself from her Allies in her attitude towards "this treacherous step." The British reply was conveyed by Mr Lloyd George, who had succeeded Mr Asquith as Prime-Minister at the beginning of December and had created a War Cabinet to deal with the urgent problems of the conflict, unhampered by the routine business of legislation and administration.

"To enter, on the invitation of Germany, proclaiming herself victorious, without any knowledge of the proposals she has to make, into a conference is to put our heads into a noose. Before we can consider such an invitation we ought to know that she is prepared to accede to the only terms on which it is possible for peace to be obtained and maintained—complete restitution, full reparation, effectual guarantees. What hope is there in the Chancellor's speech that the arrogant spirit of the Prussian military caste will not be as dominant as ever, if we patch up peace now? The very speech in which these peace suggestions are made is a long paean to the victories of Hindenburg and his legions."

After these individual rejoinders the Allied Governments of Russia, France, Great Britain, Japan, Italy, Servia, Belgium, Montenegro, Portugal and Roumania returned a collective reply on December 30th.

"A mere suggestion, without statement of terms, that negotiations should be opened, is not an offer of peace. A sham proposal, lacking all substance and precision, would appear to be less an offer of peace than a war manœuvre. It rests on a War Map of Europe alone, which represents nothing more than a superficial and passing phase of the situation, and not the real strength of the belligerents. A peace on these terms would be only to the advantage of the aggressors. The disasters caused by the German Declaration of War and the innumerable outrages committed by Germany and her Allies demand penalties, reparation and guarantees; but Germany avoids mention of any of these. The object of these overtures is to create dissension in Allied countries, to stiffen opinion in Germany, and to deceive opinion in neutral countries. The Allied Governments refuse to consider a proposal which is empty and insincere. Once again, the Allies declare that no peace is possible till they have secured reparation of violated rights, recognition of the principle of nationalities and of the free existence of small States, and a settlement calculated to end forces which have constituted a perpetual menace to the nations."

The German *démarche* was quickly followed by an appeal from the cooler atmosphere of Washington. On December 18th, the President issued an invitation to the belligerents (which, he explained, he had long had in mind, and which was in no way connected with the recent offer), to explain their views as to the terms on which the War might be concluded. "It may be that peace is nearer than we know; that the terms are not so irreconcilable as some have feared; that an interchange of views would clear the way for conference. The President is not proposing peace or even offering mediation. He is merely proposing that soundings be taken." On December 25th, Germany, who was waiting for the Allied response to her invitation, replied that direct discussion between belligerent delegates in some neutral country seemed the best road to peace, and added that she would be glad to cooperate with the United States in the work of preventing future wars after the end of the present struggle.

While Berlin thus politely declined the President's invitation to state her terms, the Allies despatched an elaborate reply, on January 10th, 1917. They associated themselves whole-heartedly with the plan of a League of Nations; but such a discussion presupposed a satisfactory settlement of the present conflict. A peace of reparation, restitution and guarantees was at present impossible. The fact of the moment was the aggressive will of Germany and Austria to ensure their mastery over Europe and their economic domination over the world. As the conflict had developed, their attitude had been a continual challenge to humanity and civilisation. The resemblance between the aims of the two belligerent groups was only apparent.

"The Allies find no difficulty in answering the request. The civilised world knows that they imply, first of all, the restoration of Belgium, Servia and Montenegro, with the compensation due to them; the evacuation of the invaded territories in France, Russia and Roumania, with just reparation; the reorganisation of Europe, guaranteed by a stable régime and based at once on respect for nationalities and on the right to full security and liberty of economic development, and upon territorial conventions and international settlements such as to guarantee land and sea frontiers against unjustifiable attack; the restitution of provinces formerly torn from the Allies by force or against the wish of their inhabitants; the liberation of the Italians, as also of the Slavs, Roumanians and Czecho-Slovaks, from foreign domination; the setting free of the populations subject to the bloody tyranny of the Turks; and the turning out of Europe of the Ottoman empire as decidedly foreign to Western civilisation. The intentions of the Tsar in regard to Poland have been indicated by his Manifesto to his armies. There is no need to say that, if the Allies desire to shield Europe from the covetous brutality of Prussian militarism, the extermination and the political disappearance of the German peoples have never formed part of their designs."

The reference to the expulsion of the Turks and partition of Turkey was plain enough; but the attitude to Austria was studiously ambiguous. The "liberation" of Italians from foreign domination could only mean annexation to Italy; but the liberation of Slavs, Roumanians and Czecho-Slovaks might denote nothing more than autonomy[1]. On the other hand the most natural interpretation of the word was adopted not only by the spokesmen of the nationalities concerned, but by the Central Powers, who pointed out to their suffering peoples that the *entente* was bent on conquest and disruption. A despatch from Mr Balfour (who had succeeded Sir Edward Grey as Foreign Secretary on the fall of the Asquith Government) to the British Ambassador at Washington restated the policy of the Government, defended the partition of Turkey, and argued that a durable peace could only be based on victory. The President had secured a statement of the war aims of the Allies; but his achievement brought peace no nearer.

Undeterred by the refusal of the Central Powers to state their terms or by the avowal of aims on the part of the *entente* which could only be secured by an overwhelming triumph, the President, expecting and desiring a peace without victory, continued his attempt at mediation. But the failure of the "Peace Offer" left the Kaiser and his Chancellor defenceless against the demand for the resumption of unrestricted submarine warfare on February 1st. It was well understood that the decision involved the entrance of the United States into the War; but the Admiralty promised the collapse of Great Britain within five months, and the Army Chiefs refused to guarantee the stability of the western front on any other terms. "It is our last card," observed the Chancellor, "the Rubicon is crossed." Washington promptly broke off diplomatic relations, and two months later the United States entered the War. The doom of the Central Powers was sealed not by the skill of *entente* diplomacy, but by their own reckless challenge to the strongest of neutral Powers.

While Germany was presenting her foes with a new and powerful Ally, the Tsardom was tottering to its fall under the strain of war and the disintegrating influences of internal corruption. A British Mission under Lord Milner failed to avert the approaching catastrophe; and, on March 15th, the feeble autocrat abdicated, after an almost bloodless Revolution. For a moment, the Allies believed that republican Russia might carry on the conflict with renewed energy; but the people were weary of the struggle, and the Coalition Government, in which Kerensky was the leading figure, was forced to abandon the

---

[1] On August 24th, 1917, Lord Robert Cecil stated that we were not pledged to any form of liberation.

vast schemes of annexation—some of them already proclaimed to the world, others recorded in Secret Treaties—of which Nicholas and his advisers had dreamed. But if Russian soldiers were no longer called upon to shed their blood for the expansion of their own frontiers, they could scarcely be expected to fight for the ambitions of their Allies. On May 30th, the Soviets appealed for a restatement of the war-aims of the *entente*, and supported a plan proposed by the Dutch Socialists for a Labour Conference in Stockholm. The project was approved by Mr Henderson, who had been despatched to Petrograd after the fall of the Tsar, on the ground that, if Russia was to be prevented from going out of the War, the confidence of the people in its purposes must be restored. The Prime-Minister, also, favoured the plan; but his colleagues were against him, and the *entente* Governments refused passports to their Labour leaders. Despite the lack of response from the Allies, Kerensky galvanised the South-Russian armies to a final offensive; but the initial success was followed by a catastrophic defeat, and the cry for peace became irresistible. Kerensky announced that a Conference would be held at which Russian Representatives would seek to reach an understanding "on the basis of the principles proclaimed by the Revolution." But the Allies were in no mood for a peace without annexations and indemnities, and, in November, the Kerensky Government was swept away by the Bolshevists, who threw the obligations of inter-Allied loyalty to the winds.

Despite the contemptuous rejection of the Peace Offer of the Central Powers, the Emperor Charles, who had succeeded Francis Joseph in November, 1916, continued to seek peace for his suffering dominions[1]. Immediately after his accession he had invited his brother-in-law, Prince Sixte of Bourbon, who was fighting for Belgium, to come to Vienna and explore the possibilities of peace. Germany, declared the young Emperor, was certain of victory; but, if she refused a reasonable settlement, he would make peace without her. The just claims of France to Alsace-Lorraine should be met; while Austria would surrender Galicia to a reconstituted Poland and afford Servia access to the Adriatic. Germany was informed of the general outlines of the negotiations, and was warned that he could not fight beyond the autumn. The Prince, bearing an autograph letter, was received in a friendly spirit by Poincaré and Mr Lloyd George. "We would gladly shake hands with Austria if she would

[1] See Manteyer, *The Austrian Peace Offer*.

leave Germany," declared the Prime-Minister; "but Italy entertains rather bitter feelings towards her, and we cannot make peace without Italy." It was suggested that the King of Italy should be asked to visit the French and British armies, where King George, the President and the two Premiers could meet him; but the invitation was declined by Sonnino, and in consequence no formal reply to the Emperor's letters was returned by the *entente*.

The war-weariness of Austria, though not her negotiations with the *entente*, became known throughout Germany at a moment when the hopes of early victory from the submarine war were fading. On July 6th, Erzberger, who had read a despairing Memorandum by Count Czernin, the Austrian Foreign Minister, expressed the opinion that the War could not be won, and urged that Germany should publicly renounce all plans of annexation. The effect was electrical, and Bethmann-Hollweg was forced by the Army chiefs to resign. On July 19th, the *Reichstag* passed a Resolution, by 212 to 126, declaring that it strove for a peace of compromise and the permanent reconciliation of the peoples. "With such a peace forced acquisitions of territory, and political, economic and financial oppressions are inconsistent. It also rejects all schemes which aim at economic barriers after the War. The Freedom of the Seas must be made secure. So long, however, as the enemy Governments threaten Germany and her allies with conquests and oppression, the German nation will fight till its own and its allies' right to life and development is secured." The effect was weakened by the statement of Michaelis, the new Chancellor, that his aims were attainable within the limits of the resolution, "as I understand it"; for, unlike his predecessor, he was *persona grata* to the military chiefs.

The Allies took no notice of the Resolution; but an appeal from the Pope, on August 1st—"in the name of the Prince of Peace"— could not be wholly ignored. The struggle, he argued, was becoming more and more a useless massacre, and ought to be ended by a peace without annexations or indemnities, and followed by the reduction of armaments and a system of arbitration. President Wilson replied that the rulers of Germany could not be trusted; but Great Britain, like Italy and France, made no official response. The view of the Cabinet was conveyed in a letter of August 21st from the Foreign Secretary to Count de Salis, our Special Envoy at the Vatican.

"The Government, not having as yet been able to take the opinion of their Allies, cannot say whether it would serve any useful purpose to offer a reply, or, if so, what form any such reply should take. Though the Central Powers have admitted their guilt in regard to Belgium, they have never definitely intimated that they intend either to restore her to her former state of entire independence or to make good the damage she has suffered. Till they and their Allies state officially how far they are willing to go in the matter of reparation and restoration, have announced their war aims, and put forward suggestions as to the measures which may offer an effective guarantee that the world will not again be plunged into the horror by which it is at present devastated, the Government consider it unlikely that any progress towards peace can be made. It appears to be useless to endeavour to bring about an agreement between the belligerents until the points of difference between them are clearly known, and neither Germany nor Austria has as yet made any statement corresponding to that issued by the Allies in answer to the note of President Wilson. You should point this out to His Eminence."

The Pope asked for and received a copy of the letter, and the Cardinal Secretary remarked to Count de Salis that Germany had already announced her intention to restore the independence of Belgium. "On my objecting to this statement, he recalled the resolution in favour of peace without annexation. I answered that the Assembly did not rule Germany." Cardinal Gasparri answered that he would reply after having received from the German Government the official declaration as to Belgium for which he had asked.

"I desired to avoid any statement," reported Count de Salis, "which might seem to give encouragement to any kind of discussions with the German Government, and therefore, on his enquiring my views, I replied that a declaration on the question of Belgium appeared desirable. This point was only one of many at issue; but it was of special importance to us."

Even these judicious observations brought a caution from Downing Street. "In the event of your opinion being asked, you should decline to express any views. It is not desirable to intervene in the negotiations between the Pope and the German Government in any way." A day or two later, Mr Balfour informed the British Ministers abroad that the Government, in view of President Wilson's Note, considered no further reply to the Papal Note to be necessary.

Despite the chilling response from the *entente*, the Pope continued his efforts. The Cardinal Secretary forwarded Mr Balfour's letter to Berlin, and suggested that a definite promise of independence and compensation for Belgium would be an important step toward negotiations. The German Government replied that conversations were only possible on the basis that neither side was beaten, and it was therefore useless to publish terms. In forwarding the German

and Austrian replies to London on September 28th, Cardinal Gasparri observed that the document left open the door for an exchange
of ideas; "and, if the Entente will not decline to enter into negotiations, the Holy See is prepared to ask, on its own initiative, for
further explanations and more precise definitions on such points as
may be indicated." To this invitation Mr Balfour replied by a formal
acknowledgment. When, about the same time, Baron Kühlmann,
the Foreign Minister, asked through Madrid on what terms the
British Government would enter into negotiations, Mr Balfour, after
consulting the *entente* Ministers in London, replied that they were
ready to receive any communication which the German Government
desired to send, and to consider it with their Allies.

Though nobody suggested the surrender of the essential aims
with which Great Britain had entered the War, the political atmosphere at the end of 1917 was different from that at the beginning,
despite the victorious progress of General Allenby in Asiatic Turkey.
The approaching conclusion of peace with Russia, the Ukraine and
Roumania enabled Germany to mass her whole strength on the west,
where French and British offensives had again failed to break the
line. Italy had suffered a catastrophic defeat at Caporetto, which
galvanised the failing energies of Austria and necessitated the despatch
of French and British troops to the Venetian plain. American troops
were arriving slowly, and a fourth winter in the trenches increased
the longing among the soldiers for an early peace. And, finally, Lord
Lansdowne, in a letter of November 28th, argued that the indefinite
prolongation of the War would spell ruin for the civilised world. It
was under the influence of these considerations that the Prime-
Minister on January 5th, 1918, in a speech to the Trade Unions, set
forth the War aims of Great Britain more fully and more authorita-
tively than they had ever been explained before. The programme had
been submitted to Mr Asquith and Lord Grey, the leaders of Labour,
and Representatives of the Dominions. He, therefore, stated that he
was speaking for the nation and the empire as a whole, and claimed
"national agreement as to the character and purpose of our War
aims and peace conditions." The moderation of tone was in marked
contrast to the challenging self-confidence of the Allied reply to
President Wilson a year earlier.

The British, began the Prime Minister, were not aiming at the
destruction or disruption of Germany, and would not fight merely to
alter or destroy the Constitution; but military autocracy was a

dangerous anachronism. The adoption of a really democratic Constitution would be the most convincing evidence that the old spirit of military domination had died and would make it easier to conclude a broad democratic peace.

"The first requirement always put forward by the British Government and their Allies has been the complete restoration, political, territorial and economic, of the independence of Belgium, and such reparation as can be made for the devastation of its towns and provinces. Next comes the restoration of Servia, Montenegro, and the occupied parts of France, Italy and Roumania. We mean to stand by the French democracy to the death in the demand they make for a reconsideration of the great wrong of 1871. We shall be proud to fight to the end side by side with the new democracy of Russia. But, if her present rulers take action which is independent of the Allies, we have no means of intervening to arrest the catastrophe which is assuredly befalling their country. Russia can only be saved by her own people. We believe, however, that an independent Poland, comprising all those genuinely Polish elements who desire to form part of it, is an urgent necessity for the stability of Western Europe."

The "reconsideration" of the problem of Alsace-Lorraine suggested something less than the integral restoration of these provinces; and the reference to Austria in like manner revealed the shrinkage of our demands. "The break-up of Austria-Hungary is no part of our war-aims; but genuine self-government must be granted to those Austro-Hungarian nationalities who have long desired it." In one case, however, complete emancipation was essential. "We regard as vital the satisfaction of the legitimate claims of the Italians for union with those of their own race and tongue." The declaration as to Roumania was studiously vague. "We also mean to press that justice be done to men of Roumanian blood and speech in their legitimate aspirations."

If the reference to Austria defined and limited the ambiguous formula of 1917, the new Turkish policy was a frank recantation. The Tsar had fallen; Russia was about to conclude peace; her new rulers had no wish for Constantinople, and the Secret Treaties of 1915 and 1916 were out of date. "We are not fighting to deprive Turkey of its capital," declared Mr Lloyd George, "nor of the rich and renowned lands of Asia Minor and Thrace, which are predominantly Turkish in race." The Straits, however, were to be internationalised and neutralised. Arabia, Armenia, Mesopotamia, Syria and Palestine were entitled to a recognition of their separate national conditions.

"What the exact form of that recognition in each particular case should be need not be here discussed; but it would be impossible to restore these territories to their former sovereignty. Much has been said about the arrangements we have entered into with our Allies on this and on other subjects. I can only say that as new circumstances, like the Russian collapse and the separate Russian negotiations, have changed the conditions under which those arrangements were made, we are, and always have been, perfectly ready to discuss them with our Allies."

The German Colonies would be held at the disposal of a conference, whose decision must have primary regard to the wishes and interests of the native inhabitants. The governing consideration should be "to prevent their exploitation for the benefit of European capitalists or Governments. The general principle of national self-determination is, therefore, as applicable in their cases as in those of other occupied European territories."

After dealing with territorial problems, the Prime-Minister turned to other considerations. There must be reparation for injuries inflicted in violation of International Law, such as those to our seamen. In the world shortage of raw materials, those countries which controlled them would naturally help themselves and their friends first; but, as circumstances changed, the settlement would change also. Finally, a great attempt must be made to establish by some international organisation an alternative to war as a means of settling international disputes. Three conditions were essential to permanent peace—the reestablishment of the sanctity of treaties, a territorial settlement based on the right of self-determination or the consent of the governed, and the creation of some international organisation to limit the burden of armaments and diminish the probability of war. "On those conditions the British empire would welcome peace; to secure those conditions its peoples are prepared to make even greater sacrifices than those they have yet endured."

The change of tone was recognised by the Central Powers. "Mr Lloyd George no longer indulges in abuse," commented Count von Hertling, the German Chancellor. The forcible incorporation of Belgium, he added, had never been contemplated; but, until the *entente* accepted the integrity of the possessions of Germany and her Allies, the Belgian Question could not be eliminated from discussion. Though President Wilson's summary of American policy in Fourteen Points, three days after the Prime-Minister's speech, breathed a similar spirit, the gulf was still too wide to be bridged; and, on February 4th, the Supreme War Council at Versailles issued a statement which brought the discussion to a close. The speeches of Hertling and Czernin, it declared, offered no basis for the conclusion of peace, and the Treaty of Brest-Litovsk revealed plans of conquest and spoliation. Consequently, the only immediate task was the prosecution of military effort till its pressure should have brought about a change of temper in the enemy Governments and peoples. This blunt declaration was reiterated at the opening of Parliament, when the Prime-Minister declared that insistence on the integrity of the possessions of the four Allies made negotiation impossible.

The attack on the western front for which the world was waiting with bated breath was launched on March 21st, 1918, and the Allied armies reeled beneath the blow. The Prime-Minister instantly appealed to Washington to accelerate the flow of American troops, and the Allied armies were at last placed under the supreme command of General Foch[1]; but the spring and early summer of 1918 were the most critical period of the War since Paris was saved at the battle of the Marne. A speech of General Smuts on May 17th reflected the anxiety of the War Cabinet and sounded like an echo of Lord Lansdowne's voice.

"When we talk of victory we do not mean marching to the Rhine or Berlin, and we do not mean going on till we have smashed Germany and the German Empire and are able to dictate peace to the enemy in his capital. We shall continue the War till the objects for which we set out are achieved. I do not think that an out-and-out victory is possible any more for any group of nations in this War, because it will mean an interminable campaign. It will mean that decimated nations will be called upon to wage war for many years to come, and the result may be that the civilisation we are out to save may be jeopardised itself. But, if you are not going to fight the war out to a smash-up, then surely it is necessary sometimes to find out how things are going and what your opponent is thinking. We shall not have a peace secured merely by the unaided efforts of armies in this war. We will have to use all our diplomacy and all the forces at our disposal to bring it to a victorious end. I can conceive that you have fought up to a stage when the enemy is prepared to concede your principal terms. But if there is no informal conference, how are you to know?"

The limited victory which had seemed probable to the War Cabinet in May was transformed into a knock-out blow by the irresistible advance of the Allies, which began on August 8th. The desperate plight of the Central Powers was revealed by Austria's appeal, on September 15th, for an exchange of views in a neutral country, and by the unconditional surrender of Bulgaria, on September 26th. On September 30th, Ludendorff informed the Kaiser that hostilities must end, and, on October 5th, Prince Max of Baden, who

[1] He was made a Marshal on August 6th of this year.

had succeeded Hertling as Chancellor and formed a Ministry representative of the several *Reichstag* parties, requested President Wilson to initiate the discussion of peace on the basis of the Fourteen Points. An exchange of Notes followed between Washington and Berlin; and, on November 5th, the *entente* announced their readiness to negotiate.

"The Allies have given careful consideration to the correspondence. Subject to the qualifications which follow, they declare their willingness to make peace with the Government of Germany on the terms of peace laid down in the President's Address of January 8th, and the principles of settlement enunciated in his subsequent Addresses. They must point out that Clause II, relating to what is usually described as the freedom of the seas, is open to various interpretations, some of which they could not accept. They must therefore reserve to themselves complete freedom on this subject when they enter the Peace Conference. Further, the President declared, on January 8th, that the invaded territories must be restored as well as evacuated and freed, and the Allied Governments feel that no doubt ought to be allowed to exist as to what this provision implies. By it they understand that compensation will be made by Germany for all damage done to the civilian population of the Allies and their property by the aggression of Germany by land, by sea, and from the air."

The President added that he was in agreement with this interpretation, and that Marshal Foch had been authorised to receive Representatives of the German Government and to communicate the terms of an Armistice. The conditions were accepted, and, at 11 a.m. on November 11th, the carnage ceased. In the closing hours of the struggle revolution had swept over Germany; the Kaiser had been forced to abdicate and had fled to Holland; a Socialist President and a Socialist Chancellor ruled in Berlin, and every dynasty in the country was chased from its Throne. Turkey had already surrendered unconditionally, and the realm of the Habsburgs had been dissolved into its component parts. The greatest of this country's Wars had ended in the greatest of her triumphs.

II. THE PEACE, 1918–1919

Directly the guns had ceased to thunder, the Prime-Minister dissolved Parliament; but, in seeking authority to represent the country in the councils of the Allies, he increased his difficulties by promises hastily made and impossible of fulfilment. Apart from glittering forecasts of a Great Britain fit for heroes, the main planks of his platform, though only adopted in response to the public demand as the electoral conflict developed, were the punishment of the Kaiser and the recovery from Germany of the cost of the War; and the

constituencies confirmed his leadership by an unexampled tribute
of gratitude and confidence. Armed with this mandate, the British
Plenipotentiaries, Mr Lloyd George, Mr Balfour, Mr Bonar Law and
Mr Barnes, arrived in Paris on January 11th, 1919. The Dominions
were represented by their own leading statesmen, of whom General
Smuts, Mr Hughes and Sir Robert Borden took the most active part
in the work of the Conference, and who occupied a dual position as
members of the British Empire Delegation and as spokesmen and
Signatories for their respective countries. The immense services of
India, though not yet an equal partner in the British firm, were also
recognised by separate Representation.

   While Castlereagh had taken fourteen assistants to Vienna in
1814, the responsible rulers of the British empire in 1919 were
accompanied by nearly two hundred officials, with an equal number
of clerks and typists. A strong Foreign Office contingent was present
under Lord Hardinge, the Permanent Under-Secretary, and Sir
Eyre Crowe; and an army of experts was at hand to advise on technical
problems. Sir Henry Wilson took a leading part in the military discussions, and Sir Hubert Llewelyn Smith rendered valuable service
in the economic field. In dealing with the problem of reparations,
the Prime-Minister depended less on his official advisers in the
Treasury than on Lord Cunliffe, the Governor of the Bank of England, and Lord Sumner, a Lord of Appeal. A position of special
importance was assigned to Sir Maurice Hankey, Secretary of the
Committee of Imperial Defence and of the War Cabinet, who was
the British Representative on the Secretariat of the Conference and
also, from April onwards, acted as Secretary to the Council of Four.
The exhausting labours of the Conference were lightened by the
Drafting Committee of Legal Advisers, on which Mr (now Sir Cecil)
Hurst, was the British Representative. Lord Robert Cecil, though
no longer a member of the Government, accepted the invitation to
represent it in the deliberations on a League of Nations. From the
outset, however, the Prime-Minister, whose personal prestige was
now at its height, pursued his own path. No Plenipotentiary ever
approached the supremely difficult task of rebuilding a world in ruins
with a less perfect equipment of precise knowledge; but he learned
quickly, and he brought a fresh mind to the bewildering array of
problems which confronted the peacemakers.

   The completeness of the victory relieved the Allies of the necessity
of haggling with the enemy, but at the same time complicated the

problem of adjusting competing claims. The British Delegation entered on its arduous task without a detailed programme, but with a few fixed principles. Germany must be rendered permanently incapable of renewed offence by land and sea, must sacrifice her Colonies, pay for the War up to the measure of her ability, and surrender her War criminals for trial. On the other hand the Fourteen Points had been accepted, subject to two exceptions, on November 5th, 1918. Moreover, the terms imposed must be of a character which the German Government would be willing to sign; for, if it were to fall, it was feared that central Europe might stagger towards Bolshevism. Great Britain, however, was in no position to dictate to her Allies, and her hands were not altogether free, since she was bound by Agreements into which she had entered during the course of the long and fluctuating struggle. It was, indeed, argued by President Wilson that the acceptance of the Fourteen Points abrogated *ipso facto* all the previous Secret Agreements. But this point of view could not be accepted without direct disregard of written engagements. The result was a compromise; for the existence of the Treaties prevented a discussion of several important problems on their merits. A more subtle difficulty confronting the British Delegation arose from the selection of Paris for a task particularly requiring cool deliberation. Bombed and bombarded without respite for many months, twice threatened with capture, and almost within sight of the devastated area, the atmosphere of the French capital was naturally charged with overstrained emotion. Hot with anger and bleeding from a thousand wounds, France sought support for her claims in her sufferings not less than in her achievements, while her geographical position and long traditions of conflict enabled her to argue with some plausibility that she understood the "*Boche*" better than did any of her guests.

The first task was to discuss the number of Representatives for each State; but the decision was of little practical importance, since the Five Great Powers—Great Britain, France, Italy, the United States and Japan—allowed the minor Allies to do little more than present their case. On January 18th, 1919, the first plenary session was opened by the President of the French Republic, after which M. Clemenceau was chosen President of the Conference. Five more plenary sessions followed; but they merely registered decisions already reached. Authority was in the hands of the Council of Ten, consisting of the Prime-Ministers and Foreign Secretaries of the Five

Great Powers; and its deliberations were continually interrupted by the necessity of dealing with executive issues such as Bolshevism in Russia and Hungary, or the relaxation of the Blockade. They met twice daily, surveying the vast field and creating Committees to deal with particular problems, till the middle of February, when the three principal actors withdrew for a brief period. Mr Lloyd George and President Wilson returned to London and Washington, respectively, to deal with domestic politics, and M. Clemenceau was wounded on February 19th. The main result of these preliminary deliberations had been to discover the extent of the differences between the French and the Anglo-American attitude towards the territorial redistribution of Europe.

The second act of the drama opened with the return of the protagonists to Paris early in March. Precedence was now given to the German Treaty; but so little progress was made that Mr Lloyd George wisely suggested the reduction of the Council of Ten to a Council of Four; the Foreign Ministers continuing to sit as a Court of Appeal on secondary questions. The new arrangement came into force on March 25th. During the temporary absence of the Italians, the Council was reduced to three. The Japanese Representative attended occasionally. For the remainder of the Conference the issues were threshed out between the Four, who met twice a day at each other's houses or the Ministry of War. Since Clemenceau spoke English fluently, most of the discussions took place in that language; but Professor Mantoux, the accomplished interpreter of the French Delegation, was at hand to assist the Italian Premier, and Sir Maurice Hankey informally recorded the decisions. The new plan worked well, and during the next six weeks the settlement with Germany was mapped out in detail.

"The tone was conversational," writes M. Tardieu, the trusted adviser of the French Premier, "no pose, no show[1]. Orlando spoke little. It was a dialogue of three—an astonishing contrast of natures the most opposite one could meet or conceive. The dialogue was at times tragic in its grave simplicity; at other times almost gay—always sincere and direct. That one duped the other is a legend. From beginning to end they discussed with a profound desire to agree. Wilson argued like an academician who criticises a thesis, sitting upright in his armchair, developing his ideas with the clarity of a didactic logician. Lloyd George discussed like a sharpshooter, with sudden cordialities and equally sudden explosions, his knee in his hands, armed with a prodigious indifference to technical arguments, drawn

[1] Tardieu, *La Paix*, pp. 113–14.

instinctively towards unexpected courses, dazzling in verve and inventiveness, responsive only to the great permanent reasons of solidarity and justice, in constant apprehension of Parliamentary repercussions. Clemenceau's dialectic, instead of being built on syllogisms like Wilson's, or exploding like that of Lloyd George, proceeded by massive affirmations, often animated by fascinating emotion."

The greatest constructive achievement of the Peace Congress presented the fewest difficulties. A League of Nations was one of the Fourteen Points, and President Wilson was determined that such a League should be created at the earliest moment. At the second plenary session, on January 25th, the Conference decided that a League should be established to promote international cooperation, to ensure the fulfilment of international obligations, and to provide safeguards against war; that it should form an integral part of the Treaty of Peace; that it should be open to every civilised nation which could be relied on to promote its objects; that its members should meet periodically and should have a permanent organisation and secretariat; and that a Committee should be appointed to work out the details of its constitution and functions. On February 14th, the Covenant, which had been framed by a Commission appointed by the Plenary Session, was laid before the Conference, and on April 28th, at the fifth plenary session, President Wilson explained the changes of detail made in the draft and secured its acceptance[1].

The most difficult question confronting the Peace-makers was the defence of the eastern frontier of France. The policy embodied in the Secret Franco-Russian Agreement of March, 1917, had been sharply repudiated by Mr Balfour, when it was revealed by the Bolshevists[2]; but the separation from Germany of the Left Bank of the Rhine appeared to the majority of Frenchmen the only solid guarantee against future invasions. Shortly after the conclusion of the Armistice, Marshal Foch urged Clemenceau to insist on the Rhine frontier; and in January, 1919, he addressed a similar appeal to the Allied Generals. The French Premier, accordingly, instructed Tardieu to prepare a full statement of the French case. Germany's capacity for attack, ran the argument, rested on the strategic network of railways on the Left Bank in combination with the Rhine fortresses. France had no desire to annex the Left Bank, wishing only that the Rhine should be Germany's western frontier, with Allied occupation

[1] This was the only part of the Treaty which was never discussed by the Council of Ten or the Council of Four.
[2] See Cocks, *The Secret Treaties*, ch. 6.

of the bridge-heads. To this scheme the British Delegation offered unrelenting opposition. "At my first visit to Paris," observed Mr Lloyd George, "my strongest impression was the statue of Strassburg in mourning. Do not let us make another Alsace-Lorraine." To separate seven million Germans from their Fatherland would be wrong in itself, had never been demanded in any of the separate or joint declaration of war-aims, and was moreover unnecessary, since Germany was disarmed. Great Britain, at any rate, would refuse to take part in garrison duty. The recovery of Alsace-Lorraine was enough.

On March 14th, the day of the President's return from America, the two Anglo-Saxon statesmen proposed a joint Military Guarantee as an alternative. The French Premier expressed a desire for the Guarantee in addition to, not as a substitute for, the Occupation, since a treaty might ensure victory but would not prevent an invasion. Negotiations lasted without interruption till April 22nd, and were complicated by other grave differences of opinion. The views of the Prime-Minister were embodied in a comprehensive Memorandum of March 26th, inspired by the loftiest statesmanship, which set forth the conditions, not of a temporary settlement, but of a lasting Peace[1].

"You may strip Germany of her colonies, reduce her armaments to a mere police force and her Navy to that of a fifth-rate Power; all the same, in the end, if she feels that she has been unjustly treated in the Peace of 1919, she will find means of exacting retribution from her conquerors. The deep impression made upon the human heart by four years of unexampled slaughter will disappear with the hearts upon which it has been marked by the terrible sword of the Great War. The maintenance of peace will then depend upon there being no causes of exasperation constantly stirring up the spirit of patriotism, of justice, or of fair play. To achieve redress our terms may be severe, they may be stern and even ruthless; but at the same time they can be so just that the country on which they are imposed will feel in its heart that it has no right to complain. But injustice, arrogance, displayed in the hour of triumph, will never be forgotten or forgiven. For these reasons I am, therefore, strongly averse to transferring more Germans from German rule to the rule of some other nation than can possibly be helped. I cannot conceive any greater cause of future war than that the German people, who have certainly proved themselves one of the most vigorous and powerful races in the world, should be surrounded by a number of small States, many of them consisting of people who have never previously set up a stable government for themselves, but each of them containing large masses of Germans

---

[1] This important document, first published in Nitti's *Peaceless Europe*, 1921, was issued as a White Paper, Cd. 1614 (1922).

clamouring for reunion with their native land....From every point of view, therefore, it seems to me that we ought to endeavour to draw up a peace settlement as if we were impartial arbiters, forgetful of the passions of the War."

A just and far-sighted Peace with Germany, he added, must be supplemented by a League of Nations, a limitation of the armaments of the victors no less than of the vanquished, and the admission of Germany to the League after accepting the Allied terms and establishing a stable and democratic government[1].

The French reply to the British Memorandum argued that to create new States without frontiers enabling them to live would cause them to turn Bolshevist, and that the contrast between the security obtained by Great Britain and the insecurity of France resulting from the British proposals would poison the relations between the Allies. The Prime-Minister now endeavoured to satisfy the French demand for security without abandoning his resolve to tolerate no fresh Alsace-Lorraines. It was agreed to reduce the German Army to 100,000 men, to abolish Conscription[2], and to demilitarise the Right Bank of the Rhine to a depth of fifty kilometres; but as to the permanent separation of the Left Bank he was adamant, and President Wilson agreed that nothing more was possible or necessary than the joint Guarantee. The French Premier caustically rejoined that the German Fleet had disappeared and that the United States were far off. Foch and the Allied Generals were summoned to address the Four; but the Marshal found no support, and even King Albert, who was called into council, did not ask for prolonged occupation. It was announced that the President had ordered his ship to Brest. France stood alone, and with a heavy heart Clemenceau withdrew his demand. On April 20th, President Wilson approved Allied occupation for fifteen years, and on April 22nd Mr Lloyd George followed suit. It was agreed that the period might be prolonged, if the guarantees for the security of France at the end of the term were insufficient, and that the Allies might reoccupy the territory, if Germany failed to pay her debts. The compromise reached with such difficulty satisfied neither Great Britain nor France. Marshal Foch complained of the limitation of time, arguing that "if one is master of the Rhine one is master of Germany; and if we are not on the Rhine we have lost

[1] The substance of this Memorandum was repeated in an interview with "a high personage" published in *The Westminster Gazette*, March 31st.
[2] The prohibition of Conscription was due to Great Britain, the French, supported by the Italians, making a formal protest.

everything." Mr Lloyd George was equally dissatisfied, and, after receiving the German comments on the original form of the Peace Treaty, attempted, though without success, to reopen the question.

In addition to their demands for the separation of the Left Bank from Germany, the French strongly urged their claim to the district on the eastern border of Lorraine which, having been assigned to them in 1814, was taken away in 1815. This claim was stoutly opposed by both the British and the Americans. The French eventually withdrew it; but it was agreed that they should receive compensation in the control and ownership of the Saar coalfield for the wanton damage done during the War to the French mines. It appeared, however, on investigation that effective control must entail the temporary separation of this district from Germany, and to this the President, who at first would approve nothing beyond a tribute of coal, eventually gave his assent. An agreement was finally reached by which this district, which included all and more than that assigned to France under the frontiers of 1814, was placed for fifteen years under an administrative commission to be appointed by the League of Nations; a plebiscite was to be taken after fifteen years as to the ultimate destination of the country. On the other hand, the French claim to the town of Landau was refused. A further problem closely, and indeed tragically, associated with the political problem of the Left Bank was settled at the same time. The obligation imposed on Belgium in 1839 to maintain permanent neutrality was removed, and she became a fully independent State.

While the British Delegation stood for a moderate settlement of the problems of the Left Bank and the Saar, its attitude on two other questions appeared to one or more of the Allies severe and even vindictive. The trial of the Kaiser was an election pledge; and, despite the opposition of the United States and Japan and the disapproval of Generals Botha and Smuts, his extradition was demanded from Holland, but demanded in vain. On the issue of Reparations, again, the British demands appeared to the American Delegation not only excessive, but unwarrantable. The Fourteen Points included the "restoration" of occupied territories, and the Note of November 5th spoke of "compensation for all damage done to the civilian population of the Allies and their property by the aggression of Germany by land, by sea and from the air." British and French politicians, however, had subsequently declared Germany liable for the whole cost of the War. Clemenceau declared that, whatever sum the experts might fix, it would still fall short of French expectation, and Mr Lloyd George added that he, too, would fall if a sum were fixed. The American Delegation, on the contrary, was unanimous for a fixed sum, in order to restore settled conditions and to encourage Germany to work. The question what claims should be made under the category of Reparation led to prolonged discussion. Mr Hughes bitterly assailed the American view that the costs of the War could not be described as reparation to civilians. President Wilson was informed by wireless of the controversy when on his way back from America in March, and replied that "the inclusion of war costs was clearly inconsistent with what we deliberately led the enemy to expect and cannot now honourably alter simply because we have the power." The President, however, though not the American Delegation, was subsequently, by a Memorandum of General Smuts, converted to the inclusion of pensions. The United States themselves did not claim a penny. The British demand was due to the fact that our claim for material damage by submarines and air-raids was relatively small, that the fruits of victory needed to be brought into some relation towards election promises, and that otherwise the Dominions would receive no pecuniary compensation. While the controversy was in progress, 360 Members of Parliament despatched a warning telegram to Paris. "Our constituents have always expected that the first action of the Peace Delegates would be, as you repeatedly stated in your election speeches, to present the Bill in full and make the Germans acknowledge the debt." Mr Lloyd George paid a flying visit to St Stephen's, where he fiercely denounced Lord Northcliffe, in whom he saw the instigator of the campaign of criticism. The final result, which was a compromise between "the cost of the War" and the formula of November 5th, included war pensions and separation allowances, and demanded a thousand million pounds within two years, before the expiration of which a scheme of payments extending over thirty years was to be worked out by an Inter-Allied Commission.

Agreement on the problems presented by Fiume, Shantung and Poland proved as difficult as with regard to the Rhineland, the Saar and Reparations. The first, indeed, was not solved till long after the Peace Congress had concluded its labours. The second was decided in favour of Japan. In neither of these cases did President Wilson receive effective support from his British colleague; but, in the third, Mr Lloyd George fought single-handed against the full Polish programme. Poland, declared M. Pichon, the French Foreign Minister, must be "*grande et forte, très forte*"; and he appeared to think that her strength must increase with her size. An Inter-Allied Commission proposed to transfer to her almost the whole of the Russian provinces of Posen and West Prussia, which had formed part of the ancient kingdom of Poland including both banks of the Vistula, the city of Danzig and the district of Marienwerder so as to secure control of the railway from Warsaw to Danzig. In addition, they also proposed to assign to Poland the greater part of Upper Silesia, which had not been Polish for some five hundred years. When the report of the Commission was presented to the Council of Ten, the Prime-Minister strongly urged the unwisdom of a settlement by which over two million Germans would be subject to Polish government. In particular he put his finger on the district of Marienwerder and the city of Danzig. In consequence of his urgent representations it was resolved to allow a plebiscite in Marienwerder, and to make Danzig a Free City under the League of Nations, though subject to Poland in customs and foreign relations. Poland was also empowered to use the docks, the river and the railways within the Danzig area. The distribution of the German Colonial empire, on the other hand, was settled without difficulty. German South-West and the larger part of German East Africa fell to the British empire, while France secured the major part of the Cameroons and Togoland. The territories in the Pacific were divided between the British empire and Japan, the former taking those south of the equator, the latter those to the north.

The Treaty was formally delivered to the German Delegates on May 7th at the Trianon Palace Hotel at Versailles. The conflict, declared Clemenceau in opening the ceremony, had cost the victors too much for them not to take all necessary precautions that the Peace should be a lasting one. On receiving the bulky volume containing the terms, Count Rantzau, the Foreign Minister, without rising from his place, read a Declaration repudiating the charge that Germany or her Allies had been solely responsible for the War. President Wilson desired oral discussion with the German Delegates; but Clemenceau insisted that all comments should be in writing, and Mr Lloyd George, with some reluctance, followed his lead. The German reply, presented on May 29th, argued that President Wilson's principles, on the basis of which Germany had laid down her arms, had been violated; that the new Government was thoroughly democratic; that Germany could only fulfil her obligations if permitted to retain Upper

Silesia; that after her losses of territory, coal and iron, millions of her citizens would be unable to live; that she ought at once to enter the League of Nations with equal rights; and that the reduction of armaments should be general, not unilateral. The "rape" of Danzig and the cession of Memel were denounced, and the retention of the Colonies under a mandate was proposed.

The German reply, which merely stiffened the back of the French Premier, produced a profound effect on Mr Lloyd George; and what M. Tardieu describes as "the second and worst crisis" began.

"They were atrocious days. He (Mr Lloyd George) was scared by the consequences of a refusal to sign or a crisis in Germany. On all questions —disarmament, occupation, reparations, Danzig, Upper Silesia—he proposed inadmissible concessions, apologised for doing it so late, and talked of consulting Parliament. 'Our demands will upset the Government, and we shall have nobody to sign. The Peace must be signed. We cannot remain two or three years in a condition which is neither peace nor war. If France wishes to do so, she can.' The work of two months threatened to collapse."

Clemenceau replied that France knew the Germans best, and that concessions would only encourage their resistance, while depriving the Allies of their rights. He added satirically that British opinion did not object to making Germany surrender her Colonies and her Fleet. Though the American Delegation was in general sympathy with the British Premier, the President himself demanded no change in the fundamental clauses. Deprived of his support, Mr Lloyd George was unable to gain all his points; but the changes announced in the Allied reply of June 16th were of considerable importance for Germany. A plebiscite was conceded in Upper Silesia; the western frontier of Poland was slightly modified; communications with East Prussia were improved; the rate of reduction for the Army was retarded; and the method of paying the indemnity was to be discussed with a German Commission. Without these changes, no German Government could have signed; and it was the unanimous desire of the German Delegates at Paris to decline even the amended terms. The German Cabinet was divided; but the persistence of Erzberger won over a majority of the National Assembly at Weimar, and on Scheidemann's resignation a new Cabinet was formed, with a Mandate to sign. A final effort to secure the omission of the Articles providing for the surrender of the Kaiser and other offenders, and declaring Germany the sole author of the War, had brought a telegraphic refusal from the Four and a demand for immediate compliance. The time-limit expired at 7 p.m. on June 23rd, and by 5.20 it was known that Germany had submitted. On June 28th the Treaty was signed by Germany and by all the Allies except China, in the Galerie des Glaces, in which the German empire had been proudly proclaimed half a century earlier. On July 2nd the formal proclamation of peace took place at St James's Palace and in the City, according to historic precedent. The Treaty was ratified by Great Britain on October 10th, and came into force on January 10th, 1920. On the same historic day, June 28th, Mr Lloyd George and Mr Balfour, Clemenceau and Pichon signed the Guarantee arranged in April; and a corresponding document was signed by President Wilson. The Guarantee included the following provisions:

Article 1. In case Articles XLII and XLIII, neutralising the Left Bank and fifty kilometres on the Right Bank, may not at first provide adequate security and protection to France, Great Britain agrees to come immediately to her assistance in the event of any unprovoked movement of aggression by Germany.

Article 2. The Treaty will only come into force when the corresponding Treaty with the United States is ratified.

Article 3. The Treaty must be submitted to the Council of the League of Nations and must be recognised by it as consistent with the Covenant. It will continue in force till, on the application of one of the parties, the Council agrees that the League itself affords sufficient protection.

Article 4. The Treaty shall before ratification be submitted to Parliament and the French Chambers for approval.

Article 5. The Treaty shall impose no obligation on any Dominion unless approved by the Parliament of such Dominion.

On July 3rd, the Prime-Minister introduced a Bill for carrying the Treaty into effect, and took occasion to review the handiwork of himself and his colleagues. The terms, he declared, were terrible but just, since all the territorial adjustments were reparations. The plotters of the War and offenders against the laws of war must be punished, not for revenge, but to discourage crime, and the Kaiser would be tried in London. The German nation must be punished; for it had applauded its rulers. He challenged any pretension to point to a single clause not in accordance with the demands of justice and fair play. The Anglo-French Treaty, he added, only engaged us in the event of wanton aggression. The Army of Occupation was a second Guarantee. The League of Nations was the greatest safeguard; but it was of no value unless the strong nations behind it were prepared to stop aggression.

The satisfaction professed by the Prime-Minister was not shared by all his Anglo-Saxon colleagues. To Mr Lansing, the terms appeared "immeasurably harsh and humiliating, while many of them seem to me impossible of performance." Mr J. M. Keynes, who had resigned his post as a Representative of the Treasury in protest against the Reparation settlement, proceeded to denounce the "Carthaginian Peace" in a volume which was read all over the world. A Declaration issued by General Smuts gave eloquent expression to the mixed feelings with which most thoughtful men regarded the achievement.

"I have signed the Treaty, not because I consider it a satisfactory document, but because it is imperatively necessary to close the War. We have not yet achieved the real peace to which our peoples were looking. The promise of the new life, the victory for the great human ideals for which the peoples have shed their blood and their treasure without stint, the fulfilment of their aspirations towards a new international order, are not written in this Treaty, and will not be written in treaties. A new heart must be given, not only to our enemies but to ourselves. A new spirit of generosity and humanity, born in the hearts of the peoples in this great hour of common suffering and sorrow, can alone heal the wounds inflicted on the body of Christendom."

After the German Treaty had been signed and Mr Lloyd George and President Wilson had left Paris, Mr Balfour and Mr Lansing remained to carry through the settlement with the other belligerents. The Austrian Treaty had been delivered to the Chancellor, Dr Renner, on June 2nd, in an incomplete form; and, after the Austrian Delegates had pointed out the impossibility of fulfilling the economic conditions, it was presented in a modified form on July 20th. It was not, however, till September 10th that the Peace of St Germain was signed. The Habsburg empire had broken in pieces before the conflict had ceased, and the victors had merely to register accomplished facts. On the other hand, they took no steps to secure the necessary conditions of existence for the republican remnant, burdening it with impossible economic exactions, vetoing (at the instigation of France) its union with Germany, and exerting no pressure on its neighbours to supply it with the food and raw materials without which it was doomed to a living death. By the Treaty of Neuilly, signed on November 27th, 1919, Bulgaria, where Boris had succeeded his discredited father, was cut off from the Aegean, compelled to surrender territory on her western frontier, and burdened with an indemnity of eighty millions, while her Army was limited to 20,000 men. By the Treaty of Trianon, signed on June 4th, 1920, the Republic of Hungary was reduced to a third of its former territory and population. Finally, the liquidation of Turkey was postponed in the vain hope that the United States would undertake a mandate for Armenia. The Treaty of Sévres, signed on August 10th, 1920, leaving to the Ottoman empire nothing but a precarious foothold in Europe and the larger part of Asia Minor, remained unratified, owing to the opposition of Mustapha Kamel's independent Government in Angora, the evident wrath of Mohammedans in India, and the substitution of King Constantine for Venizelos as the ruler of Greece. This fact, however, did not prevent Great Britain from retaining her conquests in Mesopotamia and Palestine, in the latter of which Mr Balfour, on behalf of the Government, had in 1917 promised to provide "a national home" for the Jews.

The British empire emerged from the titanic struggle with a large accession of territory, and with the German Navy at the bottom of the sea; but Great Britain is burdened by debt, and her best European customers are temporarily ruined. The Balance of Power has ceased to exist; for the supremacy of France on land is as unchallengeable as British supremacy at sea. The Triple Entente, like the Triple Alliance, has disappeared. In a new world, where familiar landmarks have been swept away by the raging tempest, British statesmen have discovered that the highest interests and the abiding prosperity of their country are bound up with the vitality and authority of the one operative organisation for the preservation of Peace—the League of Nations.

CHAPTER VIII

THE FOREIGN OFFICE

INTRODUCTORY

FOREIGN AFFAIRS are not a common British study, nor is diplomacy a characteristically British art. The people of these Islands have supposed it part of their great inheritance to be insular; and the sense of the splendour of isolation is inconveniently apparent even in the distant Continents inhabited by the Island-race. Great Britain has sometimes enjoyed, but has seldom sought, a dominant position in the counsels of Europe. None of her Foreign Ministers has seemed to mankind to be quite of the first eminence, though there have been several of the first quality. None fascinates the imagination like Talleyrand or Metternich; nor is there any whose policy abroad is so closely related to policy at home as that of Bismarck or Cavour. It is, indeed, significant of the place of Foreign Affairs among English political interests that only one Prime-Minister[1] has thought fit to choose the Foreign Office for his own Department; and that this Prime-Minister should have stood noticeably aloof from the current of popular opinion and have seemed peculiarly insensible to its pressure. And it is no less significant that throughout the nineteenth century, for all the march of democracy, the Foreign Secretary should have been selected from among the members, actual or prospective, of the House of Lords—that is, if we neglect the cases of Fox and Russell and Palmerston that only just fail to show the rule, and the case of Canning that by exception proves it. A veil was, in fact, allowed by mutual consent to fall between the mass of the people and the statesmen to whom it was given to open and to shut the doors of the Temple of Janus. Neither did the nation desire to be disturbed in its ignorant bliss, nor the Foreign Secretary in his delicate business. But, though public opinion has not been vigorous enough to be habitually consulted on Foreign Affairs, it has not been apathetic enough to be safely ignored. At critical times—and especially if the Temple-gates begin to swing upon their hinges to let pass out the god of war—it can awake, lay hold of the national destinies, and exact from public servants a strict, if not a just account of their stewardship. It is then that men

[1] Salisbury.

will be found to use hard words about the Foreign Office, to reflect that, while diplomatists tread the smooth and easy road that leads to war, those who are not diplomatists must hack their way out of it, and to remember that the Foreign Service of the country has been manned by young men of fortune, though perhaps to forget that the labour of these has gone some while unpaid and still goes a great while underpaid. British troops, a provincial chemist once assured the writer, were the bravest in the world; but in our Foreign Office, he continued, there was more 'brass' than brains.

A philosophical student of political affairs might probably be disposed to meet such vigorous criticism by observing that, since nations tend, according to one of the best-established laws of natural justice, to have the Government they deserve, the British Foreign Secretary, the British Foreign Office Clerk and the British Diplomatist, alike in their weakness and their strength, are very much what their countrymen have made them, if not what their countrymen would have them to be. The Foreign Service, dominated, though it has unquestionably been, by the influence of our largest English public-school and our oldest English University, has, not the less for that, been representative of Great Britain as she was wont to look out upon the world in all her lazy strength—capable, easy-going, contemptuous, inordinately fond of carrying the form and temper of a game into the pursuit of the business of life. Such an institution, like the remnant of the age that fostered it, is ill-suited to a world driven on by the desire for efficiency and driven mad by the rage for equality; and the light sarcasm of the witty undergraduate that the Foreign Office was "the last choice preserve of administration practised as a sport," when some twenty years later it reached the ears of a Royal Commission as the dictum of a professor[1], was on the point of becoming, if indeed it had not even then become, a lament over the grace of a day that is gone. The history of the Foreign Service, as it will be presented here, is, therefore, in one aspect the record of a finished phase of its existence—the account of an organisation which has travelled out of the province of privilege into that of open, if not yet of equal, competition.

Some such reflexions as these may, then, serve to introduce a sketch of what has seemed to all eyes, whether friendly or the reverse, to wear the blue ribbon amongst the Departments of State. Like

---

[1] Prof. J. S. Phillimore, quoted by Mr Hirst. *Appendix to the 5th Report Royal Commission on the Civil Service*, 1914, Minutes of Evidence, Q. 40,579.

most British institutions, it was generated, not of logic and method, but of inconvenience and disorder. Foreign Affairs, so late as the reign of George III fell within the sphere of those things that were administered by a dual State Secretariate, owing its duplication, though not its origin, to the energy of Henry VIII. The Secretaries of his days and of many days afterwards, were secretaries indeed. At the close of the seventeenth century the Sovereign was still his own Foreign Minister; and William III was, in fact, better fitted to be so than any man in his kingdom. There were secrets in his keeping, which, perhaps, never found their way into public offices and at which, for all we know, Secretaries of State may not have guessed. Marlborough took the King's place in the great days of Queen Anne; and Marlborough had as smooth a tongue and as sweet a temper as ever graced a diplomatist. But, when Queen Anne was dead, the Throne lost at once its hedge of divinity and its central situation. The English Revolution was consummated; and Foreign Policy, like all things political, began to revolve around the Prime-Minister, whom the Constitution had borne in secret, and the Cabinet, which it had nurtured in seclusion.

Foreign Affairs thus fell into the hands of the two Secretaries of State[1], acting as principals rather than as agents; and they shared them oddly. Foreign Policy was directed by the one or the other, according as the country concerned lay to the north or the south of Europe. What circumstance determined the exact line of division is a matter for speculation. Probably, some casual arrangement between the two Secretaries with nothing more to guide them than the unimaginative consideration that north is north, and south south—but, possibly, a more studied appreciation of the fact that the hegemony of Europe was in issue between the Bourbons and the Habsburgs. Anyway, when the elder Pitt took office in 1756, intending to save the country, he found as embarrassing a confusion of the Foreign business of the State as can well be imagined. The Southern Department of the Secretariate, which was his own, had, besides the control of Irish, American and Home Affairs, the direction of British policy in respect of France, Spain, Italy, Turkey, and the Barbary States, with the Portuguese and Swiss correspondence thrown in. All the rest of the Continent lay in the province of the Northern Secretary. It might naturally be supposed that this division of labour would have produced

[1] There was also a Secretary for Scotch Affairs from 1708–46; and for the American, or Colonial Department from 1768–82.

divided counsels and conflicting combinations. But Pitt's personality was capable of making one office out of two; and from his chambers in Cleveland Row he effectively dominated the proceedings of his colleague at the Cockpit in Whitehall. It must not, however, be concluded that the localities named had any inseparable connexion with the two spheres of administration[1]. A man might very well preside in Whitehall over the diplomatic relations between Great Britain and the countries round the Mediterranean, or in Cleveland Row over those with Germany, Russia, the Low Countries and Scandinavia; and presumably the papers and *personnel* were shifted as was required. Pitt, however, increased a hundredfold the efficiency of his clerks. Abstracts of the negotiations on hand were made for him; and a new system established of recording their progress. But his staff was conceived on a scale of Lilliputian size. This greatest of War Ministers, whose duties covered the administration of the greater part of Home and Foreign Affairs, had for his exclusive use no more than two Under-Secretaries and nine Clerks, though some further assistance was given by persons whose services the Northern and Southern Departments owned in common[2].

Such, then, was the Foreign Office in embryo. It was only brought to birth, however, as an independent institution twenty years after Pitt's famous Ministry, during that admirable Administration of Rockingham's, which, inspired by the genius of Burke, accomplished a maximum of reform in a minimum of time. In 1782, the Southern Department became the Home Office with the charge of Irish affairs and of such Colonial business as remained after the secession of the United States. The Northern was converted into the Foreign Department[3]; and Charles James Fox became the first Secretary of State for Foreign Affairs.

I

Of no statesman of a date so distant is it necessary to say less. Everyone knows about Fox's vices and defects. In the Foreign Department, they noticed chiefly his virtues—his facility and industry, his constant good-temper, his unaffected bearing, and above all, his commonsense[4]. "He shines," said Horace Walpole, "as greatly in Place as he did in Opposition, though infinitely more difficult a task."

[1] Hertslet, *Recollections of the Old Foreign Office*, p. 251.
[2] B. Williams, *Life of William Pitt*, I. 327, 328.
[3] Sir W. Anson, *Law and Custom of the Constitution*, II. 166.
[4] See Horace Walpole's letter to Mann of May 5th, 1782.

For all that, he did not retain office so long as four months; and it was an interdepartmental dispute that drove him out. The reconstruction of the administrative machine had left Anglo-American affairs hanging between heaven and earth. To Fox, who viewed American Independence as a thing conceded, the revolted Colonies appeared as foreign a State as any other. To Shelburne, who, as Home Secretary, had charge of the Colonial business of the Government, they seemed, until peace was signed, to be nothing more than what they had been before. Both Ministers, therefore, employed separate agents to negotiate a settlement; and, when a majority of the Cabinet supported the view of his rival, Fox resolved to resign. The illness of Rockingham delayed this event; and his death obscured its origin. But to those who were behind the scenes it must have been apparent that the great schism between the Shelburne and Portland Whigs, which opened the way for the famous, or infamous, Coalition between Fox and North, owed its first beginnings to the establishment of the Foreign Office.

On Fox's resignation, the Foreign Office was given to Lord Grantham, "a very agreeable, pleasing man[1]," but a Minister of no importance; for Shelburne, in his new capacity as Premier, tended to monopolise the functions of government. The Peace of 1783 with France and America was, in fact, the work of the Prime-Minister, not of the Foreign Secretary; and one of its negotiators was Oswald, whose mission to Franklin had been a leading incident in the dispute between Fox and Shelburne. It may have been as good a peace as could be made, but it was not as good a peace as was wanted. Fox coalesced with North, and, having brought about the downfall of Shelburne, resumed his place at the Foreign Office. But Fortune gave him no chance of elaborating a policy. We know only that, although he was aware of the inclination of the Court and the Country for an alliance with Austria, his own preference in favour of the character of the King of Prussia as against that of the Emperor, and his sense of the importance to Great Britain of the Baltic armaments led him to desire an alliance or understanding with the Baltic Powers —Russia, Prussia, and most important of all, Denmark[2]. For this he worked with all his former brilliancy of address during the eight brief months of Coalition Government between April and December, 1783.

---

[1] See Horace Walpole's letter to Mann of July 21st, 1782.
[2] Malmesbury, *Diaries and Correspondence*, II. 51, 52.

"Mr Pitt is certainly an extraordinary young man," wrote Horace Walpole to Horace Mann, after the Coalition had been some months dead[1]; "but is he a supernatural one? Do not trust to me, but believe the Foreign Ministers. There is but one voice amongst them on the marvellous superiority of Mr Fox, and the unheard of facility of doing business with him. He made the peace between the Turks and the Russians; and Simonin, the latter's Minister, told the King himself so, in the drawing-room, since Fox's fall. On the contrary, those foreigners talk loudly of the extreme ignorance of the new Secretaries. Our Ambassador at Paris is a model of insufficience. Lord Shelburne said the other day, 'Upon my word, I hear that the Duke of Dorset's letters are written very well; he talks of the ceded islands, as if he knew where they are.'"

Dukes, in those days, formed a structural part of the fabric of the Constitution, and were an article rarely dispensed with in the making of Cabinets. Pitt's particular Duke was Leeds, who, when still Caermarthen, had succeeded Fox, at Pitt's urgent request, as Foreign Secretary in December, 1783. He was, as the portrait by Lawrence, presented to the Duchess by "the gentlemen of the Foreign Office" on his retirement in 1791, sufficiently discloses, a very ducal personage. His knowledge, so The Gentleman's Magazine advises us, was not profound, but miscellaneous and extensive; he was a better scholar than others of his rank; he delighted in conversation, being much disposed to take the lead in it; and he was never forgetful of his station in life[2]. Despite all this, he was not a nonentity. He had a policy of his own, resting upon an agreement between Great Britain and the two Imperial Courts[3]—Austria and Russia—though, possibly enough, he had derived his ideas from Sir James Harris, the leading British diplomatist of his day and the ancestor of a Foreign Secretary not quite so able as himself. The compulsion of circumstance, however, proved too much for them both; and Harris's large powers of persuasion and brilliant diplomatic art were in the end devoted to forming an alliance between Great Britain, Holland, and Prussia, which was initiated by the Treaty of 1788 and was the occasion of the Malmesbury peerage. Three years afterwards, Pitt's refusal to take action against Russia under the terms of this Treaty caused Leeds to resign on the ground that we were committed in honour to give assistance to Prussia[4].

[1] March 30th, 1784.
[2] See the Memoir of him in Political Memoranda of Francis, 5th Duke of Leeds, pp. ii, iii.
[3] Ibid. p. 116. Cp. Harris's letter of June 29th, 1783, to Grantham (Malmesbury, Diaries and Correspondence, II. 25).
[4] Political Memoranda of Francis, 5th Duke of Leeds, pp. x, xi.

If Malmesbury was well-informed, Lord Grenville's influence was responsible for Pitt's decision[1]. It was, at any rate, Grenville who took Leeds's place.

Leeds's Ministry deserves a paragraph in the purely Departmental history of the Foreign Office. Fox, when he took over the straggling establishment, which had stood so long with one foot in St James's and the other in Whitehall, had fixed its abode in Cleveland Row. But Leeds, in 1786, brought it back to the Cockpit—not the Royal Cockpit in Birdcage Walk, but the Whitehall Cockpit, which had for some while been converted from a habitation of fighting-cocks to the more dignified uses of the Treasury[2] and the Privy Council. The Foreign Secretary, if he chose his room with circumspection, probably looked north over the Horse Guards' Parade, and west over what is now the garden of 10 Downing Street into St James's Park. At any rate, we shall figure him best with that pleasant prospect before his windows; for he was a good, easy man, enjoying great place in comfortable times and fortunate in the hour of his resignation.

Grenville, both in respect of temperament and energy, was better fitted to face the storms of the Revolutionary and Napoleonic Era. His defects lay in his coldness, his secrecy and his reserve. It was said of him that he knew no one and was known of none[3]; and he said of himself that he was incompetent to the management of men[4]. Circumstances—ironical as ever—made him, who had brought about the fall of Leeds in the interest of non-interference, a chief instrument of British intervention in the affairs of the Continent, and a principal promoter of the Coalitions against France. He was, indeed, by disposition, far more warlike than his leader; and his attitude differed widely from that of the Prime-Minister. Pitt held it as an article of faith, both political and religious, that peace must be constantly pursued[5]; but Grenville had no delicacy about fighting and fighting to the finish. His ruling wish, if Malmesbury is right, was to free himself from his cousin[6]; but, as long as Pitt was alive, his policy was the policy that cousin imposed. He even remained in office in 1796, while Malmesbury set out on the abortive journey to Paris which

---

[1] Malmesbury, *Diaries and Correspondence*, II. 441.
[2] Sheppard, *The Old Palace of Whitehall*, p. 68.
[3] Malmesbury, *Diaries and Correspondence*, III. 590.
[4] *Courts and Cabinets of George III*, IV. 133.
[5] Malmesbury, *Diaries and Correspondence*, III. 369.
[6] Pitt. See Malmesbury, *ibid.* IV. 302.

evoked Burke's sarcasm that the progress of the Mission was doubtless slow, since the Envoy had to go all the way upon his knees. Nor did he resign when the negotiation was resumed a year later, to his certain disapproval and with no better success[1]. His conduct differed fundamentally from that of Leeds; he remained disapproving. As we go forward, we shall have occasion to notice a few cases of serious conflict between the Prime-Minister and the Foreign Secretary. This is the second of them; and in this instance, as in all the rest, the Prime-Minister prevailed.

It was in the face of the divided counsels of his leaders—in sympathy with Pitt and in antipathy to Grenville[2]—that George Canning gained his first experience of Foreign Affairs. We catch a glimpse of him just at this time, preparing Malmesbury's French correspondence for the Press, in the firm conviction that, but for the *coup d'état* in Paris of September, 1797, Pitt's patience, in spite of Grenville, would have won Pitt's peace, and resolved himself to gain what Grenville had never secured—the priceless affection of his subordinates. "I write this," he tells Malmesbury, "in the midst of a hubbub of clerks; all of whom I am taking home from their work to dine with me, that they may work again the more readily and actively after dinner[3]."

In Grenville's time the Foreign Office was moved from the Cockpit to Downing Street. The buildings leased for the purpose belonged to Lord Sheffield and Sir Samuel Fludyer, and were first occupied by their new tenant in December, 1793. In these old dwelling-houses, looking into St James's Park and standing, as was subsequently discovered, on ten thousand wooden piles, Foreign Affairs were conducted for the next seventy years. "Dingy and shabby to a degree," is Rumbold's[4] description of the building, "made up of dark offices and labyrinthine passages—four houses at least tumbled into one, with floors at uneven levels and wearying corkscrew stairs that men cursed as they climbed—a thorough picture of disorder, penury and meanness !" In the attics of this agreeable tenement were presently installed the Foreign Office printers, their heavy machines imperilling the existence of those who inhabited the floors below them; in the basement lived the bookbinders; and in the labyrinthine passages there died that famous cat which buried itself by passing in behind the shelves

[1] See Malmesbury, *Diaries and Correspondence*, III. 369.
[2] See Malmesbury, *ibid.* III. 591. "Canning more out of sorts with Grenville than ever."
[3] *Ibid.* III. 593.   [4] Sir H. Rumbold, *Recollections of a Diplomatist*, I. 109.

after one volume of *The Times* had been temporarily removed, and whose skeleton was sent up to Lord John Russell in a red despatch-box some time after its corpse had set the sanitary authorities hunting for malodorous drains[1]. Literal sepulchre as the place may have proved in its inmost recesses, it was at least metaphorically a whited one without. Here there were to be seen certain modest old-time elegancies in the shape of pediments, brick facings and standard lamps, not to speak of the sentries, whose sentry-boxes are still to be detected in the obituary sketches that Scharf executed whilst the auctioneer's strident voice was actually winding up the tale of the old Foreign Office in the late October days of 1861[2]. And there were, too, though Rumbold had, perhaps, in his early years little occasion to enter them, some very presentable rooms in the side of the building touching the Park— spacious apartments in which Canning had once entertained, and where the Secretary of State, and his Private Secretaries, and the Under-Secretary of State, and the Foreign Ambassadors, when kept waiting, all found adequate accommodation. Here, on the first-floor, was the room used for Cabinet meetings, to which during the recess Ministers could at any time repair to read the more important despatches. This last circumstance was not without its Constitutional significance; for there was nothing, perhaps, which distinguished the Foreign Office from other Departments of State more than this—that its affairs were considered to be in a peculiar degree the special concern of the Cabinet as a whole, and not simply or mainly that of the Foreign Secretary.

Into the quarters just described there moved with Grenville a staff of two Under-Secretaries and eleven Clerks. At the head of these there had stood, since 1790, as Permanent Under-Secretary one, George Aust, destined, five years later, to be succeeded by George Hammond, whose name is kept in remembrance by the more recent Under-Secretaryship of his more celebrated son. As regards salaries, the Under-Secretaries—the Parliamentary and the Permanent —Bland Burges and Aust, were paid £1500 a year; the Chief Clerk had £1000; the two Senior Clerks £650 and £480; and the nine Junior from £80 to £300. These officials did not represent quite all the labour at command. There were certain persons whose abilities were the common property of the Secretaries of State—a Gazette-writer and Printer, for example, a Latin Secretary, a Keeper and two

---

[1] See the story in Hertslet, *Recollections of the Old Foreign Office*, p. 38.
[2] See for these sketches, Hertslet, *Recollections of the Old Foreign Office*.

Deputy-keepers of State Papers, a Decipherer of Letters and an Interpreter of Oriental Languages. The salaries of some of these gentlemen are set out in the *Royal Kalendars* of the respective dates. The Gazette-writer received £300 a year; the Latin Secretary only £200. To the Decipherer of Letters there was paid a more liberal wage—£500 a year[1].

Grenville is responsible for making, in the year 1800, an important change in British diplomatic procedure. Before his time, French had been used in diplomatic conversations between the British Foreign Secretary and Foreign Representatives accredited to the Court of St James's. He introduced the use of English[2]. The employment of the vernacular in written documents had, indeed—Edmund Hammond's evidence before a Select Committee in 1861, notwithstanding[3] —been actually prescribed as early as 1753[4]; but it was Canning, perhaps inspired by his early association with Grenville, who, in 1823, compelled the British Minister at Lisbon to abide by the regulation; and it was Palmerston, the inheritor of the Canning tradition in Foreign Affairs, who, in 1851, finally vindicated the practice in dealing with the Germanic Diet. The same rule, if Sir Ernest Satow is right[5], should govern diplomatic intercourse by word of mouth; but it is a rule which, so far as the British Foreign Office is concerned, must be proved mainly from its exceptions. It was, indeed, followed in our own time by Lord Grey of Fallodon; but more generally French, though sometimes English, has been used by both parties, the decisive factor being of course in reality the convenience and linguistic attainments of the two actual negotiators.

Grenville left the Foreign Office when Pitt resigned on the question of Catholic Emancipation. In the Addington Ministry Lord Hawkesbury—the Liverpool of the longest premiership of the century, and the "arch-mediocrity" of the Beaconsfield novels, but in those days, as it seemed to Pitt and to others, a remarkably gifted young man[6]—became Foreign Secretary. He proved popular in the Office[7], though the King declared he had neither head for business, nor method, nor punctuality[8]; and he appears to have been well served

---

[1] See the *Royal Calendar* for 1792, p. 104, and the *5th Report Civil Service Comm.* 1914 (Cd. 7748, p. 8).　　　　[2] Satow, *Diplomatic Practice*, I. 65.
[3] *Report of the Select Committee on the Diplomatic Service*, 1861, Min. of Ev., Q.235.
[4] Satow, *Diplomatic Practice*, I. 65.
[5] *Ibid.* I. 67. "The general usage is that diplomatists address the Foreign Minister in their own language and that he uses his own in reply."
[6] See Yonge, *Life and Administration of Lord Liverpool*, I. 18.
[7] *Ibid.* p. 150.　　　　[8] Malmesbury, *Diaries and Correspondence*, IV. 63.

by his spies outside it. Every day, so his biographer asserts, there lay upon his table the copied or deciphered despatches which the Foreign Ambassadors in England had that same day sent off or received[1].

Hawkesbury came into power as one of a Government intent on making peace; and he made it—a Peace, as Sheridan, himself an old Parliamentary Under-Secretary for Foreign Affairs[2], acutely observed, of which everyone was glad and no one proud, but which Pitt and Fox and Grey united to support. It was a truce rather than a treaty. Hawkesbury, as he required Whitworth, in his capacity of British Ambassador in Paris, most explicitly to inform Bonaparte, had no thought of surrendering the claim of England to interfere at will in the affairs of the Continent[3]. War followed inevitably, and, with war, Pitt, whose influence at the Foreign Office[4], as elsewhere, had remained paramount during Addington's lease of power, as inevitably returned.

In the new Government, Harrowby, a good linguist, but reluctant to leave his retirement and only persuaded to do so by the solicitations of the Prime-Minister, was entrusted with the conduct of Foreign Affairs. He was wise enough to begin his activities by a very long talk with Malmesbury, and modest enough to assure that eminent diplomatist of his intention to take him for his political tutor. In regard to policy, Malmesbury told his pupil to form connexions and alliances abroad, without which Europe could never be secure against France; and, in respect to diplomacy, he counselled him "to hear more than to speak," to meet the enquiries of foreign representatives at their interviews with "neutral unmeaning civilities," unless indeed, there happened to be real business to be done, in which case he should get them to put their ideas on paper. Ministers from the Minor Courts of Europe, were, as Malmesbury observed, always on the look-out for "copy" for despatches[5]. Wise, if obvious words, whose range extends from one generation to another!

Harrowby's term of power, however, ran only from May to December. In the last month of 1804, he fell downstairs in his house in Park Lane and injured himself too badly to continue at the Foreign Office. On his recovery, he reentered the Cabinet and was given a

---

[1] Yonge, *Life and Administration of Lord Liverpool*, I. 239.
[2] In 1782 under Fox.
[3] Yonge, *Life and Administration of Lord Liverpool*, I. 94.
[4] See Malmesbury, *Diaries and Correspondence*, IV. 69. "I will tell Lord Hawkesbury of it," Pitt said to Malmesbury, speaking of some negligence on the part of the Foreign Office, "and it shall be set right." [5] *Ibid.* IV. 313, 314.

kind of roving authority over British Diplomatists on the Continent, while himself accredited only to the Court of Berlin. At the time of Harrowby's accident, Malmesbury offered to act for a time as Foreign Secretary, provided that it was only business and not patronage that he had to deal with. Pitt took the suggestion in good part, but appointed Mulgrave, who, as an agreeable nonentity, probably met his requirements at the moment considerably better. He had had too much trouble with Grenville not to wish for a pliable character in control of Foreign Policy.

On Pitt's death, when the Ministry of All the Talents was formed, the Foreign Office reverted to Fox. It was the third time he had held it; and on this occasion Death made his tenure what the vicissitudes of politics had made it before—a thing of months. He had, in fact, only just time to seek peace with Bonaparte and to find it unattainable. We know that he was capable of being a great Foreign Secretary, but we do not know whether he would have been one; for his life had been the most brilliant of failures. Howick—the Lord Grey of the Reform Bill—reigned in his stead until the Ministry broke up. The new Minister was probably guided, as his biographer thinks, by the experienced hand of Grenville, though in the matter of Foreign subsidies, which he reduced to a minimum, his policy was widely different from that of Pitt's Administrations[1].

II

To Grey Canning succeeded. He was the first man of consummate ability to control Foreign Affairs for any appreciable time after the Foreign Office had come into being in 1782; and his two periods of administration were of more than usual importance, both in regard to the interior development of the Office itself and of its Constitutional relations with the Crown and with Parliament. He had to bear the usual reproach of an innovator; and old diplomatists, no doubt, shook their heads over his doings. Malmesbury notes with disapproval Canning's "new habit" of laying a lot of papers before the House of Commons[2]; it did not consort with the prudent and secret ways of the diplomacy to which he had been accustomed. Great man as he had been in his craft—great as Stratford de Redcliffe and Lyons and Ampthill were great in the next century—his own day was done, and he knew it. He refused Canning's offer to stand aside in his favour and let him take the Foreign Office; and Canning

[1] G. M. Trevelyan, *Lord Grey of the Reform Bill*, p. 150.
[2] Malmesbury, *Diaries and Correspondence*, IV. 404.

then paid him the graceful compliment of making his son—FitzHarris —into his Under-Secretary. It proved both an unhappy and an instructive appointment.

For Canning's administration of Foreign Affairs was responsible for the one clear violation of neutral rights of which British Governments have been guilty. Learning—according to Malmesbury, through the Prince-Regent of Portugal[1]—that the secret clauses of Napoleon's agreement with Alexander included the project of seizing the Danish fleet, and using it against Great Britain to enforce the Berlin and Milan Decrees, Canning resolved to require, and, if necessary, to compel the Danes to surrender it. The Danish Minister suspected this intention; and Lord FitzHarris[2], who as Under-Secretary was left by Canning to answer his enquiries, was, of course, aware of it. There appeared to be no way of keeping the intention secret but that of denying its existence. The Under-Secretary made the denial required, but was unable to get over what he had done[3], and presently resigned his post. Canning's conscience was not so nice. As he wrote at the time to Boringdon, his intimate friend, that he would "do nothing wicked[4]," he must be reckoned, in view of what occurred, a catechumen in the vast school of politicians, who suppose, with varying reserves, that the end justifies the means. It is worth noticing that his standard falls below, not only that of FitzHarris's innocent instinct, but of Malmesbury's ripe experience. "No occasion," declared that famous diplomatist, "no provocation, no anxiety to rebut an unjust accusation, no idea, however tempting, of promoting the object you have in view, can need, much less justify, a falsehood. Success obtained by one is a precarious and baseless success. Detection would ruin, not only your own reputation for ever, but deeply wound the honour of your Court[5]." And this, though Malmesbury did not scruple on occasion to give bribes or make use of spies[6]!

During his two years' tenure of office, George Canning introduced into the Foreign Office his cousin, Stratford, whose life was presently to exemplify a brilliant diplomatic career in the nineteenth century as appositely as Malmesbury's had in the eighteenth. Stratford Canning was still a Cambridge undergraduate, twenty years of age, when he

[1] Malmesbury, *Diaries and Correspondence*, IV. 400.
[2] Afterwards second Earl of Malmesbury.
[3] Malmesbury, *Memoirs of an Ex-Minister*, I. 2.
[4] Stapleton, *George Canning and his Times*, p. 133.
[5] Malmesbury, *Diaries and Correspondence*, IV. 414.
[6] *Ibid*. IV. 412.

entered the public service as précis-writer to the Foreign Secretary. He got his place by favour, for his cousin put him in, and held it without security, for his cousin's retirement might have thrown him out. His duties were confidential, but, like those of other young men of ability employed by the Foreign Office for a long while afterwards, not responsible. He made summaries of the official correspondence between the Foreign Secretary and British Representatives abroad; and he wrote out fair copies of the Instructions sent by the one to the others. But, within a year, Fortune began to give him chances, and he was presently appointed Secretary to the Mission which, in 1808, under Robert Adair, was despatched to open peace negotiations with the Turks. The Mission was successful; and Adair became the head of the British Embassy at Constantinople, with Stratford Canning as its Secretary and in actual possession of a dormant commission as Minister Plenipotentiary, which was to come into effect should Adair be transferred, as seemed possible, to Vienna. Thus, at the age of twenty-two, the young diplomatist was in receipt of a salary of over £1000 gross, besides the usual £300 granted as equipage money and the customary allowance of 300 oz. of plate[1]. Nor did Fortune delay further favours. Becoming head of the Embassy in 1810, he negotiated in 1812 the Peace of Bucharest—a Treaty which did England the incalculable service of enabling Russia to enter the final Coalition against Napoleon unshackled by the exigencies of a Turkish War. Wellington, reviewing the course of events which led to Napoleon's downfall, went so far as to argue that this Treaty was "the most important service that ever fell to the lot of any individual to perform," and went on to claim the merit for his brother, Wellesley, who had succeeded George Canning as Foreign Secretary in December, 1809. It was, as we shall see, a most unwarrantable boast.

The occasion of George Canning's resignation had been his duel with Castlereagh—a duel, if we look beneath the surface, between the Foreign and the War Offices, and illustrating their intimate, necessary connexion. Canning, as Foreign Secretary, had at that time to consider the interests of our Allies, the Austrians and the Portuguese. The ill-conceived Walcheren Expedition, upon which the delays of the second Chatham and of Sir Richard Strachan have conferred an immortal name, was of no assistance to Austria in her third and most heroic effort to overthrow Napoleon; and the clause of the

[1] Lane-Poole, *Life of Stratford Canning*, I. 57 footnote.

Convention of Cintra, which left to the French the plunder they had taken in Portugal, violated the elementary obligations of an honest ally. Canning told Portland that he could no longer serve with a War Minister responsible for such diplomatic blunders. His temporary retention of office in these circumstances, without making known to the colleague more particularly concerned his decision ultimately to resign, even though it sprang from nothing else than the Prime-Minister's wish, seemed, when it afterwards became known to Castlereagh, an act disloyal enough to require a challenge. The affair stamped itself upon the page of history far more deeply than the duel, for example, between Wellington and Winchilsea, and, in fact, deserved to do so. For among the conditions of successful Cabinet-making and Cabinet-preserving there are, perhaps, few more vital than the existence of a continuous, sympathetic understanding between the Minister responsible for the conduct of Foreign Policy and the Ministers at the head of Naval and of Military Affairs.

After an interregnum, during which Bathurst administered the business of the Foreign Office, Wellesley took over its direction. It was reasonable to suppose that an ex-Governor-General of India, whose place as an empire-builder is hardly less assured than that of Clive and Hastings, would prove an energetic Foreign Secretary not indifferent to Near Eastern affairs. Wellington, as we have seen, did, in fact, feel sure that his brother had been nothing less. But the publication of Stratford Canning's *Life* revealed the ugly circumstance that at no time has the Foreign Office been more negligently administered than under the elder Wellesley. The young man, not yet twenty-five years of age, who at Constantinople was shouldering the burden of British Diplomacy in the most critical years of the struggle with Napoleon, wrote repeatedly and urgently for Instructions and for what he needed even more than Instructions—the moral support of his chief in dealing with the Turks. But, from the summer of 1810 to the spring of 1812, Wellesley—that brilliant and delicate scholar to whom writing should have been rather a pleasure than a toil—sent his anxious subordinate no more than sixteen despatches in all, of which the contents of no single one bore any relation to the pregnant and momentous business in which that subordinate was engaged[1]. Excuses for the neglect are impossible to make; and the most reasonable explanation involves the most damaging of admissions. Owing to the long reach of Napoleon's arm, the Court

[1] Lane-Poole, *Life of Stratford Canning*, 1. 128.

of Palermo was the only place besides the Porte at which a working Embassy could be maintained; and the Foreign Secretary had so little official correspondence left, that he would appear to have ignored or forgotten the existence even of that which remained to him.

Castlereagh succeeded Wellesley as Foreign Secretary in 1812, when Liverpool followed the murdered Perceval in the Premiership. His capacity for business stood high, according to the standard of his time. He was at his office by eleven o'clock and remained there till three or four. All despatches of any consequence were written by his own hand; he replied to those he received with regularity; and he never allowed the business of one day to encroach upon that of the next[1].

The unsuccessful Secretary for War proved a capable Foreign Minister, and was responsible for the British share in the Treaty of Vienna, which had the merit of pacifying Europe for forty years[2], and localising European Wars for a century. In the course of that negotiation there occurred an incident worth notice. Castlereagh, in spite of his official assurances to the contrary[3], was not reluctant to maintain the Partition of Poland. Edward Cooke, the Permanent Under-Secretary of State, a man of character and ability, did his utmost to dissuade his chief from a policy so cynical, failed to get his way, and resigned his post[4]. The doctrine that a public servant has no public opinions was not yet established.

On the spot, and in the middle of the Congress, Castlereagh offered Cooke's place to another member of his modest staff—to his Private Secretary, Joseph Planta[5]—though this appointment does not appear to have been officially recognised till 1817[6]. The incoming Under-Secretary was an Etonian, a friend of Stratford Canning's, and an official of good business capacity. He became devoted to Canning[7]; and it is natural to credit him with a leading part in the Departmental reforms which took effect under Canning's administration.

Castlereagh's Foreign Secretaryship had a noticeable effect upon the custom of the Constitution in regard to that office. No two

---

[1] Alison, *Lives of Castlereagh and Stewart*, III. 176, 193, 200.

[2] This is, of course, speaking loosely. The Russo-Turkish War of 1829 is an exception; and rebellions are left out of the reckoning.

[3] The alleged discovery, after Castlereagh's death, in a drawer of the Foreign Office of some letters containing evidence of a secret understanding between Castlereagh and Metternich, carried on through the medium of Sir Charles Stewart, the British Representative at Vienna, ought to be mentioned in this connexion. See on this Greville, *Memoirs*, I. 107, and Spencer Walpole, *Foreign Relations*, p. 33.

[4] Stapleton, *George Canning and his Times*, p. 356. Stapleton spells the name "Cook." The F.O. List is followed here.

[5] *Ibid.*   [6] F.O. List.   [7] Lane-Poole, *Life of Canning*, II. 21.

Ministers, perhaps, have, at any time since Cabinet Government begun, exhibited greater differences of character and temperament than Castlereagh and Canning; yet it was in their day that the doctrine of continuity in the conduct of Foreign Affairs may plausibly be said to have been brought to birth. Canning had entered Liverpool's Government as President of the Board of Control in 1816; and he remained in office until the question of Queen Caroline's rights caused his resignation in 1820. It was then that Castlereagh wrote to him in terms which show how close had become the cooperation in public affairs of the former adversaries.

"As the individual member of the Government who must feel your loss the most seriously, both in the House of Commons and in the business of the department," so wrote the Foreign to the ex-Foreign Secretary, "…allow me most cordially to thank you for the uniform attention with which you have followed up and the kindness with which you have assisted me, in the business of the department for the conduct of which I am more immediately responsible[1]."

The results of this generous collaboration were apparent two years later. Though between Castlereagh and Canning there lay the whole difference between the Old and the New Toryism, and though, consequently, they reached their conclusions in regard to Foreign Affairs by different roads, those conclusions were in effect the same. Castlereagh's diplomacy was based upon the theory that every successful Revolution on the Continent advanced the power of France and every unsuccessful one the power of Russia[2]; and he shrank, as a result, from Continental entanglements. Canning's policy rested on a deeper insularity and a broader nationalism, which, after Castlereagh's death, sensibly increased the distance between Great Britain and the Powers of the Holy Alliance. But, in practice, there was no vital difference between them; and the Instructions which Castlereagh gave, a little before he died, to Wellington as prospective British Envoy at the Congress of Verona, might have been penned by Canning.

"As to the form of government," he wrote, "which Spain has of late established for herself in Europe, that is a matter with which, in the opinion of the English Cabinet, no foreign Power has the smallest right to interfere.... The case of the revolted Colonies[3] is different. It is evident from the course which events have taken that their recognition as independent States has become merely a question of time[4]."

---

[1] Stapleton, *George Canning and his Times*, p. 319.
[2] Alison, *Lives of Castlereagh and Stewart*, ii. 633.
[3] The Spanish Colonies in the Americas.
[4] Alison, *Lives of Castlereagh and Stewart*, iii. 170.

The recognition of the independence of the republics of Spanish America, which was Canning's proudest boast, had entailed a struggle between the Crown and the Foreign Secretary. George IV held the view that the policy proposed would embroil him with his Allies; he was studiously encouraged in this belief by the Russian and Austrian Ambassadors; and of the Cabinet, which included Wellington, all were of a like opinion, except the Prime-Minister and, of course, Canning himself. Castlereagh had raised no objection to the occurrence of interviews between the Sovereign or the Prince-Regent in the absence of the Foreign Secretary; but the abuse of this concession by Esterházy and Lieven, the Ambassadors in question, caused Canning to resolve to reassert the constitutional doctrine that it was the duty of the British Foreign Minister to be present at every meeting between the King and a foreign Envoy—a doctrine from which he maintained George III had never departed.

The crisis in the Cabinet came to a head before the crisis in the Constitution; and the issue of the first resolved the problem of the second. The Prime-Minister and the Foreign Secretary confronted their colleagues with a Memorandum setting out their reasons for recognising the revolted Spanish Colonies as independent States, threatened to resign if their policy was not accepted, and reduced their colleagues to submission. It was in these circumstances that Wellington, then as always the unflinching disciple of necessity, informed the King that his choice lay between surrender and the resignation of a united Cabinet. George decided to give way, but did it with a sufficiently ill grace. Canning thereupon renewed his threat of resignation and compelled the unwilling Sovereign to be gracious. Tact completed what firmness had commenced. So soon as the policy of recognition had been vindicated by results, the Minister proceeded to give the credit for his diplomacy to the King, who had no great difficulty in believing that he was responsible for the more notable achievements of his subjects.

Bulwer, with the astuteness of an old diplomatist, has observed that a Foreign Minister possesses a better opportunity of attracting the regard of royal personages than the Heads of other Departments, since Foreign Politics, being a rivalry between kings, are the most interesting of all politics to a Sovereign[1]. The observation, no doubt, savours of the old diplomacy; but Canning had enough of the old Adam in him to vindicate its exactitude. His ascendancy over George IV grew

[1] Bulwer, *Historical Characters*, I. 364.

with the continued suggestion that the success of British policy abroad was due to the King's prescience. And there were, besides, little services that Canning was not above rendering and subtle influences that he was not above invoking. He appointed Lord Francis Conyngham, the son of the King's mistress, to be Under-Secretary for Foreign Affairs; and he disposed of Lord Ponsonby, her lover, by sending him as Minister to Buenos Ayres. His intimacy, too, with Princess Lieven, the wife of the Russian Ambassador and an *intrigante* of some influence at the Court, was a political asset of a certain importance[1]. Thus it came about that, when Liverpool had a stroke in 1826, the King was not unwilling to see the Minister, whom he had formerly so much disliked, exchange the Foreign Office for the Premiership.

Of Canning's habits as Foreign Secretary some slight memorials have come down to us through Lord George Bentinck[2]. His powers of thought and expression were singularly rapid; and, living as he did before the age of typists and impatient as he was at the slowness of scribes, he fell into the way of writing everything himself. Even so, his rapid pen lagged behind his mind; and it needed only the occasion afforded by an injury to his hand to set him dictating, with a ready command of the thread of each argument in turn, to two secretaries at the same time. He possessed at that period of dignified deportment the capacity of unbending; and his subordinates, if tried by the supreme test of the love of officials—the willingness to risk an act of disobedience—are shown to have been devoted to his service. Stapleton tells the story of how, in spite of Canning's express instructions, he once held back an indiscreet letter, induced his Chief, after a moment's annoyance, to read it again, and was told in the end that he had acted quite rightly. "These were the sort of things," concludes the secretary, "which created such a warm feeling of attachment towards him in those by whom he was surrounded[3]."

It is worth while, before we pass on, to try to form some idea of the constitution of Canning's Foreign Office—of the Foreign Office, that is, as it was in Canning's day. At the head of the edifice stood, of course, the Foreign Secretary with a salary of £6000 a year[4]. Immediately below him there were, in 1822, two Under-Secretaries, with salaries of £2500, but by 1827 these had been increased to three

---

[1] Bulwer, *Historical Characters*, I. 266.   [2] Greville, *Memoirs*, I. 109.
[3] Stapleton, *George Canning and his Times*, p. 530.
[4] It was Grey's Administration of 1830 which fixed the salaries of the Secretaries of State at £5000.

—the chief Under-Secretary receiving £2500, the others only £1000 each. The Chief Clerk, who came next, was assigned a salary of £1811 in 1822, but this was reduced to £1100 in 1827. The pay, on the other hand, of the Senior Clerks, of whom there were twelve, was raised. It averaged between £1149 and £314 in 1822, but between £1400 and £350 in 1827. Meanwhile, the three Supernumerary Clerks receiving from £100 to £180 in 1822, had grown by the later date into seven Junior Clerks receiving from £150 to £170[1].

There remains to be mentioned an official whose importance in the Office, partly on account of growing duties and partly of individual diligence, rose steadily throughout the century—the Librarian. It was only in 1812 that Wellesley had put him on the footing of other Foreign Office Clerks as from 1801[2]; and his salary was brought up from £700 in 1822 to £850 in 1827.

The Librarian had, however, another source of income. He was Superintendent of the Establishment of Foreign Service Messengers; and about that distinguished corps it is proper here to say a few words, since the changes in its organisation formed a not inconsiderable feature of the Canning reforms. On July 31st, 1824, Joseph Planta wrote a minute to the effect that "though it may be impracticable to appoint gentlemen to the situation, yet that a better description of persons than those at present to be retired should be selected for the Foreign Messengers[3]"; and we may pause without irrelevance to look at that romantic side of Foreign Office work, which was devoted to the safe-delivery of State Papers passing between the Foreign Secretary and British Representatives abroad.

A King's Foreign Messenger in those days was liable to suffer most, if not all, of the pains and perils which were set down in detail by the Apostle of the Gentiles as the habitual accompaniment of his missionary travels—pains of scarcity, fatigue and cold; perils of waters and of robbers; perils in the sea and in the city, and from false brethren. Edward Hertslet, the younger of the two Foreign Office Librarians of that name, collected indeed, some twenty years ago, a little list of horrors illustrating the ugly possibilities of the Messenger-service in the beginning of the nineteenth century, and ranging from a death by drowning off Calais Sands to a death from cold or Asiatic cholera in Petersburg. His own grandfather—a King's Messenger of the Napoleonic era—knew what it was to have to make the long

---

[1] For the above figures see F.O. General (Librarian's Dept.) 1801–54.
[2] *Ibid.*   [3] F.O. 351/10/88 (in the Record Office).

crossing from the Continent by Cuxhaven to Great Yarmouth—a passage in any case of some days' and, perhaps, if there were ice-floes, of a week's duration—and to have to travel for four months on end with fifty-two days out of them in the saddle[1]. This was a Messenger's life at the worst. By 1822 we may presume that matters had rather improved. Up to that year, the King's Messenger Service had been maintained for the common benefit of the Home, Foreign and War Departments; and of the £30,000 a year spent upon the thirty Messengers, prescribed by the arrangement of 1795, the Foreign Service work was estimated to cost £18,000[2]. In 1822 the number of the corps was raised to thirty-eight. Eighteen of these were placed under the immediate orders of the Foreign Office for foreign service only. They were required to be British subjects, not over thirty-five years of age, good linguists and good horsemen; and the choosing of them rested in turn with each of the three Secretaries of State[3].

A Messenger, of course, was placed under a rigid discipline during

[1] Hertslet, *Recollections of the Old Foreign Office*, p. 160.
[2] These are the rough figures. The actual figures are £29,567. 19s. 8d. and £18,573.
[3] A foreign-service Messenger, by the regulations of 1795, received a salary of £60 a year, besides 7s. 6d. a day board wages while on home service and 13s. 4d. while abroad. This represented, however, only about half his emoluments, for he was allowed besides to make a profit on the mileage of his journeys, amounting in 1820, according to Hertslet's estimate, to £200, so that, altogether, his income came to about £400 a year. Colonel Townley, however, speaking of the period between 1840 and 1859, put it at twice this figure, while pointing out that under the system then in use a Messenger's income might vary by as much as £500 from year to year (*Report Select Comm. Diplom. Service*, 1861, Min. of Ev., Q. 3058 & 3067). His travelling allowance was proportioned to the cost of travelling in the different countries he had to pass through. He journeyed as a rule in his own carriage, which he had probably had built for him at a cost of £200 or £250, and which he kept on the Continent, post-horses and postilions being, of course, hired by stages. A pair of horses for a French "post"—that is, five English miles—cost three francs; the postilion's fee was two francs five sous; and in addition, the King's Messenger was entitled to charge 6d. a mile profit for himself and 3d. a mile for the estimated cost of the carriage. A German "post" was just twice the distance of a French one; but the relative cost approximated closely. Posting in Russia was, as might be guessed, a good deal cheaper. The merit of this elaborate system of calculating expenses lay in its precision; for the Messenger was paid exactly in proportion to the length of journey he performed; and the more obvious but, from this point of view, less satisfactory plan of leaving it to the Government to supply the conveyance was, therefore, for a long while, rejected. The Messenger, besides, sometimes got something very substantial out of the ownership of his own travelling-carriage in the shape of a paying companion who was accommodated with the spare seat; and Palmerston, in 1837, failed to stop a practice which had the additional recommendation of suiting the convenience of Members of Parliament or other persons travelling to and from the Continent. He succeeded, however, in putting some limitation on the use of post-chaises by King's Messengers at home. A Memorandum of 1831 enjoins the use of gigs in the case of single stages from town and, except where orders have been received to the contrary, or the hours of departure prevent, the use of mails and stage-coaches for longer distances.

the period between the receipt and delivery of his despatches. Under the regulations of 1829, he might neither call at the residence of any private person till his trust was executed, nor let his packet out of his custody except for fumigation, in his presence, by the quarantine officer. No letters nor articles other than such as bore the official seal might be carried; and no intelligence bearing upon his professional business might be communicated to friends or acquaintance. On board ship, provision was made for him to mess alone or with a warrant-officer; and at every town entered, where a British Consul or Agent was present, he must have his certificate endorsed with the date and hour of his arrival and departure. In any capital, the endorsement of the British Representative was required as well as that of the Consul. Mention in the newspapers of the arrival or departure of a Foreign Office Messenger was strictly forbidden; and his movements were treated as official confidences. If not actually on service, he was required to continue in attendance at the Foreign Office until the close of the business of each day; and the first three Messengers on the list for employment had to leave word as to their whereabouts, if absent from their homes at night.

The Messenger's uniform in 1829 consisted of a dark-blue coat or jacket with scarlet collar and cuffs and a piping of gold lace; a blue waistcoat similarly edged; grey trousers with a line of scarlet cloth on the seams; gilt buttons bearing the royal cypher and a blue cloth cap with a gold lace band. An enamelled badge carrying the figure of a silver greyhound, which hung by a blue ribbon from his neck, gave the Messenger precedence in the matter of post-horses both at home and abroad. This dress was modified, though not appreciably, in 1851, and again later, but gradually fell into disuse. It had, in fact, its indisputable inconveniences. During the Franco-Prussian War the British Government wished to arrange for the appointment of a Special Envoy to the Prussian Court then re-sident at Versailles; and Captain Robbins, a Messenger in whom great confidence was placed, was entrusted with the correspondence relating to the negotiation. He travelled, as was prescribed, in full dress, and, as he returned, was taken, in virtue apparently of the gold band round his cap, for a Prussian spy. The silver greyhound had no magic for the *franc-tireurs* who had made him prisoner; and it was only at the intercession of the innkeeper that his execution was deferred till dawn. Things looked ugly enough; he thought that at any moment his captors might make a rush at him;

and, having had a fire lit at the inn on the pretext of feeling cold, he spent the night crouching over it, resolved at least, if he could not save himself, to burn his confidential packet, which included letters from Bismarck to Granville and from the Crown-Prince of Prussia to Queen Victoria. However, as the night wore on, the guard, which had been furnished with wine and cigars at his expense, withdrew; and, after giving orders in a loud voice for his carriage to be round at a comparatively late hour in the morning, he slipped quietly away before daybreak. "Do beg Mr Hammond," he said to Mr Sanderson[1] on his return, "not to insist upon our wearing that d——d uniform."

The story, still to be heard at first-hand, furnishes a fitting finale to that long chronicle of the perils and adventures of the Foreign Messenger Service which adds to the Court poetry of diplomatic life something of the primitive vigour of the *chanson de geste*. The telegraph and the train had indeed, long before Robbins's affair, been playing havoc with the more ordinary romances of his profession; and Colonel Townley's famous ride from Belgrade to Constantinople—a ride of a little over eight hundred miles undertaken to assure the Turkish Government of British support if they declined to surrender to the Austrian Emperor the political refugees of 1849—was even then some twenty years old. It was left to Malmesbury, who reduced the number of Foreign Service Messengers from eighteen to fifteen, to deal a final blow at the chance and hazard which had hitherto played so large a part in a Foreign Messenger's affairs. During his second term of office in 1858–9, he put an end to what he called "the sort of gambling transaction" regulating salaries. Instead of being allowed to make profits which roughly corresponded to the length and difficulty of their journeys, Foreign Messengers were thenceforward paid a fixed salary of £525 a year and their travelling expenses estimated by the Foreign Office. No Messenger could hope any more to clear, like Colonel Townley, over £1000 profit in a single year. Townley, indeed, described the new plan as "very harsh and unjust," and Russell, when he became Foreign Secretary, by way of putting things straight, reduced the fixed salary to £400, separated personal from travelling expenses and allowed Messengers £1 a day to cover the former while on service abroad[2], thus giving them an income of about £550 a year.

Improving methods of communication continued to undermine the romance, and seemed even to threaten the existence, of the Foreign

[1] Now Lord Sanderson.
[2] *Report Select Comm. Diplom. Service*, 1890, Min. of Ev., Q. 3514.

Messenger Service. In 1890 there were but ten Messengers employed, and these were so jealously regarded that the Chief Clerk at that date hastened to assure a Royal Commission that they would soon be only nine[1]. By the time the 1914 Commission was sitting, their number had sunk to seven[2], the reduction being facilitated by the practice, which was then more common than it is now, of entrusting bags to casual travellers of unexceptionable qualifications. The *personnel* of the present Department of the King's Foreign Messengers and Communications, has risen to sixteen; but it must be remembered that, with a view to affording change of employment, the duties of a King's Messenger to-day have been enlarged and now alternate between the conveyance of despatches abroad and the coding or decoding of telegrams at home.

It has already been said that there existed an incongruous connexion between the Foreign Messenger Service and the Foreign Office Library. The arrangement came about in this way. In 1801 the Messengers required someone to make out their bills of expenses; and the Librarian was not sorry to enlarge his meagre income by becoming their private agent for the purpose. The link was strengthened later by the presence in the Library of Louis Hertslet, himself a Messenger converted into a Keeper of Books; and in 1824, during the Canning reforms, Hertslet's dual personality was officially recognised by appointing him to be Superintendent of the Foreign Messengers' Establishment[3].

III

When Canning became Prime-Minister, Lord Dudley and Ward took over the Foreign Office, where he continued during the whole of the "transient and embarrassed" Administration of Goderich and during part of the more durable, but scarcely less embarrassed Administration of Wellington. It is usual to regard Dudley as a cipher; and both Canning and the Duke treated him as such. He was, in fact, a rather clever, eccentric, unpractical personage, whom the King was glad to have in office, for the sake of his entertaining conversation[4]. Lieven even supposed him to be very astute, because he once made the

[1] *4th Report Civil Establ. Comm.* 1890, Min. of Ev., Q. 26,645.
[2] *Appendix to the 5th Report Civil Establ. Comm.* 1914, Min. of Ev., Q. 43,548.
[3] For the preceding sketch of the Foreign Messenger Service the writer has drawn upon F.O. 351 (Record Office), upon Townley's and Malmesbury's evidence before the Select Committee on the Diplomatic Service of 1861, and upon Hertslet's *Recollections of the Old Foreign Office.* And attention should also be drawn to the article by Bergne, "The Queen's Messenger," in *The Quarterly Review* for April, 1892.
[4] Ellenborough, *Political Diary,* I. 72.

mistake of slipping a letter, intended for the French Representative and containing some information which, if it became known, was calculated to prove damaging to France, into an envelope addressed to the Russian Ambassador[1]. But the French themselves took his measure more accurately, for they discovered his absence of mind and declared that he had been entrusted with the care of foreign affairs *"parceque ses affaires lui ont été toujours étrangères*[2]." Ellenborough, who, being a personal friend of Dudley's and at the same time Lord Privy Seal with more leisure on his hands than he cared about, helped a good deal with the business of the Foreign Office, found the Foreign Secretary a slow worker in his Department, and in the Cabinet a rare speaker without clear principles of policy[3]. During Wellington's Ministry, indeed, Dudley was kept in strict tutelage. "Good God!" the Duke told the Prince Consort, "there never was a paper (from the Foreign Department) which I had not brought to me first[4]." Of all the Foreign Secretaries of the nineteenth century he may safely be placed the lowest.

It is far otherwise with Lord Aberdeen, who followed him. That profoundly good man, whose sun set so sadly amidst the muddles and misfortunes of the Crimean War, brought to the Foreign Office a knowledge of European affairs derived from his large experience as the British Representative at the Austrian Court during the advance of the Allies in 1813–14, an acquaintance with the principal statesmen of the Continent, which included the friendship of Metternich, and, last, but not least, a character perfectly disinterested and a disposition perfectly pacific. Wellington, who was aware that an incompetent Foreign Secretary is of all public officials the one most capable of running the country into a vast expense, could have found no better Minister to handle matters like those of the Independence of Greece and the Succession in Portugal. For Aberdeen, brought up in Pitt's house and educated by Pitt's example, believed in letting other nations alone to the utmost of his ability. It is true that he found a severe critic in Ellenborough, whom he had generously allowed to continue to assist in the work of the Foreign Office; but a good deal must be allowed for the feelings of an observer, eagerly desirous to hold the Foreign Secretaryship himself and utterly convinced that he could do the work better than the Foreign Secretary[5]. To Ellenborough's eye it

---

[1] *Gentleman's Magazine* (1833), I. 368. [2] Escott, *Story of British Diplomacy*, p. 265.
[3] Ellenborough, *Political Diary*, I. 41, 109. [4] Martin, *Life of the Prince Consort*, II. 427.
[5] Ellenborough, *Political Diary*, I. 149.

seemed that Aberdeen was unable to "grasp the argument on a great question," though equal to discharging "very well" "all the ordinary work" of his Department[1]. And Ellenborough's *Diary* accuses Aberdeen of substituting essays for diplomatic instructions[2]; of using expressions stronger than his meaning and even sufficient to "make the Emperor of Russia jump six feet high[3]," and, finally, of depending for the whole substance of his despatches upon Wellington, being himself unfit for all the higher parts of his duty[4]. But, though Ellenborough felt sure that the Duke would be unable to retain such a man as Aberdeen at the Foreign Office, Aberdeen held his post to the end of the Administration, and resumed it at Peel's request in 1841, and left it only, to Queen Victoria's great regret, in 1846. He was, in fact, a man without ambition, without partiality and without hypocrisy.

The year 1830, owing to the death of George IV and the subsequent resignation by William IV of the hereditary revenues of the Crown, saw the charges of the Diplomatic Establishment transferred from the Civil List to the Consolidated Fund. Parliament, in other words, became the paymaster of the Diplomatic Service instead of the Sovereign. The change, slight as it was, heralded an extension of Parliamentary control over Foreign Affairs. According to the new arrangement, the Foreign Office was to have the free disposal of £180,000 for the maintenance of the Diplomatic Service of the country; but there were other diplomatic charges which were expected to fall outside this sum and required to be met by an annual vote in Parliament.

The nation, however, can hardly be expected to have observed these signs of the times and the increase of its hold upon Foreign Policy. A much more noticeable event was the displacement of Aberdeen by Palmerston on the return of the Whigs to power. The new Foreign Secretary was as great a contrast to the old as can well be imagined. Boisterous and bellicose, rough and resolute, he left a deep impression upon his Office, whether we look at its internal organisation, its position in the country, or its policy abroad.

In spite of some fond suppositions of Princess Lieven's, it was Lansdowne and not herself to whom Palmerston owed his appointment to the Foreign Office[5]. Circumstances furnished him with an immediate opportunity of asserting himself; and his tenure of power,

---

[1] Ellenborough, *Political Diary*, 1. 171.   [2] *Ibid*. 1. 188.
[3] *Ibid*. 1. 235.   [4] *Ibid*. 1. 171, 265.
[5] G. M. Trevelyan, *Lord Grey of the Reform Bill*, p. 243.

which, but for the brief administration of Wellington between November, 1834, and April, 1835, continued until 1841, disclosed that vigorous tendency to interfere in the domestic politics of other countries, which the progressive forces of the world approved and the stable forces denounced. In Belgium, in Portugal and in Spain he took sides with the popular, or at least the Liberal, party, giving them effective moral assistance, very much as Canning had done in Greece some years earlier. His politics pleased many of his country-men, who had begun to believe in the principles of self-determination and nationality, at least for Europe and outside Ireland; his activity was well-calculated to attract attention to his country; and his methods, though challenged by Aberdeen, who knew the value of a quiet and scrupulous diplomacy, did not immediately reveal their final conse-quences. He enjoyed, too, in the first part of his term of office the aid of Grey—an old, experienced Foreign Secretary—to whom the administration of Foreign Affairs appeared the most interesting branch of the art of government.

In the Foreign Office itself, Palmerston was both hated and esteemed. When he lost his election in Hampshire in 1835, his sub-ordinates were in a mood to illuminate the scene of his official activities —so much did he make himself disliked by his unpunctuality, his in-considerateness, his asperity and his precision[1]. What they could not but respect in him, however, was his diligence—a diligence astonishing to that age of easygoing public servants—and his capacity. "Eight hours work, when little is doing," so he told Granville, "must be your daily minimum." In fact, he commonly devoted to the public service some two hours more. A reader of little else, he read all his official papers; and, if it came to writing, no man in the office wrote better or a better hand. He had, indeed, a facility on paper which he did not equal in debate. Besides possessing a complete mastery of French, he was able to read German and had some acquaintance with Italian. And to these attainments he added the equipment, the promptitude, the energy, the push of a successful man of business.

Nevertheless, Palmerston was disliked—disliked by the Diplomatic Corps, with Talleyrand, who first despised, but eventually recognised, his ability[2], at their head; disliked by the Great Powers, who felt the pressure of his personality, as well as by the weak States, whom he

---

[1] See Greville, *Memoirs*, III. 139, 203, 216; Lorne, *Palmerston*, pp. 146, 219. Cf. Malmesbury, *Memoirs of an Ex-Minister*, p. 310, with reference to this and some of the following remarks.

[2] Greville, *Memoirs*, III. 58, 367.

lectured and coerced; disliked, as we have seen, by the Clerks, who served him fearfully and whom he chastised with cutting minutes and rough rebukes. Sometimes, like other driving personalities, he had the worst of it; more often he got his way; always, or almost always, he was imperturbable and unabashed. There was an appearance of rude justice in some of his proceedings obscuring, as in the famous case of General Haynau, about which a word will be said presently, their real want of equity, and inducing the majority of Englishmen to make a hero out of one who behaved at times perilously like a bully. Nothing in his nature served him, indeed, so well with the public as his freedom from all the niceties and formalities of competent bureaucracy; and it was characteristic of him that a mail carrying out the official censure of the Admiralty upon an officer who, at the point of a naval gun, had coerced the Governor of Macao, into releasing from prison an indiscreet English clergyman, carried also a letter from the Foreign Secretary approving and commending what had been done[1]. His native vigour of action impressed and partially misled critics of no mean importance. Talleyrand called him the only statesman in Grey's Government[2]; Peel, though his opponent, declared on a famous occasion that everyone was proud of him; and Lady Granville, "a woman," according to Greville, "expert in judging," pronounced him to be of first-rate capacity bordering on greatness, by virtue of his power of decision, distance of view, contempt for clamour and, above all, indifference to abuse[3].

Such, then, if the anecdotes of Whitehall and the opinions of St James's can be relied upon, was "Protocol Palmerston" (to revive the name he received from his Clerks after they had drafted no less than seventy-eight protocols respecting the affairs of Holland and Belgium); a man who both for merit and defect, for length of administration and strength of will, must always rank as one of the foremost figures in British diplomatic history. One would like, indeed, to penetrate still deeper into the dingy recesses of that old-world building, in which he did his work, to rouse all the spectres of his staff, to see again the diligent Backhouse; the courteous, conservative Addington; that famous Mellish who together with Palmerston and the Prince Consort was alone credited with understanding the Schleswig-Holstein question[4]; and those other latent figures of the early-Victorian

[1] Lorne, *Viscount Palmerston*, pp. 141–3.   [2] Greville, *Memoirs*, III. 367.   [3] *Ibid*.
[4] Only three men in England, so Palmerston once declared, had thoroughly understood all the complicacions of that affair—the Prince-Consort who was dead, Mellish who had retired and disappeared, and himself who had forgotten them.

Foreign Office whose names are not remembered and whose praises have gone unsung. But it would be a hopeless adventure. Ghosts may still be sought in the doomed mansions of Mayfair; but for these shadows of fleeting shades there does not remain so much as the background of their old habitation.

What may fairly be called the Palmerston touch in diplomacy— so different is it from the fine fingering of the diplomatist of tradition —appears first in connexion with the appointment of Stratford Canning as Ambassador at the Russian Court. It is an established point of diplomatic usage that some information, usually verbal, as to the personality and antecedents of any proposed Representative abroad, should be submitted to the Foreign Sovereign immediately concerned. Palmerston had omitted to do this in the instance of Lord Durham in 1831[1]; and Lieven, the Russian Ambassador in England, remonstrated, though without pressing his objection. In Stratford Canning's case there was, therefore, the reminiscence of an affront to be reckoned with, as well as the probability that the Emperor Nicholas might dislike the presence at his Court of one who, though he does not appear to have had, as was alleged, any inauspicious meeting with Nicholas before his accession, had been at least notoriously active in thwarting Russian designs at Constantinople. But Palmerston cared nothing for prudence or propriety. He gazetted Canning's nomination to Petersburg ten days before he announced it to Lieven; and he affirmed, in face of Lieven's remonstrances, that the King of Great Britain could appoint whom he pleased to represent him, and that the Emperor was without rights in the matter. Eventually, he was told that Canning, if he came, would not be received at Court, while the place of Russian Ambassador at St James's would, at the same time, be taken by a Chargé d'affaires. Palmerston maintained his attitude for eight months longer, and during this period sent Canning on a special Mission to Spain with the title of "Ambassador to the Emperor of all the Russias." But the Emperor of all the Russias proved too many for Lord Palmerston; and in July, 1835, Durham was reappointed to the Embassy at Petersburg.

The *envoi* to this episode is supplied by the observation of Joseph Planta, by this time a retired official, brooding, no doubt over the changes that could not be called improvements in the Office he had left. He could not understand, he said[2], how any Foreign Power

---

[1] See on this Satow, *Diplomatic Practice*, I. 190.
[2] Lane-Poole, *Life of Stratford Canning*, II. 18.

should have been allowed to act as Russia had done, or how things should not have been so managed as to prevent it. For bluff, and drive, and the high hand can produce heavy rebuffs and humiliating withdrawals as well as successful aggressions and proud reflexions upon the range and power of British citizenship.

Palmerston, as might have been expected, employed the Press a good deal; and the character of his relations with it was peculiar. He set the limit of discretion at the written word, and, while wary and reserved in his dealings with Lemarchant and Drummond, who worked the Press on behalf of the Government, would see any editor who wanted to see him, and impart confidences on the most delicate affairs[1]. His particular organ was *The Morning Chronicle*, whose owner, John Easthope, created a baronet for his services in 1841, was accustomed to attend daily at the Foreign Office to receive information, sometimes perhaps fully prepared in article form, on Foreign Affairs[2]. Power was at that time passing, if it had not already passed, from the quarterlies to the dailies; and Palmerston was not the man to neglect the exploration of new avenues to popular support. It seems to have been, however, Aberdeen, oddly enough, who first made the Press the instrument of a memorable diplomatic stroke.

The Conservatives had returned to power in 1841, and Aberdeen to the Foreign Office. In 1845 it happened that, while the Cabinet was torn with dissensions about Free Trade, the Americans were hesitating to settle the Oregon Boundary dispute. Aberdeen was persuaded that the conversion of Great Britain to the principles of Cobden would determine the doubts of America in the way he desired. He, therefore[3], communicated to Delane, the enterprising young editor of *The Times*, the fact that the Government was changing its economic policy, though he did not communicate the circumstance that the Government was about to fall. His confidences effected his purpose; and, on the day the Government resigned, he was able to announce the conclusion of the Oregon Treaty. This incident (out of which Meredith, seeking a woman where no woman was, fashioned the story of *Diana of the Crossways*), proved the foundation of that intimacy between Delane and Aberdeen which has to be reckoned with in studying the inner history of British Foreign Policy in the years that followed.

[1] Greville, *Memoirs*, IV. 123.
[2] Maxwell, *Life and Letters of the 4th Earl of Clarendon*, I. 213.
[3] It is proper to say that Reeve's explanation has been challenged (see E. T. Cook, *Delane of the Times*, p. 27).

There was another Foreign Question engaging Aberdeen's attention in 1845, the course of which was fatally prejudiced by his fall from power. One of the chief props of the Franco-British understanding, towards which, from 1815 onwards, the constant compulsion of circumstances, and the best consideration of statesmen repeatedly drove two unwilling and uncongenial nations, was Aberdeen's friendship with Guizot. The two Ministers enjoyed the rare and inestimable benefit of mutual confidence; and it is as certain as such things can be that the negotiations between Great Britain and France respecting the marriages of the Queen of Spain and her sister could never have had their actual discreditable issue, if Aberdeen's place had not been taken by Palmerston at the very crisis of the affair. For there can be little or no doubt that it was the suspicions entertained of the incoming British Foreign Secretary which induced Guizot to propose and Louis-Philippe to consent to that sudden *démarche* in August, 1846, which seemed to the British people to amount to a most deliberate breach of a most explicit undertaking. It was left to Aberdeen's son to bring out, at a later date, what Aberdeen himself never apparently guessed[1], how well-founded those suspicions had been. The contents of Palmerston's letters to Bulwer[2], the British Ambassador at Madrid, were all the while coming to the knowledge of the French Government through the medium of Queen Christina, to whom Bulwer communicated them; and those letters urged the British Ambassador, in the words of the well-informed, impartial authority just alluded to, "to effect and carry out at once the double marriage of the sisters to the Duke of Seville and Prince Leopold, leaving it an open question whether the latter married the Queen or the Infanta[3]." This was in direct violation of the condition upon which Louis-Philippe's promise had been given—the condition that Queen Isabella should marry within the House of Bourbon.

There are two points in these transactions of which a student of British diplomatic methods may find it worth while to take notice. The first is that Palmerston's private correspondence with Bulwer had passed into the category of secret diplomacy. It differed, that is, not by mere elaboration of detail or prescription of method, from what was laid before Parliament, but in principle and vitally. The French Government, though they could not produce their evidence, knew

[1] Stanmore, *The Earl of Aberdeen*, p. 170.
[2] Afterwards Lord Dalling and Bulwer.
[3] Stanmore, *The Earl of Aberdeen*, p. 168.

what was not within the knowledge of the British people—that Palmerston was not, as the phrase is, "playing straight." His use of private correspondence for public purposes went, indeed, so far as one can arrive at an opinion on so obscure a subject, beyond that of all other Foreign Secretaries of the nineteenth century. When Wellington had taken over the business of the Foreign Office for some months in 1834, pending Peel's return from abroad and the formation of a Cabinet, he could find no trace amongst the official papers of his Department of an offer on the part of Great Britain to mediate between France and the United States, the acceptance of which by the latter was notified during his Administration. Palmerston, he then discovered, had done everything by private correspondence, leaving no official trace behind; and to Palmerston, therefore, application had to be made for information on the issue[1]. But the use of private letters for public purposes, which involves one of the most vexed questions of Foreign Office procedure, is, of course, older than Palmerston. Hamilton Seymour, who was on Clancarty's staff at Brussels in the early years of the nineteenth century, declared that "there was always an active private correspondence between Lord Clancarty and the Secretary of State," and that he had, himself, as a Minister, followed the precedent with every successive chief at home[2]. Ellenborough, on the other hand, during Aberdeen's first Administration, had taken exception to this unofficial method of communicating Instructions as causing gaps in the public records[3]; and the two schools of opinion remain and contend with one another to this day. But we shall presently come upon what may fitly be called the Clarendon canon, on the subject; and any further discussion of it may be deferred till then.

The other point worth noticing is the totally different conception of diplomatic aims and practice disclosed by Aberdeen on the one hand and Palmerston on the other. Aberdeen became aware of Bulwer's earlier intrigue to marry the young Queen to Prince Leopold of Coburg; and no false consideration for his country's honour or his subordinate's reputation prevented him from disavowing these proceedings on behalf of the British Government. And, to Bulwer himself, he wrote, neither mincing words nor mixing morals: "Depend upon it that, as you have discovered the intrigue of Bresson (the French

[1] Martin, *Life of the Prince Consort*, II. 427, 428.
[2] *Report Select Comm. Diplom. Service*, 1861, p. 211.
[3] *Political Diary*, I. 150.

Ambassador), he would inevitably have discovered yours[1]." Aberdeen knew on principle, what men of the world often have to learn from hard experience, that in the long run, though sometimes only in the long run, honesty really pays. Palmerston, indeed, in the affairs of the Spanish Marriages had not, as things turned out, even the satisfaction of transient success. He had, however, too good a conceit of himself to learn anything from this or any other rebuff. Assured, as an Englishman, of the efficacy of a Liberal Constitution, he desired to impose its blessing upon Spain; and in 1848 we find him instructing the British Representative at Madrid to advise Queen Isabella to widen the basis of her Government by calling Liberals to her counsels. His despatch was communicated to the Spanish Premier, who returned it as containing observations insulting to the dignity of an independent nation. The return of the despatch of a British Foreign Secretary as unfit for reception or retention had, as Aberdeen remarked, seemed till then inconceivable; and he was probably justified in characterising the affair as an indignity without precedent[2]. Such incidents, however, are of little more than antiquarian importance. In every generation, high-minded men are found to say that their country has been eternally dishonoured, or that its liberties have been irreparably violated; but the liberties that have been lost are seldom long lamented, and the dishonour that has been done is rarely remembered for a decade.

It was in the course of his third Administration of Foreign Affairs that Palmerston started that extraordinary conflict with the Crown which must be reckoned to be easily the first event in the Constitutional history of the Foreign Office. The relations between the Sovereign and the Foreign Secretary are necessarily peculiar. So long as Monarchy survives, the form and fashion, if not the substance, of Foreign Policy are partly entangled with the intimacies and relationships and sentiments of the Heads of States; and an English King to-day, though he cannot be his own Foreign Secretary, can still, if he chooses, be the first diplomatist in his country's service. In Queen Victoria's time, however, partly on account of the greater strength of the monarchical idea abroad, partly because the political power of the British Sovereign was of more consequence at home than it is now, but chiefly because the Prince Consort was a man of rare knowledge and sagacity especially in relation to Foreign

[1] Stanmore, *The Earl of Aberdeen*, p. 166.
[2] Quoted in Martin, *Life of the Prince Consort*, ii. 66.

Affairs, something more than diplomacy—something approximating rather to statesmanship—was aimed at by the Crown. It was not surprising, indeed, that a Prince to whom Melbourne had advised the Queen from the first to communicate Foreign despatches[1], and whom Palmerston himself privately described in 1855 as "far greater and more extraordinary than Napoleon III[2]," should have sought to bring the wisdom of Stockmar and the talent for diplomacy native in the House of Coburg, to the service of his adopted country. So early as 1845, Greville reported, on the authority of Lord John Russell and Lord Lansdowne, that the Queen no longer received her Ministers alone, and that both she and the Prince always said "we" in conversation; the inference drawn being that "while she has the title, he is really discharging the functions of the Sovereign[3]." And it cannot be too much emphasised that the Prince, by his great personal ability and integrity, gave the Crown a position in regard to Foreign Policy, which the Queen continued to occupy after his death, but of which the Constitution was hardly any longer patient.

In that same month of 1845, when Peel was seeking to pass "the poisoned chalice" of Free Trade over to Russell, the Queen informed Lord John of her aversion to the practically inevitable reappointment of Palmerston as Foreign Secretary, and resolved, in agreement with the prospective Prime-Minister, to intimate to its intended head, that the Foreign Office was a Department of which the affairs required to be treated in consultation with his colleagues and not according to his own fancy[4]. Though she chose the point of Palmerston's unconstitutional tendencies, her objection probably reached behind method to policy. "The Queen and myself," so the Prince Consort told Napoleon III in 1854, "had long been at variance with Lord Palmerston as to the main principle of his foreign policy, which was even an exaggeration of that laid down in Mr Canning's celebrated speech in December, 1826[5]." In the event, Russell's attempt to form a Government failed, and failed precisely because Lord Grey disapproved, quite as much as the Queen, of Palmerston's being placed in control of Foreign Affairs, and was in a better position than she was to enforce their view. In the next year, however, Peel fell; and Russell entrusted the Foreign Office to Palmerston.

It only needed time and opportunity for the Queen's fears to

[1] Martin, *Life of the Prince Consort*, I. 95. [2] *Ibid.* II. 429.
[3] Greville, *Memoirs*, V. 330. [4] *Ibid.* V. 129.
[5] Martin, *Life of the Prince Consort*, III. 112.

be realised. With twenty-eight thousand despatches passing in or out[1] of the Foreign Office during 1849—that year of Revolution —the pressure of work was prodigious; and Palmerston yielded once again to the old temptation of settling things himself. "These 28,000 despatches in the year," the Prince Consort wrote warningly to Russell in 1849, "Lord Palmerston must recollect, come to you and to the Queen as well as to himself[2]." The Constitutional rule, indeed, required that the outgoing despatches, before being sent, should pass first to the Prime-Minister and be sent on, with his criticisms, if there were any, to the Sovereign for alteration or assent[3]. It was an obvious objection that all this took time, and that events no more waited upon a monarch's pleasure than the sea-waves were stayed by the command of Canute. The Queen, however, was reasonable in her demands. She asked for twenty-four hours, or at the least for twelve, to consider State Papers, instead of the few minutes which Palmerston sometimes allowed her, if he gave her any minutes at all. And he agreed to these conditions, though, when it came to the point, he paid no more attention to them than suited his convenience, playing fast and loose with the whole business of his Office, concealing the Instructions issued, and altering the despatches she had returned to him otherwise than in the manner indicated, or even back to what they had been before[4]. In April, 1850, the Prince protested to Russell in the Queen's name against these proceedings, as being the consequence, not of negligence or oversight, but of principle and deliberation. Palmerston, quite indifferent, went on as before. Then, in August, came the Queen's famous Memorandum—in its principal features the work of Stockmar—which was not, however, made public until Palmerston's fall a year later. Since it defines the Constitutional relations between the Crown and the Foreign Office as they were then understood, it is best reproduced here, not in paraphrase, but verbatim.

OSBORNE, *August 12th*, 1850.

"With reference to the conversation about Lord Palmerston, which the Queen had with Lord John Russell the other day, and Lord Palmerston's disavowal that he ever intended any disrespect to her by the various neglects of which she has had so long and so often to complain, she thinks it right, in order to prevent any mistake about the future, to explain what it is she expects from the Foreign Secretary.

---

[1] Martin, *Life of the Prince Consort*, II. 64.   [2] *Ibid.*
[3] *Ibid.* II. 302.   [4] *Ibid.* II. 303.

She requires:

1. That he will distinctly state what he proposes in a given case, in order that the Queen may know as distinctly to what she has given her Royal sanction.

2. Having once given her sanction to a measure, that it be not arbitrarily altered or modified by the Minister. Such an act she must consider as failure in sincerity towards the Crown, and justly to be visited by the exercise of her Constitutional right of dismissing that Minister. She expects to be kept informed of what passes between him and the Foreign Ministers, before important decisions are taken based upon that intercourse; to receive the Foreign despatches in good time, and to have the drafts for her approval sent to her in sufficient time to make herself acquainted with their contents before they must be sent off. The Queen thinks it best, that Lord John Russell should show this letter to Lord Palmerston[1]."

Palmerston received his chastisement with his usual appearance of good temper and told the Prime-Minister that he would not fail to observe its directions. Pressure of business had caused unfortunate delays; but thenceforward the old practice of copying important despatches for the Queen's immediate use, so soon as they came in, should be resumed. This might mean an extra clerk or so, but the Treasury would, doubtless, be liberal.

The Foreign Secretary was not, however, on this occasion, so thick-skinned as he appeared to be. A day after his letter to Russell, shaking with agitation, tears in his eyes and excuses on his lips, he had an audience of the Prince Consort. The custom of the Constitution was then further defined. The Queen—so the Prince stated—had constantly differed from Palmerston's policy; but, after urging her objections, she had submitted in accordance with Constitutional theory to the will of her Ministers, not in recent years without suffering the severe penalty of being associated in the public eye with their mistakes. But she was at least within her rights in insisting that, before any course was decided upon, she should be put in possession of all the pertinent facts. As regards what passed between the Foreign Secretary and the Foreign Diplomatic Representatives and in Cabinet discussions, she claimed to know, not the details debated, but the conclusions arrived at. This would save her un-profitable controversies with Russell and Palmerston over the actual wording of despatches. Palmerston, by way of defence, attributed these verbal debates to the fact that he had no easy, direct access to the Sovereign, since the Queen had laid it down that every draft for

[1] Cf. Martin, *Life of the Prince Consort*, II. 305–6.

despatch must pass to her through the hands of the Prime-Minister. The Prince, however, justified this arrangement on the ground that nothing prevented Palmerston from communicating with the Queen by letter as fully as he pleased, and so giving her any information she ought to have. And he instanced the British policy regarding Schleswig-Holstein—a matter pregnant with consequences for Europe, and about which the Queen's views differed from those of her Ministers—as Foreign business of the developments of which she ought to be kept fully and carefully informed.

Russell fondly hoped that this frank exchange of views had cleared the air; but before the end of the year there had arisen the case of General Haynau. A distinguished soldier, discredited in England by the severity with which he suppressed the Hungarian insurrection of 1849, Haynau, while privately visiting Barclay's Brewery, was attacked by a crowd of rough fellows and shamefully handled. Palmerston drafted an apology for the incident in terms which suggested that the General was too obnoxious to British opinion to deserve the protection of British law, and, before the Queen had passed the Note, despatched it to the Austrian Government. This was intolerable; and Russell, who himself thought the phrases of the Note ill-chosen, compelled its author, after some pretence of resignation, to substitute another. The incident was closed, but not the episode; for, a twelvemonth later, Palmerston had offended again, by consenting to receive at the Foreign Office addresses thanking him for his benevolence towards the defeated Hungarian revolutionaries and taking occasion to call the Russian and Austrian Emperors despots and assassins—names, which, of course, when applied to friendly rulers, were unsuitable for the ears of a Foreign Secretary. The affair annoyed the Queen and provoked the censure of the Cabinet. But it was scarcely closed when Palmerston had committed himself even more deeply than before. In spite of express Instructions from the Sovereign not to depart from an attitude of strict passivity in regard to the French *coup d'état* of December, 1851—Instructions which he had himself acknowledged and conveyed to the British Ambassador in Paris—he declared in conversation with the French Ambassador in London his entire approval of Louis Napoleon's act, and described it as inevitable. His language was naturally quoted by the French Foreign Minister in conversation with Lord Normanby[1], and was revealed to the Queen in one of that

[1] The British Ambassador in Paris.

Ambassador's despatches. She applied to Russell for an explanation; and Russell, in his turn, applied to Palmerston. The Foreign Secretary let two days go by, then repeated his views in a despatch to Normanby, and on the same day defended them in a letter to Russell. But the issue was not, as he pretended, whether Louis Napoleon was right in violating the French Constitution by arresting his political opponents; but whether he was, himself, right in violating the British Constitution by expressing an official opinion on the subject without consultation with his colleagues. He claimed, indeed, that his opinion was not more than personal and private; but, as the Prince Consort wrote to Russell when all was over, this distinction was perfectly untenable in practice. Lord John, however, had not waited for advice from the highest quarters to dismiss his turbulent colleague; and his action was unhesitatingly endorsed by the Cabinet at its next meeting and by Parliament in a full-dress debate.

In reviewing the whole episode, Palmerston's biographer could not resist the temptation to represent him as the victim of a cabal of absolute Sovereigns[1]. Even had it been so, it would be obvious to reply that the cause for which he had fought was not the cause in which he fell, since Liberalism had no worse enemy than the Second Empire. But, in fact, his downfall was essentially a domestic matter, Constitutional and Departmental. The most powerful contemporary support that he received is to be found in some words of Clarendon's, who can be quoted as saying that the Queen and the Prince Consort were claiming "a right to control, if not to direct, the foreign policy of England[2]." This judgment, however, was probably, not a considered one; and, whatever general truth may lie in the suggestion, he would be a rash historian who should accept it in regard to Palmerston's last administration of Foreign Affairs, the more so since the Prime-Minister at the time was a Whig and yet supported the attitude of the Crown throughout. All that can be fairly urged is that the Queen regarded the issue rather from the Constitutional, and Palmerston more from the Departmental, point of view. And, since the spirit of the Constitution deserves to prevail over the convenience of a Department, the Sovereign must be held to have acted with wisdom and justice in insisting upon her rights, which, as will be seen more clearly when we reach the period of Palmerston's Premiership, were to prove a prop for those of the Cabinet.

[1] Ashley, *Life of Lord Palmerston*, I. 308.
[2] Maxwell, *Life and Letters of the 4th Earl of Clarendon*, I. 341.

The pressure of Science is stronger than the spirit of the Constitution; and the battle that Palmerston lost was gradually won by the growing momentum of Foreign Affairs. The decorous delays of the *ancien régime* are impossible in a world conditioned by the telegraph. Action, to be effective, has sometimes to be immediate; business grows every year in volume; labour cannot afford to be multiplied. In consideration for the Queen as she aged, something of a veil was thrown over the facts; and a document submitted for her approval bore always the legend "Draft," even when at times it was no more nor less than the copy of a despatch on its way to its destination. In the latter case, however, it was understood that important Instructions were sent subject to subsequent confirmation by telegram. But the change was the thin end of a wedge which has since been driven further into this fragment of the old Constitution.

It only remains to notice that Palmerston consolidated, if he did not precisely originate, the two main traditions of British Foreign Policy, which, subject, of course, to occasional modifications, were to dominate the Foreign Office for the next half century or more—the traditions of friendship with France and of the protection of Turkey. In countenancing Louis Napoleon Palmerston was ahead of his countrymen, but not ahead of their needs. A decade earlier, in connexion with the affair of Mehemet Ali in 1840 he had, in spite of a remarkable Memorandum of Clarendon's[1], given British policy in the Near East that decided twist into line with the Porte, which made an alliance with the Third Napoleon practically indispensable. Thus it came about that two diplomatic posts acquired a superiority over all the rest—the Embassy in Paris, and the Embassy in Constantinople; and it is, perhaps, no mere accident that, of the only British *diplomates de carrière*, whose translation from the conduct of an Embassy to the office of Foreign Secretary was ever contemplated by a British party-leader, one[2] was at the time Ambassador in Turkey and the other[3] Ambassador in France. As a rule, at any rate, the more eminent British Diplomatists of the century will be found to have made their names in one of those countries—Stratford de Redcliffe and White, Cowley and Lyons and Dufferin[4]. But, after the proclamation of the German

---

[1] Printed in Maxwell, *Life and Letters of the 4th Earl of Clarendon*, I. 186–93.
[2] Stratford de Redcliffe.   [3] Lyons.
[4] It has been suggested to the present writer by a very eminent authority that Cromer's name should be added to these, since technically he worked under the direction of the Foreign Office. His work, however, was rather administrative than diplomatic, and on this account it has not been taken account of here.

empire, one considerable reputation—Lord Odo Russell's[1]—was made at Berlin, while Morier, a great figure, though gifted rather with diplomatic insight than diplomatic talent, had specialised in German studies. It must not, however, be supposed from this that the opportunities of professional distinction usually determined the tastes and preferences of the members of the British Diplomatic Corps. Malmesbury, on taking office in 1852, was warned by Palmerston that, as Foreign Secretary, he would be struck with "a very curious circumstance—namely, that no climate agrees with an English diplomatist excepting that of Paris, Florence or Naples[2]."

The fall of Palmerston brought a very charming personality back to the Foreign Office. Granville, who had been Under-Secretary of State during 1840 and 1841, was the son of a distinguished Ambassador, and the second husband of that daughter of the Dalbergs who was, also, the first Lord Acton's mother. The choice had lain between him and Clarendon; and circumstances had weighed the scales against the abler man of the two. Though Clarendon had, early in life and on Palmerston's nomination, been for some years Minister at Madrid and, therefore possessed diplomatic experience to which Granville could not pretend, yet his original debt to Palmerston, coupled with the false suggestion, constantly insinuated, that he had desired to supplant him, to say nothing of his comparative, but only comparative, insufficiency as a courtier, and his abiding disinclination to take office, told against him. No one, perhaps, was better pleased than Clarendon at Granville's appointment, unless it were Aberdeen, who declared that of all Lord John's Government the new Minister was the man he would himself have selected for the Foreign Office[3]. It was high praise; but the sands of "the last Whig Ministry" were running out too fast for it to be immediately tested, though, on the fall of the Administration in 1852, Russell made so bold as to claim that the country would "lose one of the best foreign secretaries it ever had[4]." Granville had, in fact, poured a great deal of oil on troubled waters; and the Queen was satisfied. In another direction, his intimacy with Henry Reeve, who managed the foreign department of *The Times*[5], enabled him to put some slight restraint upon the energetic animosity towards Louis Napoleon displayed by that vast

[1] Afterwards Lord Ampthill.
[2] Malmesbury, *Memoirs of an Ex-Minister*, I. 318.
[3] Fitzmaurice, *Life of the 2nd Earl Granville*, I. 46.   [4] *Ibid.* I. 78.
[5] *Ibid.* I. 68, 69.

engine of opinion, which, as Clarendon said, alone of all the English newspapers signified something abroad[1].

The nomination to the Embassy at Paris became vacant during Granville's term of office; and it fell to him to acquaint Stratford Canning with the fact that the Government had decided against giving it to the most eminent Englishman in his profession[2]. Before Canning had had time to reply to Granville's note, he had lost an even greater prize. Derby had sounded him, a year before, as to whether, if it were offered him in the next Conservative Administration, he would accept the post of Foreign Secretary; and he had returned a favourable answer. But when, in fact, the Russell Ministry fell, Derby, either because, as he affirmed, the times did not admit delay, or because, as might be suspected, to appoint Canning was tantamount to a declaration of ill-will towards Russia, nominated Malmesbury instead.

The new Foreign Secretary was without experience of the administration of Foreign Affairs, except such as he had gleaned in editing the *Diaries and Correspondence* of his celebrated ancestor. This, however, was not an acquisition to be despised, as the Foreign Office Clerks were presently to discover; and he was assisted, besides, by that freemasonry which tends to grow up between the past and present heads of a Department where patriotism has generally held its own against party. It was, indeed, only according to etiquette[3] for Granville to call on his successor and explain the position of affairs abroad. But from Palmerston, also, Malmesbury received a visit and a dissertation which he characterised as "a masterly sketch of the European situation"; and he went, besides, to see Wellington, then a very deaf, old man in the last months of his life. Though one of these counsellors was the conqueror of the First Napoleon and the other the friend of the Third, they both gave him the same advice—to keep well with France[4]. Palmerston warned him that the French and English Governments were like men in love with the same woman, desiring, both of them, to dominate the East; while Wellington bade him distrust the Emperor Nicholas as he would have distrusted a Greek of the Lower empire. He had one other important adviser—perhaps the most important of all. The Prince Consort gave him information, particularly with regard to the German Courts, which no one else in England could have supplied.

---

[1] Maxwell, *Life and Letters of the 4th Earl of Clarendon*, I. 330.
[2] Fitzmaurice, *Life of the 2nd Earl Granville*, I. 69.
[3] Malmesbury, *Memoirs of an Ex-Minister*, I. 320.   [4] *Ibid.* I. 317, 318.

37—2

All the Foreign Ministers in London, Palmerston told his successor, would try to get out of him the things which had been refused them by previous Governments. Malmesbury had not been two days in office before he had evidence of the justice of this observation. Buol, the Austrian Ambassador, had been eager to induce Granville to accept from his hands diplomatic Notes emanating from the Governments of Rome and Modena and relating to the right of asylum accorded by Great Britain to political refugees—a course which, had it been taken, would have implied a recognition of the Austrian hegemony in Italy. Granville, just on the point of resigning office, refused and, what was more, to Buol's great vexation, returned the Notes to the Austrian Embassy. As soon as Malmesbury appeared at the Foreign Office, Buol renewed his solicitations and, being again refused, "behaved in the most coarse and insolent manner." Malmesbury asked him if he was in the habit of addressing English Ministers in that style, and warned him that he should report his conduct to his Government[1]. Eventually, the Ambassador was recalled and his demands repudiated; but the incident, of course embellished and exaggerated not to Malmesbury's advantage, became the talk of the town.

IV

The Derby Ministry had the supreme misfortune to lack a majority in Parliament; and, before the year 1852 was out, Malmesbury had been succeeded by Lord John Russell. The new Foreign Secretary was not intended to be permanent; and, in fact, vacated his post in February, 1853. Before he left the Foreign Office, however, Russell had taken the momentous step of sending Lord Stratford de Redcliffe (as Stratford Canning had now become) back to Constantinople. The "Great Elchi"—to adopt Kinglake's immortal inaccuracy[2]—was uncongenial both to Aberdeen, the new Prime-Minister, and to Clarendon, the new Foreign Secretary, who, though in different degrees, shunned the cause of the Turks. Clarendon's Memorandum of 1840, already referred to[3], had suggested that British interests in the Near East were focussed in Egypt rather than Turkey—a sally of judgment altogether beyond the capacity of other statesmen of the time; and Aberdeen, who in his youth had seen the slaughter at Leipzig, hated war as good men hate the Devil.

[1] Malmesbury, *Memoirs of an Ex-Minister*, I. 313–4, 320.
[2] The title had nothing distinctive or personal about it; it was common to all Ambassadors in Turkey.
[3] See above, p. 43.

If, perhaps, there is one rule more than another which Foreign Secretaries should inscribe upon the secret tablets of their hearts, it is, when once they have, to the best of their ability, located the centre of the next European storm, to place upon that spot, at all costs and before all other considerations, a man with whom they have established the closest attainable understanding. Constantinople was such a centre in Clarendon's time; but Stratford de Redcliffe was not the diplomatist who ought, in the circumstances, to have been found there. How deep ran the conflict of temperament between the Foreign Secretary and the Ambassador can best be judged from the former's lively description of the latter as a "pest[1]." But it was Clarendon's great misfortune that, during the negotiations preceding the Crimean War, he feared Stratford de Redcliffe unchained more even than he feared him at his post. "If I recalled him," he wrote, "he would make peace impossible[2]." Thus it came about that, with one of the greatest of British Foreign Secretaries in Downing Street and one of the greatest of British Diplomatists at Constantinople, our Diplomacy on the eve of the Crimean War was, perhaps, at its worst during the whole course of the century.

Clarendon was four times Foreign Secretary—between 1853 and 1855 in Aberdeen's Ministry; between 1855 and 1858 in Palmerston's; between 1865 and 1866 under Russell; and, again in 1868 until his death in 1870. The continuity is broken by Malmesbury's fifteen months of office in 1858–9, by Russell's six years from 1859 to 1865, and by Stanley's year and a half from 1866 to 1868. Of Malmesbury sufficient has already been said; of Stanley something will be added presently; and as we trace the path of Clarendon some side-lights will be thrown upon Russell. But in regard to the last-named it is best to note at once that his presence at the Foreign Office was a compliment to his political position rather than to his diplomatic abilities, and that he was to be found there only so long as Palmerston was alive to keep him out of the Premiership. As there was nothing in his character to remind one of that "furious spirit of the House of Bedford[3]" of which Junius had once spoken, so there was nothing in his foreign policy to catch the popular imagination. One thing, indeed, he had in common with Palmerston: he lectured. But he lectured sharply, drily, without grace or fervour. "Lord Russell,'

---

[1] Maxwell, *Life and Letters of the 4th Earl of Clarendon*, II. 68.
[2] *Ibid.* II. 261.
[3] Letter I, January 21st, 1769.

observes Bagehot[1], "hardly conducted a foreign controversy in which the extreme intelligibility of his words did not leave a sting behind them." His diplomacy was, indeed, not unlike himself—slight and thin and somewhat shrill[2]. He lacked the power to please either the Courts abroad or the populace at home; and his term of administration must be regarded as an unhappy encroachment upon the usefulness of the ablest of the Liberal Foreign Secretaries.

It was in Russell's time that the influence of the Prince Consort upon Foreign Policy was probably most salutary and perhaps most marked. His wisdom saved the Government from the worst embarrassments in which the Austrian antipathies of Palmerston and the Italian sympathies of Russell might otherwise have involved them[3]; and in 1861, when his last illness had him actually in its grip, his hand reshaped Russell's Note in the famous case of Slidell and Mason after such a fashion as to make it possible for the American Federal Secretary to recommend his Government to accept it and close an incident which, if left open, might have meant the victory of the South in the American Civil War. But neither by the personality of the Prince, nor yet by that of Russell, can we afford to be long detained here; for by neither the one nor the other was the mind of the mid-Victorian Foreign Office shaped.

It is the figure of Clarendon that dominates our stage in the period roughly corresponding to that of the Second Empire in France; and it was his hand that was mainly responsible for the development of the understanding with the Third Napoleon, commended by Palmerston and Wellington to Malmesbury as the cornerstone of British Foreign Policy. The Prince Consort left him a most valuable legacy in the confidence of the Queen; and he retained this to so full a degree that, when the Derby Government was formed in 1866, she begged him, a member of the fallen Ministry, to waive all considerations of party and continue at his post[4]. He had too high a sense of political propriety to consent; but he gave Stanley, his successor, two and a half hours of carefully considered counsel, and the promise of as much cordial assistance as if he were a colleague[5]. The doctrine

---

[1] *Biographical Studies*, "The Earl of Clarendon."
[2] Compare Sir H. Rumbold's *Recollections of a Diplomatist*, II. 106, 107.
[3] See Martin, *Life of the Prince Consort*, ch. xcv.
[4] Maxwell, *Life and Letters of the 4th Earl of Clarendon*, II. 318. It is proper to mention that the Queen's attitude towards him changed subsequently and that in 1868 she tried to prevent his nomination as Foreign Secretary.
[5] *Ibid.* II. 320, 324.

of continuity in Foreign Policy was thus holding its ground even at a time of highly developed party conflict.

One of Clarendon's leading characteristics was his nice appreciation of the proper relations between the Foreign Secretary and the Cabinet. During the period from 1859 to 1865, when Russell, as we have seen, usurped the Foreign Office and Clarendon, much to his own satisfaction, found himself in retirement, he criticised with severity the unconstitutional proceedings of his supplanter.

"I feel," he wrote to his brother-in-law, "so strongly because I soon became aware how easy it was for a Foreign Secretary to act dishonestly towards his colleagues without being detected; and I, therefore, always took especial care never to write or say a word that I did not wish them to know. I have no doubt that a deep game is now playing which may succeed with the Court but which will utterly fail with L. Napoleon and other Governments[1]."

In fact, Russell—perhaps, as Granville supposed, mainly from want of method—came near in 1860 to disavowing those sound conventions which had led him to dismiss Palmerston in 1851. The struggle with the Court concerning Foreign Policy carried on in the last years of the Prince Consort's life by "those two old ringleaders," as Clarendon called them, was, indeed, acute and important. Russell even went so far as to declare that one "might as well live under a despotism," because the Queen set her face against intervention in the War between France and Austria. The majority of the Cabinet were, however, satisfied that she had, as Sidney Herbert put it, "come to their rescue," and that the despotism they had to fear was not that of the Crown but of the Prime-Minister and the Foreign Secretary acting in collusion[2]. Against anything of this kind Ministers were secure when Clarendon had charge of Foreign Affairs; and the little note, which, when he had resumed their direction after Palmerston's death, was slipped by Granville at a Cabinet Council across the table under Russell's very eye, tells its own tale.

"I hope," his colleague and successor wrote to him, "you will not abandon us. You communicate more openly with your colleagues, and act more thoroughly with them in the line of policy you adopt, than any Foreign Secretary I remember. If you go to a conference (abroad) we shall be in the dark; we shall not always see what you write, and certainly

---

[1] Maxwell, *Life and Letters of the 4th Earl of Clarendon*, II. 214 (May 21st, 1860, to Sir G. C. Lewis).
[2] See the story in Fitzmaurice's *Life of the 2nd Earl Granville*, II. 356, 357.

be ignorant of many instructions, approvals, suggestions, etc., which will be poured upon you without you[r] having the means of knowing whether they are personal or representing [sic] the opinions of the Cabinet[1]."

In Parliament, Clarendon, though his pen was extremely ready and his English extremely good, was not more than an adequate speaker. Foreign Affairs, in his day, were still left much to the care of the House of Lords, even though they were ceasing to be, as Greville had affirmed of them in writing to him in 1839, its exclusive property for the purpose of discussion[2]. Outside Parliament, his close relationship with Sir George Lewis and his close friendship with Henry Reeve enabled him to make use on occasion of *The Edinburgh Review* and *The Times*; though Reeve prided himself upon maintaining a perfect freedom of opinion and declared that, if his articles "did, as was often the case, express the opinions of Sir Robert Peel or Lord Aberdeen or Lord Clarendon, it was because he commonly found that he took the same view that they had formed on public affairs[3]." Where they differed, however, Clarendon was quite as capable as Granville of letting *The Times* know pretty plainly how much mischief it sometimes caused to the best interests of the country[4].

Within his Department Clarendon possessed an unusual claim to popularity. He is one of the very few men—perhaps the only man— with a right to be called a *diplomate de carrière*, who ever held the seals of the Foreign Office. In early life he had been for some while Minister at Madrid; and he must have felt some of those rubs and pricks of the Diplomatic Service as a profession, which are lightly viewed by, or perhaps largely hidden from, the eyes of professional politicians. Also, as his affection for tobacco bore witness, he knew how to run his business on easy lines. Smoking is strictly prohibited in office-hours, he was informed by the conservative Addington, who hated the habit. "Oh! indeed!" he replied, "Can I offer you a cigar[5]?"

The Clarendon period of Foreign Office history originated, or at least coincided with, some considerable changes in Departmental economy, of which the present appears to be the proper place to take account. In 1852, when Malmesbury had been but a few days

[1] Maxwell, *Life and Letters of the 4th Earl of Clarendon*, II. 312.
[2] *Ibid.* I. 173: "As Foreign Affairs are never discussed except at the House of Lords, you will be much more the public organ of Government than the Foreign Minister himself."
[3] *Memoirs of the Life of Henry Reeve*, II. 339, and see pp. 323, 325.
[4] Maxwell, *Life and Letters of the 4th Earl of Clarendon*, II. 103.
[5] Hertslet, *Recollections of the Old Foreign Office*, p. 121.

in office, the ceiling of the room in which he was accustomed to sit, descended upon the table at which he might have been writing. In less civilised communities than our own the incident would probably have been referred to more occult causes than the decay of the structure; but this was, in fact, the explanation of the circumstance. The buildings of the Old Foreign Office were giving out, and new ones had become urgently necessary. Four years later, the authorities had resolved what to do. In 1856, with Clarendon as Foreign Secretary, it was decided that his Department should be housed in the north-west block of a building designed to shelter the Home, Colonial, India and Local Government Offices; and, twelve years afterwards and a few months before Clarendon entered upon his last Administration, Foreign Affairs began to be conducted in their existing quarters. While the old Downing Street houses were being swept away—and with them the State Paper Office, a costly and convenient stone building, still at that time in good preservation and standing where the India Office stands now—business was carried on at Pembroke House, No. 7 Whitehall Gardens, and at No. 8, Lord Malmesbury's house adjoining. In the meantime, on the site thus freed, Gilbert Scott, who had wished to build after the Gothic manner, raised under Palmerston's orders the present Venetian palace; and there, in 1868, Disraeli, the professed enemy of Venetian oligarchies, gave, in his capacity as Prime-Minister, a grand inaugural party to celebrate the house-warming of the Foreign Secretary and his staff.

Such, in the Clarendon period, were the changes in the outward appearance of the Foreign Office. In the *personnel* of the Department there had been changes also. Henry Unwin Addington, who had succeeded Backhouse as Under-Secretary in 1842, had himself retired in 1854. He had slipped away one evening, so he told Aberdeen, without causing any trouble to his colleagues and without any notice being taken of his withdrawal. "Scarcely very flattering to you, Mr Addington!" was Aberdeen's caustic comment. Evidently he was a man of no great mark, bearing indeed the name of "Pumpy" in the Office; but he had more diplomatic experience than Backhouse, whom Canning, doubtless with his eye on the requirements of a nation of shopkeepers, had turned from a commercial agent into a précis-writer!

As Pitt had been to Addington, so was Hammond to Addington's nephew. Edmund Hammond is the Permanent Under-Secretary of the Clarendon period—a Whig, like his chief, but rough as Clarendon never was, and ungracious as public officials have no right to be; yet, on the other side, forcible, capable, immensely industrious and, they say, at bottom, kindly. The world, having little time for detailed study of the lives of public servants, remembers him chiefly by an anecdote which shows him to have been rather a clerk than a prophet. Granville, on taking office after Clarendon's death in the summer of 1870 had turned to the Permanent Under-Secretary to put him in touch with the detail of current business, and, on July 3rd, according to the account he afterwards gave to the House of Lords, that "able and experienced" man, "Mr Hammond, at the Foreign Office...it being then three or four o'clock," told him that, with the exception of the recent murder of British subjects by Greek brigands, "he had never, during his long experience, known so great a lull in foreign affairs, and that he was not aware of any important question that he (Lord Granville) should have to deal with[1]." It happened, unfortunately for Hammond's reputation, that this incident occurred on the day on which Prince Leopold of Hohenzollern-Sigmaringen accepted the Crown of Spain; and it was not three weeks later that France declared war upon Prussia.

The anecdote is worth comparing with another. "Never in my life," said Bismarck in 1871 to Clarendon's daughter, Lady Emily Russell, "was I more glad to hear of anything than I was of your father's death." And then, when she recoiled from a compliment too subtle to be obvious, he added, "Ach! dear lady, you must not take it like that. What I mean is that, if your father had lived, he would have prevented the War[2]." The remark, whatever its actual value in the sphere of speculation, at least gives the measure of Clarendon's reputation for insight and influence. Things that were hidden from Hammond, Bismarck was probably right enough in supposing not to be equally obscure to Hammond's chief. In that vanished society of kings and emperors, there lay between the mere expert in diplomacy and the accomplished man of the world in power a gulf not easily to be filled in by surreptitious or second-hand information, however carefully collated, nor bridged over by mere training, however fully finished. "Your very interesting letters," Russell had written to Clarendon in 1863, "confirm what I always thought—that a hundred spies cannot ascertain so much as an English gentleman whom Princes and Ministers believe that they can safely trust[3]."

---

[1] Fitzmaurice, *Life of the 2nd Earl Granville*, II. 32.
[2] Maxwell, *Life and Letters of the 4th Earl of Clarendon*, II. 366.
[3] *Ibid.* II. 282.

The system of privilege which formed part and parcel of a diplomatic career in the nineteenth century possesses, and perhaps requires, no better defence. Hammond retired from work in 1873 with a peerage[1], and a pension of £2500. Towards the close of his career, a bust, which faces the fine marble staircase of the new Foreign Office, was put up in his honour. It satisfies a nice sense of proportion that within view there stands also a full-length statue of Clarendon.

Of the witnesses who appeared before the Select Committee on the Diplomatic Service, which sat in 1861, Hammond and Clarendon were among the most important; and their evidence furnishes a comprehensive view of the Foreign Office and the Diplomatic Service as they appeared in the middle of the nineteenth century. Hammond's Memorandum drawn up for the Committee on the organisation of the Office, is, indeed, a primary authority for this period of its history.

At the apex of the structure stood, of course, the Foreign Minister with his Private Secretary, the latter not yet quite so influential a person as he was later to become. Next after the Foreign Secretary followed the two Under-Secretaries. These cannot be sufficiently distinguished from each other, though old Foreign Office Lists class them together as if their relation had been of the closest. One was a permanent and a public official; the other, a Member of Parliament, subject, like other politicians, to the changes and chances of political fortune. Though they stood upon a supposed equality, there was no comparison in their influence, since the one knew his work and the other had to learn it; nor was there any similarity in their aims, since the Permanent Under-Secretary, with his eye upon Foreign Governments, best attained his ends by suppressing all mention of successes, while the Parliamentary Under-Secretary, with his eye upon Parliament, was hardly less concerned to advertise the triumphs of his Chief's diplomacy. The work of these ill-paired functionaries, each controlling, as he did at this time, one half of the business of the Office, and drafting the despatches relating to that half in accordance with the Secretary of State's minutes, was connected always by formal, and at will by informal, means. In the course of its many peregrinations, each despatch-box, just before it found its way to the Prime-Minister, was required to pass through the hands of the Under-Secretary not directly concerned with the affairs of the country to which the contents of the box related. But,

[1] Conferred in 1874.

in addition, prudent Under-Secretaries would meet morning by morning to compare notes about the events of the preceding day and to take counsel about the eventualities of the coming one[1].

In 1858, during Malmesbury's Administration, the work of the Office was held to have become so considerable as to justify the appointment of an Assistant Under-Secretary—an official whose prototype was already to be found at the Colonial, India and War Offices. There had, in fact, been a great multiplication of business in the Department of Foreign Affairs, for which the troubled condition of Europe was, no doubt, to blame as well as the increase in population, trade and facilities of communication. As Malmesbury sat beside Lady Clarendon at dinner one night in 1853, he took occasion to contrast the exertion required of himself with that required of Canning. He had had a census taken, so he said, of the despatches sent out in 1828 and had found them to number 5000. During his own year of office, the incoming and outgoing despatches together were something like seven times as numerous. From this figure they rose further under Clarendon's Administration, numbering over 35,000 in 1853 and nearly 49,000 the year after[2]. Delegation of authority, unfortunately, failed to keep pace with these encroachments on the Foreign Secretary's time; and the bad system which required him to read and initial such masses of documents seemed to a close observer to have been a contributory cause of Clarendon's death[3].

In the Foreign Office hierarchy the Chief Clerk follows next after the Secretaries. In Hammond's time the post was held by Lenox-Conyngham, whose temper in stormy weather, owing to his loss of a leg, was famous for rising as the glass fell. He had worked his way up from a supernumerary Clerkship in 1812 to the Chief-Clerkship and a salary of £1450 a year in 1841; and he remained a Foreign Office character for some twenty years after that. But his Department was one delivered over to the routine of audits, estimates and accounts; and of him and the three Clerks who served his tables there is no further need to speak. Next below him on the ladder stood the eight Senior Clerks, each with a division of

---

[1] See Lord Wodehouse's Evidence. *Report Select Committee on the Diplom. Service*, 1861, p. 95.
[2] See for these figures Maxwell, *Life and Letters of the 4th Earl of Clarendon*, II. 11. Footnote.
[3] *Report of the Select Committee on the Diplomatic and Consular Service*, 1871, p. 58. Sir A. Otway's Evidence.

business—the Consular service; or the Slave Trade correspondence, which in those days bulked large; or the political and commercial affairs of the six geographical sections into which the world, for convenience, was divided[1]. To each Senior Clerk, with his £700 to £1000 a year, there was allotted an Assistant Clerk with from £550 to £650. And then, at the bottom of the pyramid, there were placed twenty-five Junior Clerks, with salaries varying from £100 to £545 a year, among whose names were to be found about this time those of Abbott and Currie and Sanderson, all later to be distinguished Permanent Under-Secretaries, but in those days, apart from some précis-writing, docketing and drafting, too modestly employed in decoding telegrams in cipher, a task which requires but little ability, or in copying despatches, a task which requires no ability at all.

Each of the eight Divisions dealt with all kinds of correspondence relating to its own business, whether it came from British Ministers abroad or Foreign Ministers at home, or Government Departments, or private persons. At night, that is out of office hours, one of four resident Clerks, appointed for the purpose, was engaged in docketing the new material, as it came in, and despatching it, where of sufficient political consequence, in a locked box to the Under-Secretary to whose division it related. After being sifted afresh in the Under-Secretary's hands, important matter would pass upwards to the Secretary of State, and then downwards again, with his comments and directions, to the Under-Secretary, who gave instructions in regard to everything sent for his inspection, to the one of the eight Senior Clerks concerned. The Senior Clerk in question, after causing the document to be registered under the heading of the country to which it related, would set the Junior Clerks to work to prepare copies or drafts, or whatever might be required in connexion with it. In the next stage of the transaction the papers were returned to the Under-Secretary for approval. According as the subject-matter was important or the reverse, he would deal with it himself or send it on to the Secretary of State. In the final stage, the Division responsible was required to produce a fair copy for signature. In cases, however, of trifling consequence this elaborate procedure was evaded by the authority of the Senior Clerk, who could approve the drafting of a letter for signature without any reference at all to the Under-Secretary.

[1] (1) The Central Powers and Denmark. (2) The Near East. (3) Russia, Greece, Sweden, and the Italian States. (4) France, Switzerland and the West Indies. (5) The Netherlands, Spain, Portugal and the South American States. (6) North and Central America, China and Japan.

The communication to the Queen and the Prime-Minister of important incoming despatches was arranged by the Senior Clerk of each Division after the Secretary of State had minuted his Instructions upon them. The Prime-Minister received them first; then the Sovereign; and they were subsequently circulated amongst the members of the Cabinet. As already explained, they passed through the hands of the Under-Secretary not especially concerned on their way to the Prime-Minister. Outgoing despatches, if relating to important matters requiring the Sovereign's assent, were submitted to the Queen in draft-form before being sent off. In cases of less significance, copies of the answers sent by the Secretary of State were furnished to the Queen and the Prime-Minister after the answers themselves had been despatched. If we ask what time was needed for all this circumvolution, we shall probably be surprised to learn that it could sometimes be compressed within the hours of a single day, though, more generally, the circle was completed within two or three days.

Foreign Office hours were nominally six, beginning at eleven or noon[1], and ending at five or six o'clock; but officials were liable to be called upon to stay till seven or eight, or, in fact, till the pressing work of the day was finished; and it was on this understanding that they were allowed two months' holiday, with easy hours of attendance and leave of absence. The discipline of the Office rested, in fact, upon the idea that you get much more out of educated men by treating them as reasonable beings and not as machines—by asking much of them at times of stress, and letting them go lightly when occupation is slack.

Two important Departments lay outside the current of the ordinary work of the Office—the Library and the Treaty Department. Eighteen months or two years after they had been finished with, papers were removed from the Division interested, and consigned to the care of the Librarian, who, with his Sub-Librarian and five Clerks, divided the despatches sent from those received, and arranged them for binding in separate volumes. Letters, on the other hand, were bound up without distinction of origin. The contents of these volumes of correspondence were then noted in a register; and an index of persons and subjects was compiled. The sufficiency of this registration to meet sudden calls for information or for precedents was, of course, a concern of the utmost consequence to the Librarian. To him, applicants, from the Prime-Minister downwards, were accustomed to turn, at any time and any notice, for historical memoranda on all such matters

[1] Strictly they were supposed to run from noon to 6 p.m.

as lay between China and Peru or had once fallen within the scope of British Foreign Relations. Beaconsfield, for example, in the crisis of 1879, startled his Cabinet by a dissertation of exceptional profundity upon the difference between a truce and an armistice, the substance of which had been supplied to him by the Foreign Office Librarian of the day[1]. This was Edward Hertslet; and in the annals of the Foreign Office Library, that name stands foremost. There were two of the family who held the post in succession—Lewis and Edward, father and son; and there was also a brother of Lewis's who acted as Sub-Librarian. Lewis began and Edward continued the famous collection of Treaties, which bears their name. And to the collaboration of Edward is due, also, the Foreign Office List.

The idea of this publication originated, however, with Francis Cavendish, whose diplomatic recollections reflect the portrait of an easy-going, agreeable man of society. In 1851, it struck him that a record of the careers of living members of the Foreign Services might be of use; and he was not deterred from his enterprise by the execrations of Lenox-Conyngham. The experienced aid of Hertslet was presently invoked; and, before many years were out, the annual was in Hertslet's hands. It has run from 1852 to the present time; and for a good many years, though the copyright is privately owned, access to Foreign Office Records has been willingly conceded to its compilers. In Cavendish's time, however, it was published by subscription at the price of two shillings a copy and, for fear of giving offence, contained no mention of official salaries. Only as we look back now over a period of seventy years can we see clearly that Cavendish and Hertslet stand out as the pioneers of a dictionary of diplomatic biography.

Another important section of Foreign Office activity remains to be mentioned. The Treaty Department, where protocols were first drafted and then put through the various stages corresponding with the progress of a negotiation, owed very nearly as much to the Bergnes as the Library owed to the Hertslets[2]. They laboured, and others whose names are not to be found on the page of history entered into their labours. But it needs a rascal to make a Department famous: and one was found, though not until some years after Clarendon's death. Charles Marvin, a copying-clerk not on the Foreign Office staff and earning 10d. an hour, betrayed to *The*

---

[1] Hertslet, *Recollections of the Old Foreign Office*, p. 202.
[2] J. B. Bergne, Sir J. H. G. Bergne, Superintendents of the Treaty Dept. 1854–73, 1881–94 respectively. See for both the *D.N.B.*

Globe newspaper, for the sake of a little gold, the secrets of the Anglo-Russian Agreement of 1878. He was put on his trial; but the law, as it then stood, was insufficient to convict him of so much as a misdemeanour. He was, therefore, acquitted and eked out his reduced means by a little volume of tattle, more bitter than amusing, which, for lack of anything better, remains to the present time a kind of authority for the inner life of the Foreign Office in the age of Victoria. In these days, he would have been quickly silenced under the provisions of the Official Secrets Acts[1].

The affair of Marvin offered a strange commentary upon the jealous secrecy in which the most confidential of public Departments had long shrouded its business. Caution had, in fact, overreached itself; and the theoretical restriction of even the most mechanical political work to clerks of the best standing had, apparently[2], enabled a man of no standing at all to slip in and become acquainted with an important State-secret. The problem was always how to secure a body of confidential clerks at modest salaries who would do Marvin's class of work, though not in Marvin's kind of way; and this point should be remembered in connexion with the reforms of some twenty years earlier.

In 1856 Clarendon had established a qualifying entrance examination for the Foreign Office[3]. The tests proposed would not have satisfied a philosopher or a pedant; but they were good enough to distinguish the intelligent from the stupid. As things were then ordered, they were, in fact, rather more than sufficient for some of the work required of the candidates accepted. A young man of from eighteen to twenty-five years old—and these were the age-limits of candidature—who could understand French, both written and spoken, make a good précis, and write a decent hand and style, deserved better than to be set down to produce copies of documents—not probably, for the most part of any very great secrecy—especially if one recollects that he had generally received the most expensive education that the country afforded and was a repository of the best traditions of a gentleman, when those traditions still went for much

---

[1] *Official Secrets Acts*, 1889 and 1911.
[2] Salisbury (see his *Life* by Lady Gwendolen Cecil, II. 285) was of opinion that the text of the Anglo-Russian Agreement had been supplied to Marvin from Russian sources.
[3] I see no reason to follow the author of the valuable article on the Foreign Office in *The British Year-Book of International Law*, 1920, pp. 97–108, in supposing that there may have been some sort of qualifying examination previous to 1856. Clarendon's own evidence (*Report Select Comm. Diplom. Service*, 1861, Q. 956) seems to me conclusive against this notion.

in public estimation. Clarendon perceived and resented the wastefulness of the system, and fought zealously for his Clerks against the petty economy of the Treasury. But it needed nothing less than a threat of resignation and the intervention of the Prime-Minister to enable him to get his way. Even then, his way did not lead very far. Supplementary Clerks, selected by competition or in some cases only by a qualifying examination on the Foreign Secretary's nomination[1], were grudgingly introduced to discharge some of the routine work in the non-political Departments—the Library, the Treaty, the Chief Clerk's and the Commercial; but the institution of Second Division Clerks did not occur till the 'eighties, and even in the early years of the twentieth century men of first-rate ability were to be found doing work of a very modest and mechanical kind.

There was one function of the Foreign Office Clerk of this period which has since disappeared. He was accustomed, under the title of "agent," to act as a kind of patron or trustee of the fortunes of one or more British diplomatists stationed abroad. It became his business to collect his client's pay, from which he took a percentage for his trouble; to send him on his letters and parcels; to warn him when diplomatic appointments were likely to fall vacant; to see that he was not passed over for lack of remembrance; and, in a word, to look after the interests of one whom distance forbade to look after his own. These agencies were not mere private arrangements. They were legalised by Order in Council in 1795, were officially regulated in 1816, became the subject of legal compensation after their abolition in 1870, and in this fashion appear to have remained a source of profit to the holders till about the end of the century[2].

Between the Diplomatist abroad and the Foreign Office Clerk at home there was, apart from this, a correspondence of function, which made it desirable that each should have an inside knowledge of the work of the other; and authorities were generally agreed that, while, after a certain time of life or degree of promotion, a man should remain fixed in the Home or Foreign section of the Foreign Service in accordance with his proved abilities, the utmost possibility of interchange should exist in the earlier stages of his career. And interchange, though not properly compulsory until 1862[3]—and then only

---

[1] *4th Report Civil Establ. Comm.* 1890, Qs. 26,006, 26,007.
[2] See *Report Select Comm. Diplom. Service*, 1861, Min. of Ev., p. 192, and *4th Report Civil Establ. Comm.* 1890, Min. of Ev., Qs. 26,547 to 26,553.
[3] *5th Report Civil Service Comm.* 1914, p. 4. Cp. *4th Report Civil Establ. Comm.* 1890, p. 8.

theoretically and temporarily—has always been practised by arrangement. Among the figures we have come across, Addington and Hammond and Mellish[1], to say nothing of Stratford de Redcliffe himself, who pined, as a young man, for a snug post in England and passed all the best years of his life in Constantinople, all had experience both at home and abroad. And there was actually a rule, more honoured, perhaps, in the breach than the observance, that two Foreign Office Clerks should always be employed at some Foreign Mission[2]. Still, when enough has been said to emphasise the community of science between the two branches of the profession, the diversity of art remains. And about the Diplomatic Service, therefore, it is now proper to say a word or two.

Whether Ferdinand of Aragon, who is said to have been the first to turn his spies into Envoys, ought really to be regarded as the founder of the Diplomatic Corps, is not a question convenient for discussion here. It is enough to start with Hammond's observation, given in evidence before the Select Committee on the Diplomatic Service, which sat in 1861 with Monckton Milnes[3] in the Chair, and John Russell, Disraeli, Layard and Acton on the Board, that diplomacy was never recognised as a profession, even in a limited sense of the word, in this country, before the peace of 1815[4]. Stratford de Redcliffe was of the same opinion. "The Diplomatic Service," he said, "when I went into it, was no profession at all[5]." When the century opened, an Ambassador was, in fact, allowed by the British Government no more staff than one Secretary[6]. All the rest of his establishment consisted of friends of his own choosing—young men, presumably anxious to see something of the world, qualified by fortune to work without pay, and qualified by birth and education to move without effort in that *beau monde* of Society which in those times mostly governed the world, and here and there is able to govern it still. They lived, as it was natural in the circumstances that they should live, at the Ambassador's expense, lodging in his house and feeding at his table. An Embassy resembled a household, and a Legation a family. Of two leading Diplomatists who gave evidence in 1861, one told the Committee that, at the outset of his career, he had gone unpaid for five years, and another spoke of having done so for eight. The Government, indeed,

---

[1] See the *Report Select Comm. Diplom. Service*, 1861, p. 158.
[2] *Ibid.* p. xiv.   [3] Afterwards Lord Houghton.
[4] See the *Report Select Comm. Diplom. Service*, 1861, Min. of Ev., Q. 30.
[5] *Ibid.* Q. 1658.   [6] *Ibid.* Q. 30.

carefully guarded itself from any suspicion of incurring an initial obligation. An Attaché, in the despatch which regularised his position,
was warned that it gave him no claim to promotion. Sir Andrew
Buchanan, who subsequently went as Ambassador to Petersburg,
told the Committee that he was employed sixteen years before he
received the Queen's Commission, which, in fact, was never given
before a man had attained the rank of Secretary[1], and, further, that,
at the end of over twenty-five years' service, he was still not entitled
to a pension, even though he had been appointed to the post of
Minister at Madrid[2]. A diplomatic career, at any rate in its earliest
and latest phases, was an occupation for a man with a competency.
A candidate for nomination, so Malmesbury told the Committee,
had to be assured of an income from parents or relatives of at least
£200 a year. And the old diplomatist, mounting the last rungs of
the diplomatic ladder and representing his country at Vienna, Petersburg or Paris, had still to depend upon his private purse to find the
last thousand or so of his expenditure. The salary of the British
Ambassador at the Court of the Tuileries, in those brilliant days of the
Second empire, was raised from £8000 to £10,000; but Cowley had
to make it up to £13,000 out of his own pocket before he could provide
for the large hospitality and considerable display required of him[3].
Hamilton Seymour at Vienna and Petersburg, where the salaries had
been put up to £6000 a year, besides £800 or £900 allowed for
house-rent, had fared better than this, but, nevertheless, declared it
impossible to live within his official means[4]. Only in the middle stage
of his career, as a Minister at a small Court, had he found the salary
adequate and the profession a paying one. The Committee were
impressed, and recommended that the official income of the British
Ambassador in Paris be raised to £12,000 and that of the Ambassadors
in Vienna and Petersburg to £9000 each. These were then the three
imperial capitals. Elsewhere, Embassies should, they thought, carry
salaries of £5000, and Legations of the first class of from £3000 to £4000,
and of the second class of from £1000 to £2500; but these figures
were to be independent of certain allowances for house-rent and
other purposes.

The Committee sat at an interesting moment in the history of
the Diplomatic Service. A few years earlier[5], and contemporaneously
with the establishment of the entrance examination at the Foreign

---

[1] *Report Select Comm. Diplom. Service*, 1861, Min. of Ev., Q. 2457.
[2] *Ibid.* Q. 1116.   [3] *Ibid.* Q. 2511.   [4] *Ibid.* pp. 202, 203.   [5] Between 1855 and 1857.

Office, Clarendon had instituted "a qualifying test" for the Diplomatic Service. As in the case of the Foreign Office Clerkships, he selected the subjects with care on the advice of competent authorities, submitted the list to Palmerston, who was then Prime-Minister, and passed it on to the Civil Service Commissioners[1]. Accordingly, a candidate for the Diplomatic Service was required to turn English into French, to speak French with fluency and exactitude, to translate Latin, German, Spanish or Italian, and to possess a good knowledge of geography, of history since the French Revolution and of the Constitutional and Foreign relations of the country for which he was destined[2]. But success in his candidature brought him no more than the honour of passing into the unpaid class of Attachés. Before he was qualified for a salary, another examination lay in front of him, which Malmesbury, however, afterwards, allowed him to pass at the end of two years instead of waiting till a paid-Attachéship fell vacant and incurring the expense and inconvenience of returning from a distant station to be examined. Though Stratford de Redcliffe, with an old man's scepticism of change, professed to have seen little or no improvement resulting from the substitution of the qualifying test for the old three months' trial at practical work in the Foreign Office, upon which an Attaché had formerly been judged, Cowley declared that insistence upon a thorough acquaintance with French had appreciably raised the diplomatic quality of the young men who came under his notice and whose predecessors had, within his recollection, sometimes appeared at an Embassy abroad without any command of French at all[3].

There is a danger of taking a false measure of Clarendon's reforms. In thinking of him as the founder of the Foreign Office and Diplomatic Service examinations, we may forget that he did not abolish the system of privilege. A nomination from the Foreign Secretary had been a very real favour before examinations were introduced; and it remained a very real favour afterwards. It had, indeed, been considered so great a favour in the early "fifties" of the last century that Morier's father, who considered himself to have been injured by Palmerston, would not stoop to ask it for his son, until Palmerston's place had been taken by Russell; while Aberdeen, though Prime-Minister at the time and his friend, would not presume to solicit it on

[1] *Report Select Comm. Diplom. Service*, 1861, Q. 956.
[2] *British International Law Year-Book*, 1920, p. 98.
[3] *Report Select Comm. Diplom. Service*, 1861, Qs. 2469, 2470.

his behalf until Russell, an ex-Premier, had made way for Clarendon[1]. But neither in 1856 nor even in 1870, after an Order in Council had introduced, subject to the consent of the Minister concerned, the system of open competition throughout the Civil Service, did Clarendon sweep away from his Department the old system of selection and influence; and his policy was approved by the Select Committee on the constitution of the Diplomatic and Consular Services which reported in May, 1871[2]. What he had really done was to give to the Foreign Service the stamp of a profession, and to introduce, by the side of the principle of privilege, a principle of competition, which, given the democratic drift of the times, was likely by degrees to efface its rival. In this as in other points, and notably in that exceptional interest in commerce and statistics, which may, as Bagehot thought, have been a legacy from his early training in the Dublin Excise Office, Clarendon showed himself, to use the words of the same critic, "a Minister singularly suited to the transition-age in which he lived[3]."

The Committee of 1861 was curious to know whether, to the eyes of old diplomatists, the character of the Diplomatic Service seemed to have greatly changed. Stratford de Redcliffe was of opinion that it had: not, as he explained, in the class of persons recruited or in the habit of business displayed, but in the "personal qualities" of its members, which were higher on the whole, as he thought, than they had been. Other changes, too, had occurred in consonance with the fall and rise of nations. Embassies had sunk to be Missions[4]; Missions had risen to be Embassies; and over South America, which George Canning supposed he had called into diplomatic existence, there had been scattered, during Stratford Canning's days, a small army corps of British diplomatic officials—Agents, Consuls-General or Chargés d'affaires as the case might be[5]. But there was a greater change to be observed than these. In 1849, Stratford de Redcliffe had, as we have seen, been no more closely connected with

[1] Wemyss, Memoirs and Letters of Sir Robert Morier, I. 124, 125.
[2] "That the admission of Members into the Service by nomination upon a test examination is a plan of which your Committee approves, and, without expressing any opinion generally as to the merits of a system of open competitive examination, they think the present plan preferable to it for this branch of the Public Service."
[3] Bagehot, Biographical Studies, "The Earl of Clarendon."
[4] The Embassy at Petersburg was suppressed in 1844, and revived in 1861 (1st Report Select Comm. Diplom. and Cons. Service, 1871, p. 12).
[5] On the other hand, by 1871, the complaint is that professional advancement has been blocked by the suppression of Missions—four in Germany, two in Italy, two in South America, and others in Monte Video and the Bolivias. (Ibid. p. 19.)

the Government at home than a good rider and a fleet horse could make him. But the electric telegraph was everywhere stretching out long coils; and, about the time of the Crimean War, the Foreign Office was pretty generally issuing Instructions by wire, though messages for Constantinople had still in the critical days of 1853 to be transmitted from Vienna by the time-honoured methods[1]. One who had known both systems and had seemed to his critics to arrogate to himself powers greater than any other English Ambassador has ever possessed, might have been expected to complain that the progress of science had ruined the profession of diplomacy; for even now the opinion is common that an Ambassador at the end of the telegraph has no initiative. But Stratford de Redcliffe did not hold this view. To his eyes it seemed that the scope for diplomatic talent had actually been increased by the advance of scientific discovery. An Ambassador in the first half of the nineteenth century, he argued, received his instructions in so great detail by means of a written despatch that little was left him to do but to read them out to the Sovereign or the Representative of the Sovereign to whom he was accredited. But a telegram necessarily left much unsaid; there was consequently much to be supplied and much to be modified by the tact, the insight, the experience and the courage of the man on the spot[2].

The Committee whose sittings in 1861 have provided so large a mirror of diplomatic life made certain recommendations, of some of which it was fortunate in obtaining the embodiment, at least to some degree, in the Foreign Office Regulations of 1862. The probationary period of Attachéship which the Committee would have fixed at two years[3], was limited to four; and at its termination a commission as Third Secretary, with a salary of £150 a year, was granted to Attachés who could speak and understand two foreign languages, of which French was one. The former class of Paid Attachés was converted into Second Secretaries; and the Foreign Secretary was empowered to compel temporary exchanges between the two branches of the Foreign Service, though this compulsory power appears never to have been exercised[4].

[1] I gather this from Lane-Poole, *Life of Stratford Canning*, II. 290, where Clarendon will be found transmitting his orders to Stratford Canning through the British Ambassador at Vienna.
[2] *Report Select Comm. Diplom. Service*, 1861, p. 168.
[3] The authors of the 5th *Report Civil Service Comm.* 1914 (p. 3) give "four" as the recommendation of the 1861 Committee. The Committee really said "two years at the most." The same *Report* appears to be, also, incorrect in its paraphrase of the second recommendation of the 1861 Committee.
[4] 4th *Report Civil Establ. Comm.* 1890, p. 8.

Some years after this—in 1869—the Diplomatic Establishment was brought more completely under the control of Parliament by putting its charges upon Parliamentary votes instead of upon the Consolidated Fund. The change was the occasion of the appointment in 1871 of another Select Committee, whose effective recommendations included the exemption of candidates possessing a University degree from all further examination except in handwriting, précis-writing and French; the institution of annual reports from the heads of Missions upon the work of the Second and Third Secretaries and Attachés; and the introduction of £100 per annum allowances in favour of Third Secretaries who could prove before the Civil Service Commission that they possessed a competent knowledge of public law, or, if stationed in countries where Russian or certain non-European languages were spoken, a working knowledge of those languages.

Here we may take leave of the early and mid-Victorian age of diplomacy—an age not overridden like its predecessors by diplomatic forms and follies, but just easy enough to be agreeable, just ceremonious enough to be dignified, just privileged enough to possess distinction, and just industrious enough to do its work. The nearer past, which we have now to traverse in review, possesses, or seems to possess, no similar attraction. The mists of time have neither softened its rigid lines, nor grouped its arid detail: reminiscence is timid, criticism has to be discreet, and statistics become obtrusive. To all appearance, the features of this period are improved organisation, advancing mechanism, growing momentum, and diminished personality, terminating in the greatest diplomatic catastrophe in the history of the world. Whether the British Foreign Office, or the British Diplomatic Service, or all the leading Foreign Ministries of Europe together, are to be held responsible in any appreciable degree for so prodigious a disaster, depends, however, upon the view we take of human fatalities.

There is a letter from Jowett, written in 1873 and printed now in Morier's *Life*[1], where the philosopher adjures the diplomatist by his preeminence in his profession, by the accident of his friendships with the Crown-Prince of Prussia, with Gortchakoff and with the Duc d'Aumale, by the time that remains to the world before the impending crisis arrives, and by the power of England, still as great at least as it was in the days of Chatham, to make the avoidance of a Continental war the motive and religion of his life. "You," Jowett says, "could prevent a war in Europe, if you devoted your

[1] Wemyss, *Life of Sir Robert Morier*, II. 288, 289.

whole mind to this object." But Morier replies that no such ideal is to be realised or even approached by a diplomatic agent; that no such idea could be assimilated by any English statesman without stamping himself as a "useless and dangerous" man; that there are worse things than war; and that, in effect, the Foreign Office is hopeless, bound hand and foot to the politicians and dominated at the moment by the malignant influence of those whom together he used to stigmatise as "Gee-Gee"—Gladstone, that is, and Granville.

It is a sombre picture—such as Morier's pictures of the Foreign Office tend to be; and we are left to speculate what he would have made of the Permanent Under-Secretaryship, if, as Derby had half promised[1], it had been offered to him instead of to Abbott in that year of 1873, when he wrote and when Hammond resigned. He was known for a great reformer, deeply in earnest—too deeply, as it seemed to Derby who held that "earnest men with ideas and great abilities were sometimes unsafe men[2]," to be convenient. It was not, however, in Derby's time that the vacancy actually occurred.

Granville, as we have seen, took up the reins of Foreign Policy, when in the year of the Franco-Prussian War they fell from Clarendon's hand. Gladstone was in his first Premiership; and the old difficulty, never finally cleared up to this day, as to the Prime-Minister's exact place in the control of Foreign Policy, reasserted itself. Foreign Ministers in England were all too ready to exploit Gladstone's indomitable eloquence. They led him on to talk, and turned what Granville called his "original and large ideas" into copy for their despatches. To Granville this proved excessively inconvenient; and even his smooth pen could not avoid a slight asperity in laying down the Constitutional principle governing the relations of the Prime-Minister and the Foreign Secretary. "I imagine," he wrote to his Chief, "that the Prime-Minister has an undoubted right to communicate directly either with our representatives abroad or with Foreign Ministers in London. But I think it is in his interest as much as in that of the Foreign Secretary, that he should only appear as the *deus ex machina*[3]." We do not learn what the Prime-Minister replied; but it is significant that in 1880, when the Liberals returned to power, Queen Victoria informed Beaconsfield that he might be at his ease as regards Foreign Affairs, since Granville managed them entirely and they were never mentioned to her by Gladstone[4].

[1] Wemyss, *Life of Sir Robert Morier*, II. 287.   [2] *Ibid.* II. 287.
[3] Fitzmaurice, *Life of the 2nd Earl Granville*, II. 64.
[4] Buckle, *Life of Disraeli*, VI. 543.

V

Granville's theory about this part of the Constitution was to be more fully tested during the Conservative Administration of 1874–80. Beaconsfield's Foreign Minister was Derby, a man of wide perceptions and nicely balanced judgment, invaluable so long as calm and caution were the qualities required, but too profoundly pacific to risk the quick decisions that diplomacy sometimes requires. Pleasant as a Chief, frank and trustworthy as a diplomatist, terse and sagacious as a speaker, he was unfortunate in the time of his Administration. During the various phases of the Near Eastern crisis of 1876–78, when for two troubled years Foreign Policy became a domestic preoccupation, Beaconsfield is to be found first approving, and then condemning, the Foreign Secretary[1]. The Constitutional tangle was increased by the action of the Queen. She held strongly that Russia ought to be opposed without delay, and showed all a woman's tenacity in asserting the special interest of the Sovereign in Foreign Politics. She "writes every day and telegraphs every hour... almost literally," was the Prime-Minister's description of her activity in the middle of the crisis[2]. Any other man might, indeed, have felt that the royal prerogative was being strained. But Beaconsfield's special veneration for the Crown as an institution, coupled with his special regard for the Queen as a person and his general agreement with her decided opinions as against the Fabian and pacific policy of some of his most influential colleagues, disposed him in favour of what amounted to a secret diplomacy on the part of the Prime-Minister and the Sovereign, carried on behind the back of the Foreign Secretary. On his instructions and with the Queen's authority, Colonel Wellesley was despatched with a message to the Emperor of Russia to make it clear that Great Britain would intervene, if the Russo-Turkish War ran into a second campaign. This policy, which had never received, and could probably never have obtained, the sanction of the Cabinet, was, as Wellesley's Memorandum explicitly stated, "on no account to be mentioned at the Foreign Office[3]." The natural safeguards of the Constitution were thus swept away by excluding from the management and even the cognisance of Foreign Affairs both the Minister responsible to Parliament and the expert advisers whom he was understood to consult; and something

---

[1] Buckle, *Life of Disraeli*, VI. 72, 77, 194.
[2] *Ibid*. VI. 150.   [3] *Ibid*. VI. 174.

very like an autocracy of the Prime-Minister necessarily ensued. It was an arrangement which no Foreign Secretary ought to tolerate, and no self-governing people ought to permit. For the Foreign Office as it was in Derby's time, and indeed, for the Diplomatic Service which carried out its instructions, Beaconsfield, however, entertained a great contempt. The criticism which appears in his published correspondence is quite ungilded. "I must," he writes to Derby in May, 1876, "again complain of the want of order and discipline in your Office[1]." And, two months later, the reproof is even more peremptory. "I must again complain of the management of your Office, and request your personal attention to it[2]." Then, of the Diplomatists— Harris, Buchanan, Odo Russell and others: "I wish we could get rid of the whole lot. They seem to me quite useless[3]."

It was during Derby's term of office, therefore, and with Beaconsfield's countenance, that Queen Victoria must be reckoned to have asserted most overtly that theory of her place in the direction of Foreign Affairs which she had learnt from the Prince Consort and the Prince Consort from Stockmar; and it may probably be no exaggeration to say that at no time during the nineteenth century was the conduct of Foreign Affairs regulated on lines so monarchical. It is not the Wellesley incident alone that has to be considered. At one of the most critical Cabinet discussions—that of January 12th, 1878—the debate was initiated by a letter from the Queen, in which she urged that the national honour required an immediate decision to defend Constantinople, and claimed that "the feeling of the nation" was behind her—and this, it must be remembered, at a time when opinion in the country was sharply divided and opinion in the Cabinet far from unanimous[4]. Even if we prefer to put the matter the other way and argue that the Queen was only sustaining the views of the Prime-Minister, this makes no considerable difference. The Sovereign does not exist to lead a party in the Cabinet. Whatever the actual rights and wrongs of the particular issue, the position of the Foreign Secretary would appear to be unfairly prejudiced if the authority and prestige of the Crown are used against him. Beaconsfield's action had, in fact, extended, not only the power of the Crown, but the function of the Prime-Minister. As his biographer puts it: "Since the crisis at the end of January (1878)...the Prime-Minister himself openly conducted the

---

[1] Buckle, *Life of Disraeli*, VI. 23.   [2] *Ibid*. VI. 44.
[3] *Ibid*. VI. 178.   [4] *Ibid*. VI. 219.

Eastern policy of the country in the Cabinet, leaving to the Foreign Secretary the part, for which he was pre-eminently fitted, of critic-in-chief, sometimes captious, but often helpful[1]."

In such circumstances no one could have expected the Foreign Office to give satisfactory expression to the wishes of the Government; and Beaconsfield's discontent had, in fact, from an early stage, reached, as we have seen, beyond Derby to the permanent officials. When Derby was gone, there still remained "the Hammonds and the Tenterdens[2]"; and the Prime-Minister welcomed Salisbury's famous Circular Despatch as a blow at that "Foreign Office jargon," in which Foreign Policy had been expressed for the last decade. Thus, when reviewing the results of his own Administration as it closed in 1880, Beaconsfield esteemed it the special merit of Salisbury's first Foreign Secretaryship that the permanent officials had not had their way, but had been brought into subjection by one who "acted for himself[3]."

Salisbury's method of showing himself master in his own house entailed, however, nothing in the nature of petty interference. If the Prime-Minister was right in thinking him the author of a new and better régime, he brought this about by example rather than by precept, by doing his own work and leaving others to do theirs. The Foreign Office Clerks, if Marvin is to be believed[4], had expected at his coming to be chastised with the whips and scorpions of the Palmerston system, but found him in fact as easy-going as Derby had been before him. The general impression that Salisbury gave to his staff, or at least to the junior members of it, is probably best described as Olympian. He did not concern himself much with the smaller matters of administration; and carping critics complained that his Private Secretary had grown too powerful[5]. Certainly, Philip Currie was an important person, even in the days when "Monty" Corry was extending the influence and reputation of Private Secretaries beyond anything known before; and, in his time, and pretty certainly on his Chief's suggestion, appointments appear to have been based upon other considerations than length of service[6]. Salisbury would certainly have set the interests of the country before those of the individual; and it may be suspected that he rated the average British diplomatist of his time rather low. But there appears to be little or nothing in his nominations of which the Diplomatic Service, as a Service, had

[1] Buckle, *Life of Disraeli*, VI. 247.
[2] *Ibid.* VI. 282.   [3] *Ibid.* VI. 254.
[4] *Our Public Offices*, p. 235.   [5] *Foreign Office Sketches*, p. 37.
[6] See for the current gossip of the time *Foreign Office Sketches*, pp. 37, 38.

any occasion to complain. Lytton was a diplomatist by profession and Drummond Wolff at any rate by experience, while Macdonald, who went to Peking, had the soldier's training and disposition which were required by the time and place. The case of Dufferin, whom Salisbury sent to Petersburg in 1879, is the likeliest to be quoted against him; but there have been instances in our own time of men of far less eminence receiving posts of as great consequence. And upon the principal British Representatives abroad he lavished those infinite pains which have been quaintly suggested as the test and attribute of genius. In the vast private correspondence which he carried on with the Ambassadors of his time, there is apparent a desire to convince as well as an obligation to instruct. He probably felt that, in order to put a case well or push it thoroughly, an agent generally needs to feel assured of its merits; and not the less if he serves a principal who expects men to exercise judgment and take responsibility. But, however this may be, there can be no doubt that Salisbury considerably developed a practice which, as we have seen, had been common in Palmerston's day and before it.

Clarendon, in his evidence before the Select Committee of 1861, had declared that it was totally impossible to carry on the business of the Foreign Office with British Ministers abroad except by writing private letters; but he had at the same time laid down the canon that those private letters should "never supersede the public instructions, or take the place of them, or be in any respect a substitute for them[1]." Salisbury's practice, involving as it does the recognition of a class of communications intermediate between private letters in Clarendon's sense and despatches eventually published, is not in perfect accord with the latter clauses of this theory of procedure. Confidential instructions, conveyed as a rule by letter, played in his time an immensely important part in the conduct of foreign business; and in his private correspondence the Historical Manuscripts Commission of a century hence will find material for several new volumes of Cecil Papers, Salisbury's own personal contribution representing, perhaps, twenty or twenty-five per cent. of the whole[2]. He had

[1] *Report Select Comm. Diplom. Service*, 1861, Min. of Ev., Q. 988. It is open to dispute whether Clarendon really adhered to his own canons in practice. The important proposals for disarmament in 1870 were conveyed to Bismarck through the medium only of a private letter (see Newton, *Life of Lord Lyons*, 1. pp. 251–6).

[2] Lord Lyons, among diplomatists, was also responsible for developing the system of private letters. Dilke (*4th Report Civil Establ. Comm.* 1890, Min. of Ev., Q. 29,158) says but, I am assured, with some exaggeration: "He (Lord L.) carried on his work chiefly by private letters in his own hand."

always written easily and with distinction; and one may doubt whether, even if inclination were to prompt, time and circumstance will ever agâin allow a Foreign Secretary to write in the same manner or in the same measure. None of his successors, at all events—neither Lord Rosebery nor Lord Lansdowne, nor Lord Grey, nor Lord Balfour —appears to have attempted to carry on a correspondence on the same scale; and in Lord Grey's case certainly, the burden of this delicate branch of diplomatic work was largely left in the hands of the Permanent Under-Secretary. It only remains to add, in this connexion, that private letters falling under this head can be, and sometimes are, converted into public despatches for presentation to Parliament, but of course with the consent and subject to the revision of the Ambassador or Minister concerned[1].

Just as the bent of Salisbury's mind was against interference with individuals, so the character of his policy was towards isolation among nations. He rejected, as we now know, an Alliance with Germany, in 1879, soon after he came into office; he had not concluded the *Entente* with France when he left office in 1901; while, as was apparent during the Boer War, the Concert of Europe, which was much spoken of in his time, acted rather as an instrument for the castigation of the Smaller Powers of the Continent than as an insurance against the hostility of the Greater. Isolation was, therefore, a policy not without risks, though justified by the event. In the Near East Salisbury's attitude, as he was himself to point out, had at the beginning been influenced by the traditional anti-Russian and pro-Turkish policy which, as we have seen, Clarendon had reluctantly taken over from Palmerston. But later, after Beaconsfield's death, and perhaps in the light of that fuller knowledge of Balkan affairs which he derived from his intimacy with Sir William White, he seemed disposed to favour the creation of autonomous Christian States around the Lower Danube rather than Elliot's and Layard's attempt to reform and resuscitate the Turks. Always, however, the motive of his policy was to be found in the political interests as opposed to the political sympathies of Great Britain; and in this way his treatment of Foreign Affairs is at the opposite pole from that of Palmerston or Gladstone.

It is an apparent rather than a real descent to turn from these high issues to notice certain little commonsense changes which Salisbury effected in the habits of the Foreign Office. A war seems greater

[1] *4th Report Civil Establ. Comm.* 1890, p. 135.

than a milk-bill, though the thousands immediately slain by the one are as nothing to the millions ultimately preserved by the other. And an extension of the use of the printing press, or the introduction of typists and typewriters, may fairly be reckoned, by the historian of an Office, to be stupendous events beside the forgotten incidents and forsaken policies which once seemed all-important in the high circles of the diplomatic world. It was possibly the prolonged Cabinet crisis of 1876–8, with its attendant urgency of information, which caused Salisbury to introduce the practice of printing Foreign Office telegrams for circulation to the Cabinet. The Office had for years possessed its own confidential printers—Messrs Harrison; and to a Department manned by their staff, and managed by that same P. S. King whose name subsequently became familiar to purchasers of Government publications, were confided such secrets of State as passed into print. The measure of their virtue as a firm, or perhaps of our virtue as a nation, is to be read in Hertslet's account of the visit of two French gentlemen, sent by their Government, sometime in the 'eighties of the last century, to study these particular domestic arrangements of "perfidious Albion."[1] With cries of surprise and uplifted hands, the strangers expressed their wonder at what they found, and were above measure astonished that such confidence should be successful. Since 1843, when apparently the first series of confidential print for the use of the Foreign Office was issued under the title of "Affairs of Serbia," the practice of printing confidential matter had in fact been steadily advancing. But it was Salisbury's decision which gave it extra-Departmental importance; and, since his time information, disseminated discreetly according to the dignity or the special interests of the Minister or official concerned, has travelled round Whitehall within a few hours of its reception.

There was another little innovation which Salisbury tried—the use by his Private Secretary of a printed stamp with his monogram on it in order to relieve him from the obligation of putting his initial to innumerable documents of inconsiderable importance[2]. A labour-saving device of more far-reaching consequence appeared in 1889. That which Lord Bryce, when Under-Secretary, had desired to see but had not seen[3]—a typist—Salisbury was bold enough to brave convention and introduce. Her name[4] is still remembered,

---

[1] Hertslet, *Recollections of the Old Foreign Office*, p. 50.
[2] *4th Report Civil Establ. Comm.* 1890, Min. of Ev., Q. 29,252.
[3] *Ibid.* Q. 27,907.   [4] Mrs Fulcher.

the better that she lived to become the head of a Typists' Department. Printing was hardly a greater benefit to the world than typewriting has been to the Foreign Office. All the need for those clear, clerkly hands upon which Palmerston had so much insisted, disappeared, and with it the labour of copying the same document three or four times over if occasion required. Salisbury, though a Conservative, had proved himself, in fact, to be one of the most radical of administrative reformers. Not so the Queen! To the end, Victoria required papers sent for her inspection to be inscribed with a pen, unless, indeed, they were already in print.

Granville returned to the Foreign Office with the restoration of Gladstone to power in 1880. He was assisted by two capable lieutenants, of whom a word must now be said. Sir Charles Dilke was Parliamentary Under-Secretary between 1880 and 1882, Sir Julian (afterwards Lord) Pauncefote Permanent Under-Secretary from 1882 to 1889. The abilities of the former were recognised by Granville as being on the Cabinet level[1]; and it was doubtless in order to give him a larger sphere of influence, as well as to satisfy the demand in Parliament for a more capable exponent of commercial matters, that the Commercial Department of the Foreign Office was placed very much under his control[2]. This Department had sprung into importance in that unlucky hour of 1872 when the advice of Sir Louis Mallet, a very distinguished Civil Servant and the author, with Morier, of the Anglo-Austrian Commercial Treaty of 1865, was accepted, and the work of the Board of Trade relating to commerce overseas was transferred to the Foreign Office. Mallet had dreamed that concentration would spell energy, and that the elimination of rivalry, or at least of overlapping, would promote the policy of cosmopolitan Free-trade, whose prospects in France, in Germany and in Austria have never been more fair than in the 'sixties and the 'seventies of the last century[3]. He was to be disappointed. The puzzle, which still torments Whitehall, how to apportion business, at once Foreign and Commercial, between the Ministries of Trade and of Foreign Affairs, was not to be solved by mere administrative shuffles. Perhaps, if he had himself been moved to the Foreign Office, together with the fine library of economics of which the Board of Trade was possessed, things might have fallen

---

[1] Gwynn and Tuckwell, *Life of Sir Charles Dilke*, I. 311.
[2] *Ibid.* p. 349.
[3] For an account of Mallet's theories see B. Mallet's *Sir Louis Mallet*, ch. ii, and Wemyss, *Memoirs of Sir Robert Morier*, II. 6, 7.

out otherwise. As it was, in spite of the efforts of Spring-Rice[1] and others, coma presently attacked the new Department; and, in the end, the old dualism was revived.

Dilke came on the scene too late to save the situation. He did not expect his industrious negotiations for a new commercial treaty with France to prove successful; and in fact they failed with the fall of Gambetta. A year later he was himself transferred to the Local Government Board, retaining, however, a kind of watching brief in Parliament on behalf of the Foreign Office[2], which had known how to value his wide information and painfully thorough grasp of detail. It was one of his services to the Department that he had forced the administration of Cyprus, then lately acquired, upon the Colonial Office, in spite of the opposition of Currie, who, as head of the Turkish branch of Foreign business, appears to have enjoyed the exercise of such administrative functions as those for which the island afforded occasion. The matter would not call for notice here, were it not that it illustrates the ill-defined borderland that exists between Colonial and Foreign Affairs. Granville had to pay in reputation the price of this uncertainty before he ceased to be Foreign Secretary. His diplomacy brought Egypt, in the years between 1881 and 1885, within the sphere of British influence; but it was rather Departmental confusion than Constitutional justice which caused the blame for the events culminating in the death of Gordon to be laid at Granville's door; and, though the exact point at which Diplomatic responsibility ends and Administrative responsibility begins may be as hard to ascertain precisely as the point of time where day dissolves into night, still it is true that the burden of Egypt was even then, and much more afterwards, in the nature of a Colonial rather than a Foreign Affair. And it is, perhaps, true to say that of the four Departments of State, with which the Foreign Office is thrown into the closest contact—the Admiralty, the War Office, the Board of Trade, and the Colonial Office—the last is that to which its relation is the most obscure and the worst-defined.

Pauncefote, a man, like Dilke, of vast industry and much solid distinction, became the Permanent in the same year in which Dilke ceased to be the Parliamentary Under-Secretary for Foreign Affairs. A barrister by profession, he had been brought over by Derby from

[1] Hon. T. C. W. Spring-Rice, appointed Superintendent of the Commercial and Consular Dept. of the F.O. in 1866.
[2] Gwynne and Tuckwell, *Life of Sir Charles Dilke*, I. 325.

the Colonial to the Foreign Office in 1876 to fill the position of Legal Assistant Under-Secretary—a post newly created in accordance with the recommendations of the Committee on Legal Establishments of 1875. Up to this time, it had been the custom to refer matters of Law to the Queen's Advocate; and, where cases involve important principles of international law or are likely to become the subject of debate in Parliament and consequently to require the advocacy of the Attorney or Solicitor-General, they are, to this day, referred to the Law Officers of the Crown. But, for the transaction of less important business, there was an obvious convenience in having a lawyer in the Department, and, after Pauncefote's promotion to be Permanent Under-Secretary and in view of the increasing legal business of the Office in connexion with the interests of British subjects abroad (such as claims for injury to person or property or the vindication of trade-concessions), the post of "Counsel[1]," or more popularly and incorrectly of "Legal Assistant" to the Foreign Office, was established in 1886, the style being changed, about 1893, to that of Legal Adviser.

The Foreign Office officials of the 'eighties of the last century are said to have feared the introduction of a lawyer into the Department; and they had some reason for their apprehension. Pauncefote, with his tact, his capacity for work, his knowledge of law and gift for languages, soon showed himself to be as good a man as there was in the Office. So, when Tenterden went, Granville gave him the vacant post of Permanent Under-Secretary. He held it for the next six years until, in 1889, he was appointed Ambassador at Washington. His promotion created a precedent and marked another stage in the growing importance of the Permanent Under-Secretary. The succession fell to Currie, who, however, presently followed along the same path as his predecessor, being nominated as Ambassador to Constantinople in 1894, and subsequently to Rome. His place was taken by Lord Sanderson, of whom, when still in the Turkish department, Salisbury had written to Beaconsfield that he was "the best clerk in the office[2]." The principle of interchangeability was now becoming so well-established that the case of Lord Sanderson, who never left the Foreign Office after he became a Senior Clerk, appears anomalous rather than regular. Even Assistant Under-Secretaries began to be appointed to high diplomatic posts; Bertie went to Paris, and Sir Francis Villiers

---

[1] *Report Civil Establ. Comm.* 1890, Q. 28,664.
[2] Salisbury to Beaconsfield, May 12th, 1879. (Unpublished.)

to Brussels. It might have been conjectured that Dilke's opinion[1] that an abler class of men entered the Foreign Office than the Diplomatic Service was gaining ground. But the diplomatists were to have their revenge in 1906 on Lord Sanderson's retirement, when Sir Charles Hardinge[2] became Permanent Under-Secretary with a rather increased concentration of power in his hands; and again, after Lord Hardinge had been .appointed Viceroy of India, when Sir Arthur Nicolson[3], of whom M. Sazonoff had said that no foreigner had ever exercised so great an influence in Russia[4], was given the post thus rendered vacant. But, from whatever source nominees were selected, it was at least plain enough that the office of Permanent Under-Secretary for Foreign Affairs had, by the beginning of the twentieth century, grown to be second to very few, if to any, others in dignity and consequence; and, had there remained any doubt upon this point, it must have been finally dispelled by the reappointment to the post of Lord Hardinge on the termination of his viceroyalty in India in 1916.

Granville's third Foreign Secretaryship was distinguished by one or two Departmental changes which deserve notice in passing. The most important, at least at the time, was the reorganisation of the business of the Office. From 1881 the work of the eight Divisions or Departments of the Office was arranged in this way. The Library, the Chief Clerk's, the Commercial, the Consular and the Treaty Departments continued to do much what they had done before, the Consular Department carrying on all the business connected with the suppression of the Slave Trade and undertaking, besides, the affairs connected with the East and West Coasts of Africa. But the geographical considerations which governed the distribution of business in the more strictly political Departments were vastly simplified by dividing the world under the headings of Eastern, Western and American; the Eastern including, besides Eastern Europe, Asiatic Turkey, Persia, Central Asia, Egypt and Tripoli; the Western, besides Western Europe, Morocco, Algiers, Tunis, and the Pacific Islands; and the American, besides the Americas, China, Japan and Siam. By 1900, however, these three last-named countries had been separated off and formed into a Far

---

[1] 4th Report Civil Establ. Comm. 1890, Min. of Ev., Q. 29,197.
[2] Now Lord Hardinge of Penshurst.
[3] Now Lord Carnock.
[4] "No foreigner ever exercised so great an influence in Russia, and this influence had its power in his moral nature. I had this from M. Sazonoff himself." *Mirrors of Downing Street*, p. 32.

Eastern Department; while part, though not all[1], of the African business, both East and West, had been assembled in an African Department.

We are now drawing towards the end of the story; but, for the sake of continuity and comparison, it seems worth while to pass, for a moment, beyond our furthest limit and to notice how the arrangements of 1881 have been modified by time and the Great War. In the Foreign Office of 1922, the Chief Clerk's Department, the Treaty Department, the Library, and the Consular Department remain as before, but Commercial business has, as we shall see, largely migrated to the Department of Overseas Trade, though the various territorial Departments still deal with the broad principles of British Commercial policy and sometimes even afford assistance to British firms operating in foreign countries by diplomatic intervention. For the rest, the Eastern Department has become Eastern and Egyptian. The Far Eastern has annexed Cambodia. The Western has added the business relating to the League of Nations. The American, while excluding from its sphere negotiations with foreign Colonies, has absorbed the African. And, besides, there has come into being a Central European Department concerned with the affairs of Germany, Austria, Hungary, Italy, Albania, Czecho-Slovakia, Jugo-Slavia, Roumania, Bulgaria and Greece; and a Northern Department occupied with Russia, Finland, Sweden, Norway, Denmark, Poland and the Baltic States. To furnish these services there were required in 1919 well over a hundred officials, of whom some seventy were in the First, and over forty in the Second, Division. But some relief of business has since been afforded by the removal of certain countries in the Middle East from the sphere of the Foreign to that of the Colonial Office—a step which illustrates once again the confusion existing as to their proper spheres of business.

In the year (1881) in which Granville regrouped the work of his Office there was introduced into it the class of Lower or Second Division Clerks. They must be distinguished from the Supplementary Clerks, whom they eventually supplanted, and who, since Clarendon's time, had discharged much of the non-confidential work of the Office. The Chief Clerk's Department, where they performed the work of accountants, was the first to use them[2]; and within a decade they numbered seventeen as against sixteen Supplementary Clerks and thirty-six Clerks "on the establishment," or, which is

---

[1] Egypt, Abyssinia, Somaliland and Tunis were excepted.
[2] 5th Report Civil Service Comm. 1914, Min. of Ev., Q. 36,858.

the same thing, of the First Division[1]. Their advent had been instigated by economy; and they were not so well paid as the Supplementary Clerks, whose business, in the capacity and under the title of Staff Clerks, they gradually took over at reduced salaries. A Supplementary Clerk in 1881 might be getting £650 a year; no Staff Clerk in 1914 was receiving more than £500[2], nor could he look to promotion into the First Division as anything but a remote possibility. The terms were, perhaps, not unreasonable, and the candidates for Second Division Clerkships were certainly aware of them; but the dissatisfaction with the conditions of their service of this class of officials, forming, as they did a generation after they were instituted, one half of the Foreign Office Staff, is one of the most striking features of the evidence brought before the Royal Commission on the Civil Service of 1914. They had evidently outgrown that stage of development when the routine of a trade or profession appears agreeable, and security of employment, with a pension attached, appears sufficient. They wished to do more interesting work and to receive better pay; and they have now so far attained their object that promotion into the First Division has become for them a possible, if an infrequent, contingency.

There was another change in the Foreign Service arrangements for which Granville was responsible. From the beginning of his last term at the Foreign Office and on his initiative, the examination for the Diplomatic Service became competitive among the nominees of the Foreign Secretary. In other words, a selection was made from among, as a rule, three or four[3] young men, possessed of incomes of not less than four hundred a year, the knowledge of two or three foreign languages, some familiarity with the Graces, and a nodding acquaintance with the Muses. It was a system not seriously challenged till our own time.

Granville's more prominent connexion with the Egyptian policy of the Government affected, as we have seen, the public opinion of his capacity; and, when, after Salisbury's brief tenure of the Foreign Secretaryship in that Administration which is known significantly as the "Ministry of Caretakers," the Liberals returned to power, it was Lord Rosebery, and not Granville, whom Gladstone placed at the head of Foreign Affairs. The incoming Minister had little time, and

---

[1] 4th Report Civil Establ. Comm. 1890, Min. of Ev., Q. 26,220. Besides those mentioned in the text, the F.O. Staff in 1889 included ten temporary Clerks.
[2] 5th Report Civil Service Comm. 1914. App. pp. 311, 312.
[3] 5th Report Civil Service Comm. 1914, p. 7.

perhaps less opportunity, either in the six months of 1886 or in the eighteen months from August, 1892, during which he was Foreign Secretary for the second time, to make any deep impression upon the Foreign Policy of the country. Like Fox, the object of his admiration, this latest offspring of the Whigs was, at the least, a chief in whom his staff could not fail to be interested and who could fascinate them at will. His immediate successor formed in every way a contrast. Lord Iddesleigh, if not a dying man, was at least one from whom life was fast receding, when he came to the Foreign Office in the late summer of 1886. And he was offered the post only on peculiar terms; for Salisbury seems to have reserved to himself a right of supervision exceeding that generally exercised by a Prime-Minister[1]. It proved an unhappy and unsuccessful arrangement; and the Premier took the opportunity of the reconstruction of the Ministry, on Lord Randolph Churchill's resignation in December, to resume direct control of Foreign Affairs, at once in his eyes the most congenial and the most important business of Government.

Salisbury's third tenure of the Foreign Secretaryship is of some importance in the history of the Foreign Office. It was the period, in the first place, when the Diplomatic Service really justified itself in the sight of all men by the negotiation of a bloodless division of the African Continent in harmony with France and Germany—an achievement which owed much to the extreme efficiency of Sir Percy Anderson, a man once of great, but now of rather forgotten, reputation. But the interest of Departmental history, at this time, centres principally in the Ridley Commission, which sat, between 1886 and 1890, to consider the general condition of the Civil Service. It was not in point of *personnel* a very distinguished Commission, nor did all its suggestions perhaps disclose remarkable insight; but it showed an appreciation of the drift of the time-spirit by recommending the amalgamation of the Foreign Office and the Diplomatic Service. This last measure would have involved an entrance examination common to both, and the abolition of the £400 a year income-qualification required of candidates for diplomacy. Attachés and Foreign Office Clerks would thenceforward have alike received £100 during a first year of probation. Attachés of over a year's standing and Second and Third Secretaries would have been graded with Junior Clerks at a salary of £200, rising annually by £20 till £500 was reached. And, on the same principle, Secretaries of Legation would have

[1] W. S. Churchill, *Life of Lord Randolph Churchill*, p. 556.

ranked with First Division Clerks in the second grade and have received from £600, rising by £25 a year, to £800; while Secretaries of Embassy would have been bracketed with First Division Clerks of the highest grade and have been in receipt of salaries rising by £50 a year from £850 to £1000. By the time this latter point in his career was reached, the idea was that a man's qualities would have determined his future, and that he would be finally told off for service at home or abroad as might seem best. For the rest, the Committee showed a great regard for economy, expedited the extinction of the Supplementary Clerk, advised the use of typewriters, foretold a reduction of staff owing to the increased mobility of labour, if the amalgamation of the two branches of the Foreign Service was decided on, and expressed satisfaction at the distribution of business between the Departments concerned with foreign trade—a distribution based upon the theory that the Foreign Office should occupy itself with the negotiation of commercial treaties and the Board of Trade with the publication of commercial information. Of all the plans of the Commission, a very trifling part was at that time put into effect. In 1892, however, the examinations for Foreign Office Clerkships and the Diplomatic Service became identical, the lists of candidates remaining distinct.

In that same year Lord Rosebery became Foreign Secretary for the second time; but, when he accepted the Premiership on Gladstone's retirement, Kimberley took his place at the Foreign Office. As Lord Wodehouse, Kimberley has already crossed our path; and it was presumably because of his earlier services, that he was thought to be the proper person to direct Foreign Affairs. The Parliamentary Under-Secretaryship was tending, with the growing interest of the House of Commons in Foreign Policy, to become, more frequently than it had been, the road to the Foreign Secretaryship. Lord Grey, who was Under-Secretary from 1892 to 1895, and Lord Curzon who followed him, were both presently to be Foreign Secretaries. In Kimberley's case the appointment fulfilled for fifteen months the ambition of a lifetime[1], and discovered, to those who were close enough to him to perceive it, a capacity for business in its holder of which the public had no real appreciation.

When the Unionist Government was formed in 1895, Salisbury again took the Foreign Office into his own hands, relinquishing it, however, on account of failing health in the last year or two of his public life, in favour of Lord Lansdowne. It fell, therefore, to this fine

[1] Fitzmaurice, *Life of the 2nd Earl Granville*, 1. 180.

French scholar, with French blood running in his veins, to reach that understanding with France, for which much of the diplomacy of the nineteenth century had been a preparation and of which the history of Europe since 1914 has been a partial vindication. To Continental and journalistic observers it sometimes seemed, indeed, that the Anglo-French *Entente* was the work of the Crown and not of the Cabinet. In reality, King Edward's part in the enterprise was that of an Ambassador, not of a Foreign Secretary—diplomatic, that is, as distinguished from political. By the time he ascended the Throne, the power to initiate or to obstruct a foreign policy had passed irrecoverably beyond the reach of the Crown. And his own influence upon Foreign Affairs fell, probably, as much short of that of his mother as it exceeded that of his son. The change reflected one side of that vast movement away from privilege and towards democracy which is the unexhausted commonplace of the age we live in.

The success of that movement seems to depend to a degree we have still imperfectly measured upon the wide extension and application of what passes at present for an academic outlook on life among people in general and men of affairs in particular; and Lord Lansdowne was only working along the line of sound contemporary development in directing his efforts towards the establishment of a liberal education as a *sine qua non* in the case of candidates for the diplomatic profession. His dominant idea in 1905, when, in consultation with the University authorities at Oxford and Cambridge, he caused the Foreign Service Examination to be assimilated to that common to the rest of the Civil Service, was "to eliminate the crammer[1]." And, though it was an assimilation and not an identification, the new rule, attended as it was by the raising of the minimum age of entry to twenty-two, had the effect of causing an honours degree at a University to become in practice assured. It was a corollary of this bid for the best abilities a University could provide, that in 1906 all the filing and registering of papers had been transferred to Second Division Clerks and all the copying to typists. A good education was no longer to be wasted on the serving of tables, and full confidence was at last reposed in the integrity of the once jealously excluded, and afterwards not less jealously admitted, class of auxiliary scribes.

[1] *App. 5th Report Civil Service Comm.* 1914, Min. of Ev., Q. 40,880.

VI.

Lord Lansdowne had made his tenure of the Foreign Office memorable, both in respect of Departmental and international history, and in both respects his successor completed and crowned his work. Departmentally, Sir Edward Grey[1] was responsible for the final blow at patronage. In 1907, the power to give nominations for the Diplomatic Service was placed in the hands of a Board of Selection, consisting always of the Permanent Under-Secretary of State and of the Private Secretary to the Secretary of State at the moment, but containing, besides, other members appointed specially for each of the biennial sittings[2]. Any young man, thenceforward, was allowed, on application to the Foreign Secretary, to present himself before the Board of Selection; and any young man who could show good recommendations—from the Head of his College, for instance, or other people of standing—would thenceforward be allowed by the Foreign Secretary, acting on the advice of the Board of Selection, to come up for examination, regardless of the social position of his parents[3]. There was a reservation left in regard to the children of aliens.

Patronage was gone; a fragment of privilege remained. The candidate for the Diplomatic Service was still required to possess an income of £400 a year; and it was against this requirement in particular that the Civil Service Commission of 1914 set its face. The principal, though not quite unanimous[4], recommendation of the Commissioners was that this property qualification should be abolished. It is to be presumed that they had counted the cost—£50,000 or £60,000 a year, perhaps[5], with money values where they stood when the Report was drawn up, but in these days very much more. Whether, however, the tradition, which has so long caused the Diplomatic Service to be closely associated with the greater Public Schools and the older Universities can be destroyed by the removal of a financial disability, is a matter which stands or falls with the truth or falsehood of the aphorism that it is the world of fashion which governs the world of men. The evidence, such as it is and so far as it goes, suggests that the connexion which Democracy would sever is not to be cut with the knife of finance; for the Foreign Office itself, where there is

[1] Now Viscount Grey of Fallodon.
[2] App. 5th Report Civil Service Comm. 1914, Min. of Ev., Qs. 40,783, 40,796.
[3] Ibid. Qs. 40,785, 40,799.
[4] See for the other view Mr Arthur Boutwood's thoughtful remarks on p. 43 of the 5th Report Civil Service Comm. 1914 (Cd. 7748).
[5] Ibid. Min. of Ev., Q. 36,680.

no property qualification, was still, in the years between 1908 and 1914, recruiting its Clerks mainly among Etonians[1].

All this is something of a digression, and we have still to touch on one or two other features of Lord Grey's administration of the Foreign Office. Circumstances made it much less easy for him to pursue a Liberal policy on the wide sea of Foreign Affairs than in the narrow waters of Departmental organisation, where the current was flowing easily and steadily in the desired direction. The gradual enlargement of the understanding with France involved an understanding also with the great enemy of Liberalism—the Government of Russia—and this, by a curious irony, was Lord Grey's special contribution to the regrouping of European forces that was going on. Time had not failed of its revenges; and British Diplomacy was falling into line with that of those very two countries in whose advancement Castlereagh a century before had discerned the chief peril of Europe[2]. So necessary is it to remember that the foe of yesterday may be the friend of to-morrow, and that the national vices we mark down for reprobation in one age may seem no more than the negligible defects of out-balancing qualities in the next!

But Lord Grey was very much more than Lord Lansdowne's successor. If his diplomatic appointments were not above criticism and his consistency not beyond discussion, the broad effect of his presence at the Foreign Office served greatly to strengthen the higher tradition of the British Foreign Service. He prepared the way for that new orientation of policy which is implicit in the establishment and maintenance of the League of Nations. In spite of what the Foreign Press is accustomed to say, British Foreign Policy, from the day when Palmerston fell in 1851 until the exigencies of the Great War scattered all the principles of international ethics, had moved on a higher plane than that either of the friends or enemies of England. Thus the secret Department of the Post Office, which came into evidence in 1844 in connexion with the opening of Mazzini's letters and which was really an annexe, though an unacknowledged one, of the British Foreign Office, disappeared at that time; the amount of Secret Service money placed by Parliament at the disposal of the Foreign Office in the latter part of the nineteenth century was trifling; and there is reason to believe that during this period it was not employed for purchasing or otherwise obtaining political information. The

[1] 5th Report Civil Service Comm. Min. of Ev., Q. 40,792.
[2] Alison, Lives of Castlereagh and Stewart, II. 633.

sentiment, indeed, of English Foreign Secretaries and Ambassadors alike ran counter to such methods perhaps more often than not.

"I can state from my own personal knowledge," says Sir Horace Rumbold, writing in 1903, "that at one of the most important Courts of Europe certain sources of absolutely accurate information which we had procured with difficulty and commanded for a short period many years ago were lost to us through the conscientious scruples of an ambassador (now long since dead) who deliberately declined to sanction the means that were requisite to keep them flowing as they were doing to our great advantage[1]."

And Count Herbert Bismarck, who had no bad opportunity for judging, considered this scrupulous temper of mind to be not the idiosyncrasy of an individual, but the characteristic of a nation. In conversation with Granville, he expressed his inability to understand how English diplomacy worked at all, seeing, as he said, that "you never bribe and...never give decorations[2]." The answer is that true diplomacy takes long views. Sometimes defeated and seemingly stultified in its generation, it bides its time and is avenged. For no immediate advantage is permanently so valuable as keeping faith; no diplomatic asset so precious as the reputation of honour and justice; nor does any national interest finally supersede the importance of international solidarity.

VII.

It was a strong sensibility to such considerations on Lord Grey's part, coupled with a special regard for the friendship of America— in which, by a happy coincidence, his successor, Mr Balfour[3], concurred—that made his Foreign Policy, in some sense, a preparation for the idea of the League of Nations—an idea which he afterwards championed with passionate conviction as the only hope of the world, but which, it is clear, demands a standard of disinterestedness and fair-dealing probably unknown to any existing Foreign Ministry. The British Foreign Office may perhaps be said to have treated it more seriously or at least more practically than any other. It was from the ranks of English diplomatists that the Secretary of the League[4] was chosen, and in the person of a very distinguished ex-Premier and ex-Foreign Secretary that the first British Representative on the Council of the League was found[5]; while some of the drafting of the League's Constitution, and much of the advocacy of the League's principles devolved upon a lawyer, who had been

[1] Sir H. Rumbold, *Further Recollections of a Diplomatist*, p. 274.   [2] *Ibid.*
[3] Now Earl of Balfour.   [4] Sir Eric Drummond.   [5] Lord Balfour.

Lord Grey's Under-Secretary and had subsequently, while retaining the Under-Secretaryship, entered the Cabinet as Minister of Blockade[1]. But over the relationship of the League of Nations and the Foreign Office there still hangs an obscurity, which it is rash to seek to penetrate, at least until war-time conditions have wholly passed away, and we can see how far "diplomacy by conference[2]" is going to prove a substitute for the old diplomacy through accredited agents. Both on this head and in respect to that development of our Imperial Constitution to which Lord Grey gave explicit expression in the statement, made in 1921, that "the British Government have given up the practice which they formerly exercised of deciding foreign policy for themselves, without consultation with the Dominions[3]," there is much need of further elucidation.

It fell to Lord Robert Cecil on July 31st, 1918, to introduce to the notice of the House of Commons, in so far as they affected the Foreign Office, the recommendations of the Civil Service Commission—the Macdonnell Commission—which had reported in December, 1914. These recommendations—some trivial and some far-reaching—covered a wide range of suggestion. Among the larger changes that were advised was the fusion of the Foreign Office and Diplomatic Establishments into a single Foreign Service; the institution of a Promotions Committee, upon whose judgment the Foreign Secretary should rely when appointing to the higher posts in the profession; the substitution of a Senior and a Junior Clerical Class for the existing system of Second Division and Boy Clerks; the abolition, already alluded to, of the £400 a year property qualification for candidates for the Diplomatic Service; and the devolution of routine work at Embassies abroad to less highly trained officials. Of these five recommendations all but the second have now (1922) been acted upon. The principles underlying the Report were expounded in Lord Robert Cecil's speech, which contains the pregnant admission that Diplomacy, once a question between Court and Court, had now become a question between People and People, and might thus be said to mark the conclusion of one period of Foreign Office history and the initiation of another.

In that coming and probably more socialistic age, there is every

---

[1] Lord Robert Cecil. He was ultimately (July 19, 1918) created Assistant Secretary for Foreign Affairs—a post not previously known to the Constitution.
[2] See Sir M. Hankey, *Diplomacy by Conference*.
[3] Lord Grey at Berwick, *The Times*, October 11th, 1921.

reason to suppose that, among the Foreign Affairs of this country, trade must be a paramount concern; and there was, perhaps, no more important passage in Lord Robert's speech than the one in which he foreshadowed an increased attention on the part of the Foreign Office to British commercial interests. The Macdonnell Commission had, indeed, pressed the same point by recommending the promotion of the Clerk in control of Commercial and Consular affairs to the rank of an Assistant Under-Secretary with a salary of £1200; and it would be negligent to close this slight sketch of the development of Foreign Office organisation without some reference, however inadequate, to the British Consular Service. This branch of the Foreign Service had grown, as English institutions are apt to grow, largely unperceived—or at least so little perceived as to induce a high authority to assert, not long ago, that only so late as 1903 did it really become "a service[1]." And, if this is hyperbole, it is at least significant of the past relations between the State and Commerce that such a statement can be plausibly advanced. A historian, however, with any eye for development in his composition, would doubtless discover the ancestry of the General Consular Service amidst the commercial disputes and difficulties of the fifteenth century. The nationalisation of the Levant and Far Eastern Consular Services can be dated with less fear of dispute. The first was reconstituted by Currie in 1876 from the relics of the Levant Company which had perished in 1825; and the second was a legacy from the East India Company, which lost its monopoly of trade with China in 1834. These two auxiliary Consular organisations, operating originally the one in the Turkish empire, Persia, Greece and Morocco, the other in China, Japan and Siam, have afforded in the nature of things greater openings to talent than the General Service. The rigid line which the British Foreign Office, unlike the Foreign Offices of France and Germany, has endeavoured to draw between Diplomatic and Consular work, cannot easily be maintained in primitive countries where private interests and commercial business easily acquire the importance of political affairs; and, even if it could, a Consul-General, with a life's experience behind him of the language and customs of an oriental or uncivilised State, must, other things being approximately equal, always possess an immense advantage over a Diplomatist, dominated by Western culture and distracted by constantly shifting spheres of activity, even though the very insight he has gained may make him so much the less

[1] *British Year-Book of International Law*, 1920, p. 104.

acceptable to the Foreign Government affected. It is, anyhow, in the East that the romances of the Consular Services must be mostly looked for. Sir Rutherford Alcock, Sir Thomas Wade, Sir Harry Parkes, and Sir Robert Hart[1] among the dead; Sir Ernest Satow and Sir John Jordan among the living, made their way as Consuls or Student-interpreters in China and ended their careers as British Representatives at Pekin; and Mr G.H.Fitzmaurice, another Student-interpreter, after passing through a series of Consular appointments in the Levant, gained, as First Dragoman of the Embassy at Constantinople, something of the position of an *éminence grise* behind the successive figures of his Chiefs. Such cases can only with difficulty, if at all, be paralleled further west, where conditions are different and the inner circle of diplomatic appointments is more highly prized and more jealously guarded. Sir Joseph Archer Crowe, for example, admittedly a singularly able man, was never transferred from Consular to political business proper. And even Sir William White, whose diplomatic talent was perhaps the most remarkable at any time disclosed by the members of the Consular Services, moved eastwards as his career advanced and made his reputation where perhaps he could alone have made it, as Ambassador to the Porte. To the vast mass of Consular officials Fortune, of course, offers as a rule no such prize as his. Their duties revolve mainly round the troubles of travellers, the needs of merchants and—in seaports—the engagement, discharge, or misconduct of merchant-seamen.

Consuls were recruited, until 1856, when Clarendon introduced a qualifying test, on no particular principle. There were no exact restrictions in the matter of age, or specific requirements in that of education. A merchant —and since the salaries were small, not probably a very successful merchant —would be given a consulship by the favour of the Foreign Secretary. He could count upon no promotion or rise of salary, but his opportunities for plunder were enormous; and he sometimes used them[2]. Vice-Consuls, though equally in theory nominees of the Secretary of State, were generally foreigners selected by the Consul from among the merchants of the district, and were often paid by him out of the fees he levied. In 1825 the Consular Act made an attempt to restrict both fees and rights of trading, but it proved abortive, as appears clearly enough from the recommendations of a Select Committee of 1858, which were themselves for the most part only made

---

[1] Hart, though best known as Inspector-General of the Chinese Customs, was British Minister from May to August, 1885.

[2] The Consul-General in the Brazils is alleged for instance in *The Times* of July 12th, 1822, to have made £57,567 in six years and apparently acknowledged to £43,500 clear profit.

effective nearly twenty years later, after another Committee had sat and brought them back to recollection. Under the system obtaining in the 'seventies of the last century, the Levant and Far Eastern Services were thrown open to competition. In the General Consular Service, however, patronage continued, and was on occasions not unmixed with jobbery[1]. The patronage system was indeed, modified, in the case of the *Consuls de carrière*, by the qualifying test; but this was itself modified by the right reserved to the Secretary of State of appointing to Consular positions suitable persons of some standing. At relatively unimportant places, such persons would be chosen from among British or well-disposed native residents and, receiving honour instead of money for their services, would be allowed to engage in private trading—a privilege denied after 1877 to the *Consuls de carrière*.

This system was accepted in its main features by the Ridley Commission of 1890; but it fell under Parliamentary criticism, and pressure from this quarter induced Lord Lansdowne in 1903 to appoint a Departmental Committee, under the chairmanship of Sir W. H. Walrond, including Mr Bonar Law, Lord Cranborne, then Parliamentary Under-Secretary for Foreign Affairs. It was this Committee which has been credited[2] with converting the Consular establishment into a real Service by the substitution of the principle of limited competition for that of nomination and the qualifying test.

The Committee recommended that, in judging a man's qualifications, a certain preference should be accorded to candidates who had had the advantage of some business experience; but the difficulty of estimating in any direct manner the value of commercial training in any individual case, coupled with the evident disinclination of men with prospects in business to limit their ambitions to £1200 a year and residence abroad, appears to have rendered this suggestion in the main unfruitful[3]. It was the more unfortunate, because the absence from the Consular Service of men with commercial experience was, as the then President of the Associated Chambers of Commerce informed the Civil Service Commission of 1914, "the almost universal complaint and the chief criticism" brought by the Chambers against that Service[4]. Sir Algernon Firth went on to recommend as a remedy a return to patronage nominations, an official system of training after nomination and an increase of salaries. The latter two recommendations have received attention. After the report of the Walrond Committee the salaries of the General Consular Service had been elaborately graded: Consuls-general receiving, according to their class, £1200, £1000, or £800; Consuls £800 or £600; Vice-Consuls from £500 to £300 and from £450 to £350; salaries not inclusive, in the case of Vice-Consuls, of special local allowances at expensive posts[5]. This revised scale of pay, however, proved inadequate, particularly in view of rising prices, to enable

---

[1] See *The Quarterly Review*, 197, p. 602.
[2] *British Year Book of International Law*, 1920, p. 104.
[3] *5th Report Civil Service Comm.* 1914, Min. of Ev., Qs. 37,341, 41,948.
[4] *Ibid.* Q. 41,965.   [5] App. *5th Report Civil Service Comm.* 1914, p. 322.

Consuls to keep up such a standard of living as was required to enable them to study local trade conditions and to mix in leading mercantile circles to the best advantage. In 1912, another Departmental Committee, under the chairmanship of Sir Algernon Law, then at the head of the Commercial and Consular Department of the Foreign Office, recommended that a year's training at some large shipping-centre should be instituted in the case of probationer Vice-Consuls, and that Consuls in the lower grade should receive salaries rising by increases of £20 to £700, besides local allowances, on the understanding that men in this category, being still young and possibly unmarried, should be regularly allotted to the more unhealthy and less desirable posts. On passing out of the lower grade, at about the age of forty-five, and entering the grade carrying, after fifteen years' service, a salary of £800 a year, a Consul would thus be entitled to expect a more agreeable appointment and to feel himself finally relieved of the fear of an insanitary one. The Committee further advised the transfer of a considerable number of desirable posts, hitherto filled by Consuls receiving only £600, to the higher list; and a similar recommendation was made in the case of posts allotted to Consuls-General, so that a larger number of these functionaries would be stationed where salaries of £1200 and £1000 were to be earned, whilst the pay of even the lowest grade was, at the same time, to be raised from £800 to £900. All this was accepted, together with other changes too detailed for mention here[1], and there appears to be some reason to anticipate in due course a higher standard of Consular efficiency, even though Sir Algernon Law's drastic recommendation, based on large experience, that Consuls should be retired on pensions at the age of fifty, or at least fifty-five[2], is unlikely to be followed by an exhausted Exchequer.

At the heart of the whole question, however, there seems to some minds to lie a wider issue. It will be remembered that, under the influence of Mallet's large conception of a Free-Trade policy gradually to be forced upon the world by the conclusion of commercial treaties, analogous to the Anglo-French Treaty of 1860 and the Anglo-Austrian Treaty of 1865, the care of overseas commerce had been transferred from the Board of Trade to the Foreign Office in 1872. Of this arrangement the Ridley Commission of 1890 expressed approval.

"The Commercial Department of the Foreign Office," they said, "is one for negotiating commercial treaties; that of the Board of Trade for the publication of information. The Foreign Office by its reports from Secretaries of Legation and Consuls supplies the Board of Trade with a good deal of the material which the latter works up for publication, and the Board of Trade gives advice to the Foreign Office with regard to the negotiation of commercial treaties. There are daily communications between the two Offices on shipping and commercial questions, and the practice which at present prevails upon all these points only requires a little more extension to be completely satisfactory[3]."

[1] They will be found in the *App. 5th Report Civil Service Comm.* 1914.
[2] *App. 5th Report Civil Service Comm.* 1914, Q. 43,097.
[3] *4th Report Ridley Comm.* 1890, p. 7.

The Commissioners were mistaken. The representative functions of the Foreign Office and the Board of Trade, in relation to foreign commerce have never, from that day to this, been perfectly adjusted; and the Consul is the victim of their discord. Sometimes his work touches politics so closely as to make it difficult to remove him from the diplomatic organisation and the control of the local Embassy; and it is probable enough that, if he were so removed, he would lose much of the advantage in regard to matters of commerce which the countenance and aid of the Embassy now afford him[1]. On the other hand, his commercial energy would be likely to increase and his statistical information might, probably, be more up-to-date, if the Foreign Office were no longer to play the part of what has been described as a "post-office[2]" to his communications on matters of trade. As things are, he is the servant of two masters; but he is appointed, paid and promoted only by one, and there can be little doubt which, as a rule, he will serve the better. "The responsibility of the Foreign Office for the *personnel* of the Consular Service and its no more than political responsibility for its work," says a distinguished authority[3], "is the real vice of our Consular system, and, if the Board of Trade is to become solely responsible for the commercial work of the Consular Service, it must also become responsible for the *personnel* of that service."

Thus, as things were until recently, the commercial interests of the country suffered in fact all the disadvantages of a divided command. There were no less than three different centres of activity. There was, first, the Commercial Department of the Board of Trade—no Argus perhaps, but, as far as numbers were concerned, hundred-headed, which in the strong hands of Sir H. Llewellyn-Smith developed a formidable will of its own. Then, in the City was located the Advisory Committee on Commercial Intelligence ·attached to this Department—a mixed body composed of Board of Trade and Foreign Office officials, with some capable business-men as their colleagues. And finally, there was the Consular and Commercial Department of the Foreign Office—a body of eight or nine First Division Clerks, with a Controller at their head, on whose shoulders there was laid a most astonishing variety of business. Three members of the staff dealt with specifically Consular affairs, which included correspondence with the Consuls on practically all subjects other than political, commercial and matrimonial, and provided for the discipline and direction of the Consular service itself as well as for the administration of the Merchant Shipping Act[4]. The other half-dozen manned the Commercial and Sanitary Section, whose range of work extended over the most formidable array of matters from the general defence and support of British commercial interests, and the collection and distribution to other Government Departments of information on the finances, trade and industries of foreign countries, down to the

---

[1] *5th Report Civil Service Comm.* 1914, Q. 38,213.
[2] *5th Rep. Civil Service Comm.* 1914, Q. 38,213, pp. 165, 242. In some matters, however, the Consul communicates directly with the Board of Trade.
[3] Lord Eustace Percy, in *The New Europe*, May 15th, 1919, p. 104.
[4] App. *5th Report Civil Service Comm.* 1914, Min. of Ev., Q. 37,318.

protection abroad of wild birds and their plumage[1]. Business so multifarious cannot have left any great spirit of enterprise in the five or six industrious public servants who had to deal with it. And, in fact, behind the complimentary criticisms of the commercial experts who gave evidence in 1914, there is apparent the sense of something wanting, of some expectation unfulfilled, which finds, perhaps, its most cogent expression in the demand of Mr Hirst, then Editor of *The Economist*, that the Foreign Office should be itself, and not in cooperation with the Board of Trade, "a mirror of the nation...an intelligence department for foreign commerce...a kind of meteorological office for publishing conditions in foreign countries[2]." It was in the hope, therefore, of obviating organic defects, which became more sensible as the strain of the Great War increased, that—Mr Balfour being at the time at the Foreign Office, Sir Albert Stanley at the Board of Trade, and reconstruction in the air[3]—the Department of Overseas Trade—a mixed concern with a composite staff and a dual allegiance—was set up in 1917, and Sir Arthur Steel-Maitland placed at its head, with the rank of an additional Parliamentary Under-Secretary in both the Offices concerned.

Generally speaking, it seems clear that the Foreign Office has done either too much or too little in the matter of foreign trade. The creation of the Overseas Trade Department, was, at best, a doubtful compromise between the majority and minority reports of an inter-departmental Committee under the Chairmanship of Lord Faringdon. It may have been the best thing to be done, but it was not the best thing that could have been thought of. The commercial business of a nation of shop-keepers desiderates something better than divided counsels or distributed energy in the Government. It is, if we are candid with ourselves, in peace-time the greatest of all its Foreign Affairs, and, in time of War, as events were even then showing, the greatest of all its weapons, both of offence and of defence. To have realised the ideas of Mallet; to have made the Foreign Secretary an interested apostle of commercial treaties; to have brought under the roof of the Foreign Office, or into its nearest vicinity, that part of the Commercial Intelligence Branch of the Board of Trade concerned with the affairs of foreign countries; to have strengthened the Commercial and Consular Department of the Foreign Office both numerically and by the inclusion in it of some Consular officers; and to have stimulated the collection of commercial intelligence by the creation of "Commercial Counsellors" of diplomatic rank, resident abroad and connecting the Consulates with the Embassies and the Embassies with the Commercial Department—this was a policy, as some critics thought, from which more considerable results might have been expected than from the plan actually adopted.

It remains to make mention of two classes of officials, both reckoned, indeed, to belong to the Diplomatic and not the Consular Service, and both strings in the network designed to catch information about trade overseas—

[1] App. *5th Report Civil Service Comm.* 1914, Min. of Ev., Q. 37,339.
[2] *Ibid.* Qs. 40,610–11.
[3] See the Memorandum on the Further Organisation of Commercial Intelligence (Cd. 8715).

the Commercial Attaché and the Commercial Secretary. Joseph Archer Crowe, of whom we have already spoken, was the first Commercial Attaché and the originator of the idea of his office[1], which was actually established by Salisbury in 1879. The aim in view was to get comprehensive reports, both special and general, upon the commercial affairs of a foreign country which should be as different from the report of a Consul as the whole is different from its part. Originally the Commercial Attaché, himself probably an ex-Consul, or perhaps a Foreign Office Clerk[2], was attached to a particular Mission as one of the staff; but quite recently the sphere of his operations has been extended to cover a group of countries, and, in order to enable him to keep in close touch with English business houses, he remains resident in England during the great part of the year. This later development has produced the Commercial Secretary, a diplomatist told off to study the trade-returns and trade-openings of the country where he is stationed and to deal with the current commercial business of the Mission. He, too, reports to the Foreign Office, being responsible for the commercial section appended to his chief's annual report on the political condition of the country concerned, just as the Naval and Military Attachés are responsible for the naval and military sections.

There we may—indeed, for reasons of space we must—take leave of the Consular and Commercial side of Foreign Office work, only noticing that the Civil Service Commission of 1914 has recommended the introduction of open competition in all branches of the Consular Service; the recruitment of candidates at an age when they would still be susceptible of training, instead of looking for a finished product as proposed by the Walrond Committee; and the adoption of a Secondary Education standard for the General and Levant Services and the maintenance of the University standard, with three years subsequent training in Oriental languages—one at a home university and two in the Far East—for the Far Eastern Service.

Changes of the kind suggested in the Diplomatic and Consular Services do not promise immediate economies; but, if the abolition of the old privileged system with its attendant obligation of sacrifice to public duty, is bound to be costly, it is not less true that the more democratic countries of the Continent have in the past known how to conduct their Foreign Affairs on the whole more cheaply than those attached to the *ancien régime*. A return made for the Foreign Office for the year 1904-5 showed Germany and Russia leading with an expenditure of £130,995 and £102,118 respectively, while France spent £42,520 and Italy £27,028. Great Britain stood midway with

---

[1] *5th Report Civil Service Comm.* 1914, Min. of Ev., Q. 43,584.
[2] *Ibid.* Q. 37,065.

£65,771, a figure which had not appreciably changed since 1870[1]; and Austria a little lower with £61,137. It is worth noticing as we pass, that the British Foreign Secretary, though not provided with a house as in the case of the Foreign Ministers of Germany, Austria, and Russia, was considerably the best-paid of all his equals in point of salary, receiving £5000 as compared with the Austrian Foreign Minister's £3800. France and Italy had, of course, adopted a far lower scale of ministerial remuneration[2].

The figures quoted have of course now no value except to show how the expenditure of the various Foreign Services compared in recent, settled times and with steady exchanges. For, in a world altered out of all recognition by the Great War, all our calculations have been revolutionised. Thus, the administrative cost of the British Foreign Office for the year 1921–2 was estimated at £215,520. Throughout the Foreign, including the Consular, Service considerable advances in salary, which can be examined in detail in the Foreign Office List, have been granted. At the one end, for example, the pay of the Permanent Under-Secretary has been raised from £2500 to £3000 a year; at the other a Third Secretary in the now amalgamated Foreign Service receives at least £300 a year, besides representation and house-rent allowances which double his income. And the plan of dividing off that part of a man's salary which he is expected to spend, so to speak, professionally from that which he is entitled to regard as remuneration—a plan obviously fair and necessary where there is high taxation and a super-tax besides—is applied equally to the salaries of the other grades of Diplomatic and Consular agents; so that a modern Ambassador, for example, receives £2500 for himself, but a great deal more for the maintenance of his house and table.

The Great War caused the creation at the Foreign Office of at least three[3] important new Departments—the Ministry of Blockade, with the War Trade Intelligence Department annexed to it, and the Political Intelligence Department. The first was an obvious war-measure, and, though a brilliant administrative achievement for an Office of no great administrative experience, was transient both in its international purposes and Departmental effects; and the second had only a *raison d'être* so long as the Commercial Intelligence Department of the Board of Trade proved unequal to the work required of it. But the

[1] For the year 1869–70 it was £63,079.   [2] £2400 and £1000.
[3] The Historical Section of the Foreign Office also came into being (in 1918) under the control of Dr, afterwards Sir George Prothero, to work up historical matter for the Peace Conference.

Political Intelligence Department, which, under the direction of Sir William Tyrrell, assisted by Mr Headlam-Morley, was created in the first instance to make good, so far as possible, the absence of information from enemy countries through the ordinary diplomatic channels, seemed, to some eyes, though the event has been disappointing[1], to promise to supply something beyond the urgent needs of the hour. Its members were in many cases expert students of their subjects—publicists accustomed to look at international affairs not through the traditions, however good, of an Office, but with clear and independent eyes—and as a body they were not, perhaps, so very far from realising that ideal which one of the witnesses before the Civil Service Commission of 1914 had tried to express by saying, as we have seen, that the Foreign Office ought to be "a mirror of the nation."

It was in this same connexion that Mr Hirst had pleaded for a disinterested understanding between the Foreign Office and the Press—an understanding such as exists in Sweden, where a journalist can walk into a certain room in the Foreign Ministry and obtain, without any expressed or tacit agreement to support the official policy on the subject, such information as he may be in want of, provided always that the information is not of a secret character[2]. Something of this sort seemed in a fair way to be established in England during the Great War. Lord Robert Cecil used to hold a kind of weekly reception for American journalists, when they were at liberty to question him on Foreign Affairs; and these interviews succeeded admirably. Information too secret to be communicated was frankly withheld; and confidences, if made, were studiously respected. The same plan was afterwards tried with English journalists, but failed—partly through lack of interest on the part of high newspaper authorities, and partly (which is, perhaps, only the same thing from a different point of view) because the English journalistic tradition is exclusive and runs counter to such democratic practices. Powerful organs of opinion have been accustomed to get their foreign information privately and from the fountain-head, and, though a News Department still exists for the benefit of foreign pressmen in England, the strong waters of knowledge have fallen back into their accustomed channels—the Private Secretary of the Secretary of State and, sometimes, the Secretary of State himself.

[1] The Department no longer exists (1922).
[2] 5th Report Civil Service Comm. 1914, Min. of Ev., Q. 40,611.

There is some reason to regret the failure. How to instruct public opinion, how to retain public attention are, or ought to be, most urgent problems for the Foreign Office in the world we live in. Something might have been hoped, if it had not perished untimely, of *The New Europe*, a weekly periodical started during the Great War, by the private enterprise and public spirit of Dr Seton-Watson, and devoted exclusively to a discussion of foreign questions. Something may still be hoped of the British Institute of International Affairs, established when the War was over—a select body of some seven hundred members or more, qualified by study or experience to debate foreign policy and seeking to form, by means of lectures and debates, and the facilities of a special library, an educated criticism of Foreign Affairs. But to construct a broad highway of knowledge, upon which the vast mass of the Electorate may set their feet, remains an unsolved problem; and David Urquhart, that impracticable dreamer of the mid-Victorian era, with his working-class associations and committees for the study and investigation of Foreign Affairs[1] and his singular power of bringing home to wayfaring men, even if fools, a conviction of the value and necessity of public law and international obligation, is still the only explorer of a region where others have lacked the faith or the fire to follow.

But for the Foreign Office, at any rate, exposed to a fiercer light than ever before, embarrassed if not supplanted during Mr Lloyd George's Premiership by the existence of a rival Secretariate under the Prime-Minister's aegis, and in process of being swept by the energy of Time into the full current of Democracy, it is plainly an important matter to capture the confidence of the vast crowds who have learnt by the experience of the last few years that within the walls of that seemingly remote Department of State lie the issues of life and death, of peace or war. And perhaps this will not be captured until Morier's profound aspiration that the Diplomatic Service might be nationalised and the Foreign Office internationalised[2] is—if it ever is—more adequately fulfilled. Not until the England we idealise has been interpreted abroad in terms that foreigners can understand—terms that exclude for ever the notion of "*Perfide Albion!*"—nor until we ourselves have learnt the meaning and implication of the idea of Christendom, will the Foreign Services, or the Foreign Secretaries upon whom they depend, have deserved

[1] See on this Robinson, *David Urquhart*, chaps. v, vi, vii, viii.
[2] Quoted in Callières, *Practice of Diplomacy* (ed. Whyte), p. xviii.

the full confidence of their country—of Great Britain and of the Greater Britains that lie beyond the Seas.

Upon the roofing over the great staircase in the new Foreign Office they wrote: "Let the people praise Thee, O God; yea, let all the people praise Thee; for Thou shalt judge the folk righteously and govern the nations upon earth." The inscription was, doubtless, the work of some dreamer of the 'sixties; and for sixty years since, every cynic whose eyes could reach so high has, doubtless, had his fling at it. In a world like ours, where statesmen not uncommonly suppose that the end justifies the means, it would be presumptuous to say that the idealist will ever avenge himself of his adversary.

BIBLIOGRAPHIES

BOOK IV

FROM THE THIRD MINISTRY OF LORD DERBY TO THE FIRST MINISTRY OF LORD SALISBURY, 1866–1886

CHAPTER I

NEUTRALITY, 1866–1874

A. NEUTRALITY IN CONTINENTAL AFFAIRS, 1866–1874.

See Bibliographies in vol. XI of *The Cambridge Modern History* (1908).

Acton, Lord. "The causes of the Franco-Prussian War." In Historical Essays and Studies, 1907.

Bourgeois, E., and Clermont, E. Rome et Napoléon III. Paris, 1907.

Buckle, G.E. Life of Benjamin Disraeli, Earl of Beaconsfield. Vols. IV–V. 1916–1920.

Egerton, H. E. A short history of British Foreign Policy in Europe. 1918.

Goriainoff, S. Le Bosphore et les Dardanelles. Études historiques sur la question des Détroits. Paris, 1910.

Hymans, P. Frère-Orban. Sa vie et correspondance. 2 vols. Brussels, 1905–10.

Lavisse, E. Histoire de France contemporaine. Vol. VII, par Ch. Seignobos. Paris, 1921.

Maxwell, Sir Herbert. Life of Lord Clarendon. Vol. II. 1913.

Mowat, R. B. Select Treaties and Documents to illustrate the development of the modern European states system, 1815–1916. With an Introduction. Enlarged edition. Oxford, 1916.

Newton, Lord. Lord Lyons. A Record of British Diplomacy. Vol. I. 1913.

Oakes, Sir A., and R. B. Mowat. The Great European Treaties of the 19th Century. With an Introduction by Sir H. E. Richards. 2nd impression. Oxford, 1921.

Ollivier, E. L'Empire Libéral. Vols. VIII–XVI. Paris, 1903–1912.

Robertson, C. G. Bismarck. 1918.

Sanger, C. P., and Norton, H. T. England's guarantee to Belgium and Luxemburg, with full Text of Treaties. 1915.

Seignobos, Ch. See Lavisse, E.

Ward, Sir A. W., and Wilkinson, S. Germany, 1815–1890. Vol. II. Cambridge, 1917.

Wemyss, Mrs Rosslyn (Lady Wester Wemyss). Memoirs and Letters of Sir Robert Morier. Vol. II. 1911.

B. SEA POLICY AND THE ALABAMA CLAIMS.

See Bibliographies in *The Cambridge Modern History*, vols. VII (1907), XI (1908), and XII (1910).

Hall, J. A. The Law of Naval Warfare. 1914.

Hall, W. E. Treatise on International Law. Oxford, 1880. Ed. by A. Pearce Higgins. 1917.

Walker, T. A. The Science of International Law. Cambridge, 1893.

Wolf, Lucien. Life of the First Marquis of Ripon. 2 vols, 1921. (Vol. I, ch. XI.)

CHAPTER II

FORWARD POLICY AND REACTION, 1874–1885

This chapter is largely based on the Diplomatic Despatches of the period in the Public Record Office and on the Blue Books and Parliamentary Papers, Treaties and Conventions, preserved there and at the Foreign Office. For both Documents and Secondary Authorities used cf. the Bibliographies in vol. XII of *The Cambridge Modern History*. See also the preceding Bibliography (ch. I).

BOOK V

THE SECOND AND THIRD SALISBURY ADMINISTRATION, AND AFTER

CHAPTER III

IMPERIAL POLICY IN THE OLD AND THE NEW WORLD, 1885–1899

This chapter is largely based on the published Diplomatic Despatches of the period, and on the Blue Books and Parliamentary Papers, Treaties and Conventions, preserved at the Foreign, Colonial and India Offices. For both Documents and Secondary Authorities used cf. the Bibliographies in vol. XII of *The Cambridge Modern History*. See also the preceding Bibliography (ch. I).

Balfour, Lady Betty. History of Lord Lytton's Indian Administration, 1876 to 1880. Compiled from letters and official papers. 1899.
Bismarck, Prince O. von. Gedanken und Erinnerungen. Ed. H. Kohl. Vols. I and II. Stuttgart, 1898. English trans. 2 vols. 1898.
—— Anhang zu Ged. und Erin. 2 vols. Stuttgart, 1901.
Blunt, W. S. Secret History of the English Occupation of Egypt. 1907.
—— My Diaries, 1888–1914. 2 vols. 1919.
Buckle, G.W. Life of Benjamin Disraeli, Earl of Beaconsfield. Vols. V and VI. 1920.
Bülow, Prince B. von. Deutsche Politik. Berlin, 1914. (In Deutschland unter Kaiser Wilhelm II.) Revised ed. 1916. English trans. by M. A. Lewenz. 1914 and 1916.
Cecil, Lady Gwendolen. Life of the Marquis of Salisbury. Vols. I and II. 1921.
[Cook, Sir E. T.]. The Foreign Policy of Lord Rosebery. 1901.
Cromer, Earl of. Modern Egypt. 2 vols. 1908.
—— Abbas II. 1915.
Dawson, W. H. The German Empire, 1867–1914. 2 vols. 1919.
Deschanel, P. E. L. Gambetta. 1920.
Durand, Sir H. M. Life of Sir A. C. Lyall. 1913.
Eckardstein, Hermann Freiherr von. Lebenserinnerungen und Politische Denkwürdigkeiten. Vols. I and II. Leipzig, 1919–20.
Edwards, H. S. Sir William White, his life and correspondence. 1902.
Elliot, Sir Henry G. Some Recollections and other Diplomatic Experiences. Edited by his daughter. 1922.
Elliot, A. R. D. Life of Viscount Goschen. 2 vols. 1911.
Eversley, Lord. The Turkish Empire from 1288 to 1914; and from 1914 to 1922 by Sir Valentine Chirol. 2nd ed. 1922.
Fitzmaurice, Lord E. Life of the second Earl Granville. 2 vols. 1905.
Freycinet, C. de. La Question d'Égypte. Paris, 1905.
—— Souvenirs, 1878–93. Paris, 1914.
German Policy. Die Grosse Politik der Europäischen Kabinette, 1871–1914. Sammlung der Diplomatischen Akten des Auswärtigen Amtes. Vols. I–VI. Berlin, 1922.
Gooch, G.P History of Modern Europe (1878–1919). 1923.
Gwynn, S. L., and Tuckwell, G. M. Life of Sir Charles W. Dilke. 2 vols. 1917.
Hake, A. E. The Story of Chinese Gordon. 1884.
—— The Journals of Major-General C. G. Gordon, C.B. at Kartoum. 1885.
Hammann, Otto. Der missverstandene Bismarck. Berlin, 1921.
Hanna, Col. H. B. The Second Afghan War, 1878–80. 2 vols. 1899 and 1904.
Hanotaux, G. Histoire de la France contemporaine, 1871–1882. 4 vols. Paris, 1903–8. English trans. 1903–1909.
—— Fachoda (Le Partage de l'Afrique). Paris, 1909.
Hohenlohe-Schillingsfürst, Fürst C. zu. Denkwürdigkeiten. 2 vols. Stuttgart and Leipzig, 1907. English trans. 1907.

Jacobi, Hugo. Fürst Herbert von Bismarck. In Biogr. Jahrbuch und Deutscher Nekrolog. Vol. IX. pp. 101–118. [An excellent account of an underrated diplomatist, and especially of his mission to London.]
Johnston, Sir H. H. The Colonisation of Africa. 1899.
Keltie, J. Scott. The Partition of Africa. 1895.
Koschitzky, M. von. Deutsche Kolonialgeschichte. 2 vols. Leipzig, 1887–8
Lémonon, E. L'Europe et la politique britannique, 1882–1909. 1910.
Loftus, Lord Augustus. Diplomatic Reminiscences. 4 vols. 1892–4.
Lyall, Sir Alfred. Life of the Marquis of Dufferin and Ava. 2 vols. 1905. (Vols. I, ch. III, and II, ch. II: Egypt. Vol. II, ch. II: India.)
Mallet, Bernard. Life of Thomas George, first Earl of Northbrook. 1908.
Miller, W. The Ottoman Empire, 1801–1913. 1913.
Milner, Viscount. England in Egypt. 1892.
Morley, Lord. Life of William Ewart Gladstone. 3 vols. 1903.
Newton, Lord. Lord Lyons: a Record of British Diplomacy. 2 vols. 1913.
Palamenghi-Crispi, Thomas. Memoirs of Francesco Crispi. Translated by Mary Prichard-Agnetti. 3 vols. 1912–14.
Rambaud, A. Jules Ferry. Paris, 1903.
Rawlinson, Sir H. England and Russia in the Near East. 1875.
Reventlow, Count E. zu. Deutschlands Auswärtige Politik, 1888–1914. 3rd ed. Berlin, 1916.
—— Der Vampir des Festlandes. Eine Darstellung der Englischen Politik. 9th ed. Berlin, 1916.
Rose, J. H. The Development of the European Nations, 1870–1900. 1905.
Schefer, C. D'une Guerre à l'autre (1871–1914). Essai sur la Politique Extérieure de la Troisième République. Paris, 1920.
Schelking, E. de. The game of diplomacy. 1918.
Sosnosky, T. von. Die Balkanpolitik Oesterreich-Ungarns seit 1866. 2 vols. 1913–14.
—— England's Danger. The Future of British Army Reform. English trans. by M. Sinclair. 1901.
Tirpitz, Alfred von. Erinnerungen. New ed. Leipzig, 1920. English trans.: My Memoirs. 2 vols. 1919.
Trapp, R. The Reconciliation between Germany and England. Berlin, 1920.
Ward, Sir A. W. Germany, 1815–1890. Vol. III. Cambridge, 1918.
Wertheimer, Eduard von. Graf Julius Andrássy, sein Leben und seine Zeit. Nach ungedruckten Quellen. 3 vols. Stuttgart, 1913.
Wilson, Sir C. Rivers. Chapters from my official life. Ed. Everilda MacAlister.
Wingate, Sir F. R. Mahdism and the Egyptian Soudan. 1891.
Wolff, Sir H. D. Rambling Recollections. 2 vols. 1908.

CHAPTER IV

THE BOER WAR AND THE INTERNATIONAL SITUATION. 1899–1902

See also the preceding Bibliography, and the Bibliographies to vol. XII of *The Cambridge Modern History*.

Asakawa, K. The Russo-Japanese Conflict. 1904.
Brinkley, Captain F. Japan and China. 12 vols. 1903–4.
Hammann, Otto. Zur Vorgeschichte des Weltkrieges. Berlin, 1918.
Hayashi, Viscount. Secret Memoirs. Ed. A. M. Pooley. 1915
Köhler, W. Zweibund; Englisch-Deutscher Gegensatz. In Amtlichem Auftrage bearb. von W. K. In vol. I (1897–1904) of Unveröffentlichte Dokumente in amtlichem Auftr. bearb. unter Leitung von B. Schwertfeger. Berlin, 1919.
Liman, Dr Paul. Der Kaiser. New ed. Leipzig, 1909.
Okuma, Count. Fifty Years of New Japan. 2 vols. 1909.
Pan-Germanic Doctrine, The. 1904.

Robertson, Charles Grant. Bismarck. Makers of the 19th century. 1918.
South African War, *The Times* History of the. 7 vols. 1900–9.
Usher, Roland G. Pan-Germanism. 1913.
William II. Kaiserreden. Leipzig, 1902.
—— Ex-Kaiser William II's Memoirs. English trans. 1922.

CHAPTERS V, VI AND VII

CONTINENTAL AGREEMENTS (1902–1907); TRIPLE ALLIANCE
AND TRIPLE *ENTENTE* (1907–1914); AND EPILOGUE, THE WAR
AND THE PEACE (1914–1919)

I. 1902–1914

Bagdad Railway Negotiations. In The Quarterly Review, October, 1917.
Barclay, Sir T. Anglo-French Reminiscences. 1914.
Begbie, H. The Vindication of Great Britain. 1916.
Belgische Aktenstücke, 1905–1914. Berlin, 1915.
Bernstein, H. The Willy-Nicky Correspondence. New York, 1918.
Bishop, J. B. Theodore Roosevelt. 2 vols. 1921.
Blunt, W. S. Diaries. Vol. II. 1920.
Bogitchevich, M. Causes of the War. 1920.
Bourgeois, E., and Pagès, G. Les Origines et les Responsabilités de la Grande Guerre.
    Paris, 1922.
Brailsford, H. N. Macedonia. 1906.
Browne, E. G. The Persian Revolution, 1905–1909. 1910.
Bülow, Prince B. von. Imperial Germany. English trans. 1916 (see above).
—— Reden. 3 vols. 1907–1909.
Caillaux, J. Agadir: ma politique extérieure. Paris, 1919.
Churchill, W. S. The World Crisis. Vol. I. 1923.
Cocks, F. Seymour. E. D. Morel. 1920.
Conrad von Hötzendorf, F. Aus meiner Dienstzeit. Vols. I–III, 1921. Vienna,
    1921–22.
Cook, Sir E. T. How Britain strove for Peace. 1915.
Dawson, W. H. The German Empire. Vol. II. 1919.
Debidour, A. Histoire diplomatique de l'Europe, 1878–1916. 2 vols. Paris, 1916.
Dillon, E. J. The Eclipse of Russia. 1918.
Durham, Edith. Twenty Years of Balkan Tangle. 1920.
Eckardstein, H. Freiherr von. Lebenserinnerungen. Vol. III. Leipzig, 1921.
Esher, Lord. The Influence of Edward VII and other Essays. 1914.
Eversley, Lord. The Turkish Empire from 1288 to 1914; and Sir Valentine Chirol,
    The Turkish Empire from 1914–1922, 1922.
Farrer, J. A. England under Edward VII. 1922.
Fisher, Lord. Memories. 1920.
Fraser, David. Persia and Turkey in Revolt. 1910.
Fraser, Lovat. India under Lord Curzon. 1911.
Friedjung, H. Das Zeitalter des Imperialismus. Vol. II. Berlin, 1922.
Gauvain, A. L'Europe au jour le jour. Vols. I–VI. Paris, 1917–18.
Giolitti, G. Mémoires de ma Vie. Paris, 1923.
Gooch, G. P. History of Modern Europe, 1878–1919. 1923.
—— Life of Lord Courtney. 1920.
Gueshoff, I. E. The Balkan League. 1915.
Gwynn, S. and Tuckwell, G. Life of Sir Charles Dilke. Vol. II. 1917.
Haldane, Viscount. Before the War. 1920.
—— Great Britain and Germany. A Study in Education. 1902. (German trans.
    by R. Eisler. 1911.)
Haller, Johannes. Die Aera Bülow. Stuttgart, 1922.

Hammann, Otto. Der neue Kurs. Erinnerungen. Berlin, 1918.
—— Zur Vorgeschichte des Weltkrieges. Berlin, 1919.
—— Um den Kaiser. Berlin, 1919.
—— Der missverstandene Bismarck. Berlin, 1921;
—— Bilder aus der letzten Kaiserzeit. Berlin, 1922.
Hanotaux, G. La Politique de l'Équilibre, 1907–1911. Paris, 1912.
—— La Guerre des Balkans et l'Europe. Paris, 1914.
Helfferich, Karl. Die Vorgeschichte des Weltkrieges. Berlin, 1919.
Huldermann, B. Albert Ballin. 1922.
Izvolsky, A. P. Memoirs. 1921.
Keith, A. B. The Congo State and the Berlin Act. 1920.
Kennedy, A. L. Old Diplomacy and New. 1922.
Laloy, Émile. Les Documents secrets publiés par les Bolcheviks. Paris, 1920.
Larmeroux, J. La Politique Extérieure de l'Autriche-Hongrie. 2 vols. Paris, 1918.
Lémonon, E. L'Europe et la Politique Britannique. Paris, 1912.
Lichnowsky, Prince. My Mission to London. 1918.
Loreburn, Earl. How the War Came. 1919.
Maurice, Louis. La Politique Marocaine de l'Allemagne. Paris, 1916.
Mévil, A. De la Paix de Francfort à la Conférence d'Algésiras. Paris, 1909.
Millet, R. Notre Politique Extérieure, 1898–1905. Paris, 1905.
Molden, B. Graf Aehrenthal. Stuttgart, 1917.
Moltke, H. von. Erinnerungen, Briefe, Dokumente. Stuttgart, 1922.
Morel, E. D. Morocco in Diplomacy. 1912.
Moore, Arthur. The Orient Express. 1914.
Murray, Gilbert. The Foreign Policy of Sir Edward Grey. 1915.
Nekludoff, A. Diplomatic Reminiscences. 1920.
Poincaré, R. The Origins of the War. 1921.
Pribram, A. F. The Secret Treaties of Austria-Hungary. English edition by A. C. Coolidge. 2 vols. Harvard University Press, 1920–1.
Repington, Colonel. Vestigia. 1919.
Reventlow, Count E. zu. Politische Vorgeschichte des Grossen Krieges. Berlin, 1919.
Rosen, Baron. Forty Years of Diplomacy. 2 vols. 1922.
Russell, Bertrand. The Policy of the Entente, 1904–1914. 1915.
Russia. Un Livre Noir. Diplomatie d'avant-Guerre d'après les documents des Archives Russes. 1910–1914. 2 vols. Paris, 1922 and 1923.
Schefer, C. D'une Guerre à l'autre. Paris, 1920.
Schiemann, T. Deutschland und die Grosse Politik. 14 vols. Berlin, 1901–14.
Schmitt, B. E. England and Germany, 1740–1914. Princeton, 1918.
Schön, Freiherr von. Memoirs of an Ambassador. (English trans. by C. Vesey.) 1922.
Schwertfeger, B. Zur Europäischen Politik, 1897–1914. Vols. I–IV. Berlin, 1919.
Shuster, M. The Strangling of Persia. 1912.
Siebert, B. von. Diplomatische Aktenstücke zur Geschichte der Ententepolitik der Vorkriegsjahre. Berlin, 1921.
Sosnosky, T. von. Die Balkanpolitik Oesterreich-Ungarns seit 1866. Vol. II. Stuttgart, 1914.
Spender, J. A. The Foundations of British Policy. 1912.
Steed, H. W. The Hapsburg Monarchy. 1913.
Stuart, G. H. French Foreign Policy, 1898–1914. New York, 1920.
Sykes, Sir P. History of Persia. Vol. II (edition of 1921).
Tardieu, A. La France et les Alliances. Paris, 1908.
—— La Conférence d'Algésiras. Paris, 1909.
—— Le Mystère d'Agadir. Paris, 1912.
Thayer, W. R. Life and Letters of John Hay. Vol. II. 1919.
Tirpitz, Admiral von. Erinnerungen. 2 vols. Leipzig, 1919. English trans.: My Memoirs. 2 vols. 1919.
Tittoni, T. Italy's Foreign and Colonial Policy. 1914.

Trubetzkoi, Fürst G. Russland als Grossmacht. Stuttgart, 1913.
Valentin, Veit. Deutschlands Aussenpolitik, 1890–1918. Berlin, 1921.
Weissbuch, das deutsche, über die Schuld am Kriege. Berlin, 1919.
William II. Letters to the Tsar. 1920.
—— Vergleichende Geschichtstabellen von 1878 bis zum Kriegsausbruch 1914. (Compiled by the Ex-Emperor William II.) Leipzig, 1921. Eng. trans. F. A. Holt. 1922.
Witte, Count S. J. Memoirs. English trans. by A. Yarmolinski. 1921.
Younghusband, F. India and Tibet. 1910.

II. THE OUTBREAK OF THE WAR

Austrian Red Book. 3 vols. Vienna, 1920.
Bethmann-Hollweg, T. von. Betrachtungen zum Weltkriege. Vol. I. Berlin, 1919. English trans. by G. Young: Reflections on the World War. 1920. Vol. II. Berlin, 1922.
Beyens, H. L'Allemagne avant la Guerre. Brussels, 1915.
Bourgeois, E., and Pagès, G. Les Origines et les Responsabilités de la Grande Guerre. Paris, 1922.
Bülow, B. von. Die Grundlinien der diplomatischen Verhandlungen bis zum Kriegsausbruch. Charlottenburg, 1920.
Dirr, P. Bayerische Dokumente zum Kriegsausbruch. 1922.
Dobrorolski, General Sergei. Die Mobilmachung der russischen Armee. Berlin, 1922.
Dumaine, A. La dernière Ambassade de France en Autriche. Paris, 1921.
Fay, Sidney. New Light on the Origins of the War. In American Historical Review, July and October, 1920, and January, 1921. New York.
Gooss, R. Das Wiener Kabinett und die Entstehung des Weltkrieges. Vienna, 1919.
Headlam, J. W. The Twelve Days. 1915.
—— The German Chancellor and the Outbreak of War. 1917.
Jagow, G. von. Ursachen und Ausbruch des Weltkrieges. Berlin, 1919.
Kautsky, Karl. Die deutschen Dokumente zum Kriegsausbruch. 4 vols. Berlin, 1919.
Oman, C. The Outbreak of the War. 1919.
Pevet, A. Les Responsables de la Guerre. Paris, 1921.
Poincaré, R. The Origins of the War. English trans. 1921.
Pourtalès, Count L. F. W. J. von. Am Scheidewege zwischen Krieg und Frieden. Charlottenburg, 1919.
Romberg, G. von. Die Fälschungen des russischen Orangebuches. Berlin, 1922.
Scott, J. B. Diplomatic Documents relating to the outbreak of the European War. 2 vols. New York, 1916.
Viviani, R. Réponse au Kaiser. Paris. 1923.

III. EPILOGUE, 1914–1919. THE WAR AND THE PEACE

i. THE WAR, 1914–1918

Abbott, G. F. Greece and the Allies, 1914–1922. 1922.
Arthur, Sir G. Life of Lord Kitchener. Vol. III. 1920.
Asquith, H. H. The Genesis of the War. 1923.
Bernstorff, Count. My Three Years in America. English trans. 1920.
Bethmann-Hollweg, T. von. Betrachtungen zum Weltkriege. Vol. II. Berlin, 1922.
—— Kriegsreden. Berlin, 1921.
Buchan, John. History of the Great War. 4 vols. 1922.
Buchanan, Sir G. My Mission to Russia and other Diplomatic Memories. 2 vols. 1923.
Cocks, F. Seymour. The Secret Treaties. 1918.

Czernin, Count Ottokar von. In the World War. English trans. 1919.
Dickinson, G. Lowes. Documents and Statements relating to Peace Proposals and War Aims. 1919.
Encyclopaedia Britannica. 12th ed. Vols. xxx–xxxii. 1922.
Erzberger, M. Erlebnisse im Weltkriege. Stuttgart, 1920.
Esher, Lord. The Tragedy of Lord Kitchener. 1921.
Eversley, Lord, and Chirol, Sir Valentine. The Turkish Empire, 1288–1922. 1923.
Gerard, J. W. My Four Years in Germany. 1917.
Helfferich, Karl. Der Weltkrieg. 2 vols. Berlin, 1919.
Hendrick, B. J. Life and Letters of Walter H. Page. 2 vols. 1922.
Hertling, Carl von. Ein Jahr in der Reichskanzlei. Freiburg, 1919.
Kennedy, A. L. Old Diplomacy and New. 1922.
Lavisse, E. Histoire de France Contemporaine. Vol. ix. Paris, 1922.
Ludendorff, General E. von. My War Recollections. 2 vols. 1919.
—— The General Staff and its Problems. 2 vols. 1920.
Manteyer, G. The Austrian Peace Offer. 1921.
Paléologue, M. La Russie pendant la Grande Guerre. 3 vols. Paris, 1922.
Pollard, A. F. A Short History of the Great War. 1920.
Repington, Colonel. The First World War. 2 vols. 1921.
Robertson, Sir W. From Private to Field-Marshal. 1921.
Roch, W. Mr Lloyd George and the War. 1919.
Scheidemann, P. Der Zusammenbruch. Berlin, 1920.
Stuart, Sir C. The Secrets of Crewe House. 1921.
Wright, P. At the Supreme War Council. 1921.

ii. The Peace, 1918–1919

Baker, R. S. Woodrow Wilson and World Settlement. 3 vols. 1923.
Baruch, B. The Making of the Reparation and Economic Sections of the Treaty. 1920.
Dillon, E. J. The Peace Conference. 1919.
Hanotaux, G. Le Traité de Versailles. Paris, 1919.
Harris, H. Wilson. The Peace in the Making. 1919.
Haskins, C. H., and Lord, R. H. Some Problems of the Peace Conference. Harvard University Press, 1920.
Hearings before the Committee on Foreign Relations of the Senate. Washington, 1919.
Huddleston, Sisley. Peace-making at Paris. 1919.
Keynes, J. M. The Economic Consequences of the Peace. 1919.
Lansing, R. The Peace Negotiations. Boston, 1921.
—— The Big Four and Others of the Peace Conference. Cambridge, Mass. 1922.
Materialien betreffend die Friedensverhandlungen. 10 Parts. Berlin, 1919.
Rothbarth, M. Die Grossen Vier am Werk. Berlin, 1921.
Tardieu, A. La Paix. Paris. 1921.
Temperley, H. A History of the Peace Conference at Paris. 6 vols. 1920–3.
What really happened at Paris. Edited by Colonel House and C. Seymour. 1921.

CHAPTER VIII

THE FOREIGN OFFICE

Report from the Select Committee on the Diplomatic Service, together with Minutes of Evidence, etc., 1861 (459).
Reports from H.M.'s Representatives respecting the British and Foreign Diplomatic Services, 1869–70 (C. 49).
First and Second Reports from the Select Committee on the Diplomatic and Consular Services, together with Minutes of Evidence, 1871 (238, 380).

638 BIBLIOGRAPHIES

Fourth Report of the Royal Commission to inquire into the Civil Establishments of the different Offices of State at home and abroad, 1890 (C. 6172).
Minutes of evidence relating to the above Report (C. 6172–i).
Report of the Committee to inquire into the Constitution of the Consular Service, 1903 (Cd. 1634).
Fifth Report of the Royal Commission on the Civil Service, 1914 (Cd. 7748).
Appendix to the above Report (containing the Minutes of Evidence) (Cd. 7749).
Memorandum by the Board of Trade and the Foreign Office with respect to the future organisation of Commercial Intelligence, 1917 (Cd. 8715).
Foreign Office Lists from the earliest in 1852.

Anson, Sir W. R. Law and Custom of the Constitution. Vol. II, ch. 4. Oxford, 1896.
British Year-Book of International Law, 1920–21, pp. 97–108.
Chambers's Journal, LXX, 705: "The British Foreign Office."
Cavendish, F. W. H. Society, Politics and Diplomacy, 1820–64 (London, 1913).
Cecil, Lord Robert. Speech in the House of Commons, July 31st, 1915.
Foreign Office Sketches, from Vanity Fair (1883).
Hall, H. Byng. The Queen's Messenger. 1865.
Hankey, Sir M. Diplomacy by Conference. 1920.
Hertslet, E. Recollections of the Old Foreign Office (1901).
Machray, R. The Foreign Office. In Cassell's Magazine, December, 1898.
Marvin, C. Our Public Offices (1879).
Percy, Lord E. Responsibilities of the League. In The New Europe, May 1st, 8th, 15th, 22nd, 29th, of 1919. In War and Democracy, ed. by A. E. Zimmern. 1914, pp. 208–237.
Quarterly Review, The. April, 1892: Art. "The Queen's Messenger."
Quarterly Review, The. April, 1903: Art. "The Consular Service and its wrongs."
Remarks on a National Style in reference to the proposed Foreign Office. 1860.
Satow, Sir Ernest. A Guide to Diplomatic Practice (1917). 2nd (revised) ed. 1922.
Scott, G. Gilbert. Explanatory Remarks on the designs for the New Foreign Office. 1860.
Walpole, Spencer. Foreign Relations. English Citizen Series. 1882.

INDEX